Paul McFedries

Microsoft® Windows®
Home Server 2011

UNLEASHED

Third Edition

 800 East 96th Street, Indianapolis, Indiana 46240 USA

Microsoft® Windows® Home Server 2011 Unleashed, Third Edition

ISBN-13: 978-0-672-33540-2

ISBN-10: 0-672-33540-9

Library of Congress Cataloging-in-Publication Data

McFedries, Paul.

  Microsoft Windows Home Server 2011 unleashed / Paul McFedries. — 3rd ed.

     p. cm.

  Includes index.

  ISBN 978-0-672-33540-2

  1. Microsoft Windows server. 2. Operating systems (Computers) 3. Home computer networks—Computer programs. I. Title.

  QA76.76.O63M398173 2011

  005.4'476—dc22

2010049345

Printed in the United States of America

First Printing: March 2011

Trademarks

Warning and Disclaimer

Bulk Sales

Que Publishing offers excellent discounts on this book when ordered in quantity for bulk purchases or special sales. For more information, please contact

  U.S. Corporate and Government Sales

  1-800-382-3419

  corpsales@pearsontechgroup.com

For sales outside of the U.S., please contact

  International Sales

  international@pearson.com

Associate Publisher
Greg Wiegand

Acquisitions Editor
Rick Kughen

Development Editor
Mark Reddin

Technical Editor
Tim Barrett

Managing Editor
Kristy Hart

Project Editor
Betsy Harris

Copy Editor
Gill Editorial Services

Indexer
Erika Millen

Proofreader
Williams Woods
Publishing Services

Publishing Coordinator
Cindy Teeters

Book Designer
Gary Adair

Compositor
Nonie Ratcliff

Contents at a Glance

Introduction 1

Part I Unleashing Windows Home Server Configuration
1   Setting Up Your Windows Home Server Network 7
2   Setting Up and Working with User Accounts 29
3   Adding Devices to the Windows Home Server Network 49
4   Configuring Windows Home Server 75
5   Setting Up and Using Home Server Storage 99

Part II Unleashing Windows Home Server Networking
6   Sharing Folders and Files on the Home Server 117
7   Making Connections to Network Computers 147
8   Streaming and Sharing Digital Media 183
9   Backing Up and Restoring Network Computers 209
10 Monitoring Your Network 239
11 Implementing Windows Home Server Security 257
12 Setting Up a Windows Home Server Website 293
13 Running a SharePoint Site on Windows Home Server 321
14 Patching Home Computers with WSUS 357

Part III Unleashing Windows Home Server Performance and Maintenance
15 Tuning Windows Home Server Performance 369
16 Maintaining Windows Home Server 407
17 Troubleshooting Windows Home Server 427

Part IV Unleashing Windows Home Server Advanced Tools
18 Working with the Windows Home Server Registry 455
19 Using Windows Home Server's Command-Line Tools 477
20 Using Other Windows Home Server Power Tools 533
21 Scripting Windows Home Server 585

Part V   Appendixes

A   Glossary 625

B   Windows Home Server Keyboard Shortcuts 639

C   Windows Home Server Online Resources 649

Index 653

Table of Contents

Introduction   **1**

Part I   **Unleashing Windows Home Server Configuration**

1   **Setting Up Your Windows Home Server Network**   **7**

Configuring Windows Home Server for Networking 8
    Do You Need to Change the Windows Home Server
      Workgroup Name? 8
    Configuring Windows Home Server with a Static IP Address 8
    Setting Up Windows Home Server as a DHCP Server 11
Connecting Windows Home Server to a Windows 7 Homegroup 13
Viewing the Windows Home Server Network 14
Troubleshooting Network Problems 14
    Checking Connection Status 15
    Checking Network Utilization 17
    Repairing a Network Connection 17
    Working with the Network and Internet Troubleshooter 19
    Troubleshooting Cables 20
    Troubleshooting the Network Interface Card 21
Handling Multiple Network Subnets 24
Making a Remote Desktop Connection to the Server 26
    Making Sure That Windows Home Server Is Ready to Host 26
    Making the Connection to the Server 27
    Disconnecting from the Server 27
From Here 28

2   **Setting Up and Working with User Accounts**   **29**

Understanding Security Groups 29
Adding a New User 32
    Setting the Password Length and Complexity 32
    Customizing the Password Length Requirement 33
    Building a Strong Password 34
    Changing the Password on the Client 35
    Adding the User Account 36
Automating Client Logons 39

Modifying User Accounts 41
    Viewing Account Properties 42
    Changing the Account Password 43
    Disabling a User Account 44
    Enabling a User Account 45
    Removing a User Account 46
    Adding a User to a Group 46
    Allowing a User to Log On to the
       Windows Home Server Desktop 47
From Here 48

3   Adding Devices to the Windows Home Server Network   49

Installing Windows Home Server Connector
  on the Client Computers 49
    Supported Operating Systems 50
    Preparing to Install Windows Home Server Connector 51
    Running the Windows Home Server Connector Setup Program 51
Using a Mac on Your Windows Home Server Network 53
    Connecting to the Windows Home Server Network 54
    Running the Windows Home Server MacConnector Setup
       Program on Your Mac 55
    Mounting a Windows Home Server Shared Folder 56
    Using a Mac to Make a Remote Desktop Connection
       to Windows Home Server 59
    Letting Windows Computers See Your Mac Shares 61
Using a Linux Client on Your Windows Home Server Network ... 65
    Viewing the Windows Home Server Network in Ubuntu ... 65
    Letting Windows Computers See Your Ubuntu Shares ... 66
Adding Other Devices to the Network 72
Adding an Xbox 360 to the Network 72
From Here 73

4   Configuring Windows Home Server   75

Running the Windows Home Server Launchpad 76
Running the Windows Home Server Dashboard 77
Changing the Date and Time on Windows Home Server 79
    Setting the Current Date and Time 79
    Synchronizing the Date and Time with a Time Server 81
Selecting the Windows Home Server Region 83
    Changing the Region in the Windows
       Home Server Dashboard 83
    Customizing the Region Formats 83

Configuring Windows Update 85
   Configuring Windows Update 85
   Updating Windows Home Server 87
Changing the Windows Home Server Password 88
Restarting or Shutting Down Windows Home Server 89
Configuring the Windows Home Server Startup 89
   Configuring Startup with the Advanced Boot Options Menu 90
   Configuring Startup with the System Configuration Editor 92
   Launching Applications and Scripts at Startup 94
From Here 98

5 Setting Up and Using Home Server Storage   **99**

Understanding Storage in Windows Home Server 2011 99
   Server Storage on a One-Drive System 100
   Server Storage on a System with Two or More Drives 102
Working with Server Backup Drives 103
   Adding a Drive for Server Backups 103
   Removing a Server Backup Drive 106
Who Needs Drive Extender? Implementing Spanning, Mirroring,
  and RAID 107
   Creating a Storage Pool Using a Spanned Volume 107
   Creating Data Redundancy Using Mirrored Volumes 111
   Mimicking Drive Extender by Creating a RAID 5 Volume 112
Repairing Storage 115
From Here 116

Part II Unleashing Windows Home Server Networking

6 Sharing Folders and Files on the Home Server   **117**

Examining the Predefined Windows Home Server Shares 118
   Setting User Permissions on Shared Folders 118
   Modifying Permissions for a Windows
    Home Server Shared Folder 119
   Sharing Server Folders Outside the Dashboard 120
Working with Shared Folders 123
   Creating a New Shared Folder 123
   Moving a Shared Folder 124
   Accessing Previous Versions of Shared Folders or Files 125
   Deleting a Shared Folder 127
Accessing the Windows Home Server Shared Folders 127
   Understanding the Universal Naming Convention 128
   Mapping a Shared Folder to a Local Drive Letter 130

Disconnecting a Mapped Network Folder 132

Creating a Network Location in Windows 7
and Windows Vista 132

Creating a Network Place in Windows XP 133

Accessing Shared Folders on Your Mac 135

Copying Files to a Shared Folder 135

Publishing a Windows Vista Calendar to the Server 136

Publishing Your Calendar 137

Subscribing to a Calendar 138

Working with Shared Calendars 140

Searching the Shared Folders 140

From Here 145

7   Making Connections to Network Computers   147

Configuring a Computer as a Remote Desktop Host 148

Configuring a Windows 7 or Vista Host 149

Configuring an XP Host 150

Restricting the Computers That Can Connect to the Host 151

Connecting via Remote Desktop Connection 153

Getting the Client Computer Ready 153

Making the Connection to the Remote Desktop 153

Disconnecting from the Remote Desktop 158

Connecting via Windows Home Server Remote Web Access 158

Configuring Users for Remote Access 159

Activating Remote Web Access on the Server 160

Displaying the Remote Web Access Page 160

Making the Connection 162

Disconnecting from the Host 163

Connecting via the Internet 163

Connecting with Your Router's IP Address 164

Connecting with a Domain Name Maintained
by a Dynamic DNS Service 168

Connecting with a Domain Name Maintained
by Windows Home Server 169

Displaying the Remote Web Access Home Page 172

Connecting to a Network Computer 173

Working with Windows Home Server Shares
in the Web Browser 173

Enabling Drag-and-Drop Uploading 176

Customizing the Remote Web Access Pages 177

Customizing the Logon Page 178

Adding Web Page Links 179

From Here 182

8   Streaming and Sharing Digital Media   **183**

Streaming Digital Media 184
    Getting Your Devices Ready 184
    Activating the Windows Home Server Media Server 186
    Playing Streamed Media in Windows Media Player 188
    Playing Streamed Media in Windows Media Center 190
    Streaming Digital Media Over the Internet 191
Sharing Photos 193
    Customizing the Pictures Share with a Template 193
    Using Server Pictures as a Screensaver Slideshow 194
    Adding the Pictures Folder to Windows Media Player 195
    Adding the Pictures Folder to Windows
      Live Photo Gallery 196
    Adding the Pictures Folder to Windows Photo Gallery 197
    Running a Slide Show from the Pictures Share 198
    Changing the Default Picture Import Location
      to Windows Home Server 198
Sharing Music 198
    Customizing the Music Share with a Template 199
    Adding the Music Folder to Windows Media Player 200
    Changing the Default Rip Location to Windows
      Home Server 200
Sharing Videos 201
    Customizing the Videos Share with a Template 201
    Adding the Videos Folder to Windows Media Player 202
    Archiving Recorded TV on Windows Home Server 204
From Here 207

9   Backing Up and Restoring Network Computers   **209**

Understanding Windows Home Server's Backup Technology 210
    Single Instance Storage 210
    No Backup Types 211
    Smarter Backups 211
    Client Computer Backup Retention 212
    Improvements to Client Backups in Windows
      Home Server 2011 212
Converting Client Partitions to NTFS 213
    Format the Partition as NTFS 214
    Run the CONVERT Utility 214
Configuring Windows Home Server Backups 215
    Configuring the Backup Time 215
    Configuring Client Computer Backup Retention 216

Configuring a Computer for Backup 217
    Excluding a Disk Drive from a Backup 218
    Excluding Folders from a Backup 219
    Adding a New Hard Drive to a Backup 220
    Turning Off Backups for a Computer 221
    Configuring Time Machine to Back Up Your Mac 222
Running a Manual Backup 223
    Cancelling a Running Backup 224
    Backing Up Other Systems to Windows Home Server 224
Working with Backups 224
    Viewing a Computer's List of Backups 226
    Viewing Backup Details 227
    Preventing Windows Home Server from Deleting
      a Backup 230
    Cleaning Up Old Backups 230
    Creating a Bootable USB Recovery Key 231
    Repairing a Client's Backups 232
Restoring Network Backups 232
    Restoring Backed-Up Files 233
    Restoring a Computer to a Previous Configuration 235
From Here 237

10   **Monitoring Your Network**   **239**
Monitoring the Network Status with the Launchpad Icon 239
    Monitoring the Icon Color 240
    Monitoring Network Health Alerts 240
    Monitoring Windows Home Server
      with the Alert Viewer 242
Monitoring the Windows Home Server Shares 245
    Launching the Computer Management Snap-In 245
    Viewing the Current Connections 246
    Viewing Connections to Shared Folders 247
    Viewing Open Files 248
    Closing a User's Session or File 249
Monitoring Remote Desktop Sessions 249
    Starting the Remote Desktop Services Manager 250
    Viewing Remote Desktop Sessions 250
    Sending a Message to a Remote Desktop Client 252
    Disconnecting a Remote Desktop Session 253
    Monitoring Users via Task Manager 254
From Here 256

11   Implementing Windows Home Server Security   257

Enabling Security Auditing on Windows Home Server 257
   Activating the Auditing Policies 258
   Understanding the Auditing Policies 259
   Tracking Auditing Events 266
More Ways to Secure Windows Home Server...........................270
   Renaming the Administrator Account 271
   Hiding the Username in the Log On Dialog Box 271
   Making Sure Windows Firewall Is Turned On 272
   Disabling the Hidden Administrative Shares....................274
Securing Network Computers.............................275
   Monitoring Home Computer Security 275
   Thwarting Spyware with Windows Defender 276
   Protecting Yourself Against Email Viruses.....................280
   Implementing Parental Controls 282
   Creating Accounts for the Kids.........................282
   Avoiding Phishing Scams 285
   Sharing a Computer Securely..........................288
Implementing Wireless Network Security 290
From Here...........................292

12   Setting Up a Windows Home Server Website   293

Understanding the Windows Home Server Default Website 294
   Viewing the Default Web Application Folders.....................294
   Viewing the Default IIS Website 296
   Viewing the Default Website with Internet Information
      Services Manager 297
Adding Folders and Files to the Default Website 298
   Adding a File to a Default Website Folder....................298
   Adding a Folder to the Default Website 299
Creating a New Website...........................301
   Creating a New Website Using a Different IP Address.............302
   Creating a New Website Using a Different Port 307
   Creating a New Website Using a Host Header 312
Configuring a Website...........................314
   Modifying the Website Bindings.........................314
   Giving a Website Multiple Identities 315
   Changing the Website Location 316
   Setting the Default Content Page.......................317
   Disabling Anonymous Access..........................319
From Here 320

13   **Running a SharePoint Site on Windows Home Server**   **321**

Installing and Configuring Windows SharePoint Foundation 2010 322
    Downloading and Installing Windows SharePoint
      Foundation 2010 322
    Running the Initial Windows SharePoint Foundation
      2010 Configuration 323
    Creating a New SharePoint Web Application 323
    Creating a Top-Level SharePoint Site 325
    Deleting the Default SharePoint Web Application 328
    Restarting the Windows Home Server Default Website 329
    Adding a Firewall Exception for the SharePoint Web
      Application Port 329
    Forwarding the SharePoint Port in Your Router 330
    Adding Users to the Top-Level SharePoint Site 331
    Logging On to the Top-Level SharePoint Site 332
Adding Sites to SharePoint 333
    Adding a Top-Level Site 335
    Adding a Subsite 335
Working with Site Settings 337
    Customizing a Site 337
    Working with Users 342
    Working with Groups 345
    Working with Permissions 347
    Deleting a Site 349
Creating Content for a SharePoint Site 350
    Storing Images in a Picture Library 350
    Tracking Appointments with a Calendar 352
    Maintaining a List of Contacts 353
    Keeping a List of Web Page Links 355
    Deleting Content from a Site 355
From Here 356

14   **Patching Home Computers with WSUS**   **357**

Installing WSUS 358
Configuring WSUS 359
Synchronizing Updates 361
Connecting Home Computers to WSUS 363
Approving Updates 364
    Approving Updates by Hand 365
    Approving Updates Using a Rule 365
From Here 367

Part III   Unleashing Windows Home Server Performance and Maintenance

15   Tuning Windows Home Server Performance   369

Monitoring Performance 369

    Monitoring Performance with Task Manager 370

    Monitoring Performance with Resource Monitor 382

    Monitoring Performance with Performance Monitor 384

Optimizing the Hard Disk 391

    Examining Hard Drive Performance Specifications 391

    Performing Hard Drive Maintenance 391

    Disabling Compression and Encryption 391

    Turning Off Windows Search 392

    Enabling Write Caching 392

Optimizing Virtual Memory 393

    Storing the Paging File Optimally 393

    Customizing the Paging File Size 394

    Watching the Paging File Size 394

    Changing the Paging File's Location and Size 395

Optimizing Applications 396

    Adding More Memory 397

    Optimizing Application Launching 397

    Getting the Latest Device Drivers 397

    Setting the Program Priority in Task Manager 397

More Optimization Tricks 398

    Adjusting Power Options 398

    Eliminate the Use of Visual Effects 399

    Optimizing Windows Home Server for Services 400

    Upgrading Your Device Drivers 401

From Here 405

16   Maintaining Windows Home Server   407

Checking System Uptime 408

    Displaying Uptime with the Task Manager 408

    Displaying Uptime with the SYSTEMINFO Command 408

    Displaying Uptime with Performance Monitor 408

    Displaying Uptime with a Script 409

Checking Your Hard Disk for Errors 411

    Understanding Clusters 412

    Understanding Lost Clusters 413

    Understanding Invalid Clusters 413

    Understanding Cross-Linked Clusters 413

    Understanding Cycles 413

Understanding Windows Home Server's
Automatic Disk Checking 414
Running Check Disk 414
Checking Free Disk Space on the System Drive 416
Deleting Unnecessary Files from the System Drive 419
Defragmenting the System Drive 422
Reviewing Event Viewer Logs 424
Setting Up a Maintenance Schedule 425
From Here 426

17 Troubleshooting Windows Home Server   427

Replacing Your System Hard Drive 428
Determining the System Hard Drive 428
Replacing the System Drive 429
Checking for Solutions to Problems 430
Understanding Troubleshooting Strategies 432
Did You Get an Error Message? 432
Does an Error or Warning Appear in the Event Viewer Logs? 433
Does an Error Appear in System Information? 433
Did You Recently Edit the Registry? 434
Did You Recently Change Any Windows Settings? 434
Did Windows Home Server "Spontaneously" Reboot? 434
Did You Recently Change Any Application Settings? 437
Did You Recently Install a New Program? 437
Did You Recently Install a New Device? 438
Did You Recently Install an Incompatible Device Driver? 438
Did You Recently Apply an Update
from Windows Update? 438
Did You Recently Install a Windows
Home Server Update? 439
General Troubleshooting Tips 440
Troubleshooting Using Online Resources 440
Troubleshooting Device Problems 442
Troubleshooting with Device Manager 442
Troubleshooting Device Driver Problems 445
Tips for Downloading Device Drivers 446
Verifying Digitally Signed Files 447
Troubleshooting Startup 448
When to Use the Various Advanced Startup Options 448
Using Safe Mode 448
Using Safe Mode with Networking 449
Using Safe Mode with Command Prompt 449

Using Enable Boot Logging.................................449

Using Enable VGA Mode...................................450

Using Last Known Good Configuration.................450

Using Directory Services Restore Mode................450

Using Debugging Mode.....................................451

What to Do If Windows Home Server Won't Start
in Safe Mode...451

Troubleshooting Startup Using the System
Configuration Utility...................................451

From Here...454

Part IV   Unleashing Windows Home Server Advanced Tools

18   Working with the Windows Home Server Registry   455

Starting the Registry Editor................................456

Navigating the Registry.......................................457

Navigating the Keys Pane..............................457

Understanding the Registry Settings................458

Getting to Know the Registry's Root Keys.........459

Understanding Hives and Registry Files............461

Keeping the Registry Safe..................................463

Backing Up the Registry................................463

Protecting Keys by Exporting Them to Disk.......463

Working with Registry Entries............................466

Changing the Value of a Registry Entry............466

Renaming a Key or Setting............................472

Creating a New Key or Setting........................473

Deleting a Key or Setting...............................473

Finding Registry Entries.....................................473

From Here..474

19   Using Windows Home Server's Command-Line Tools   477

Getting to the Command Line.............................477

Running CMD...478

Opening a Folder in a Command Prompt Session.......481

Working at the Command Line.............................483

Running Commands..483

Working with Long Filenames..........................484

Changing Folders Faster.................................485

Taking Advantage of DOSKEY.........................486

Redirecting Command Output and Input............488

Piping Commands..491

Understanding Batch File Basics 492
    Creating Batch Files 493
    REM: Adding Comments to a Batch File 493
    ECHO: Displaying Messages from a Batch File 494
    PAUSE: Temporarily Halting Batch File Execution 495
    Using Batch File Parameters 495
    FOR: Looping in a Batch File 496
    GOTO: Jumping to a Line in a Batch File 497
    IF: Handling Batch File Conditions 498
Working with the Command-Line Tools 501
    Working with Disk Management Tools 501
    Working with File and Folder
        Management Tools 506
    Working with System Management Tools 518
From Here 531

20   Using Other Windows Home Server Power Tools   533

Using the Local Group Policy Editor 533
    Working with Group Policies 534
    Customizing the Windows Security Screen 537
    Customizing the Places Bar 539
    Increasing the Size of the Recent Documents List 541
    Enabling the Shutdown Event Tracker 544
Getting More Out of Control Panel 546
    Reviewing Control Panel Icons 546
    Understanding Control Panel Files 550
    Alternative Methods for Opening
        Control Panel Icons 552
    Putting a Control Panel Submenu
        on the Start Menu 554
    Removing an Icon from Control Panel 554
    Showing Only Specified Control Panel Icons 556
Configuring the Microsoft Management Console 557
    Launching the MMC 560
    Adding a Snap-In 560
    Saving a Console 562
    Creating a Custom Taskpad View 562
    Controlling Snap-Ins with Group Policies 565
Controlling Services 566
    Controlling Services with the Services Snap-In 566
    Controlling Services at the Command Prompt 569
    Controlling Services with a Script 570

Setting Up a Fax Server 574

    Adding the Fax Server Role 574

    Configuring a Shared Fax Printer 575

    Starting the Fax Service Manager 576

    Configuring the Fax Modem 576

    Starting Windows Fax and Scan 577

    Sending a Fax 578

    Receiving Faxes 580

From Here 584

21 Scripting Windows Home Server   585

Understanding Windows Script Host 586

Running Scripts 587

    Running Script Files Directly 588

    Using WScript for Windows-Based Scripts 588

    Using CScript for Command-Line Scripts 590

    Script Properties and .wsh Files 590

Programming Objects 592

    Working with Object Properties 592

    Working with Object Methods 593

    Assigning an Object to a Variable 595

    Working with Object Collections 595

Programming the WScript Object 597

    Displaying Text to the User 597

    Shutting Down a Script 598

    Scripting and Automation 598

Programming the WshShell Object 603

    Referencing the WshShell Object 604

    Displaying Information to the User 604

    Running Applications 608

    Working with Shortcuts 609

    Working with Registry Entries 611

    Working with Environment Variables 613

Programming the WshNetwork Object 615

    Referencing the WshNetwork Object 615

    WshNetwork Object Properties 616

    Mapping Network Printers 616

    Mapping Network Drives 616

Programming the Windows Management Instrumentation Service 617

    Referencing the WMI Service Object 618

    Returning Class Instances 618

From Here 622

Part V   Appendixes

A   Glossary   **625**

B   Windows Home Server Keyboard Shortcuts   **639**

C   Windows Home Server Online Resources   **649**

Windows Home Server Websites 649

Windows Home Server Blogs 650

Windows Home Server for Developers 651

Index   **653**

About the Author

Paul McFedries is a Windows expert and full-time technical writer. He has been authoring computer books since 1991 and has more than 70 books to his credit, which combined have sold more than four million copies worldwide. His recent titles include the Sams Publishing book *Windows 7 Unleashed* and the Que Publishing books *Networking with Microsoft Windows Vista* and *Tweak It and Freak It: A Killer Guide to Making Windows Run Your Way*. Paul is also the proprietor of Word Spy (www.wordspy.com), a website devoted to lexpionage, the sleuthing of new words and phrases that have entered the English language. Please drop by Paul's website at www.mcfedries.com, or follow Paul on Twitter at twitter.com/paulmcf and twitter.com/wordspy.

Dedication

For Karen

Acknowledgments

That's why editors and publishers will never be obsolete: a reader wants someone with taste and authority to point them in the direction of the good stuff, and to keep the awful stuff away from their door.

—*Walter J. Williams*

Windows Home Server, like all versions of Windows, is loaded with good stuff, but it also comes with its share of awful stuff, too. One of the goals of *Microsoft Windows Home Server 2011 Unleashed* is to help you find the good portions of Windows Home Server and avoid the bad bits. I was helped tremendously in this by the editors at Sams, who not only bring terrific technical know-how to their jobs, but who can also spot chaff in a field of written wheat and aren't shy about separating the two. The result of all their efforts is a book that I think reads better, flows more logically, and has the best content possible.

My name may be the only one that adorns the cover, but tons of people had a big hand in creating what you now hold in your hands. You'll find a list of all the people who worked on this book near the front, but there are a few I'd like to thank personally:

Rick Kughen: Rick is the acquisitions editor for this book, and he was kind enough to electronically tap me on the shoulder and ask if I wanted to tackle this project. I immediately said yes (I've got to learn to be more coy about these things), and I'm glad I did because I had a blast writing this book.

Mark Reddin: Mark is the book's development editor, so it's his job to ensure that everything about the book makes sense: He ensures that the book covers every topic that it should cover—no more, no less; he ensures that the chapters are organized in a natural and sensible sequence; and he ensures that each chapter presents its information in a way that makes it easy for you to digest the material. Mark also has the rare and wonderful skill of asking the perfect question at the ideal time. If, while you're reading this book, you think of a question and I answer it in the next paragraph, that's probably because Mark thought of it, too, and asked me to include a response in the book.

Betsy Harris: Betsy is the project editor, which means she's responsible for helping the book out of its relatively casual editorial clothes and into its more formal production duds. Coordinating the work of multiple editors, graphic artists, the production team, and, of course, the always fretful author is not easy. And to pull all that off with competence, aplomb, and a sense of humor, as Betsy did with this book, is a rare and remarkable feat.

Karen Gill: The job of copy editor requires a remarkable range of skills: a saint-like patience, an obsessive attention to detail, a prodigious memory, and the ability to hold your nose and type at the same time (when you come across a technical writer whose talents lie more toward the technical end of the authorial spectrum). Karen possesses all those skills in abundance, and this book became much better thanks to her editorial ministrations.

Tim Barrett: As the book's technical editor, it was Tim's job to double-check my facts, try out my techniques, and implement my tips and tricks. This is a crucial step in the editing process because it ensures that you get a book that's accurate, easy to follow, and won't lead you astray. Tim's patience in the face of this daunting work and his unparalleled Windows knowledge make him a tremendous asset and a joy to work with. Any book he tackles becomes better thanks to his helpful suggestions and tactful corrections. This book was no exception.

Thanks to all of you for another outstanding effort. And, of course, I'd be remiss if I didn't thank you, dear reader, for purchasing this book and letting me be your guide to unleashing Windows Home Server.

Paul McFedries
February 2011

We Want to Hear from You!

As the reader of this book, *you* are our most important critic and commentator. We value your opinion and want to know what we're doing right, what we could do better, what areas you'd like to see us publish in, and any other words of wisdom you're willing to pass our way.

As an associate publisher for Que Publishing, I welcome your comments. You can email or write me directly to let me know what you did or didn't like about this book—as well as what we can do to make our books better.

Please note that I cannot help you with technical problems related to the topic of this book. We do have a User Services group, however, where I will forward specific technical questions related to the book.

When you write, please be sure to include this book's title and author as well as your name, email address, and phone number. I will carefully review your comments and share them with the author and editors who worked on the book.

Email: feedback@samspublishing.com

Mail: Greg Wiegand
            Associate Publisher
            Sams Publishing
            800 East 96th Street
            Indianapolis, IN 46240 USA

Reader Services

Visit our website and register this book at informit.com/register for convenient access to any updates, downloads, or errata that might be available for this book.

Introduction

When you think of the word *server*, you probably first imagine either a massive mainframe hulking behind locked doors in the bowels of some large corporation or a powerful and expensive desktop-like device full of esoteric hardware that helps it—and perhaps a few others like it—run the network of a medium-sized company. The common thread here is that we've always thought of servers as *business* machines. With the exception of a few hardcore geeks and technical writers (not that the two designations are mutually exclusive), having a server in your home seemed, well, *excessive*. What home needs the power of a server? What home can afford the expense of such a high-end device?

But then a funny thing happened: times changed. All those one-computer households suddenly became two-, three-, and even four-computer households. Broadband became nearly ubiquitous, and of course every family member wanted a piece of the new pipe. We began digitizing our media en masse; we wanted to share that media with other members of the family and with other devices scattered around the house, and we discovered wireless computing and became addicted to working and playing anywhere we wanted. The result has been an explosion of home networks over the past few years.

However, it didn't take long for amateur network administrators to learn something that their professional counterparts have known for many years: the larger the network, the more you need some device in the middle of it all to coordinate activities and offer a central repository for data. And our home networks have started to become quite large, with multiple computers, multiple devices such as wireless access points and network attached storage drives, and increasingly massive files, from multiple-megabyte digital audio files to multi-gigabyte digital video files. Suddenly we, too, needed a powerful machine in the middle of it all to keep things humming.

It helped significantly that extremely powerful computers had became extremely inexpensive, but one big problem remained: A server computer needs a server operating system (OS). Unfortunately, the only choices here simply weren't reasonable or practical choices for the home: the powerful but expensive Windows Server 2008 or the various flavors of Linux, all of which are far too complex and arcane for the average home network.

However, the last piece of the puzzle fell into place when Microsoft announced Windows Home Server to the world in January 2007. Now we all had access to a server OS that was designed specifically for home networks. We had access to a server OS that was easy to configure, simple to use, inexpensive, and could run on a variety of hardware. We had a server OS that not only did the usual server tasks—store data and manage users—but also went much further with automatic backups for every computer, streaming media, and easy-to-configure access to any desktop from the network or from the Internet.

Welcome, then, to *Microsoft Windows Home Server 2011 Unleashed*, Third Edition. My goal in this book is to take you beyond the basic Windows Home Server Dashboard interface and into the tremendously powerful behind-the-scenes features that enable you to get the most out of your investment without requiring an advanced networking degree.

This book also covers the new and changed features in Windows Home Server 2011, including the following:

- ▶ Windows Home Server Dashboard
- ▶ Windows Home Server Launchpad
- ▶ Windows Home Server Alert Viewer
- ▶ Improved add-in installation
- ▶ Remote Web Access
- ▶ Remote Web Access page customization
- ▶ Remote Web Access mobile browser features
- ▶ Improved router setup
- ▶ Using Remote Web Access with a custom domain name
- ▶ Easier home PC backup and restore
- ▶ Scheduling server backups

Who Should Read This Book?

For a book like this, it doesn't make much sense to have a "typical reader" in mind when writing. First, there's just no such thing as a typical reader, so you'd be writing for an audience of none. Second, home networks are as varied and unique as the families who use them. There are simple two-computer homes; there are large one-computer-per-person households; there are families who qualify as media powerhouses who create, share, and play audio and video incessantly; there's the home-office crowd who use their network for work as well as play; and finally there's the Alpha Geek family with one person who's juiced not so much about Windows Home Server itself, but about getting his hands on the powerful Windows Server 2008 engine that comes with it.

In this book, I've tried to keep all these different families and situations in mind, and there's lots of content here for everyone. As a general rule, this book is for anyone who wants more from Windows Home Server. If you want to learn more about how Windows Home Server works, if you want to get more out of the unique features in Windows Home Server, and if you want to know how to use the powerful but hidden server features that are also part of the Windows Home Server package, this book is most definitely for you.

How This Book Is Organized

To give you a sense of the overall structure of the book, the next few sections offer a brief summary of the five main parts of the book.

Part I: Unleashing Windows Home Server Configuration

The five chapters in Part I show you how to get everything configured and connected so that you can start to take full advantage of what Windows Home Server has to offer. You learn how to set up Windows Home Server for networking and how to troubleshoot basic network woes (Chapter 1). You learn how to set up and manage user accounts (Chapter 2) and how to add various computer types—Windows 7, Vista, and XP, as well as Mac and Linux—and various devices—including Windows Mobile and Xbox 360—to the Windows Home Server network (Chapter 3). You learn how to configure various Windows Home Server settings, including the computer name, the password, and various startup options (Chapter 4), and delve deep into the new Windows Home Server storage system to learn how the system works; how to add, repair, and remove storage; and more (Chapter 5).

Part II: Unleashing Windows Home Server Networking

Part II is the biggest section of the book, with nine chapters focused on various aspects of networking with Windows Home Server. You learn how to share files and folders (Chapter 6); connect to other computers, both over the network and over the Internet (Chapter 7); stream and share digital image, audio, and video (Chapter 8); use Windows Home Server's computer backup and restore features (Chapter 9); monitor your network (Chapter 10); and implement network security (Chapter 11). I close this section with three chapters that take you well beyond Windows Home Server's core capabilities: Chapter 12 shows you how to use the built-in web server to create powerful and flexible websites; Chapter 13 shows you how to download, install, configure, and use Windows SharePoint Services to run collaborative sites for your family; and Chapter 14 shows you how to implement the Windows Server Update Services to remotely patch your home computers.

Part III: Unleashing Windows Home Server Performance and Maintenance

Part III takes you into some of the features of Windows Home Server that are less glamorous but still crucially important: performance tuning (Chapter 15), system maintenance (Chapter 16), and problem troubleshooting (Chapter 17).

Part IV: Unleashing Windows Home Server Advanced Tools

The four chapters in Part IV take your Windows Home Server knowledge to a higher level with in-depth looks at some advanced tools and features. You learn how to use the Windows Home Server Registry (Chapter 18); how to use the command-line tools (Chapter 19); how to use power tools such as the Control Panel, the Local Group Policy Editor, and the Computer Management snap-ins (Chapter 20); and how to create Windows Home Server scripts, including scripts that control the incredibly powerful Windows Management Instrumentation (WMI) interface (Chapter 21).

Part V: Appendixes

To round out your Windows Home Server education, Part V presents a few appendixes that contain extra goodies. You'll find a glossary of Windows Home Server terms (Appendix A), a complete list of Windows Home Server shortcut keys (Appendix B), and a list of online resources for Windows Home Server (Appendix C).

Conventions Used in This Book

To make your life easier, this book includes various features and conventions that can help you get the most out of this book and out of Windows Home Server:

Steps	Throughout the book, I've broken many Windows Home Server tasks into easy-to-follow step-by-step procedures.
Things you type	Whenever I suggest that you type something, what you type appears in a **bold monospace** font.
Filenames, folder names, and code	These things appear in a monospace font.
Commands	Commands and their syntax use the monospace font as well. Command placeholders (which stand for what you actually type) appear in an *italic monospace* font.
Pull-down menu commands	I use the following style for all application menu commands: *Menu*, *Command*, where *Menu* is the name of the menu that you pull down and *Command* is the name of the command you select. Here's an example: File, Open. This means that you pull down the File menu and select the Open command.
Code-continuation character	When a line of code is too long to fit on only one line of this book, it is broken at a convenient place and continued to the next line. The continuation of the line is preceded by a code continuation character (➡). You should type a line of code that has this character as one long line without breaking it.

This book also uses the following boxes to draw your attention to important (or merely interesting) information.

NOTE

The Note box presents asides that give you more information about the current topic. These tidbits provide extra insights that offer a better understanding of the task.

TIP

The Tip box tells you about Windows Home Server methods that are easier, faster, or more efficient than the standard methods.

CAUTION

The all-important Caution box tells you about potential accidents waiting to happen. There are always ways to mess up things when you're working with computers. These boxes help you avoid those traps and pitfalls.

CHAPTER 1

Setting Up Your Windows Home Server Network

IN THIS CHAPTER

▶ Configuring Windows Home Server for Networking

▶ Connecting Windows Home Server to a Windows 7 Homegroup

▶ Viewing the Windows Home Server Network

▶ Troubleshooting Network Problems

▶ Handling Multiple Network Subnets

▶ Making a Remote Desktop Connection to the Server

You're almost ready to put Windows Home Server to good use storing files, sharing media, and backing up the other machines on your network. Before you get to all that, however, you need to make sure that Windows Home Server is ready to do the networking thing. To that end, this chapter takes you through a few network configuration chores that you might require to get Windows Home Server and the rest of your network on speaking terms. If you have problems, this chapter also includes an extensive network troubleshooting section (see "Troubleshooting Network Problems") that should help.

In this chapter, I assume that the basics of your home network are already in place. You have wired or wireless network interface cards (NICs) installed in each machine, you have the necessary routers and switches, you have a router or wireless access point connected to your broadband Internet service, the wired machines have the correct cable connections, and so on.

> **NOTE**
>
> If your network is either nonexistent or a work in progress, you might want to check out the book *Sams Teach Yourself Networking in 24 Hours, 4th Edition*, by Uyless Black, to get things going.

Configuring Windows Home Server for Networking

Windows Home Server's default networking setup creates a basic configuration that should work without a hitch on most home networks. However, you should know about a few small tweaks that can make Windows Home Server a bit easier to work with and that are required for certain features to work properly. For example, setting up remote access to the Windows Home Server machine is much easier if you give the computer a static Internet Protocol (IP) address. These next few sections take you through this and other network modifications.

Do You Need to Change the Windows Home Server Workgroup Name?

It used to be the case that home networking worked best when all the computers on the network used the same workgroup name. By default, Windows Home Server installs with the name WORKGROUP, which is also the default workgroup name used by Windows 7, Windows Vista, and Windows XP Professional. Therefore, if you're using any of those operating systems and you've set up your network using the default settings, all your machines should reside in the WORKGROUP group.

However, if your client machines are using some other workgroup name, you shouldn't need to modify the Windows Home Server workgroup name to match, because the client PCs should still see the Windows Home Server machine. (This will only be true if your Windows Home Server machine and your client computers reside on the same network subnet. See "Handling Multiple Network Subnets," later in this chapter.)

That's a good thing, because Windows Home Server 2011 actually locks the workgroup name, and you can't change it. Or, more accurately, you *can* change it, but only after running through a fairly convoluted and time-consuming process that involves disabling and later enabling the services that prevent you from changing the workgroup name. In my own testing, the process works, but it also breaks the local Dashboard on the server, so in my view it's not worth the hassle.

Configuring Windows Home Server with a Static IP Address

Every computer on your network requires a unique designation so that packets can be routed to the correct location when information is transferred across the network. In a default Microsoft peer-to-peer network, the network protocol that handles these transfers is Transmission Control Protocol/Internet Protocol (TCP/IP), and the unique designation assigned to each computer is the IP address.

By default, Windows Home Server obtains its IP address via Dynamic Host Configuration Protocol (DHCP). This requires a server, and in the vast majority of home broadband networks, that server is the router or wireless access point. (If you have no DHCP server on your network, you can convert Windows Home Server into one; see the next section.)

To find out the current IP address of the Windows Home Server machine, log on to the server and then use either of the following methods:

▶ Log on to the server, click Start, type **network**, and then click View Network Connections to open the Network Connections window. Double-click the local area network (LAN) icon (which is usually named Local Area Connection), and then click Details. As shown in Figure 1.1, the IP Address value appears in the Network Connection Details list as the IPv4 value.

▶ Select Start, All Programs, Accessories, Command Prompt, type **ipconfig /all**, and press Enter.

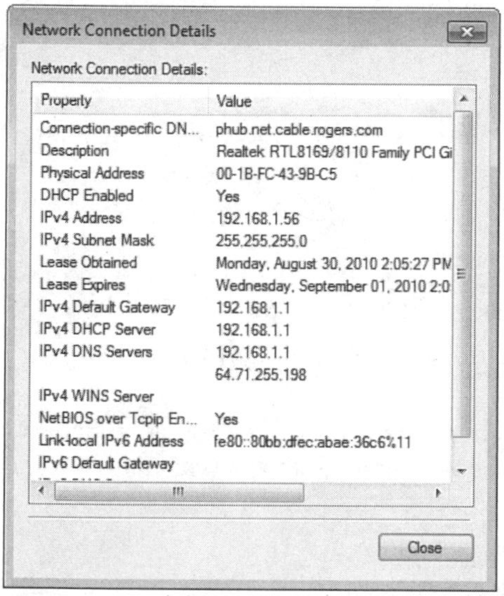

FIGURE 1.1   In the Network Connection Details dialog box, the IPv4 value displays the server's current IP address.

The DHCP server offers each client a lease on the IP address, and in most cases that lease expires after 24 hours. When the expiration time approaches, the client asks for a new IP address. In small networks, the DHCP server often assigns a client the same IP address each time, but that's not guaranteed. A changing IP address is no big deal for client computers, but it can be a problem for the Windows Home Server machine. Most importantly, remote access sessions require that you set up your router to forward remote requests to the Windows Home Server computer. You do that by specifying the server's IP address, so if that address changes, the remote access sessions won't work.

▶ SEE "Setting Up Port Forwarding on the Router," **P. 165**.

Therefore, it's a good idea to assign a static IP address to your Windows Home Server machine. Here's how:

1. Log on to Windows Home Server either locally or by using a Remote Desktop connection. (See "Making a Remote Desktop Connection to the Server," later in this chapter.)
2. Select Start, type **network**, and then click View Network Connections to open the Network Connections window.

TIP

You can also click the network icon in the notification area, click Open Network and Sharing Center, and then click Change Adapter Settings.

---

3. Double-click the icon for the connection to your LAN. The connection's Status dialog box appears.
4. Click Details.
5. Make a note of the following values (refer to Figure 1.1):
   - **Subnet Mask**—On home networks, this is usually 255.255.255.0.
   - **Default Gateway**—On home networks, this is the IP address of your router or access point.
   - **DNS Servers**—These are usually the IP address of your router and access point, as well as the IP address of the main Domain Name System server that your Internet Service Provider (ISP) uses.
6. Click Close to return to the Status dialog box.
7. Click Properties. The connection's property sheet appears.
8. On the General tab, click Internet Protocol Version 4 (TCP/IPv4), and then click Properties.
9. Click the Use the Following IP Address option.
10. Type the IP address you want to use. Be sure to use an address that won't conflict with the other DHCP clients on your network. A good idea is to use the highest possible address, such as 192.168.1.254 (if your network uses 192.168.1.* addresses) or 192.168.0.254 (if your network uses 192.168.0.* addresses).
11. Type the IP addresses for the Subnet Mask (Windows Home Server should fill this in automatically), Default Gateway, Preferred DNS Server, and Alternate DNS Server that you noted in step 5. Figure 1.2 shows a completed version of the dialog box.
12. Click OK to return to the connection's property sheet. If at this point you lose your Remote Desktop connection (because you changed the server's IP address), you can skip the next two steps.
13. Click Close to return to the Status dialog box.
14. Click Close.

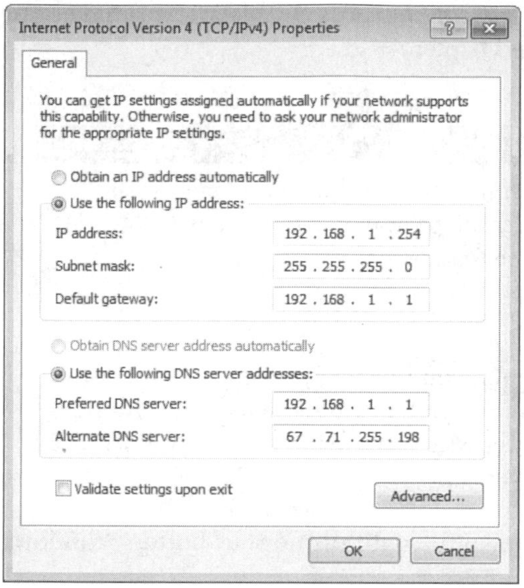

FIGURE 1.2   It's a good idea to assign a static IP address to the Windows Home Server machine.

TIP

When you specify a static IP address, you must also specify a static domain name system (DNS) server address used by your ISP. This shouldn't cause a problem with most ISPs because their DNS server addresses are constant. However, you might have trouble if your ISP changes its DNS settings. You can work around this problem by first returning Windows Home Server to getting its IP address dynamically. Then log in to your router and look for an option that enables you to map a static IP address to the server's Media Access Control (MAC; see the next Note) address. This means that each time the server requests a new DHCP lease, the router supplies the server the same IP address. Note that not all broadband routers offer this option.

NOTE

To find out your server's MAC address, open the Network Connections window, right-click the LAN icon, click Status, and then click Details. (Alternatively, select Start, Command Prompt, type **ipconfig /all**, and press Enter.) The MAC address is given by the Physical Address value.

Setting Up Windows Home Server as a DHCP Server

If your home network doesn't have a device that acts as a DHCP server, or if you want more control over DHCP on your network, you can convert Windows Home Server into a DHCP server. (The next three sections assume that you're logged on to Windows Home

Server either locally or by using a Remote Desktop connection; see "Making a Remote Desktop Connection to the Server," later in this chapter.)

CAUTION

Windows Home Server's DHCP Server service might not work if you have another DHCP server on the network. If you have a router or access point that currently has DHCP enabled, you might have to first disable DHCP on that device.

To set up Windows Home Server as a DHCP server, you must add the DHCP Server role. This role comes with Windows Home Server, but it's not added by default. Assuming you've already set up your Windows Home Server with a static IP address, as described earlier, follow these steps to add the DHCP Server role:

1. Click the Server Manager icon that appears to the right of the Start button. Windows Home Server opens the Server Manager.

2. Click Roles.

3. Click Add Roles. Server Manager launches the Add Roles Wizard.

4. Click Next.

5. Click to activate the DHCP Server check box, and then click Next. The wizard displays the DHCP Server dialog box.

6. Click Next. The wizard displays the Select Network Connection Bindings dialog box.

7. Make sure the check box beside the network connection to which you assigned a static IP address is activated, and then click Next. The wizard displays the Specify IPv4 DNS Server Settings dialog box.

8. Use the Parent Domain text box to type the name of your workgroup, and then click Next. The wizard displays the Specify IPv4 WINS Server Settings dialog box.

9. You don't need a WINS (Windows Internet Name Service) server, so click Next.

10. Click Next. The wizard displays the Add or Edit DHCP Scopes dialog box. The scope is the range of IP addresses that the server can dole out to the clients.

11. Click Add. The Add Scope dialog box appears.

12. Type a name for the scope.

13. Define the scope range:

    ▶ **Starting IP Address**—Type the starting address for the IP address range you want the server to use (for example, 192.168.1.50).

    ▶ **Ending IP Address**—Type the ending address for the IP address range you want the server to use (for example, 192.168.1.99). Make sure this address is higher than the Starting IP Address value.

14. Use the subnet Type list to select Wired. Figure 1.3 shows a completed Add Scope dialog box.

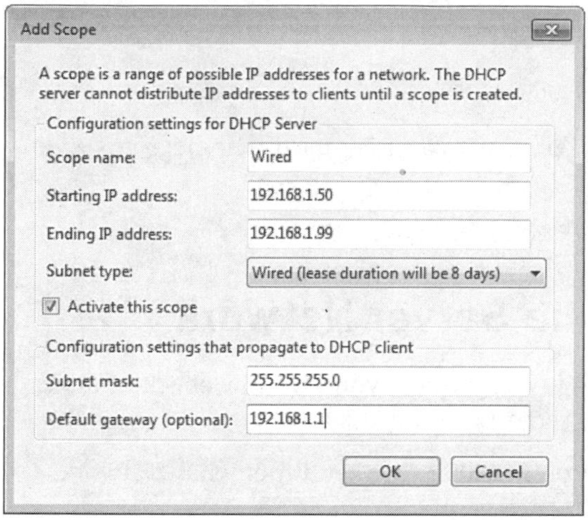

Add Scope

A scope is a range of possible IP addresses for a network. The DHCP server cannot distribute IP addresses to clients until a scope is created.

Configuration settings for DHCP Server

Scope name:	Wired
Starting IP address:	192.168.1.50
Ending IP address:	192.168.1.99
Subnet type:	Wired (lease duration will be 8 days) ▼

☑ Activate this scope

Configuration settings that propagate to DHCP client

| Subnet mask: | 255.255.255.0 |
| Default gateway (optional): | 192.168.1.1 |

OK   Cancel

FIGURE 1.3   An Add Scope dialog box, ready to go.

15. Click OK.

16. Click Next. The wizard displays the Configure DHCPv6 Stateless Mode dialog box.

17. Activate the Disable DHCPv6 Stateless Mode for This Server option, and then click Next.

18. Click Install. Server Manager installs the DHCP server.

19. Click Close.

Connecting Windows Home Server to a Windows 7 Homegroup

One of the major innovations that Windows 7 brought to the networking table was the idea of a *homegroup*. This is a collection of computers on a peer-to-peer network that use a single password to share data between them. The idea is that once you join a homegroup by entering the homegroup password, you never need to worry about networking again because Windows 7 handles all the connections for you automatically. This is in contrast to the more traditional way of managing networking connections and sharing resources, which is by setting up user accounts and passwords and then assigning user permissions for each shared resource.

In other words, homegroups are designed to make networking easier and less problematic for new and inexperienced users, particularly home users. So it's not surprising that Windows Home Server 2011 comes with support for homegroups baked in. If you already have a Windows 7 homegroup on your network, follow these steps to join Windows Home Server to the homegroup:

1. Open the Dashboard.
2. Click Server Settings.
3. Click the HomeGroup tab.
4. Click Join Now. Windows Home Server prompts you to enter the homegroup password.
5. Type the password and then click Join Now.

Viewing the Windows Home Server Network

With your Windows Home Server networking tweaks done, you can now check to make sure that the rest of the network can see the server:

▶ In Windows 7, click the Windows Explorer taskbar icon, and then click Network.

▶ In Vista, select Start, Network.

▶ In XP, select Start, My Network Places, and then click View Workgroup Computers. (If you have the Folders list displayed, open the My Network Places, Entire Network, Microsoft Windows Network branch, and then click your workgroup.)

Figure 1.4 shows Windows 7's Network window, which displays icons for the computers, devices, and shared media connections on the network (as does the Network window in Vista). (XP just displays icons for the workgroup computers.)

Notice that for the Windows Home Server machine, you might see as many as three icons:

▶ **Server Device icon**—Double-click this icon to see data about the server as a network device. The data includes the server's IP address and MAC address.

▶ **Server Shared Folders icon**—Double-click this icon to see the server's shared folders.

▶ **Server Shared Media icon**—Double-click this icon to open Windows Media Player, which then lets you access the server's shared media. This icon appears only when you configure Windows Home Server to share its Music, Photos, or Videos folders.

▶ **SEE** Chapter 8, "Streaming and Sharing Digital Media."

Troubleshooting Network Problems

Big-time corporate networking is a complex, arcane topic that taxes the patience of all but the most dedicated *wireheads* (an affectionate pet name often applied to network hackers and gurus). There are so many hardware components to deal with (from the network adapters to the cables to the routers to the hubs) and so many layers of software (from the device drivers to the protocols to the redirectors to the network providers) that big networks often seem like accidents looking for a place to happen.

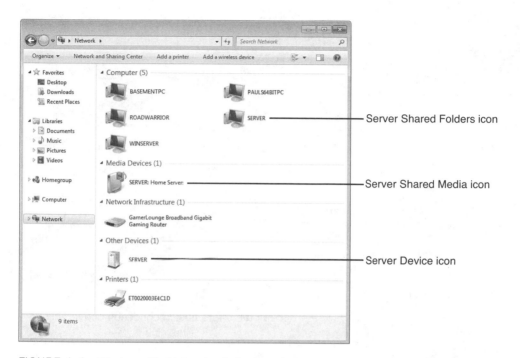

Server Shared Folders icon

Server Shared Media icon

Server Device icon

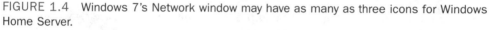

FIGURE 1.4   Windows 7's Network window may have as many as three icons for Windows Home Server.

Home networks are much simpler beasts and, more often than not, they work well right out of the box. That's not to say that home networks are bulletproof—not by a long shot. If your network has become a *notwork* (some wags also refer to a downed network as a *nyetwork*), this section offers a few solutions that might help. I don't make any claim to completeness here, however. Most network ills are a combination of several factors and are therefore relatively obscure and difficult to reproduce. Instead, I go through a few general strategies for tracking down problems and offer solutions for some of the most common network afflictions.

Checking Connection Status

A good starting point for diagnosing network problems is checking the status of the Windows Home Server network connection. This shows you things such as your connection status, connection speed, current IP address, network's default gateway addresses, DHCP server, DNS servers, and so on. Invalid entries for these and other status items could provide a hint as to where the network problem might lie.

To display the connection status, log on to Windows Home Server, select Start, type **network**, click View Network Connections to open the Network Connections window, and then double-click the connection.

FIGURE 1.5   In the Status dialog box, the General tab offers basic connection details and activity metrics.

Figure 1.5 shows the Status dialog box that appears. In the General tab are two groups to check out, as follows:

▶ **Connection**—This group shows the connection's current status: Connected or Disconnected. If the status value shows Connected, the Duration value shows how long the connection has been active, and the Speed value shows the connection speed in Mbps or Gbps.

▶ **Activity**—This group shows the number of network packets that the connection has sent and received. A low number for either value gives you a hint about the direction of the problem. For example, a low Sent value might indicate that Windows Home Server can't communicate with the client computers.

NOTE

On most Windows Home Server networks, the Received value is significantly higher than the Sent value at first because you're sending lots of data to the server. After a while, however, the two values should be fairly balanced, with one or the other being perhaps 10–40% higher than the other. On networks that do a lot of media streaming, however, the Sent value may be significantly higher than the Received value.

For other network connection data, click the Details button to see information such as the addresses of the DHCP server (this appears only if you're using a dynamically allocated IP address), DNS servers, and so on. (Refer to Figure 1.1, earlier.)

You can also click Diagnose to initiate the Windows Home Server network connection repair utility. See "Repairing a Network Connection," later in this chapter.

Checking Network Utilization

If your network feels sluggish, it could be that the computer you're working with is sharing data slowly or that network traffic is exceptionally high. To see whether the latter situation is the cause of the problem, you can check out the current *network utilization* value, which is the percent of available bandwidth that your network adapter is currently using.

To check network utilization, follow these steps:

1. Log on to Windows Home Server either locally or by using a Remote Desktop connection. (See "Making a Remote Desktop Connection to the Server," later in this chapter.)
2. Right-click an empty section of the taskbar, and then click Start Task Manager.
3. Display the Networking tab, shown in Figure 1.6.

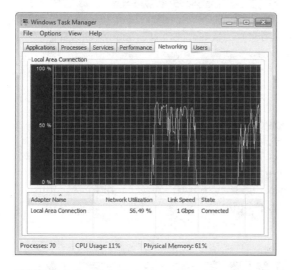

FIGURE 1.6   Use Task Manager's Networking tab to check the current network utilization percentage.

4. If you have multiple adapters, click the one you want to check in the Adapter Name list.
5. Use the graph or the Network Utilization column to monitor the current network utilization value.

Repairing a Network Connection

When a user calls Microsoft Support to resolve a networking issue, the support engineer has a list of troubleshooting steps that he takes the user through. For example, if there's a problem with a DHCP network, the engineer usually starts by telling the user to use

IPCONFIG to release (`ipconfig /release`) and then renew (`ipconfig /renew`) the IP address. Other steps include running specific commands with the ARP (Address Resolution Protocol) and NBTSTAT (NetBIOS over TCP/IP Statistics) utilities.

Someone at Microsoft realized that all these steps could be automated by creating a script that runs the various `ipconfig`, `arp`, and `nbstat` commands. The result is the network connection repair tool, which runs the following six troubleshooting steps:

1. **Broadcasts a request for the renewal of the computer's DHCP lease**—A *DHCP lease* is a guarantee that the DHCP client computer will have the IP address supplied by the DHCP server for a specified period. To avoid lease expiration, the DHCP client usually sends a request—a DHCPREQUEST message—for lease renewal to the original DHCP server after 50% of the lease time has expired. If 87.5% of its lease time has expired, the DHCP client sends a lease renewal request to all available DHCP servers. This broad request for a lease renewal is what the repair tool does.

> **NOTE**
>
> Why send a DHCPREQUEST message instead of just using IPCONFIG to release and renew the IP address? Because if the current address is functioning properly, releasing that address could cause extra problems if a new address cannot be obtained from a DHCP server. With a lease renewal request, the DHCP client keeps its current address.

2. **Flushes the ARP cache**—The *ARP* (*Address Resolution Protocol*) handles the conversion of an IP address to the MAC address of a network adapter. To improve performance, Windows Home Server stores resolved addresses in the *ARP cache* for a short time. ARP cache entries that are obsolete or incomplete cause some networking problems. The cache is normally flushed regularly, but the repair tool forces a flush. This is the same as running the following command:

```
arp -d
```

> **TIP**
>
> To see the contents of the ARP cache, run the following command:
>
> ```
> arp -a
> ```
>
> You'll see output similar to the following, which lists IP addresses and their corresponding MAC addresses:
>
> ```
> Interface: 192.168.1.254 --- 0x10003
>   Internet Address      Physical Address      Type
>   192.168.1.101         00-c0-a8-b2-e0-d3     dynamic
>   192.168.1.102         00-11-11-ce-c7-78     dynamic
>   192.168.1.108         00-0f-66-ea-ea-24     dynamic
>   192.168.1.111         00-0d-4b-04-27-2f     dynamic
> ```

3. **Flushes the NetBIOS name cache**—NetBIOS handles the conversion between the network names of computers and their IP addresses. To improve performance, Windows Home Server stores resolved names in the *NetBIOS name cache*. To solve problems caused by NetBIOS name cache entries that are obsolete or bad, this step clears the cache. This is the same as running the following command:

```
nbtstat -R
```

4. **Reregisters the computer with the network's WINS server**—The repair tool asks the WINS server to release the computer's NetBIOS names that are registered with the server and then reregister them. This is useful if you're having problems connecting to other computers using their network names. This is the same as running the following command:

```
nbtstat -RR
```

5. **Flushes the DNS cache**—DNS handles the conversion of domain names to IP addresses. To improve performance, Windows Home Server stores resolved domain names in the DNS cache. To solve problems caused by DNS cache entries that are obsolete or bad, this step clears the cache. This is the same as running the following command:

```
ipconfig /flushdns
```

6. **Reregisters the computer with the DNS server**—This is useful if you're having trouble resolving domain names or if you're having trouble with a dynamic DNS server. This is the same as running the following command:

```
ipconfig /registerdns
```

To launch the repair process, log on to Windows Home Server, and then use one of the following techniques:

▶ In the connection's Status dialog box, click Diagnose.

▶ In the Network Connections window, click the connection and then click Diagnose This Connection.

▶ Right-click the network icon in the notification area, and then click Troubleshoot Problems.

Working with the Network and Internet Troubleshooter

If you suspect you're having network trouble—such as computers on the network not being able to see each other or file transfers or other network activity behaving erratically—but you aren't sure, one easy way to find out is to run the Network and Internet Troubleshooter utility. This is a Control Panel connectivity troubleshooting tool that can aid you in isolating network problems.

To get started, log on to Windows Home Server, select Start, Control Panel, Troubleshooting, and then click Network and Internet. In the Network and Internet window (see Figure 1.7), click the type of problem you're having to launch the associated troubleshooting tool.

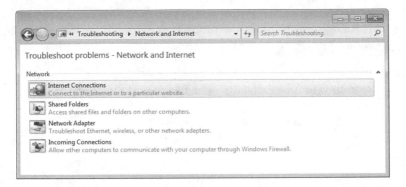

FIGURE 1.7 Use the Network and Internet troubleshooting tools to diagnose and repair connectivity problems.

Troubleshooting Cables

If one of the problems discussed so far isn't the cause of your networking quandary, the next logical suspect is the cabling that connects the workstations. This section discusses cabling, gives you a few pointers for preventing cable problems, and discusses some common cable kinks that can crop up.

Although third-party cable installers perform most large-scale cabling operations, home setups are usually do-it-yourself jobs. You can prevent some cable problems and simplify your troubleshooting down the road by taking a few precautions and "ounce of prevention" measures in advance:

- ▶ First and foremost, always buy the highest-quality cable you can find (for example, Category 5e or higher for twisted-pair cable). With network cabling, you get what you pay for.

- ▶ Good-quality cable is labeled. You should also add your own labels for things such as the cable source and destination.

- ▶ To avoid electromagnetic interference, don't run cable near electronic devices, power lines, air conditioners, fluorescent lights, motors, and other electromagnetic sources.

- ▶ Try to avoid phone lines because the ringer signal can disrupt network data carried over twisted-pair cable.

- ▶ To avoid the cable being stepped on accidentally, don't run it under carpet.

- ▶ To avoid people tripping over a cable (and possibly damaging the cable connector, the NIC port, or the person doing the tripping!), avoid high-traffic areas when laying the cable.

- ▶ If you plan to run cable outdoors, use conduit or another casing material to prevent moisture damage.

▶ Don't use excessive force to pull or push a cable into place. Rough handling can cause pinching or even breakage.

If you suspect cabling might be the cause of your network problems, here's a list of a few things to check:

▶ **Watch for electromagnetic interference**—If you see garbage on a workstation screen or experience random packet loss or temporarily missing nodes, the problem might be electromagnetic interference. Check your cables to make sure they are at least 6 to 12 inches from any source of electromagnetic interference.

▶ **Check your connections**—Loose connections are a common source of cabling woes. Be sure to check every cable connection associated with the workstation that's experiencing network difficulty, including connections to the network adapter, router, switch, and so on.

▶ **Check the lay of the line**—Loops of cable could be generating an electrical field that interferes with network communication. Try not to leave your excess cable lying around in coils or loops.

▶ **Inspect the cable for pinching or breaks**—A badly pinched cable can cause a short in the wire, which could lead to intermittent connection problems. Make sure that no part of the cable is pinched, especially if the back of the computer is situated near a wall. A complete lack of connection with the network might mean that the cable's copper core has been severed completely and needs to be replaced.

Troubleshooting the Network Interface Card

After cabling, the NIC is next on the list of common sources of networking headaches. Here are some items to check if you suspect that Windows Home Server and your NIC aren't getting along:

▶ **Make sure that Windows Home Server installed the correct NIC**—Windows Home Server usually does a pretty good job of detecting the network card. However, a slight error (such as choosing the wrong transceiver type) can wreak havoc. Double-check that the NIC listed in Device Manager (see the next section) is the same as the one installed in your computer. If it's not, click Remove to delete it, run the Add Hardware Wizard, and choose your NIC manually.

▶ **Perform a physical check of the NIC**—Open the case and make sure the card is properly seated in its slot.

CAUTION

Before touching any component inside a computer case, ground yourself to prevent electrostatic discharge. To ground yourself, touch any metal surface, such as the metal of the computer case.

▶ **Try a new NIC**—Try swapping out the NIC for one that you know works properly. (If the existing NIC is on the computer's motherboard, insert the working NIC in an open bus slot.) If the switch fixes the problem, remove the faulty interface card (if possible) and insert a new one.

▶ **Get the latest driver**—Check with the manufacturer of the NIC to see whether it has newer Windows Home Server or Windows Server 2008 64-bit drivers for the card. If so, download and install them, as described in the section after next.

Viewing the NIC in Device Manager

Windows Home Server stores all its hardware data in the Registry, but it provides Device Manager to give you a graphical view of the devices on your system. To display Device Manager, log on to Windows Home Server, click Start, right-click Computer, click Manage in the shortcut menu, click Diagnostics, and then click Device Manager.

TIP

A quick way to go directly to the Device Manager snap-in is to select Start, type `devmgmt.msc`, and press Enter. Note, too, that you can also press Windows Logo+Pause/Break to display the System window, and then click Device Manager.

Device Manager not only provides you with a comprehensive summary of your system's hardware data, but it doubles as a decent troubleshooting tool. To see what I mean, check out the Device Manager tab shown in Figure 1.8. See how the icon for the Marvell Yukon 88E8056 PCI-E Gigabit Ethernet Controller device has an exclamation mark superimposed on it? This tells you that there's a problem with the device.

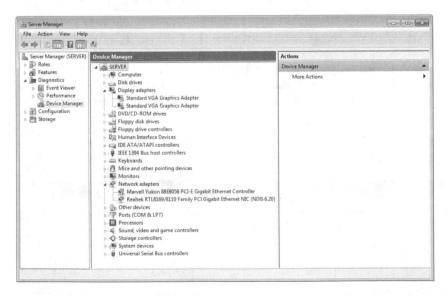

FIGURE 1.8   The Device Manager uses icons to warn you if there's a problem with a device.

If you examine the device's properties, as shown in Figure 1.9, the Device Status area tells you a bit more about what's wrong. As you can see in Figure 1.9, the problem here is that the device's driver isn't installed. Either try Device Manager's suggested remedy (in this case, click Update Driver to locate a driver for the device) or launch the hardware troubleshooter.

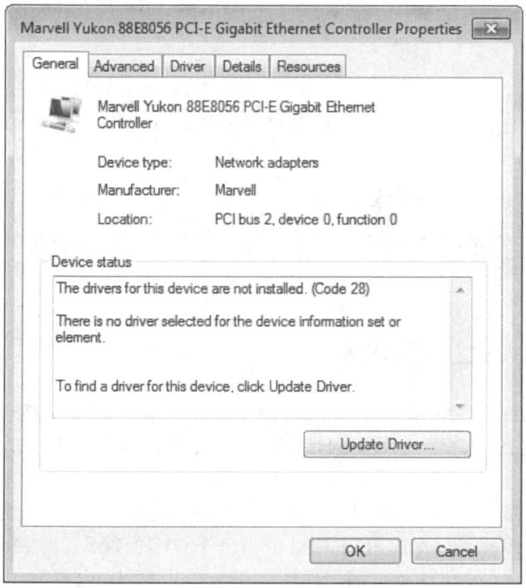

FIGURE 1.9   The Device Status area tells you if the device isn't working properly.

> **NOTE**
>
> Device Manager has several dozen error codes. See the following Microsoft Knowledge Base article for a complete list of the codes, as well as solutions to try in each case: http://support.microsoft.com/kb/310123/. (This page shows codes for XP, but they also apply to Windows Home Server.)

Device Manager uses three different icons to indicate the device's current status:

- ▶ A black exclamation mark (!) on a yellow field tells you that there's a problem with the device.

- ▶ A red X tells you that the device is disabled or missing.

- ▶ A blue i on a white field tells you that the device's Use Automatic Settings check box (on the Resources tab) is deactivated and that at least one of the device's resources was selected manually. Note that the device might be working just fine, so this icon doesn't indicate a problem. If the device isn't working properly, however, the manual setting might be the cause. (For example, the device might have a DIP switch or jumper set to a different resource.)

Updating the NIC Device Driver

If a device is flagged on your system but you don't notice problems, you can usually get away with just ignoring the flag. I've seen lots of systems that run perfectly well with flagged devices, so this falls under the "If it ain't broke..." school of troubleshooting. The danger here is that tweaking your system to try to get rid of the flag can cause other—usually more serious—problems. Otherwise, a good next step is to get an updated device driver from the manufacturer and then install it.

Follow these steps to update a device driver:

1. If you have a floppy disk or CD with the updated driver, insert the disk or CD. If you downloaded the driver from the Internet, decompress the driver file, if necessary.

2. In Device Manager, click the device you want to work with.

3. Select Action, Update Driver. (You can also open the device's property sheet, display the Driver tab, and click Update Driver.)

Handling Multiple Network Subnets

By default, Windows Home Server assumes that all the computers on your home network lie within the same *subnet*, which is a subsection of a network that uses related IP addresses. For example, suppose that your Windows Home Server computer uses the IP address 192.168.1.254 and a subnet mask of 255.255.255.0. This means that the subnet that Windows Home Server can "see" is the IP address range 192.168.1.1 to 192.168.1.254. Working from client to server, any computer on your network that has an IP address within that range can therefore "see" Windows Home Server and connect to it. Windows Home Server allows this because its Windows Firewall is configured to allow only traffic that comes from the local subnet.

This works fine in the majority of home networks. However, you may have clients on your network that aren't on the same subnet as Windows Home Server. For example, you might have clients that use IP addresses in the range 192.168.0.2 to 192.168.0.254. (The default address in some routers is 192.168.0.1, so if you have clients that get IP addresses assigned from that router, the addresses will be in the 192.168.0.*x* subnet.) This represents a different subnet, so those clients might not be able to see Windows Home Server or connect to it.

To handle this problem, you need to configure the Windows Home Server subnet mask, which is a series of numbers that looks something like an IP address, but that tells Windows Home Server which subnet it's part of. On most systems the default subnet mask is 255.255.255.0, which means that the subnet consists of those computers where the first three IP address values are identical, and that have any value in the fourth position. For example, if the router address is 192.168.1.1 and your Windows Home Server machine uses the 255.255.255.0 subnet mask, the server will only see computers with IP addresses that start with 192.168.1 (that is, 192.168.1.2 through 192.168.1.254). The server will *not* see computers that use addresses such as 192.168.0.2 and 192.168.0.3.

To broaden the subnet to include any value in the third and fourth IP address positions, you need to use the subnet mask 255.255.0.0. For example, if the router address is

192.168.1.1 and your Windows Home Server machine uses the 255.255.0.0 subnet mask, the server will see computers with IP addresses that start with 192.168.0 (that is, 192.168.0.2 through 192.168.0.254), 192.168.1 (that is, 192.168.1.2 through 192.168.1.254), and so on.

Assuming you've already configured your Windows Home Server with a static IP address, as I described earlier, follow these steps to adjust the subnet mask:

1. Log on to Windows Home Server either locally or by using a Remote Desktop connection. (See "Making a Remote Desktop Connection to the Server," later in this chapter.)

2. Select Start, type **network**, and then click View Network Connections to open the Network Connections window.

TIP

You can also click the network icon in the notification area, click Open Network and Sharing Center, and then click Change Adapter Settings.

---

3. Double-click the icon for the connection to your local area network. The connection's Status dialog box appears.

4. Click Properties. The connection's property sheet appears.

5. On the General tab, click Internet Protocol Version 4 (TCP/IPv4), and then click Properties.

6. Use the Subnet Mask field to change the mask to 255.255.0.0, as shown in Figure 1.10.

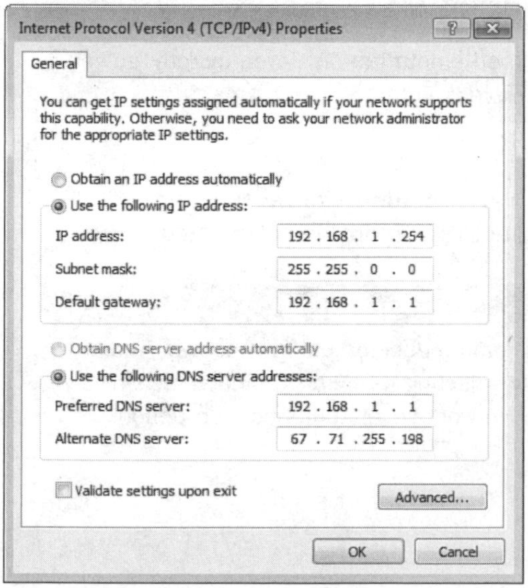

FIGURE 1.10   To handle multiple subnets, use the subnet mask 255.255.0.0.

7. Click OK to return to the connection's property sheet.

8. Click Close to return to the Status dialog box.

9. Click Close.

Making a Remote Desktop Connection to the Server

Windows Home Server's Remote Desktop feature enables you to connect to the server from a workgroup computer and use the server's desktop just as though you were sitting in front of it. This is handy if you can't leave your desk but need to tweak a setting or run a program on the server.

NOTE

This section gives you just a bare-bones look at remote desktop connections. For an in-depth treatment, **SEE** "Connecting via Remote Desktop Connection," **P. 153**.

Making Sure That Windows Home Server Is Ready to Host

Out of the box, Windows Home Server is configured to host remote desktop sessions using the Administrator account. However, just to be safe, you should run through the following steps to make sure that Windows Home Server is configured properly:

1. Select Start, right-click Computer, and then click Properties to open the System Properties window.

2. Click the Remote Settings link. The System Properties dialog box appears with the Remote tab displayed.

TIP

To open the System Properties dialog box with the Remote tab displayed directly, select Start, type **systempropertiesremote**, and then press Enter.

3. In the Remote Desktop group, make sure that the Allow Connections from Computers Running Any Version of Remote Desktop option is activated.

TIP

If your network will only connect to the server's remote desktop using Windows 7 computers, you can ensure much greater security by selecting the Allow Connections Only from Computers Running Remote Desktop with Network Level Authentication option.

4. Click Select Users to display the Remote Desktop Users dialog box.

5. Above the Add button, you should see Administrator Already Has Access. If not, click Add to display the Select Users dialog box, type **Administrator**, and click OK.

6. Click OK to return to the System Properties dialog box.

7. Click OK.

Making the Connection to the Server

On the client computer, you can now connect to the host computer's desktop. Follow these steps:

1. Select Start, All Programs, Accessories, Remote Desktop Connection. (In Windows XP, select Start, All Programs, Accessories, Communications, Remote Desktop Connection.) The Remote Desktop Connection dialog box appears.

2. In the Computer text box, type the name or the IP address of the Windows Home Server computer.

3. Click Connect. Windows prompts you to enter your security credentials.

4. If the displayed username is something other than Administrator, click Use Another Account and then type **Administrator** in the User Name text box.

5. Type the Windows Home Server Administrator account password in the Password box, and then click OK. (Note that in subsequent logons, you'll only need to type the password.)

The remote desktop then appears on your computer. If you're working in full-screen mode, move the mouse to the top of the screen to see the connection bar, shown in Figure 1.11.

If you want the connection bar to appear all the time, click to activate the Pin button. If you need to work with your own desktop, you have two choices:

▶ Click the connection bar's Minimize button to minimize the Remote Desktop window.

▶ Click the connection bar's Restore button to display the Remote Desktop window.

Disconnecting from the Server

When you finish with the Remote Desktop session, you have two choices for disconnecting:

▶ Using the Windows Home Server desktop and selecting Start, Log Off.

▶ Clicking the Close button in the connection bar. Windows displays a dialog box to let you know that your remote session will be disconnected. Click OK.

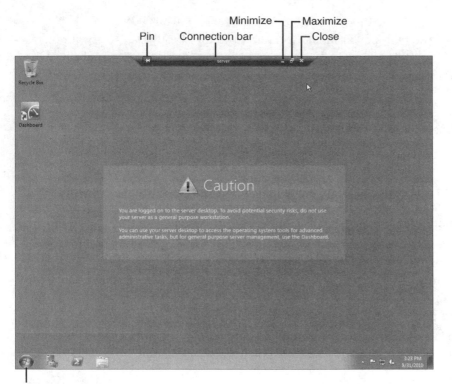

Windows Home Server Start button

FIGURE 1.11   After you've connected and the remote computer's desktop appears on your screen, move the mouse to the top of the screen to see the connection bar.

From Here

▶ For an in-depth treatment of remote desktop connections, **SEE** "Connecting via Remote Desktop Connection," **P. 153.**

▶ For the details on setting up your router for remote access sessions, **SEE** "Setting Up Port Forwarding on the Router," **P. 165.**

▶ To learn how to share a Windows Home Server media folder, **SEE** Chapter 8, "Streaming and Sharing Digital Media."

CHAPTER 2

Setting Up and Working with User Accounts

IN THIS CHAPTER

▶ Understanding Security Groups

▶ Adding a New User

▶ Automating Client Logons

▶ Modifying User Accounts

Windows Home Server doesn't really do much until you connect one or more client machines to the network by installing the Windows Home Server Connector software (as described in Chapter 3, "Adding Devices to the Windows Home Server Network"). However, the Connector software won't install properly unless Windows Home Server recognizes the current user account on the client computer. Because, out of the box, Windows Home Server really has only one working user account—the Administrator account (there are a few other built-in accounts that you can ignore)—you won't be able to connect any machines to the network right away. Instead, you need to set up user accounts for each person who'll be accessing Windows Home Server. This chapter shows you how to set up user accounts using the Home Server Dashboard. It also takes you through a few useful techniques for managing those accounts.

> ▶ **SEE** "Installing Windows Home Server Connector on the Client Computers," **P. 49**.

Understanding Security Groups

Security for Windows Home Server user accounts is handled mostly (and most easily) by assigning each user to a particular security group. For example, the default Administrator account is part of the Administrators group. Each security group is defined with a specific set of access and rights, and any user added to a group is automatically granted that group's access and rights.

Windows Home Server has three main security groups:

▶ **Administrators**—Members of this group have complete control over the server, meaning they can access all folders and files; install and uninstall programs (including legacy programs) and devices; create, modify, and remove user accounts; install Windows updates, service packs, and fixes; use Safe mode; repair Windows; take ownership of objects; and more. For safety, only the Administrator account should be a member of this group.

▶ **Remote Desktop Users**—Members of this group have access to log on to the server remotely (from inside or outside the local area network, or LAN) using the Remote Desktop feature.

▶ **SEE** "Connecting via Remote Desktop Connection," **P. 153**.

▶ **SEE** "Connecting via the Internet," **P. 163**.

▶ **Users**—Members of this group can access files only in their own folders and in the server's shared folders, change their account's password, and run programs that don't require administrative-level rights.

For each user and for each shared folder on the server, you can apply an *access level*, which determines what the user can do with the folder. There are three levels:

▶ **Full Access**—This level means that the user has read/write permissions on the share: he can traverse subfolders, run programs, open documents, make changes to documents, create new files and folders, and delete files and folders.

▶ **Read Only**—This level means that the user has read-only permission on the shared folder: He can traverse subfolders, run programs, and open documents, but he can't make changes to the shared folder or any of its contents.

▶ **No Access**—This level prevents the user from even viewing a shared folder.

Besides the main security groups I mentioned earlier, Windows Home Server defines a list of groups that specify remote web access to the server's features, such as the server Dashboard, shared folders, and the client computers:

▶ **RA_AllowAddInAccess**—Members of this group have remote access to the server's add-in programs.

▶ **RA_AllowComputerAccess**—Members of this group have remote access to the client computers on the network.

▶ **RA_AllowDashboardAccess**—Members of this group have remote access to the Windows Home Server Dashboard.

▶ **RA_AllowHomePageLinks**—Members of this group have remote access to the links that appear on the Windows Home Server remote home page.

▶ **RA_AllowMediaAccess**—Members of this group have remote access to media streaming on Windows Home Server.

▶ **RA_AllowNetworkAlertAccess**—Members of this group can view network health alert messages.

▶ **RA_AllowRemoteAccess**—Members of this group can access the server remotely via the web.

▶ **RA_AllowShareAccess**—Members of this group have remote access to the Windows Home Server shared folders.

More Windows Home Server Security Groups

For the sake of completeness, here's a list of the other security groups defined by Windows Home Server:

▶ **Backup Operators**—Members of this group can access the Backup program and use it to back up and restore folders and files, no matter what access is set on those objects.

▶ **Certificate Services DCOM Access**—Members of this group can add security certificates to the computer.

▶ **Cryptographic Operators**—Members of this group can perform cryptographic tasks.

▶ **DHCP Administrators**—Members of this group have full control of the DHCP service.

▶ **DHCP Users**—Members of this group have read-only access on the DHCP service.

▶ **Distributed COM Users**—Members of this group can start, activate, and use Distributed COM (DCOM) objects.

▶ **Event Log Readers**—Members of this group can access and read Windows Home Server's event logs.

▶ **Guests**—Members of this group have the same privileges as those of the Users group. The exception is the default Guest account, which is not allowed to change its account password.

▶ **HomeUsers Security Group**—Members of this group are assigned security privileges for accessing a Windows 7 homegroup. All Windows 7 user accounts (except the Guest account) are assigned to this group if Windows Home Server joins a homegroup.

▶ **IIS_IUSRS**—Members of this group can access an Internet Information Services (IIS) website installed on the Windows Home Server computer.

▶ **Network Configuration Operators**—Members of this group have a subset of the Administrator-level rights that enable them to install and configure networking features.

▶ **Performance Log Users**—Members of this group can use the Performance snap-in to monitor performance counters, logs, and alerts, both locally and remotely.

▶ **Performance Monitor Users**—Members of this group can use the Performance snap-in to monitor performance counters only, both locally and remotely.

▶ **Power Users**—Members of this group have a subset of the Administrator group privileges. Power Users can't back up or restore files, replace system files, take ownership of files, or install or remove device drivers. In addition, Power Users can't install applications that explicitly require the user to be a member of the Administrators group.

▶ **Print Operators**—Members of this group can administer network printers.

▶ **Replicator**—Members of this group can replicate files across a domain.

▶ **Windows Media Center**—Members of this group can access Windows Media Center on network clients as part of Windows Home Server's Media Center Connector technology.

The rest of this chapter shows you the various methods Windows Home Server offers to create, modify, disable, and remove user accounts.

Adding a New User

As I mentioned earlier, you can't access Windows Home Server shares until you configure Windows Home Server with a user account that has the same logon name as a user account on the client computer. You have two ways to go about this:

▶ If the user account already exists on the client, create a new account on Windows Home Server that uses the same username.

▶ If the user account doesn't exist on the client, create the account both on the client and on Windows Home Server. (It doesn't matter which order you do this; just make sure that both accounts have the same username and password.)

Before getting to the specifics of creating a user account on Windows Home Server, the next few sections take you through some important password-related material.

Setting the Password Length and Complexity

Windows Home Server maintains several password policies that determine the length and complexity of the passwords you can assign to the Windows Home Server accounts. Before creating an account, you should specify the policy you want to use. You have four choices:

▶ **Weak**—This is the default policy, and it has no restrictions on password length or complexity. You can specify any password you want for most users (with the exception of users granted Remote Access; see the Strong policy, which follows). Note that this policy implies that you can set up accounts without any password.

▶ **Medium**—This policy requires that all passwords be at least five characters long. This policy has no restrictions on password complexity.

▶ **Best**—This policy requires that all passwords be at least five characters long and that they contain three out of the following four character types: lowercase letters, uppercase letters, numbers, and symbols (!, @, #, $, and so on).

▶ **Strong**—This policy requires that all passwords be at least seven characters long and that they contain three out of the following four character types: lowercase letters, uppercase letters, numbers, and symbols (!, @, #, $, and so on). Note that every user who gets Remote Access must have a strong password, even if you've configured Windows Home Server to use the Weak or Medium policy.

Follow these steps to specify the Windows Home Server password policy:

1. Launch the Windows Home Server Dashboard.

2. Select the Users section.

3. Click Set the Password Policy. The Dashboard opens the Change the Password Policy dialog box, shown in Figure 2.1.

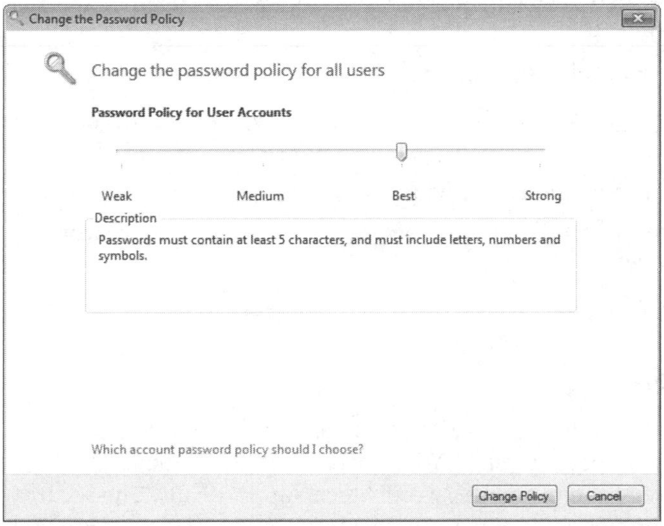

FIGURE 2.1   In the Change the Password Policy dialog box, use the Password Policy for User Accounts slider to set the user accounts password policy.

4. Click and drag the Password Policy for User Accounts slider to the policy setting you want: Weak, Medium, Best, or Strong.

5. Click Change Policy and then click OK when Windows Home Server confirms the change.

Customizing the Password Length Requirement

You saw in the previous section that each Windows Home Server password policy has a length component:

▶ **Weak**—Passwords can be any length.

▶ **Medium**—Passwords must be at least five characters.

▶ **Best**—Passwords must be at least five characters.

▶ **Strong**—Passwords must be at least seven characters.

To increase security on your Windows Home Server, you might want to override these minimums. For example, you might want to require a minimum length of 8 characters or more for all users to make your network even safer from potential Internet-based intrusions.

You can override the minimum password length using the Local Group Policy Editor. Follow these steps:

1. Log on to the Windows Home Server computer, or establish a Remote Desktop connection to the server.

2. Select Start, type **group**, and then click Edit Group Policy in the search results. The Local Group Policy Editor appears.

▶ **SEE** "Using the Local Group Policy Editor," **P. 533.**

3. Select the Computer Configuration, Windows Settings, Security Settings, Account Policies, Password Policy branch.

4. Double-click the Minimum Password Length policy.

5. Use the Password Must Be at Least text box to type your new minimum password length, and then click OK.

6. Close the Local Group Policy Editor.

Building a Strong Password

If you just use your home network locally, the passwords you assign to each user account aren't that important from a security point of view. Your goal should be to make them easy to remember and avoid those "I forgot my password!" tech support calls. The security landscape changes drastically when you add users to the Remote Desktop Users group, and thus enable them to connect to the network via the Internet. In this case, it's crucial to supply remote users with strong passwords. Ideally, when you're creating such a password, you want to pick one that that provides maximum protection without sacrificing convenience. Follow these guidelines when choosing a password:

> **TIP**
>
> The password guidelines I provide will ensure that your passwords exceed Windows Home Server's password policy complexity minimums. For an extra challenge, submit the password (or, ideally, text that's similar to your password) to an online password complexity checker. Microsoft runs such a checker at www.microsoft.com/protect/fraud/passwords/checker.aspx. You can also run a Google search on "password complexity checker" to see others.

▶ **Use passwords that are at least eight characters long**—Shorter passwords are susceptible to programs that try every letter combination. You can combine the 26 letters of the alphabet into about 12 million different five-letter word combinations, which is no big deal for a fast program. If you bump things up to eight-letter passwords, however, the total number of combinations rises to 200 *billion*, which would take even the fastest computer quite a while. If you use 12-letter passwords, as many experts recommend, the number of combinations goes beyond mind-boggling: 90 *quadrillion*, or 90,000 trillion!

▶ **Mix up your character types**—The secret to a strong password is including characters from the following categories: lowercase letters, uppercase letters, numbers, and symbols. If you include at least one character from three (or, even better, all four) of these categories, you're well on your way to a strong password.

▶ **Don't be too obvious**—Because forgetting a password is inconvenient, many people use meaningful words or numbers so that their password will be easier to remember. Unfortunately, this means that they often use extremely obvious things such as their name, the name of a family member or colleague, their birth date or Social Security number, or even their system username. Being this obvious is just asking for trouble.

CAUTION

After going to all this trouble to create an indestructible password, don't blow it by writing it on a sticky note and then attaching it to your notebook keyboard! Even writing it on a piece of paper and then throwing the paper away is dangerous. Determined crackers have been known to go through a company's trash looking for passwords. (This is known in the trade as *dumpster diving*.) Also, don't use the password itself as your Windows 7, Vista, or XP password hint. Finally, if you've thought of a particularly clever password, don't suddenly become unclever and tell someone. Your password should be stored in your head alongside all those "wasted youth" things you don't want anyone to know about.

Changing the Password on the Client

If you already have a user account on the client computer, you might want to adjust the account password before adding the account to Windows Home Server. For example, if you'll be accessing the network remotely with the account, you might want to specify a strong password when you set up the account in Windows Home Server. If you know the new password you want to use, it makes sense to update the client account with the new password in advance.

If you're running Windows 7 or Vista on the client, or if you're running XP with the Welcome screen disabled, follow these steps to change an account password:

1. Log on to the account you want to modify.
2. Press Ctrl+Alt+Delete.
3. Click Change a Password. (Click Change Password in XP.)
4. Type the old password in the appropriate box.

5. Type the new password in the appropriate box, and then type it again in the Confirm Password text box. (It's Confirm New Password in XP.)

6. Press Enter. Windows changes the password.

7. Click OK.

If your client is running XP with the Welcome screen enabled, follow these steps to change an account password:

1. Log on to the account you want to modify.

2. Select Start, Control Panel, User Accounts.

3. Click the account you want to work with.

4. Click Change My Password.

5. Use the text boxes provided to type your old password, your new password (twice), as well as an optional password hint.

6. Click Change Password.

Adding the User Account

Here are the steps to add an account to Windows Home Server:

1. Launch the Windows Home Server Dashboard.

2. Select the Users section.

3. Click Add a User Account. The Add a User Account Wizard appears.

4. Type the user's first name and last name in the appropriate boxes. (The latter is optional.)

5. Type the user's account (that is, logon) name.

NOTE

The logon name can consist of only letters, numbers, spaces, periods (.), hyphens (-), or underscores (_). The name can't end with a period, and you must use at least one letter or number. Also, the name must be unique among the Windows Home Server accounts.

---

6. Type the password and then type it again in the Confirm Password text box. Keep an eye on the following items (see Figure 2.2):

   ▶ **The Passwords Match**—You see a check mark beside this item if you typed both passwords identically.

   ▶ **The Passwords Must Be at Least X Characters Long**—If the password meets or exceeds the length requirements specified by the Windows Home Server password policy, a check mark appears beside this item. You don't see this item if you're using the Weak password policy.

▶ **The Password Must Meet Complexity Requirements**—If the password meets or exceeds the complexity requirements specified by the password policy, a check mark appears beside this item. You don't see this item if you're using either the Weak or the Medium password policy.

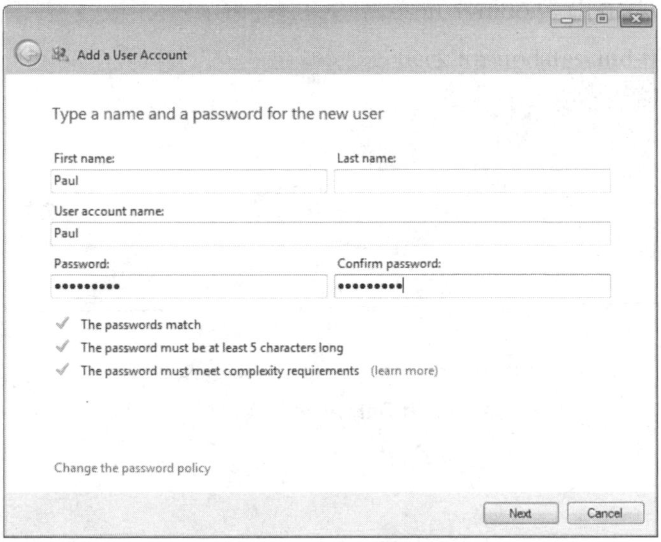

FIGURE 2.2   The password you enter must meet or exceed the length and complexity requirements of the current Windows Home Server password policy.

7. Click Next. The Add a User Account Wizard prompts you to specify the user's access to the shared folders (see Figure 2.3).

8. For each shared folder, use the list to select the option that corresponds to the access you want to give: Full Access, Read Only, or No Access.

9. Click Next. The Add a User Account Wizard prompts you to specify the user's remote web access permissions (see Figure 2.4).

10. If you want to give the user remote web access, leave the Allow Remote Web Access option selected, and then activate the check box beside each feature that you want the user to access via the web. If, instead, you don't want the user to be able to access the network over the web, select the Do Not Allow Remote Web Access option.

11. Click Create Account. Windows Home Server adds the user account, sets the shared folder access, and creates a shared folder for the user. If you left the Allow Remote Access option activated, Windows Home Server adds the user to the appropriate security groups (such as RA_AllowShareAccess).

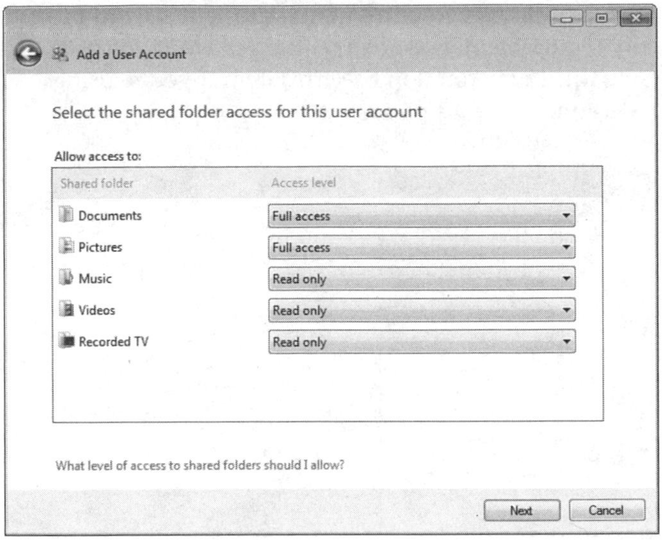

FIGURE 2.3   You can give the new user Full Access, Read Only Access, or No Access to each shared folder.

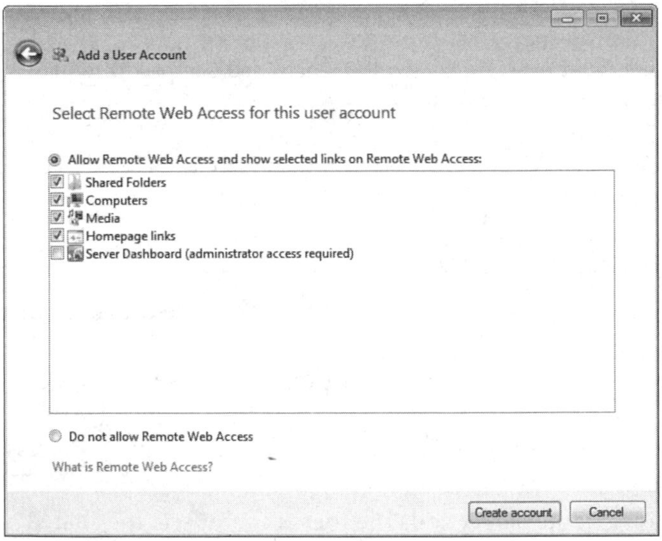

FIGURE 2.4   You can give the new user access to the network via the web, and you can specify the features the user can access.

12. Click Close. The account appears in the Windows Home Server Dashboard's Users section, as shown in Figure 2.5.

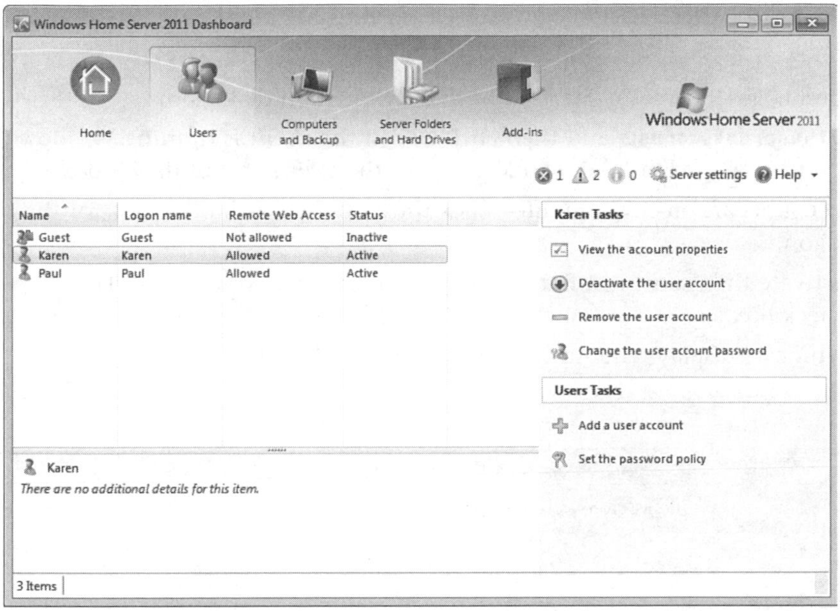

FIGURE 2.5   When you complete the wizard, the new account appears in the Windows Home Server Dashboard's Users tab.

NOTE

Remember that you can add a maximum of 10 user accounts to Windows Home Server.

Automating Client Logons

Many people run their home networks with at least one computer that doesn't use a password—that is, they have a computer that contains no personal or confidential data, just common documents (such as media files) and web access. Anyone in the family can use that PC just by starting it up. Because there's no password, Windows boots right to the desktop without prompting for a logon. That's convenient, but if you have Windows Home Server configured to use the Normal or Complex password policy, you've got a problem because these policies require accounts to have nonblank passwords.

How do you maintain the convenience of a no-logon startup and still get Windows Home Server connectivity? One solution would be to configure Windows Home Server to use the Simple password policy, which allows blank passwords. However, that won't work if the user account is configured for remote access, which requires a strong password. The best workaround I know is to set up the client machine with a password that Windows Home Server is happy with and then configure the client with an automatic logon.

After you add a password to the client machine's user account, use these steps to automate the logon:

1. Press Windows Logo+R (or select Start, Run) to open the Run dialog box.

2. Type **control userpasswords2**, and then click OK. (If the client is running Windows Vista, enter your UAC credentials.) Windows opens the User Account dialog box.

3. If multiple accounts are on the computer, click the account you want to use for the automatic logon.

4. Click to deactivate the Users Must Enter a User Name and Password to Use This Computer check box.

5. Click OK. Windows displays the Automatically Log On dialog box, shown in Figure 2.6.

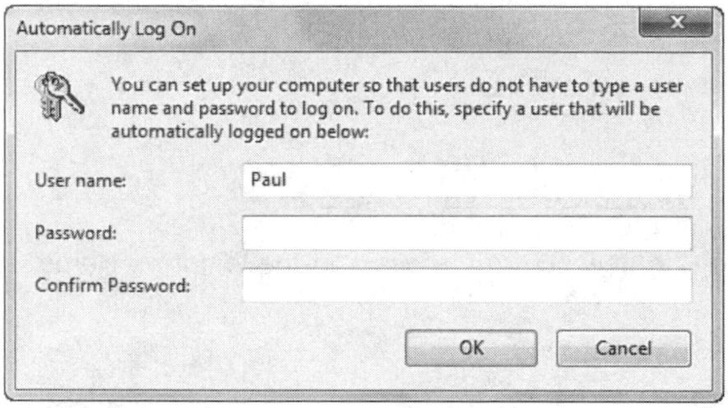

FIGURE 2.6   Use this dialog box to set up an automatic logon for a client computer.

6. Type the account's password in the Password and Confirm Password text boxes.

7. Click OK. Windows configures the automatic logon.

TIP

You can temporarily bypass the automatic logon and display the Windows logon screen by holding down the Shift key while Windows boots.

TIP

If the version of Windows 7 or Windows Vista running on the client doesn't support the User Accounts dialog box, you can still set up an automatic logon by hand using the Registry. Open the Registry Editor (see Chapter 18, "Working with the Windows Home Server Registry") and head for the following Registry key:

```
HKLM\Software\Microsoft\Windows NT\CurrentVersion\Winlogon\
```

Double-click the `AutoAdminLogon` setting and change its value to 1. Double-click the `DefaultUserName` setting and change its value to the username you want to log on automatically. Finally, create a `String` setting named `DefaultPassword` and change its value to the password of the default user.

Modifying User Accounts

After you've added a user to Windows Home Server, you can modify the account as needed via the Windows Home Server Dashboard. You can view the current account properties, change the account password, disable the account, and remove the account. These next few sections take you through these and other account chores.

Before continuing, I should point out that Windows Home Server does come with other tools for modifying user accounts. The server's Windows Server 2008 underpinnings mean that two advanced user account tools are available:

▶ **The User Accounts dialog box**—Select Start, Run, type **control userpasswords2**, and click OK (see Figure 2.7). You saw in the previous section that you can use this dialog box to set up an automatic logon. You can do the same thing for the Windows Home Server machine. You can also display the Advanced tab and then click Advanced to display the Local Users and Groups snap-in, discussed next. Other than that, however, to avoid breaking Windows Home Server's user accounts, you shouldn't use the User Accounts dialog box for any other account-related chores.

FIGURE 2.7   In Windows Home Server, you can do only a limited number of things with the User Accounts dialog box.

CAUTION

Set up Windows Home Server with an automatic logon only if security is absolutely not a problem in your house. Otherwise, you won't be able to lock out unauthorized users from the server, and the results could be catastrophic (depending on the age and rebelliousness of the users in your house).

▶ **The Local Users and Groups snap-in**—Click the Server Manager icon in the taskbar, click Configuration, click Local Users and Groups, and then click Users (see Figure 2.8). This snap-in plays a bit nicer with Windows Home Server than it does the User Accounts dialog box. For example, you can use this snap-in to disable or enable an account, change an account's full name, and give a user access to remotely access the server. You can also make an account a member of a group not used by Windows Home Server. (See "Adding a User to a Group," later in this chapter.) However, some actions—such as renaming an account—can break the account in Windows Home Server, so again you're mostly better off using the Home Server Dashboard.

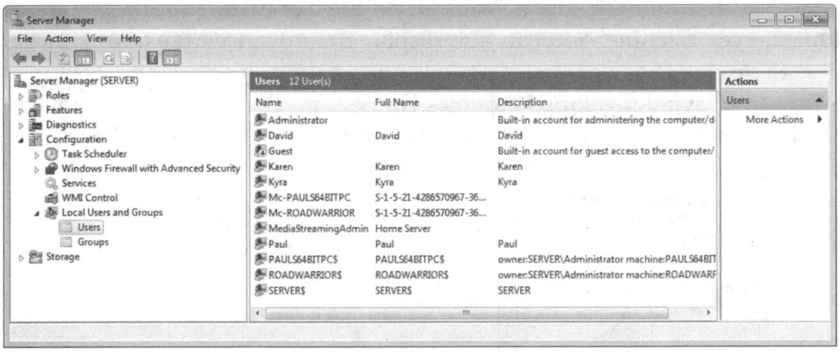

FIGURE 2.8   You can use the Local Users and Groups snap-in for some account-related chores, but use caution.

Viewing Account Properties

When you open the Home Server Dashboard and click the Users icon, you see a list of users with accounts on the server. For each user, you see the full name, the logon name, whether the user has remote access (Allowed or Not Allowed), and the current account status (Active or Inactive). To see more properties, click the account and then click View the Account Properties. Windows Home Server displays the accounts property sheet, as shown in Figure 2.9.

TIP

For faster service, you can also display the user's property sheet either by double-clicking the account or by right-clicking the account and then clicking View the Account Properties.

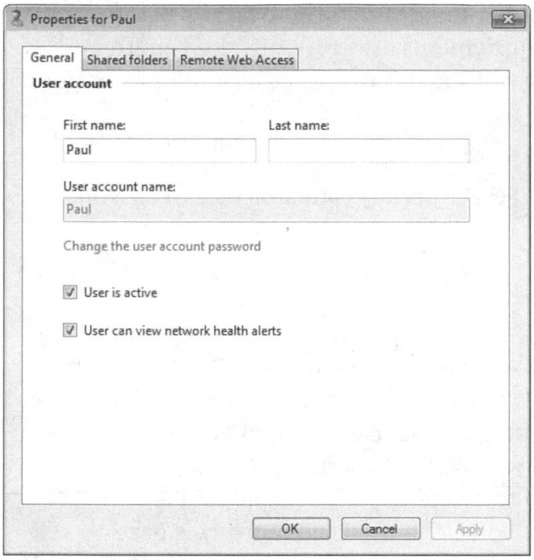

FIGURE 2.9   The property sheet for a Windows Home Server user account.

Here's a quick look at some of the more basic chores you can perform from this dialog box:

▶ **Changing the full name**—Edit the First Name and Last Name text boxes.

▶ **Configuring remote access**—Display the Remote Web Access tab. If you select the Allow Remote Access option, use the list to choose what you want the user to be able to access remotely: shared folders, home computers, and so on.

▶ **Apply shared folder access**—Display the Shared Folders tab and then use the list beside each available share to set the access level to Full Access, Read Only, or No Access.

Changing the Account Password

If you want to change a user's password, here are the steps to follow:

1. Launch the Windows Home Server Dashboard.
2. Select the Users section.
3. Click the user you want to modify.
4. Click Change the User Account Password. Windows Home Server displays the Reset User Password dialog box.

NOTE

If you happen to have the user's property dialog box open, you can also change the password by clicking Change the User Account Password in the General tab.

5. Type the new password in the Password text box. When you're done, make sure that you see check marks in the Password Requirements area for both the Length and Complexity, meaning that your new password meets or exceeds the Windows Home Server password policy requirements.

6. Retype the password in the Confirm Password dialog box.

7. Click Change Password. Windows Home Server displays a dialog box to let you know that it changed the password.

8. Click OK.

TIP

Somewhat unusually, when you change a user's password in the Windows Home Server Dashboard, the program doesn't ask you to first enter the user's current password. Although atypical, it can also come in handy if you (and the user) forget an account's password. Just follow the steps in this section to create a new password for the account. On the downside, note that you won't be able to synchronize the new password with the user's client account because Windows Home Server requires you to provide the forgotten client account password to perform the synchronization.

Disabling a User Account

If you want to prevent an account from accessing the network temporarily, you can disable it by following these steps:

1. Launch the Windows Home Server Dashboard.

2. Select the Users section.

3. Click the user you want to disable.

4. Click Deactivate the User Account. Windows Home Server asks you to confirm.

5. Click Yes.

NOTE

If you have the user's property dialog box open, you can also deactivate the user by selecting the General tab and then deactivating the User Is Active check box.

When the user tries to access the Windows Home Server shares, he sees the message shown in Figure 2.10.

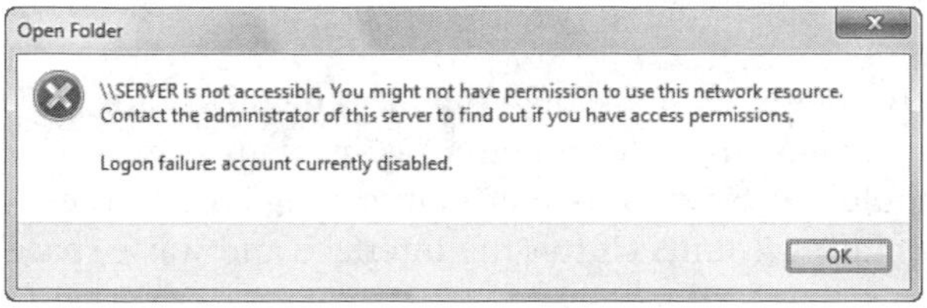

FIGURE 2.10   Disabled users see this message when they try to access the Windows Home Server shared folders.

Enabling a User Account

If you've disabled a user account in Windows Home Server, here are the steps to follow to enable the account and once again allow it to access the network:

1. Launch the Windows Home Server Dashboard.
2. Select the Users section.
3. Click the user you want to disable.
4. Click Activate the User Account. Windows Home Server asks you to confirm.
5. Click Yes.

> **NOTE**
>
> If you have the user's property dialog box open, you can also activate the user by selecting the General tab and then activating the User Is Active check box.

Enabling the Guest Account

What do you do if you have someone visiting your place and that person wants to, say, access some media on Windows Home Server with his computer? You could allow the person to log on using an existing account, but that might not be reasonable due to privacy or security concerns. Another option would be to set up a user account for that person, but that seems like overkill, particularly for a person on a short visit.

A better solution would be to enable the Guest account and allow your visitor to log on under that account. Here are the steps to follow:

1. Launch the Windows Home Server Dashboard.
2. Select the Users section.
3. Click the Guest user.
4. Click Activate the User Account. Windows Home Server asks you to confirm.
5. Click Yes.

Removing a User Account

Windows Home Server supports up to 10 user accounts, which ought to be plenty for most households, with only the odd Brady Bunch–like clan bumping up against this ceiling. Still, that doesn't mean you should just leave unused accounts lying around the Windows Home Server Dashboard. Dormant accounts clutter the interface and waste space on the server's shares.

If you have a Windows Home Server user account that you no longer need, follow these steps to delete it:

1. Open the Windows Home Server Dashboard.
2. Click the Users icon.
3. Click the user you want to delete.
4. Click Remove the User Account. The Delete a User Account dialog box appears.
5. Click Delete Account.

Adding a User to a Group

You learned earlier that Windows Home Server adds each user to the Users group and to the Remote Desktop Users group if you give that person remote access to the network. It's unlikely that you'll need to add a user to any other group defined by Windows Home Server, but it's not unheard of. For example, if you want to script the Windows Home Server machine from a client machine on the network using Windows Management Instrumentation (WMI), you need to add that user to the Administrators group. (See Chapter 21, "Scripting Windows Home Server.")

Just in case it comes up, here are the steps to follow to add a user to a security group:

1. On the server, select Start, right-click My Computer, and then click Manage to open the Computer Management snap-in.
2. Select Local Users and Groups, Users to display the list of users on the server.
3. Double-click the user you want to work with to open that user's property sheet.
4. Display the Member Of tab.
5. Click Add to display the Select Groups dialog box.
6. Type the name of the group to which you want the user added.

TIP

If you're not sure of the exact group name, click Advanced and then click Find Now to display a complete list of the available groups. Click the group you want to use, and then click OK.

---

7. Click OK. Windows Home Server returns you to the user's property sheet and adds the group to the Member Of list.
8. Click OK.

Allowing a User to Log On to the Windows Home Server Desktop

For security purposes, it's a good idea to allow just the Administrator account to access the Windows Home Server desktop. (Other users can log on to Windows Home Server remotely, but they only see the Windows Home Server Dashboard.) However, if you really need to allow another user to access the desktop, you can configure Windows Home Server to allow this. You can configure the user for a local logon (sitting at the Windows Home Server computer) or a remote logon (from another computer or over the Internet).

CAUTION

If you're going to allow a user access to the Windows Home Server desktop, be sure to assign a strong password to that user's account.

Technically, it's the Administrators group that has permission to log on to Windows Home Server locally and remotely. Therefore, the easiest way to give someone the same permissions is to add that account to the Administrators group. (Refer to the previous section "Adding a User to a Group.")

Allowing a User to Log On Locally

To give a user permission to log on locally, follow these steps:

1. Log on to Windows Home Server.
2. Select Start, Administrative Tools, Local Security Policy. The Local Security Settings snap-in appears.

TIP

You can also open the Local Security Setting snap-in by selecting Start, Run to open the Run dialog box, typing `secpol.msc`, and then clicking OK.

3. Open the Security Settings, Local Policies, User Rights Assignment branch.
4. Double-click the Allow Log On Locally policy.
5. Click Add User or Group to display the Select Users or Groups dialog box.
6. Type the user's name, and then click OK to return to the policy's property sheet.
7. Click OK.

Allowing a User to Log On Remotely

To give a user permission to log on remotely, you have two choices:

▶ Follow steps 1 through 7 from the previous section, but instead of adding the user to the Allow Log On Locally policy, add the user to the Allow Log On Through Remote Desktop Services policy.

▶ Add the user via the Remote Desktop settings.

For the latter, here are the steps to follow:

1. Log on to Windows Home Server.
2. Select Start, right-click Computer, and then click Properties.
3. Click the Remote Settings link. The System Properties dialog box appears with the Remote tab displayed.
4. Click Select Users. The Remote Desktop Users dialog box appears.
5. Click Add to open the Select Users dialog box.
6. Type the user's name, and then click OK to return to the Remote Desktop Users dialog box.
7. Click OK.

From Here

▶ For details on running the Connector software, **SEE** "Installing Windows Home Server Connector on the Client Computers," **P. 49.**

▶ To learn how to start a remote session from inside the LAN, **SEE** "Connecting via Remote Desktop Connection," **P. 153.**

▶ For the details on making remote connections via the Internet, **SEE** "Connecting via the Internet," **P. 163.**

▶ You can use Windows Home Server's monitoring tools to monitor each user's network activity. **SEE** "Monitoring Users via Task Manager," **P. 254.**

▶ To learn how to use the Registry Editor, **SEE** Chapter 18, "Working with the Windows Home Server Registry."

▶ To learn more about the Local Group Policy Editor, **SEE** "Using the Local Group Policy Editor," **P. 533.**

▶ To learn more about WMI scripting, **SEE** "Programming the Windows Management Instrumentation Service," **P. 617.**

CHAPTER 3

Adding Devices to the Windows Home Server Network

IN THIS CHAPTER

▶ Installing Windows Home Server Connector on the Client Computers

▶ Using a Mac on Your Windows Home Server Network

▶ Using a Linux Client on Your Windows Home Server Network

▶ Adding Other Devices to the Network

▶ Adding an Xbox 360 to the Network

A network consisting of just a single Windows Home Server box isn't much of a "network;" it goes without saying. To make things interesting, you need to add one or more devices to the network. By "devices," I mean other computers, first and foremost. As you'll see, Windows 7, Windows Vista, and Windows XP machines can participate in the full extent of the Windows Home Server experience by accessing the Windows Home Server shares, streaming media, and getting backed up nightly. However, that doesn't mean these are the only computers you can insert into your network. Older Windows boxes, Macs, and Linux machines can also get in on the action by accessing the Windows Home Server shared folders. In some cases, with the right software installed, you can connect remotely to the network from these machines.

By "devices," I also mean noncomputer equipment, including Xbox consoles. This chapter gives you the details on connecting these other devices to your Windows Home Server network.

Installing Windows Home Server Connector on the Client Computers

Your key to the riches of Windows Home Server from a client computer's point of view is a program called Windows Home Server Connector, which does the following:

▶ Locates the Windows Home Server on the network.

▶ Registers your computer with Windows Home Server.

▶ Configures Windows Home Server to automatically back up your computer every night.

▶ Configures your computer to receive local and network health alerts.

▶ Installs the client version of the Restore Files or Folders Wizard, which enables you to restore backed-up files and folders.

▶ Adds a desktop shortcut for the Windows Home Server shared folders.

▶ Installs the Launchpad application, which gives you quick access to manual backups, Remote Web Access, the shared folders, and the Dashboard. It also installs a notification area icon that tells you the current network status.

▶ Installs the client version of the Windows Home Server Dashboard.

Supported Operating Systems

The good news is that it's the Connector program that lets your client machine get in on the complete Windows Home Server experience. The bad news is that the Connector software only works on clients running newer versions of Windows, as follows:

▶ Windows 7 Home Basic

▶ Windows 7 Starter

▶ Windows 7 Home Premium

▶ Windows 7 Professional

▶ Windows 7 Enterprise

▶ Windows 7 Ultimate

▶ Windows Vista Home Basic with Service Pack 2

▶ Windows Vista Home Premium with Service Pack 2

▶ Windows Vista Business with Service Pack 2

▶ Windows Vista Enterprise with Service Pack 2

▶ Windows Vista Ultimate with Service Pack 2

▶ Windows Vista Starter with Service Pack 2

▶ Windows XP Media Center Edition 2005 with Service Pack 3

▶ Windows XP Home with Service Pack 3

▶ Windows XP Professional with Service Pack 3

Note that for Windows 7 and Windows Vista, both 32-bit and 64-bit versions are supported (the exceptions being Windows 7 Starter and Windows Vista Starter, which only come in 32-bit versions). Microsoft has posted no other system requirements for Windows Home Server Connector. In other words, if your system is capable of running any of the preceding operating systems and can make a wired or wireless connection to your network, you can install and run Windows Home Server Connector.

Preparing to Install Windows Home Server Connector

Before installing Windows Home Server Connector, you should make sure that your client is ready for the installation and for joining the Windows Home Server network. Here's a checklist:

- ▶ Set up a wired or wireless connection to your network.

- ▶ Make sure the client's computer name is unique on the network.

- ▶ Make sure the client's workgroup name is the same as the workgroup name that Windows Home Server uses. (As I mentioned in Chapter 1, "Setting Up Your Windows Home Server Network," however, it's actually more important to make sure the client is on the same network subnet as Windows Home Server.)

- ▶ **SEE** "Handling Multiple Network Subnets," **P. 24**.

- ▶ Make sure you can see the Windows Home Server on your network. (In Windows 7, click Windows Explorer on the taskbar, and then click Network; in Windows Vista, select Start, Network; in Windows XP, select Start, My Network Places, and then either click the View Workgroup Computers link or select Entire Network, Microsoft Windows Network, and then click your workgroup.)

- ▶ (Optional) On the client, set up the user account you want to use with Windows Home Server (if you don't want to use an existing account).

- ▶ On Windows Home Server, set up a user account with the same username and password as the client user account.

Running the Windows Home Server Connector Setup Program

With your Windows 7, Windows Vista, or Windows XP client PC ready, here are the steps to follow to install the Windows Home Server Connector:

1. Launch the web browser and navigate to http://*server*/connect, where *server* is the name (or the IP address) of your Windows Home Server machine. The Connect Your Computer to the Server page loads, as shown in Figure 3.1.

NOTE

If you're using Internet Explorer, when you navigate to http://*server*/connect, the Information bar might show up to tell you that "Intranet settings are now turned off by default." If so, click the Information bar, click Enable Intranet Settings, and then click Yes when Internet Explorer asks you to confirm.

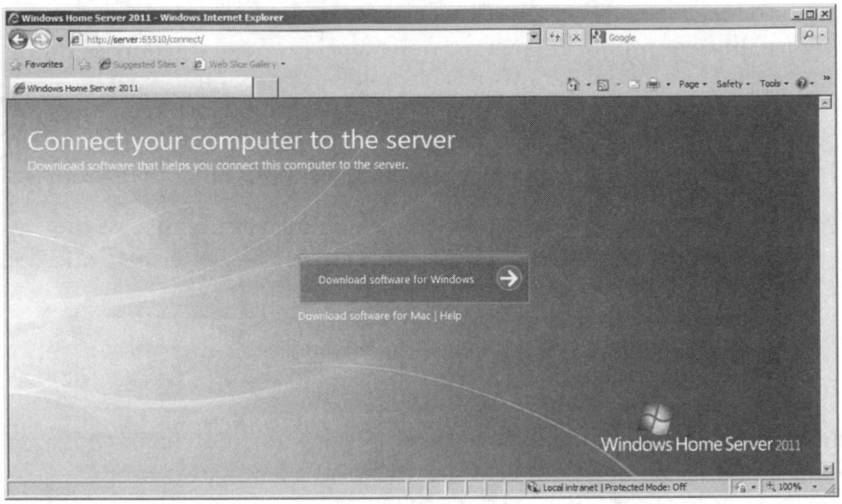

FIGURE 3.1   Surf to http://*server*/connect to access the Windows Home Server Connector software.

2. Click Download Software for Windows. What happens from here depends on your web browser:

   ▶ **Internet Explorer**—When the browser asks if you want to run or save the file, click Run, and then when you're prompted to confirm, click Run. The Connect a Computer to the Server dialog box appears.

   ▶ **Firefox**—When the browser asks if you want to save the file, click Save File, and then double-click the downloaded file.

   ▶ **Safari**—When the browser asks if you want to run or save the file, click Run, and then when you're prompted to confirm, click Run.

   ▶ **Chrome**—When the browser asks you to confirm the download, click Save, and then click the downloaded file.

3. If you see the User Account Control dialog box, enter your User Account Control credentials to authorize the installation. The Connect a Computer to the Server Wizard loads, locates your Windows Home Server, and then displays the initial dialog box.

4. Click Next. The wizard checks your system to ensure it meets the minimum requirements for using the connector software. If your PC passes muster, you see the This Computer Meets the Prerequisites dialog box.

5. Click Next. Windows Home Server installs the connector software. When the install is complete, you're prompted for the Windows Home Server password, as shown in Figure 3.2.

6. Type the Windows Home Server password, and then click Next. The wizard prompts you to review and, if needed, modify the computer's description.

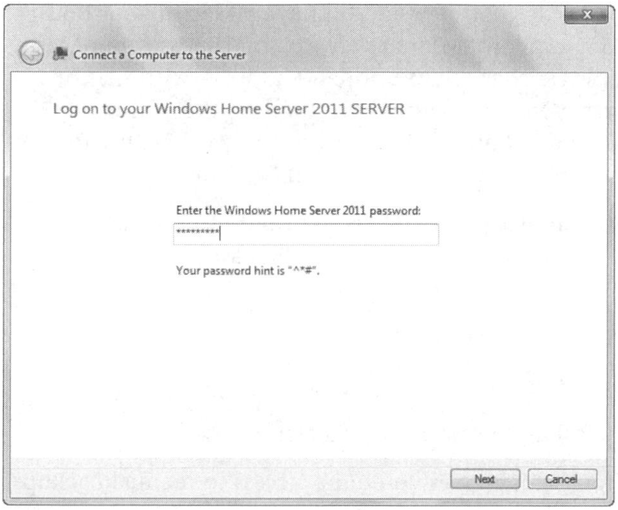

FIGURE 3.2   When the Windows Home Server Connector software is installed, you need to log on to Windows Home Server.

7. Edit the description, if you feel like it, and then click Next. The wizard asks if you want to wake up the computer to back it up.

8. Click the Yes option to have Windows Home Server wake up your sleeping computer. If you'd prefer to leave your computer in sleep mode, click the No option instead.

9. Click Next. The wizard asks if you want to participate in the Windows Customer Experience Improvement Program, which collects anonymous information about how you use Windows Home Server.

10. Click Yes or click No, and then click Next. The wizard joins your computer to the network and configures Windows Home Server to back up your computer nightly.

11. If you don't want to open the Dashboard right away, click to deactivate the Open the Dashboard to Administer Your Server check box, and then click Finish.

The wizard adds a shortcut to the server shares on your desktop. Note that this shortcut appears on the desktop for all users of the computer. Also, the Launchpad icon appears in the notification area.

Using a Mac on Your Windows Home Server Network

One of the important networking layers used by all Microsoft networks—including, of course, your Windows Home Server network—is called Server Message Block (SMB). It is via SMB that Windows PCs can share folders on the network and access folders that other Windows PCs have shared. In a very real sense, SMB *is* the network.

SMB's central role in Windows networking is good news if you have a Mac in your household. That's because all versions of OS X support SMB natively, so you can use your Mac not only to view the Windows Home Server shares, but to open and work with files on those shares. (That's provided, of course, you have permission to access the share and OS X has an application that's compatible with whatever file you want to work with.) You can even switch things around and view your Mac shares from within Windows.

Even better, Windows Home Server 2011 now supports Macs right out of the box. Specifically, Window Home Server 2011 comes with a program called MacConnector, which does the following:

- ▶ Locates the Windows Home Server on the network.
- ▶ Registers your Mac with Windows Home Server.
- ▶ Configures your Mac to receive local and network health alerts.
- ▶ Installs the Launchpad application, which gives you quick access to manual backups, Remote Web Access, and the shared folders.
- ▶ Enables you to configure Time Machine to back up your Mac to the server.

The next few sections provide you with the details.

Connecting to the Windows Home Server Network

First, connect your Mac to the Windows Home Server network. If the Mac is near your network's switch (or router, depending on your configuration), run a network cable from the device to the Mac. If you're using a wireless connection instead, follow these steps to connect your Mac to the wireless portion of your Windows Home Server network:

1. Click the System Preferences icon in the Dock.
2. Click Network to open the Network preferences.
3. Click AirPort.
4. Use the Network Name list to select your Windows Home Server wireless network ID.

TIP

OS X normally shows the AirPort status icon in the menu bar. If you see that icon, a faster way to initiate a wireless connection is to click the icon and then click the name of the network you want to join.

5. If your network is secure, make sure the Wireless Security list displays the correct security type.
6. Type the security key in the Password text box, and then click OK to return to the Network window. As shown in Figure 3.3, the Status should show Connected.
7. Close the Network preferences window.

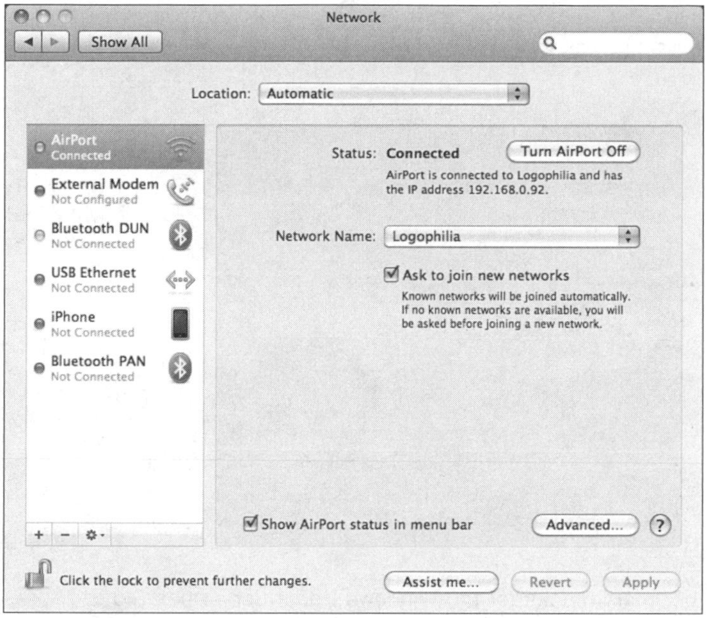

FIGURE 3.3   When you connect your Mac to the Windows Home Server network via wireless, the AirPort tab shows the connection status.

Running the Windows Home Server MacConnector Setup Program on Your Mac

With your Mac ready, here are the steps to follow to install the Windows Home Server MacConnector:

1. Launch Safari and navigate to http://*server*/connect, where *server* is the name (or the IP address) of your Windows Home Server machine. The Connect Your Computer to the Server page loads.

2. Click Download Software for Mac. Safari downloads the MacConnector software.

3. Double-click MacConnector in the Downloads window. Your Mac asks you to confirm that you want to open the application.

4. Click Open. Mac OS X prompts you for your Mac's administrator credentials.

5. Type an administrator's username and password, and then click OK. The Connect a Computer to the Network Wizard loads.

6. Click Continue. The wizard prompts you for your server name or IP address.

7. Type the name or IP address, and then click Continue. The wizard checks your system to ensure it meets the minimum requirements for using the connector software. If your Mac passes muster, the wizard next prompts you for a network name for your Mac. The default is your Mac's name, without the spaces, truncated to 15 characters, if necessary.

8. Adjust the name as needed, and then click Continue. The wizard now asks for the Windows Home Server password, as shown in Figure 3.4.

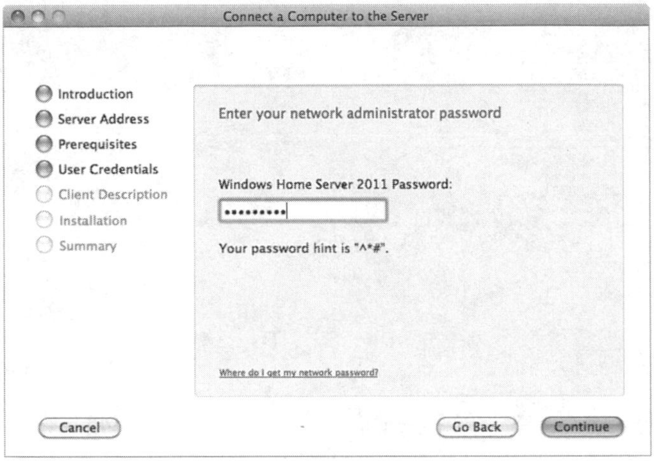

FIGURE 3.4   The MacConnector program asks for the Windows Home Server password.

9. Type the Windows Home Server password, and then click Continue. The wizard prompts you to enter a description for your Mac.

10. Type the description, and then click Continue. The wizard asks if you want to start Launchpad automatically each time your Mac starts.

11. If you don't want Launchpad to start automatically, deactivate the check box.

12. Click Close.

Your Mac opens Launchpad and prompts you to log on. Type a username and password of a Windows Home Server account, and then press Return. Launchpad appears, as shown in Figure 3.5. From here, you can back up your Mac, use Remote Web Access, or access the server's shared folders. Note, however, that if you want to use Dashboard, you must use it on the Windows Home Server machine directly, since there's no Mac version of Dashboard. See "Using a Mac to Make a Remote Desktop Connection to Windows Home Server," later in this chapter.

> **NOTE**
>
> Before you can back up your Mac, you have to configure Time Machine to use Windows Home Server as the backup location; **SEE** "Configuring Time Machine to Back Up Your Mac," **P. 222**.

Mounting a Windows Home Server Shared Folder

You can use the Mac version of Launchpad that's now installed to access the Windows Home Server shared folders. I take you through the details in Chapter 6.

FIGURE 3.5   The Mac version of Launchpad, which opens as soon as you complete the MacConnector installation.

▶ **SEE** "Accessing Shared Folders on Your Mac," **P. 135**.

However, it's also possible to access the server's shares directly through Finder. Before you get started, check that your Mac can see the Windows Home Server computer. Open Finder and then select Go, Network (or press Shift+Command+K). In the Network folder that appears, you see an icon for each network computer that your Mac can see (see Figure 3.6).

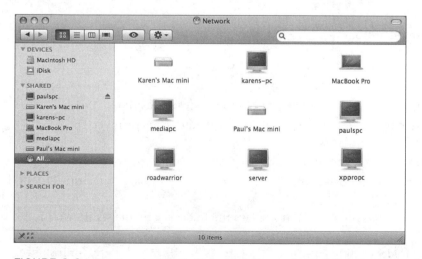

FIGURE 3.6   Check out Finder's Network folder and see if there's an icon for your Windows Home Server computer.

How you proceed depends on whether you see your Windows Home Server computer:

▶ **If you see your Windows Home Server machine**—Double-click the icon to open the server, and then click Connect As.

▶ **If you don't see your Windows Home Server box**—Select Go, Connect to Server (or press Command+K) to open the Connect to Server dialog box. In the Server Address text box, type `smb://server`, where *server* is the name or the IP address of your Windows Home Server, and then click Connect.

Either way, Mac OS X displays the logon dialog box shown in Figure 3.7.

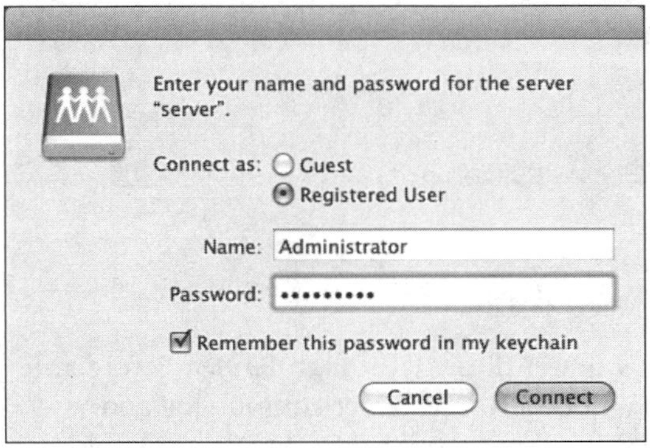

FIGURE 3.7   You need to enter your Windows Home Server Administrator password to access the shares from OS X.

Here are the steps to follow from here:

1. Make sure the Registered User option is selected.
2. Type **Administrator** in the Name text box.
3. Type your Administrator account password in the Password text box.
4. If you want OS X to remember your credentials, activate the Remember This Password in My Keychain check box.
5. Click Connect. OS X asks you to select which shared volume you want to connect to.
6. In the list, select the Windows Home Server share you want to access (Music, Photos, and so on).
7. Click OK. OS X mounts the share and displays the folder's contents, as shown in Figure 3.8.
8. Work with the folder contents using the OS X tools. In the Music share, for instance, you could play compatible music files using iTunes.

Windows Home Server's Music share

Click the server to access the other shared folders.

FIGURE 3.8   When you connect to a Windows Home Server share, OS X mounts it on the desktop, and an icon appears in the sidebar.

Using a Mac to Make a Remote Desktop Connection to Windows Home Server

You learn in Chapter 7, "Making Connections to Network Computers," how to use Windows' Remote Desktop Connection program to connect to the desktop of another computer on your network. However, it's also possible to make Remote Desktop connections to Windows computers from your Mac.

▶ **SEE** "Connecting via Remote Desktop Connection," **P. 153**.

To do this, you need to install on your Mac the Remote Desktop Connection Client for Mac, which is available from Microsoft. First, shut down Launchpad if it's still running. Go to www.microsoft.com/downloads and search for *Remote Desktop Mac*. (Note that as I write this, the latest version of the Remote Desktop Connection Client for Mac is 2.0.1.)

After you have the Remote Desktop Connection Client installed on your Mac, mount it and then follow these steps:

1. Ensure that the Windows PC to which you'll be connecting is configured to accept Remote Desktop connections.

▶ **SEE** "Getting the Client Computer Ready," **P. 153**.

2. In Finder, open the Applications folder, and then launch the Remote Desktop Connection icon.

3. In the Computer text box, type the name or IP address of the host computer.

4. If you don't want to customize Remote Desktop, skip to step 7. Otherwise, select RDC, Preferences to open the Remote Desktop Connection preferences dialog box, shown in Figure 3.9.

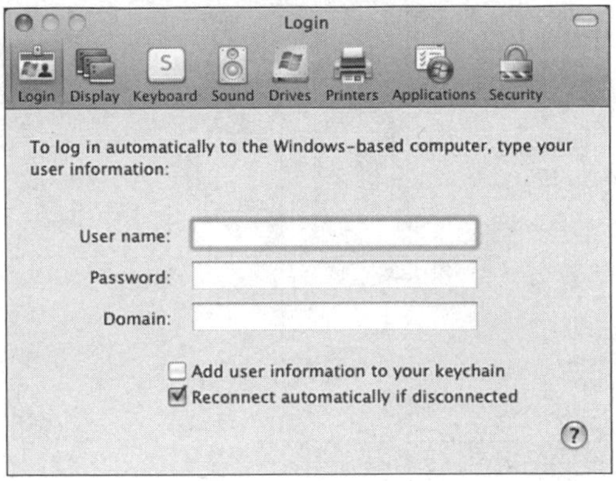

FIGURE 3.9   Use the preferences dialog box to customize Remote Desktop Connection for Mac.

5. The Login tab offers the following options:

   ▶ **User Name**—This is the username you want to use to log in to the host computer.

   ▶ **Password**—This is the password to use to log on to the host computer.

   ▶ **Domain**—Leave this text box blank.

   ▶ **Add User Information to Your Keychain**—Activate this check box to have OS X remember your logon data.

   ▶ **Reconnect Automatically if Disconnected**—Leave this check box activated to enable automatic reconnections.

6. Fill in the options in the Display, Keyboard, Sound, Drives, Printers, Applications, and Security tabs, as required, and then close the preferences dialog box.

▶ **SEE** "Making the Connection to the Remote Desktop," **P. 153**.

TIP

The default number of colors that Remote Desktop Connection Client for Mac uses is Thousands, which can make most Windows screens look hideous. In the Display tab, use the Colors list to select Millions.

---

7. Click Connect. Remote Desktop Connection Client for Mac connects to the Windows PC and prompts you for your login credentials, if you didn't add them to the Login tab. Figure 3.10 shows OS X with a connection to a Windows Home Server computer.

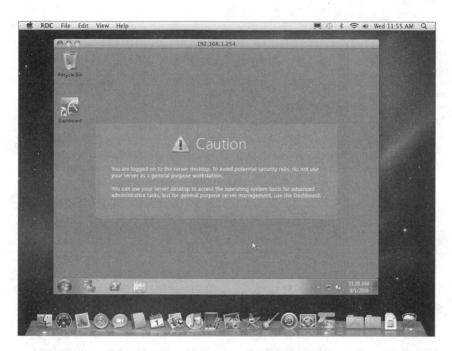

FIGURE 3.10   A Mac connected to a Windows Home Server PC using the Remote Desktop
Connection Client for Mac software.

When you're done, select RDC, Quit RDC, and then click OK when the program warns
you that you're about to disconnect from the Windows PC.

Letting Windows Computers See Your Mac Shares

SMB not only lets your Mac see shares on the Windows Home Server network, it also can
let Windows PCs see folders shared by the Mac. This feature is turned off by default in OS
X, but you can follow these steps to turn it on:

1. Click the System Preferences icon in the Dock.

2. Click Sharing to open the Sharing preferences.

3. Click to activate the File Sharing check box.

4. Click Options to open the Options sheet.

5. Click to activate the Share Files and Folders Using SMB (Windows) check box, as
   shown in Figure 3.11.

6. Click to activate the check box beside a user to enable SMB sharing for that user,
   enter the user's password when prompted, and then click OK.

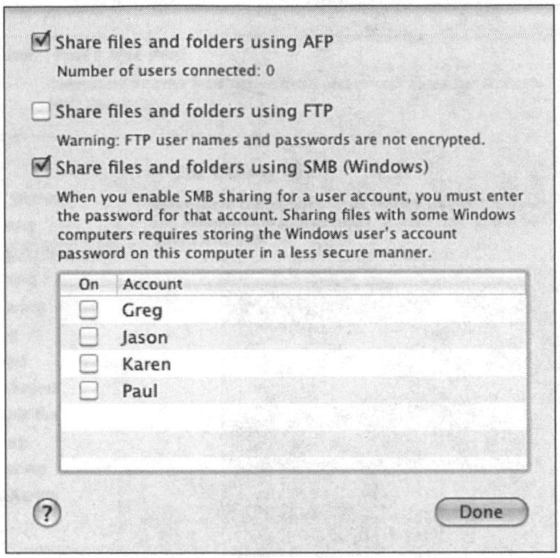

FIGURE 3.11   Activate the Share Files and Folders Using SMB check box to enable your Mac to share folders with Windows machines.

TIP

For easiest sharing, enable SMB sharing for accounts that also exist on the Windows machines.

7. Click Done. The Sharing window shows you the address that Windows PCs can use to access your Mac shares directly, as shown in Figure 3.12.

TIP

Macs often end up with long-winded computer names such as Paul McFedries' Computer. Because you need to use the computer name to log on to the share, consider editing the Computer Name field to something shorter.

8. Select System Preferences, Quit System Preferences.

One way to access the Mac shares from a Windows PC is to enter the share address directly, using either the Run dialog box or Windows Explorer's address bar. You have two choices:

```
\\IP\user
\\Computer\user
```

Here, *IP* is the IP address shown in the OS X Sharing window (see Figure 3.13), *Computer* is the Mac's computer name (also shown in the OS X Sharing window), and in both cases, *user* is the username of the account enabled for Windows Sharing. For example, I can use either of the following addresses to access my Mac:

```
\\192.168.0.92\paul
\\Pauls-Mac-mini\paul
```

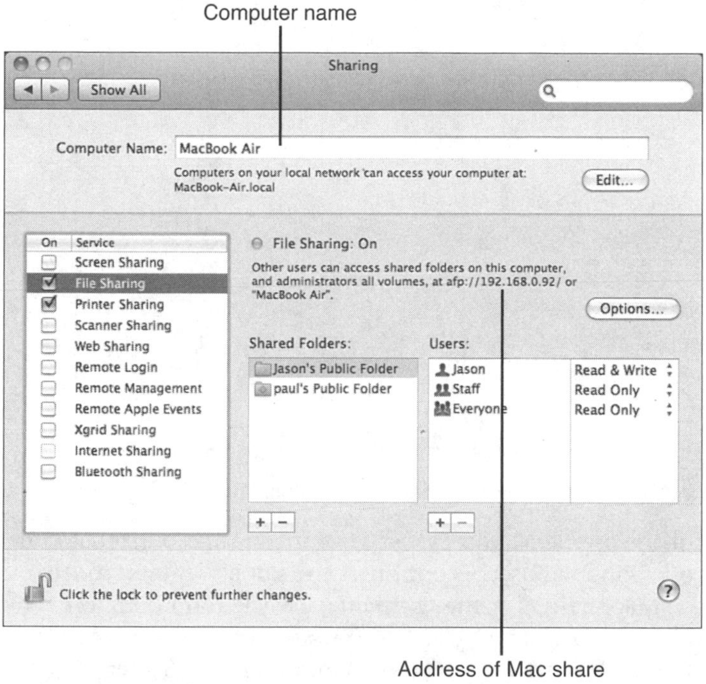

Computer name

Address of Mac share

FIGURE 3.12   The Sharing window with File Sharing activated.

Alternatively, open your workgroup as shown in Figure 3.13 and look for the icon that has the same name as the Mac's computer name (shown in Figure 3.12). Double-click that icon.

NOTE

If you don't see the icon for your Mac, it could be that the Mac isn't set up to use the same workgroup as your Windows Home Server network. (Both OS X and Windows Home Server use the name Workgroup by default, but you never know.) To check this, open System Preferences, click the Network icon, click the network interface you're using (usually either Ethernet or AirPort), and then click Advanced. Click the WINS tab, make sure the Workgroup value is the same as your Windows Home Server workgroup name, click OK, and then click Apply.

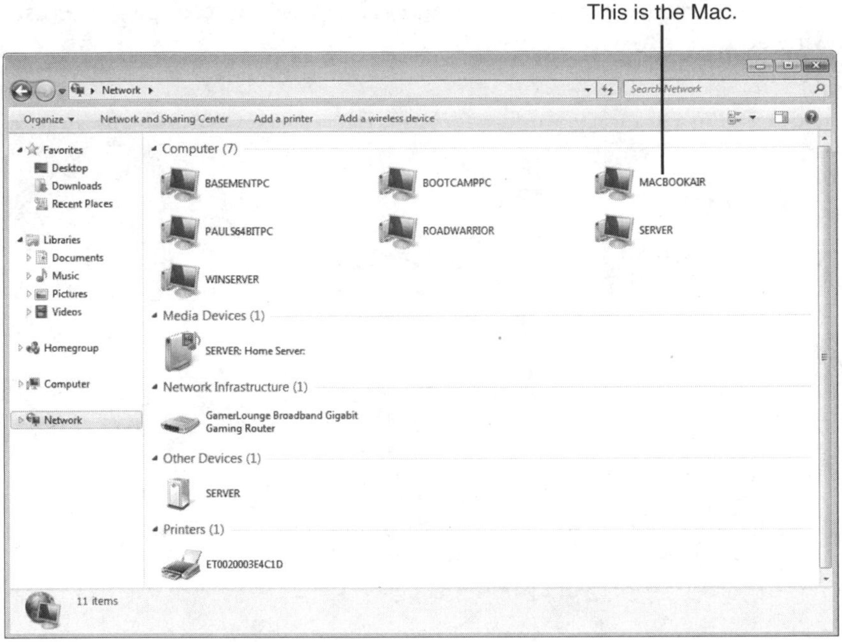

This is the Mac.

FIGURE 3.13   Look for the icon that has the same name as your Mac.

Either way, you're prompted for the username and password of the Mac account that you enabled for SMB sharing. (If your Windows user account uses the same username and password, you go directly to the Mac share.) For the username, use the form *Computer\ UserName*, where *Computer* is the name of your Mac and *UserName* is the name of the SMB sharing account. Figure 3.14 shows a Mac share opened in Windows Home Server.

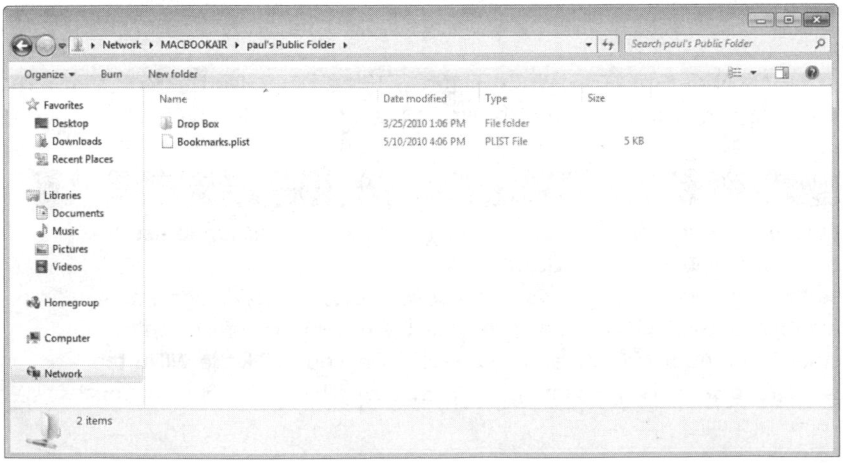

FIGURE 3.14   A shared Mac folder opened in Windows Home Server.

> **TIP**
>
> If you have trouble logging on to your Mac from Windows Vista, the problem is likely caused by Vista's use of NT LAN Manager version 2 (NTLMv2) authentication, which doesn't work properly when negotiated between some versions of Vista and some versions of OS X. To fix this, on the Vista PC, press Windows Logo+R (or select Start, All Programs, Accessories, Run), type `secpol.msc`, click OK to open the Local Security Policy snap-in, and enter your User Account Control (UAC) credentials. Open the Security Settings, Local Policies, Security Options branch. Double-click the Network Security: LAN Manager Authentication Level policy, change the authentication level to Send LM & NTLM - Use NTLMv2 Session Security If Negotiated, and then click OK.
>
> If your version of Vista doesn't come with the Local Security snap-in (it's not available in Home and Home Premium), open the Registry Editor (press Windows Logo+R, type `regedit`, and click OK), and navigate to the following key:
>
> `HLM\SYSTEM\CurrentControlSet\Control\Lsa\`
>
> Change the value of the LMCompatibilityLevel setting to 1.

Using a Linux Client on Your Windows Home Server Network

Until recently, it was a rare household that included a Linux box as part of its computer collection. That is changing rapidly, however, thanks to easy-to-use and easy-to-install Linux distributions such as Ubuntu and new Linux-based offerings from mainstream computer manufacturers such as Dell.

The good news is that Linux, like OS X, supports SMB natively (via Samba, a free implementation of the SMB protocols), so it's possible for Linux machines to coexist on your Windows Home Server network. In the sections that follow, I use the Ubuntu distribution (specifically, Ubuntu 10.10, also known as Maverick Meerkat) to access the Windows Home Server network. The procedures for your Linux distribution should be similar.

Viewing the Windows Home Server Network in Ubuntu

Ubuntu isn't set up out-of-the-box to view and work with Windows shares that use NTFS. This is a problem for Windows Home Server because all your shares are NTFS. To fix this problem, you need to install the NTFS Configuration tool in Ubuntu:

1. Select Applications, Ubuntu Software Center to open the Ubuntu Software Center window.
2. Type **ntfs** in the Search box. You should see NTFS Configuration Tool appear in the search results.
3. Click NTFS Configuration Tool, and then click Install. Ubuntu asks you to authenticate the install.
4. Enter your administrative password, and then click Authenticate.

3

Here are the steps to follow to open your workgroup and view the Windows Home Server shares:

1. Select Places, Network. The File Browser program opens and displays the Network folder. If you see your network computers, skip to step 4.

2. Double-click the Windows Network icon. You should now see the icon for your Windows Home Server workgroup.

3. Double-click the workgroup icon. You should now see icons for each computer in your workgroup, as shown in Figure 3.15.

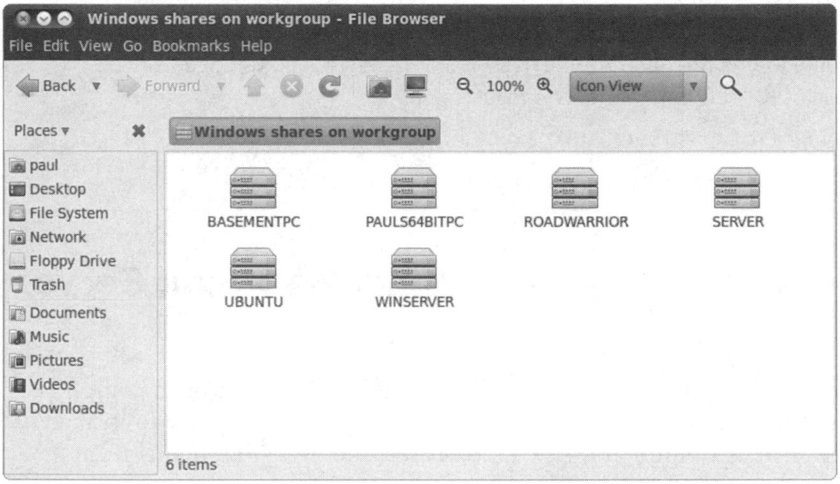

FIGURE 3.15   In Ubuntu's File browser, open the workgroup icon to see your workgroup computers.

4. Double-click the icon for the Windows Home Server computer. File Browser prompts you for your username and password.

5. Type your Windows Home Server username and password, leave the workgroup name in the Domain field, and then click Connect. File Browser displays the Windows Home Server shares, as shown in Figure 3.16.

Letting Windows Computers See Your Ubuntu Shares

The Linux support for SMB cuts both ways, meaning that not only can you see and work with Windows shares in Ubuntu, you can configure Ubuntu as a file server and enable Windows computers to see and work with Ubuntu shares. The next few sections show you how to set this up in Ubuntu.

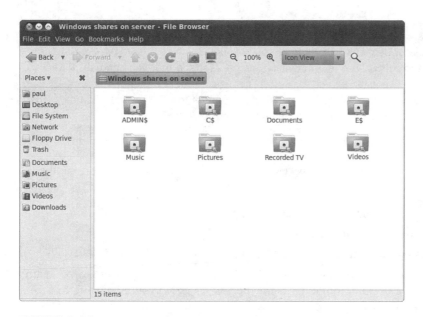

FIGURE 3.16   In Ubuntu's File browser, open the Windows Home Server icon to see the server's shared folders.

Installing Samba in Ubuntu

Your first step is to install Samba by following this procedure:

1. Select System, Administration, Synaptic Package Manager, enter your administrator password, and click OK.
2. In the Quick Search text box, type **samba**. You see a list of packages that include "samba" in the name.
3. In the Package list, click the check box beside samba and then click Mark for Installation.
4. Click Apply.
5. Synaptic Package Manager displays a list of the changes to be applied.
6. Click Apply. Synaptic Package Manager downloads and installs the software.
7. Click Close.

Defining Samba Users in Ubuntu

Next, you need to define one or more users who can access Samba shares. For this to work, you need to set up the same username and account on both the Ubuntu box and the Windows PC.

Assuming you already have your Windows users configured, follow these steps to add a user in Ubuntu:

1. Select System, Administration, Users and Groups.
2. Click Add. Ubuntu asks you to authenticate.
3. Type your administrator password, and click Authenticate.
4. Type the person's name and the account's short name (that is, the username). Again, make sure this is a username that exists on the Windows PC you'll be using to access the Ubuntu shares.
5. Click OK. Ubuntu asks for the user's password.
6. Type the user password and the password confirmation.
7. Click OK to add the user.
8. Repeat steps 2–7 to add other users.
9. Click Close.

Now you can add these users to Samba. Here are the steps to follow:

1. Select Applications, Accessories, Terminal to launch a terminal session.
2. Type the following command (where *user* is the username), and then enter your administrative password when prompted:

    ```
    sudo smbpasswd -a user
    ```

3. Ubuntu displays the following prompt:

    ```
    [sudo] password for user:
    ```

4. Type the user account's password (you won't see characters onscreen while you type), and then press Enter. Ubuntu displays the following prompt:

    ```
    New SMB password:
    ```

5. Type the user account's password, and then press Enter. Ubuntu displays the following prompt:

    ```
    Retype new SMB password:
    ```

6. Type the user account's password again, and press Enter. Ubuntu adds the user.

7. Reload Samba by typing the following command and pressing Enter:

   ```
   sudo smbd restart
   ```

8. Repeat steps 2–7 to add the other users to Samba.

You need the terminal session for the next setup task, so leave the session running for now.

Changing the Samba Workgroup Name in Ubuntu

In the latest versions of Samba, the default Samba workgroup name is WORKGROUP, which is likely to be the same as the workgroup name you use for your Windows Home Server network. However, older versions of Samba used MSHOME as the default workgroup name. If you're running an older version of Samba, or if your Windows Home Server workgroup name is something other than Workgroup, then for easier access to the Ubuntu shares, you should configure Samba to use the same workgroup name that you use for your Windows network. Here are the steps to follow:

1. If you don't already have a terminal session running from the previous section, select Applications, Accessories, Terminal.

2. Type the following command, and press Enter:

   ```
   sudo gedit /etc/samba/smb.conf
   ```

3. If you see the Password prompt, type your Ubuntu password, and press Enter. The gedit text editor loads and opens smb.conf, which is the configuration file for Samba.

4. Locate the workgroup line, and change the value of the workgroup parameter to the name of your Windows Home Server workgroup. For example, if your network uses the name workgroup, the line should appear as follows:

   ```
   workgroup = workgroup
   ```

5. Select File, Save (or press Ctrl+S or click the Save button).

6. Select File, Quit (or press Ctrl+Q) to return to the terminal session.

7. Select File, Close Window (or press Ctrl+Shift+Q).

TIP

If you want to change the name of the Ubuntu computer, you must install the gnome-network-admin package using Synaptic Package Manager. (For the general steps, see "Installing Samba in Ubuntu," earlier in this chapter.) Once that's done, select System, Administration, Network to open the Network Settings dialog box. Click Unlock, and then enter your administrative password. Display the General tab, modify the Host Name setting, and then click Close.

Sharing a Folder in Ubuntu

You're now ready to share a folder or two for Windows users to access. Use these steps:

1. Select Places, Home Folder to open File Browser and display your Ubuntu home folder.

2. Display the icon for the folder you want to share.

3. Right-click the icon, and then click Sharing Options. Ubuntu displays the Folder Sharing dialog box.

4. Click to activate the Share This Folder check box, as shown in Figure 3.17.

FIGURE 3.17   Use the Folder Sharing dialog box to set up a folder to share with your Windows Home Server network.

5. Modify the name, if necessary.

6. If you want Windows users to be able to change the contents of the folder, activate the Allow Others to Create and Delete Files in This Folder check box.

7. Click Create Share. Ubuntu lets you know that it needs to add some permissions.

8. Click Add the Permissions Automatically.

To work with the Ubuntu machine, open your workgroup as shown in Figure 3.18 and look for the icon that has the same name as the Ubuntu computer. Double-click that icon, and Windows displays the Ubuntu shares, as shown in Figure 3.19. Double-click a share icon, and then enter the username and password of a Samba account on the Ubuntu box to access the share.

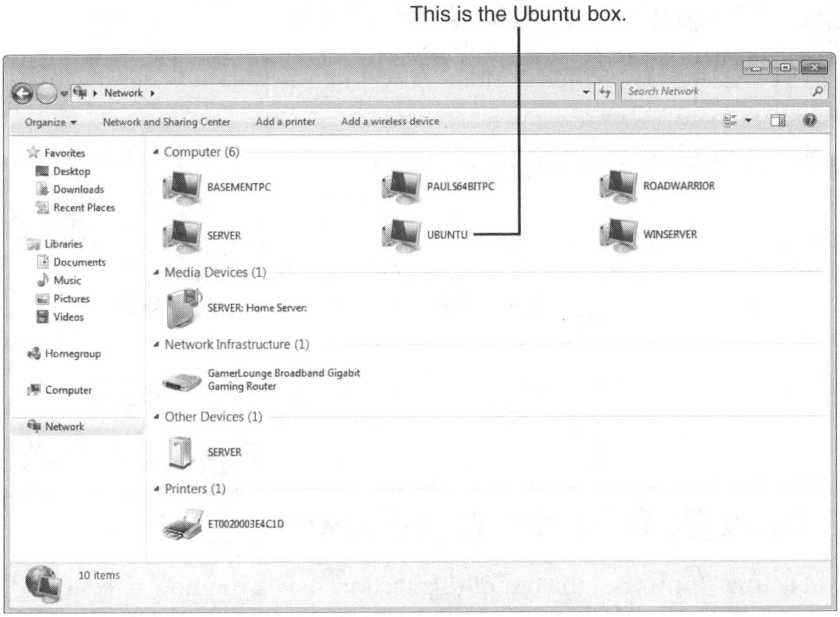

This is the Ubuntu box.

FIGURE 3.18   Look for the icon that has the same name as your Ubuntu box.

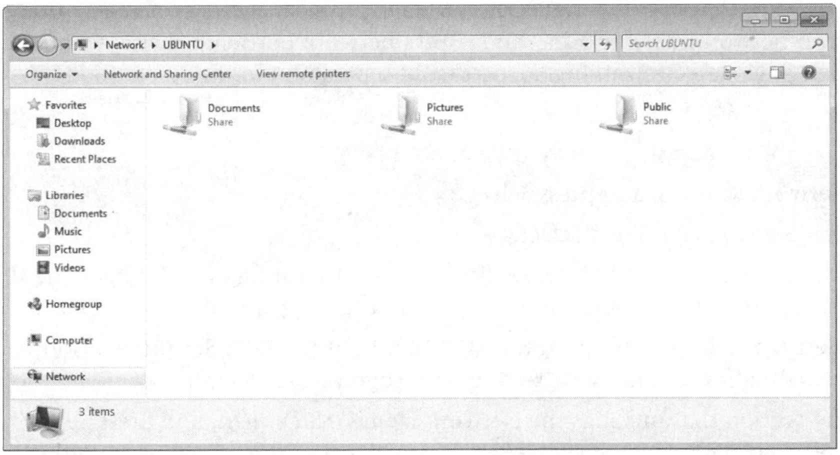

FIGURE 3.19   Open the Ubuntu box icon to see the folders it's sharing via Samba.

Adding Other Devices to the Network

Getting other devices to access your Windows Home Server network always begins with making the initial network connection:

▶ If the device has an RJ-45 jack, run a network cable from the jack to a port on your network's switch or router.

▶ If the device supports Wi-Fi, turn on the Wi-Fi option, if necessary. (Some devices have a physical switch that you must set to activate Wi-Fi.) Then use the device interface to display a list of the available wireless networks, select your Windows Home Server network, and enter the security key.

When that's done, you can usually access the Windows Home Server shares directly using the device interface.

Adding an Xbox 360 to the Network

To give you some idea how this works, the rest of this section shows you how to connect an Xbox 360. The Xbox 360 and Windows Home Server go together well because the Xbox can access and play media streamed from the server. First, you need to get the Xbox 360 connected to your network. Follow these steps:

1. Connect your Xbox 360 to the network. If you have physical access to the network, you can plug a network cable into the Xbox 360's network port. Otherwise, you need to attach a wireless networking adapter (sold separately) to the Xbox 360.

2. Turn on the Xbox 360.

3. When the Dashboard appears, display the System blade.

4. Highlight Network Settings, and press Select.

5. Highlight Edit Settings, and press Select.

6. In the Basic Settings tab, if the IP Settings field isn't set to Automatic, highlight the IP Settings section, press Select, highlight the Automatic setting, and then press Select.

7. If the DNS Settings field isn't set to Automatic, highlight the DNS Settings section, press Select, highlight the Automatic setting, and then press Select.

8. Highlight the section that includes the Network Name (SSID) field, and press Select. The Xbox 360 displays a list of available wireless networks. (I'm assuming here that you have a wireless card plugged in to your console.)

9. Highlight your network, and press Select. (Tip: If you don't see your network listed, press X to rerun the network search.)

10. If your network uses WEP or WPA security, use the onscreen keyboard to enter the security key. When you're finished, select Done. The Xbox 360 updates the network settings.

11. Highlight Test Media, and press Select. You should see Connected in the Wireless Network field and Confirmed in the IP Address field. (If not, highlight Edit Settings, press Select, and repeat steps 6–10.)

From Here

▶ For more about network subnets, **SEE** "Handling Multiple Network Subnets," **P. 24.**

▶ For the details on setting up a new share in Windows Home Server, **SEE** "Creating a New Shared Folder," **P. 123.**

▶ To learn how to use Launchpad to access the Windows Home Server shares, **SEE** "Accessing Shared Folders on Your Mac," **P. 135.**

▶ To learn how to get a computer set up for Remote Desktop connections, **SEE** "Getting the Client Computer Ready," **P. 153.**

▶ For the details on connecting via Remote Desktop, **SEE** "Connecting via Remote Desktop Connection," **P. 153.**

▶ For a complete look at the various Remote Desktop Connection options, **SEE** "Making the Connection to the Remote Desktop," **P. 153.**

▶ Before you can back up your Mac, you have to configure Time Machine to use Windows Home Server as the backup location; **SEE** "Configuring Time Machine to Back Up Your Mac," **P. 222.**

▶ For the details on the Registry and using the Registry Editor, **SEE** Chapter 18, "Working with the Windows Home Server Registry."

CHAPTER 4

Configuring Windows Home Server

IN THIS CHAPTER

▶ Running the Windows Home Server Launchpad

▶ Running the Windows Home Server Dashboard

▶ Changing the Date and Time on Windows Home Server

▶ Selecting the Windows Home Server Region

▶ Configuring Windows Update

▶ Changing the Windows Home Server Password

▶ Restarting or Shutting Down Windows Home Server

▶ Configuring the Windows Home Server Startup

Windows Home Server isn't meant to be constantly tweaked in the same way that you might always find yourself fiddling with settings in Windows 7, Windows Vista, or even Windows Server 2008. After you get through the setup (which nearly qualifies as a *forehead install*—that is, an installation so simple that theoretically you could run through each step just by hitting the spacebar with your forehead) and the simple and straightforward *OOBE* (out-of-box experience—that is, what you must do to get a computer running after you take it out of the box), there isn't much you're supposed to do with the machine. You set up your users and permissions, perhaps add a few extra shared folders, and your Windows Home Server is good to go.

Of course, this only applies to the nongeek users that Microsoft is truly targeting with Windows Home Server. For the rest of us, adjusting the settings of any operating system (OS) is a must because there has never been an OS made that satisfies and is set up for everyone. We tweak; therefore, we are.

In a sense, this book is all about tweaking Windows Home Server to get the most out of it. However, this chapter in particular takes you through some essential configuration tasks. You can accomplish most of these tasks via the Windows Home Server Launchpad and Dashboard (meaning that you can adjust the server's settings from any client machine), but some of the techniques in this chapter run outside these tools (and so require either a direct login or a Remote Desktop connection to the server).

Running the Windows Home Server Launchpad

The Launchpad is a client-side tool that's new with Windows Home Server 2011, and it's designed to give you easy access to common Windows Home Server tasks and features. On most systems, Launchpad starts automatically, but if it's not already started on your computer, you have two ways to make it so:

▶ Select Start, All Programs, Windows Home Server 2011, Windows Home Server 2011 Launchpad.

▶ Display the Launchpad icon in the notification area and then double-click the icon.

The first time you do this, you're prompted to enter your Windows Home Server username and password. If you don't want to type your username each time, activate the Remember Me on This Computer check box. (If you don't see this check box, click Options.) If you want to sign in automatically (and if other people can't access your computer), you can also activate the Remember My Password check box.

When you're ready, press Enter. Figure 4.1 shows the Launchpad window that appears.

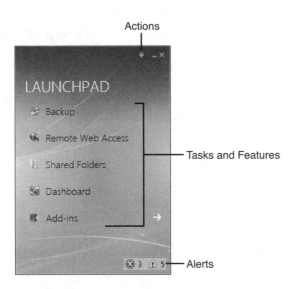

FIGURE 4.1   Launchpad is a client-side application for easy access to Windows Home Server tasks, features, and settings.

There are three sections of the Launchpad window to note:

▶ **Actions.** Click this icon (pointed out in Figure 4.1) to access the Launchpad settings or to sign out from Launchpad.

▶ **Tasks and Features.** This area gives you one-click access to five common Windows Home Server tasks and features: Backup (which enables you to run a manual backup right away); Remote Web Access; Shared Folders; Dashboard; and Add-ins (which you only see if you have any client add-ins installed).

▶ **Alerts.** This area (see Figure 4.1) lets you know if there are any health alerts that you need to take care of. Click an alert icon to open the Alert Viewer and see what the problems are.

▶ **SEE** "Monitoring Windows Home Server with the Alert Viewer," **P. 242.**

The alerts that appear in Launchpad are controlled by the scope, which defines which alerts you see. There are three possible scopes:

▶ **None**—This scope means that you don't see alerts. This is useful if you're configuring Launchpad for a novice user.

▶ **Local Only**—This scope means that you only see alerts that apply to your computer. This is useful if you're configuring Launchpad for intermediate users who may be able to either solve the problem or, more likely, know to notify you when an alert comes up.

▶ **Local and Network**—This scope means that you see not only alerts for the client computer, but any other health alerts generated by Windows Home Server or by other clients on the network. This is useful for anyone who is administering Windows Home Server.

To change the scope, follow these steps:

1. Click the Actions icon, and then click Settings. The Launchpad Settings dialog box appears.
2. In the Scope of Alerts to be Presented section, click None, Local Only, or Local and Network.
3. Click OK to put the new setting into effect.

Running the Windows Home Server Dashboard

Most of the Windows Home Server configuration chores are easily accomplished via the Windows Home Server Dashboard application (which replaces the Console application from a previous version of Windows Home Server). To ensure that you can always access this program easily, here's a list of the various methods you can use to launch it:

▶ On the Windows Home Server machine, select Start, All Programs, Windows Home Server 2011, Dashboard.

▶ On the Windows Home Server machine, double-click the Dashboard desktop icon.

▶ On a client machine, select Start, All Programs, Windows Home Server 2011, Windows Home Server 2011 Dashboard.

▶ On a client machine, open Launchpad and then click Dashboard.

▶ On the client machine, right-click the Launchpad icon in the notification area and then click Open Dashboard.

▶ On the server, select Start, Run (or press Windows Logo+R) to open the Run dialog box, type `%ProgramFiles%\Windows Server\Bin\Dashboard.exe`, and then click OK.

▶ On a client, select Start, Run (or press Windows Logo+R) to open the Run dialog box, type `%ProgramFiles%\Windows Server\Bin\DashboardClient.exe`, and then click OK.

If you're running Windows Home Server Dashboard on a client, you see the logon screen shown in Figure 4.2. Type the Windows Home Server password (that is, the password for Windows Home Server's Administrator account) in the text box, and then press Enter or click the arrow. The Windows Home Server Dashboard appears, as shown in Figure 4.3.

TIP

If your computer is secure and you want to avoid entering the Windows Home Server password each time, display the logon screen, click Options, and then activate the Remember My Password check box.

NOTE

If you can't recall the Windows Home Server password, click Options and then click Password Hint to see some text that gives you a hint about the password. See "Changing the Windows Home Server Password," later in this chapter.

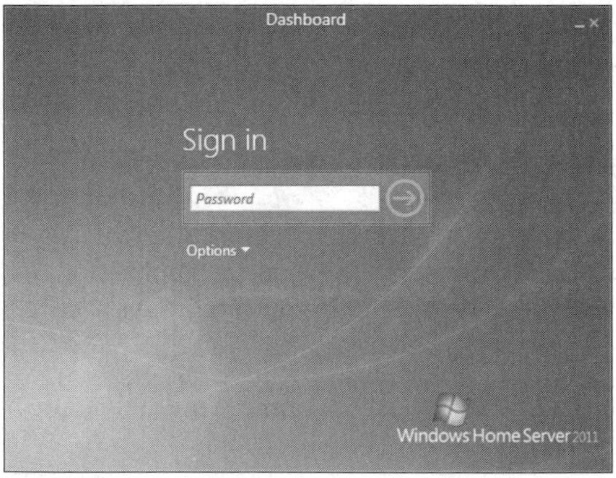

FIGURE 4.2   When you run the client version of Windows Home Server Dashboard, you must first log on to the server.

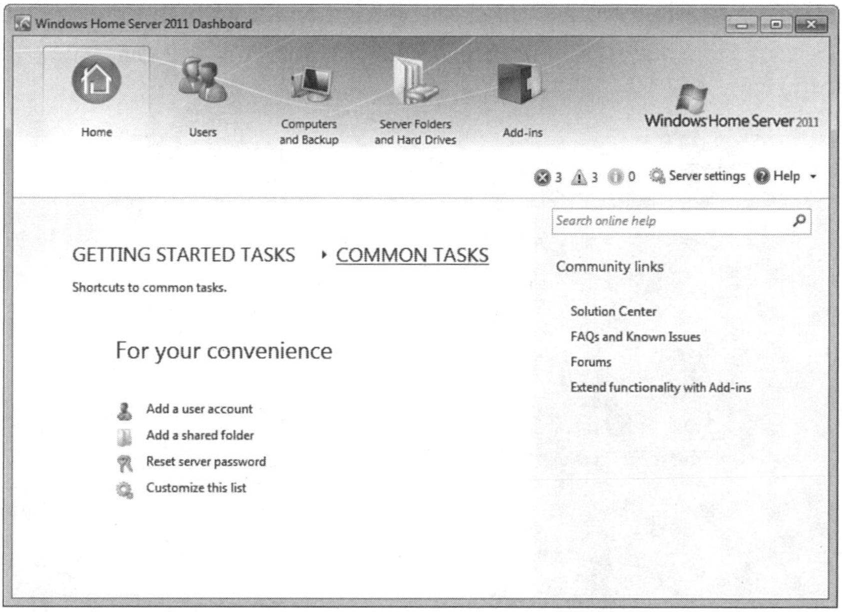

FIGURE 4.3   Use the Windows Home Server Dashboard program to configure most common server settings.

Changing the Date and Time on Windows Home Server

Windows Home Server runs the client backups each night starting around midnight. This is usually ideal because it's late enough that you or anyone in your family won't be working on a client machine, but early enough that the server has sufficient time to complete all the client backups (which it performs one client at a time). So it's important that the time is set up correctly on Windows Home Server.

The server's internal date is important, too, because Windows Home Server uses the date to organize backups. If you need to restore a file or folder, you need the date to be accurate so you can tell which version of the file or folder to restore.

Setting the Current Date and Time

If the Windows Home Server date or time is off, follow these steps to make a correction:

1. Launch the Windows Home Server Dashboard.
2. Click Server Settings to open the Server Settings dialog box.
3. Click the General tab.

4. In the Date and Time section, click Change to display the Date and Time dialog box.

5. Click Change Date and Time section to display the Date and Time Settings dialog box, shown in Figure 4.4.

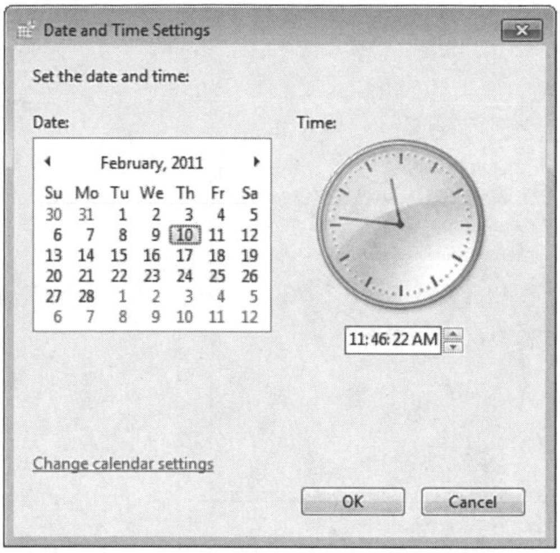

FIGURE 4.4   Use the Date and Time Settings dialog box to set the server's internal date and time.

TIP

If you're logged in to the server, a faster way to display the Date and Time dialog box is to right-click the time in the taskbar's notification area, and then click Adjust Date/Time. Alternatively, select Start, Control Panel, Date and Time.

---

6. Use the Date calendar to select the current month and day.

7. Use the spin box in the Time group to specify the current hour, minute, second, and AM or PM. These four items are separate "sections" within the text box. Either edit each section directly, or click within a section and use the up and down arrows to increase or decrease the section value.

8. Click OK to return to the Date and Time dialog box.

9. To specify a different time zone, click Change Time Zone to open the Time Zone Settings dialog box, and then use the list to select your time zone.

10. If you want Windows Home Server to adjust the time during daylight saving time changeovers, leave the Automatically Adjust Clock for Daylight Saving Time check box activated. (Note that you only see this check box if your time zone uses daylight saving time.)

11. Click OK to put the new settings into effect.

> **TIP**
>
> If you're working with a client machine and you just want to know the current time on the server, use the NET TIME command. Start a command prompt session on the client machine (select Start, All Programs, Accessories, Command Prompt), type the following, and press Enter:
>
>   net time \\server
>
> Replace *server* with the name of your Windows Home Server.

Synchronizing the Date and Time with a Time Server

If you want to ensure that Windows Home Server always has the accurate time, you can configure the system to synchronize with an Internet-based time server. Here are the steps to follow:

1. Launch the Windows Home Server Dashboard.
2. Click Server Settings to open the Server Settings dialog box.
3. Click the General tab.
4. In the Date and Time section, click Change to display the Date and Time dialog box.
5. Click the Internet Time tab.
6. Click Change Settings to open the Internet Time Settings dialog box.
7. Make sure the Synchronize with an Internet Time Server check box is activated.
8. Use the Server list to choose a time server (you can also type in a different server).
9. Click Update Now to synchronize the time manually. (Windows Home Server schedules the next synchronization for a week later.)
10. Click OK in each open dialog box to put the new settings into effect.

Unfortunately, the time synchronization in Windows Home Server (and, indeed, in all versions of Windows that support this feature) isn't very reliable. On my Windows machines, I usually have to configure a different time server by hand either by using a command prompt session or by modifying the list of servers in the Internet Time tab. I most often use one of the time servers that the U.S. Navy operates:

    tick.usno.navy.mil
    tock.usno.navy.mil

> **NOTE**
>
> You can find a long list of time servers at http://support.ntp.org/bin/view/Servers/ WebHome.

Specifying the Time Server at the Command Prompt
To configure a time server via the command prompt, follow these steps:

1. In Windows Home Server, select Start, All Programs, Accessories, Command Prompt.

2. Enter the following command to specify the time server you want to use. (Replace *TimeServer* with the domain name of the time server.)

   ```
   w32tm /config /manualpeerlist:TimeServer,0x1
   ```

3. Stop the Windows Time service by entering the following command:

   ```
   net stop w32time
   ```

4. Restart the Windows Time service by entering the following command:

   ```
   net start w32time
   ```

When you restart the Time service, it automatically synchronizes with the time server you specified.

Customizing the Synchronization Interval

By default, Windows Home Server synchronizes with the default time server every 15 minutes. If you'd prefer that Windows Home Server synchronize less often—for example, once a day—you can follow these steps to customize the synchronization interval:

1. Select Start, Run (or press Windows Logo+R) to open the Run dialog box, type **regedit**, and click OK to open the Registry Editor (which I discuss in detail in Chapter 18).

2. Display the following key:

   ```
   HKLM\SYSTEM\CurrentControlSet\Services\W32Time\TimeProviders\NtpClient
   ```

3. Double-click the SpecialPollInterval setting to open the Edit DWORD Value setting.

4. Click the Decimal option.

5. In the Value Data text box, type the number of seconds you want to use as the synchronization interval. For example, to synchronize every 24 hours, type **86400**.

6. Click OK.

7. Exit the Registry Editor.

To put the new setting into effect, you have two choices:

▶ Stop and then restart the Windows Time service. One way to do this is to use the net stop w32time and net start w32time commands I mentioned earlier.

▶ Select Start, Administrative Tools, Services to open the Services snap-in. Click the Windows Time service, click the Stop link (see Figure 4.5), and then click the Start link.

▶ **SEE** "Controlling Services with the Services Snap-In," **P. 566.**

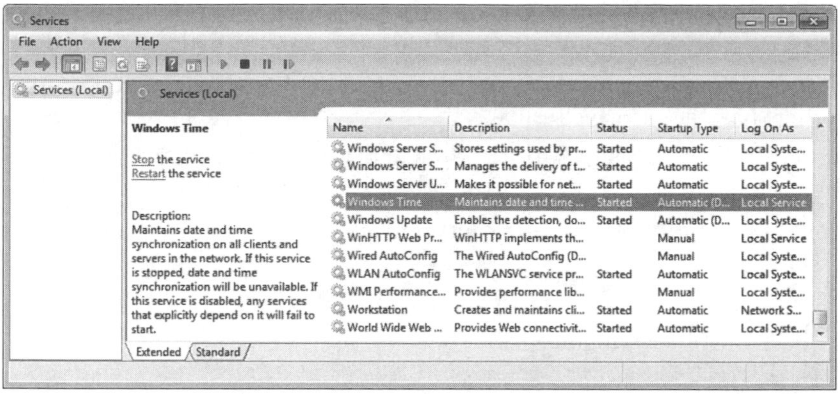

FIGURE 4.5   You can use the Services snap-in to stop and start the Windows Time service.

Selecting the Windows Home Server Region

In Windows Home Server, you can specify the region you're in. This determines how Windows Home Server formats data such as numbers, currency values, dates, and times. For example, depending on the region, Windows Home Server would display August 7, 2011 in the short date format as 8/7/2011 or as 7/8/2011.

Changing the Region in the Windows Home Server Dashboard

Here are the steps to follow to use the Windows Home Server Dashboard to change the current region setting:

1. Launch the Windows Home Server Dashboard.
2. Click Server Settings to open the Windows Home Server Settings dialog box.
3. Click the General tab.
4. Use the Country/Region Location of Server list to select the region and the language within that region.
5. Click OK to put the new setting into effect.

Customizing the Region Formats

The Windows Home Server Dashboard only enables you to switch from one region setting to another. However, you might need to customize a particular region's formats. For example, you may select a region where the short date format is d/m/yyyy but you'd rather use m/d/yyyy. Windows Home Server enables you to customize the format not only of dates, but of times, numbers, and currency values. Follow these steps:

1. Log in to the Windows Home Server machine and select Start, Control Panel, Region and Language. Windows Home Server displays the Region and Language dialog box.

2. In the Formats tab, use the Format list to select a region and language, if you want something other than the displayed value.

3. Use the Date and Time Formats lists to select the date formats and time formats you want to use.

4. Click Additional Settings. Windows Home Server displays the Customize Format dialog box, shown in Figure 4.6.

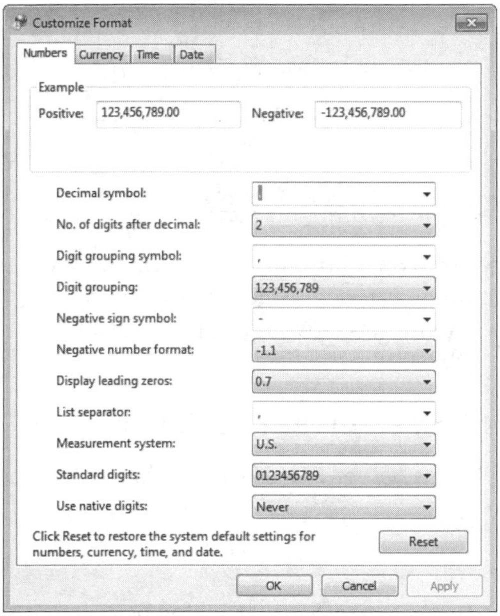

FIGURE 4.6   Use the Customize Format dialog box to set up custom formats for numbers, currency values, dates, and times.

5. Use the lists in the Numbers tab to customize how Windows Home Server displays numeric values.

6. Use the lists in the Currency tab to customize how Windows Home Server displays monetary values.

7. Use the lists in the Time tab to customize how Windows Home Server displays time values.

8. Use the lists in the Date tab to customize how Windows Home Server displays date values.

9. Click OK to return to the Region and Language dialog box.

10. Click OK to put the new settings into effect.

Configuring Windows Update

Windows Update is a feature that keeps Windows Home Server up-to-date by offering power packs, operating system fixes, security patches, enhancements, and new features for download. You can check for new updates at any time by selecting Start, All Programs, Windows Update to load the Microsoft Windows Update website into the browser.

Rather than you remembering to check for updates and then trying to figure out which ones to download and install, Windows Home Server offers the Automatic Updates feature. This takes the guesswork out of updating the server by automatically checking to see whether updates are available, downloading those that are, and then installing them, all without intervention on your part. The next few sections show you how to configure Automatic Updates and how to check for updates from within Windows Home Server.

Configuring Windows Update

When you started Windows Home Server, the OOBE program asked you to choose a Windows Update setting. If you want to change that setting, you can do it using the Windows Home Server Dashboard, as described in the following steps:

1. Launch the Windows Home Server Dashboard.
2. Click Server Settings to open the Windows Home Server Settings dialog box.
3. Click the General tab.
4. Click Change/Install Updates. The Dashboard opens the Windows Update window for the server. (This looks like your local Windows Update window, but it really is the server version.)
5. Click Change Settings to open the Change Settings window, shown in Figure 4.7.
6. Use the Important Updates list to select one of the following options:

   ▶ **Install Updates Automatically**—This option tells Windows Home Server to download and install updates automatically. Windows Home Server checks for new updates on the date (such as Every Day or Every Sunday) and time you specify. For example, you might prefer to choose a time when you won't be using your computer.

CAUTION

Some updates require your server to be rebooted to put them into effect. In such cases, if you activate the Automatic option, Windows Home Server automatically reboots your system. This might lead to problems if you have a particular program that you need to be running at all times. You can work around this problem by setting up an automatic logon and by setting up the program to run automatically at startup. (Refer to "Launching Applications and Scripts at Startup," later in this chapter.)

▶ **SEE** "Automating Client Logons," **P. 39.**

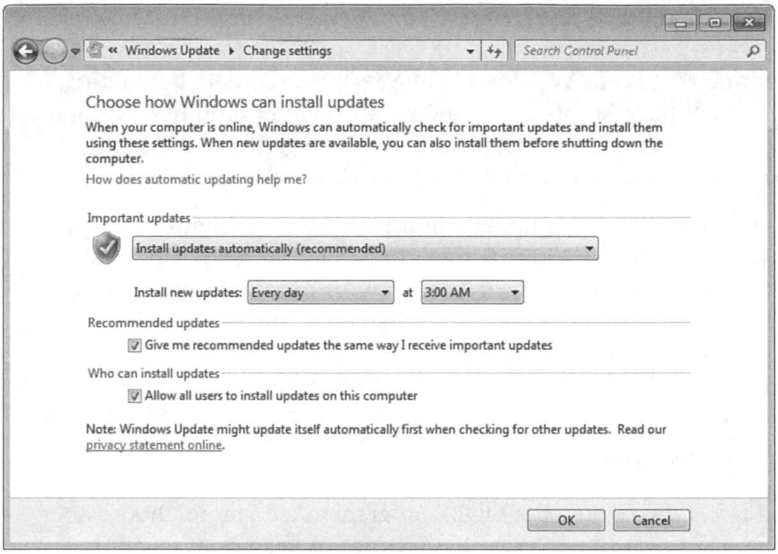

FIGURE 4.7   Use the Automatic Updates dialog box to configure Windows Home Server's automatic updating.

▶ **Download Updates but Let Me Choose When to Install Them**—If you activate this option, Windows Home Server checks for new updates and then automatically downloads any updates that are available. Windows Home Server then displays an icon in the notification area to let you know that the updates are ready to install. Click the icon to see the list of updates. If you see an update that you don't want to install, deactivate its check box. Click Install to install the selected updates.

TIP

An update that you choose not to install still appears in the Select Updates to Install window. If you'd prefer not to see that update, right-click the update and click Hide Update. If you later want to unhide the update, display the Windows Update window and click the Restore Hidden Updates link. In the Restore Hidden Updates window, activate the update's check box, and then click Restore.

▶ **Check for Updates but Let Me Choose Whether to Download and Install Them**—If you activate this option, Windows Home Server checks for new updates and then, if any are available, displays an icon in the notification area to let you know that the updates are ready to download. Click the icon to see the list of updates. If you see an update that you don't want to download, deactivate its check box. Click Start Download to initiate the download. When the download is complete, Windows Home Server displays an icon in the notification area to let you know that the updates are ready to install. Click the icon, and then click Install to install the updates.

▶ **Never Check for Updates**—Activate this option to prevent Windows Home Server from checking for new updates.

CAUTION

I strongly recommend that you *not* choose to turn Windows Update off. All recent versions of Windows have been plagued with security vulnerabilities, and Windows Home Server (or, more accurately in this case, Windows Server 2008, which underlies Windows Home Server) isn't an exception. You need to keep your server updated to avoid having your system—and, almost certainly, your entire home network—compromised or damaged by malicious hackers.

---

7. Click OK to put the new setting into effect.

Updating Windows Home Server

If you elected not to use automatic updating, you need to watch out for available updates and install the ones you want by hand. How do you watch for updates? The easiest method is to watch the alert icons either in the Launchpad or the Dashboard. When updates are ready for download, you see a warning alert (a black exclamation mark on a yellow triangle). To make sure this warning is update related, click the alert icon to open the Alert Viewer, and then look for an alert similar to the one displayed in Figure 4.8.

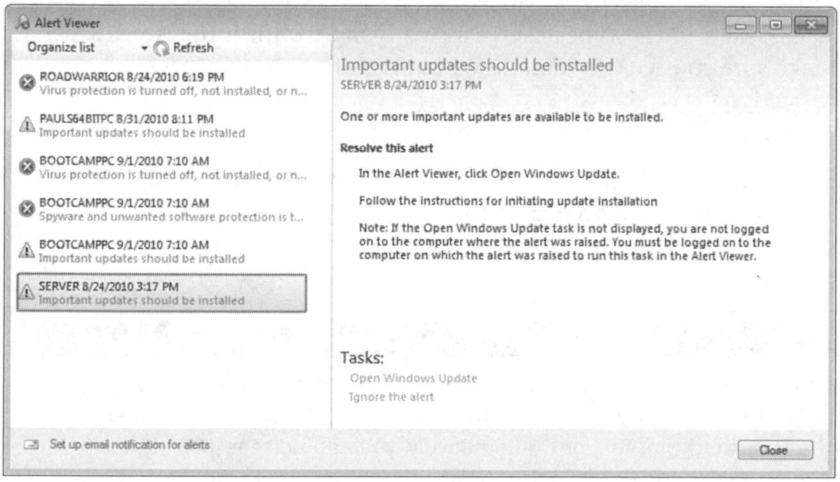

FIGURE 4.8   If updates are available, you see a warning in the Alert Viewer.

Follow these steps to update the server:

1. Launch the Windows Home Server Dashboard.
2. Click Server Settings to open the Windows Home Server Settings dialog box.
3. Click the General tab.
4. Click Change/Install Updates. The Dashboard opens the Windows Update window for the server.
5. Click Install Updates. Windows Home Server then downloads and installs the updates.

Changing the Windows Home Server Password

The Windows Home Server password—that is, the password associated with the Administrator account—must meet or exceed the current Windows Home Server password policy requirements for length and complexity. However, you may feel that you can make the password more secure by making it longer or by including characters from all four of the following sets: lowercase letters, uppercase letters, numbers, and symbols. Similarly, you might want to enhance security by changing the password regularly, as security experts urge us to do. Either way, here are the steps to follow to change the password using the Windows Home Server Dashboard:

1. Launch the Windows Home Server Dashboard.
2. Click the Home section.
3. Click Common Tasks.
4. Click Reset Server Password.
5. Use the Existing Server Password text box to type the current password.
6. Type the new password in the Type a New Password and Confirm the New Password text boxes. Make sure you see check marks beside each item in the Password Requirements section.
7. Type a password hint.
8. Click Change Password to put the new password into effect. Windows Home Server tells you that the password has been changed.
9. Click OK.

TIP

If you just want to change the password hint, follow the steps in this section, but enter the current password in the Password and Confirm Password text boxes. Then enter the new hint in the Password Hint text box. Alternatively, you can edit the hint via the Registry Editor. Log on to the server and select Start, Run to open the Run dialog box, type **regedit**, and click OK. In the Registry Editor, open the following key: HKLM\Software\Microsoft\Windows Server\Identity. Double-click the PasswordHint setting, type the new hint, and then click OK.

Restarting or Shutting Down Windows Home Server

The Windows Home Server is meant to run as an always-on appliance that should rarely need to be restarted or shut down. However, if you find that Windows Home Server is performing sluggishly or acting flaky, the standard Windows troubleshooting advice—reboot the machine!—might be in order. Similarly, if you need to add an internal circuit board or hard drive, or if you'll be going on vacation for an extended time, you need to shut down the server.

If you're logged on to the Windows Home Server, you can use the normal Windows technique of selecting Start, Shut Down to display the Shut Down Windows dialog box, choosing Restart or Shut Down in the list, and then clicking OK.

If you're on a client, you can restart or shut down the server remotely using the Windows Home Server Dashboard. Here are the steps to follow:

1. Launch the Windows Home Server Dashboard.
2. Click Server Settings to open the Server Settings dialog box.
3. Click the arrow beside the Shut Down icon.
4. Click either Restart or Shut Down. Windows Home Server asks you to confirm.
5. Click Yes.

TIP

On the client machine, you probably want to know when Windows Home Server restarts. One way to do this is to select Start, All Programs, Command Prompt to open a command prompt session. Enter the following command (replace the IP address shown with the IP address of the server):

```
ping 192.168.1.254 -t.
```

This tells Windows to repeatedly ping the server's IP address. While the server is restarting, Windows displays the following result for each ping:

```
Request timed out.
```

When the server is back up and running, you'll know because the ping result changes to something like the following:

```
Reply from 192.168.1.254: bytes=32 time=1ms TTL=128
```

Press Ctrl+C to stop the pinging.

Configuring the Windows Home Server Startup

A couple of years ago, not long after I installed a prerelease version of the original Windows Home Server, I also installed a screen capture program so that I could capture some screen shots for the first edition of this book. Unfortunately, the Windows Home Server beta and that screen capture program did *not* get along. The machine crashed, and

I mean *hard*: It wouldn't boot into Windows Home Server, nor would it boot to the Windows Home Server DVD or to *any* bootable medium I added to the machine. The server was simply dead in the water.

Fortunately, I know a few startup tricks, and I was able to use one of those tricks to get the machine back on its feet. (Hint: I ran a startup command called Last Known Good Configuration, which I'll tell you about shortly.) I hope you never have serious (or even minor) startup problems with your Windows Home Server machine. However, just in case you do, you should know about a few startup tips and techniques.

Configuring Startup with the Advanced Boot Options Menu

After you start your Windows Home Server computer, wait until the Power On Self Test (POST) is complete (this is usually signaled by a beep), and then press F8 to display the Advanced Boot Options menu. (If your computer is set up to "fast boot," it might not be obvious when the POST ends. In that case, just turn on your computer and press F8 repeatedly until you see the Advanced Boot Options menu.) Here's the menu you see:

```
Advanced Boot Options
Choose Advanced Options for: Windows Server 2008 R2
(Use the arrow keys to highlight your choice.)

    Repair Your Computer

    Safe Mode
    Safe Mode with Networking
    Safe Mode with Command Prompt

    Enable Boot Logging
    Enable low-resolution video (640x480)
    Last Known Good Configuration (advanced)
    Directory Services Restore Mode
    Debugging Mode
    Disable automatic restart on system failure
    Disable Driver Signature Requirement

    Start Windows Normally
```

The Start Windows Normally option loads Windows Home Server in the usual fashion. You can use the other options to control the rest of the startup procedure:

- ▶ **SEE** "Troubleshooting Startup," **P. 448.**

- ▶ **Safe Mode**—If you're having trouble with Windows Home Server—for example, if a corrupt or incorrect video driver is mangling your display, or if Windows Home Server won't start—you can use the Safe Mode option to run a stripped-down version of Windows Home Server that includes only the minimal set of device drivers that Home Server requires to load. You could reinstall or roll back the offending device driver and then load Home Server normally. When Windows Home Server finally loads, the desktop reminds you that you're in Safe mode by displaying Safe Mode in each corner.

NOTE

If you're curious to know which drivers are loaded during a Safe mode boot, see the subkeys in the following Registry key:

`HKLM\SYSTEM\CurrentControlSet\Control\SafeBoot\Minimal\`

▶ **Safe Mode with Networking**—This option is identical to plain Safe mode, except that Windows Home Server's networking drivers are also loaded at startup. This enables you to log on to your network, which is handy if you need to access the network to load a device driver, run a troubleshooting utility, or send a tech support request.

▶ **Safe Mode with Command Prompt**—This option is the same as plain Safe mode, except that it doesn't load the Windows Home Server graphical user interface (GUI). Instead, it runs `CMD.EXE` to load a command prompt session.

▶ **Enable Boot Logging**—This option is the same as the Start Windows Normally option, except that Windows Home Server logs the boot process in a text file named `NTBTLOG.TXT` that resides in the system root.

▶ **Enable Low-Resolution Video (640x480)**—This option loads Windows Home Server with the video display set to 640×480 and 256 colors.

▶ **Last Known Good Configuration**—This option boots Windows Home Server using the last hardware configuration that produced a successful boot. This is the option I used to get my Windows Home Server machine back on its feet after it was cut off at the knees by the screen capture program.

▶ **Directory Services Restore Mode**—This option applies only to Windows domain controllers, so it doesn't apply to Windows Home Server machines.

▶ **Debugging Mode**—This option enables the Windows kernel debugger during startup.

▶ **Disable Automatic Restart on System Failure**—This option prevents Windows Home Server from restarting automatically when the system crashes. Choose this option if you want to prevent your system from restarting so that you can troubleshoot the problem.

▶ **Disable Driver Signature Enforcement**—Prevents Windows Home Server from checking whether device drivers have digital signatures. Choose this option to ensure that Windows Home Server loads an unsigned driver, if failing to load that driver is causing system problems.

Configuring Startup with the System Configuration Editor

The Advanced Boot Options menu is useful for one-time startup tweaks. If you want to make a more permanent change to the Windows Home Server startup, you're better off using the System Configuration Editor. To start this program, log on to the server, select Start, type **msconfig**, and press Enter. When the System Configuration window appears, select the Boot tab, shown in Figure 4.9.

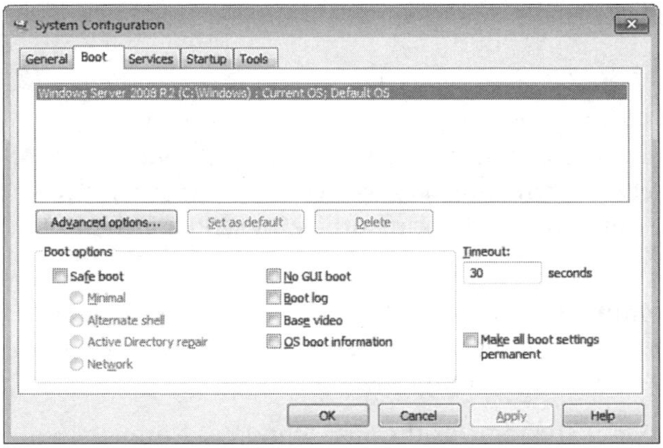

FIGURE 4.9   In the System Configuration Utility, use the Boot tab to create a custom startup.

The large box near the top of the tab displays the Windows installations on the current computer. I'm going to assume that you're not dual-booting your Windows Home Server machine with another OS, so I'll skip the multiboot options.

To create the custom startup, you use the check boxes in the Boot Options section:

▶ **Safe Boot: Minimal**—Boots Windows Home Server in Safe mode, which uses only a minimal set of device drivers. Use this switch if Windows Home Server won't start, if a device or program is causing Windows Home Server to crash, or if you can't uninstall a program while Windows Home Server is running normally.

▶ **Safe Boot: Alternate Shell**—Boots Windows Home Server in Safe mode but also bypasses the Windows Home Server GUI and boots to the command prompt instead. Use this switch if the programs you need to repair a problem can be run from the command prompt or if you can't load the Windows Home Server GUI.

NOTE

The value in the following Registry key determines the shell that the /safeboot:minimal(alternateshell) switch loads:

    HKLM\SYSTEM\CurrentControlSet\Control\SafeBoot\AlternateShell

The default value is CMD.EXE (the command prompt).

▶ **Safe Boot: Active Directory Repair**—Applies only to domain controllers, so you won't use it with Windows Home Server. It boots the OS in Safe mode and restores a backup of the Active Directory service.

▶ **Safe Boot: Network**—Boots Windows Home Server in Safe mode but also includes networking drivers. Use this switch if the drivers or programs you need to repair a problem exist on a shared network resource, or if you need access to email or other network-based communications for technical support.

▶ **No GUI Boot**—Tells Windows Home Server not to load the VGA display driver that is normally used to display the progress bar during startup. Use this switch if Windows Home Server hangs while switching video modes for the progress bar, or if the display of the progress bar is garbled.

▶ **Boot Log**—Boots Windows Home Server and logs the boot process to a text file named NTBTLOG.TXT that resides in the %SystemRoot% folder. Move to the end of the file, and you might see a message telling you which device driver failed. You probably need to reinstall or roll back the driver. Use this switch if the Windows Home Server startup hangs, if you need a detailed record of the startup process, or if you suspect (after using one of the other Startup menu options) that a driver is causing Windows Home Server startup to fail.

NOTE

%SystemRoot% refers to the folder into which Windows was installed. Windows Home Server is always installed in C:\Windows, so on Windows Home Server systems, the %SystemRoot% environment variable always refers to that folder.

▶ **Base Video**—Boots Windows Home Server using the standard VGA mode: 640×480 with 256 colors. This is useful for troubleshooting video display driver problems. Use this switch if Windows Home Server fails to start using any of the Safe mode options, if you recently installed a new video card device driver and the screen is garbled or the driver is balking at a resolution or color depth setting that's too high, or if you can't load the Windows Home Server GUI. After Windows Home Server has loaded, you can reinstall or roll back the driver, or you can adjust the display settings to values that the driver can handle.

▶ **OS Boot Information**—Displays the path and location of each device driver as it loads, as well as the operating system version and build number, the number of processors, the system memory, and the process type.

You can also click the Advanced Options button to display the BOOT Advanced Options dialog box shown in Figure 4.10. You can set the following options:

▶ **Number of Processors**—In a multiprocessor (or multicore) system, specifies the maximum processors that Windows Home Server can use. Activate this check box if you suspect that using multiple processors is causing a program to hang.

▶ **Maximum Memory**—Specifies the maximum amount of memory, in megabytes, that Windows Home Server can use. Use this value when you suspect a faulty memory chip might be causing problems.

▶ **PCI Lock**—Activate this check box to tell Windows Home Server not to dynamically assign hardware resources for PCI devices during startup. The resources assigned by the BIOS during the POST are locked in place. Use this switch if installing a PCI device causes the system to hang during startup.

▶ **Debug**—Enables remote debugging of the Windows Home Server kernel. This sends debugging information to a remote computer via one of your computer's ports. If you use this switch, you can use the Debug Port list to specify a serial port, IEEE 1394 port, or USB port. If you use a serial port, you can specify the transmission speed of the debugging information using the Baud Rate list; if you use an IEEE 1394 connection, activate Channel and specify a channel value; if you use a USB port, type the device name in the USB Target Name text box.

FIGURE 4.10   Click Advanced Options to display the dialog box shown here.

Launching Applications and Scripts at Startup

Two key features of Windows Home Server are that it's always on and that it's always available to computers and devices on the network. Many people take advantage of these features to run programs and scripts on the server. For example, one common Windows Home Server application is a home automation system. Another is a program that sends random images to a digital photo frame.

Because you want these and similar programs to be always running, you can save yourself the hassle of launching these programs manually by getting Windows Home Server to do it for you automatically at startup. Similarly, you can get Windows Home Server to automatically launch scripts or batch files at startup. As the next few sections show, you can set up a program or script for automatic startup launch using the Startup folder, the Registry, group policies, and the Task Scheduler.

Launching Items Using the Startup Folder

The Startup folder is a regular file folder, but it has a special place in Windows Home Server. You can get a program or script to run automatically at startup by adding a shortcut for that item to the Startup folder.

Note that the Startup folder appears twice in the Windows Home Server interface:

▶ Via the Start menu. (Click Start, All Programs, Startup.)

▶ Via Windows Explorer as a subfolder:

   `%AppData%:\Microsoft\Windows\Start Menu\Programs\Startup`

NOTE

%AppData% refers to the folder that contains the current users data, which in Windows Home Server is %SystemDrive%:\Users\Administrator\AppData\Roaming.

TIP

You can prevent the Startup items from running by holding down the Shift key while Windows Home Server loads. (Hold down Shift after logging on.)

Launching Items Using the Registry

The Startup folder method has two drawbacks: Anyone who has access to the server can easily delete shortcuts from the Startup and can bypass Startup items by holding down the Shift key while Windows Home Server loads. These aren't likely to be major problems on Windows Home Server. However, should the need arise, you can work around both problems by using the Registry Editor (see Chapter 18) to define your startup items.

The Registry offers two keys (note that these are in HKEY_CUURENT_USER, which is the key for the current user's settings):

▶ **HKCU\Software\Microsoft\Windows\CurrentVersion\Run**—The values in this key run automatically each time the user logs on.

▶ **HKCU\Software\Microsoft\Windows\CurrentVersion\RunOnce**—The values in this key run only the next time the user logs on; then they are deleted from the key. (This key might not be present in your Registry. In that case, you need to add this key yourself.)

To create a startup item, add a string value to the appropriate key, give it whatever name you like, and then set its value to the full pathname of the executable file or script file that you want to launch at startup.

TIP

If the program is in the %SystemRoot% folder, you can get away with entering only the name of the executable file. Also, if the program you want to run at startup is capable of running in the background, you can load it in this mode by appending /background after the pathname.

Launching Items Using Group Policies

If you prefer not to edit the Registry directly, or if you want to place a GUI between you and the Registry, Windows Home Server's Local Group Policy Editor can help. Note, however, that the Local Group Policy Editor doesn't work directly with the Run keys in the HKCU hive because these are considered to be legacy keys, meaning they're mostly used by older programs. The new key (new as of Windows 2000, that is) is the following:

`HKCU\Software\Microsoft\Windows\CurrentVersion\Policies\Explorer\Run`

This key doesn't appear in Windows Home Server by default. You see it only after you specify startup programs in the Local Group Policy Editor, as discussed in the next section. Alternatively, you can add these keys yourself using the Registry Editor.

NOTE

The startup items run in the following order:

`HKCU\Software\Microsoft\Windows\CurrentVersion\Run`

`HKCU\Software\Microsoft\Windows\CurrentVersion\Policies\Explorer\Run`

`HKCU\Software\Microsoft\Windows\CurrentVersion\RunOnce`

`Startup folder (all users)`

`Startup folder (current user).`

Adding Programs to the Run Key

To open the Local Group Policy Editor in Windows Home Server, select Start, type **gpedit.msc**, and press Enter. In the Local Group Policy Editor window, select User Configuration, Administrative Templates, System, Logon.

You see at least the following three policies:

▶ **Run These Programs at User Logon**—Use this policy to add or remove startup programs using the \Policies\Explorer\Run key in the Registry. To add a program, double-click the policy, select the Enabled option, and then click Show. In the Show Contents dialog box, enter the full pathname of the program or script you want to run at startup, and then click OK.

▶ **Do Not Process the Run Once List**—Use this policy to toggle whether Windows Home Server processes the RunOnce Registry key (which I discussed in the previous section). Double-click this policy, and then activate the Enabled option to put this policy into effect; that is, programs listed in the RunOnce key are not launched at startup.

▶ **Do Not Process the Legacy Run List**—Use this policy to toggle whether Windows Home Server processes the legacy Run key. Double-click this policy and then activate the Enabled option to put this policy into effect; that is, programs listed in the legacy Run key are not launched at startup.

Specifying Startup and Logon Scripts

You also can use the Local Group Policy Editor to specify script files to run at startup. Select User Configuration, Windows Settings, Scripts (Logon/Logoff), double-click the Logon policy, click Add, and then specify the location of the script. You can also use the Logoff policy to specify a script to run when you log off Windows Home Server.

Finally, note that Windows Home Server has policies dictating how these scripts run. For example, you can see the startup script policies by selecting User Configuration, Administrative Templates, System, Scripts. Three items affect startup scripts:

▶ **Run Logon Scripts Synchronously**—If you enable this item, Windows Home Server runs the logon scripts one at a time.

▶ **Run Startup Scripts Asynchronously**—If you enable this item, Windows Home Server runs the startup scripts at the same time.

▶ **Run Startup Scripts Visible**—If you enable this item, Windows Home Server makes the startup script commands visible to the user in a command window.

For logon scripts, a similar set of policies appears in the User Configuration, Administrative Templates, System, Scripts section.

CAUTION

Logon scripts are supposed to execute before the Windows Home Server interface is displayed to the user. However, Windows Home Server's Fast Logon Optimization can interfere with that by displaying the interface before all the scripts are done. The Fast Logon Optimization feature runs the user logon scripts asynchronously, which greatly speeds up the logon time because no script has to wait for another to finish.

To prevent this, select Computer Configuration, Administrative Templates, System, Logon and enable the Always Wait for the Network at Computer Startup and Logon setting.

Using the Task Scheduler

Yet another way to set up a program or script to run at startup is to use the Task Scheduler. (Select Start, type **task**, and then click Task Scheduler.) When you create a new task (by clicking Create Basic Task), two of the "trigger" options you'll see are the following:

▶ **When the Computer Starts**—Choose this option to run the program when your computer boots.

▶ **When I Log On**—Choose this option to run the program only when you log on to Windows Home Server.

From Here

▶ To learn how to set up an automatic logon, **SEE** "Automating Client Logons," **P. 39.**

▶ For details on running the Connector software, **SEE** "Installing Windows Home Server Connector on the Client Computers," **P. 49.**

▶ To learn more about the Alert Viewer, **SEE** "Monitoring Windows Home Server with the Alert Viewer," **P. 242.**

▶ To learn how to use the Advanced Options menu to troubleshoot startup woes, **SEE** "Troubleshooting Startup," **P. 448.**

▶ For details on the Registry and using the Registry Editor, **SEE** Chapter 18, "Working with the Windows Home Server Registry."

▶ For more information on the Services snap-in, **SEE** "Controlling Services with the Services Snap-In," **P. 566.**

▶ To learn more about WMI scripting, **SEE** "Programming the Windows Management Instrumentation Service," **P. 617.**

CHAPTER 5

Setting Up and Using Home Server Storage

IN THIS CHAPTER

▸ Understanding Storage in Windows Home Server 2011

▸ Working with Server Backup Drives

▸ Who Needs Drive Extender? Implementing Spanning, Mirroring, and RAID

▸ Repairing Storage

W indows Home Server offers the home network a wide range of capabilities that include monitoring the health of network PCs (for example, detecting whether the clients have their firewalls turned on), establishing a central fax server, and enabling remote access to any computer from outside the network. I'll go into all of these features in a satisfying amount of detail later in the book. However, just about every other Windows Home Server feature is related to storage: shared folders, media streaming, centralized backup and restore, and backups of the home server itself. In other words, it's no stretch to say that storage is at the heart of Windows Home Server and is the source of much of what makes Windows Home Server such a useful package.

With that in mind, this chapter takes you on a complete tour of all the Windows Home Server storage features. You learn some background on the technologies behind Windows Home Server storage, and you learn techniques such as adding, configuring, and removing storage, turning on folder duplication, repairing storage, and much more.

Understanding Storage in Windows Home Server 2011

Although Windows Home Server 2011 comes with many new and useful features—the Dashboard, the Launchpad, improved Mac support, easier remote access, and more—all anyone seems to talk about is what's *not* in Windows Home Server 2011. I speak, of course, of Drive Extender, the file system technology that in version 1 of Windows Home Server made disk management supremely simple by offering data redundancy in the form of folder duplication, a seamlessly expandable pool of storage data that could span multiple hard drives, and load balancing.

As I write this just before the launch of Windows Home Server 2011, it's unclear why Microsoft removed Drive Extender so abruptly, and we may never know the full story. What is clear is that Microsoft is relying on system vendors and other third parties to come up with innovative storage solutions that mimic or surpass what Drive Extender could do, and no doubt there are lots of clever people working on just that.

However, it's also clear that many of the tools you need to mimic most of the functionality of Drive Extender are already present in Windows Home Server 2011. Or, to be more accurate, those tools are present in the OS that underlies Windows Home Server 2011: Windows Server 2008 R2. Here's a summary:

▶ **Data redundancy**—You can mimic this Drive Extender feature by using the Disk Management snap-in feature called *mirroring*. See "Creating Data Redundancy Using Mirrored Volumes," later in this chapter.

▶ **Expandable storage pool**—You can mimic this Drive Extender feature by using another Disk Management feature called a *spanned volume*. See "Creating a Storage Pool Using a Spanned Volume," later in this chapter.

▶ **Redundancy, expandability, and load balancing**—You can reproduce almost everything in Drive Extender by using Disk Management to implement a *RAID 5* volume. See "Mimicking Drive Extender by Creating a RAID 5 Volume."

For now, however, let's take a quick look at how Windows Home Server 2011 handles storage without these tricks (and, of course, without Drive Extender).

Server Storage on a One-Drive System

If you have just one hard drive on your system, Windows Home Server divides the hard drive into two unnamed partitions, as shown in Figure 5.1: one for the Windows Home Server system files, which is seen as drive C: in the Computer folder, and another for the data, which is seen as drive D: in the Computer folder. Note, too, that in Windows Home Server 2011 the size of drive C: is 60GB, which is a welcome increase from the mere 20GB assigned to the system drive in previous versions of Windows Home Server.

How do you know the data gets stored on drive D:? Open the Windows Home Server Dashboard, click the Server Folders and Hard Drives icon, and then click the Server Folders tab. As you can see in Figure 5.2, the Location column shows that each Windows Home Server folder resides in `D:\ServerFolders`.

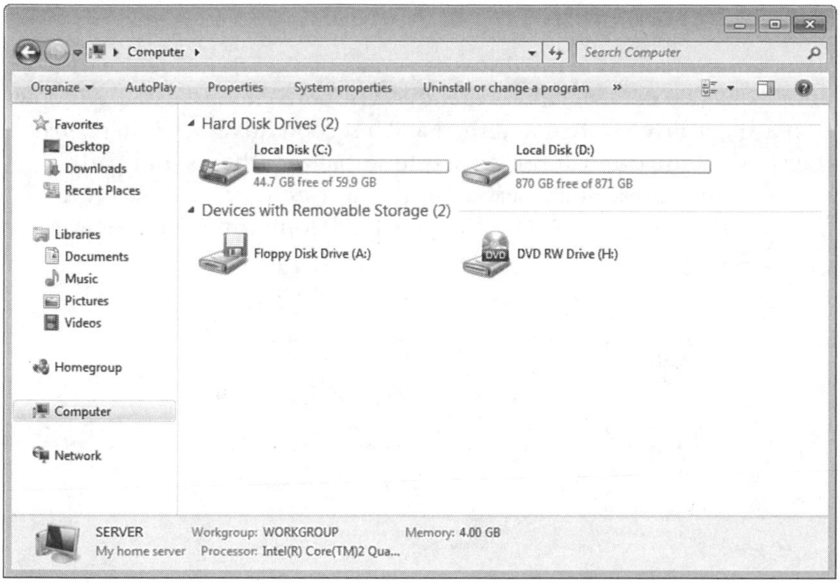

FIGURE 5.1   On a single-drive system, Windows Home Server 2011 creates two partitions C: and D: for the system and data files, respectively.

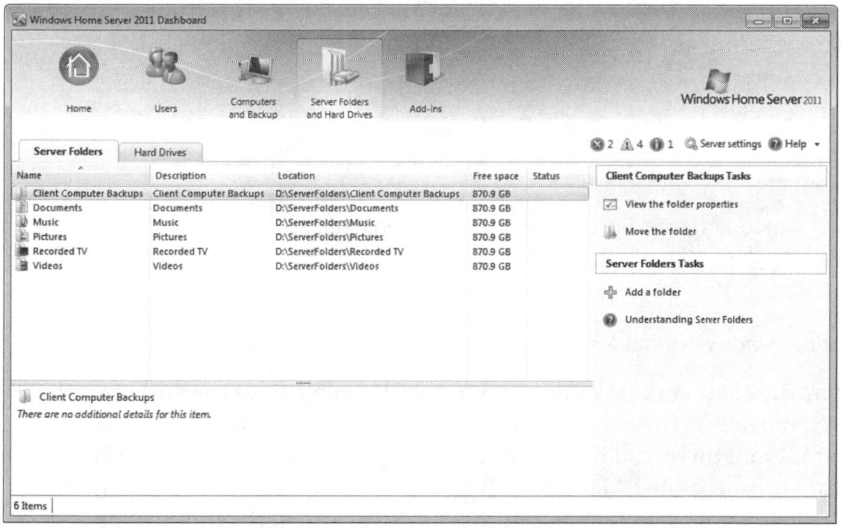

FIGURE 5.2   On a single-drive system, Windows Home Server 2011 stores its client backups and shared folders in D:\ServerFolders.

Server Storage on a System with Two or More Drives

Windows Home Server lets you add as many drives as you can either fit inside the case or plug into your system's USB (2.0 or 3.0), FireWire, and eSATA ports. If you install Windows Home Server 2011 on a single-drive system and then add a second drive, what happens next depends on the status of the drive. If the drive is uninitialized (that is, not partitioned and not formatted), Windows Home Server 2011 generates information alert for the server, which you can see in Figure 5.3. (See Chapter 10, "Monitoring Your Network," to learn more about the Alert Viewer.)

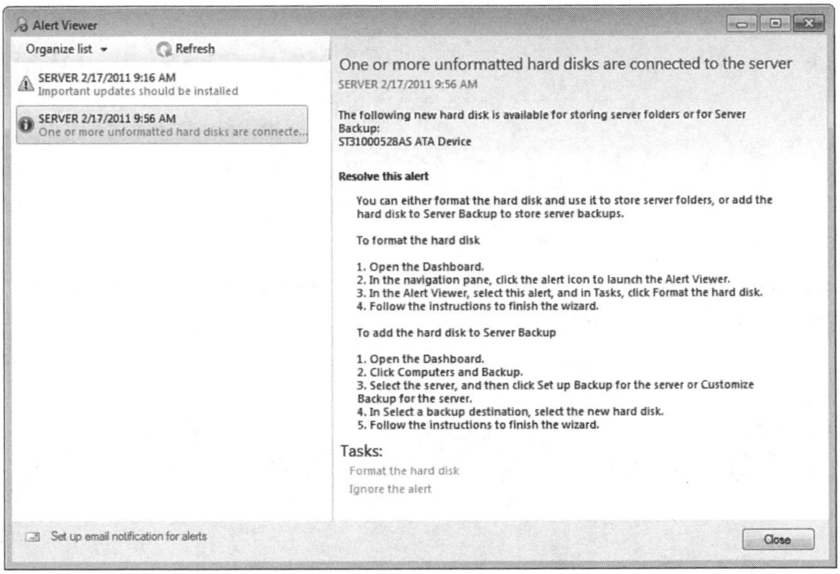

FIGURE 5.3   When Windows Home Server detects a new, uninitialized hard drive on the system, it generates an information alert similar to the one shown here.

▶ **SEE** "Monitoring Windows Home Server with the Alert Viewer," **P. 242**.

Clicking the Format the Hard Disk link at the bottom of the alert message initializes the drive and makes it available in the Dashboard's Server Folders and Hard Drives section (in the Hard Drives tab). From there you can either configure the drive for server backups (see "Adding a Drive for Server Backups," later in this chapter), or you can move any of the default Windows Home Server data folders to the new drive, as described in Chapter 6, "Sharing Folders and Files on the Home Server."

▶ **SEE** "Moving a Shared Folder," **P. 124**.

However, instead of adding a new drive to an existing Windows Home Server installation, you might instead install Windows Home Server on a system that already has two drives attached. In this scenario, Windows Home Server does a slightly odd thing. As with a single-drive install, Windows Home Server divides one hard drive into two unnamed partitions: one for the Windows Home Server system files, which is seen as drive C: in the Computer folder, and another for the data, which this time is seen as drive E: in the Computer folder (see Figure 5.4). The extra drive is formatted with a single partition and assigned drive D:.

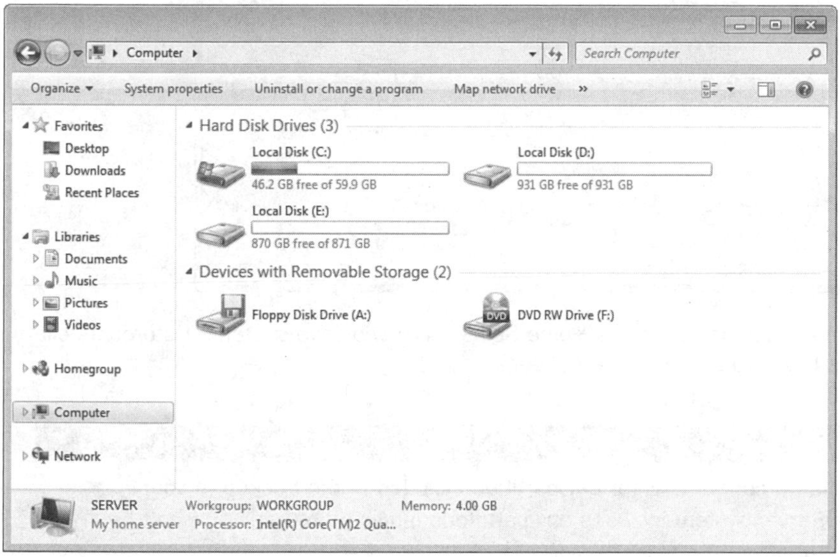

FIGURE 5.4   When you install Windows Home Server on a two-drive system, it creates two partitions C: and E: for the system and data files, respectively, and assigns drive D: to the other drive.

Again, we can confirm that the data gets stored on drive E: by opening the Windows Home Server Dashboard, clicking the Server Folders and Hard Drives icon, and then clicking the Server Folders tab. As you can see in Figure 5.5, the Location column shows that each Windows Home Server folder resides in E:\ServerFolders.

Working with Server Backup Drives

Adding a Drive for Server Backups

Windows Home Server 2011 may not have Drive Extender's folder duplication to protect the files stored on the server, but it does come with a decent Server Backup program that can backup not only the shared folder data, but also the client computer backups, and any extra hard drives you have added to the system. You can also use Server Backup to create a system image, which you can use to restore your entire system should your system drive go belly up.

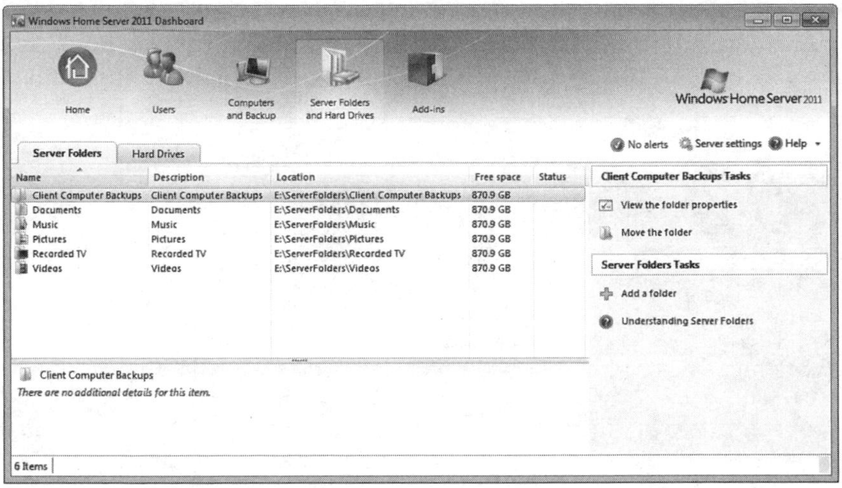

FIGURE 5.5   When you install Windows Home Server on a two-drive system, it stores its client backups and shared folders in E:\ServerFolders.

NOTE

Server Backup has a limit of 2TB for any partition included in the backup. If your Windows Home Server system includes any partitions larger than that, you won't be able to back them up.

With a new (ideally external) hard drive installed and formatted, follow these steps to add it as the Windows Home Server backup drive:

1. Open the Windows Home Server Dashboard.
2. Click Server Folders and Hard Drives.
3. Display the Hard Drives tab.
4. In the Hard Drives section, click the drive you want to add.
5. Click Add the Hard Drive to Server Backup. Windows Home Server launches the Set Up Server Backup Wizard.
6. Click Next in the wizard's initial dialog box. The wizard displays a list of hard drives that are suitable (and available) for use as server backup drives.
7. Activate the check box beside the drive you want to use, and then click Next. The wizard asks whether you want to format the new hard drive.
8. Click Yes. The wizard prompts you for a drive name.
9. Type a name for the drive, and then click Next. The wizard prompts you to specify a backup schedule, as shown in Figure 5.6.

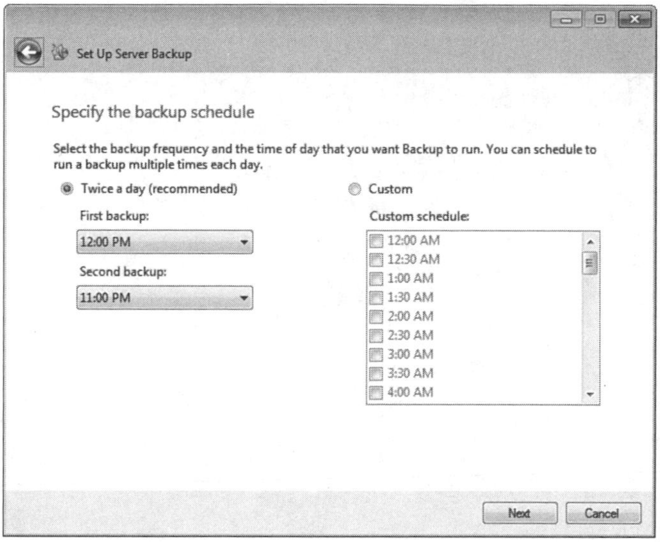

FIGURE 5.6   When you set up a hard drive to use as a server backup drive, you also need to specify a backup schedule.

10. You have two choices:

   ▶ **Twice a Day**—Select this option to run a twice-daily backup, and use the First Backup and Second Backup lists to select the backup times.

   ▶ **Custom**—Select this option if you want to run only a single backup, or if you want to run three or more daily backups. Use the check boxes in the Custom Schedule list to select the backup time or times you want to use.

11. Click Next. The wizard prompts you to select the items you want to include in the backup.

12. Activate the check box beside each item you want to include in the backup, and then click Next.

13. Click Apply Settings. The wizard sets up the server backup.

14. Click Close. Windows Home Server Dashboard creates a new section in the Hard Drives tab called Server Backup, and it displays your new drive in that section (see Figure 5.7). (Your Windows Home Server machine also now appears in the Computers and Backup section of the Dashboard.)

NOTE

You can use multiple drives with Server Backup, which is useful if a single hard drive isn't large enough to store the entire backup (particularly the Windows Home Server system image). Repeat the steps in this section to add more drives to the server backup.

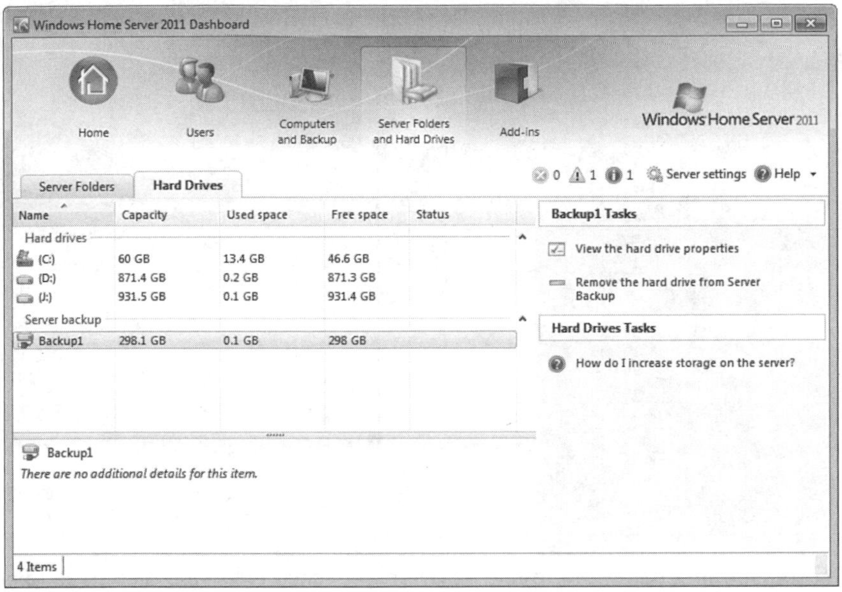

FIGURE 5.7   In the Hard Drives tab, you now see a Server Backup section that displays the hard drive (or drives) that you use for backing up Windows Home Server.

Removing a Server Backup Drive

If you have a hard drive that's currently being used as a backup device for Windows Home Server, follow these steps to remove it:

1. Launch the Windows Home Server Dashboard.

2. Click Server Folders and Hard Drives.

3. Display the Hard Drives tab.

4. Click the drive you want to remove from the system.

5. Click Remove the Hard Drive from Server Backup. Windows Home Server starts the Customize Server Backup Wizard.

6. Click Next. The wizard displays the Configuration Options dialog box.

7. Click Change Server Backup Settings. The wizard displays the Select the Backup Destination dialog box.

8. Deactivate the check box beside the drive you want to remove.

9. Click Next until you reach the Confirm the Backup Settings dialog box.

10. Click Apply Settings. Windows Home Server removes the hard drive from the server backup pool.

11. Click Close to shut down the wizard.

Who Needs Drive Extender? Implementing Spanning, Mirroring, and RAID

People loved Drive Extender because of its seamlessness and set-it-and-forget-it nature. It was and remains the easiest drive maintenance tool that Microsoft (or, really, anyone) has ever built. Its loss is a blow, to be sure, but as I said earlier in this chapter it's not a catastrophic one. There are plenty of good reasons to use Windows Home Server 2011, and there are plenty of tools that you can wield to implement most of what Drive Extender could do. The next few sections show you how to use those tools.

Creating a Storage Pool Using a Spanned Volume

One of the best features of Drive Extender (indeed, one of the best features in all of Windows Home Server version 1) was the dynamic storage pool. If you installed a new hard drive on the server, you could then add that drive to the existing drives and instantly get a larger storage pool for client backups and shared folder data.

Alas, Drive Extender now resides in the trash bin of technology history, so you have to deal with fixed disk sizes in Windows Home Server 2011. This can be a particular problem with client backups because they tend to take up a lot of disk space, and if the server drive that stores the backups gets full, subsequent backups will fail.

That is, to say the least, not good, so you're forced to look for other solutions. Fortunately, one such solution sits right under your nose as a feature of Windows Server 2008 R2: a spanned drive. This is a kind of virtual drive—or *volume*, as Windows Server calls it—that combines two or more physical hard drives into a single storage area with two main characteristics:

▶ The new volume is *dynamic* because if you install more drives on the server, you can add those drives to the volume to instantly increase the storage area without losing any existing data.

▶ The new volume is *spanned* because data is seamlessly stored on all the physical hard drives without your having to worry about where the data is stored. If one of the hard drives fills up, Windows Server automatically writes new data to one of the other drives in the volume.

In other words, a dynamic, spanned volume is a reasonable facsimile of the storage pool feature of Drive Extender. Is there a downside to using spanned volumes? Yes, unfortunately, there are two:

▶ If one of the hard drives dies, you lose all the data stored in the spanned volume, even data that resides on the remaining functional drives.

▶ If the total size of the spanned volume exceeds 2TB, you won't be able to back up the volume using the Server Backup feature of Windows Home Server 2011 (because Server Backup has a 2TB maximum for any volume).

In other words, if you go this route, I strongly recommend that you come up with some other way to back up the spanned volume to prevent data loss (for example, by installing a third-party backup program on the server).

Converting Hard Drives to Dynamic Disks

To get started, your first chore is to take the hard drives that you want to use for the spanned volume and convert them to dynamic disks:

1. Log on to the Windows Home Server machine.
2. In the taskbar, click Server Manager to open the Server Manager window.
3. Select Storage, Disk Management to display the Disk Management snap-in.
4. In the list of hard drives in the lower half of the Disk Management pane, right-click one of the drives you want to convert to a dynamic volume. Be sure to right-click on the left side of the drive display (where you see the disk designations, such as Disk 1, Disk 2, and so on).
5. Click Convert to Dynamic Disk. Disk Management displays the Convert to Dynamic Disk dialog box.
6. Make sure the check box beside the disk is activated, as shown in Figure 5.8, and then click OK. Disk Management displays the Disks to Convert dialog box.

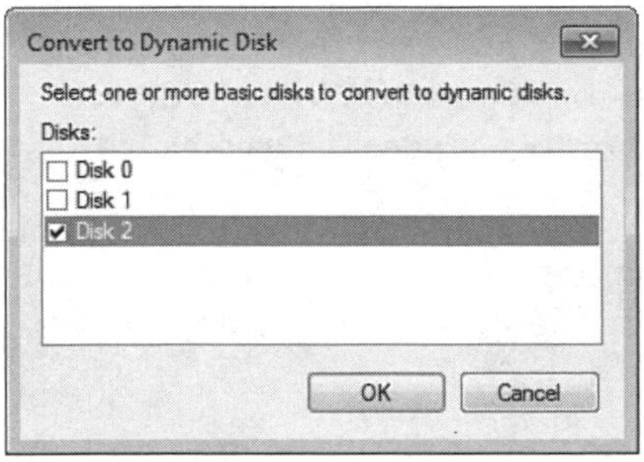

FIGURE 5.8   Your first task is to convert to dynamic disks those drives you want to include in the spanned volume.

7. Click Convert. Disk Management asks you to confirm.
8. Click Yes. Disk Management converts the drive to a dynamic disk.
9. Repeat steps 4–8 to convert any other drives you want to include in the spanned volume.

Combing Dynamic Disks into a Spanned Volume

With your dynamic disks converted, you can now combine them into a spanned volume by following these steps:

1. Log on to the Windows Home Server machine.
2. In the taskbar, click Server Manager to open the Server Manager window.

3. Select Storage, Disk Management to display the Disk Management snap-in.

4. In the list of hard drives in the lower half of the Disk Management pane, right-click one of the drives you want to include in the spanned volume. Be sure to right-click on the left side of the drive display (where you see the disk designations, such as Disk 1, Disk 2, and so on).

5. Click New Spanned Volume. Disk Management runs the New Spanned Volume Wizard.

6. Click Next. The Select Disks dialog box appears.

7. In the Available list, click a dynamic disk you want to include in the volume, and then click Add.

NOTE

You don't have to include the entire dynamic disk in the spanned volume. For example, you might want to set aside a portion of the dynamic disk for other storage uses. In that case, click the disk in the Selected list, and then use the Select the Amount of Space in MB spin box to set the amount of space you want to assign to the spanned volume.

---

8. Repeat step 7 to add any other drives you want to include in the volume. Figure 5.9 shows a spanned volume with two dynamic disks added.

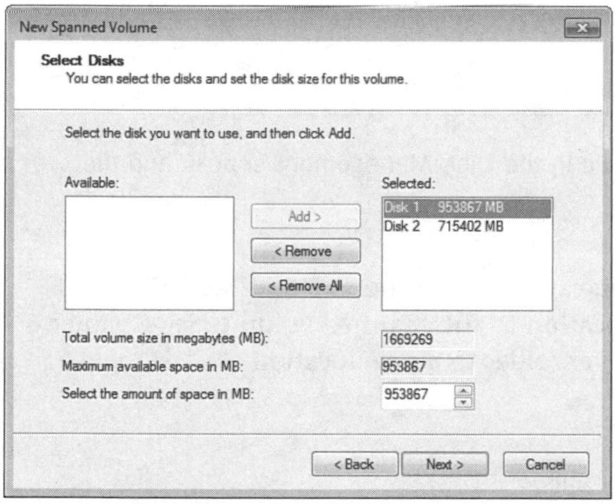

FIGURE 5.9   Add the dynamic drives that you want to include in the new spanned volume.

9. Click Next. The Assign Drive Letter or Path dialog box appears.

10. Choose a drive letter (the default will probably be D:, which is fine), and then click Next. The Format Volume dialog box appears.

11. Assign a Volume Label, if needed, leave the other options as is, and then click Next. The last wizard dialog box appears.

12. Click Finish. Disk Management creates the spanned volume.

Figure 5.10 shows how the new spanned volume (drive D:, in this case) appears in Disk Management (the top window) and in the Computer folder (bottom window).

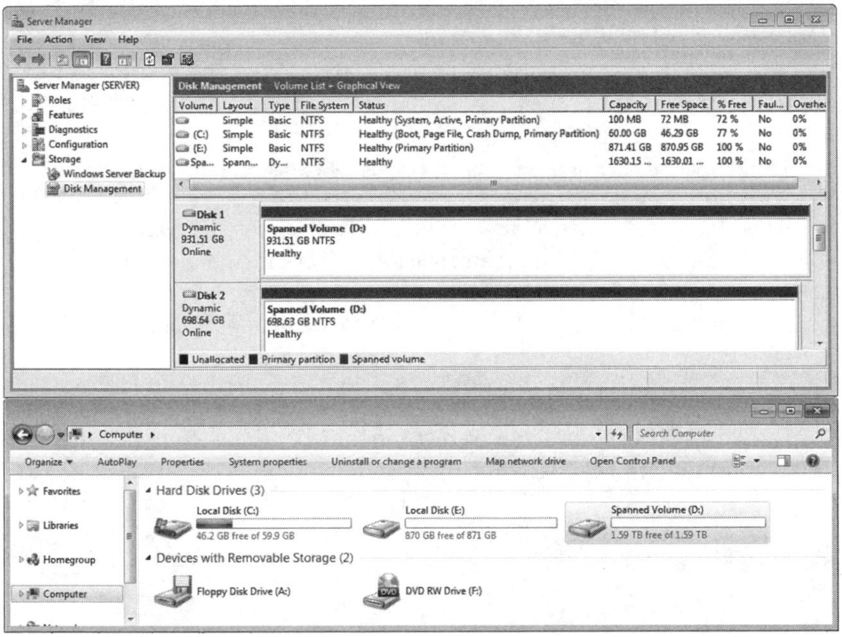

FIGURE 5.10   The new spanned volume shown in the Disk Management snap-in and the Computer folder.

With your spanned volume at the ready, you can move Windows Home Server's Client Computer Backups folder from its default location to the spanned volume. See Chapter 6 to learn how to move a Windows Home Server folder to a new location.

▶ **SEE** "Moving a Shared Folder," **P. 124**.

Adding another Dynamic Disk to the Spanned Volume

If you install a new hard drive on the server, you can add that drive to the spanned volume. Open the Disk Management snap-in and convert the new drive to a dynamic disk, as I described earlier. Now follow these steps to add the new dynamic disk to the spanned volume:

1. In the list of hard drives in the lower half of the Disk Management pane, right-click one of the disks in your current spanned volume. Be sure to right-click on the right of the drive display (where you see the spanned volume drive letter).

2. Click Extend Volume. Disk Management runs the Extend Volume Wizard.

3. Click Next. The Select Disks dialog box appears.

4. In the Available list, click the new dynamic disk, and then click Add.

5. Click Next. The last wizard dialog box appears.

6. Click Finish. Disk Management adds the dynamic disk to the spanned volume.

Creating Data Redundancy Using Mirrored Volumes

A spanned volume is an easy way to set up a dynamic storage pool using multiple drives, which is great if you don't want your data needs being cramped by a single hard drive. However, what if your concerns are more about data redundancy? That is, if you want to minimize server downtime, then the best way to do that is to have a redundant set of data on another hard drive. That way, if the original hard drive goes down for the count, you can still keep the server running off the redundant data on the other drives.

Drive Extender accomplished this by using folder duplication to maintain two copies of any shared folder file on multiple hard drives. You can replicate this data redundancy fairly well by setting up another drive or partition as a *mirror* of the original. Windows Home Server maintains exact copies of the data on the mirror drive, and if the original drive dies, the server still continues to function by using the mirrored data.

There are a couple of ways you can go about this:

▶ If you have a single hard drive and plan on leaving your system files and data on that drive, then you can add a second hard drive of the same size (or larger) and use this new hard drive as a mirror for your original data.

▶ If you've added a second hard drive and are using it to store important data (such as ripped movies or recorded TV shows), then you can add a third drive of the same size (or larger) and use this new drive as a mirror of the data drive.

Of course, there's nothing stopping you from combining both techniques, depending on your data needs (and your hard drive budget!).

Here are the steps to follow to mirror a partition:

1. Log on to the Windows Home Server machine.

2. In the taskbar, click Server Manager to open the Server Manager window.

3. Select Storage, Disk Management to display the Disk Management snap-in.

4. Make sure the disk you want to use for the mirror has no current partitions. If it does have partitions, then for each one right-click the partition and click Delete Volume.

5. In the list of partitions in the lower half of the Disk Management pane, right-click the partition you want to mirror, and then click Add Mirror. The Add Mirror dialog box appears.

6. Click the disk you want to use for the mirror, and then click Add Mirror. Disk Management warns you that the disk to be mirrored must be converted to a dynamic disk and asks you to confirm this conversion.

7. Click Yes. Disk Management converts the disk to dynamic and then starts mirror the partition to the other hard drive.

8. Repeat steps 5 to 7 for any other partitions you also want to mirror. Figure 5.11 shows the Disk Management snap-in with two mirrors: On Disk 0, drives C: and E: are being mirrored to same sized partitions on Disk 1. The original sync might take as little as a few minutes or as much as a few tens of hours, depending on how much data is to be mirrored.

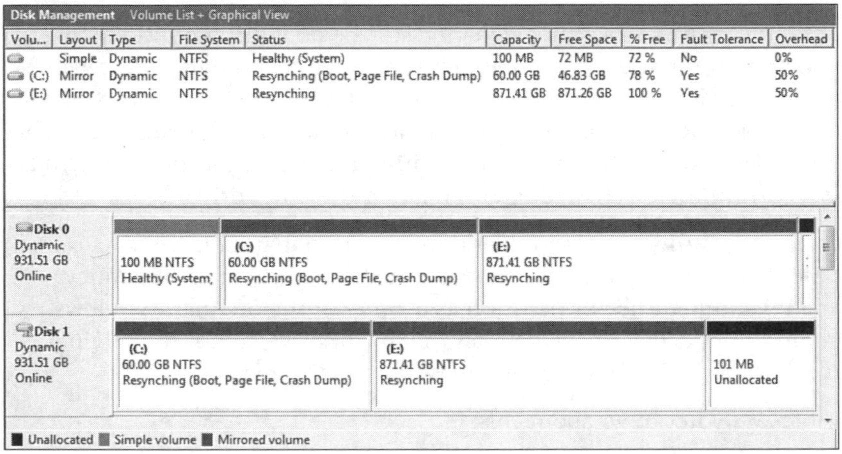

FIGURE 5.11   Disk Management showing mirrors for drives C: and E:.

Mimicking Drive Extender by Creating a RAID 5 Volume

So far you've seen that you can mimic Drive Extender's expandable storage pool by creating a spanned volume that stores data in a single storage area that encompasses two or more hard drives (see "Creating a Storage Pool Using a Spanned Volume"). Similarly, you saw that you can mimic Drive Extender's folder duplication by creating mirrored volumes that store each file and folder on two or more hard drives (see "Creating Data Redundancy Using Mirrored Volumes"). These are easy-to-implement techniques that can be really useful, depending on your data and safety needs.

However, there's a third technique that I want to show you that combines spanning and mirroring, and also includes a bit of load balancing (writing to a second hard drive if one hard drive is busy), so it comes closest to mimicking all the features of Drive Extender. This is called RAID (Redundant Array of Inexpensive Disks) level 5, and it has the following characteristics:

▶ **Three-drive minimum**—The implement a RAID 5 volume, you require at least three empty drives.

▶ **Expandable storage pool**—A RAID volume is expandable, so you can add more drives to increase the size of the storage pool. In a three-drive RAID setup, the total available storage space in the volume will be twice the size of the smallest drive, in a four-drive setup it will be three times the smallest drive, and so on. Therefore, it's best to use drives that are the same size to maximum the available storage area.

▶ **Data protection**—One of the RAID drives is used as a so-called *parity* volume, means which it monitors data integrity to prevent data corruption.

▶ **Data redundancy**—The other RAID drives are used to store data, with each file and folder being stored multiple times. This means that if one of the data drives fails, you don't lose any data.

▶ **Load balancing**—RAID monitors drive activity, and if one of the data drives is busy reading or writing data, RAID uses the other drive to perform the current read or write operation.

▶ **Fault tolerance**—In a RAID setup, if any hard drive goes down, the entire array remains operational and you don't lose any data. However, it's always best to replace the faulty drive as soon as possible, because if a second drive goes down, you lose everything.

Are there negatives to consider? Yes, as usual:

▶ **Not applicable to the system drive**—You can't incorporate the Windows Home Server system drive into a RAID volume, so the RAID advantages don't apply to the system files partition (drive C:). However, once you've built the array, you can move the Windows Home Server client backups and shared folders to the RAID volume.

▶ **Slow**—The type of RAID we're talking about here is called *software RAID* because the entire array is maintained and utilized by a software program. Software is inherently slower that hardware, so you might see quite a performance drop when you use a RAID volume, particularly for things like streaming media files.

5

TIP

What's the solution to slow software RAID? Speedy *hardware RAID*! This means that you add a RAID-dedicated hardware device to your server, and that device manages the array. Because the device works directly with the drives (bypassing the CPU), hardware RAID is many times faster than software RAID. Although several types of hardware RAID are available, the most common solution is to insert a RAID controller card inside your server. These cards usually come with multiple SATA ports (usually 2, 4, or 8) and you attach your hard drives directly to these controller card ports instead of the mother-board SATA ports. When you start your server, you see an option to invoke the controller card setup routine, which enables you to choose the disks you want in the array and what type of RAID level you prefer.

▶ **Expensive**—Since RAID 5 requires a minimum of three hard drives (*not* including the Windows Home Server system drive), it can get quite expensive.

▶ **Possibly not available for backup**—If your RAID 5 volume exceeds 2TB, Windows Home Server won't include it in the server backup.

With all that in mind, if you want to implement a RAID 5 volume on your server, follow these steps to set it up:

1. Log on to the Windows Home Server machine.

2. In the taskbar, click Server Manager to open the Server Manager window.

3. Select Storage, Disk Management to display the Disk Management snap-in.

4. In the list of hard drives in the lower half of the Disk Management pane, right-click one of the drives you want to include in the RAID 5 volume and then click New RAID-5 Volume. Disk Management runs the New RAID-5 Volume Wizard.

5. Click Next. The Select Disks dialog box appears.

6. In the Available list, click a disk you want to include in the volume, and then click Add.

7. Repeat step 6 to add any other drives you want to include in the volume. Figure 5.12 shows a RAID 5 volume with three disks added (the minimum).

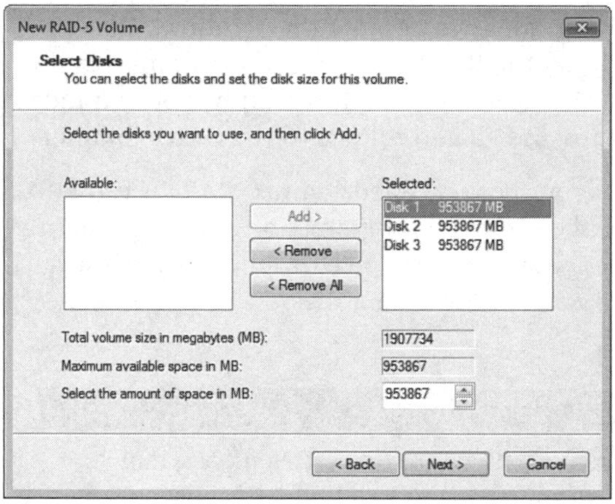

FIGURE 5.12   You must add at least three disks to the RAID 5 volume.

8. Click Next. The Assign Drive Letter or Path dialog box appears.

9. Choose a drive letter and then click Next. The Format Volume dialog box appears.

10. Assign a Volume Label, if needed, leave the other options as is, and then click Next. The last wizard dialog box appears.

11. Click Finish. Disk Management warns you that it must convert the disks to dynamic disks and asks you to confirm.

12. Click Yes. Disk Management creates the RAID 5 volume.

Figure 5.13 shows how the new RAID 5 volume (drive R:, in this case, combining Disk 1, Disk 2, and Disk 3) appears in Disk Management.

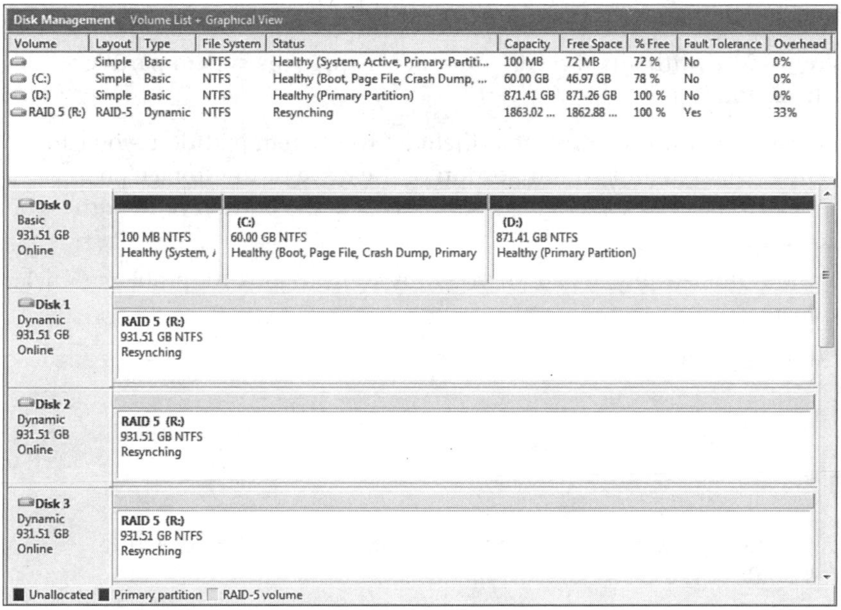

Disk Management	Volume List + Graphical View								
Volume	Layout	Type	File System	Status	Capacity	Free Space	% Free	Fault Tolerance	Overhead
▭	Simple	Basic	NTFS	Healthy (System, Active, Primary Partiti...	100 MB	72 MB	72 %	No	0%
▭ (C:)	Simple	Basic	NTFS	Healthy (Boot, Page File, Crash Dump, ...	60.00 GB	46.97 GB	78 %	No	0%
▭ (D:)	Simple	Basic	NTFS	Healthy (Primary Partition)	871.41 GB	871.26 GB	100 %	No	0%
▭ RAID 5 (R:)	RAID-5	Dynamic	NTFS	Resynching	1863.02 ...	1862.88 ...	100 %	Yes	33%

▭ **Disk 0**			
Basic 931.51 GB Online	100 MB NTFS Healthy (System, /	**(C:)** 60.00 GB NTFS Healthy (Boot, Page File, Crash Dump, Primary	**(D:)** 871.41 GB NTFS Healthy (Primary Partition)

▭ **Disk 1**	
Dynamic 931.51 GB Online	**RAID 5 (R:)** 931.51 GB NTFS Resynching

▭ **Disk 2**	
Dynamic 931.51 GB Online	**RAID 5 (R:)** 931.51 GB NTFS Resynching

▭ **Disk 3**	
Dynamic 931.51 GB Online	**RAID 5 (R:)** 931.51 GB NTFS Resynching

■ Unallocated ■ Primary partition ▭ RAID-5 volume

FIGURE 5.13 The new RAID 5 volume shown in the Disk Management snap-in.

With your RAID 5 volume at the ready, you can move Windows Home Server's Client Computer Backups folder and its shared folders from their default locations to the RAID 5 volume. See Chapter 6 to learn how to move a Windows Home Server folder to a new location.

▶ **SEE** "Moving a Shared Folder," **P. 124**.

Repairing Storage

You saw in the previous section that Windows Home Server can detect data corruption and other hard drive problems. When this happens, Windows Home Server changes the drive's status to Failing. In that case, you should run Windows Home Server's Check and Repair feature on the drive. Here's how it works:

1. Launch the Windows Home Server Dashboard.
2. Click Server Folders and Hard Drives.
3. Display the Hard Drives tab.
4. Click the hard drive.
5. Click View the Hard Drive Properties (or just double-click the drive). The drive's Properties dialog box appears.
6. Click the Check and Repair tab.

7. Start the process as follows:

   ▶ If you're working with any drive that doesn't include the system partition, click Check and Repair.

   ▶ If you're working with the drive that includes the system partition, you can check either the system partition portion of the drive or the storage pool portion. Click the Check and Repair button beside the portion of the drive you want to work with.

8. Click Check and Automatically Repair. (If you only want to look for problems, click Check Only, instead.)

9. Follow the wizard's prompts to repair the hard drive.

10. Click Close.

From Here

▶ To learn how to add shared folders to Windows Home Server, **SEE** "Creating a New Shared Folder," **P. 123.**

▶ To learn how to move a Windows Home Server share to a new location, **SEE** "Moving a Shared Folder," **P. 124.**

▶ For details on copying data to a Windows Home Server share, **SEE** "Copying Files to a Shared Folder," **P. 135.**

▶ For information on using the Windows Home Server media shares, **SEE** Chapter 8, "Streaming and Sharing Digital Media."

▶ To learn how to replace your primary hard drive, **SEE** "Replacing Your System Hard Drive," **P. 428.**

CHAPTER 6

Sharing Folders and Files on the Home Server

IN THIS CHAPTER

▶ Examining the Predefined Windows Home Server Shares

▶ Working with Shared Folders

▶ Accessing the Windows Home Server Shared Folders

▶ Copying Files to a Shared Folder

▶ Publishing a Windows Vista Calendar to the Server

▶ Searching the Shared Folders

Sharing data with other people is one of the principal benefits of networking. Whether you want to collaborate with someone on a document or just make a document accessible for reference purposes, you can place that file in a shared network folder. Unfortunately, network file sharing is marred by the time and complexity it entails. You have to set up the shared folder, give users secure access to that folder, and upload the data to the folder. IT types are old pros at this, but the average user—particularly the average home user—usually doesn't want to bother with such geeky chores.

Fortunately, Windows Home Server takes almost all of the geekiness out of sharing files over the network. Windows Home Server comes with several predefined shares for common file types, such as music and photos, and it presents a simple interface for giving users secure access to each share. And if your local username and password are the same as your Windows Home Server username and password, logging in to Windows automatically logs you in to Windows Home Server, so you can access the shared folders with just a few clicks. Best of all, everything happens on the server, so you don't have to bother creating separate shares on the users' computers, which could leave your home network vulnerable to possible security threats.

This chapter takes you through Windows Home Server's file sharing features. You learn about the predefined shares, how to create your own shares, how to set user permissions, how to access shares, how to search the shared folders, and much more.

Examining the Predefined Windows Home Server Shares

You learn how to create new shares on Windows Home Server a bit later in this chapter. (See "Creating a New Shared Folder.") However, it's entirely possible (albeit unlikely) that you won't have to create new shares. That's because Windows Home Server comes with a few predefined shared folders. Here's a summary of what's on the system by default:

▶ **Documents**—Use this shared folder for nonmedia files.

▶ **Music**—Use this shared folder for music and other digital audio files.

▶ **Pictures**—Use this shared folder for digital photos, images, artwork, and other graphics files.

▶ **Recorded TV**—Use this shared folder to store TV shows that you've recorded.

▶ **Videos**—Use this shared folder to store digital video files, movies, and animations.

If you have access to the server (either directly via monitor, mouse, and keyboard, or indirectly via a Remote Desktop connection), you can access the shares using either the `D:\ServerFolders` folder (if Windows Home Server 2011 is installed on a machine with a single hard drive) or the `E:\ServerFolders` folder (if Windows Home Server 2011 is installed on a multi-drive system).

Setting User Permissions on Shared Folders

The first thing you should do with the existing Windows Home Server shared folders is set user permissions on those shares. Permissions specify the level of access that each user has to the folder. As you learned in Chapter 2, "Setting Up and Working with User Accounts," Windows Home Server defines three types of access, as follows:

▶ **SEE** "Understanding Security Groups," **P. 29**.

▶ **Read/Write**—This level of access means that the user has both read and write permission on the share. The user can open subfolders, launch programs, open documents, edit documents, create new files and folders, and delete files and folders.

▶ **Read**—This level of access means that the user has read-only permission on the shared folder. The user can open subfolders, launch programs, and open documents, but he can't make changes to the shared folder or any of its contents. If a user with Read access tries to create a new file or folder, the user sees an error message similar to the one shown in Figure 6.1. If the read-only user changes a file and then attempts to save it, an error message appears, and what that message says depends on the editing program. For example, Notepad displays the `Access is denied` error, as shown in Figure 6.2.

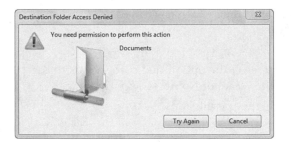

FIGURE 6.1   A read-only user sees an error similar to this when trying to create a file or folder.

FIGURE 6.2   A read-only user sees an error similar to this when trying to save a modified file.

▶ **No Access**—This level of access means that the user can't view a shared folder. If the user double-clicks the shared folder to open it, he receives a `Windows Cannot Access Share` error (see Figure 6.3).

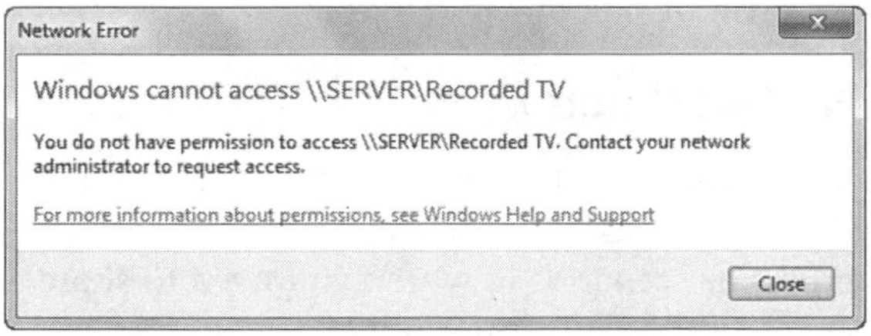

FIGURE 6.3   If a user's access level for a folder is set to No Access, Windows Home Server doesn't even let the user open the folder.

Modifying Permissions for a Windows Home Server Shared Folder

Here are the steps to follow to modify the user access levels for a shared Windows Home Server folder:

1. Launch the Windows Home Server Dashboard.

2. Select the Server Folders and Hard Drives section.

3. Display the Server Folders tab.

4. Click the folder you want to work with, and then click View the Folder Properties. The folder's Properties dialog box appears.

5. Display the Sharing tab.

6. For each user, use the Access Level list to select the option that corresponds to the access level you want to apply: Read/Write, Read, or No Access (see Figure 6.4).

7. Click OK. Windows Home Server sets the new permissions.

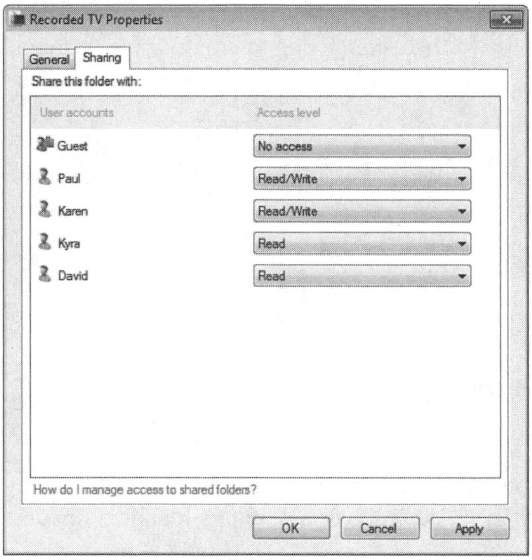

FIGURE 6.4   In Windows Home Server Dashboard, open a shared folder's Properties dialog box and use the Sharing tab to set the permissions.

Sharing Server Folders Outside the Dashboard

As I mentioned at the beginning of this chapter, the shared folders that Windows Home Server maintains will in most cases mean that home users need not share other folders, particularly on the server. However, there might be scenarios in which you need to share a server folder outside the Windows Home Server Dashboard. For example, if you use the server for development work, you might store scripts, code, and other files in the Administrator account's My Documents folder, and you might need to share those files with one or more client machines. Because you can't include My Documents with the Windows Home Server shares, you need to set up a regular share for that folder.

Follow these steps to share a folder outside the Dashboard:

1. Log on to the server.

2. In Windows Explorer, right-click the drive or folder, and then click Properties. (Make sure you right-click a folder and not a library; you can't share libraries.) Windows Home Server displays the object's property sheet.

3. Select the Sharing tab.

4. Click Advanced Sharing to open the Advanced Sharing dialog box.

5. Activate the Share This Folder check box, as shown in Figure 6.5.

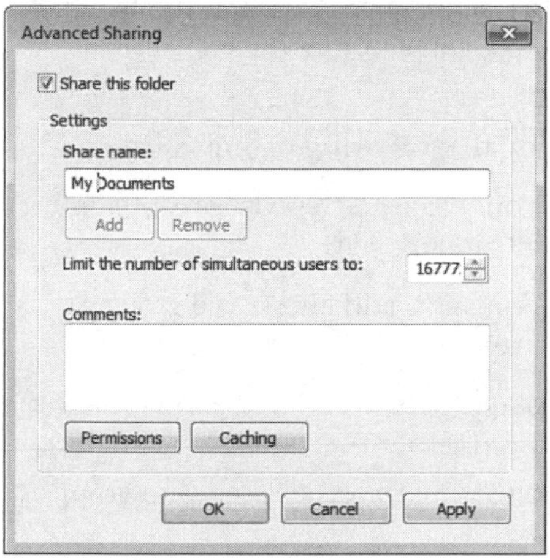

FIGURE 6.5   Activate the Share this Folder check box to enable sharing on the folder.

6. Edit the Share Name, if desired, and add a comment. (The latter is optional.)

7. Click Permissions to display the Permissions dialog box, shown in Figure 6.6.

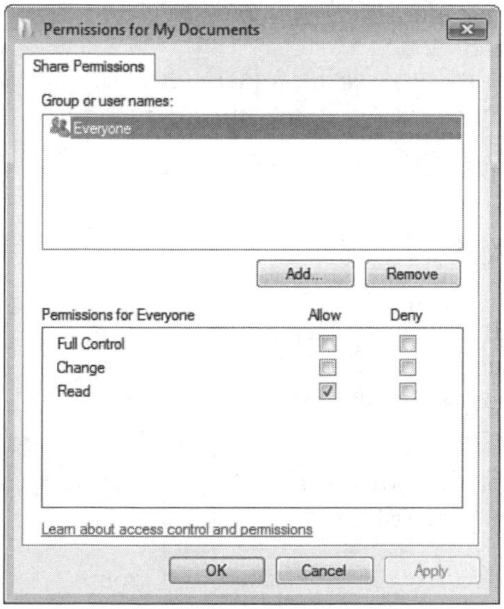

FIGURE 6.6   Use the Permissions dialog box to specify file permissions for the shared resource.

 8. Select the Everyone group in the Group or User Names list, and then click Remove.

 9. Click Add to display the Select Users or Groups dialog box.

10. In the Enter the Object Names to Select text box, type the name of the user or group you want to give permission to access the shared resource. (Separate multiple user-names or group names with semicolons.) Click OK when you're done.

11. Select an item in the Group or User Names list.

12. Using the Permissions list, you can allow or deny the following permissions:

> **Read**—Gives the group or user the ability only to read the contents of a folder or file. The user can't modify those contents in any way.

> **Change**—Gives the group or user Read permission and allows the group or user to modify the contents of the shared resource.

> **Full Control**—Gives the group or user Change permission and allows the group or user to take ownership of the shared resource.

13. Repeat steps 9 through 12 to add and configure sharing for other users and groups.

14. Click OK to return to the folder's property sheet.

15. Display the Security tab.

16. Click Edit.

17. Repeat steps 9 through 12 to add the same users and groups that you earlier added to the Sharing tab.

18. Using the Permissions list, you can allow or deny the following permissions:

> **Full Control**—Gives the group or user the ability to perform any of the actions listed. The group or user can also change permissions.

> **Modify**—Gives the group or user the ability to view the folder contents, open files, edit files, create new files and subfolders, delete files, and run programs.

> **Read and Execute**—Gives the group or user the ability to view the folder contents, open files, and run programs.

> **List Folder Contents**—Gives the group or user the ability to view the folder contents.

> **Read**—Gives the group or user the ability to open files but not edit them.

> **Write**—Gives the group or user the ability to create new files and subfolders and open and edit existing files.

> **Special Permissions**—Gives the group or user advanced settings for permissions, auditing, ownership, and effective permissions.

19. Repeat steps 17 and 18 to add and configure security for other users and groups.

20. Click OK to share the resource with the network.

Working with Shared Folders

The Windows Home Server Dashboard gives you quite a few ways to work with the server's shared folders, including adding new shared folders, moving a shared folder, accessing shadow copies, and deleting a folder. The next few sections take you through all of these shared folder tasks.

Creating a New Shared Folder

Windows Home Server's predefined shared folders should suit most needs, but you might require other folders to hold different file types. For example, you might want a folder for scripts, a folder for downloaded programs, or a folder to hold user calendars. (See "Publishing a Windows Vista Calendar to the Server," later in this chapter.) Windows Home Server allows you to create as many shared folders as you need. Again, it's possible to create and share folders outside of the Dashboard, but if you want use the simple permissions system, you need to create and share the folder within the Windows Home Server Dashboard.

Follow these steps to create a new shared folder:

1. Launch Windows Home Server Dashboard.
2. Select the Server Folders and Hard Drives section.
3. Display the Server Folders tab.
4. Click Add a Folder. Windows Home Server launches the Add a Folder Wizard, shown in Figure 6.7.

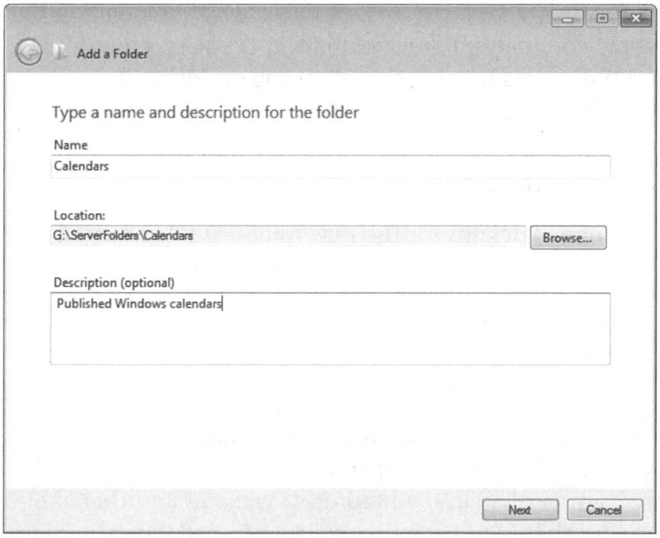

FIGURE 6.7   In the initial Add a Folder Wizard dialog box, type a name and description for the new shared folder.

5. Type a name for the folder.

NOTE

The folder name must consist of only letters, numbers, spaces, hyphens (-), under-scores (_), or periods (.), and it must end with a letter or number.

6. Type an optional description. (This text appears in the Description column of the Server Folders tab.)

7. Click Next. The wizard asks you to set the access level for the users.

CAUTION

Note that the default access level for all users is Read (except for the Guest user, which is set to None). If you want a particular user to have full control over the new share, be sure to change that user's access level to Full.

8. Click an access level command:

   ▶ **Everyone (Full Access)**—Click this command to give all users Full Access (Read/Write) permission on the new folder. Skip to step 12.

   ▶ **Everyone (Read Access)**—Click this command to give all users Read Only permission on the new folder. Skip to step 12.

   ▶ **Specific People**—Click this command if you want to apply different access levels to different users.

9. If you clicked the Specific People command, the wizard prompts you to choose the access level. For each user, use the Access Level list to select the option that corresponds to the access level you want to apply: Read/Write, Read, or No Access.

10. Click Add Folder. Windows Home Server creates the folder and applies the access permissions. The new folder appears in the Server Folders tab.

11. The wizard prompts you to configure backups for the new folder. You learn how to do that in Chapter 9, "Backing Up and Restoring Network Computers," but for now you can just click Close.

Moving a Shared Folder

Because Windows Home Server 2011 no longer comes with Drive Extender, it no longer maintains a storage pool, so the server hard drives now operate much like hard drives on any other Windows operating system. In particular, if a hard drive gets full and there are no old or unnecessary files to clean out, then you have no choice but to add another hard drive to the system and use it to store any new files you add to the server.

Of course, even without Drive Extender, Windows Home Server isn't quite the same as any other Windows OS. In particular, there are those built-in shared folders that are just so easy to configure, access, share, and stream. If you add a new hard drive to the server and the old hard drive containing the shared folders is full, don't you effectively lose access to the shared folders (at least as far as adding new files goes)?

On the face of it, the answer is a disappointing "Yes." Fortunately, however, Windows Home Server 2011 enables you to move a shared folder to a new location. So if your original 500GB hard drive is bursting at the seams and you add a shiny, new 2TB drive to the server, you can move all the Windows Home Server shared folders to the new drive and carry on with your life just as it was before.

Here are the steps to follow to move a shared folder to another drive:

1. Launch the Windows Home Server Dashboard.
2. Select the Server Folders and Hard Drives section.
3. Display the Server Folders tab.
4. Select the folder you want to move.
5. Click Move the Folder. Windows Home Server runs the Move a Folder Wizard.
6. Select the hard drive destination for the folder.
7. Click Move Folder. Windows Home Server moves the folder to the new location.
8. When the operation is complete, click Close.

Accessing Previous Versions of Shared Folders or Files

Windows Home Server 2011 implements an interesting new technology called Shadow Copies of Shared Folders. The idea is that, twice a day (at 7:00 a.m. and at 12 noon), Windows Home Server creates copies of all its shared folders, as well as the files in those shared folders. These files are called *shadow copies*, and each one is essentially a snapshot of the folder's or file's contents at a particular point in time. Because each shadow copy of a shared folder or file is a version of that object, any shadow copy that was taken prior to the current version of a folder or file is called a *previous version*.

Windows Home Server offers three different scenarios for using previous versions of shared folders and files:

► **Recovering an overwritten file**—If you copy a file to a shared folder that already contains a file with the same name, you might overwrite the existing file. If you later decide you need the original file, you can restore a previous version of the file.

► **Recovering an accidentally deleted file**—If you use a client PC to delete a file from a shared folder, that deletion is permanent. If you then realize that you deleted the file accidentally, you can restore a previous version of the file.

► **Recovering a higher-quality version of a file**—If you open a file from a shared folder, make lots of edits, formatting changes, and other modifications, and then save the file, you might later decide that your changes were for the worse. You can use the file's shadow copies to recover an earlier version of the file that doesn't include your changes.

To revert to a previous version of a shared folder or file, right-click the folder or file, and then click Restore Previous Versions. This opens the object's Properties dialog box with the Previous Versions tab displayed, as shown in Figure 6.8.

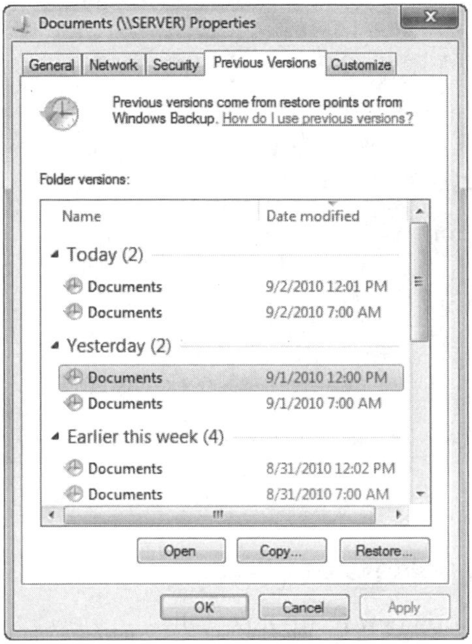

FIGURE 6.8   Right-click a shared folder or file and then click Restore Previous Versions.

Clicking a version activates the following three command buttons:

▶ **Open**—Click this button to view the contents of the previous version of the folder or to open the previous version of the file. This is useful if you're not sure which previous version you need.

▶ **Copy**—Click this button to make a copy of the previous version of the folder or file. This is useful if you're not sure that you want to restore the whole object. By making a copy, you can restore just part of the object (say, a few files from a folder or a section of a file).

▶ **Restore**—Click this button to roll back changes made to the folder or file to the previous version.

Deleting a Shared Folder

If you no longer need a shared folder, you should delete it so that it doesn't clutter the Server Folders tab. Windows Home Server enables you to delete any folder that you've created yourself. (You can't remove the predefined shares, such as Music and Documents.) Follow these steps to delete a shared folder:

1. If you have any data in the shared folder that you want to preserve, open the folder and copy or move it to another location.

2. If the shared folder is open either on the server or on a client, close the folder. (Technically this step isn't strictly necessary because Windows Home Server closes all open instances of the folder automatically. However, if any files from that folder are open, you must close them.)

3. Launch the Windows Home Server Dashboard.

4. Select the Server Folders and Hard Drives section.

5. Display the Server Folders tab.

6. Click the folder you want to delete.

7. Click Delete the Folder. Windows Home Server asks you to confirm and warns you that the deletion will be permanent.

8. Activate the I Understand That the Folder and Its Contents Will Be Permanently Deleted check box.

9. Click Yes. Windows Home Server deletes the folder.

Accessing the Windows Home Server Shared Folders

To add files to a shared folder or open and edit files in a shared folder, you first need to access the share from a client PC. You have several choices:

▶ In Windows 7, Vista, or XP clients that have the Windows Home Server Connector software installed, check to see if your desktop has a Shared Folders on *Server* icon (in which *Server* is the name of the Windows Home Server machine). If so, double-click that icon.

▶ In Windows 7, Vista, or XP clients that have the Windows Home Server Launchpad installed, log in to Launchpad and then click Shared Folders.

TIP

On a Windows 7, Windows Vista, or Windows XP client with the Windows Home Server Connector installed, an often easier way to open a server share is to run Windows Home Server Dashboard, select the Server Folders and Hard Drives section, click the Server Folders tab, and then double-click the shared folder you want to work with.

▶ In Windows 7, click Windows Explorer in the taskbar, click Network, and then double-click the icon for the Windows Home Server.

▶ In Windows Vista, select Start, Network, and then double-click the icon for the Windows Home Server.

▶ In Windows XP, select Start, My Network Places. If you don't see the server shares, click View Workgroup Computers, and then double-click the icon for the Windows Home Server.

▶ In Windows XP or Windows Me, launch Windows Explorer and, in the Folders list, select My Network Places, Entire Network, Microsoft Windows Network. Click your workgroup, and then double-click the icon for the Windows Home Server.

▶ In Windows 2000, double-click the desktop's My Network Places icon, double-click the Computers Near Me icon, and then double-click the icon for the Windows Home Server.

NOTE

Windows Home Server doesn't have a limit on the number of users who can access a shared folder. However, because Windows Home Server only allows you to add up to 10 user accounts, the practical limit on share access is 10 users (plus the Guest account, if you activate it). The Advanced Sharing dialog box (see "Sharing Server Folders Outside the Dashboard," earlier in this chapter) has a Limit the Number of Simultaneous Users value that you can use to restrict a folder to less than 10 simultaneous users if you like.

In all cases, you end up with a folder window that displays the Windows Home Server shared folders, as shown in Figure 6.9. (Note that this figure includes an extra Calendars folder that I added to my Windows Home Server.) From here, you double-click the icon of the shared folder you want to work with.

Understanding the Universal Naming Convention

If you examine the address bar with a share open, you see an address that uses the following format:

\\HOMESERVER\Share

Here, *HOMESERVER* is the name of the Windows Home Server computer, and *Share* is the name given to the shared resource. This is the universal naming convention (UNC). For example, the following UNC path refers to a shared resource named Music on a computer named SERVER:

\\SERVER\Music

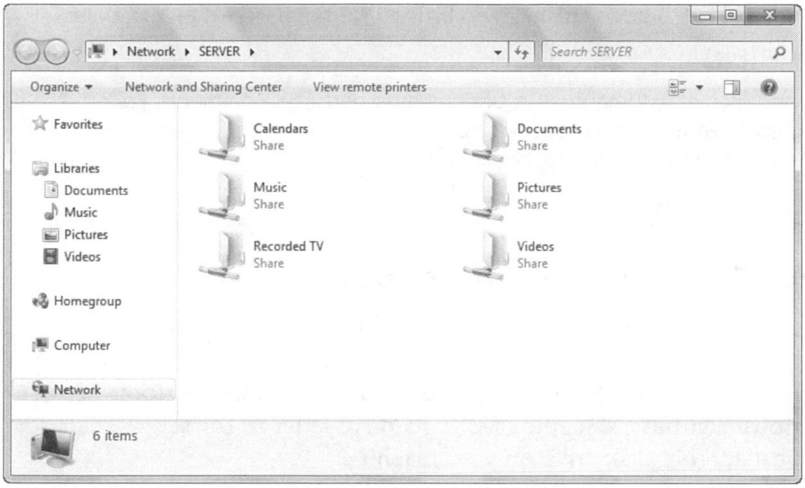

FIGURE 6.9   When you access the Windows Home Server over the network, the resulting folder window displays the server's shared folders.

NOTE

The Windows 7 and Windows Vista address bars show a "breadcrumb" path to the server share: Network > *HOMESERVER* > *Share*. To see the UNC address, either right-click the address and then click Edit Address, or click the icon that appears on the left side of the address bar (or click an empty spot within the address bar).

(UNC paths aren't case sensitive, so you can enter a path using any combination of uppercase and lowercase letters; however, it's traditional to write computer names in all-uppercase.) If the UNC path refers to a drive or folder, you can use the regular path conventions to access subfolders on that resource. For example, if the resource Music on SERVER has a Wilco subfolder, you can refer to that subfolder as follows:

\\SERVER\Documents\Wilco

TIP

The UNC offers you several alternative methods of accessing shared network resources:

▶ In Windows Explorer, click inside the address bar, type the UNC path for a shared resource, and then press Enter.

▶ Press Windows Logo+R to open the Run dialog box. Type the UNC path for a shared resource, and then click OK to open the resource in a folder window.

▶ In a 32-bit application's Open or Save As dialog box, you can use a UNC path in the File Name text box.

▶ At the command prompt, type **start** followed by the UNC path. Here's an example:

```
start \\SERVER\Public
```

▶ At the command prompt, you can use a UNC path as part of a command. For example, to copy a file named `Wilco.mp3` from `\\SERVER\Music\Wilco\` to the current folder, you'd use the following command:

```
COPY "\\SERVER\Music\Wilco\Wilco.mp3"
```

Mapping a Shared Folder to a Local Drive Letter

One networking conundrum that comes up repeatedly is the problem of referencing network resources (in, say, a script or command). You can reference UNC paths, but they're a bit unwieldy to use. To avoid the hassle, you can map a Windows Home Server shared folder to your own computer. Mapping assigns a drive letter to the server share so that it appears to be just another disk drive on your machine.

> **NOTE**
>
> Another good reason to map a Windows Home Server share to a local drive letter is to give certain programs access to the shared folder. Some older programs aren't network aware, so if you try to save files to a Windows Home Server share, the program might display an error or tell you that the location is out of disk space. In most cases, you can solve this problem by mapping the folder to a drive letter, which fools the program into thinking it's dealing with a local folder.

To map a Windows Home Server shared folder, follow these steps:

1. Select Start, right-click Computer (in Windows 7), Network (in Vista) or My Network Places (in XP), and then click Map Network Drive. (In any folder window, you can also select Tools, Map Network Drive; in Windows 7 and Vista, you need to first press Alt to display the menu bar.) The Map Network Drive dialog box appears.

2. The Drive drop-down list displays the last available drive letter on your system, but you can pull down the list and select any available letter.

> **CAUTION**
>
> If you use a removable drive, such as a memory card or Flash drive, Windows assigns the first available drive letter to that drive. This can cause problems if you have a mapped network drive that uses a lower drive letter. Therefore, it's good practice to use higher drive letters (such as X, Y, and Z) for your mapped resources.

3. Use the Folder text box to type the UNC path to the Windows Home Server shared folder, as shown in the example in Figure 6.10. (Alternatively, click Browse, select the shared folder in the Browse for Folder dialog box, and then click OK.)

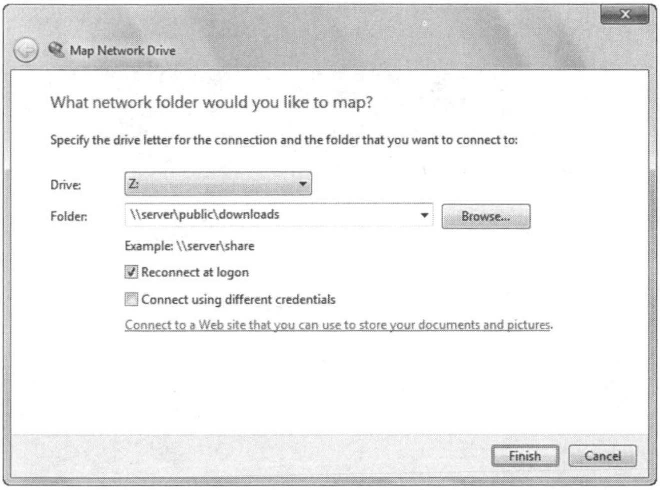

FIGURE 6.10   Use the Map Network Drive dialog box to assign a drive letter to a Windows Home Server shared folder.

4. If you want Windows to map the server share each time you log on to the system, leave the Reconnect at Logon check box activated.

5. If you prefer to log on to the server share using a different account, use one of the following techniques:

   ▶ **Windows 7**—Click to activate the Connect Using Different Credentials link. After you click Finish in step 6, Windows 7 prompts you to enter the username and password.

   ▶ **All other versions of Windows**—Click the Different User Name link, type the username and password, and click OK.

   Either way, make sure you specify a username and password that correspond to an existing Windows Home Server account.

6. Click Finish. Windows adds the new drive letter to your system and opens the shared folder in a new folder window.

To open the mapped server folder later, select Start, Computer (or My Computer in XP), and then double-click the drive in the Network Location group.

Mapping Folders at the Command Prompt

You can also map a shared Windows Home Server folder to a local drive letter by using a Command Prompt session and the NET USE command. Here's the basic syntax:

NET USE [*drive*] [*share*] [*password*] [/USER:*user*] [/PERSISTENT:[YES ¦ NO]] ¦ /DELETE]

   ▶ ***drive***—The drive letter (following by a colon) of the local drive to which you want the shared folder mapped.

> ▶ *share*—The UNC path of the Windows Home Server shared folder.
>
> ▶ *password*—The password required to connect to the shared folder (that is, the password associated with the username, specified next).
>
> ▶ */USER:user*—The username you want to use to connect to the shared folder.
>
> ▶ */PERSISTENT:*—Add YES to reconnect the mapped network drive the next time you log on.
>
> ▶ */DELETE*—Deletes the existing drive letter for the share that you previously mapped to *drive*.
>
> For example, the following command maps the shared folder \\SERVER\Music\Wilco to drive W:
>
> ```
> net use w: \\server\music\wilco \persistent:yes
> ```

Disconnecting a Mapped Network Folder

If you no longer need to map a Windows Home Server share, you should disconnect it by following these steps:

1. Select Start, Computer (or My Computer in XP).

2. Right-click the mapped drive, and then click Disconnect.

3. If files are open from the server share, Windows displays a warning to let you know that it's unsafe to disconnect the share. You have two choices:

   ▶ Click No, close all open files from the mapped folder, and then repeat steps 1 and 2.

   ▶ If you're sure there are no open files, click Yes to disconnect the share.

Creating a Network Location in Windows 7 and Windows Vista

When you map a Windows Home Server shared folder to a drive on your computer, Windows 7 and Windows Vista create an icon for the mapped drive in the Computer folder's Network Locations group. You can also add your own icons to this group. These are similar to the network places you can create in Windows XP (as described in the next section). That is, after you create a network location, you can access that location by double-clicking the icon. This is usually a lot faster than drilling down through several layers of folders on the server, so create network locations for those Windows Home Server shares you access most often.

Follow these steps to create a network location in Windows 7 and Vista:

1. Select Start, Computer to open the Computer window.

2. Right-click an empty section of the Computer folder, and then click Add a Network Location. Windows launches the Add Network Location Wizard.

3. Click Next in the initial wizard dialog box.

4. Click Choose a Custom Network Location, and then click Next.

5. Type the UNC address of the Windows Home Server shared folder (see Figure 6.11; you can also click Browse to use the Browse for Folder dialog box to select it), and then click Next.

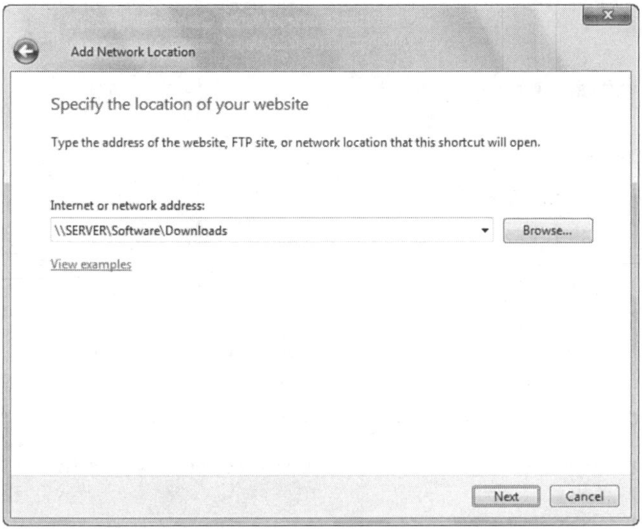

FIGURE 6.11 In Windows 7 and Vista, you can create network locations for Windows Home Server shares that you use frequently.

6. Type a name for the network location, and click Next.

7. Click Finish.

Creating a Network Place in Windows XP

In Windows XP, a *network place* is a shared folder on a network computer. (It can also be a location on a web or FTP server.) The name of each network place uses the following format:

`Share on Description (Computer)`

Here, `Share` is the name of the shared resource, `Description` is the description of the computer where the network place resides, and `Computer` is the name of that computer. For Windows Home Server 2011 (which, unlike earlier versions of Windows Home Server, does come with a description), the name of each network place appears as follows. (See Figure 6.12; again, I created the extra Calendars share on my Windows Home Server.)

`Share on My home server (Server)`

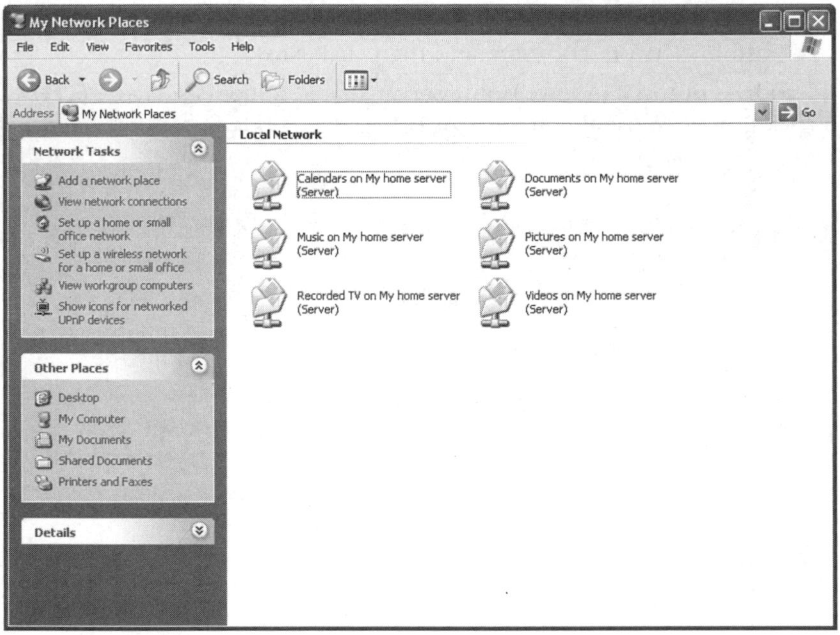

FIGURE 6.12   Windows XP's My Network Places folder showing icons for Windows Home Server shared folders.

Whenever a workgroup computer shares a folder, Windows XP detects the new share and adds it automatically to My Network Places. This means that the main Windows Home Server shares should appear in My Network Places. However, you might want to create a new network place for a subfolder of a server share. To do this, follow these steps:

TIP

You can tell Windows XP not to add new shared resources to My Network Places automatically. To do this, launch Control Panel's Folder Options icon, display the View tab, and then deactivate the Automatically Search for Network Folders and Printers check box.

---

1. In the My Network Places (or any network folder) task pane, click Add a Network Place to launch the Add Network Place Wizard.

2. Click Next.

3. Click Choose Another Network Location, and click Next.

4. Either use the Internet or Network Address text box to type the UNC address of the shared Windows Home Server folder, or click Browse to select the folder using the Browse for Folder dialog box. Click Next.

5. Modify the name in the Type a Name for This Network Place, if desired, and then click Next.

6. To open the network place in a folder window, leave the Open This Network Place When I Click Finish check box activated.

7. Click Finish.

Accessing Shared Folders on Your Mac

In Chapter 3, "Adding Devices to the Windows Home Server Network," you learned how to access the Windows Home Server shared folders directly using Finder on your Mac. However, if you have the MacConnector software installed on your Mac, you can use the Launchpad to access a shared folder. Follow these steps:

1. Open Launchpad on your Mac.

2. Type the username and password of a Windows Home Server account.

3. If you want Launchpad to save your credentials, click Options and then click Remember Me on This Computer.

4. Press Return. The Launchpad window appears.

5. Click Shared Folders. If this is the first time you've connected to the shared folders, your Mac asks you to log on.

6. Type the username and password for a Windows Home Server account, activate the Remember This Password in My Keychain, and then click Connect. Your Mac displays a list of the Windows Home Server shared folders, as shown in Figure 6.13.

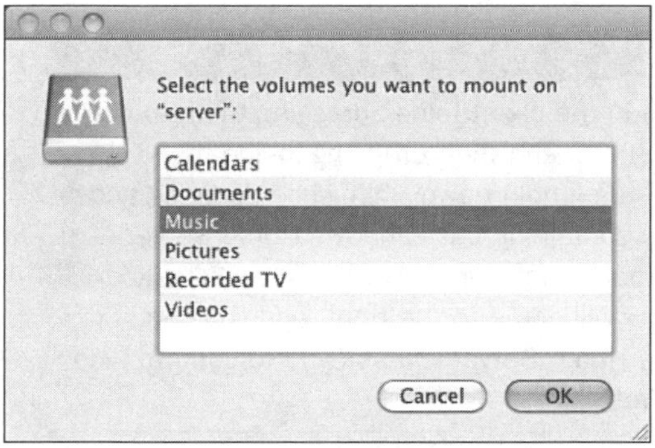

FIGURE 6.13   Your Mac displays a list of the Windows Home Server shared folders.

7. Click the shared folder you want to access.

8. Click OK. Your Mac opens a Finder window for the shared folder.

Copying Files to a Shared Folder

Most of the Windows Home Server shares are empty after the initial installation. To make these shares useful, you need to copy (or move) files from a client machine to the server. It's quite common to load up Windows Home Server with a huge number of media files—music, photos, videos, and so on—to give other people on the network access to those files to stream to an Xbox 360 or other network media device.

Before you initiate such a large copy operation, you need to check to see whether the destination folder is included in the Windows Home Server media library. If it is, Windows Home Server starts indexing the media while the file transfer is in progress which, again, only slows everything down. Temporarily remove the folder from the media library before starting the file transfer, and then add it back again afterward.

▶ **SEE** "Streaming Digital Media," **P. 184**.

Follow these steps to copy or move files from a client machine to a Windows Home Server shared folder:

1. On the client or server, double-click the desktop's Shared Folders on *Server* icon (where *Server* is the name of your Windows Home Server).

2. Open the Windows Home Server shared folder or subfolder you want to use as the file destination.

3. On the client or server, open Windows Explorer, and navigate to the client folder that contains the files you want to work with.

4. Select the client files, and then press either Ctrl+C (if you're copying them) or Ctrl+X (if you're moving them).

5. Switch to the window containing the Windows Home Server share.

6. Press Ctrl+V to paste the files.

TIP

It's often easier to copy files by selecting them in the client folder, dragging them to the window containing the Windows Home Server share, and then dropping inside the shared folder. (If you want to move the files instead, hold down Shift while dragging and dropping the files.) If you can't see the window containing the Windows Home Server share, first drag the mouse pointer to the taskbar and hover it over the share's taskbar button. After a second or two, the share window will come to the front, and you can then drop the files inside the window. Windows Home Server will ask you to confirm that you want to move or copy the files. Click Yes.

Publishing a Windows Vista Calendar to the Server

One of the pleasant surprises in Windows Vista was a new program called Windows Calendar. It's not as powerful as Outlook's Calendar feature, but it does all the basic jobs that a calendar should: You can create appointments (one-time and recurring), set up all-day events, schedule tasks, apply reminders to appointments and tasks, and view appointments by day, week, or month. For our purposes, Windows Calendar even does something that Outlook's Calendar can't: It can publish a calendar to a network share. (With Outlook, you need to be on a Microsoft Exchange network to do this.) You can set things up so that the published calendar is updated automatically, so the remote calendar always has current data. Your family members can then subscribe to the calendar to see your appointments (and, optionally, your notes, reminders, and tasks).

This means that you can create a new shared folder—called, say, `Calendars`—and publish your calendar to that folder. After you've done that, start Windows Calendar using any of the following methods:

- ▶ Select Start, All Programs, Windows Calendar.
- ▶ Press Windows Logo+R (or select Start, All Programs, Accessories, Run) to open the Run dialog box, type `wincal`, and click OK.
- ▶ In Windows Mail, select Tools, Windows Calendar, or press Ctrl+Shift+L.

Publishing Your Calendar

Here are the steps you need to follow in Windows Calendar to publish your calendar:

1. In the Calendars list, click the calendar you want to publish.
2. Select Share, Publish to open the Publish Calendar dialog box.
3. Edit the calendar name, if necessary.

TIP

After the calendar publishes, you have the option of sending an email message that includes the address of the shared calendar. Most email clients display this address as a link. However, if the address includes spaces, the link stops at the first space. Therefore, consider changing the calendar name to remove any spaces.

---

4. Use the Location to Publish Calendar text box to type the address of the shared folder you created on Windows Home Server (see Figure 6.14).
5. If you want Windows Calendar to update your calendar whenever you make changes to it, activate the Automatically Publish Changes Made to This Calendar check box. (If you leave this option deactivated, you can still publish your changes by hand, as described later; see "Working with Shared Calendars.")
6. In the Calendar Details to Include section, activate the check box beside each item you want in your published calendar: Notes, Reminders, and Tasks.
7. Click Publish. Windows Calendar publishes the calendar to Windows Home Server by creating a file in the iCalendar format (`.ics` extension) and copying that file to the share. Windows Calendar then displays a dialog box to let you know the operation was successful.
8. To let other people know that your calendar is shared and where it can be found, click Announce. Windows Calendar creates a new email message that includes the following in the body (where *address* is the address of your published calendar; see Figure 6.15 for an example):

    You can subscribe to my calendar at *address*
9. Click Finish.

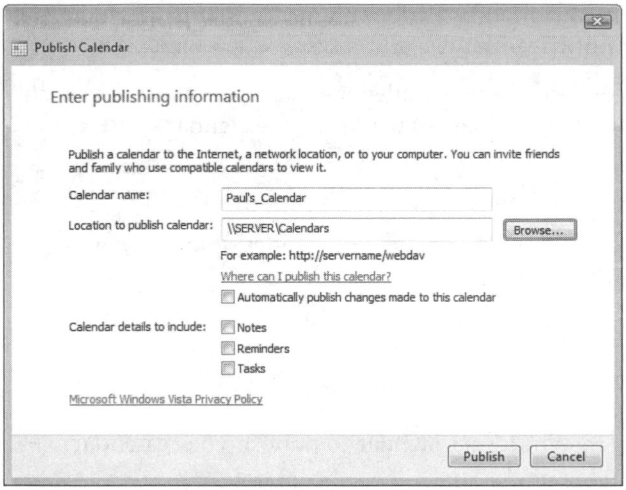

FIGURE 6.14   Use the Publish Calendar dialog box to publish your calendar to a shared Windows Home Server folder.

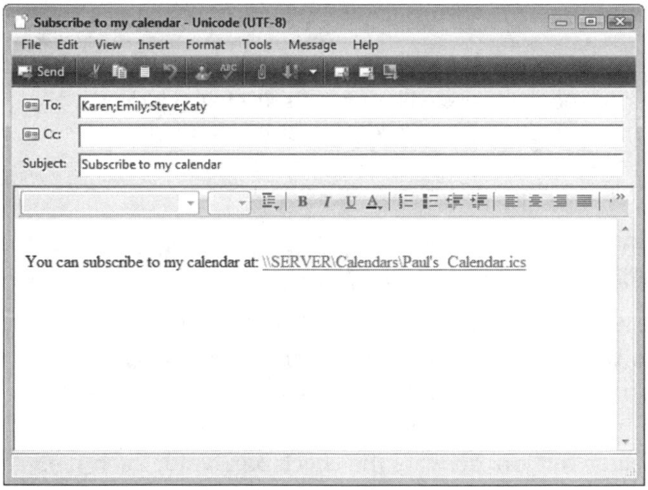

FIGURE 6.15   You can send an email message to let everyone know that you've published your calendar on Windows Home Server.

Subscribing to a Calendar

You can add another person's published calendar to your Calendars list. How you do this depends on whether you've received a subscription invitation via email.

If you have such a message, follow these steps:

1. Open the invitation message.

2. Click the link to the published calendar. Windows Mail asks you to confirm that you want to open the iCalendar file.

TIP

If the calendar address contains a space, you won't be able to click the link because it will be broken. In that case, select the address text and press Ctrl+C to copy it. Press Windows Logo+R (or select Start, All Programs, Accessories, Run) to open the Run dialog box, press Ctrl+V to paste the calendar address, and then click OK.

---

3. Click Open. Windows Calendar opens and displays the Import dialog box, shown in Figure 6.16.

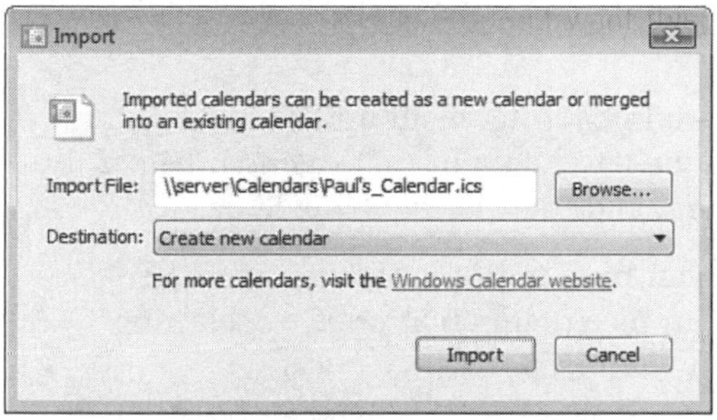

FIGURE 6.16 If you receive an email inviting you to subscribe to a calendar, click the link to import the calendar into Windows Calendar.

4. If you want to merge the published calendar into your own calendar, use the Destination list to select the name of your calendar; otherwise, the published calendar appears as a separate calendar.

5. Click Import. Windows Calendar adds the published calendar.

If you don't have a subscription invitation message, follow these steps instead:

1. Select Share, Subscribe to open the Subscribe to a Calendar dialog box.

2. Use the Calendar to Subscribe To text box to type the address of the published calendar.

3. Click Next. Calendar subscribes you to the published calendar and then displays the Calendar Subscription Settings dialog box.

4. Edit the calendar name, if necessary.

5. Use the Update Interval list to select the interval at which you want Calendar to update the subscribed calendar: Every 15 Minutes, Every Hour, Every Day, Every Week, or No Update.

6. If you want to receive reminders in the calendar, activate the Include Reminders check box.

7. If you also want to see the published calendar's tasks, activate the Include Tasks check box.

8. Click Finish. The published calendar appears in your Calendars list.

Working with Shared Calendars

After you publish one or more of your calendars and subscribe to one or more remote calendars, Windows Calendar offers a number of techniques for working with these items. Here's a summary:

▶ **Changing a calendar's sharing information**—When you select a published or subscribed calendar, the Details pane displays a Sharing Information section, and you use the controls in that section to configure the calendar's sharing options.

▶ **Publishing calendar changes**—If your published calendar isn't configured to automatically publish changes, you can republish by hand by selecting the calendar and then selecting Share, Sync.

▶ **Updating a subscribed calendar**—If you didn't configure an update interval for a subscribed calendar, or if you want to see the latest data in that calendar before the next update is scheduled, select the calendar and then select Share, Sync.

▶ **Synchronizing all shared calendars**—If you have multiple shared calendars (published and subscribed), you can synchronize them all at once by selecting Share, Sync All.

▶ **Sending a published calendar announcement**—If you didn't send an announcement about your published calendar, or if you want to send the announcement to different people, select the calendar and then select Share, Send Publish E-Mail.

▶ **Stopping a published calendar**—If you no longer want other people to subscribe to your calendar, select it and then select Stop Publishing. When Calendar asks you to confirm, click Unpublish. (Note, however, that if you want your calendar file to remain on the server, you first need to deactivate the Delete Calendar on Server check box.)

▶ **Stopping a subscribed calendar**—If you no longer want to subscribe to a remote calendar, select it and then press Delete. When Calendar asks you to confirm, click Yes.

Searching the Shared Folders

After you've used Windows Home Server for a while, you could easily end up with thousands—heck, even tens of thousands—of files on the server shares. This is particularly true if you have a large amount of data stored on the Windows Home Server shares (remember the old computing law that data expands to fill the space available for storage), several Windows clients, and several users. Of course, it's perfectly acceptable to treat the Windows Home Server shares as a kind of virtual basement where you toss a bunch of files and folders; however, there will almost certainly come a day when you need to actually find a particular file or folder in that mess. Assuming you have a life, you probably don't want to waste valuable chunks of that life by scouring the server shares manually.

Instead, you need to put the powerful Windows Home Server Search feature to work for you. You can use Search to scour the shared folder not only for filenames, but file contents and metadata (such as file size and properties such as the artist name and music genre). You might think you could only do this on the Windows Home Server itself, but if you have the Connector software installed in a Windows 7, Vista, or XP client, you can perform these powerful searches right from the client!

Windows Home Server Search works by indexing the entire contents of just the following locations on the server:

- ▶ **Users**—This is Windows Home Server's user profiles folder (C:\Users), which in most cases contains only a single profile for the Administrator user. (By default, Windows Search also indexes the All Users profile.)

- ▶ **Internet Explorer History**—The Administrator account's list of visited websites.

- ▶ **Start Menu**—The contents of the Start menu folders.

- ▶ **Shares**—The Windows Home Server shared folders: Documents, Music, Pictures, Recorded TV, and Videos, as well as the Shadow Copies folder.

These strike me as sensible defaults because there isn't likely to be anything else on your server that you'd want to search. However, you can control what Windows Search indexes and force a rebuild of the index. Log on to the server and select Start, Control Panel, Indexing Options. This displays the Indexing Options dialog box shown in Figure 6.17. To customize the search engine, you have two choices:

- ▶ **Modify**—Click this button to display the Indexed Locations dialog box, which enables you to change the locations included in the index. Activate the check box for each drive or folder you want to include.

- ▶ **Advanced**—Click this button to display the Advanced Options dialog box, which enables you to index encrypted files, change the index location, specify the file types (extensions) that you want include in or exclude from the index, and even add network shares to the index. You can also click Rebuild to re-create the index, which is useful if you find that Windows Search doesn't seem to be returning the correct results.

NOTE

The Windows Search Engine takes a long time to index even a relatively small amount of data. If you're asking WSE to index dozens of gigabytes of data, wait until you're done working for the day and let the indexer run all night.

To run a search, open the shared folder on the client PC, and then use the Search feature (such as the Search box in Windows 7 and Vista) to type your search text.

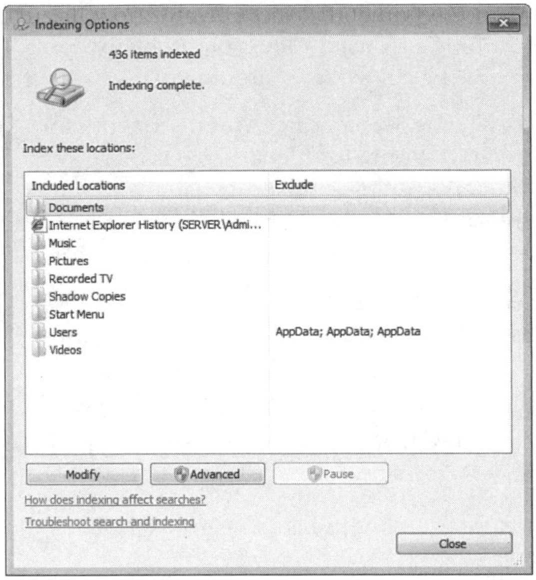

FIGURE 6.17   Use Control Panel's Indexing Options to configure Windows Search.

Simple text searches aren't going to radically boost anyone's productivity or help you find a file needle in a hard disk haystack. To take searching to the next level, you need to know about another powerful search feature: Windows Search syntax.

When you run a standard text search, Windows Search looks for matches not only in the filename and the file contents, but in the file metadata: the properties associated with each file. That's cool and all, but what if you want to match only a particular property? For example, if you're searching the Music share for albums that include the word "Rock" in the title, a basic search on "rock" will also return music in which the artist's name includes rock and the album genre is Rock. This is not good.

To fix this kind of thing, you can create powerful and targeted searches by using a special syntax in your search queries. For file properties, you use the following syntax:

```
property:value
```

Here, *property* is the name of the file property you want to search on, and *value* is the criteria you want to use. The property can be any of the metadata categories used by Windows Home Server. For example, the categories in a music folder include Name, Track Number, Title, Artist, Album Title, and Bit Rate. Right-click any column header in Windows Explorer's Details view to see more properties such as Genre and Duration, and you can click More to see the complete list.

Here are a few things to bear in mind:

▶ If the property name is a single word, use that word in your query. For example, the following code matches music in which the Artist property is Coldplay:

```
artist:coldplay
```

▶ If the property name uses two or more words, remove the spaces between the words, and use the resulting text in your query. For example, the following code matches pictures in which the Date Taken property is August 23, 2011:

```
datetaken:8/23/2011
```

▶ If the value uses two or more words and you want to match the exact phrase, surround the phrase with quotation marks. For example, the following code matches music in which the Genre property is Alternative & Punk:

```
genre:"alternative & punk"
```

▶ If the value uses two or more words and you want to match both words in any order, surround them with parentheses. For example, the following code matches music in which the Album property contains the words "Head" and "Goats" in any order:

```
album:(head goats)
```

▶ If you want to match files in which a particular property has no value, use empty braces, [], as the value. For example, the following code matches files in which the Tags property is empty:

```
tags:[]
```

You can also refine your searches with the following operators and wildcards:

▶ >—Matches files in which the specified property is greater than the specified value. For example, the following code matches pictures in which the Date Taken property is later than January 1, 2011:

```
datettaken:>1/1/2011
```

▶ >=—Matches files in which the specified property is greater than or equal to the specified value. For example, the following code matches files in which the Size property is greater than or equal to 100MB (use m for MB, and g for GB):

```
size:>=100m
```

▶ <—Matches files in which the specified property is less than the specified value. For example, the following code matches music in which the Bit Rate property is less than 128 (kilobits per second):

```
bitrate:<128k
```

▶ <=—Matches files in which the specified property is less than or equal to the specified value. For example, the following code matches files in which the Size property is less than or equal to 1024 bytes:

```
size:<=1024
```

▶ ..—Matches files in which the specified property is between (and including) two values. For example, the following code matches files in which the Date Modified property is between and including August 1, 2011 and August 31, 2011:

```
datemodified:8/1/2011..8/31/2011
```

▶ *—Substitutes for multiple characters. For example, the following code matches music in which the Album property includes the word "Hits":

```
album:*hits
```

▶ ?—Substitutes for a single character. For example, the following code matches music in which the Artists property begins with "Blu" and includes any character in the fourth position:

```
artists:blu?
```

For even more sophisticated searches, you can combine multiple criteria using Boolean operators:

▶ **AND (or +)**—Use this operator to match files that meet all your criteria. For example, the following code matches pictures in which the Date Taken property is later than January 1, 2011 and the Size property is greater than 1000000 bytes:

```
datetaken:>1/1/2011 AND size:>1000000
```

▶ **OR**—Choose this option to match files that meet at least one of your criteria. For example, the following code matches music in which the Genre property is either Rock or Blues:

```
genre:rock OR genre:blues
```

▶ **NOT (or –)**—Choose this option to match files that do not meet the criteria. For example, the following code matches pictures in which the Type property is not JPEG:

```
type:NOT jpeg
```

NOTE

The Boolean operators AND, OR, and NOT must appear with all-uppercase letters in your query.

From Here

- ▶ To learn about security groups and their associated permissions, **SEE** "Understanding Security Groups," **P. 29.**

- ▶ For information on viewing Windows Home Server shared folders using a Mac, **SEE** "Using a Mac on Your Windows Home Server Network," **P. 53.**

- ▶ For information on viewing Windows Home Server shared folders using Linux, **SEE** "Using a Linux Client on Your Windows Home Server Network," **P. 65.**

- ▶ To learn how to use Windows Home Server's media sharing feature, **SEE** "Streaming Digital Media," **P. 184.**

CHAPTER 7

Making Connections to Network Computers

IN THIS CHAPTER

▶ Configuring a Computer as a Remote Desktop Host

▶ Connecting via Remote Desktop Connection

▶ Connecting via Windows Home Server Remote Web Access

▶ Connecting via the Internet

▶ Customizing the Remote Web Access Pages

You saw in Chapter 6, "Sharing Folders and Files on the Home Server," that Windows Home Server offers a number of predefined folders that you can use to store documents as well as media such as music, photos, and videos. Of course, you're also free to share folders on any client computer, and those folders will show up when you open the computer's folder from the Network window (in Windows 7 or Vista) or My Network Places (in XP).

However, having access to shared folders may not be sufficient in some cases:

▶ You want to edit a document, but only another computer on your network has the required application.

▶ You want to read or respond to an email message that you received on another network computer.

▶ You want to access files in any folder on another network computer, not just a shared folder.

▶ You want to visit an Internet site that you've set up as a favorite in Internet Explorer on another network computer.

All of these scenarios require a higher level of connection to the network computer: the computer's desktop. If you can't physically sit down in front of the computer, or if it's just not convenient to use the computer directly right now, you need to access the computer's desktop remotely. As you learn in this chapter, you actually have three options for getting a network computer's desktop to appear on your screen:

▶ You can connect directly using the Remote Desktop Connection feature found in Windows 7, Windows Vista, and Windows XP.

▶ You can use Windows Home Server's Remote Web Access to access a network computer's desktop through a web browser and a local area network (LAN) connection.

▶ You can use Remote Web Access to access a network computer's desktop through a web browser and an Internet connection.

In each case, you get full access to the network computer's desktop, which enables you to open folders, run programs, edit documents, and tweak settings. In short, almost anything you can do while physically sitting in front of the other computer you can now do remotely from your own computer. The responsiveness of the remote session depends a great deal on the speed of the connection. For a LAN connection, an Ethernet (10Mbps) connection or 802.11b (11Mbps) wireless connection is just too slow, whereas a Fast Ethernet (100Mbps) or 802.11g (54 Mbps) connection will give you adequate performance for most tasks. If you want to play games or perform other graphics-intensive tasks, you really need a Gigabit Ethernet (1Gbps) or 802.11n (248Mbps) connection. Over the Internet, don't even try to connect using dial-up; instead, you need a cable or DSL broadband (1Mbps or better) link, and even then you'll want to avoid large files and heavy-duty graphics tasks.

Configuring a Computer as a Remote Desktop Host

Remote Desktop is easy to configure and use, but it does require a small amount of prep work to ensure trouble-free operation. Let's begin with the remote computer, also called the *host* computer.

The first thing you need to know is that not all versions of Windows 7, Vista, and XP can act as Remote Desktop hosts. The only versions that support this are Windows 7 Professional, Windows 7 Enterprise, and Windows 7 Ultimate; Vista Business, Vista Enterprise, and Vista Ultimate; XP Pro, and XP Media Center Edition 2005. Yes, you read that right: The five versions of Windows most likely to be used in the home and therefore most likely to be clients on a Windows Home Server network—Windows 7 Starter, Windows Home Premium, Vista Home Basic, Vista Home Premium, and XP Home—*can't* act as Remote Desktop hosts. This is a mind-numbingly shortsighted move on Microsoft's part, and it may prevent many home users from making the move to Windows Home Server.

All that aside, on machines that *can* act as hosts, by default the user currently logged on to the host machine has permission to connect remotely to the host. Other users with default remote connection permissions are members of the host's Administrators and Remote Desktop Users groups. (In all cases, only users with password-protected accounts can use Remote Desktop.) If you want to connect to the host remotely, you first need to set up an account for the username with which you want to connect from the client. (Again, you must assign a password to this account.)

Configuring a Windows 7 or Vista Host

If the host machine is running Windows 7 Professional, Enterprise, or Ultimate, or Vista Business, Enterprise, or Ultimate, you have to do two things to prepare the computer for its Remote Desktop hosting duties:

▶ Disable Sleep mode.

▶ Activate the Remote Desktop service.

Most Windows 7 and Vista machines are configured to go into Sleep mode after one hour of inactivity. Sleep is a low-power mode that turns everything off except power to the memory chips, which store the current desktop configuration. When you turn the machine back on, the desktop and your open programs and documents appear within a few seconds. However, remote clients won't be able to connect to the host if it's in Sleep mode, so you have to disable this feature. Here are the steps to follow:

1. Select Start, Control Panel, click either System and Security (in Windows 7) or System and Maintenance (in Windows Vista), and then under Power Options click Change When the Computer Sleeps.

2. In the Put the Computer to Sleep list, select Never.

3. Click Save Changes.

Now follow these steps to activate the Remote Desktop service:

1. Select Start, right-click Computer, and then click Properties to open the System window.

2. Click the Remote Settings link. (In Windows Vista, you must enter your UAC credentials at this point.) Windows opens the System Properties dialog box with the Remote tab displayed, as shown in Figure 7.1.

TIP

Another way to open the System Properties dialog box with the Remote tab displayed is to press Windows Logo+R (or select Start, All Programs, Accessories, Run), type **systempropertiesremote** (or **control sysdm.cpl,,5**), click OK, and (in Vista) enter your UAC credentials.

3. In the Remote Desktop group, you have two choices:

▶ **Allow Connections from Computers Running Any Version of Remote Desktop**—Select this option if you want people running previous versions of Remote Desktop to be able to access the host.

▶ **Allow Connections Only from Computers Running Remote Desktop with Network Level Authentication**—Select this option if you only want the most secure form of Remote Desktop access. In this case, Vista checks the client computer to see if its version of Remote Desktop supports Network Level Authentication (NLA). NLA is an authentication protocol that authenticates the user before making the Remote Desktop connection. NLA is built into every version of Windows 7 and Windows Vista, but it is not supported on older Windows systems.

4. If you didn't add more users earlier, skip to step 7. Otherwise, click Select Users to display the Remote Desktop Users dialog box.

5. Click Add to display the Select Users dialog box, type the username, and click OK. (Repeat this step to add other users.)

6. Click OK to return to the System Properties dialog box.

7. Click OK.

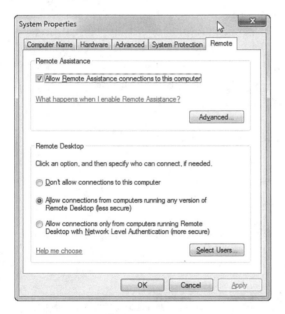

FIGURE 7.1   In Windows 7 or Vista versions that can act as remote hosts, select an option in the Remote Desktop group to enable remote connections to the computer's desktop.

Configuring an XP Host

If the host machine is running XP Pro, here are the steps to follow to set it up to host Remote Desktop sessions:

1. Log on to the host as an Administrator.

2. Launch Control Panel's System icon to open the System Properties dialog box. (Alternatively, click Start, right-click My Computer, and then click Properties.)

3. Display the Remote tab.

4. In the Remote Desktop group, activate the Allow Users to Connect Remotely to This Computer check box, as shown in Figure 7.2.

5. If you didn't add more users earlier, skip to step 8. Otherwise, click Select Remote Users to display the Remote Desktop Users dialog box.

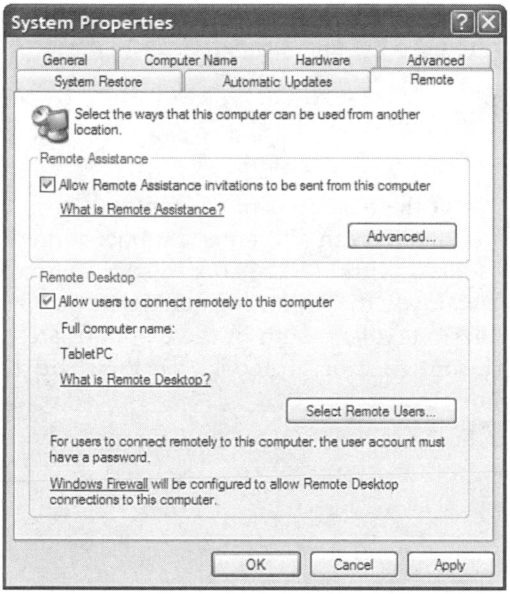

FIGURE 7.2   In XP Pro, the Allow Users to Connect Remotely to This Computer check box must be activated to enable Remote Desktop sessions on the computer.

6. Click Add to display the Select Users dialog box, type the username, and click OK. (Repeat this step to add other users.)

7. Click OK to return to the System Properties dialog box.

8. Click OK.

Restricting the Computers That Can Connect to the Host

When you configure a computer to be a host, Windows adds the Remote Desktop service to Windows Firewall's Exceptions list and, in Windows 7 and Windows Vista, it creates a Windows Firewall rule that allows incoming connections using the Remote Desktop Protocol (RDP) on port 3389. You can increase the security of the Remote Desktop connection by modifying this rule using Windows Firewall with Advanced Security (WFAS), which is a Microsoft Management Console snap-in. Specifically, you can specify the IP addresses of the computers that are allowed to connect to the host. You might do this, for example, if you want to be able to connect the host from your desktop computer and your notebook, but you don't want the kids' computers to be able to connect.

Here are the steps to follow:

1. Press Windows Logo+R (or select Start, All Programs, Accessories, Run), type `wf.msc`, and then click OK.

2. In Windows Vista, enter your User Account Control credentials. The WFAS snap-in appears.

3. Click Inbound Rules. After a few seconds, the list of Inbound Rules appears.

4. Double-click the Remote Desktop (TCP-In) rule. (If you see two of these rules, double-click the one with the green check mark.) The rule's property sheet appears.

5. Display the Scope tab.

6. In the Local IP Address group, select These IP Addresses.

7. Click Add to open the IP Address dialog box.

8. In the This IP Address or Subnet text box, enter the IP address of a computer that can connect to the host, as shown in Figure 7.3. (You can also enter a subnet address such as 192.168.0.0/24, which allows any address in the 192.168.0.x subnet; alternatively, you can click This IP Address Range and type the beginning address in the From text box and the ending address in the To text box. Both of these options are useful for networks that use Dynamic Host Configuration Protocol (DHCP), where the client IP addresses may change over time.)

FIGURE 7.3   Use the property sheet for the Remote Desktop (TCP-In) rule to customize security for incoming Remote Desktop connections.

9. Click OK.

10. Repeat steps 7–9 to add other IP addresses to the Scope tab.

11. If you also want to restrict access to only wired or wireless connections, display the Advanced tab, click Customize in the Interface Types group, and then click These Interface Types. Activate the check box beside the type you want to allow: Local Area Network (wired) or Wireless. Click OK.

12. Click OK.

Connecting via Remote Desktop Connection

Although, as I mentioned earlier, only certain Windows 7, Vista, and XP machines can act as Remote Desktop hosts, *all* Windows 7, Vista, and XP computers can initiate a Remote Desktop connection to a host (that is, they can act as Remote Desktop *clients*). In this section, you learn how to prepare the clients and make the connection.

Getting the Client Computer Ready

You must install the Remote Desktop Connection software on the client computer. This software is already installed in all versions of Windows 7 and Windows Vista. If you're running Windows XP on the client, you can install the Remote Desktop Connection software from the Windows XP CD (if you have one):

1. Insert the Windows XP CD, and wait for the Welcome to Microsoft Windows XP screen to appear.
2. Click Perform Additional Tasks.
3. Click Set Up Remote Desktop Connection.

TIP

You can also download the latest client software from Microsoft at www.microsoft.com/windowsxp/downloads/tools/rdclientdl.mspx.

In addition, you can use this client if you're running Windows XP and don't have access to the XP install disc.

If you have a Mac machine running OS X connected to your network, you can initiate a session with any Remote Desktop host and even share files between the two computers. The Remote Desktop Connection Client for Mac is available from Microsoft at www.microsoft.com/mac/remote-desktop-client.

If you have a Linux box on your network, you can use rdesktop as a Remote Desktop Protocol client. You can download the software at www.rdesktop.org/.

▶ **SEE** "Using a Mac to Make a Remote Desktop Connection to Windows Home Server," **P. 59**.

Making the Connection to the Remote Desktop

On the client computer, you can now connect to the host computer's desktop. Follow these steps:

1. Select Start, All Programs, Accessories, Remote Desktop Connection. (In Windows XP, select Start, All Programs, Accessories, Remote Desktop Connection.) The Remote Desktop Connection dialog box appears.
2. In the Computer text box, type the name or the IP address of the host computer.

3. If you don't want to customize Remote Desktop, skip to step 10. Otherwise, click Options to expand the dialog box to the version shown in Figure 7.4.

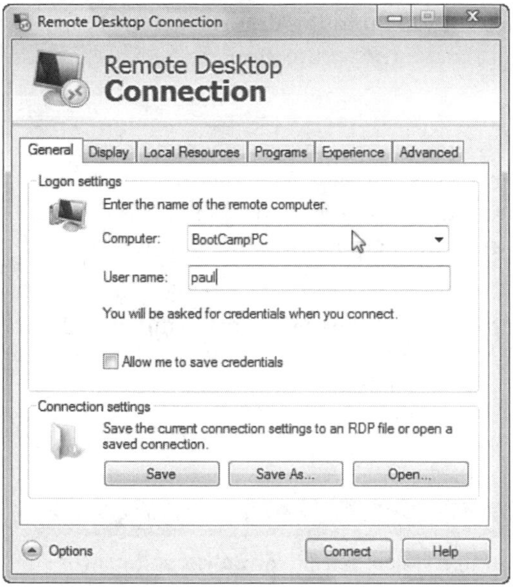

FIGURE 7.4   Clicking the Options button expands the dialog box so that you can customize Remote Desktop.

4. The General tab offers the following additional options:

   ▶ **Computer**—The name or IP address of the remote computer.

   ▶ **User Name**—The username you want to use to log in to the host computer.

   ▶ **Password**—(Windows XP Service Pack 2 or earlier only) The password to use to log on to the host computer.

   ▶ **Allow Me to Save Credentials**—Activate this check box to enable the Remember My Credentials option in the login dialog box.

   ▶ **Save**—Click this button to have Windows remember your current settings so that you don't have to type them again the next time you connect. This is useful if you only connect to Windows Home Server.

   ▶ **Save As**—Click this button to save your connection settings to a Remote Desktop (.rdp) file for later use. This is useful if you regularly connect to other hosts.

   ▶ **Open**—Click this button to open a saved .rdp file.

5. The Display tab offers three options for controlling the look of the Remote Desktop window:

   ▶ **Remote Desktop Size**—(Display Configuration in Windows 7) Drag this slider to set the resolution of Remote Desktop. Drag the slider all the way to the left for a 640×480 screen size; drag the slider all the way to the right to have Remote Desktop take up the entire client screen, no matter what resolution the host is currently using.

   ▶ **Colors**—Use this list to set the number of colors used for the Remote Desktop display. Note that if the number of colors on either the host or the client is fewer than the value you select in the Colors list, Windows uses the lesser value.

   ▶ **Display the Connection Bar**—When you activate this check box, the Remote Desktop Connection client displays a connection bar at the top of the Remote Desktop window, provided you selected Full Screen for the Remote Desktop Size setting. You use the connection bar to minimize, restore, and close the Remote Desktop window. If you find that the connection bar just gets in the way, deactivate this check box to prevent it from appearing.

6. The Local Resources tab offers three options for controlling certain interactions between the client and host:

   ▶ **Remote Computer Sound**—(Remote Audio in Windows 7) Use this list to determine where Windows plays the sounds generated by the host. You can play them on the client (if you want to hear what's happening on the host), on the host (if you want a user sitting at the host to hear the sounds), or not at all (if you have a slow connection). In Windows 7, you can also choose to enable remote audio recording.

   ▶ **Keyboard**—Use this list to determine which computer is sent special Windows key combinations—such as Alt+Tab and Ctrl+Esc—that you press on the client keyboard. You can have the key combos sent to the client, to the host, or to the host only when you're running the Remote Desktop window in full-screen mode. What happens if you're sending key combos to one computer and you need to use a particular key combo on the other computer? For such situations, Remote Desktop offers several keyboard equivalents:

     Windows Key Combo—Remote Desktop Equivalent

     Alt+Tab—Alt+Page Up

     Alt+Shift+Tab—Alt+Page Down

     Alt+Esc—Alt+Insert

     Ctrl+Esc or Windows Logo—Alt+Home

     Print Screen—Ctrl+Alt+– (numeric keypad)

     Alt+Print Screen—Ctrl+Alt++ (numeric keypad)

> **TIP**
>
> Here are three other useful keyboard shortcuts you can press on the client computer and have Windows send to the host:
>
> Ctrl+Alt+End   Displays the Windows Security dialog box. This is equivalent to pressing Ctrl+Alt+Delete, which Windows always applies to the client computer.
>
> Alt+Delete   Displays the active window's Control menu.
>
> Ctrl+Alt+Break   Toggles the Remote Desktop window between full-screen mode and a regular window.

> ▶ **Local Devices and Resources**—Leave the Printers check box activated to display the client's printers in the host's Printers and Faxes window. The client's printers appear with the syntax *Printer (*from *COMPUTER)*, where *Printer* is the printer name and *COMPUTER* is the network name of the client computer. In Windows 7 and Vista, leave the Clipboard check box activated to use the client's Clipboard during the remote session. You can also connect disk drives and serial ports, which I describe in the next step.

7. Click More to see the Remote Desktop Connection dialog box. Use the following check boxes to configure more client devices and resources on the host. (Click OK when you're done.)

   > ▶ **Smart Cards**—Leave this check box activated to access the client's smart cards on the host.

   > ▶ **Serial Ports**—(Ports in Windows 7) Activate this check box to make any devices attached to the client's serial ports (such as a barcode scanner) available while you're working with the host.

   > ▶ **Drives**—Activate this check box to display the client's hard disk partitions and mapped network drives in the host's Computer (or My Computer) window. (You can also open the branch to activate the check boxes of specific drives.) The client's drives appear in the window's Other group with the syntax *D* on *Computer*, where *D* is the drive letter and *Computer* is the network name of the client computer.

   > ▶ **Supported Plug and Play Devices**—Activate this check box to make some of the client's Plug and Play devices, such as media players and digital cameras, available to the host. (You can also open the branch to activate the check boxes of specific devices.)

8. Use the Programs tab to specify a program to run on connection. Activate the Start the Following Program on Connection check box, and then use the Program Path and File Name text box to specify the program to run. After connecting, the user can work with only this program. When he quits the program, the session also ends.

9. Use the Experience tab (the Windows 7 version is shown in Figure 7.5) to set performance options for the connection. Use the Choose Your Connection Speed to
   Optimize Performance drop-down list to set the appropriate connection speed.
   Because you're connecting over a network, you should choose the LAN (10 Mbps or
   higher) option. Depending on the connection speed you choose, one or more of the
   following check boxes will be activated. (The faster the speed, the more check boxes
   Windows activates.)

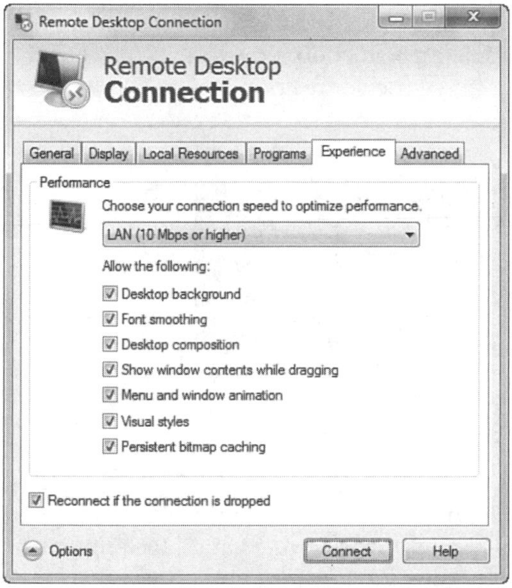

FIGURE 7.5   Use the Experience tab to set performance options for the connection.

▶ **Desktop Background**—Toggles the host's desktop background on and off.

▶ **Font Smoothing**—(Windows 7, Vista, and XP Service Pack 3 only) Toggles the
   host's font smoothing on and off.

▶ **Desktop Composition**—(Windows 7, Vista, and XP Service Pack 3 only)
   Toggles the host's desktop composition engine on and off.

▶ **Show Windows Contents While Dragging**—Toggles the display of window
   contents when you drag a host window with your mouse.

▶ **Menu and Windows Animation**—Toggles on and off the animations that
   Windows normally uses when you pull down menus or minimize and maximize windows.

▶ **Visual Styles**—(Themes in Windows Vista and XP) Toggles the host's current
   visual theme on and off.

▶ **Persistent Bitmap Caching**—Improves performance by storing frequently used
   host images on the client computer.

10. Click Connect. Windows Vista prompts you to enter your security credentials.

11. In Windows 7 or Vista, type the username and password of the host account you want to use for the logon, and then click OK. (Note that in subsequent logons, you'll only need to type the password.)

12. If you activated the Disk Drives or Serial Ports check boxes in the Local Resources tab, a security warning dialog box appears. If you're sure that making these resources available to the remote computer is safe, activate the Don't Prompt Me Again for Connections to This Remote Computer check box. Click OK.

The remote desktop then appears on your computer. If you choose to work in full-screen mode, move the mouse to the top of the screen to see the connection bar, shown in Figure 7.6.

FIGURE 7.6   After you've connected and the remote computer's desktop appears on your screen, move the mouse to the top of the screen to see the connection bar.

If you want the connection bar to appear all the time, click to activate the Pin button. You can also grab the connection bar and drag it left or right if it's pinned and blocking something on the screen. If you need to work with your own desktop, you have two choices:

▶ Click the connection bar's Minimize button to minimize the Remote Desktop window.

▶ Click the connection bar's Restore button to display the Remote Desktop window.

Disconnecting from the Remote Desktop

When you finish with the Remote Desktop session, you have two choices for disconnecting:

▶ Using the host desktop, select Start, Log Off.

▶ Click the Close button in the connection bar. Windows displays a dialog box to let you know that your remote session will be disconnected. Click OK.

Connecting via Windows Home Server Remote Web Access

You can use the Remote Desktop Connection program to connect to *any* Remote Desktop host, even hosts that don't have the Windows Home Server Connector software installed. A second method you can use to connect to Remote Desktop hosts is to go through the Windows Home Server network. With this method, which is a bit easier than running

Remote Desktop Connection directly, you can only connect to hosts that have Windows Home Server Connector installed.

This method runs Remote Desktop Connection behind the scenes via Windows Home Server. That is, instead of connecting directly to the remote host, Remote Desktop Connection takes you to the Windows Home Server, which then shows you the remote computer's desktop. Up front, Windows Home Server gives you a simple interface that lists the available computers to which you can connect. This interface is part of Windows Home Server Remote Web Access. This is the same interface that you use to connect to your network via the Internet, as described a bit later (see "Connecting via the Internet"). However, you also use it to connect to a Remote Desktop host over your LAN, which is what I discuss in this section.

For this to work, you must enable the Remote Desktop service on the host, as described earlier (see "Configuring a Computer as a Remote Desktop Host"), and then be sure to reboot the host PC.

CAUTION

Windows Home Server's Remote Web Access feature is *not* compatible with Network Level Authentication. Therefore, when you're setting up a Windows 7 or Windows Vista host, don't select the Allow Connections Only from Computers Running Remote Desktop with Network Level Authentication option. Instead, select the Allow Connections from Computers Running Any Version of Remote Desktop option.

NOTE

It's crucial that you reboot the host PC after you enable Remote Desktop; otherwise, Windows Home Server won't recognize the PC as being configured for Remote Desktop duties.

Configuring Users for Remote Access

You need to configure Windows Home Server to allow remote access for the user account that you'll be using to log on to the Remote Desktop host. Here are the steps to follow:

1. Log in to the Windows Home Server Dashboard.
2. Select the Users tab.
3. Double-click the user you want to configure. The user's property sheet appears.
4. In the Remote Web Access tab, click to activate the Allow Remote Web Access check box.
5. Click to activate the check box beside each item you want the user to see as a link on the Remote Web Access page. In particular, activate the Computers check box to give the user remote access to the network computers.
6. Click OK.

Activating Remote Web Access on the Server

Your final bit of prep involves turning on the Remote Access service in Windows Home Server. Here's how it's done:

1. Log in to the Windows Home Server Dashboard.
2. Click Server Settings.
3. Click the Remote Web Access tab.
4. Click Turn On. Windows Home Server runs the Turn on Remote Web Access Wizard.
5. You don't need your router configured at this point (we get into that a bit later; see "Connecting via the Internet"), so click to activate the Skip Router Setup check box, and then click Next. Windows Home Server configures Remote Web Access on your network and then prompts you to set up a domain name. I discuss this in detail a bit later (see "Connecting with a Domain Name Maintained by Windows Home Server"), so you can ignore this for now.
6. Click Close.
7. Click OK.

Displaying the Remote Web Access Page

Before you can connect to a remote computer, you need to log on to Windows Home Server's Remote Web Access page. This is a page on the Windows Home Server website that gives you access to the Remote Desktop hosts on your network, as well as to the Windows Home Server shared folders. Here are the steps to follow to display the Remote Web Access page:

1. On the client, launch the Internet Explorer web browser.

TIP

You can use most modern web browsers—including Firefox, Safari, and Chrome—to display the Remote Web Access pages, but you can only remotely access computers using Internet Explorer. To fix this in Firefox, install the IE Tab add-on (available from ietab.mozdev.org). When you get to the Remote Web Access logon page, right-click the page and then click View Page in IE Tab.

---

2. Type the following address into the address bar (where *server* is the name of your Windows Home Server):

   `http://server`

3. Press Enter. Windows Home Server redirects you to the Remote Web Access logon page (see Figure 7.7) at the following address:

   `https://server/Remote/logon`

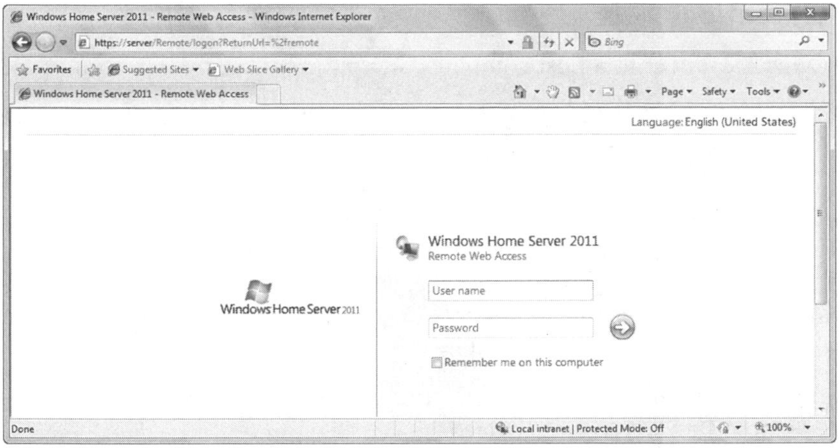

FIGURE 7.7   The logon page for Remote Web Access.

4. Type the username and password of your Windows Home Server account, and then press Enter or click the Go arrow. Windows Home Server displays the Remote Web Access Home page (see Figure 7.8) at the following address:

   https://*server*/remote/

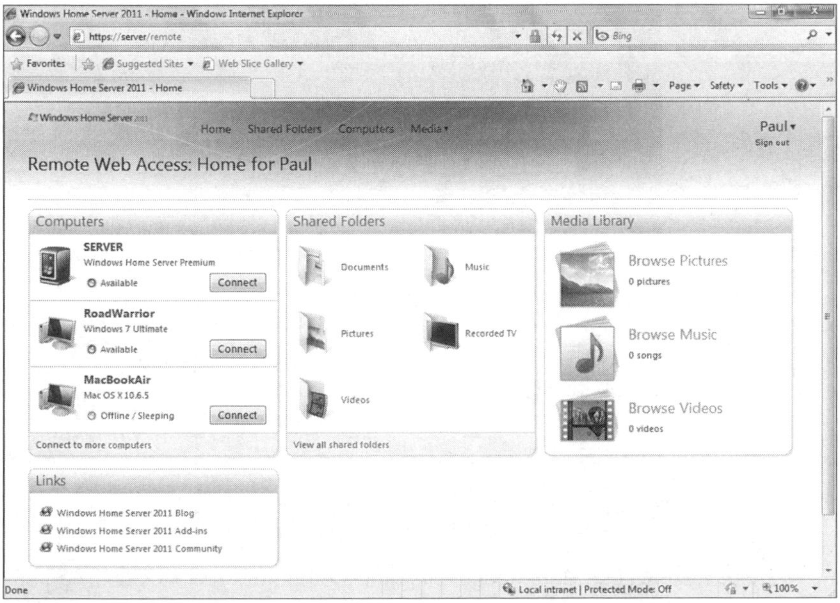

FIGURE 7.8   Windows Home Server's Remote Web Access Home page.

Making the Connection

With that done, you can connect to a host computer on your network by following these steps:

1. Display the Remote Web Access Home page.
2. The Computers section shows three machines on your network: the server and two clients. If you want to connect to one of these machines, click its Connect button; if you don't see the client you want to connect to, click the Computers link at the bottom of the list to display the Computers page, which displays a list of the computers on your Windows Home Server network, as shown in Figure 7.9. Note that the Status column shows one of the following four values:

   ▶ **Available**—The computer is capable of acting as a Remote Desktop host, and it has the Remote Desktop service enabled.

   ▶ **Connection Is Disabled**—The computer is capable of acting as a Remote Desktop host, but it doesn't have the Remote Desktop service enabled.

   ▶ **Offline / Sleeping**—The computer either is not connected to the network or is in sleep mode.

   ▶ **Not Supported on This Operating System**—The computer is not capable of acting as a Remote Desktop host. That is, the computer is running Windows7 Starter, Windows7 Home Premium, Vista Home Basic, Vista Home Premium, or XP Home.

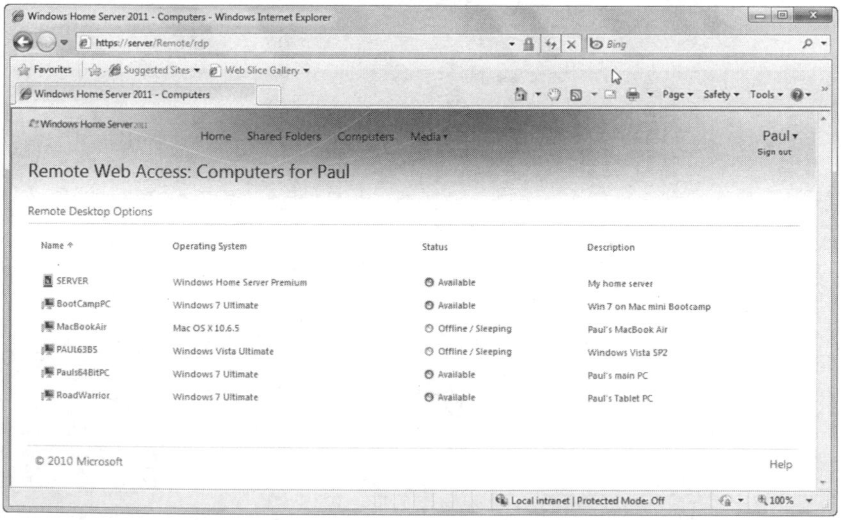

FIGURE 7.9   In the Remote Web Access Home page, click the Computers link to display a list of the Windows Home Server clients.

3. If the computer you want to connect to shows Available in the Status column, click the computer. (If Internet Explorer prompts you to install an ActiveX control, be sure to install it.) The Remote Desktop Connection dialog box appears, as shown in Figure 7.10.

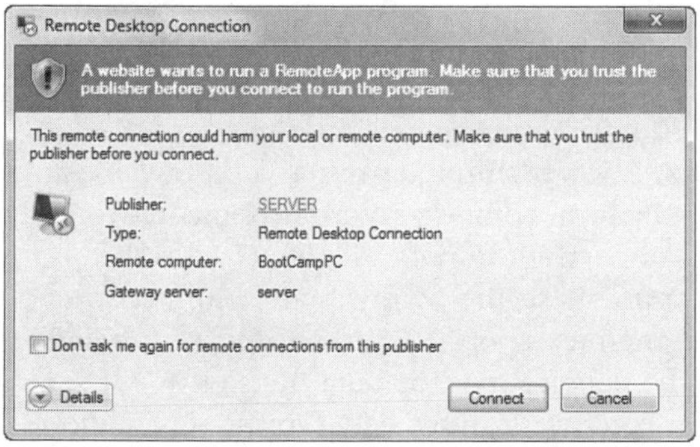

FIGURE 7.10   Use the Remote Desktop Connection dialog box to initiate the connection to the remote host.

4. Click Connect. Windows Home Server prompts you to log on to the client.

5. Log on to the remote computer.

> **NOTE**
>
> If you connect to the Windows Home Server machine, you end up at the Dashboard, not the Windows Home Server desktop.

Disconnecting from the Host

When you finish with the Remote Desktop session, you have two choices for disconnecting:

▶ Using the host desktop, select Start, Log Off.

▶ Display the Connection bar and click the Close button.

When you return to the Windows Home Server Remote Access page, click Sign Out to end your session.

Connecting via the Internet

One of the most significant features in the Windows Home Server package is the capability to securely connect to a computer on your home network via an Internet connection. So, for example, if you're in a coffee shop before a big meeting and you remember that you forgot to copy to your notebook the updated presentation file you were working on last night, you can connect to the Internet using the merchant's Wi-Fi access, connect to your home machine, and then download the file.

In fact, there are all kinds of useful ways to take advantage of remote Internet connections: You can check your home email; upload a file you've been working on as a quick-and-dirty backup system; transfer files from the office; or start a program such as a backup or defrag so that it's done by the time you get home. The possibilities are endless.

Windows enables you to connect to a remote computer via the Internet, but it did this using the Remote Desktop Protocol (RDP), and setting up the machines to connect securely wasn't straightforward. Windows Home Server simplifies things a bit by *not* using RDP for the initial Internet connection from the local computer to your home network. Instead, Windows Home Server initiates the connection on port 443, which uses the Secure Sockets Layer (SSL) protocol to create a highly secure point-to-point connection between you and Windows Home Server and then uses port 4125 to set up a secure RDP channel. The port that provides the bulk of the Remote Desktop data transfers is 3389, but Windows Home Server only uses that port for communications between the server and the network client. This means that port 3389—the standard RDP port that all malicious hackers know about—is *not* exposed to the Internet.

Windows Home Server 2011 gives you three ways to connect to your home network over the Internet:

▶ Using your router's IP address.

▶ Using a domain name that is set up and maintained using a dynamic DNS service.

▶ Using a domain name that is set up and maintained with Windows Home Server.

The next few sections take you through the details for each method.

Connecting with Your Router's IP Address

Setting up your system to allow remote connections through the Internet using the router's IP address is easier with Windows Home Server than it is with Vista or XP, but you still have a few hoops to jump through. Here's a summary of the steps involved. (The sections that follow fill in the details for each step.)

1. Determine the IP address of the Windows Home Server.
2. Configure your network router or gateway to forward data sent on ports 443 and 4125 to the Windows Home Server.
3. Determine your router/gateway's IP address.

Determining the Windows Home Server IP Address

To ensure that the incoming data gets to Windows Home Server, you need to know the server's IP address. Ideally, you configured Windows Home Server with a static IP address, as described in Chapter 1, "Setting Up Your Windows Home Server Network." This is the best way to go because if you use DHCP on the server instead, you have to modify the gateway/router port forwarding (discussed in the next section) every time the server's IP address changes.

▶ **SEE** "Configuring Windows Home Server with a Static IP Address," **P. 8.**

If you didn't set up Windows Home Server with a static IP address, or if you don't remember the static IP address, you can get the address via the Windows Home Server Dashboard (see "Letting Windows Home Server Configure the Router," later in this chapter) or by following these steps:

1. Log on to Windows Home Server.
2. Select Start, Command Prompt.
3. Type **ipconfig** and press Enter. Windows Home Server displays its current IP address.
4. Write down the address, and then close the Command Prompt window.

Setting Up Port Forwarding on the Router

If your network uses a router, gateway, or other hardware firewall, you need to configure it to forward to the Windows Home Server computer and data sent on the following ports:

▶ Port 443 (SSL) using the TCP protocol

▶ Port 4125 (RDP) using the TCP protocol

This is *port forwarding*, and you can either get Windows Home Server to configure this for you, or you can do it by hand.

Letting Windows Home Server Configure the Router

If your router or gateway supports Universal Plug and Play (UPnP), Windows Home Server may be able to configure it for you automatically. Here are the steps to follow:

NOTE

Most routers that support UPnP also come with options that enable and disable UPnP. Before asking Windows Home Server to configure your router, access the router's setup pages and make sure that UPnP is enabled.

---

1. Open the Windows Home Server Dashboard.
2. Click Server Settings to open the Server Settings dialog box.
3. Select the Remote Web Access tab.
4. In the Router section, click Set Up. (I'm assuming here that you've already turned on Remote Web Access as I described earlier. If not, click Turn On, instead.) Windows Home Server attempts to configure your router, as shown in Figure 7.11.

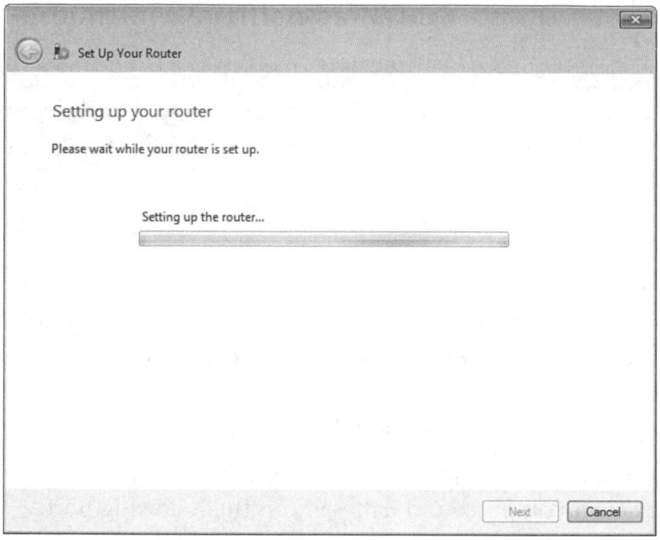

FIGURE 7.11   The Turn On Remote Web Access Wizard configures your router for remote access.

5. Click Close. If the configuration was successful, the Remote Web Access tab's Router section shows the router IP address and model, the Windows Home Server IP address, and the Windows Home Server physical address (that is, the Media Access Control—MAC, for short—address), as shown in Figure 7.12.

6. Click OK.

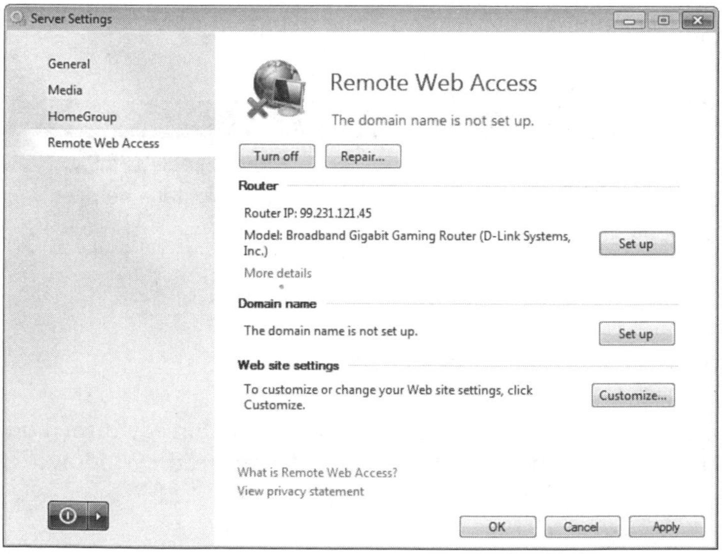

FIGURE 7.12   With Remote Web Access turned on and the router configured, Windows Home Server Dashboard shows the router and server addresses.

> **TIP**
>
> If Windows Home Server fails to configure your router, consider upgrading the router's firmware. This seems to solve many UPnP problems, particularly with Linksys routers. To upgrade the firmware, go to the router manufacturer's site, find the support or downloads section, and then download the latest firmware version of your device. Then access the router's setup page (use a wired connection, not a wireless one) and look for the page that enables you to apply the new firmware version.

Configuring the Router By Hand

If Windows Home Server couldn't configure the router, you can always do it yourself, although the steps you follow depend on the device. Figure 7.13 shows the Port Forwarding screen of the router on my system. In this case, I've forwarded the two ports— 443 and 4125—so that any data sent to them over TCP is sent automatically to the address 192.168.1.254, which is the static IP address of my Windows Home Server. Consult your device documentation to learn how to set up port forwarding.

VIRTUAL SERVERS LIST

Enable	Name	IP Address	Protocol Private Port/Public Port	Inbound Filter	Schedule		
☑	RPD 4125	192.168.1.254	TCP 4125/4125	Allow All	Always	🖹	🗑
☑	RDP 443	192.168.1.254	TCP 443/443	Allow All	Always	🖹	🗑

FIGURE 7.13   On your router/gateway, forward ports 443 and 4125 to the Windows Home Server IP address.

Determining the Router's External IP Address

To connect to your network via the Internet, you need to specify an IP address instead of a computer name. (You can bypass this if you get a Windows Home Server domain name; see "Connecting with a Domain Name Maintained by Windows Home Server," later in this chapter.) The IP address you use is the address that your ISP assigns to your router when that device connects to the Internet. This is called the router's *external* IP address (to differentiate it from the router's *internal* IP address, which is the address you use to access the router locally). Although some ISPs provide static IP addresses to the router, it's more likely that the address is dynamic and changes each time the gateway connects.

Either way, you need to determine the router's current external IP address. One way to do this is to log on to the router's setup pages and view some sort of status page. However, Windows Home Server 2011 makes this easier by showing you the router's current IP address in the Dashboard. Open the Dashboard, click Server Settings, and then click Remote Web Access. In the Router section, the Router IP value tells you the router current external IP address (see Figure 7.12, earlier).

When you set up your remote connection, you'll connect to the router's IP address, which will then forward your connection (thanks to your efforts in the previous section) to Windows Home Server.

TIP

Another way to determine your router's IP address is to navigate to any of the free services for determining your current IP. Here are two:

▶ WhatIsMyIP (www.whatismyip.com)

▶ DynDNS (checkip.dyndns.org)

Connecting with a Domain Name Maintained by a Dynamic DNS Service

If you want to use Remote Desktop via the Internet regularly, constantly monitoring your router's dynamic IP address can be a pain, particularly if you forget to check it before heading out of the office. A useful solution is to sign up with a dynamic DNS service, which supplies you with a static domain name. The service also installs a program on your computer that monitors your IP address and updates the service's dynamic DNS servers to point your domain name to your IP address. Here are some dynamic DNS services to check out:

▶ DynDNS (www.dyndns.org)

▶ TZO (www.tzo.com)

▶ No-IP.com (www.no-ip.com)

To give you some idea how to go about this, here's a summary of the steps I took to set up dynamic DNS with DynDNS:

1. Sign up for one of the company's services. In my case, I already had a domain name, so I signed up for the Custom DNS service so that DynDNS could handle the DNS duties for my domain. If you don't have a domain, you can sign up for the Domain Registration service.

2. After confirming my account, I used one of the excellent "how-to" articles found on DynDNS to determine the domain names of their DNS servers.

3. With those names in hand, I logged in to my account on the registrar that handles my domain. I then changed the DNS servers for my domain so that they pointed to the DynDNS servers.

4. I downloaded the DynDNS Updater, a program that runs on your local computer and monitors your gateway's dynamic IP address. When that address changes, DynDNS Updater passes the new address to the DynDNS system so that my domain name always points to the correct IP address.

5. I waited for about a day for the DNS changes to propagate throughout the Internet.

Connecting with a Domain Name Maintained by Windows Home Server

Using a domain name instead of an IP address is better because domain names are easier for everyone in the family to remember, and they don't change the way the IP address assigned by your ISP probably does. Using a dynamic DNS service as described in the previous section enables you to never worry about your router's IP address again. However, if there's a downside to using these services, it's that they add an extra layer of maintenance to your remote access duties, and you can never be sure how long the company might be in business.

You can simplify connecting with a domain name by letting Windows Home Server handle the dynamic DNS details for you. (And you can sleep better at night knowing that Microsoft will probably be around for a while!) The Windows Home Server dynamic DNS service gives you three options:

▶ **Use a subdomain name from Microsoft.** Whereas a domain name takes the form *domain*.com, a subdomain name takes the form *mydomain.domain*.com. Here, *domain*.com is the domain name of the company providing the service, and *mydomain* is a unique name that you provide. With Windows Home Server, the subdomain takes the form *mydomain*.homeserver.com, and the domain is administered by Microsoft's Windows Live Custom Domains service via the homeserver. com site, the official home of Windows Home Server. The subdomain is free, although it does require you to have a Windows Live ID, such as a Hotmail, Live, or MSN account.

▶ **Use an existing domain name.** This is the way to go if you already have a domain name that you want to use to access your home network via the Internet. Note, however, that Windows Home Server requires you to transfer your domain name to a provider that works with Windows Home Server.

▶ **Set up a new domain name.** This is the route to take if you don't already have your own domain name, or if you prefer to use a new name to access your home network over the Internet. In this case, Windows Home Server connects you with a domain name provider in your area, and you use that third-party service to create your new domain. (Note that the third-party service will charge you a small annual fee to maintain the domain name.)

No matter which method you choose, this is a dynamic DNS service, so even if your router's IP address changes, your subdomain or domain will be updated to point to the new address. (Windows Home Server periodically polls the router for its current IP address and sends that address to the Microsoft dynamic DNS server. The server then updates its DNS database with the current IP address of your router.)

Setting Up a Subdomain from Microsoft

Follow these steps to set up a Windows Home Server subdomain:

1. Open the Windows Home Server Dashboard.
2. Click Server Settings to open the Server Settings dialog box.
3. Select the Remote Web Access tab.

4. In the Domain Name section, click Set Up to launch the Set Up Your Domain Name Wizard. (If you don't have Remote Access turned on, click Turn On instead; once Windows Home Server has configured your router, click the Set Up Domain Name link to launch the Set Up Your Domain Name Wizard.)

5. Click Next. The wizard asks you to choose which method to use to set up the domain name.

6. Click I Want to Set Up a New Domain Name, and then click Next. The wizard asks what type of domain name you want.

7. Click Get a Personalized Domain Name from Microsoft, and then click Next. The wizard asks you to sign in to your Windows Live ID account.

8. Type your Windows Live email address and password, and then click Next. What happens next depends on whether you already have a subdomain registered with Microsoft:

   ▶ If you already have a subdomain registered with Windows Live and you want to use that subdomain, select Choose a Registered Name, choose the subdomain from the list, click Next, and then skip to step 10.

   ▶ If you already have a subdomain registered with Windows Live but you want to use a new subdomain, select Create a New Domain Name, click Next, and proceed with step 9.

   ▶ If you don't have a subdomain registered with Windows Live, proceed with step 9.

9. Type your subdomain name and then click Check Availability to confirm that it's available. If the name is available, click Set Up. The wizard sets up your subdomain name.

NOTE

Your subdomain name can be any length, but it must contain only letters, numbers, or hyphens, and it must begin and end with a letter or number.

10. Click Close. The wizard returns you to the Server Settings dialog box and displays a link for your new domain name. (You can click this link to access your Windows Home Server over the Internet.)

11. Click OK.

Setting Up an Existing Domain

Follow these steps to set up an existing domain name:

1. Open the Windows Home Server Dashboard.

2. Click Server Settings to open the Server Settings dialog box.

3. Select the Remote Web Access tab.

4. In the Domain Name section, click Set Up to launch the Set Up Your Domain Name wizard. (If you don't have Remote Access turned on, click Turn On instead; once Windows Home Server has configured your router, click the Set Up Domain Name link to launch the Set Up Your Domain Name Wizard.)

5. Click Next. The wizard asks you to choose which method to use to set up the domain name.

6. Click I Want to Use a Domain Name I Already Own, type the domain name, and then click Next. The wizard either displays your current domain provider (in which case, you can skip to step 9), or it displays a list of domain name providers in your area (in which case, continue with step 7).

7. If the provider that currently maintains your domain name is on the list, select that provider; otherwise, select the provider you want to use. Click Next. The wizard warns you that transferring a domain will take some time and asks if you want to proceed.

8. Click Yes. The wizard displays the domain name and provider you chose.

9. Click Go to *Provider*, where *Provider* is the name of the domain name provider you chose in step 7. The wizard launches your web browser and connects you with the domain name provider.

10. Proceed through the steps required to transfer your domain name.

11. Switch back to the wizard and click Next. The wizard sets up your domain name.

12. Click Close. The wizard returns you to the Server Settings dialog box and displays a link for your new domain name. (You can click this link to access your Windows Home Server over the Internet.)

13. Click OK.

Setting Up a New Domain

Follow these steps to set up a new domain name:

1. Open the Windows Home Server Dashboard.

2. Click Server Settings to open the Server Settings dialog box.

3. Select the Remote Web Access tab.

4. In the Domain Name section, click Set Up to launch the Set Up Your Domain Name Wizard. (If you don't have Remote Access turned on, click Turn On instead; once Windows Home Server has configured your router, click the Set Up Domain Name link to launch the Set Up Your Domain Name Wizard.)

5. Click Next. The wizard asks you to choose which method to use to set up the domain name.

6. Click I Want to Set Up a New Domain Name, and then click Next. The wizard asks what type of domain name you want.

7. Click Purchase Professional Domain Name from a Supported Provider, and then click Next. The wizard displays a list of domain name providers in your area.

8. Select the provider you want to use, and then click Next. The wizard asks you to select your new domain name.

9. Type the domain name, select an extension (such as .com) from the list, and then click Next. The wizard checks with the provider to make sure the domain name is available.

10. Click Register Now. The wizard launches your web browser and connects you with the domain name provider.

11. Proceed through the steps required to register and create your domain name.

12. Switch back to the wizard and click Next. The wizard sets up your domain name.

13. Click Close. The wizard returns you to the Server Settings dialog box and displays a link for your new domain name. (You can click this link to access your Windows Home Server over the Internet.)

14. Click OK.

Displaying the Remote Web Access Home Page

As with LAN connections through Windows Home Server, before you can connect to a computer via the Internet, you need to log on to Windows Home Server's Remote Web Access Home page.

If you configured a Windows Home Server domain, you have two choices:

▶ Log on to the Windows Home Server Dashboard, click Server Settings, click the Remote Web Access tab, and then click the link in the Domain Name section.

▶ Run Internet Explorer and enter the address **https://*domain***, where *domain* is the domain name you configured; if you signed up for a subdomain, remember to use the address **https://*subdomain*.homeserver.com**, where *subdomain* is the subdomain you registered with Microsoft.

If you don't have a subdomain, you need to use your router's external IP address. Launch Internet Explorer and enter **https://*RouterIP*** (where *RouterIP* is the external IP address of your router. (If you see a message telling you that the website's security certificate is invalid, you can ignore the error and continue loading the page.)

NOTE

Whether you use a subdomain or an IP address, note that you use `https` as the protocol instead of `http`.

Windows Home Server redirects you to the Remote Web Access logon page at https://*Address*/Remote/logon (where *Address* is your domain or your router's external IP address).

Type the username and password of your Windows Home Server account, and then press Enter or click the Go arrow. Windows Home Server redirects you to the Windows Home Server Web Site Remote Access page (see Figure 7.14) at https://*Address*/remote.

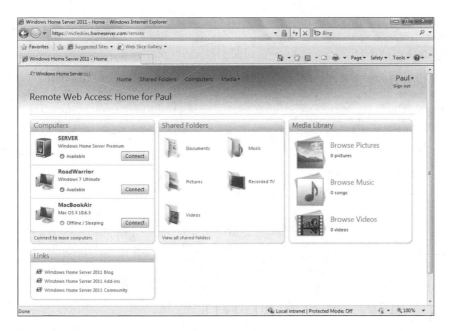

FIGURE 7.14   Windows Home Server's Remote Web Access Home page accessed over the Internet.

Connecting to a Network Computer

After you're logged on to Remote Web Access, connecting to a network computer running the Remote Desktop service is as easy as clicking a client's Connect button in the Computers section, or clicking the Computers link and then clicking the computer in the list. For the details, see "Making the Connection," earlier in this chapter.

> **TIP**
>
> If you're using Firefox, remember that you can't connect to a network computer unless you install the IE Tab add-on (available from ietab.mozdev.org).

> **NOTE**
>
> If you connect to the Windows Home Server machine, you end up at the Dashboard, not the Windows Home Server desktop.

Working with Windows Home Server Shares in the Web Browser

Besides connecting to Remote Desktop hosts and to Windows Home Server, you can use Remote Web Access to work with the server's shared folders via the Internet. You can access the built-in shares and any nonuser shares that you've created. Within each shared folder, you can create subfolders, rename and delete files, upload files from your computer to the server, and download files from the server share to your computer.

When you log on to Remote Web Access, click Shared Folders. As you can see in Figure 7.15, this displays a file interface for the available shares, with a tree view on the left and a contents view on the right. Select a shared folder, and you see the file management interface shown in Figure 7.16.

Here's a summary of the actions you can perform in this page:

▸ **Select items**—Use the check boxes to select files and subfolders, or click the Select All check box (the one at the top of the file list) to select all the files shown in the current page.

▸ **Create a subfolder**—Navigate to the folder in which you want the subfolder created, and click the New Folder button to open the Add a Folder dialog box. Type the folder name, and then click OK.

▸ **Rename a file or folder**—Select the file or folder, and then select Organize, Rename to open the Type a New File Name dialog box. Type the new name, and then click OK.

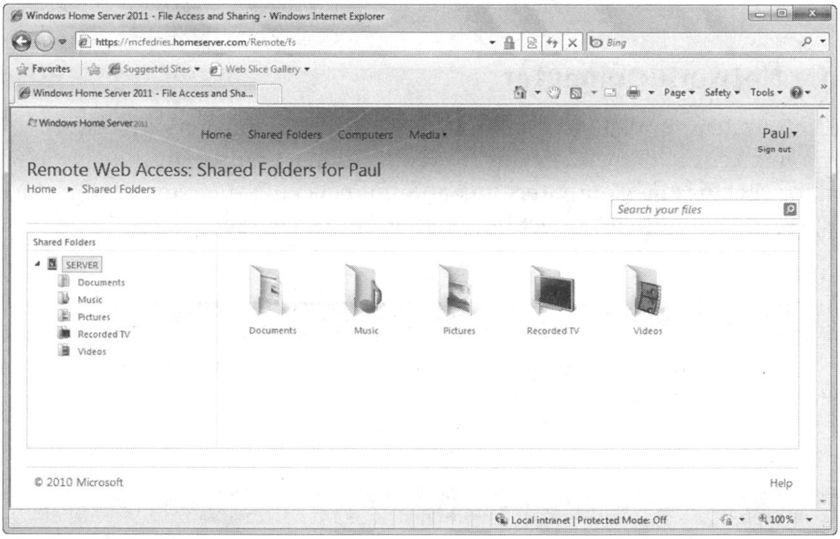

FIGURE 7.15   The Shared Folders page contains icons for the Windows Home Server shared folders that are accessible to your user account.

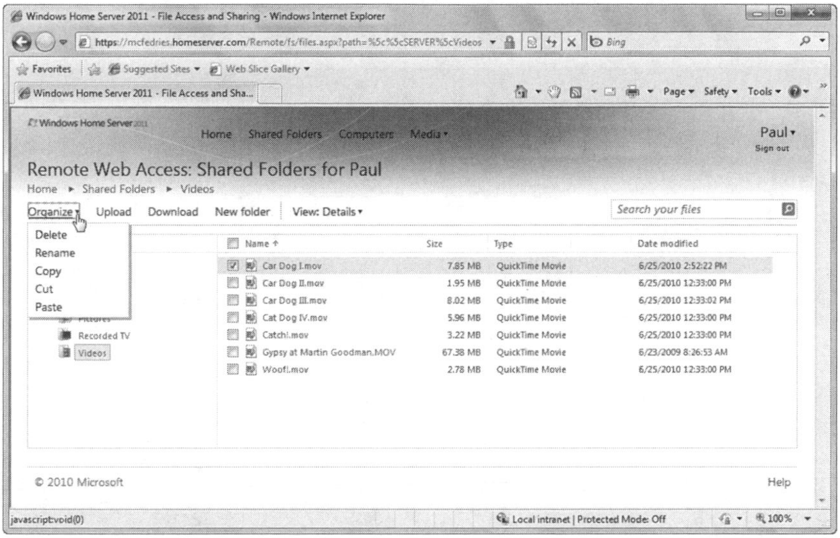

FIGURE 7.16   Use this file management interface to work with the files and folders in the share.

▶ **Upload items from your computer to the server**—Click Upload to display the Upload page, shown in Figure 7.17. Click Browse to open the Choose File to Upload dialog box, select the file or folder, and then click Open to add the item to the Upload page. Repeat for other items you want to send to the share, and then click Upload.

▶ **Download items from the server share to your computer**—Select the items you want to download, and then click the Download button. If you selected multiple items, Windows Home Server asks whether you want the selected items downloaded as a self-extracting executable file or as a compressed ZIP file. Click the option you prefer, and then click OK. Windows Home Server inserts the selected items into a compressed file named either *share.exe* or *share.zip* (where *share* is the name of the shared folder) and then displays the File Download dialog box. Click Save, use the Save As dialog box to choose a download location (and, optionally, rename the download files), and then click Save.

NOTE

Windows Home Server imposes a 30-minute limit on creating the ZIP file, so don't try to cram too much data into the download.

▶ **Delete a file or folder**—Select the objects you want to work with, and then select Organize, Delete. When Windows Home Server asks you to confirm the deletion, click Yes.

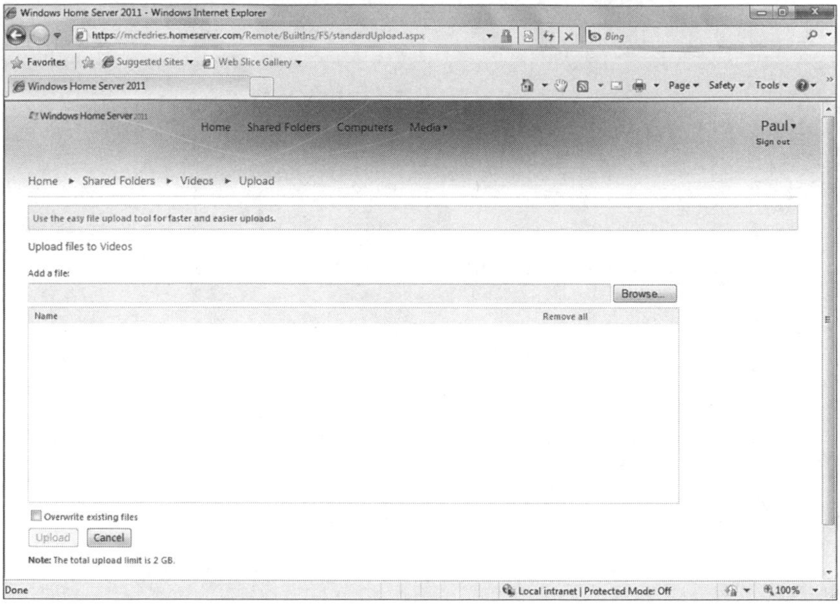

FIGURE 7.17   Use the Upload page to send files from your computer to the server share.

Enabling Drag-and-Drop Uploading

The Remote Web Access Upload page is a decent-enough interface for uploading, but we're used to dragging and dropping files in Windows, and the web browser is mouse-oriented, so it would be nice to be able to upload files using drag-and-drop. Happily, that functionality is built in to Windows Home Server 2011, but it's turned off by default. To enable it, follow these steps:

1. Click the Upload button to open the Upload Files page.

2. Click Install the Easy File Upload Tool. Windows 7 and Vista prompt you for your User Account Control credentials.

3. Enter your User Account Control credentials.

You now see an upload area in the Upload page, and you can drag files (up to 2GB in size) from Windows Explorer and drop them in the area. Each time you drop a file, Windows Home Server adds it to the list, as shown in Figure 7.18 (which also shows an image file about to be dropped in the upload area). When you're done, click Upload.

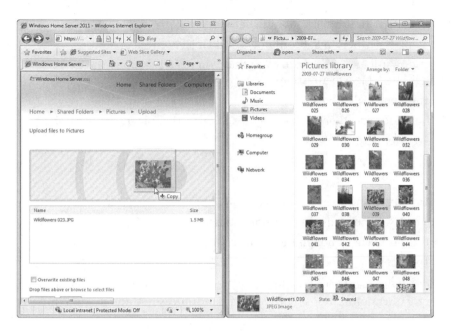

FIGURE 7.18   With drag-and-drop enabled, you can drag files from Windows Explorer and drop them inside the Upload page.

Customizing the Remote Web Access Pages

Much of what you see in the Remote Web Access web pages is ASP.NET code found in text files that reside in the following folder:

```
%ProgramFiles%\Windows Server\Bin\WebApps\RemoteAccess
```

If you know ASP.NET, HTML, and cascading stylesheets (CSS), you can customize the Remote Web Access pages in any way you see fit. However, if you make changes to any of these files, you must first take ownership of them. Here are the steps to follow:

1. Log on to Windows Home server and use Windows Explorer to display %ProgramFiles%\Windows Server\Bin\WebApps.
2. Right-click the RemoteAccess folder, and then click Properties to open the folder's property sheet.
3. Display the Security tab.
4. Click Advanced to open the Advanced Security Settings dialog box.
5. Display the Owner tab.
6. Click Edit.

7. In the Change Owner To list, click Administrator.

8. Activate the Replace Owner on Subcontainers and Objects check box.

9. Click OK. Windows Home Server warns you that you need to reopen the property sheet to change the folder's permissions.

10. Click OK in the open dialog boxes.

11. Right-click the folder, and then click Properties to open the folder's property sheet.

12. Display the Security tab.

13. Click Edit.

14. Click Add.

15. Type **administrator** and then click OK.

16. In the Group or User Names list, click Administrator.

17. Click the Full Control check box in the Allow column.

18. Click OK in the open dialog boxes.

I won't go into the details of editing these files here. However, the next three sections take you through a couple of customizations that you can perform easily through the Windows Home Server Dashboard.

CAUTION

Take some care when modifying the Remote Access files to avoid breaking Windows Home Server. Before modifying anything in the `Inetpub` folder, it's a really good idea to make backups of the files so that you can restore the defaults should anything go awry.

Customizing the Logon Page

You can customize the Remote Web Access logon page by changing the following:

▶ The page title, which appears in the browser title bar, the browser tab, and above the User Name and Password text boxes.

▶ The logon logo, which is the small icon that appears to the left of the page title.

▶ The logon background image, which is the image that appears behind the page title and the User Name and Password text boxes.

Here are the steps to follow:

1. Open the Windows Home Server Dashboard.

2. Click Server Settings to open the Server Settings dialog box.

3. Select the Remote Web Access tab.

4. In the Web Site Settings section, click Customize to open the Customize Remote Web Access dialog box with the Logon Page tab displayed, as shown in Figure 7.19).

5. Use the Web Site Title text box to type a new title.

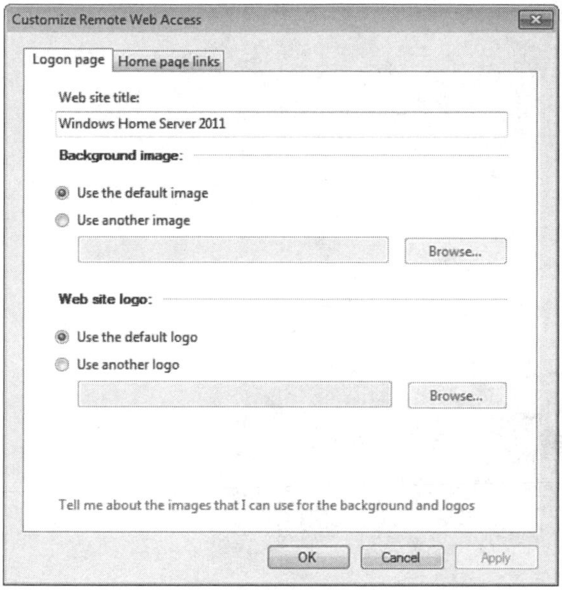

FIGURE 7.19   In the Customize Remote Web Access dialog box, use the Logon Page tab to change the page title, background, and logo.

6. To set the background, select the Use Another Image option, click Browse, and then select the image. If possible, select an 800x500 Bitmap, GIF, JPEG, or PNG image file.

7. To set the logo, select the Use Another Logo option, click Browse, and then select the image. Ideally, choose a 32x32 image file.

8. Click OK.

9. Click OK.

Figure 7.20 shows the Remote Web Access logon page with a new title, background, and logo.

Adding Web Page Links

The Remote Web Access Home page contains a Links section that out of the box contains a few links to some Windows Home Server 2011 resources. You can customize the Links box by adding your own links, removing any existing links you don't need, and rearranging the links. Here's how it works:

1. Open the Windows Home Server Dashboard.

2. Click Server Settings to open the Server Settings dialog box.

3. Select the Remote Web Access tab.

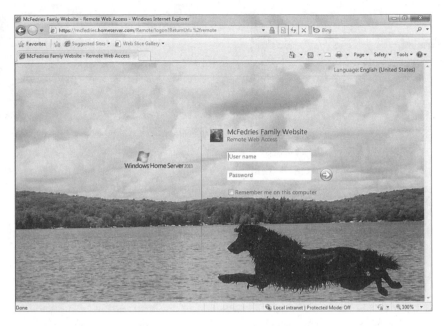

FIGURE 7.20   Windows Home Server's Remote Web Access logon page showing the new title, background, and logo.

4. In the Web Site Settings section, click Customize to open the Customize Remote Web Access dialog box.

5. Click the Home Page Links tab.

6. To add a new link, type the link text in the Name text box, the link address in the Address text box, and then click Add.

7. To delete a link, select it and then click Remove.

8. To reorder the links, click each link you want to move and then click either Move Up or Move Down. Figure 7.21 shows a Home Page Links tab with some custom links added and reordered.

9. Click OK.

10. Click OK.

Figure 7.22 shows the Remote Web Access Home page with the customized Links box.

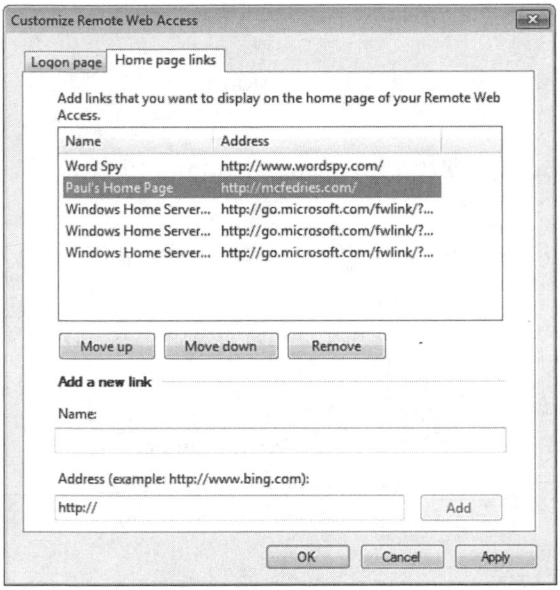

FIGURE 7.21   In the Customize Remote Web Access dialog box, use the Home Page Links tab to add, remove, and reorder the links.

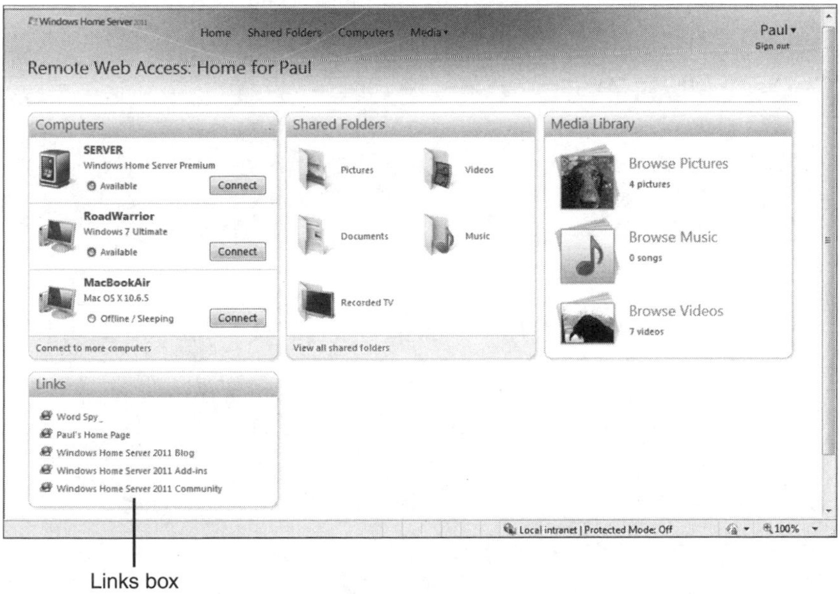

Links box

FIGURE 7.22   The Remote Web Access Home page showing the customized Links box.

From Here

Here are some other sections in the book where you'll find information related to the topics in this chapter:

- ▶ For details on setting a static IP address, **SEE** "Configuring Windows Home Server with a Static IP Address," **P. 8.**

- ▶ To learn how to view the properties of a Windows Home Server user account, **SEE** "Viewing Account Properties," **P. 42.**

- ▶ For details on Mac-based Remote Desktop connections, **SEE** "Using a Mac to Make a Remote Desktop Connection to Windows Home Server," **P. 59.**

- ▶ For information on other ways to take advantage of Windows Home Server's built-in web server, **SEE** Chapter 12, "Setting Up a Windows Home Server Website."

CHAPTER 8

Streaming and Sharing Digital Media

IN THIS CHAPTER

▶ Streaming Digital Media

▶ Sharing Photos

▶ Sharing Music

▶ Sharing Videos

Windows Home Server comes with support for Windows Media Connect, which is software that streams digital media from (in this case) the server to programs and devices that support Windows Media Connect. Supported programs include digital media players such as Windows Media Player and devices such as the Xbox 360 and Kodak Wireless Digital Picture Frame. The latter two are examples of *digital media receivers* (DMRs), or devices that can access a media stream being sent over a wired or wireless network connection and then play that stream through connected equipment such as speakers, audio receivers, or a TV. In Windows Home Server 2011, the server now supports Microsoft's Play To functionality, which enables the server to act as a *digital media server* (DMS).

Note, too, that Windows Media Connect uses standard protocols—specifically Hypertext Transfer Protocol (HTTP) and Universal Plug and Play (UPnP)—so, theoretically, any device that supports these protocols should also be able to receive Windows Home Server media streams. (Most UPnP devices have options to disable and enable UPnP, or "network control" as it's sometimes called. Access the device settings, and make sure that UPnP is enabled.)

Windows Home Server offers four media streams: music, pictures, recorded TV, and videos. This chapter shows you how to get your devices ready for streaming and how to activate streaming via Windows Home Server. You also learn nonstreaming techniques for sharing photos, music, and videos via Windows Home Server.

Streaming Digital Media

The ability to stream music over the network is one of Windows Home Server's most attractive features. Yes, you can activate the Media Streaming feature in Windows Media Player 12 (or the Media Sharing feature in Windows Media Player 11) and share your library over the network, but that sharing is limited to the media on your computer. Throw Windows Home Server's centralized storage into the mix, and you suddenly have a much wider variety of media to stream.

If you're in the market for a new DMR device, make sure it's a certified Digital Living Network Alliance (DLNA) device, because Windows Home Server 2011 now supports DLNA out of the box. This means that a DLNA-compatible device—it could be a Blu-ray player, a TV, a digital picture frame, or an Xbox 360 in Windows Media Center mode—will automatically find your server and stream content from it. If it's a Wi-Fi device, make sure it supports 802.11n for maximum wireless bandwidth.

CAUTION

Before purchasing a DMR, check the device's wireless capabilities. Some older and less expensive devices can only connect to wireless networks that use Wired Equivalent Privacy (WEP) security. However, WEP has been superseded by Wi-Fi Protected Access (WPA), which is much more secure than WEP. If you use WPA or WPA2 (a more secure version of WPA) on your wireless network (as you should), make sure any DMR you purchase either supports WPA out of the box or can be updated to support WPA with a firmware upgrade.

Getting Your Devices Ready

Getting a device ready to receive and play streaming media is a fairly straightforward affair that usually encompasses just the following steps:

1. Get the device ready for networking:

   ▶ If the device is physically near a network router or switch, run a network cable from the device to the router or switch.

   ▶ If you need to use a wireless connection, check to see if the device has built-in wireless (at least 802.11b) support. Many devices—including the Xbox 360— require separate wireless components to be plugged in to the device.

2. Turn on the device.

3. If you're using a wireless connection, set up the device to connect to your wireless network.

   ▶ **SEE** Chapter 3, "Adding Devices to the Windows Home Server Network."

4. Use audio or video cables to connect the device to the appropriate output equipment, such as powered speakers, a receiver, a display, or a TV set.

After you have the device on the network, you should see an icon for it in Windows 7's Network folder, or Windows Vista's Network window. For example, Figure 8.1 shows a Network window with two media devices: an Xbox 360 and a Roku SoundBridge.

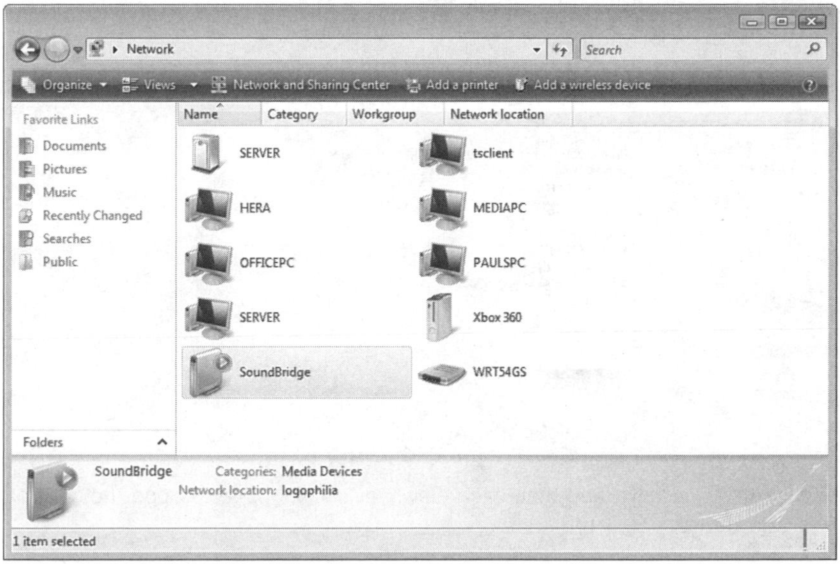

FIGURE 8.1   Devices that support Windows Media Connect should also appear in the Network window.

TIP

Whatever device you use, it's always a good idea to install the latest firmware to ensure that you're using the most up-to-date version of the device interface. See the device documentation to learn how to upgrade the firmware.

NOTE

You can also see many digital media devices in Windows XP with Service Pack 2 or later. Select Start, My Network Places, and then click the Show Icons for Networked UPnP Devices link in the Network Tasks section. (XP may install support for this feature at this point.) The devices appear in My Network Places in a new Local Network group.

Note, too, that some devices offer a link to their built-in control and settings pages. Right-click the device icon, and look for the View Device Webpage command. For example, Figure 8.2 shows the pages that appear for the Roku SoundBridge device.

8

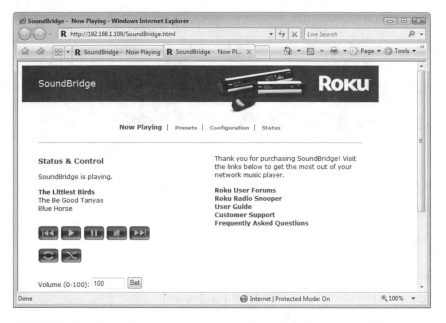

FIGURE 8.2   Right-click a device icon, and then click View Device Webpage to open the control and settings pages for the device.

TIP

If you don't see the View Device Webpage command, you can also try opening the device directly in a web browser. Find the device's IP address (right-click the device icon and then click Properties) and then enter **http://address** in the web browser (where *address* is the device's IP address).

Activating the Windows Home Server Media Server

The next step in getting media streaming up and running in Windows Home Server is to enable the server's built-in media server, and then enable Media Library Sharing for some or all of the shared media folders. You can stream any of the shared folders, but the four media folders are the most common: Music, Pictures, Recorded TV, and Videos. Before getting to the specifics, here are some notes to bear in mind:

▶ Media Library Sharing doesn't work with most copy-protected media, because generally you can only play that media on the computer or device that you used to purchase the media in the first place. You're still free to place copies of such media on the Windows Home Server shares, but you can only use the purchase device to play back the media stream.

▶ Media Library Sharing isn't related to sharing the files themselves through \\server and the Windows Home Server user accounts. With the latter, you can assign permissions such as Full Access or Read Only to tailor the access that a specific user has to the folder contents. When you enable Media Library Sharing on a folder, however, *any* program or device that supports DLNA or Windows Media Connect can access the library and play the media it contains.

▶ As a consequence of the previous point, note that Media Library Sharing overrides any user restrictions that you've placed on a media folder. Even if the folder access level that you've assigned to a particular user is No Access, after you enable Media Library Sharing for that folder, the user can stream the folder contents to a DLNA or Windows Media Connect media player on his computer. If you have media in a folder that you don't want others to stream, you must move the files into a folder that doesn't have Media Library Sharing activated.

CAUTION

A further consequence to the open nature of Media Library Sharing is that any computer or device that can access your network can also stream the media. Therefore, if your wireless network is not secured, anyone within range of the network has access to your streamed media. If you don't want this, secure your wireless network.

Here are the steps to follow to stream some or all of the Windows Home Server shared media folders:

1. Log on to the Windows Home Server Dashboard.
2. Click Server Settings to open the Server Settings dialog box.
3. Click the Media tab.
4. If the media server is currently off, click Turn On to activate it.
5. In the Video Streaming Quality section, use the list to select the streaming video level: Low, Medium, High, or Best.

TIP

The higher the video streaming quality, the better the playback, but the greater the burden it puts on the server's processor. How do you know which level to choose? That's a bit tricky, because it depends on the horsepower of your server's processor. Microsoft's guidelines are, oddly, based on the processor score that you see in the Windows Experience Index, which is part of Windows 7 and Vista, but *not* Windows Home Server! Your best bet is to search the Web for processor scores for your server's processor. If you find it, choose low for a score less than 3.6; Medium for a score between 3.6 and 4.1; High for a score between 4.2 and 5.9; or Best for a score of 6.0 or better.

---

6. In the Media Library section, click Customize to open the Customize Media Library dialog box.
7. Select Yes for each media folder you want to stream, as shown in Figure 8.3.

8

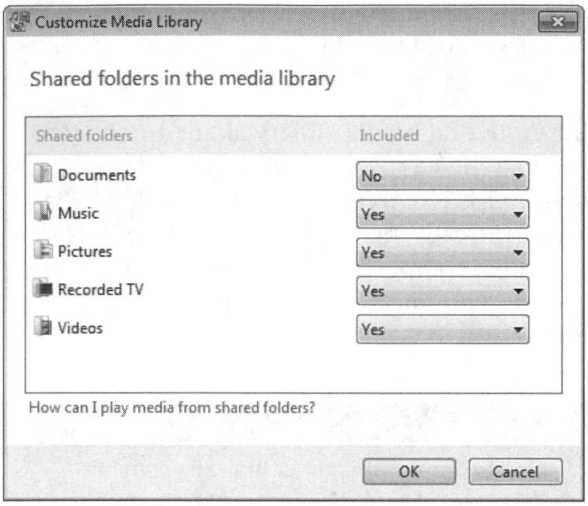

FIGURE 8.3   In the Customize Media Library dialog box, select Yes for each media share you want to stream over the network.

8. Click OK, and then click OK again. Windows Home Server immediately starts sharing the selected media folders.

When you turn on media streaming, Windows Home Server activates a new media server "device," which appears in the list of network devices, as shown in Figure 8.4.

Playing Streamed Media in Windows Media Player

After you activate Media Library Sharing on a Windows Home Server share, Windows Media Player (which supports DLNA in version 12 and Windows Media Connect in versions 11 and later) immediately recognizes the new streams and adds them to its library.

To play the streamed media, follow these steps:

1. Select Start, All Programs, Windows Media Player (or click the Windows Media Player icon in the taskbar).

2. In Media Player 11, click the Library tab.

3. In Media Player 11, pull down the Library menu and select a media category: Music, Pictures, or Video.

4. In the Navigation pane, click the Windows Home Server shared media library, the name of which in Media Player 12 always takes the following form (where *server* is the name of the Windows Home Server computer; see Figure 8.5. In Media Player 11, the library name is Home Server on server):

   Home Server (*server*)

5. Use the library properties (such as Artist and Album in the Music category) to open the media you want to view.

6. Play the media.

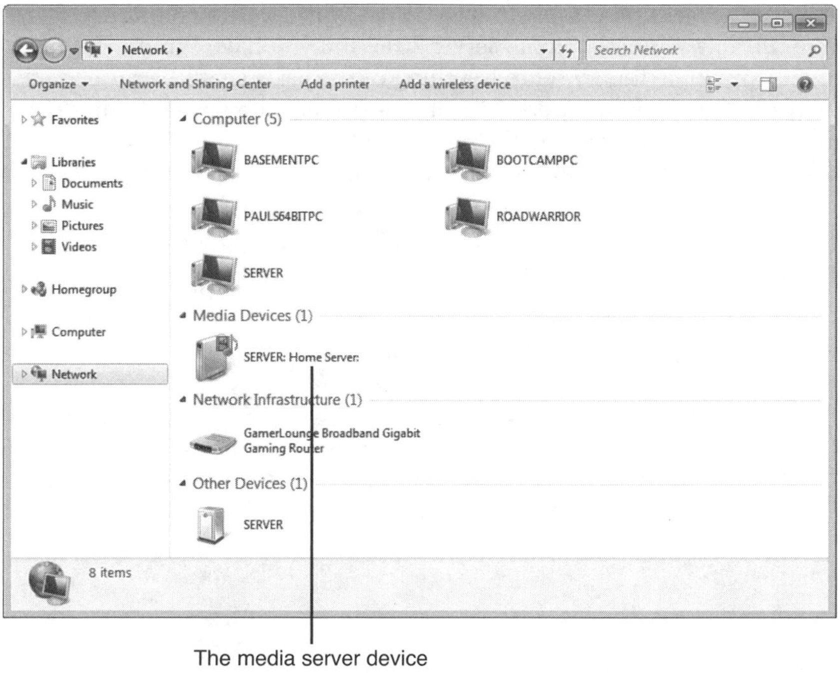

The media server device

FIGURE 8.4   When you turn on media streaming, the server's media server device appears in the list of network devices.

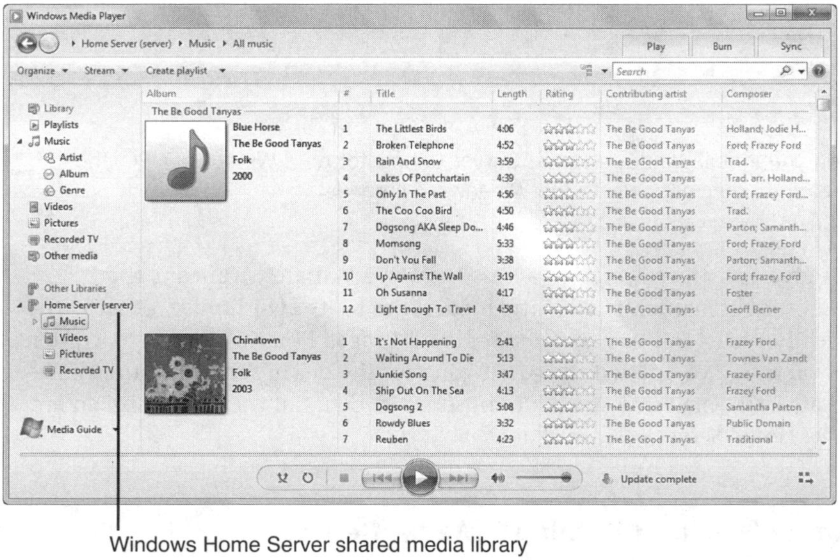

Windows Home Server shared media library

FIGURE 8.5   Windows Media Player automatically adds the shared Windows Home Server media libraries to its own library.

This all works fine, but it's a bit cumbersome to have to deal with multiple libraries. Fortunately, if you're running Windows Home Server 2011 and you have Windows 7 on the client PC, the whole multiple library setup is a thing of the past. That's because Windows Home Server 2011 supports Windows 7's libraries, which are virtual folders that can gather content from multiple folders, including (crucially for our purposes here) network shares. When you install the Windows Home Server Connector on your Windows 7 PC, the program automatically adds the server shares to the appropriate Windows 7 libraries. For example, the server's Music folder gets added to Windows 7's Music library (see Figure 8.6), and the Pictures share appears in the Pictures library.

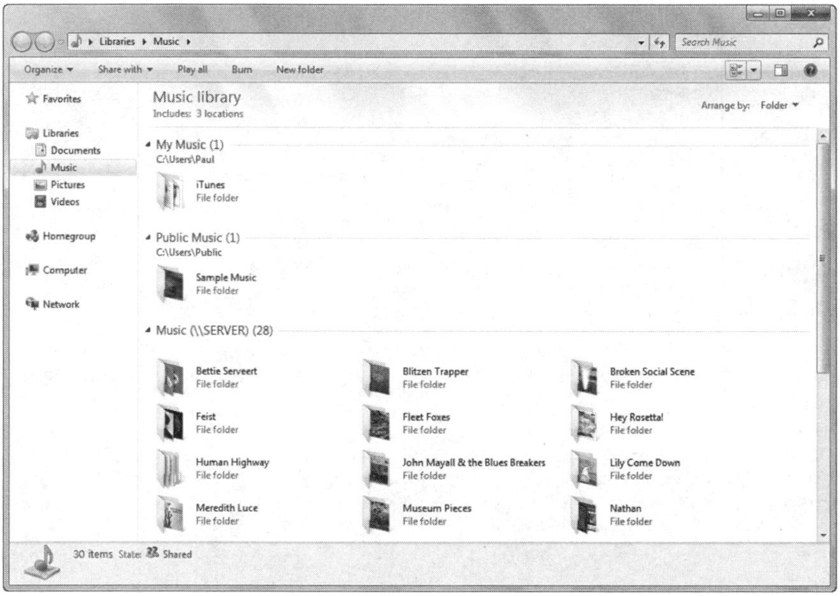

FIGURE 8.6   When you install Windows Home Server Connector on a Windows 7 PC, the server's shares are added automatically to the Windows 7 libraries.

Not only does this give you an easy way to access the server's shares, it means that Windows Media Center automatically adds the media files to its own library, because the program automatically scours the Music, Pictures, and Videos libraries for media content. In Figure 8.7, for example, I've opened the Artist genre of the Music section of the Media Center library. Because this machine stores no music of its own, all the artists shown are located in Windows Home Server's Music share.

Playing Streamed Media in Windows Media Center

As with Windows Media Player, Windows Media Center (another DLNA and Media Connect application) automatically recognizes Windows Home Server's shared media libraries and sets them up in the Media Center interface.

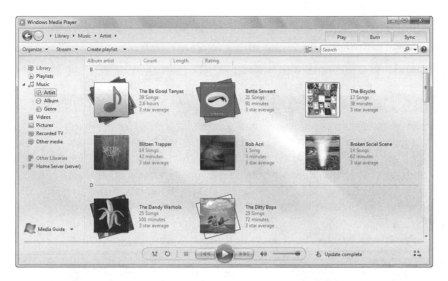

FIGURE 8.7   On a Windows 7 PC, Media Center automatically loads the Windows Home Server media shares into the library for easier access.

> **NOTE**
>
> For some reason, Media Center takes quite a bit longer to add all the Windows Home Server media to its libraries. Whereas Media Player usually populates its libraries with Windows Home Server media within a few minutes (depending on how much media exists on the shares), Media Center can take considerably longer, even a few hours.

To play the streamed media, follow these steps:

1. Select Start, All Programs, Windows Media Center.

2. Select a media library:

   ▶ For Windows Home Server music, select Music, Music Library.

   ▶ For Windows Home Server photos, select Pictures + Videos, Picture Library.

   ▶ For Windows Home Server TV recordings, select Home Server, TV Archive.

   ▶ For Windows Home Server videos, select Pictures + Videos, Video Library.

3. Use the Media Center interface to open and play the media you want.

Streaming Digital Media Over the Internet

One of the awesome new features in Windows Home Server 2011 is the capability to stream media—photos *and* videos—over the Internet. This happens through the Remote Web Access feature, and a special Silverlight plug-in renders high-quality video to the remote device. It's a sweet setup, but it does require three things:

▶ A fast Internet connection (DSL or cable)

▶ Remote Web Access turned on and set up with a domain name

▶ Silverlight installed on the client's web browser

NOTE

Windows Home Server 2011 also includes welcome support for a range of video formats, including the following: 3GP, AAC, AVCHD, MPEG-4, WMV, and WMA, as well as most AVI, DivX, MOV, and Xvid files. As I write this, Windows Home Server 2011 doesn't support MPEG2 and AC3, but Microsoft has promised that these codecs will be supported when Windows Home Server 2011 is officially released. Note, too, that if a device doesn't have the proper codec to play back a video, the server will transcode the stream to different formats (and different resolutions, if necessary) on the fly to make the stream playable on the device.

To try this out, open the remote computer's web browser, navigate to your Remote Web Access domain name, and then log in. In the Remote Web Access Home page, use the Media Library section to select the media type you want to stream:

▶ **Browse Pictures**—Click this item to open the Pictures library, which shows thumbnail images of all the files in the server's Pictures share. Click Play Slideshow or double-click an image to view it (see Figure 8.8).

FIGURE 8.8   Open a picture to view it, and click Play to start the slide show.

▶ **Music**—Click this item to open the Music library, which shows thumbnail images of all the albums in the server's Music share. You can use the View menu to choose a different library view, such as Artists or Genre. Double-click an album (or whatever) to play it. Windows Home Server opens a separate window with the playback controls, as shown in Figure 8.9.

FIGURE 8.9 Double-click a music item to open this separate playback window, which includes the playback controls.

▶ **Videos**—Click this item to open the Videos library, which shows thumbnail images of all the items in the server's Videos share. Click a video to play it. Windows Home Server opens a separate window with the playback controls.

Sharing Photos

Whether or not you activate Media Library Sharing for Windows Home Server's Pictures folder, you can still use this share as the central repository for some or even all of your family's photos. The next few sections take you through a few techniques that should make the shared Pictures folder easier to work with.

Customizing the Pictures Share with a Template

When you access your user account's Pictures library (in Windows 7), Pictures folder (in Windows Vista), or My Pictures folder (in Windows XP), you see a few features that aren't part of the regular folder view, as follows:

▶ You get access to image-related file metadata, such as the date an image was taken and the image dimensions.

▶ In Windows 7 and Windows Vista, the task pane includes extra commands such as Slide Show and E-Mail.

▶ In Windows XP, the task pane includes a Picture Tasks group with links such as View as a Slide Show, Order Prints Online, and Print Pictures.

These extra features come from a special template that Windows applies to this type of folder. However, when you access the Windows Home Server `Pictures` share, Vista and XP treat it just like any other folder. (In Windows 7, if you access the `Pictures` share through the `Pictures` library, you get the extra image-related features; if you access the share via the `Network` folder, you don't see those features.) If you want access to the extras that you see in the local `Pictures` (or `My Pictures in XP`) folder, follow these steps to customize the `Pictures` share to use a picture folder template:

1. Open the folder containing the Windows Home Server shares.

2. Right-click the `Pictures` folder, and then click Properties to open the folder's property sheet.

3. Display the Customize tab.

4. In the list, select the template you want to apply:

   ▶ **Picture and Videos**—(Windows Vista) Choose this template to give the folder the same features as Vista's `Pictures` folder.

   ▶ **Pictures**—(Windows 7 and Windows XP) Choose this template to give the folder the same features as Windows 7's `Pictures` library or XP's `My Pictures` folder.

   ▶ **Photo Album**—(Windows XP only) Choose this template to give the folder the same features as XP's `My Pictures` folder and display the folder in Filmstrip view by default.

5. If you want Windows to apply this template to all the subfolders in the `Pictures` share, click to activate the Also Apply This Template to All Subfolders check box.

6. (Windows XP only) If you also want to change the image used for the folder icon, click Choose Picture, choose a new picture in the Browse dialog box, and then click Open.

7. Click OK.

Using Server Pictures as a Screensaver Slideshow

In the old days (a few years ago) when everyone was still using CRT monitors, you had to be careful to avoid *burn-in*, which is permanent damage to areas of the screen caused by continuously displaying a particular image over a long period. Whatever the image—it could be a menu bar, the Windows taskbar, or an application toolbar—if it was onscreen long enough, it eventually became a permanent part of the screen as a ghostly reflection of the original.

Now that most of us are using LCD monitors, burn-in is a thing of the past, but that doesn't mean that continuously displayed images are no longer a worry. LCDs suffer from a similar problem called *persistence*, in which a long-displayed image persists onscreen as a faint version of the original. Fortunately, LCD persistence is usually temporary and can often be remedied just by turning off the monitor for a while (say, half an hour or so). However, persistence does become permanent on occasion, so further preventative measures are necessary.

The best of these measures is configuring a screensaver to kick in after an extended period of computer idleness. Windows 7, Vista, and XP come with built-in screensavers, but you can also set up a screensaver that displays a slideshow of images from a folder. If you have lots of pictures stored on Windows Home Server's Pictures share, this folder is perfect for a screensaver. Here are the steps to follow to set this up:

1. Use one of the following methods to display the Screen Saver tab:

   ▶ In Windows 7 and Windows Vista, right-click the desktop, click Personalize, and then click Screen Saver. (Alternatively, select Start, Control Panel, Appearance and Personalization, Change Screen Saver.)

   ▶ In Windows XP, right-click the desktop, click Properties, and then display the Screen Saver tab. (Alternatively, select Start, Control Panel, Display, Screen Saver.)

2. In the Screen Saver list, select Photos (in Windows 7 or Vista) or My Pictures Slideshow (in XP).

3. Click Settings.

4. Click Browse, use the Browse for Folder dialog box to select the *SERVER**Pictures* folder, and then click OK.

5. Configure any other screensaver options you want to use (such as the slide show speed), and then click Save (in Windows 7 or Vista) or OK (in XP).

6. Click OK to put the new screensaver into effect.

Adding the Pictures Folder to Windows Media Player

If you're not streaming the Pictures share, you can still add it to Windows Media Player so that you can access it in the Pictures portion of the Media Player library. Note, however, that you don't have to bother with this in Windows 7 if you have the Windows Home Server Connector software installed, because the Connector automatically adds the *SERVER**Pictures* share to Windows 7's Pictures library.

Here are the steps to follow in Windows Media Player 11:

1. Select Start, All Programs, Windows Media Player.

2. Pull down the Library menu and select Add to Library. Media Player displays the Add to Library dialog box.

3. If you don't see the Monitored Folders list, click Advanced Options to expand the dialog box.

4. Click Add to display the Add Folder list.

5. Select Windows Home Server's `Pictures` share, and then click OK. Media Player adds the folder to the Monitored Folders list.

6. Click OK. Media Player begins adding the contents of the `Pictures` share to the library.

7. Click Close. (Note that you don't have to wait until Media Player has added all the pictures to the library; the process continues in the background, although it might take a bit longer than if you had left the dialog box open.)

To view the folder contents in Media Player, pull down the Library menu and select Pictures. In the Navigation pane, click Library, and then double-click the Folder view. You then see an icon for `\\SERVER\Pictures`, as shown in Figure 8.10. Double-click that icon to view the images.

FIGURE 8.10   Double-click `\\SERVER\Pictures` to view the contents of the `Pictures` share in Media Player 11.

Adding the Pictures Folder to Windows Live Photo Gallery

By default, Windows Live Photo Gallery includes the contents of your Windows 7 Pictures library. If you want to use the extensive Photo Gallery tools—fixing image problems, burning images to DVD, ordering prints online, and so on—with your server images, you need to add the Windows Home Server `Pictures` share to the program's Folders list. Here are the steps to follow:

1. Select Start, All Programs, Windows Live Photo Gallery.

2. Select File, Include a Folder. The Picture Library Locations dialog box appears.

3. Click Add to open the Include Folder in Pictures dialog box.

4. Select Windows Home Server's `Pictures` share. (In Windows 7, you can add the share either via your user account's `Pictures` library or via the network.)

5. Click Include Folder. Photo Gallery adds the folder to the library.

6. Click OK.

To view the folder contents in Windows Live Photo Gallery, click Pictures in the Folders pane, as shown in Figure 8.11.

Pictures share

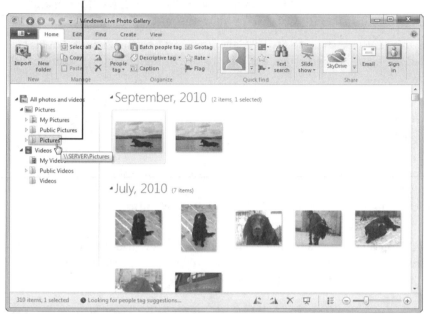

FIGURE 8.11   Click Pictures to view the contents of the `Pictures` share in Windows Live Photo Gallery.

Adding the Pictures Folder to Windows Photo Gallery

By default, Vista's Windows Photo Gallery program includes your user account's `Pictures` and `Videos` folders, as well as the `Public Pictures` and `Public Videos` folders. To add the Windows Home Server `Pictures` share to the program's Folders list, follow these steps:

1. Select Start, All Programs, Windows Photo Gallery.
2. Select File, Add Folder to Gallery. The Add Folder to Gallery dialog box appears.
3. Select Windows Home Server's `Pictures` share.
4. Click OK. Photo Gallery asks you to confirm that you want to add the folder.
5. Click Add. Photo Gallery confirms that it has added the folder.
6. Click OK.

Running a Slide Show from the Pictures Share

You saw earlier that you can configure a screensaver–based slide show that uses Windows Home Server's Pictures share as the image source. If you don't want to wait until the screensaver kicks in, you can run a slide show anytime you like. Windows 7, Vista, and XP give you several ways to run a slide show based on images from the Pictures share:

▶ If you added the Pictures share to Media Player (see "Adding the Pictures Folder to Windows Media Player," earlier), open the User 1 (*server*) branch, select Pictures, and then click Play.

▶ If you added the Pictures share to Windows Live Photo Gallery (see "Adding the Pictures Folder to Windows Live Photo Gallery," earlier), open Photo Gallery's Folders branch, select Pictures, and then click the Slide Show button. (You also can press F12 or Alt+S.)

▶ If you added the Pictures share to Photo Gallery (see the previous section "Adding the Pictures Folder to Windows Photo Gallery"), open Photo Gallery's Folders branch, select Pictures, and then click the Play Slide Show button. (You also can press F11.)

▶ If you applied a picture template to the Pictures share earlier (see "Customizing the Pictures Share with a Template"), open the share and either click Slide Show (in Windows 7 or Vista) or View as a Slide Show (XP).

Changing the Default Picture Import Location to Windows Home Server

Both Windows Live Photo Gallery and Windows Photo Gallery come with a feature that enables you to import images from a digital camera or a document scanner. (Select File, Import from Camera or Scanner.) By default, the program imports the images to a subfolder in your user account's Pictures folder. If you prefer to import the images directly to Windows Home Server's Pictures share, follow these steps:

1. Select File, Options. The program's Options dialog box appears.

2. Select the Import tab.

3. Use the Settings For list to select the type of import you want to customize: Cameras, Video Cameras, or CDs and DVDs.

4. Click Browse to open the Browse for Folder dialog box.

5. Select Windows Home Server's Pictures share, and then click OK.

6. Repeat steps 3–5 to customize the other import types, if necessary.

7. Click OK to put the new options into effect.

Sharing Music

When you think of the word *streaming*, you probably think about music, because it's the medium that's most closely associated with streaming and that's most easily streamed (because music files generally contain less information than, say, video files). However, even if you don't activate Media Library Sharing for Windows Home Server's Music folder, you can still use this share to store your family's digital music files. To help make this easier, the next few sections show you some techniques for using and managing the Music share.

Customizing the Music Share with a Template

Earlier you learned about the folder template that applies special features to the Pictures folder. There is also a template associated with the Music library (in Windows 7), the Music folder (in Windows Vista), and the My Music folder (in Windows XP). This template gives you a few features that aren't part of the standard folder view:

▶ You get access to music-related file metadata such as the Artists, Album, and Genre.

▶ In Windows 7 and Vista, the task pane includes extra commands such as Play and Play All.

▶ In Windows XP, the task pane includes a Music Tasks group with links such as Play All, Play Selection, and Shop for Music Online.

However, when you access the Windows Home Server Music folder, Vista and XP treat it like a regular folder. (In Windows 7, if you access the Music share through the Music library, you get the extra image-related features; if you access the share via the Network folder, you don't see those features.) If you want to see the extras that are part of the local Music (or My Music) folder, follow these steps to customize the Music share to use a music folder template:

1. Open the folder containing the Windows Home Server shares.

2. Right-click the Music folder, and then click Properties to open the folder's property sheet.

3. Display the Customize tab.

4. In the Use This Folder as a Template list, select the template you want to apply:

   ▶ **Music Icons**—(Windows Vista) Choose this template to give the folder the same features as the Music folder. The folder opens in Large Icons view.

   ▶ **Music Details**—(Windows Vista) Choose this template to give the folder the same features as the Music folder. The folder opens in Details view.

   ▶ **Music**—(Windows 7 and Windows XP) Choose this template to give the folder the same features as the My Music folder.

   ▶ **Music Artist**—(Windows XP) Choose this template for a folder that holds music by a single artist. This gives the folder the same features as the My Music folder and opens the folder in Thumbnails view, which displays an album art icon for each folder that holds an album by the artist.

   ▶ **Music Album**—(Windows XP) Choose this template for a folder that holds music from a single artist. This gives the folder the same features as the My Music folder and opens the folder in Tiles view, which displays an icon for each track from the album.

8

5. If you also want Windows to apply this template to all the subfolders in the Music share, click to activate the Also Apply This Template to All Subfolders check box.

6. (Windows XP only) If you also want to change the image used for the folder icon, click Choose Picture, choose a new picture in the Browse dialog box, and then click Open.

7. Click OK.

Adding the Music Folder to Windows Media Player

You saw earlier that when you activate Media Library Sharing for Windows Home Server's Music folder, it appears in Media Player's Navigation pane in the User 1 (server) branch (or the User 1 on server branch), where server is the Windows Home Server name. (See the earlier section "Playing Streamed Media in Windows Media Player.") However, even if you don't stream the Music share, you can still add it to Windows Media Player so that you can access it in the Music portion of the Media Player library. Note, however, that you don't have to bother with this in Windows 7 if you have the Windows Home Server Connector software installed, because the Connector automatically adds the \\SERVER\Music share to Windows 7's Music library.

Just follow these steps in Windows Media Player 11:

1. Select Start, All Programs, Windows Media Player.

2. Pull down the Library menu, and select Add to Library. Media Player displays the Add to Library dialog box.

3. If you don't see the Monitored Folders list, click Advanced Options to expand the dialog box.

4. Click Add to display the Add Folder list.

5. Select Windows Home Server's Music share, and then click OK. Media Player adds the folder to the Monitored Folders list.

6. Click OK. Media Player begins adding the contents of the Music share to the library.

7. Click Close. (Note that you don't have to wait until Media Player has added all the songs to the library; the process continues in the background, although it might take a bit longer than if you had left the dialog box open.)

To view the folder contents in Media Player, pull down the Library menu and select Music. In the Navigation pane, click Library, and then double-click the Folder view. You then see an icon for \\SERVER\Music, as shown in Figure 8.12. Double-click that icon to view the music.

Changing the Default Rip Location to Windows Home Server

When you rip music from an audio CD in Windows Media Player, the resulting digital audio files are stored in a subfolder of your user profile's Music library (in Windows 7), Music folder (in Windows Vista), or My Music folder (in Windows XP). If you then want to stream those files over your network, you need to copy them to Windows Home Server's Music share.

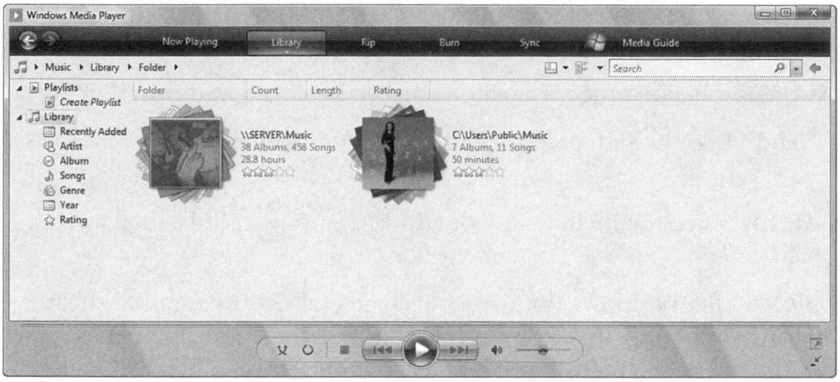

FIGURE 8.12   Double-click *SERVER*\Music to view the contents of Windows Home Server's Music share in Media Player.

This two-step process is fine if you always want to maintain a local copy of the audio files. However, if you only access the music on Windows Home Server, having to both rip and move the audio files is a waste of time. A better idea is to rip your audio CDs straight to Windows Home Server.

Here are the steps to follow to change Media Player's rip location to Windows Home Server's Music folder:

1. Select Start, All Programs, Windows Media Player.
2. Select Tools, Options. (If you don't see the Tools menu, press Alt.) The Options dialog box appears.
3. Select the Rip Music tab.
4. In the Rip Music to This Location group, click Change to open the Browse for Folder dialog box.
5. Select *SERVER*\Music, and then click OK to return to the Options dialog box.
6. Click OK to put the new setting into effect.

Sharing Videos

The rest of this chapter takes you through a few techniques to make Windows Home Server's shared Videos folder easier to use and manage.

Customizing the Videos Share with a Template

In previous sections of this chapter, you learned about the folder templates that apply special features to the Pictures and Music folders (My Pictures and My Music in Windows XP). There is also a template associated with the Videos library (in Windows 7), the

Videos folder (in Windows Vista), and the My Videos folder (in Windows XP). This template provides some features that aren't part of the normal folder view:

▶ You get access to video-related file metadata, such as Date Taken and Duration.

▶ In Windows 7 and Vista, the task pane includes extra commands such as Play and Slide Show.

▶ In Windows XP, the task pane includes a Video Tasks group with links such as Play All and Copy to CD.

However, when you access the Windows Home Server Videos folder, Vista and XP treat it like a normal folder. (In Windows 7, if you access the Videos share through the Videos library, you get the extra video-related features; if you access the share via the Network folder, you don't see those features.) If you want to see the extras that are part of the local Videos (or My Videos) folder, follow these steps to customize the Videos share to use a video folder template:

1. Open the folder containing the Windows Home Server shares.

2. Right-click the Videos folder, and then click Properties to open the folder's property sheet.

3. Display the Customize tab.

4. In the Use This Folder as a Template list, select the template you want to apply:

   ▶ **Picture and Videos**—(Windows Vista) Choose this template to give the folder the same features as Vista's Videos folder.

   ▶ **Videos**—(Windows 7 and Windows XP) Choose this template to give the folder the same features as XP's My Videos folder.

5. If you also want Windows to apply this template to all the subfolders in the Pictures share, click to activate the Also Apply This Template to All Subfolders check box.

6. (Windows XP only) If you also want to change the image used for the folder icon, click Choose Picture, choose a new picture in the Browse dialog box, and then click Open.

7. Click OK.

Adding the Videos Folder to Windows Media Player

If you turn on Media Library Sharing for Windows Home Server's Videos share, that folder appears in Media Player's Navigation pane as part of the User 1 (server) branch (or the User 1 on server branch), where server is the Windows Home Server name. (See "Playing Streamed Media in Windows Media Player.") If you're not streaming the Videos share, you can still add it to Windows Media Player's library in the Video section. Note, however, that you don't have to bother with this in Windows 7 if you have the Windows Home Server Connector software installed, because the Connector automatically adds the \\SERVER\Videos share to Windows 7's Videos library.

Here are the steps to follow in Windows Media Player 11:

1. Select Start, All Programs, Windows Media Player.
2. Pull down the Library menu, and select Add to Library. Media Player displays the Add to Library dialog box.
3. If you don't see the Monitored Folders list, click Advanced Options to expand the dialog box.
4. Click Add to display the Add Folder list.
5. Select Windows Home Server's Videos share, and then click OK. Media Player adds the folder to the Monitored Folders list.
6. Click OK. Media Player begins adding the contents of the Videos share to the library.
7. Click Close. (Note that you don't have to wait until Media Player has added all the videos to the library; the process continues in the background, although it might take a bit longer than if you had left the dialog box open.)

To view the folder contents in Media Player, pull down the Library menu and select Video. In the Navigation pane, click Library, and then double-click the Folder view. You then see an icon for \\SERVER\Videos, as shown in Figure 8.13. Double-click that icon to view the video files.

FIGURE 8.13   Double-click \\SERVER\Videos to view the contents of Windows Home Server's Videos share in Media Player.

If the Windows Home Server Videos share contains recorded TV shows, Media Player displays them separately. Pull down the Library menu and select Recorded TV. Figure 8.14 shows a Media Player icon for a Windows Home Server folder that contains some recorded TV content.

FIGURE 8.14   Media Player shows Windows Home Server's recorded TV shows in the
Recorded TV section of the library.

Archiving Recorded TV on Windows Home Server

When you record TV in Windows Media Center, the program stores the resulting files—
which use the Microsoft Recorded TV Show file type with the .dvr-ms extension—in the
following folder:

%SystemDrive%\Users\Public\Recorded TV

If you want to stream your recorded TV shows to Windows Media Connect programs and
devices on your network, you need to move or copy the Recorded TV files to Windows
Home Server's Recorded TV share.

As with ripping music (see "Changing the Default Rip Location to Windows Home
Server," earlier), this extra step is a hassle, particularly because Recorded TV files are often
multigigabyte affairs that can take quite a while to transfer. A better solution is to record
TV shows directly to Windows Home Server. In previous versions of Windows Home
Server, this wasn't as simple as tweaking a folder value, because by default Media Center
has no such setting. It was possible to work around this problem by modifying some
Media Center services and Registry settings (as I explained in the previous edition of this
book), but it was a hassle.

Fortunately, it's a hassle that's now history. Windows Home Server 2011 comes with a new
Windows Media Center Connector feature, which adds a Home Server menu item to the
Media Center interface. The Home Server menu item includes a tile called TV Archive that
enables you to configure Media Center to record TV shows directly to the server. Finally!

CAUTION

Recording a TV show is incredibly bandwidth-intensive, so the modification in this section stretches your home network to its limit. So, although it's possible to record shows to Windows Home Server on a 100Mbps wired or 54Mbps wireless connection, for best results, you really should do this only on a network that uses 1Gbps wired or 802.11n (248Mbps) wireless connections.

Assuming you've installed Windows Media Center Connector, follow these steps to configure TV archiving in Media Center:

1. In Windows Media Center, select Home Server, and then click TV Archive.

2. Click Settings. Media Center shows the TV archiving settings, as shown in Figure 8.15.

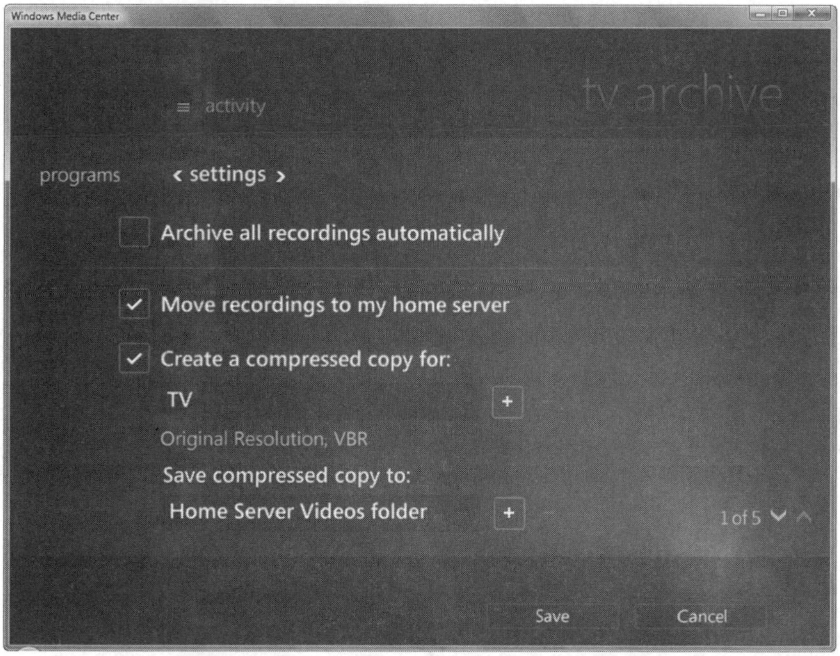

FIGURE 8.15   With Windows Home Server 2011's Windows Media Center Connector installed, use the TV Archive Settings tab to configure TV recording directly to the server.

3. If you want Media Center to archive all your TV shows—that is, shows you've already recorded and shows you record in the future—to Windows Home Server's Recorded TV share, activate the Archive All Recordings Automatically check box.

4. If you want Media Center to record TV shows directly to Windows Home Server's Recorded TV share, activate the Move Recordings to My Home Server check box.

NOTE

Actually, it's not really accurate to say that, if you activate the Move Recordings to My Home Server check box, Media Center records TV shows "directly" to the server. Instead, Media Center creates a temporary copy of the recorded TV show locally, and it then moves that copy to the server.

---

5. If you want Media Center to also create a compressed version of each recorded TV show, activate the Create a Compressed Copy For check box, and then choose a format and location:

   ▶ **Create a Compressed Copy For**—Use this list to choose one of the following three formats: TV (uses the original resolution of the recording); Windows Mobile (320×240, 500Kbps bitrate); or Zune (720×480, 1,500Kbps). Note that in all cases, the resulting file uses the Windows Media Audio/Video (.wmv) format.

   ▶ **Save Compressed Copy To**—Use this list to select a location for the compressed copies. The default is Home Server Videos folder, and you should leave that as is if you want your compressed copies on the server. Otherwise, you can choose either Public Videos Folder or Let Me Use a Different Folder. (The latter requires a path to the save location.)

6. Click Save to put the new settings into effect.

If you left the Archive All Recordings Automatically check box deactivated, you can select which of your existing recordings get archived to the server. In Media Center, select the Home Server item, and then click the TV Archive tile. You have two choices from here, as follows:

▶ **Series**—Click this tab to see a list of your recorded TV series. Activate the check box beside each series that you want to archive.

▶ **Programs**—Click this tab to see a list of your recorded TV programs. Activate the check box beside each program that you want to archive.

Click Save to put the settings into effect. Remember that how your existing series and programs are archived depends on the options you configured in the Settings tab:

▶ If you activated the Move Recordings to My Home Server check box, your selected series and programs are moved to the server's Recorded TV share.

▶ If you activated the Create a Compressed Copy for Server check box, Media Center creates compressed copies of your selected series and programs and stores the copies in the server's Videos share.

From Here

▶ To learn how to add a user to Windows Home Server, **SEE** "Adding a New User," **P. 32.**

▶ For information on connecting various devices to your Windows Home Server network, **SEE** Chapter 3, "Adding Devices to the Windows Home Server Network."

▶ For details on changing user permissions, **SEE** "Modifying Permissions for a Windows Home Server Shared Folder," **P. 119.**

▶ To learn how to work with the Registry, **SEE** Chapter 18, "Working with the Windows Home Server Registry."

8

CHAPTER 9

Backing Up and Restoring Network Computers

IN THIS CHAPTER

▸ Understanding Windows Home Server's Backup Technology

▸ Converting Client Partitions to NTFS

▸ Configuring Windows Home Server Backups

▸ Configuring a Computer for Backup

▸ Running a Manual Backup

▸ Working with Backups

▸ Restoring Network Backups

Backing up your computer is a "spinach" task. By that, I mean that it's a task that, like the vegetable, is good for you but not particularly palatable. (This will no doubt seem a libelous association to anyone who enjoys spinach.) The reasons why people don't like backing up are legion: It's too complicated, it's too time-consuming, my computer will never die, and so on. Whatever the excuse, most people simply don't bother backing up their system, much less their precious and irreplaceable documents. Now apply this backup negativity to your home network, where the difficulty is multiplied by the number of computers on the local area network (LAN), and you're left with a major problem.

Fortunately, it's a problem that Windows Home Server was designed to solve. As soon as you connect a computer to the network, Windows Home Server automatically adds the machine to its list of computers to back up. This means that the computer gets backed up every night, no questions asked. It's as simple and as painless as backups can be, and it means you may never have to worry about (or even think about) backing up again.

Of course, this is *Windows* we're talking about, so the initial simplicity is a front that hides a fairly complex bit of technology that you can tweak and tune to fit your needs. This chapter takes you behind the scenes of Windows Home Server's backups and tells you a bit about the underlying technology, how to take advantage of the backup settings, and how to restore files, folders, and even entire systems should something go wrong down the road.

Understanding Windows Home Server's Backup Technology

Backups seem like such straightforward things: You take all the files that exist on a computer, and you make copies of them somewhere else. In the case of Windows Home Server backups, however, there's a lot more going on under the hood. This section provides you with a few notes that give you some idea of the efficiencies and power that Windows Home Server implements.

> **NOTE**
>
> If it occurred to you that the server should be backed up as well, that's certainly not a bad idea. If you want to learn how to back up Windows Home Server itself, **SEE** Chapter 16, "Maintaining Windows Home Server."

Single Instance Storage

Unlike almost every other backup system, Windows Home Server does *not* back up at the file level (by, say, storing copies of files on the server). Instead, it backs up data at the *cluster* level. (A cluster, you'll recall, is the fundamental unit of storage in the file system. That is, every file is really a series of clusters, each of which is usually 4KB.) When Windows Home Server backs up a file, it performs a cluster-by-cluster check to see if the same data has already been backed up. If it finds an identical cluster already on the system, it doesn't include the redundant cluster in the backup. Instead, it leaves the existing cluster on the system and makes a note about which files that cluster belongs to. This technology is new to Windows Home Server, and it's called *Single Instance Storage*.

Note that this applies not just to the backups for a single computer, but for *every* machine on the network. For example, suppose that a popular song resides on your computer and on two other computers on your home network. If your computer is the first to be backed up, Windows Home Server will include the song in that backup. When it backs up the other two computers, it will see that song on each one, but it won't add the redundant data to the backup.

You might think the space savings generated by cluster-level backups will be minimal because, after all, how many songs (or whatever) do multiple computers have in common? However, remember that Windows Home Server doesn't just back up your data. It also backs up the %SystemRoot% folder, which contains the Windows system files, many of which are identical across multiple machines (depending on the versions of Windows each is running). It also backs up the %ProgramFiles% folder, so popular applications such as Microsoft Office and Internet Explorer also have lots of common files across the network. As a result, the storage space used by the backups on Windows Home Server is a mere fraction of the size of all the original files put together.

No Backup Types

Other backup systems muddy the waters by offering numerous backup types: Full, Incremental, Differential, Daily, and so on. Part of the reluctance many people have to setting up a backup regimen is trying to figure out the differences between these various types.

Windows Home Server does away with all that by having no backup types. Instead, Windows Home Server's backups use a simple two-stage system:

▶ For a computer's first backup, Windows Home Server backs up everything on the machine (with a few exceptions, as you'll see a bit later).

▶ On subsequent backups for the same machine, Windows Home Server only backs up data that has been added or that has been changed since the last backup.

This sounds like an incremental (or is it differential?) backup, but that's not the case. Instead, Windows Home Server treats *every* backup as a full backup. So even if Windows Home Server only had to back up a single file last night, if you look at that backup, you see all your files. In other words, with Windows Home Server, you never run into the situation where you need to restore one file from yesterday's backup, a second file from last week's backup, and so on.

The other (not insignificant) advantage to this backup strategy is that, although a computer's initial backup may take several hours, subsequent backups for that machine may take just a few minutes.

> **CAUTION**
>
> To avoid an extremely long initial backup for a computer, make sure that the machine has a wired connection to the network. Even a 100Mbps wired connection is twice as fast as the typical 54Mbps wireless connection, and gigabit wired connections are closer to 20 times faster. Of course, that's assuming your wireless connection can even achieve 54Mbps, which is rare due to interference, shared bandwidth, and so on.

Smarter Backups

Single Instance Storage is a pretty smart technology, but Windows Home Server also implements a few other features for intelligent backups:

▶ To avoid conflicts, Windows Home Server never backs up more than one computer at a time. When the backup time comes around (the default time is midnight), Windows Home Server puts the network clients in a queue and backs them up one at a time. Even if you initiate a manual backup during that time, Windows Home Server still puts that machine in the queue.

▶ Windows Home Server backs up the entire computer by default, but it doesn't back up every last file. Intelligently, it avoids unnecessary files, such as the paging file (used by Windows to swap oft-used data to disk rather than having to retrieve it from its original location); the Recycle Bin (where Windows stores your deleted files); the hibernation file (where Windows stores the current contents of memory when the system goes into hibernation mode); and file system shadow copies (the previous versions of files and folders maintained by Windows).

▶ If a computer is in Sleep or Hibernate mode when the scheduled backup time occurs, Windows Home Server pings the computer to let it know that it's time for backup, and the server puts the machine into the queue. When the backup completes, Windows Home Server tells the computer to put itself back into Sleep or Hibernate mode. For notebooks, this only happens if the computer is running on AC; if it's on batteries, the machine skips the "wakeup call" to avoid using too much battery life during the backup.

TIP

Windows Home Server only wakes up the computer if you enabled that option during the Windows Home Server Connector setup process, as I described in Chapter 3. If you want to change whatever option you chose during setup, open Launchpad, click Backup to open the Backup Properties dialog box, and then use the Automatically Wake This Computer check box to set the state you prefer.

▶ **SEE** "Installing Windows Home Server Connector on the Client Computers," **P. 49**.

Client Computer Backup Retention

Some backup systems accumulate backups until there's no space left for new ones! Windows Home Server's Single Instance Storage technology means that this is less likely to happen. However, storage is always finite, so even Windows Home Server's backups can't accumulate indefinitely. Fortunately, as part of Windows Home Server's commitment to a fully automated backup system, even the process of removing old backups happens behind the scenes. This is called *Client Computer Backup Retention*, (it was called Automated Backup Management in previous versions of Windows Home Server), and it means that Windows Home Server deletes old backups after a preset time has elapsed.

For dedicated tinkerers, you can customize the frequency with which Windows Home Server removes old backups. (See "Configuring Client Computer Backup Retention," later in this chapter.)

Improvements to Client Backups in Windows Home Server 2011

The client backup system in previous versions of Windows Home Server was excellent, but not perfect. For example, you couldn't protect client PC backups by including them with the server backup, and the wizards used to exclude folders (as well as choose files and folders for recovery) were a bit clunky to use. In Windows Home Server 2011, Microsoft has addressed these and a few other issues to improve client backups:

▶ **Backup backups**—Windows Home Server introduced backups of the server in Power Pack 3, but those backups didn't include the database of backups associated with each network computer. That shortcoming has been rectified in Windows Home Server 2011, which now gives you the option of including the client computer backups in the server backup.

▶ **Easier folder exclusions**—In previous versions of Windows Home Server, excluding a folder from a client's backup was a bit of a chore, particularly if you had multiple folders to exclude. Windows Home Server 2011 makes this much easier by providing standard check boxes for each folder, so you exclude a folder simply by deactivating its check box.

▶ **Backup resume**—In previous versions of Windows Home Server, if a backup was interrupted, it just failed, and a completely new backup wouldn't start until the next scheduled backup time. Windows Home Server 2011 now tracks the client backup process, and if the backup is interrupted for any reason (for example, losing the network connection), Windows Home Server 2011 resumes the backup from where the interruption occurred.

▶ **Support for Mac clients**—Windows Home Server 2011 adds support for Time Machine backups, so you can back up your Mac computers to Windows Home Server.

▶ **Easier file and folder recovery**—Windows Home Server 2011 comes with a new restore wizard that makes it much easier to choose individual files and folders to restore from a backup.

▶ **USB client recovery key**—You can now use a USB flash drive to create a bootable computer recovery key. If you can no longer boot a client PC, you can boot to its recovery key and then restore the client from a Windows Home Server backup.

Converting Client Partitions to NTFS

Windows Home Server only supports backing up client partitions that use the NT File System (NTFS). If you have partitions that use FAT16 or FAT32, they won't be included in the backups. If you need such a partition backed up, you must convert it to NTFS. (Doing this has other benefits as well. NTFS is your best choice if you want optimal hard disk performance because, in most cases, NTFS outperforms both FAT16 and FAT32. This is particularly true with large partitions and with partitions that have lots of files. Also, NTFS enables you to encrypt files for maximum security.)

You can use two methods to convert a partition to NTFS:

▶ Format the partition as NTFS.

▶ Run the CONVERT utility.

6

Format the Partition as NTFS

Formatting the partition as NTFS is the best way to go because it maximizes NTFS performance, which means faster backups. Note, however, that formatting wipes all the data from the partition, so you need to store important files in a safe place (say, on a Windows Home Server share) before formatting.

Here are the steps to follow:

1. If the drive contains important files, copy or move those files to another partition, an external drive or memory card, a recordable CD or DVD, or a network share.
2. Select Start, Computer (or My Computer in Windows XP).
3. Right-click the partition you want to work with, and then click Format.
4. In Windows Vista, enter your UAC credentials to continue.
5. In the Format dialog box, select NTFS in the File System list.
6. (Optional) Enter a volume label. (This is the partition name that appears in the Computer or My Computer window.)
7. Click Start. Windows warns you that all data on the partition will be erased.
8. Click OK. Windows formats the partition.
9. When you see the Format Complete message, click OK.
10. Click Close to shut down the Format dialog box.

Run the CONVERT Utility

If you have data on the partition that you can't store in a safe place, you can preserve the data and convert the partition to NTFS by using the CONVERT command-line utility:

```
CONVERT volume /FS:NTFS [/V] [/CvtArea:filename] [/NoSecurity] [/X]
```

volume	Specifies the drive letter (followed by a colon) or volume name you want to convert.
/FS:NTFS	Specifies that the file system is to be converted to NTFS.
/V	Uses verbose mode, which gives detailed information during the conversion.
/CvtArea:*filename*	Specifies a contiguous placeholder file in the root directory that will be used to store the NTFS system files.
/NoSecurity	Specifies that the default NTFS permissions are not to be applied to this volume. All the converted files and folders will be accessible by everyone.
/X	Forces the volume to dismount first if it currently has open files.

For example, running the following command at the command prompt converts drive G to NTFS:

```
convert g: /FS:NTFS
```

Configuring Windows Home Server Backups

Before I cover the specifics of running backups, you should configure the Windows Home Server backup settings to suit your needs. In keeping with the overall simplicity of the backup feature, there are only two things you can configure: the backup time and when Windows Home Server performs Client Computer Backup Retention.

Configuring the Backup Time

When the backup time occurs, Windows Home Server does three things:

▶ It backs up all the connected computers, one machine at a time.

▶ If you have automatic updates turned on, Windows Home Server installs any pending updates and then restarts the system if an update requires a reboot.

▶ **SEE** "Configuring Windows Update," **P. 85.**

▶ Every Sunday, Windows Home Server runs the Backup Cleanup feature, which deletes old backups according to the schedule maintained by the Client Computer Backup Retention policy (discussed in the next section).

Windows Home Server's default backup time runs from midnight to 6:00 a.m.

Note that if Windows Home Server hasn't completed its backups or maintenance by 6:00 a.m., it finishes whatever task it's currently running, and then it cancels the remaining operations and reschedules them for the next backup period. If this is a problem on your network, you might want to extend the backup time. Windows Home Server supports backup periods as long as 23 hours (or as short as one hour).

Here are the steps to configure Windows Home Server's backup time:

1. Log on to the Windows Home Server Dashboard.
2. Click Computers and Backup.
3. Click the Additional Client Computer Backup Tasks link to open the dialog box shown in Figure 9.1.
4. Use the Start Time box to set the time you want Windows Home Server to begin its backup and maintenance period.
5. Use the End Time box to set the time you want Windows Home Server to stop its backup and maintenance period.

9

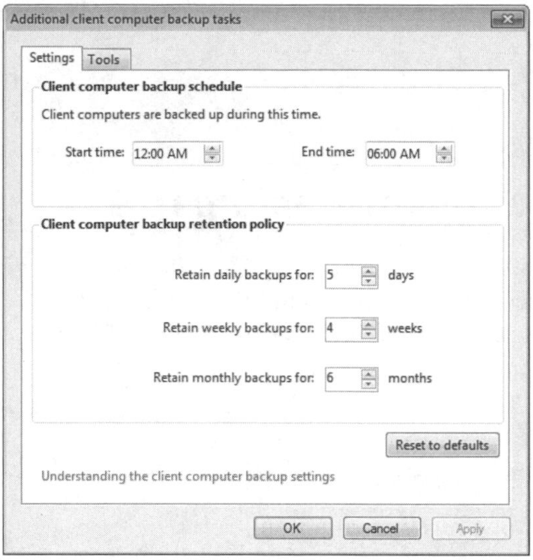

FIGURE 9.1   Use this dialog box to configure the start and end time for the backup and maintenance period.

NOTE

Make sure the End Time value is at least one hour later and at least one hour before the Start Time value. For example, if you leave the Start Time at 12:00 a.m., the End Time can't be earlier than 1:00 a.m. or later than 11:00 p.m.

---

6. Click OK to put the new settings into effect.

Configuring Client Computer Backup Retention

To avoid the unwelcome scenario of old backups gradually usurping all your storage space, Windows Home Server regularly deletes old backups. This Client Computer Backup Retention policy keeps old backups under control by maintaining three deletion schedules:

▶ The number of days to keep the first backup of the day. (There is, by default, just one backup per day, but you can also add backups by running them manually; see "Running a Manual Backup," later in this chapter.) The default value is five days.

▶ The number of weeks to keep the first backup of the week. The default value is four weeks.

▶ The number of months to keep the first backup of the month. The default value is six months.

The default values should be fine for most people, but they could cause you to lose data in some relatively rare scenarios. For example, suppose you create a document on Tuesday and then permanently delete it (by pressing Shift+Delete to bypass the Recycle Bin) on Wednesday. Assuming Tuesday wasn't the first of the month, the file will only reside in the daily backups (since it didn't make it into the first backup of the week on Monday). Windows Home Server's Client Computer Backup Retention will delete the Tuesday backup on Sunday (because, by default, it only keeps five days' worth of daily backups), which means that if you suddenly yearn to have the file back on Sunday (or later), you're out of luck.

If you or your family members generate a lot of new content, and if your Windows Home Server is swimming in storage space, you might want to bump up the default values for extra safety. For example, bumping up the value for the daily backup to 14, and the monthly backup to 12, will make it less likely that you'll lose important information.

> **CAUTION**
>
> Even if you have tons of storage space on the server, bumping up the number of saved backups can eat disk space in a hurry, even with Single Instance Storage doing its duty. If you drastically increase the number of saved backups, be diligent about keeping an eye on how much space the backups are using. In the Windows Home Server Dashboard, display the Storage Space tab, and check the PC Backups value.

Follow these steps to configure Windows Home Server's Client Computer Backup Retention Policy:

1. Log on to the Windows Home Server Dashboard.
2. Click Computers and Backup.
3. Click the Additional Client Computer Backup Tasks link.
4. In the Client Computer Backup Retention Policy group, use the following controls to set the number of backups you want to keep (see Figure 9.1, shown earlier):
    - **Retain Daily Backups For**—Specify the number of days to keep the first backup of each day. The maximum number of days is 99.
    - **Retain Weekly Backups For**—Specify the number of weeks to keep the first backup of the week. The maximum number of weeks is 99.
    - **Retain Monthly Backups For**—Specify the number of months to keep the first backup of the month. The maximum number of months is 99.
5. Click OK to put the new settings into effect.

Configuring a Computer for Backup

By default, Windows Home Server always backs up all the computer's drives (or, more accurately, it backs up all the computer's NTFS drives). This is ideal because it means that if a computer crashes and can't be recovered, you can still get the machine back on its feet by using a bootable USB recovery drive to restore one of the complete backups. (For the details on this, see "Creating a Bootable USB Recovery Key" and "Restoring a Computer to a Previous Configuration," later in this chapter.) However, there may be situations in which you don't want or need certain parts of a computer included in the backups:

▶ You have a folder that contains some extremely large files (for example, ripped DVDs), and you don't want those files taking up space in the backups.

▶ You have a folder that contains files you're going to delete anyway. For example, most people delete recorded TV shows after viewing them. Because these files tend to be huge, it's a good idea to exclude the Recorded TV folder from the backups to save space. (If you have shows you want to save, consider moving them to a separate folder that *does* get backed up.)

▶ You have an external hard drive that you occasionally bring home from work or borrow from someone else. Because the files on this drive aren't really yours, you probably don't want them backed up.

▶ You have an external hard drive that gets swapped among your family members. This could cause problems with Windows Home Server if it expects the drive to be on one computer and finds it "missing" the next time it tries to back up that machine.

For these and similar scenarios, you can exclude one or more drives and folders from a computer's backup configuration. The next two sections show you how to do this. (Note that Windows Home Server does let you exclude all the drives on a system or all the folders on a drive. However, if you want to stop Windows Home Server from backing up a client, see "Turning Off Backups for a Computer," later in this chapter.)

Excluding a Disk Drive from a Backup

To exclude one or more hard disk drives or hard disk partitions from a computer's backup configuration, follow these steps:

1. Log on to the Windows Home Server Dashboard.
2. Display the Computers and Backup tab.
3. Click the computer you want to work with.
4. Click Customize Backup for the Computer. Windows Home Server launches the Customize Backup for *Computer* Wizard (where *Computer* is the name of the computer you're configuring).
5. Click Add or Remove Backup Items. The wizard examines the computer and then displays a list of disk drives and partitions, as shown in Figure 9.2.
6. Deactivate the check box for each partition that you want to exclude from the backup.
7. Click Next. The wizard displays a summary of what will and won't be backed up for the computer.
8. Click Save Changes to complete the configuration.

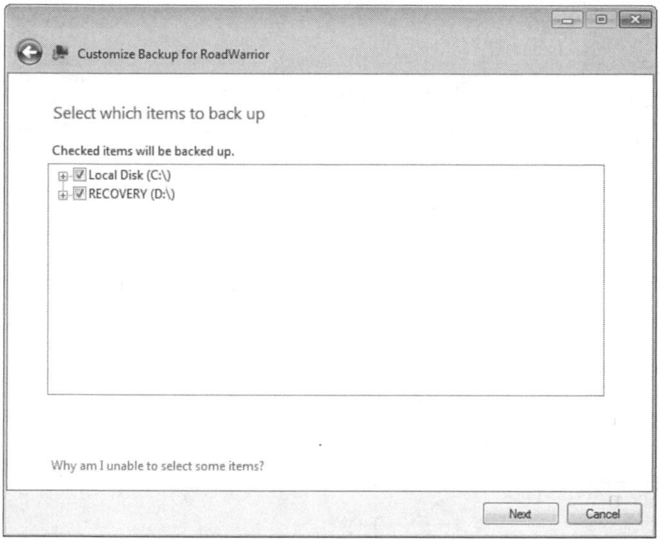

FIGURE 9.2 Use the Customize Backup Wizard to exclude one or more drives or partitions from a computer's backups.

Excluding Folders from a Backup

To exclude one or more folders from a computer's backup configuration, follow these steps:

1. Log on to the Windows Home Server Dashboard.
2. Display the Computers and Backup tab.
3. Click the computer you want to configure.
4. Click Customize Backup for the Computer. Windows Home Server launches the Customize Backup for *Computer* Wizard (where *Computer* is the name of the computer you're configuring).
5. Click Add or Remove Backup Items. The wizard examines the computer and then displays a list of disk drives and partitions.
6. Click the plus sign (+) beside the drive that contains the folder or folders you want to exclude. A list of the folders on that drive appears.
7. Repeat step 6 until you drill down to the folder you want to exclude. (You may need to drill down into various levels of subfolders to find the one you want.)
8. Deactivate the check box for each folder that you want to exclude from the backup, as shown in Figure 9.3.
9. Repeat steps 6–8 to exclude other folders, as needed.
10. Click Next. The wizard displays a summary of what will and won't be backed up for the computer.
11. Click Save Changes to complete the configuration.

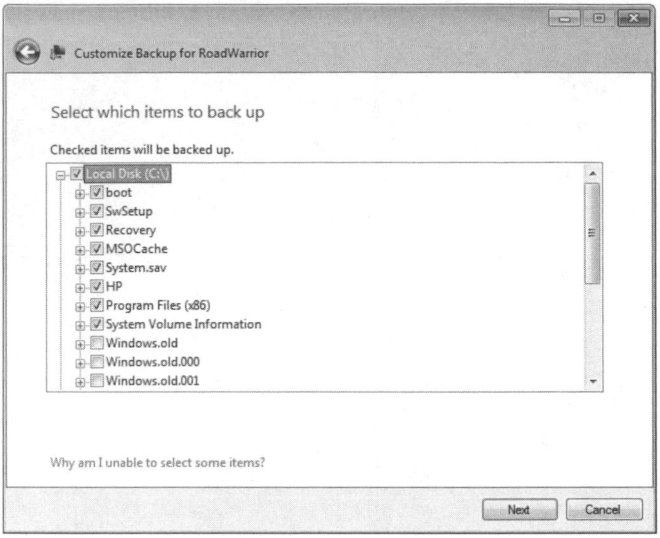

FIGURE 9.3   Deactivate the check box for each folder that you want Windows Home Server to exclude from the backups.

Adding a New Hard Drive to a Backup

If you add a hard drive to a computer, Windows Home Server eventually detects the new drive, changes the network status to At Risk, and displays the alert shown in Figure 9.4 on each client.

FIGURE 9.4   When you add a hard drive to a computer, Windows Home Server broadcasts a warning alert to add that drive to the computer's backups.

If you don't want to include this drive in the computer's backups, follow these steps to handle the warning:

1. Click the alert. (If the alert no longer appears, right-click the Launchpad icon in the notification area, and then click View Alerts.) The Alert Viewer appears.
2. Select the warning, as shown in Figure 9.5.
3. Click Ignore the Alert. Windows Home Server asks you to confirm.
4. Click Yes.
5. Click Close.

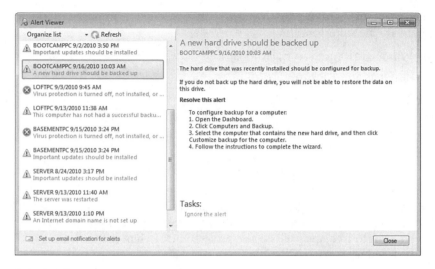

FIGURE 9.5   You can tell Windows Home Server to ignore the new drive.

On the other hand, you might prefer to include the new drive in the computer's nightly backups. In that case, you need to work through the following steps to reconfigure the computer:

1. Log on to the Windows Home Server Dashboard.

2. Display the Computers and Backup tab.

3. Click the computer that has the new drive.

4. Click Customize Backup for the Computer. Windows Home Server launches the Customize Backup for *Computer* Wizard (where *Computer* is the name of the computer you're configuring).

5. Click Add or Remove Backup Items. The wizard examines the computer and then displays a list of disk drives and partitions.

6. Activate the check box for the new drive.

7. Click Save Changes. Windows Home Server adds the new drive to the computer's backup configuration.

Turning Off Backups for a Computer

There might be times when you don't want a particular computer to get backed up:

▶ You might know that you'll be using the computer during the backup time, and you don't want the backup process to slow down your work.

▶ You might need the computer to run an all-night job (such as compiling a large application or rendering a 3D image), and you don't want the backup to interfere.

▶ The computer might be a backup or spare with no important information on it.

▶ You might be running out of storage space on the server, and you want to prevent backups until you can add more storage.

9

For these and similar situations, you can tell Windows Home Server not to back up one or more computers. Here are the steps to follow:

1. Log on to the Windows Home Server Dashboard.

2. Display the Computers and Backups tab.

3. Click the computer you want to configure.

4. Click Customize Backup for the Computer. Windows Home Server launches the Customize Backup for *Computer* Wizard (where *Computer* is the name of the computer you're configuring).

5. Click Disable Backup for This Computer. The wizard asks what you want to do with the computer's existing backups.

6. If you're disabling the computer's backups only temporarily, click Keep the Existing Backups for This Computer; if you're turning off the computer's backups permanently (or if you want to free up space on the server), click Delete the Existing Backups for This Computer, instead.

7. Click Save Changes.

8. Click Close. Windows Home Server changes the computer's backup status to Not Set Up. (You can see what this looks like in Figure 9.7.)

To tell Windows Home Server to resume backing up the computer, follow steps 1–4, click Back Up All of My Files and Folders for the Computer, and then click Save Changes.

Configuring Time Machine to Back Up Your Mac

One of the great new features in Windows Home Server 2011 is support for Macs right out of the box. This not only includes using Launchpad on your Mac to access shared folders and Remote Web Access, but it includes the welcome capability to configure Time Machine to back up your Mac to Windows Home Server. Here's how you set this up:

1. On your Mac, open Launchpad.

2. Click the drop-down icon in the upper-right corner of the Launchpad window.

3. Click Settings to open the Launchpad Settings dialog box.

4. Click the Time Machine tab.

5. Click Configure Time Machine. Launchpad launches the Time Machine preferences dialog box.

6. Click Select Backup Disk. Time Machine displays a list of available backup volumes.

7. Click the Windows Home Server volume.

8. Click Use for Backup.

Running a Manual Backup

Windows Home Server's nightly backups ought to suit the needs of most people. However, at times you may want even more assurance that your data is safe:

▶ You just installed the Windows Home Server Connector on a client PC, and you don't want to wait until midnight to get it backed up.

▶ You spent the morning creating, modifying, or downloading a large number of files, and you want them backed up now.

▶ You turned off backups for a computer the previous night, and now you want a backup for the current day.

▶ The previous backup failed for some reason, so you want to try again.

▶ You just installed a major program (such as Microsoft Office), and you want to back it up.

▶ You added a new hard drive full of important files, and you want to get them backed up right away.

▶ You're getting ready to leave town and would like to back up your notebook computer before your trip.

▶ You're more paranoid than most.

Whatever the reason, Windows Home Server lets you make as many backups as you want, as long as it has the free space to store them.

Here are the steps to follow to launch a backup manually:

1. Log on to the Windows Home Server Dashboard.
2. Display the Computers and Backups tab.
3. Click the computer that you want to back up.
4. Click Start a Backup for the Computer. Windows Home Server displays the Backup Now dialog box, shown in Figure 9.6.

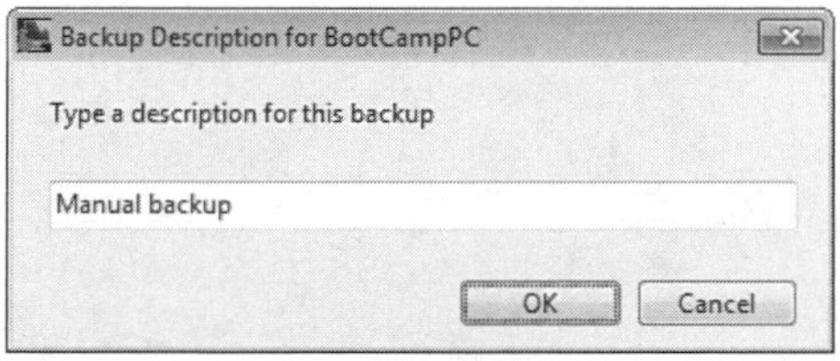

FIGURE 9.6   Type a description for your manual backup.

TIP

A faster way to launch a manual backup is to open Launchpad on the client and then click Backup. In the Backup Properties dialog box that appears, click Start Backup.

5. Type a description for the backup. Just in case you need to use this backup later on to restore some files, make your description useful and unique (for example, Just Installed Microsoft Office or Retrying Failed Backup).

6. Click Backup Now. Windows Home Server begins backing up the computer.

If you're in the Windows Home Server Dashboard, the Status column in the Computers and Backup tab displays the progress of the operation, as shown in Figure 9.7. If you initiated the manual backup from the client, click Backup in the Launchpad to open the Backup Properties dialog box, shown in Figure 9.8.

Cancelling a Running Backup

You might be busy with the computer and don't want the backup to run just now. In that case, you can cancel the backup:

▶ On the client, open Launchpad, click Backup to open the Backup Properties dialog box, and then click Stop Backup.

▶ In the Windows Home Server Dashboard, display the Computers and Backup tab, click the computer that's being backed up, and then click Stop Backup for the Computer.

Backing Up Other Systems to Windows Home Server

Because the Windows Home Server Connector software only works on Windows 7, Vista, and XP PCs, the automatic backup feature of Windows Home Server isn't available for other systems on your network. If you need to back up an older Windows machine, a Mac, or a Linux box, you need to do it the old-fashioned way: You need to run the computer's built-in (or third-party) backup software.

The good news is that you don't have to worry about *where* you store the backups for these other systems because you've got your Windows Home Server shares ready to do the job. On my network, I created a Backups subfolder in the Public share:

\\SERVER\Public\Backups

When configuring backups on your other systems, use this Windows Home Server shared folder as the backup destination.

Working with Backups

As your network computers are backed up nightly, Windows Home Server maintains a database of the backups that it's currently storing for each computer. The number of backups in the database depends on the Client Computer Backup Retention settings you specified for saving daily, weekly, and monthly backups. (See "Configuring Client

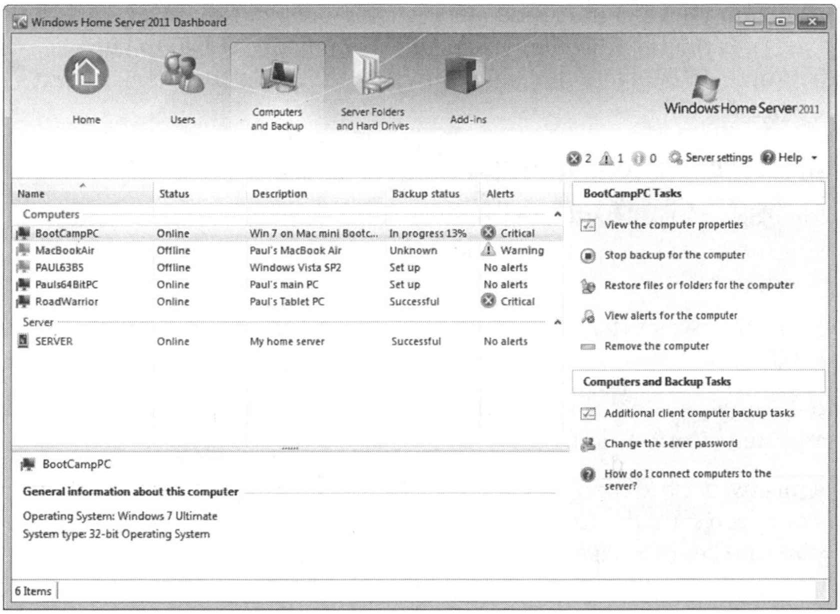

FIGURE 9.7   In the Computers and Backup tab, the Status column shows the progress of the backup.

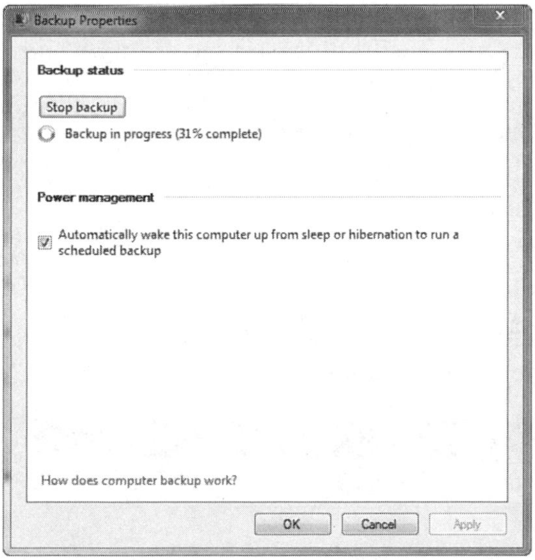

FIGURE 9.8   On the client, the Backup Properties dialog box shows the progress of the backup.

Computer Backup Retention," earlier in this chapter.) Windows Home Server enables you to access this database of backups and see the status of each backup, view a backup's details, prevent a backup from being deleted, and browse the files in a backup. The next few sections provide the details.

Viewing a Computer's List of Backups

In the Windows Home Server Dashboard, the Computers and Backup tab has a Status column that tells you the current state of the backups for each computer. You can see five values in the Status column:

- ▶ **Successful**—This means that the computer's most recent backup completed without a hitch.

- ▶ **Unsuccessful**—This means that the computer's most recent backup failed. This status also generates a Critical alert.

- ▶ **Set Up**—This means that the computer is on the list of clients to get backed up, but a backup has not yet occurred, probably because the computer is sleeping (and you didn't configure the client to wake up for backups) or not connected to the network.

- ▶ **Not Set Up**—This means that you've disabled backups for the computer (as explained earlier in the "Turing Off Backups for a Computer" section).

- ▶ **Unknown**—This status means that Windows Home Server can't determine the computer's current backup status.

Note that seeing Unsuccessful for a computer doesn't necessarily mean that Windows Home Server has never been able to back up the computer; it just means that the most recent backup attempt failed; Windows Home Server might still have a successful backup stored, so it might be possible to restore the computer if the need arises.

If you want to know the status of the individual backups, you need to display the computer's list of backups. Here are the steps to follow:

1. Log on to the Windows Home Server Dashboard.
2. Display the Computers and Backup tab.
3. Click the computer you want to work with.
4. Click View the Computer Properties. The computer's Properties dialog box appears.
5. Click the Backup tab, which displays the backups. Figure 9.9 shows an example.

TIP
You can also double-click a computer to see its list of backups.

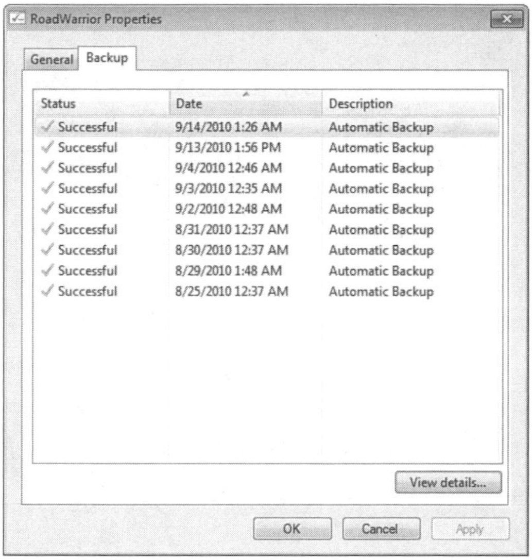

FIGURE 9.9   The Backup tab shows the list of stored backups on the computer.

The list of backups has three columns:

▶ **Status**—This column tells you the status of the backup. There are three possibilities (see Figure 9.10):

   ▶ **Successful**—Windows Home Server successfully backed up the entire computer.

   ▶ **Incomplete**—Windows Home Server backed up some, but not all, of the computer. In other words, this status tells you that at least one drive on the computer was not backed up properly.

   ▶ **Unsuccessful**—Windows Home Server backed up zero drives on the computer.

▶ **Date**—This column tells you the date of the backup or backup attempt.

▶ **Description**—This column shows either Automatic Backup (for the nightly Windows Home Server backups) or the description of a manual backup you ran.

Viewing Backup Details

The View Backups window tells you some useful information about each backup, but there is more data available. For example, it's also possible to see the partitions included in the backup, the size of the backed up files, and the folders that were excluded from each partition during the backup.

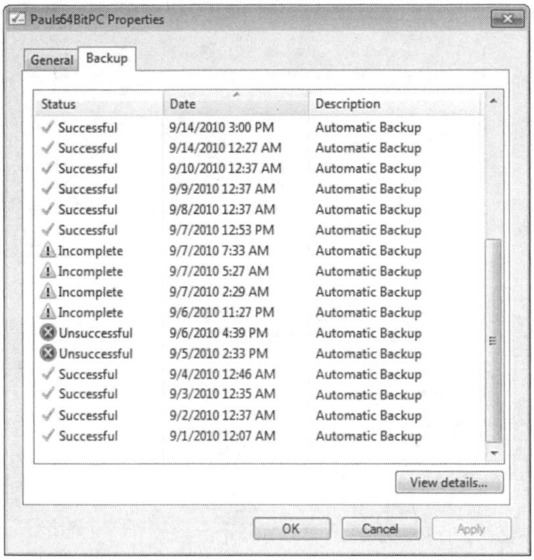

FIGURE 9.10   The Status column can have three values: Successful, Incomplete, or Unsuccessful.

To view this extra detail for a backup, follow these steps:

1. Log on to the Windows Home Server Dashboard.
2. Display the Computers and Backup tab.
3. Click the computer you want to work with.
4. Click View the Computer's Properties. The computer's Properties dialog box appears.
5. Click the Backup tab.
6. Click the backup you want to view.
7. Click View Details. The Backup Details dialog box appears, as shown in Figure 9.11.

TIP

You can also double-click a backup to see its details.

Note that in the Volumes in Backup list, Windows Home Server shows the partition name (drive letter and partition label), capacity, and location (internal or external). It also shows the status for each partition, which will be either Successful or Unsuccessful. So if the overall status of the backup is either Incomplete or Unsuccessful, you can view the details and see which partition is causing the problem. Click the failed volume backup to see the Failure Details, as shown in Figure 9.12.

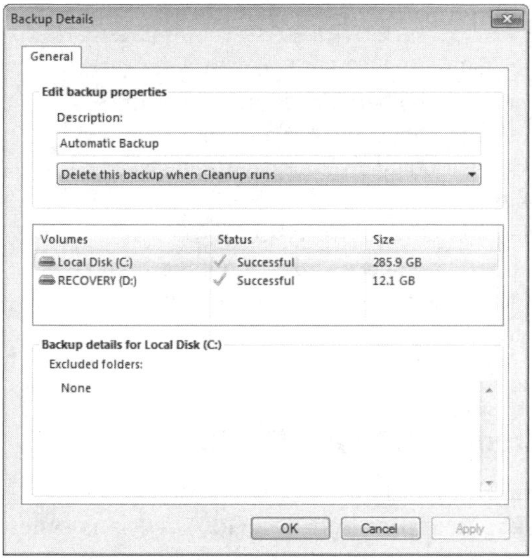

FIGURE 9.11   The Backup Details dialog box provides extra information about each backup.

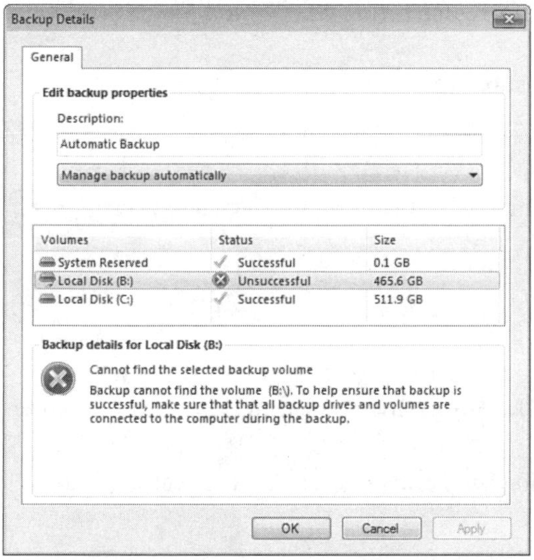

FIGURE 9.12   If the overall backup status is Incomplete or Unsuccessful, the Backup Details dialog box tells you which partition (or partitions) failed.

9

NOTE

What should you do if a particular partition is failing routinely? First, just try rebooting the client computer to see if that helps. If it's an external hard drive, make sure the drive is powered up and connected to the PC. It's also possible that a drive error could be causing the problem, so run Windows' Check Disk utility on the drive. (Right-click the partition, click Properties, display the Tools tab, and then click Check Now. Note that this operation requires Administrator credentials in Windows Vista.) If you still can't get Windows Home Server to back up the partition successfully and if the partition doesn't contain important files, exclude it from the backups. (See "Excluding a Disk Drive from a Backup," earlier in this chapter.)

Preventing Windows Home Server from Deleting a Backup

As I mentioned earlier in this chapter, Windows Home Server deletes old backups every Sunday according to the Client Computer Backup Retention settings. However, sometimes you might not want Windows Home Server to remove a particular backup during the cleanup process. For example, you may know that a backup contains an important version of a file or folder, and you always want the ability to restore that version if necessary.

For such situations, you can tell Windows Home Server not to delete a particular backup. Follow these steps:

1. Log on to the Windows Home Server Dashboard.
2. Display the Computers and Backup tab.
3. Click the computer you want to work with.
4. Click View the Computer's Properties. The computer's Properties dialog box appears.
5. Click the Backup tab.
6. Click the backup you want to keep.
7. Click View Details.
8. In the Edit Backup Properties section, use the list to select the Keep This Backup item. The next time it runs the backup cleanup, Windows Home Server won't delete the backup.
9. Click OK to return to the Properties dialog box, and then click OK to return to the Dashboard.

Cleaning Up Old Backups

Windows Home Server's backup cleanup process should prevent each computer's list of backups from getting unwieldy. Even so, there are situations in which you might want to accelerate the cleanup process:

▶ You have a number of manual backups that you no longer need.

▶ The list of backups includes many failed or incomplete backups that you no longer need to see (because, for example, you've solved whatever problem was causing the unsuccessful backups).

▶ You're running low on storage space in Windows Home Server.

Here are the steps to follow to schedule a backup to be deleted the next time Windows Home Server performs the backup cleanup:

1. Log on to the Windows Home Server Dashboard.
2. Display the Computers and Backup tab.
3. Click the computer you want to work with.
4. Click View the Computer's Properties. The computer's Properties dialog box appears.
5. Click the Backup tab.
6. Click the backup you want to keep.
7. Click View Details.
8. In the Edit Backup Properties section, use the list to select the Delete This Backup When Cleanup Runs item. The next time it runs the backup cleanup, Windows Home Server deletes the backup.
9. Repeat steps 6–8 to schedule other backups for deletion.
10. Click OK.

Creating a Bootable USB Recovery Key

The worst-case scenario for PC problems is a system crash that renders your hard disk or system files unusable. Your only recourse in such a case is to start from scratch with either a reformatted hard disk or a new hard disk. This usually means that you have to reinstall Windows and then reinstall and reconfigure all your applications. In other words, you're looking at the better part of a day or, more likely, a few days, to recover your system.

Fortunately, with just a bit of foresight on your part, you can avoid all that by recovering your entire PC using a Windows Home Server backup of that system. The only foresight required (besides making sure that Windows Home Server is successfully backing up your computer) is creating a Windows Home Server recovery key on a USB flash drive. By inserting the drive in your down-and-out PC, the drive boots automatically and takes you through the recovery steps. (See "Restoring a Computer to a Previous Configuration," later in this chapter.)

Here are the steps to follow to create a USB recovery key:

1. Using the computer you want to protect, log on to the Windows Home Server Dashboard.
2. Click Computers and Backup.

3. Click the Additional Client Computer Backup Tasks link.

4. Click the Tools tab.

5. Click Create Key. Windows Home Server launches the Create Computer Recovery Key Wizard.

6. Insert a USB flash drive into the server, and give the drive a minute or so to mount.

CAUTION

The USB flash drive you use must have a capacity of at least 512MB. Also, creating the recovery key deletes any existing files on the drive, so make sure the drive contains no data you want to keep. (If it does, copy the files to a safe location before proceeding.)

---

7. Click Next. The wizard asks you to select the USB flash drive.

8. Use the list to select the drive, activate the check box (to indicate your understanding that the wizard will delete all files on the drive), and then click Next. The wizard creates the computer recovery key on the drive. Note that this takes a few minutes.

9. When the wizard is done, click Close.

Repairing a Client's Backups

If you're having trouble accessing a client backup, it's possible that the database that Windows Home Server uses to store the backups has become corrupted. In that case, you can use Windows Home Server's repair tool to fix the problem. Here's how it works:

1. Using the computer you want to repair, log on to the Windows Home Server Dashboard.

2. Click Computers and Backup.

3. Click the Additional Client Computer Backup Tasks link.

4. Click the Tools tab.

5. Click Repair Now. Windows Home Server runs the Repair the Backup Database Wizard.

6. Activate the check box (to indicate your understanding that the wizard might have to delete one more existing backups during the repair), and then click Next. The wizard begins the repair process.

7. When the wizard is done, click Close.

Restoring Network Backups

Like any type of insurance, backups are something you hope you never have to use. Unfortunately, in the real world, stuff happens:

► Important information inside a document is deleted or edited.

► Important files are permanently deleted by accident.

► Hard drives and entire systems kick the digital bucket.

These and similar situations are when you thank your lucky stars (or your deity of choice) that Windows Home Server has been on the job making nightly backups, because now you can restore the file, folder, or system and get back to more important things. The rest of this chapter takes you through various techniques for restoring files via Windows Home Server.

Restoring Backed-Up Files

Follow these steps to restore a file or folder on a client computer:

1. Using the computer you want to use to store the recovered file or folder (which could be the original computer or another client), Log on to the Windows Home Server Dashboard.

> ### NOTE
>
> One of the remarkable things about Windows Home Server is that you can restore objects from computers other than your own. For example, if an image, song, or video was backed up on your media PC, you can access that PC's backups and then restore the file to a folder on your own computer.

2. Display the Computers and Backup tab.

3. Click the computer you want to work with.

4. Click Restore Files or Folders for the Computer. The Restore Files or Folder Wizard appears.

5. Click the backup you want to use for the restore, and then click Next. If the backup includes two or more partitions, the Choose a Volume dialog box appears. (If the backup includes only a single partition, skip to step 7.)

6. Select the partition that contains the file or folder you want to restore, and then click Next. The wizard gathers the partition data.

7. Navigate to the folder that contains the data you want to restore.

8. Select the file or folder. To select multiple items, hold down Ctrl, and click each file or folder.

9. Click Next. The wizard prompts you to select a restore location. The default location depends on which computer you're using to run the restore:

   ► **The original computer**—In this case, the default restore location is the original location of the file or folder.

▶ **Another computer**—In this case, the default restore location is a folder named `Restored Items` that the wizard creates on your desktop.

10. Adjust the restore location, if needed, and then click Next. If some or all of the objects already exist in the destination folder, Windows asks how you want to handle the conflict:

▶ Windows XP displays a dialog box asking whether you want to replace the existing file or folder. Click Yes to replace the existing file with the backup copy. (If you don't want the existing file to be replaced, click No, instead.)

▶ Windows 7 and Vista display a Copy File dialog box like the one shown in Figure 9.13. You have three choices: Click Copy and Replace to have the backup copy replace the existing item; click Don't Copy to bypass copying the backup version and leave the existing item as is; or click Copy, But Keep Both Files to leave the existing file as is and add the backup copy to the folder with (2) appended to the file's primary name.

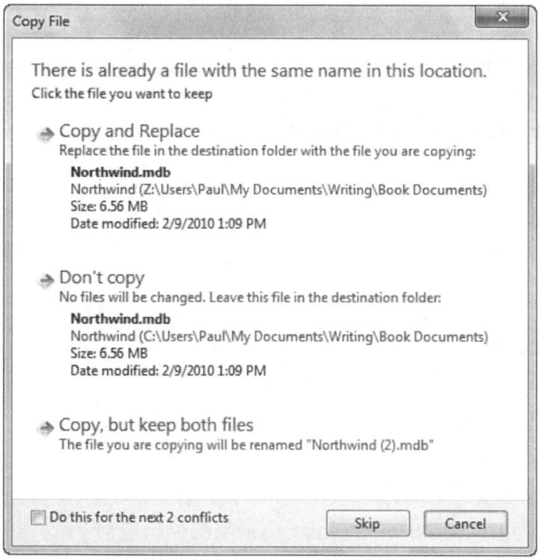

FIGURE 9.13   If one or more of the objects already exist in the destination folder, use the Copy File dialog box to decide which objects you want to restore.

TIP

If Windows 7 or Vista detects multiple conflicts, you can save time by activating the Do This for the Next *X* Conflicts check box (see Figure 9.13) to resolve the conflict in the same way with each file.

Restoring a Computer to a Previous Configuration

Losing a file or two or even an entire folder is no big deal because, as you saw in the previous section, recovering the data requires nothing more than a simple copy-and-paste operation. It's a much more serious problem when your entire system goes south due to a hard drive crash, a virus, or some other major problem.

Before Windows Home Server, restoring a computer was a day-long affair that involved reinstalling the operating system and all your programs, reconfiguring Windows, re-creating email accounts, and salvaging as much of your data as you could.

With Windows Home Server, however, restoring a computer is pretty close to painless because it already has your entire computer backed up, so its main chore is to take that backup and apply it to the computer. Because the backup includes not only your data, but Windows, your applications, and your settings, at the end of the restore you have your computer back up and running. You may lose a bit of work or changes that you made since the most recent backup, but that's a small price to pay for having your system back on its feet without much fuss on your part.

Before attempting the recovery, you should, of course, remedy whatever problem caused the system crash in the first place. If your hard drive died, replace it with one that's as big or bigger than the original. If your system was infected by a virus, purchase a good antivirus program and run a scan of your computer after the restore, because there's a possibility that restoring the computer could also restore the virus. Also, because the restore process requires access to Windows Home Server, make sure your computer has a physical connection to the network router or switch.

> **NOTE**
>
> The recovery will almost certainly fail without a wired connection to your network, because the recovery program won't be able to locate your server over a wireless connection.

With your hardware ready to go, here are the steps to follow to restore your computer:

1. Turn off the computer, if it isn't off already.
2. Insert the bootable USB flash drive that contains the computer's recovery key.
3. Start the computer.
4. Access your computer's setup or BIOS configuration, locate the boot options, and then configure the computer to boot to the USB flash drive.
5. Restart the computer, which now boots to the USB flash drive.
6. Select either Full System Restore (32-Bit Operating System) or Full System Restore (64-Bit Operating System), and then press Enter. After a few minutes, the Full System Restore Wizard appears and prompts you for the regional and keyboard settings you want to use.

7. Change the settings as needed (the defaults are probably fine for most folks), and then click Continue. The wizard asks whether you need to install additional drivers.

8. If you don't need to install additional device drivers, click Continue and skip to step 13. Otherwise, click Load Drivers to view the list of devices that the wizard found.

TIP

Windows Home Server includes all of a computer's device drivers as part of the computer backup. If you notice that a device is missing, you can load those drivers onto a USB drive. Using another computer, insert a USB flash drive and then run through steps 1–7 from the previous section to open the most recent backup from the computer you're trying to restore. Select the Drivers for Full System Restore folder (it's part of the system root folder; usually C:\), and then restore that folder to the USB drive. You can then use that USB drive to install extra drivers, as described here in steps 9–11.

---

9. Copy the device driver files to a USB flash drive, and then insert the flash drive.

10. Click Install Drivers.

11. Click Scan. Windows Home Server locates the drivers on the flash drive or floppy and then installs them. When you see the message telling you that the drivers were found, click OK.

12. Click Continue. Windows Home Server restarts the Full System Restore Wizard.

13. Click Next. The wizard locates Windows Home Server on your network and then prompts you to enter the Windows Home Server password. (If the wizard fails to find your home server, click Find My Home Server Manually, click Next, type the server name, and then click Next.)

14. Type the password, and click Next. The wizard logs on to Windows Home Server.

15. How you proceed from here depends on whether the wizard recognizes your computer:

    ▶ If the wizard thinks it recognizes your computer, the option for the computer's name is activated. If that option is not correct, click Another Computer, and then use the list to select the computer you're restoring.

    ▶ If the wizard doesn't recognize your computer, it displays a list of computers that have available backups on Windows Home Server. Select the computer you're restoring, and click Next.

16. The wizard now displays a list of the computer's stored backups. Select the backup you want to use for the restore. (If you're not sure, you can click Details to see more information about the selected backup.) Click Next. The wizard asks you to choose the volumes (partitions) that you want to restore.

17. Select the Let the Wizard Fully Restore the Computer option, and then click Next. The wizard displays a summary of the partitions it will restore.

> **NOTE**
>
> There's no rule that says you must restore the entire system. For example, if your computer has two hard drives and only one of them crashed, you need to restore only the crashed drive. To prevent Windows Home Server from restoring a drive, select I Will Select the Volumes to Restore, click Next, and then select the partitions you want to restore.

> **TIP**
>
> If you need to perform disk maintenance of any kind, click the Run Disk Manager button. This loads the Disk Management snap-in, which enables you to format partitions, change partition sizes, delete partitions, change drive letters, and more. Right-click the partition you want to work with, and then click the command you want to run.

18. Click Next. Windows Home Server begins restoring the computer. After a few seconds, it displays an estimate of how long the restore might take. (The length of the restore depends on the size of the partitions and the amount of data you're restoring; it could take as little as 15 minutes or as much as an hour or two.)

When the restore is complete, the wizard shuts down and then restarts your computer. Note that your computer might require a second reboot after Windows Home Server detects the machine's devices and installs their drivers.

From Here

▶ To learn how to enable automatic updating, **SEE** "Configuring Windows Update," **P. 85.**

6

CHAPTER 10

Monitoring Your Network

IN THIS CHAPTER

▸ Monitoring the Network Status with the Launchpad Icon

▸ Monitoring the Windows Home Server Shares

▸ Monitoring Remote Desktop Sessions

Even a humble home network with just a few computers is still a fairly large and unwieldy beast that requires a certain amount of vigilance to keep things running smoothly. If you're the one around the house who wears the hat that says "Network Administrator," it's your job to keep an eye on the network to watch for things going awry.

Fortunately, Windows Home Server makes network monitoring about as easy as this kind of chore can get. For one thing, Windows Home Server comes with its own set of features that enable you to quickly monitor the network and be alerted to problems. For another, the Windows Server 2008 R2 code that underlies Windows Home Server 2011 means that you have a few other powerful tools at your disposal for monitoring the network.

This chapter takes you through all these tools and shows you how to use them to keep tabs on various aspects of your home network.

Monitoring the Network Status with the Launchpad Icon

Before getting to the remote administration tools that you implement yourself, let's take a second to look at Windows Home Server's built-in monitoring tool, the Launchpad icon, which appears in the Windows notification area. The purpose of this icon is to visually indicate the current health status of the Windows Home Server network. There are two types of indications: the icon color and the network health alerts.

Monitoring the Icon Color

The simplest way to monitor your network's health status is to examine the color of the Status icon. Table 10.1 presents the four icon colors and what they mean.

TABLE 10.1   Colors Used by the Windows Home Server Status Icon

Icon Color	Status	Description
Green	Healthy	The network is healthy. All the clients are backed up and have their security settings set up correctly, and Windows Home Server has all available updates installed.
Yellow	Warning	The network has a problem. For example, one of the client computers might not have successful backups.
Red	Critical	The network has a serious problem. For example, one of the client computers might not have its firewall turned on, or Windows Home Server might not have an available update installed.
Gray	Not Connected	The client computer can't find Windows Home Server. For example, a network cable might be unplugged, or there might be no wireless connection.

Monitoring Network Health Alerts

When the network health status changes from green to any other color, the Windows Home Server Status icon displays a *network health* alert, a fly-out message that tells you why the status changed. Windows Home Server has all kinds of these messages. To give you some idea what to expect, Table 10.2 lists a few of the more common network health notifications that you're likely to see.

TABLE 10.2   Common Network Health Alerts Displayed by the Launchpad Icon

Notification	Description
	The specified computer has a new hard drive that has not yet been added to the computer's backup configuration.
	At least one service on the home server is not started.

TABLE 10.2   Common Network Health Alerts Displayed by the Launchpad Icon

Notification	Description
⊗ SERVER — The router is not configured correctly	The network router has a configuration problem.
⚠ ROADWARRIOR — Important updates should be installed	Windows Home Server has detected new updates that must be installed on the specified computer.
⚠ BOOTCAMPPC — Restart the computer to apply updates	The specified computer must be restarted to apply the installed updates.
⊗ BOOTCAMPPC — The Network Firewall is turned off.	Windows Firewall has been turned off on the specified computer.
⊗ BOOTCAMPPC — Spyware and unwanted software protection is turned off, not installed, or not up-to-date.	The antispyware program on the specified computer has either been turned off, or its spyware definitions are out-of-date.
⚠ BOOTCAMPPC — Computer Monitoring Error — 2:24 PM 9/2/2010	Windows Home Server is having trouble monitoring the health of the specified computer.
⊗ ROADWARRIOR — Virus protection is turned off, not installed, or not up-to-date.	The antivirus program on the specified computer has been turned off, is not installed, or its virus definitions are out-of-date.
⊗ PAULS64BITPC — This computer was not successfully backed up	The specified computer's most recent backup failed.
⊗ PAULS64BITPC — This computer has not had a successful back up recently	The specified computer has not been backed up recently.

10

TABLE 10.2   Common Network Health Alerts Displayed by the Launchpad Icon

Notification	Description
	The Remote Web Access domain name has been successfully configured on the server.

> **NOTE**
>
> If you don't want Windows Home Server to display these health alerts, you can turn them off. Click the Show Hidden Icons arrow in the notification area, click Customize, and then in the Launchpad list, select Hide Icon and Notifications.

> **NOTE**
>
> The security-related health alerts are only available for Windows 7 and Windows Vista PCs. The Windows 7 and Vista Security Center has an internal feature that enables other programs to poll its current status. The Security Center in Windows XP doesn't have this feature.

Monitoring Windows Home Server with the Alert Viewer

The Launchpad icon color is a reflection of the current network health alerts generated by Windows Home Server:

▶ If Windows Home Server has detected at least one critical alert, the icon appears red.

▶ If Windows Home Server has detected no critical alerts, but at least one warning alert, the icon appears yellow.

▶ If Windows Home Server has detected no critical alerts and no warning alerts, the icon appears green (assuming the computer has a connection to the server).

However, seeing a red or yellow icon doesn't necessarily mean that Windows Home Server has detected a single alert. In fact, there could be multiple critical or warning alerts that await your attention. How do you know? Windows Home Server gives you two easy ways to tell:

▶ When you log in to Launchpad, you see alert icons in the lower-right corner. If there's at least one critical alert, you see the critical icon (a red circle with a white X inside it) and the number of critical alerts. If there's at least one warning alert, you see the warning icon (an yellow triangle with a black exclamation mark inside it) and the number of warning alerts. Figure 10.1 shows an example.

FIGURE 10.1   Launchpad displays the current number of critical and warning alerts in the lower-right corner of the window.

TIP

You can configure Launchpad to show only alerts that apply to the client computer. Click the drop-down arrow in the upper-right corner, and then click Settings. In the Launchpad Settings dialog box, select the Local Only option. If you want to hide the alerts altogether from, say, a novice user, select the None option, instead.

▶ When you log in to the Dashboard, you see alert icons in the toolbar, to the left of the Server Settings button. If there's at least one critical alert, you see the critical icon and the number of critical alerts; if there's at least one warning alert, you see the warning icon and the number of warning alerts. The Dashboard also shows the number of informational alerts next to the information icon (a blue circle with a white i inside it). Figure 10.2 shows an example.

Knowing the number of alerts that are current is one thing, but if you want to do anything about them you need to know what those alerts are. In Windows Home Server 2011, that's the job of the Alert Viewer, which displays information on each outstanding network alert. To open the Alert Viewer, you have four choices:

▶ If the Launchpad icon is currently displaying a network health alert, click the alert.

▶ Right-click the Launchpad icon, and then click View Alerts.

▶ In Launchpad, click the critical or warning icons.

▶ In the Dashboard, click the critical or warning icons.

10

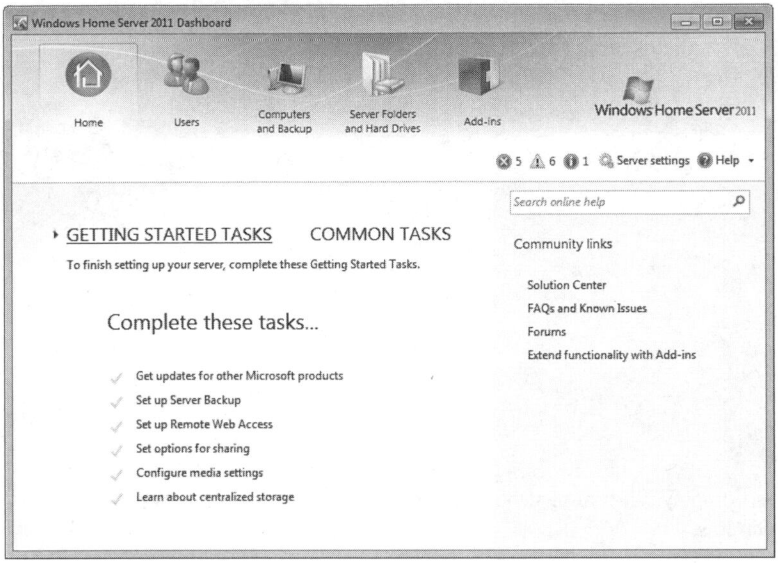

FIGURE 10.2   The Dashboard displays the current number of critical, warning, and informational alerts in the toolbar.

Figure 10.3 shows the Alert Viewer, which displays the current alerts on the left and information about the selected alert on the right.

TIP

If there are a lot of alerts, you can make life a tad easier by filtering them by computer or alert type. To filter by computer, select Organize List, Filter By Computer, and then click a computer; to filter by type, select Organize List, Filter By Alert Type, and then click a type (Critical, Warning, or Informational).

To handle an alert, you have two options:

▶ To fix the problem, read the alert text and follow the instructions provided (if any). For some alerts, you also see a Try to Repair the Issue link, so you can try clicking that.

▶ To tell Windows Home Server to no longer bother with the alert, click Ignore the Alert.

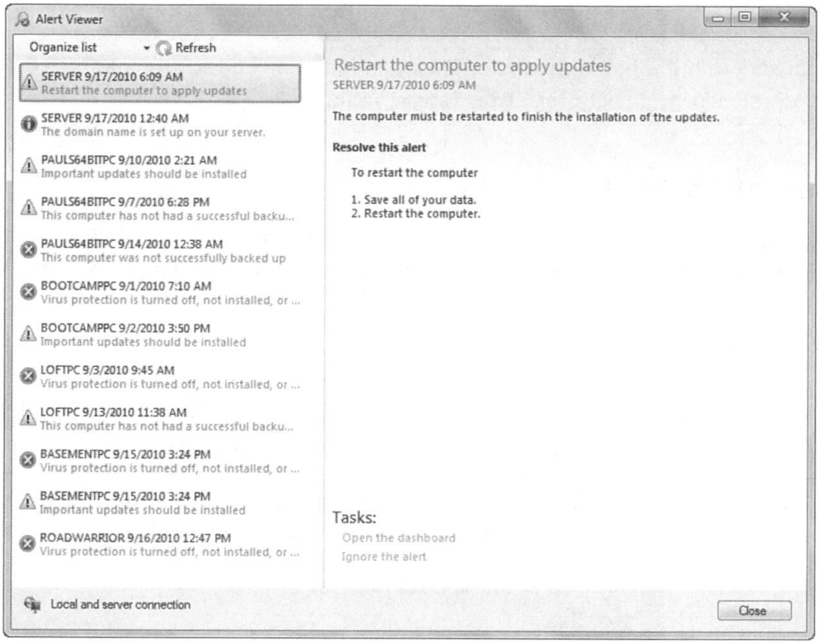

FIGURE 10.3   The Alert Viewer displays the current alerts as well as information about the selected alert.

Monitoring the Windows Home Server Shares

The Computer Management snap-in is a great tool for managing many different aspects of your system, from devices to users to services and much more. But Computer Management also enables you to monitor the Windows Home Server shared folders. For example, for each shared folder, you can find out the users who are connected to the folder, how long they've been connected, and the files they have open. You can also disconnect users from a shared folder or close files that have been opened on a shared folder. The next few sections provide the details.

Launching the Computer Management Snap-In

To get started, you need to open the Computer Management snap-in. Here are the steps to follow:

1. Log on to Windows Home Server.
2. Select Start, type **computer**, and then click Computer Management. The Computer Management snap-in appears.
3. Open the Shared Folders branch.

10

> **TIP**
>
> If you don't want to work with the entire Computer Management snap-in, you can load just the Shared Folders snap-in. Select Start, type `fsmgmt.msc`, and press Enter.

Viewing the Current Connections

To see a list of the users connected to any Windows Home Server shared folder, select System Tools, Shared Folders, Sessions. Figure 10.4 shows an example. For each user, you get the following data:

User	The name of the user.
Computer	The name of the user's computer. If Windows Home Server doesn't recognize the computer, it shows the machine's IP address instead.
Type	The type of network connection. Windows Home Server always shows this as Windows (even if the user is connected from a Mac or from Linux).
Open Files	The number of open files in the shared folders.
Connected Time	The amount of time that the user has been connected to the remote computer.
Idle Time	The amount of time that the user has not been actively working on the open files.
Guest	Whether the user logged on using the Guest account.

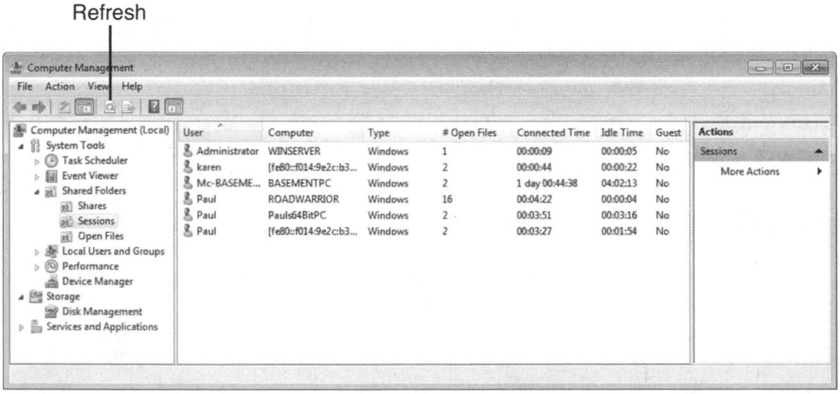

Refresh

FIGURE 10.4   The Sessions folder shows the users currently connected to shared folders on the remote computer.

NOTE

To ensure that you're always viewing the most up-to-date information, regularly select the Action, Refresh command, or click the Refresh toolbar button (pointed out in Figure 10.4).

Viewing Connections to Shared Folders

The Computer Management snap-in also makes it possible for you to view the connections to Windows Home Server by its shared folders. To get this display, select System Tools, Shared Folders, Shares. As you can see in Figure 10.5, this view provides the following information:

Share Name	The name of the shared folder. Note that the list includes the Windows Home Server hidden shares.
Folder Path	The drive or folder associated with the share.
Type	The type of network connection, which Windows Home Server always shows as Windows.
# Client Connections	The number of computers connected to the share.
Comment	The description of the share.

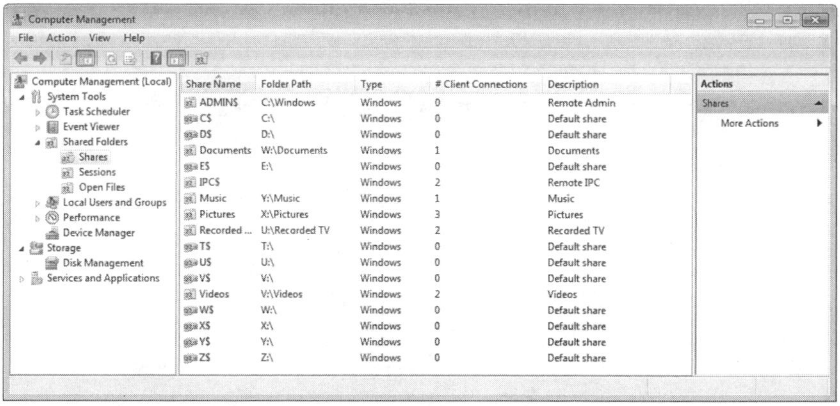

FIGURE 10.5 The Computer Management snap-in can display a server's connections by its shared folders.

10

CAUTION

The Shares branch includes commands that enable you to change the properties of a share, disable sharing for a folder, and create a new shared folder. However, you should not use these commands. In Windows Home Server, always manage shares either via the Windows Home Server Console or by using each share's UNC path (for example, *SERVER*\Pictures).

Viewing Open Files

The Computer Management snap-in can also display the files that are open on the Windows Home Server shares. To switch to this view, select System Tools, Shared Folders, Open Files. Figure 10.6 shows the result. Here's a summary of the columns in this view:

Open File	The full pathname of the file.
Accessed By	The name of the user who has the file open.
Type	The type of network connection, which Windows Home Server always shows as Windows.
# Locks	The number of locks on the file.
Open Mode	The permissions the user has over the file.

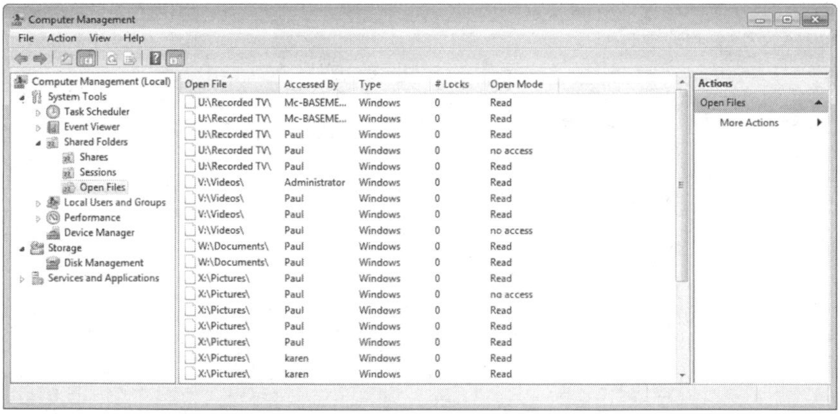

FIGURE 10.6   The Computer Management snap-in can also display a remote computer's open files in its shared resources.

Closing a User's Session or File

Although in the interest of network harmony you'll want to let users connect and disconnect as they please, at times you might need to boot someone off a machine. For example, you might see that someone has obtained unauthorized access to a share. To disconnect that user, follow these steps:

1. In the Computer Management snap-in, select System Tools, Shared Folders, Sessions.
2. Right-click the name of the user you want to disconnect.
3. Click Close Session. Windows Home Server asks you to confirm.
4. Click Yes.

Similarly, you'll usually want to let users open and close files themselves so that they don't lose information. However, you might find that a user has a particular file open and you would prefer that the user not view that file (for example, because you want to work on the file yourself or because the file contains information you don't want the user to see). To close a file opened by a user, follow these steps:

> **NOTE**
>
> If you have a file in a shared folder and you don't want other users to see that file, it makes more sense to either move the file to a protected folder or change the permissions on the file's current folder.

1. In the Computer Management snap-in, select System Tools, Shared Folders, Open Files.
2. Right-click the name of the file you want to close.
3. Click Close Open File. Windows Home Server asks you to confirm.
4. Click Yes.

> **NOTE**
>
> The remote user doesn't see a warning or any other indication that you're closing the file. For example, if the user is playing a music file, that file just stops playing and can't be started again (except by closing all open shared files and folders and starting a new session).

Monitoring Remote Desktop Sessions

There are three ways you can remotely connect to Windows Home Server.

From any network client computer, you can connect to the Windows Home Server desktop via the Remote Desktop Connection feature, as described in Chapter 1, "Setting Up Your Windows Home Server Network."

▶ **SEE** "Making a Remote Desktop Connection to the Server," **P. 26**.

Also from a network computer, you can connect to Windows Home Server using the Windows Home Server Dashboard as described in Chapter 4, "Configuring Windows Home Server," which creates a special kind of Remote Desktop session.

▶ **SEE** "Running the Windows Home Server Dashboard," **P. 77**.

Additionally, from the Internet, you can connect to Windows Home Server using the Remote Web Access page, as described in Chapter 7, "Making Connections to Network Computers."

▶ **SEE** "Connecting via the Internet," **P. 163**.

As your network's administrator, you might want to monitor such connections so you know which PC is connected and when that person logged on. You can also send messages to logged on users and disconnect sessions. You do all this using Windows Home Server's Remote Desktop Services Manager, described in the next few sections.

Starting the Remote Desktop Services Manager

To get the Remote Desktop Services Manager onscreen, follow these steps:

1. Log on to Windows Home Server.
2. Select Start, Administrative Tools, Remote Desktop Services, Remote Desktop Services Manager.
3. If you see a dialog box telling you that Remote Control and Connect only work from a client session, click OK.

TIP

Another way to launch the Remote Desktop Services Manager is to select Start, Run (or press Windows Logo+R) to open the Run dialog box, type **tsadmin.msc**, and click OK.

Viewing Remote Desktop Sessions

In the Remote Desktop Services Manager, you see an item for your Windows Home Server. Click this item to see three tabs: Users, Sessions, and Processes. The Users tab (shown in Figure 10.7) has the following columns:

User	The name of the user who initiated the session.
Session	The session type. For Remote Desktop connections, the session is RDP Tcp#*n*, where *n* is an integer that increments with each new session. For anyone logged on directly to Windows Home Server, the session is Console.
ID	A number that uniquely identifies each session.

State   The current state of the session: Active (the Remote Desktop session has started), Connected (the client has connected to the server, but the Remote Desktop session hasn't yet started), or Disconnected (the Remote Desktop session has ended).

Idle Time   For a disconnected session, the time that the session has been closed.

Logon Time   For an active session, the time the user logged on.

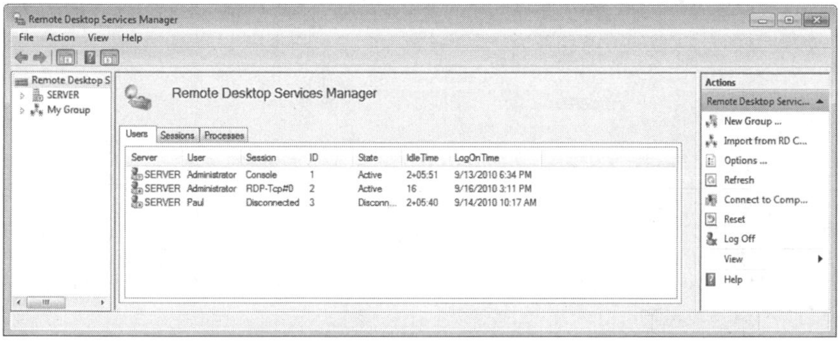

FIGURE 10.7   In Remote Desktop Services Manager, the Users tab shows information about the users with active or disconnected Remote Desktop sessions.

TIP

If you don't want to see a disconnected session in the Remote Desktop Services Manager, right-click the session, click Reset, and then click OK when Remote Desktop Services Manager asks you to confirm.

The Sessions tab (shown in Figure 10.8) has the following columns:

Session   The session type. (This is the same as in the Users tab.)

User   The name of the session's user.

ID   A number that uniquely identifies each session.

State   The current state of the session: Active, Connected, Disconnected, or Listen. The latter refers to the RDP Listener, a Remote Desktop Services component that detects and processes incoming requests for new RDP sessions.

Type   The session type, which will either be Console (which refers to the local logon session) or Microsoft RDP 5.2 (which refers to any RDP-related session).

Client Name   The name of the client computer on which the RDP session was initiated.

10

Idle Time	For a disconnected session, the time that the session has been closed.
Logon Time	For an active session, the time the user logged on.
Comment	Text that describes the session.

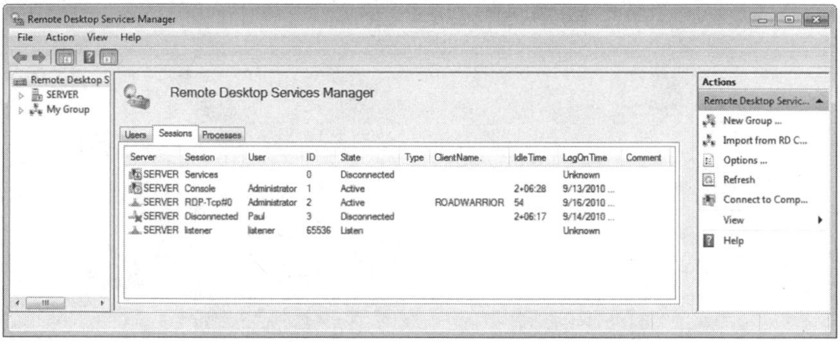

FIGURE 10.8   In Remote Desktop Services Manager, the Sessions tab provides data about the various Remote Desktop sessions.

The Processes tab lists the programs and services that are active in each session, as shown in Figure 10.9.

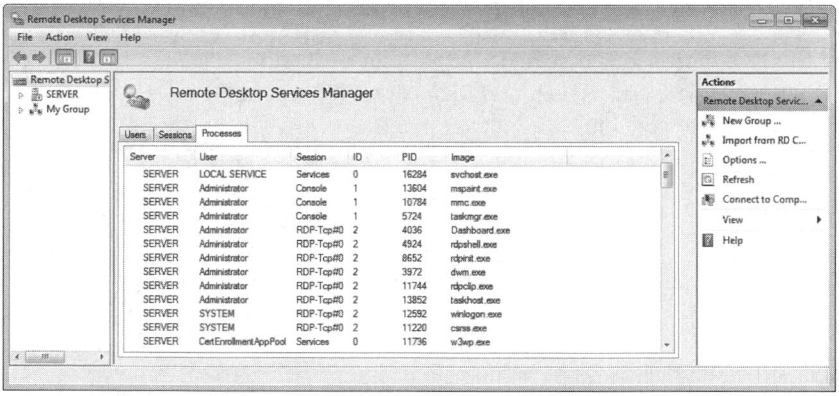

FIGURE 10.9   In Remote Desktop Services Manager, the Processes tab shows you the programs and services in use in each session.

Sending a Message to a Remote Desktop Client

There may be situations in which you find it necessary to send a message to a user with an active Remote Desktop session. For example, you may need to shut down the server for maintenance or restart the server after applying an update. Ideally, it's best if the user disconnects the Remote Desktop session correctly to avoid losing data or damaging open files. This is no big deal if the user is in the next room because you can easily tell the person to disconnect the session. It's a bit more of a hassle if you're in the basement and the user is a floor or two above you.

When you need to let connected users know something important, but it's not convenient to convey that information face-to-face, you can do the next best thing: You can send the user a message. Here's how it works:

1. Start Remote Desktop Services Manager, and display the list of sessions.
2. In either the Users tab or the Sessions tab, select the user or users to whom you want to send the message. (To select multiple users, hold down Ctrl and click each user.)
3. Right-click the selection, and then click Send Message. Remote Desktop Services Manager displays the Send Message dialog box.
4. Type your message (see Figure 10.10), and then click OK. Remote Desktop Services Manager sends the message to each user. The message appears in a dialog box inside the remote session window, as shown in Figure 10.11.

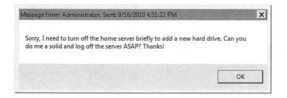

FIGURE 10.10   You can use Remote Desktop Services Manager to send a message to one or more users with active Remote Desktop sessions.

FIGURE 10.11   On the Remote Desktop client computers, the message appears in a dialog box.

Disconnecting a Remote Desktop Session

If you need to shut down or restart Windows Home Server, you should make sure that all Remote Desktop sessions are disconnected. The best way to do this is to send a message to each user with an active session, as described in the previous section. If that doesn't work, you can either access the computer physically (if it's a network session) and log off Windows Home Server, or you can force the session off by disconnecting it from Remote Desktop Services Manager. Here's how you do the latter:

1. Start Remote Desktop Services Manager, and display the list of sessions.

2. In either the Users tab or the Sessions tab, select the user or users you want to disconnect. (To select multiple users, hold down Ctrl and click each user.)

3. Right-click the selection, and then click Disconnect. Remote Desktop Services Manager asks you to confirm.

4. Click OK. Remote Desktop Services Manager disconnects the sessions.

Monitoring Users via Task Manager

Much of the information displayed by Remote Desktop Services Manager's Users tab is also available in Windows Task Manager, which is sometimes more convenient to use. To launch Task Manager, log on to Windows Home Server and use either of the following techniques:

▶ Right-click the taskbar, and then click Task Manager.

▶ Press Ctrl+Alt+Delete, and then click Task Manager.

TIP

You can also open Task Manager directly by pressing Ctrl+Shift+Esc.

The Users tab (shown in Figure 10.12) has the following columns:

User	The name of the user who initiated the session.
ID	A number that uniquely identifies each session.
Status	The current state of the session: Active (the Remote Desktop session has started), Connected (the client has connected to the server, but the Remote Desktop session hasn't yet started), or Disconnected (the Remote Desktop session has ended).
Client Name	The name of the client computer on which the RDP session was initiated.
Session	The session type. For Remote Desktop connections, the session is RDP Tcp#n, where n is an integer that increments with each new session. For anyone logged on directly to Windows Home Server, the session is Console.

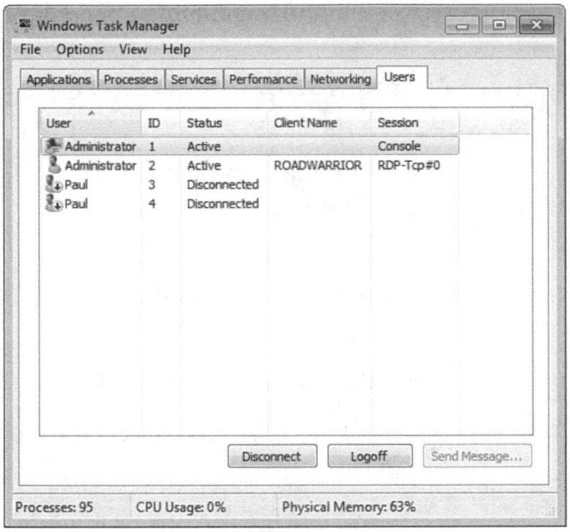

FIGURE 10.12   You can view Remote Desktop sessions from the Task Manager's Users tab.

You can also use the following buttons in the Users tab:

Disconnect   Click this button to disconnect the selected user or users.

Logoff   If the user disconnected the session (so he appears with the status Disconnected), click Logoff to remove that user from the list.

Send   Click this button to broadcast a message to the selected users. This is similar to
Message   sending a message from Remote Desktop Services Manager (see "Sending a Message to a Remote Desktop Client," earlier in this chapter), except that the Task Manager method also enables you to specify the message title, as shown in Figure 10.13.

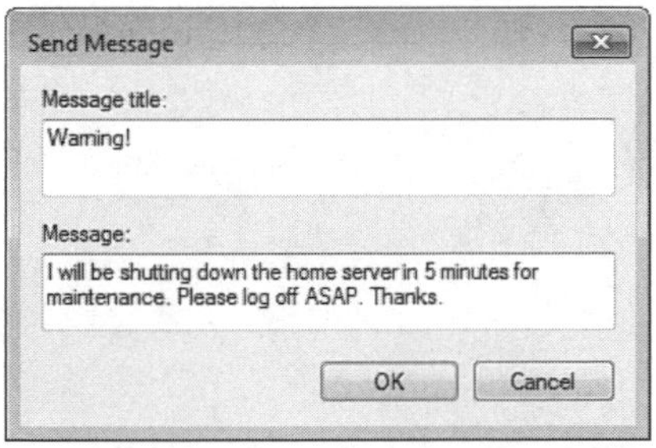

FIGURE 10.13   When you send a message from Task Manager, you can specify both the title and text.

From Here

▶ For the specifics of using Remote Desktop to connect to Windows Home Server, **SEE** "Making a Remote Desktop Connection to the Server," **P. 26.**

▶ For information on using the Windows Home Server Dashboard to connect to Windows Home Server, **SEE** "Running the Windows Home Server Dashboard," **P. 77.**

▶ To learn how to connect to Windows Home Server from the Internet, **SEE** "Connecting via the Internet," **P. 163.**

▶ For the details on monitoring the performance of Windows Home Server and your network, **SEE** "Monitoring Performance," **P. 369.**

CHAPTER 11

Implementing Windows Home Server Security

IN THIS CHAPTER

▸ Enabling Security Auditing on Windows Home Server

▸ More Ways to Secure Windows Home Server

▸ Securing Network Computers

▸ Implementing Wireless Network Security

Networking your home computers offers lots of advantages: easy and fast file swapping, simple hardware sharing, a single Internet connection for all computers, the ability to work or play anywhere in your house (if you have a wireless connection), and many more. If networking has a downside, it's that computers that can easily share resources can also easily share malicious resources, such as viruses, Trojan horses, and spyware. Also, cobbling your home PCs into a network—particularly a wireless network—opens up a few extra avenues that nefarious users can take advantage of to try to infiltrate your network.

Fortunately, you don't need a degree in electrical engineering to safeguard your Windows Home Server network from all these threats. As you see in this chapter, all it takes is a healthy dose of paranoia and a few techniques for battening down the hatches on the Windows Home Server and on your network clients.

Enabling Security Auditing on Windows Home Server

A big part of keeping any computer secure involves examining what users do with the computer. For Windows Home Server, this means tracking events such as logon failures (repeated failures might indicate a malicious user trying different passwords) and account changes (in which someone changes some aspect of a user account). This type of tracking is called *auditing*.

> **NOTE**
>
> Since Windows Home Server 2011 is built upon Windows Server 2008 R2, you see the same auditing policies as you would if you were working with a pure Windows Server 2008 R2 system. However, there are many Windows Server 2008 R2 auditing policies that don't apply to Windows Home Server; for example, it's useless to audit accesses to Active Directory (AD) objects because Windows Home Server doesn't support AD.

In the next section, I show you how to enable the security auditing policies in Windows Home Server, and then I explain how to track auditing events.

Activating the Auditing Policies

To enable Windows Home Server's security auditing policies, follow these steps:

1. Log on to Windows Home Server.
2. Select Start, Administrative Tools, Local Security Policy. The Local Security Policy window appears.

> **TIP**
>
> You can also open the Local Security Settings window by selecting Start, typing **secpol.msc**, and pressing Enter.

3. Open the Local Policies branch, and click Audit Policy. Windows Home Server displays the audit policies, as shown in Figure 11.1.

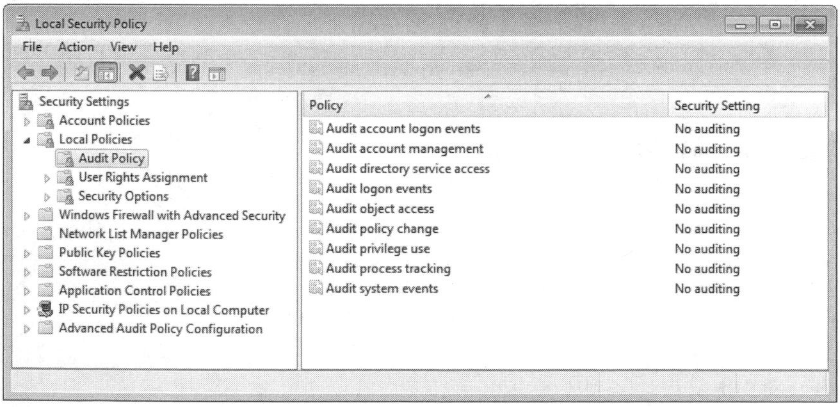

FIGURE 11.1   Windows Home Server's audit policies.

4. Double-click the policy you want to work with.
5. If you want to know when someone uses the policy event successfully, activate the Success check box.

6. If you want to know when someone uses the policy event unsuccessfully, activate the Failure check box.

7. Click OK.

8. Repeat steps 4–7 for the other events you want to audit.

Understanding the Auditing Policies

To help you decide which auditing policies to use, the next few sections give you a bit of detail about some of them. Note that several of these policies require AD to return meaningful or useful results. This means they don't apply to Windows Home Server, so I don't discuss them here.

Audit Account Logon Events

The Audit Account Logon Events policy enables you to track when users log on to their account on the Windows Home Server computer. If you track failures for this policy, the resulting Failure Audit event returns an Error Code value, as shown in Figure 11.2. (To learn how to view these events, see "Tracking Auditing Events," later in this chapter.) Table 11.1 tells you what the various error codes mean.

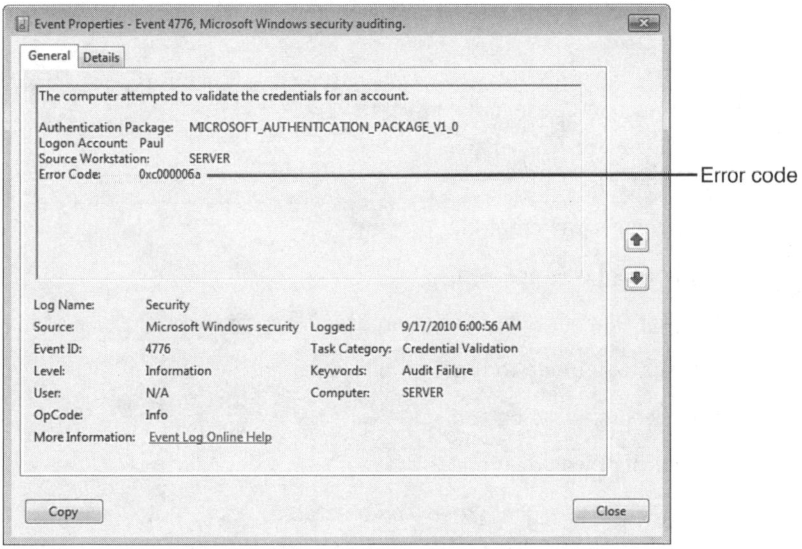

FIGURE 11.2   An example of a failed Account Logon event.

TABLE 11.1   Error Codes Returned for Account Logon Failure Events

Error Code	Description
0xC0000064	The user tried to log on with a misspelled or invalid username.
0xC000006A	The user tried to log on with a misspelled or invalid password.
0xC000006D	The user tried to log on with an unknown username or bad password.

TABLE 11.1   Error Codes Returned for Account Logon Failure Events

Error Code	Description
0xC000006F	The user tried to log on outside the account's authorized hours.
0xC0000070	The user tried to log on from an unauthorized computer.
0xC0000071	The user tried to log on with an expired password.
0xC0000072	The user's account is disabled.
0xC0000193	The user's account is expired.
0xC0000224	The user was supposed to change his password at the next logon, but he didn't.
0xC0000234	The user's account is locked.

Audit Account Management

The Audit Account Management policy enables you to track events related to managing groups and user accounts on Windows Home Server. Events include creating new groups or users, modifying or deleting groups or users, changing user passwords, or renaming or disabling users. Table 11.2 lists the possible event IDs for the Audit Account Management category.

TABLE 11.2   Event ID Values for Account Management Events

Account Management Event ID	Description
4720	A user account was created.
4722	A user account was enabled.
4723	An attempt was made to change an account's password.
4724	An attempt was made to reset an account's password.
4725	A user account was disabled.
4726	A user account was deleted.
4727	A security-enabled global group was created.
4728	A member was added to a security-enabled global group.
4729	A member was removed from a security-enabled global group.
4730	A security-enabled global group was deleted.
4731	A security-enabled local group was created.
4732	A member was added to a security-enabled local group.
4733	A member was removed from a security-enabled local group.
4734	A security-enabled local group was deleted.

TABLE 11.2   Event ID Values for Account Management Events

Account Management Event ID	Description
4735	A security-enabled local group was changed.
4737	A security-enabled global group was changed.
4738	A user account was changed.
4739	Domain Policy was changed.
4740	A user account was locked out.
4741	A computer account was created.
4742	A computer account was changed.
4743	A computer account was deleted.
4754	A security-enabled universal group was created.
4755	A security-enabled universal group was changed.
4756	A member was added to a security-enabled universal group.
4757	A member was removed from a security-enabled universal group.
4758	A security-enabled universal group was deleted.
4765	SID History was added to an account.
4766	An attempt to add the Security ID (SID) History to an account failed.
4767	A user account was unlocked.
4780	The Access Control List (ACL) was set on accounts that are members of administrators groups.
4781	The name of an account was changed.
4782	The password hash for an account was accessed.

Figure 11.3 shows a sample event that occurred when a user's account was disabled (event ID 4725).

Audit Logon Events

The Audit Logon Events policy enables you to track when users log on to the Windows Home Server network. These events always occur in conjunction with Account Logon events. That is, first Windows Home Server processes the logon to the user's account on the server; then it processes the logon to the network. Table 11.3 lists the possible event IDs for the Audit Logon Events category.

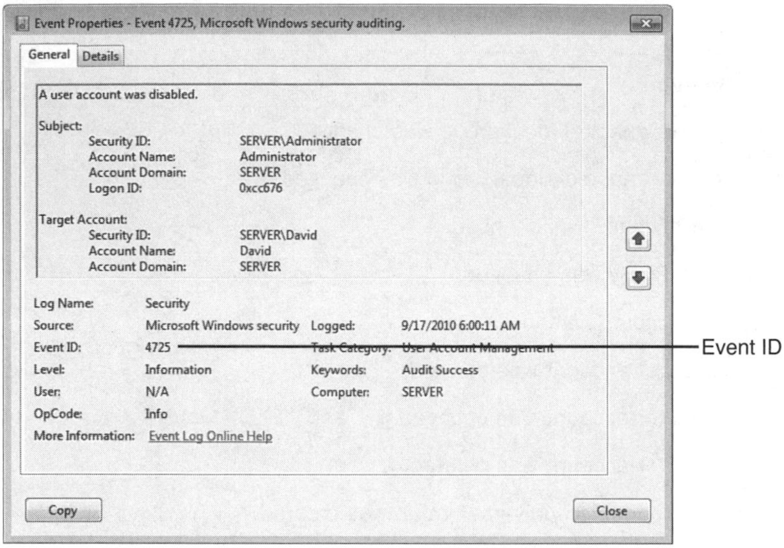

FIGURE 11.3   An example of an Account Management event.

TABLE 11.3   Event ID Values for Logon Events

Logon Event ID	Description
4624	An account was successfully logged on.
4625	An account failed to log on.
4634	An account was logged off.
4647	A user initiated logoff.
4648	A logon was attempted using explicit credentials.
4649	A replay attack was detected.
4675	SIDs were filtered.
4778	A session was reconnected to a window station.
4779	A session was disconnected from a window station.
4800	The workstation was locked.
4801	The workstation was unlocked.
4802	The screensaver was invoked.
4803	The screensaver was dismissed.
5378	The requested credentials delegation was disallowed by policy.
5632	A request was made to authenticate to a wireless network.
5633	A request was made to authenticate to a wired network.

If you're auditing failures for this category, each Failure Audit event tells you the reason for the failure, as shown in Figure 11.4.

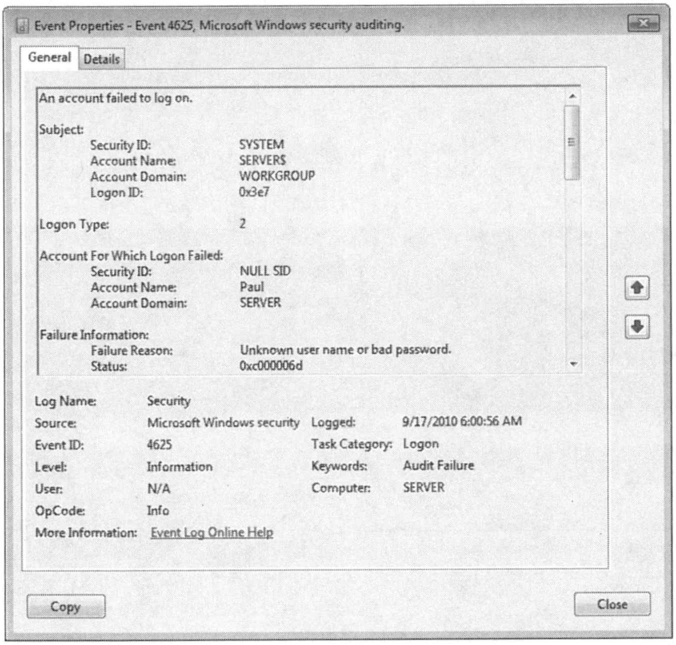

FIGURE 11.4   An example of a failed Logon event.

Audit Policy Change

The Audit Policy Change policy enables you to track when users make changes to group policies. The resulting event shows you what policy was changed and what the new policy setting is. For example, Figure 11.5 shows an event generated by modifying the auditing policies.

Audit Process Tracking

The Audit Process Tracking policy enables you to track the starting and stopping of processes, including programs. For example, you might want to track when scripts run on the server. Most scripts are handled by wscript.exe, so the program runs each time a script is launched. Figure 11.6 shows an example event created when a script starts.

Audit System Events

The Audit System Events policy enables you to track system events such as shutdown and startup, security changes, and system time changes. Figure 11.7 shows an example event, and Table 11.4 lists the possible event IDs.

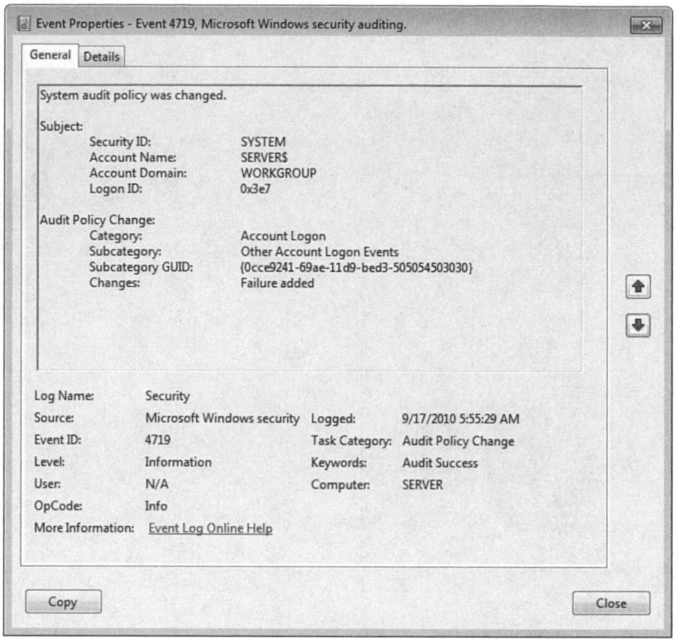

FIGURE 11.5 An example of a Policy Change event.

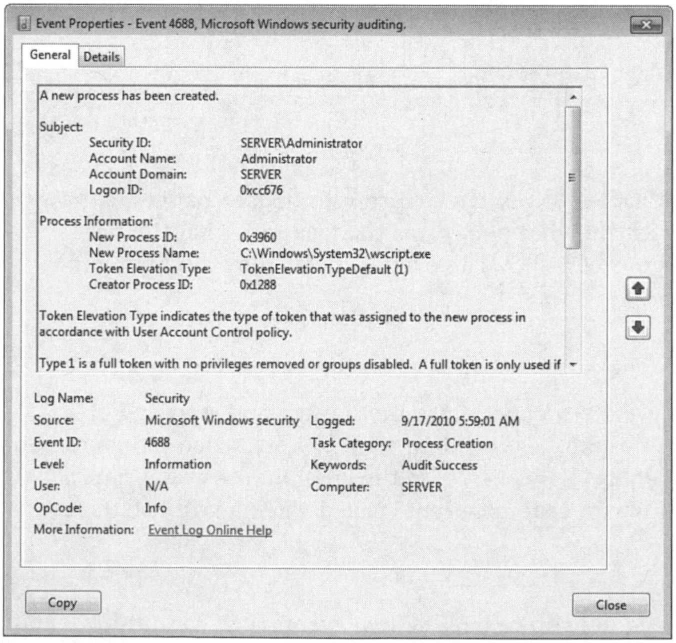

FIGURE 11.6 An example of an Audit Process Tracking event.

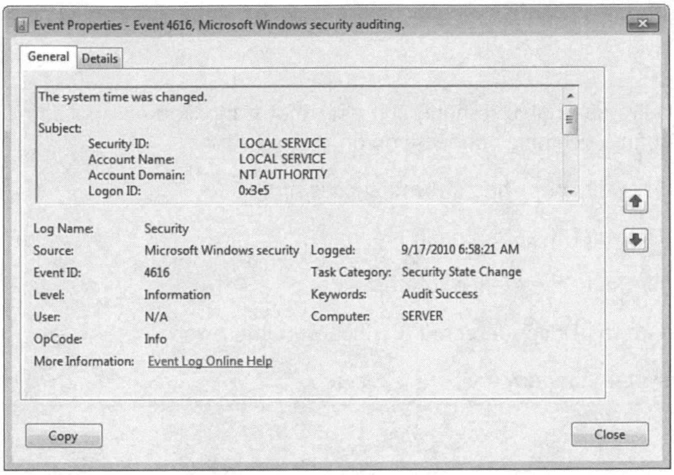

FIGURE 11.7   An example of a System event.

TABLE 11.4   Event ID Values for System Events

System Event ID	Description
4608	Windows is starting up.
4609	Windows is shutting down.
4616	The system time was changed.
4618	A monitored security event pattern has occurred.
4621	The administrator recovered the system from CrashOnAuditFail. Users who are not administrators will now be allowed to log on. Some auditable activity might not have been recorded.
4697	A service was installed in the system.
5024	The Windows Firewall Service has started successfully.
5025	The Windows Firewall Service has been stopped.
5027	The Windows Firewall Service was unable to retrieve the security policy from the local storage. The service will continue enforcing the current policy.
5028	The Windows Firewall Service was unable to parse the new security policy. The service will continue with currently enforced policy.
5029	The Windows Firewall Service failed to initialize the driver. The service will continue to enforce the current policy.
5030	The Windows Firewall Service failed to start.

TABLE 11.4   Event ID Values for System Events

System Event ID	Description
5032	Windows Firewall was unable to notify the user that it blocked an application from accepting incoming connections on the network.
5033	The Windows Firewall Driver has started successfully.
5034	The Windows Firewall Driver has been stopped.
5035	The Windows Firewall Driver failed to start.
5037	The Windows Firewall Driver detected a critical runtime error.
6008	The previous system shutdown was unexpected.

Tracking Auditing Events

After you've enabled the security auditing policies that you want Windows Home Server to monitor, you can start tracking them to look for suspicious behavior. You do this using Windows Home Server's Event Viewer. Unfortunately, the Security event log (which is where the auditing events appear) likely has tens of thousands of items. How do you look for suspicious behavior in such a large database?

Viewing Auditing Events with a Filter

The trick is to filter the log to show just the events you want. Here are the steps to follow:

1. Log on to Windows Home Server.

2. Select Start, Administrative Tools, Event Viewer. Windows Home Server opens the Event Viewer.

3. Open the Windows Logs, Security branch.

4. In the Actions pane, click Filter Current Log. Windows Home Server opens the Filter Current Log dialog box with the Filter tab displayed.

5. In the Logged list, select the time frame you want to use, such as Last 24 Hours.

6. In the Includes/Excludes Event IDs text box, type the event ID you want to find, if any. You can also enter a range (such as 4720–4782), or you can exclude an ID by preceding it with a minus sign.

7. In the Keywords list, activate the check boxes for just the events you want to see (such as Audit Failure). Figure 11.8 shows a sample filter.

8. Click OK. Event Viewer filters the Security log using your criteria. Figure 11.9 shows an example.

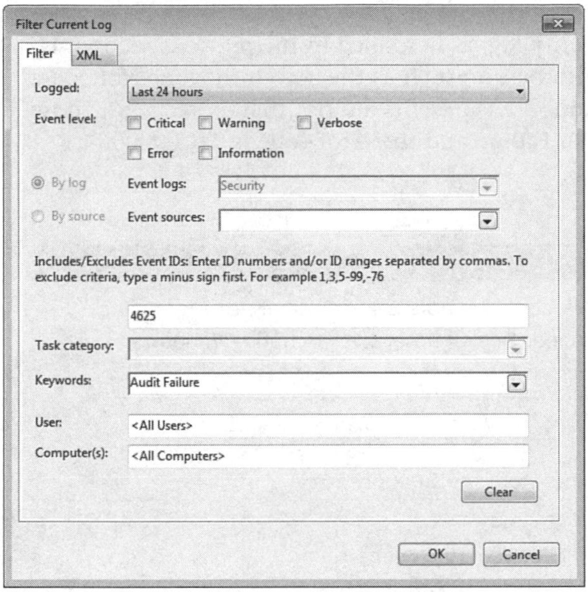

FIGURE 11.8   Use the Filter tab to specify exactly the events you want to see.

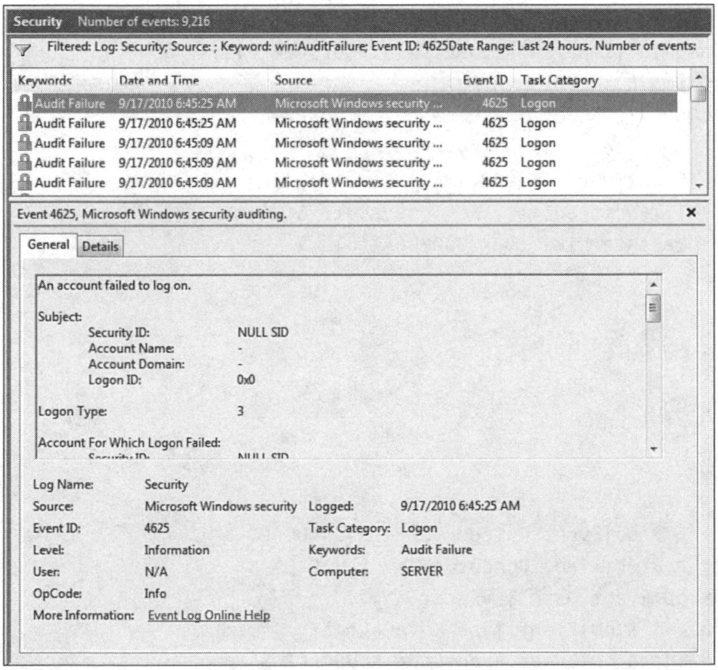

FIGURE 11.9   The results of the filter specifying Audit Failure shown in Figure 11.8.

Viewing Auditing Events with a Script

The only problem with filtering the Security log, as described in the previous section, is that you can't filter based on detailed information such as the account logon error code. To do that, you need to use a script. Listing 11.1 presents a script that extracts just those Security events in which the type is Audit Failure and the error code is 0xC000006A (which represents an incorrect password).

> **NOTE**
>
> You can find the VBS files containing this book's scripts on my website at www.mcfedries.com/HomeServer2011Unleashed. See Chapter 21, "Scripting Windows Home Server," to learn how to run scripts on the server.

LISTING 11.1   A Script That Extracts Events from the Security Log

```
'
' Use WMI to extract events from the Security log where:
'  - The type is "Audit Failure" (5)
'  - The date is today
'  - The error code points to an incorrect password (0xC000006A)
'
compName = "localhost"
Set objWMI = GetObject("winmgmts:{impersonationLevel=impersonate}!//" & _
                    compName & "\root\cimv2")
Set colSecLog = objWMI.ExecQuery("SELECT * FROM Win32_NTLogEvent Where " & _
                    "LogFile = 'Security' And " & _
                    "EventType = 5 And " & _
                    "TimeWritten > '" &  TodaysDate & "' And " & _
                    "Message Like '%0xC000006A%'")
'
' Run through the returned events
'
i = 0
For Each objEvent in colSecLog
    '
    ' Display the event data
    '
    WScript.Echo "Category: " & objEvent.CategoryString & VBCrLf & _
                "Computer: " & objEvent.ComputerName & VBCrLf & _
                "User: " & objEvent.User & VBCrLf & _
                "Event Type: " & objEvent.Type & VBCrLf & _
                "Event Code: " & objEvent.EventCode & VBCrLf & _
                "Source Name: " & objEvent.SourceName & VBCrLf & _
                "Time Written: " & ReturnLogDate(objEvent.TimeWritten) & _
                VBCrLf & VBCrLf & _
```

```
                     "Message: " & VBCrLf & VBCrLf & objEvent.Message
        i = i + 1
Next
'
' Check for no events
'
If i = 0 Then
        WScript.Echo "No events found!"
End If
'
' Release objects
'
Set wmi = Nothing
Set secLog = Nothing
'
' This function creates a datatime string based on today's date
`
Function TodaysDate()
        strYear = Year(Now)
        If Month(Now) < 10 Then
                strMonth = "0" & Month(Now)
        Else
                strMonth = Month(Now)
        End If
        If Day(Now) < 10 Then
                strDay = "0" & Day(Now)
        Else
                strDay = Day(Now)
        End If
        TodaysDate = strYear & strMonth & strDay & "000000.000000-000"
End Function
'
' This function takes the event datetime value and converts
' it to a friendlier date and time format
'
Function ReturnLogDate(logTime)
        eventYear = Left(logTime, 4)
        eventMonth = Mid(logTime, 5, 2)
        eventDay = Mid(logTime, 7, 2)
        eventHour = Mid(logTime, 9, 2)
        eventMinute = Mid(logTime, 11, 2)
        eventSecond = Mid(logTime, 13, 2)
        ReturnLogDate = DateSerial(eventYear, eventMonth, eventDay) & " " & _
                        TimeSerial(eventHour, eventMinute, eventSecond)
End Function
```

The script uses WMI to query the `W32_NTLogEvent` database, which consists of all the events on the system. The query extracts just those events in which the following is true:

- The `LogFile` property equals `Security`.

- The `EventType` property equals 5, which represents Audit Failure events.

- The `TimeWritten` property contains only today's date. The values in the `TimeWritten` property use the `datetime` data type, which uses the general format `yyyymmddhhmmss.000000-000`. So, the script uses the `TodaysDate` function to return a `datetime` value that corresponds to midnight today. The query actually looks for events that were written to the log after that time.

- The `Message` property (which holds the error code, among other data) contains the error code `0xC000006A`.

Then a `For Each...Next` loop runs through all the returned events. For each event, various event properties are displayed in a dialog box, as shown in Figure 11.10. The code calls the `ReturnLogDate` function to convert the `TimeWritten` property's `datetime` value into a more readable format.

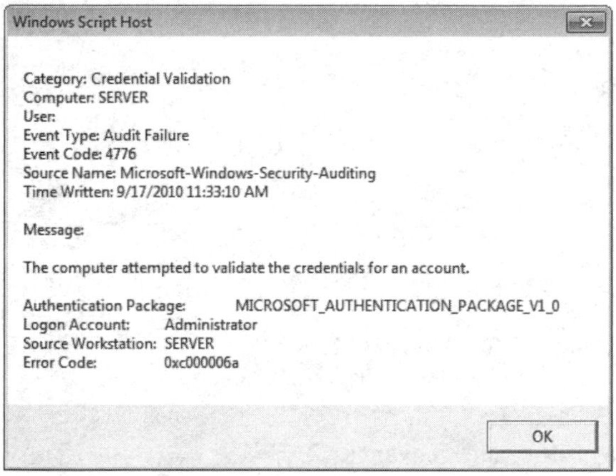

FIGURE 11.10   An example of the event data displayed by the script in Listing 11.1.

More Ways to Secure Windows Home Server

Enabling security auditing is a good start for securing Windows Home Server. However, you can take a number of other security measures, such as renaming the Administrator account, hiding the most recent username, checking the firewall status, and disabling Windows Home Server's hidden administrative shares. The next few sections take you through these and other Windows Home Server security measures.

Renaming the Administrator Account

By default, Windows Home Server sets up one member of the Administrators group: the Administrator account. This account is all-powerful on Windows Home Server (and, by extension, on your home network), so the last thing you want is for some malicious user to gain control of the system with Administrator access. Unfortunately, black-hat hackers have one foot in your digital door already because they know the default account name is Administrator; now all they have to do is guess your password. If you've protected the Administrator account with a strong password, you almost certainly have no worries.

However, you can close the door completely on malicious intruders by taking away the one piece of information they know: the name of the account. By changing the account name from Administrator to something obscure, you add an extra layer of security to Windows Home Server.

Here are the steps to follow to change the name of the Administrator account:

1. Log on to Windows Home Server.
2. Select Start, right-click Computer, and then click Manage. The Computer Management snap-in appears.
3. Open the System Tools, Local Users and Groups, Users branch.

> **TIP**
>
> You can open the Local Users and Groups snap-in directly by selecting Start, typing `lusrmgr.msc`, and then pressing Enter.

4. Right-click the Administrator account, and then click Rename.
5. Type the new account name, and then press Enter.

> **NOTE**
>
> The Guest account also has an obvious and well-known name, so if you've enabled the Guest account, be sure to rename it as well.

Hiding the Username in the Log On Dialog Box

When you log on locally to Windows Home Server, the Log On to Windows dialog box always shows the name of the most recent user who logged on successfully. It's unlikely that a malicious user would gain physical access to the server in your home, but it's not impossible. Therefore, renaming the Administrator account as described in the previous section is useless because Windows Home Server just displays the new name to anyone who wants to see it.

Fortunately, you can plug this security breach by following these steps:

1. Log on to Windows Home Server.

2. Select Start, Administrative Tools, Local Security Policy. The Local Security Setting snap-in appears.

TIP

You can also open the Local Security Setting snap-in by selecting Start, typing `secpol.msc`, and then pressing Enter.

3. Open the Security Settings, Local Policies, Security Options branch.

4. Double-click the Interactive Logon: Do Not Display Last User Name policy.

5. Click the Enabled option.

6. Click OK.

Making Sure Windows Firewall Is Turned On

Your Windows Home Server network probably connects to the Internet using a *broadband*—cable modem or DSL—service. This means that you have an always-on connection, so there's a much greater chance that a malicious hacker could find your computer and have his way with it. You might think that with millions of people connected to the Internet at any given moment, there would be little chance of a "script kiddy" finding you in the herd. Unfortunately, one of the most common weapons in a black-hat hacker's arsenal is a program that runs through millions of IP addresses automatically, looking for live connections. The fact that many cable systems and some DSL systems use IP addresses in a narrow range compounds the problem by making it easier to find always-on connections.

When a cracker finds your address, he has many avenues from which to access your computer. Specifically, your connection uses many different ports for sending and receiving data. For example, File Transfer Protocol (FTP) uses ports 20 and 21, web data and commands typically use port 80, email uses ports 25 and 110, the domain name system (DNS) uses port 53, remote connections to the network use ports 443 and 4125, and so on. In all, there are dozens of these ports, and every one is an opening through which a clever cracker can gain access to your computer.

As if that weren't enough, attackers can check your system for the installation of some kind of Trojan horse or virus. (Malicious email attachments sometimes install these programs on your machine.) If the nefarious hacker finds one, he can effectively take control of your machine (turning it into a *zombie computer*) and either wreak havoc on its contents or use your computer to attack other systems.

Again, if you think your computer is too obscure or worthless for someone else to bother with, think again. Hackers with malicious intent probe a typical computer connected to the Internet for vulnerable ports or installed Trojan horses at least a few times every day. If you want to see just how vulnerable your computer is, several good sites on the Web can test your security:

▶ **Gibson Research (Shields Up)**—www.grc.com/default.htm

▶ **DSL Reports**—www.dslreports.com/secureme_go

▶ **HackerWhacker**—www.hackerwhacker.com

The good news is that Windows Home Server comes with Windows Firewall. This program is a personal firewall that can lock down your ports and prevent unauthorized access to your machine. In effect, your computer becomes *invisible* to the Internet (although you can still surf the Web and work with email normally).

Windows Firewall is activated by default in Windows Home Server. However, it pays to be safe, so here are the steps to follow to ensure that it's turned on:

1. Log on to Windows Home Server.
2. Select Start, Control Panel, Windows Firewall. Windows Home Server displays the Windows Firewall dialog box.
3. Click Turn Windows Firewall On or Off.
4. In the Home or Work (Private) Network Location Settings group, make sure the Turn On Windows Firewall option is activated, as shown in Figure 11.11.
5. Click OK.

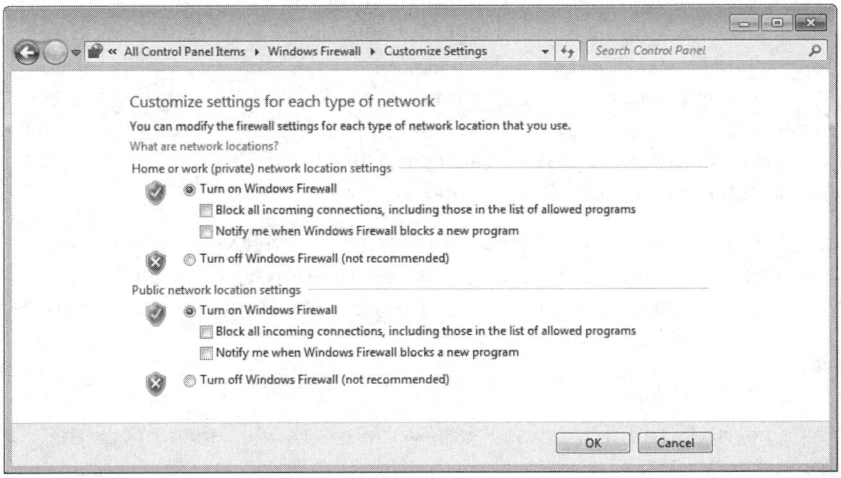

FIGURE 11.11   To ensure safe computing, make sure Windows Firewall is turned on.

CAUTION

Activating Windows Firewall on Windows Home Server only protects the server; it doesn't do anything for the security of your client computers. Therefore, it's a good idea to check your Windows 7, Vista, and XP machines to ensure that Windows Firewall is activated on each. (Note, however, that Windows Home Server lets you know if any Windows 7 or Vista machine has its firewall turned off.)

Disabling the Hidden Administrative Shares

By default, Windows Home Server sets up automatic administrative shares for the root folders of the C: and D: drives, as well as `C:\Windows`. These shares have a dollar sign ($) at the end of their names (`C$`, `D$`, and `ADMIN$`), so they're hidden from the list of shares you see when you access `\\SERVER`. To see them, select Start, Command Prompt to open a command prompt session, type **net share**, and press Enter. You'll see a listing similar to this:

```
Share name    Resource                    Remark

-------------------------------------------------------------
ADMIN$        C:\Windows                  Remote Admin
C$            C:\                         Default share
D$            D:\                         Default share
IPC$                                      Remote IPC
E$            E:\                         Default share
F$            F:\                         Default share
G$            G:\                         Default share
Documents     E:\ServerFolders\Documents  Documents
Music         E:\ServerFolders\Music      Music
Pictures      E:\ServerFolders\Pictures   Pictures
Recorded TV   E:\ServerFolders\Recorded TV  Recorded TV
Videos        E:\ServerFolders\Videos     Videos
```

Although the `C$` and `ADMIN$` shares are otherwise hidden, they're well known, and they represent a small security risk should an intruder get access to your system. To close this hole, you can force Windows Home Server to disable these shares. Here are the steps to follow:

1. Log on to Windows Home Server.
2. Select Start, type **regedit**, and then press Enter. Windows Home Server opens the Registry Editor.
3. Navigate to the following key:

    `HKLM\SYSTEM\CurrentControlSet\Services\lanmanserver\parameters`

4. Select Edit, New, DWORD (32-bit) Value.

5. Type **AutoShareServer**, and press Enter. (You can leave this setting with its default value of 0.)

6. Restart Windows Home Server to put the new setting into effect.

Once again, select Start, Command Prompt to open a command prompt session, type **net share**, and press Enter. The output now looks like this:

```
Share name  Resource                        Remark

-----------------------------------------------------------------
IPC$                                        Remote IPC
Documents   E:\ServerFolders\Documents      Documents
Music       E:\ServerFolders\Music          Music
Pictures    E:\ServerFolders\Pictures       Pictures
Recorded TV E:\ServerFolders\Recorded TV    Recorded TV
Videos      E:\ServerFolders\Videos         Videos
```

> **CAUTION**
>
> Some programs expect the administrative shares to be present, so disabling those shares may cause those programs to fail or generate error messages. If that happens, enable the shares by opening the Registry Editor and either deleting the AutoShareServer setting or changing its value to 1.

Securing Network Computers

Implementing security across a network is a "weakest link" proposition. That is, your network as a whole is only as secure as the most vulnerable of the clients. So although you may now have Windows Home Server locked down, you still have to get your security up to snuff on each computer. This section takes you through a few features and techniques that enhance the security of the rest of your network.

Monitoring Home Computer Security

I mentioned in Chapter 10, "Monitoring Your Network," that Windows Home Server displays various network health notifications via the Windows Home Server Status icon, which appears in the notification area. If you have a Windows 7 or Vista PC, the Windows Home Server Status icon can check the current Security Center settings for the computer's firewall, automatic updating, and antispyware and antivirus programs. If any of these is turned off or, in the case of antispyware and antivirus programs, out of date, the Windows Home Server Status icon displays a notification. Table 11.5 shows the four security-related notifications that you might see.

TABLE 11.5   Security-Related Network Health Notifications Displayed by the Windows Home Server Status Icon

Notification	Description
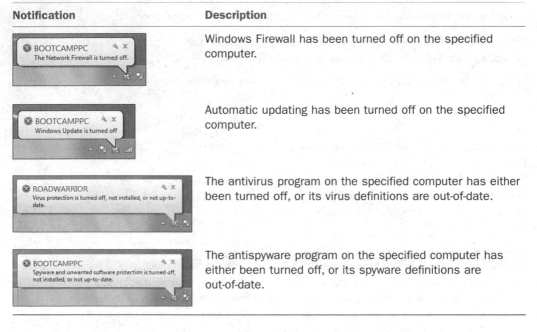	Windows Firewall has been turned off on the specified computer.
	Automatic updating has been turned off on the specified computer.
	The antivirus program on the specified computer has either been turned off, or its virus definitions are out-of-date.
	The antispyware program on the specified computer has either been turned off, or its spyware definitions are out-of-date.

▶ **SEE** "Monitoring Network Health Alerts," **P. 240**.

Thwarting Spyware with Windows Defender

Malware is the generic term for malicious software such as viruses and Trojan horses. The worst malware offender by far these days is *spyware*. It's generally defined as any program that surreptitiously monitors a user's computer activities—particularly the typing of passwords, PINs, and credit card numbers—or harvests sensitive data on the user's computer and then sends that information to an individual or a company via the user's Internet connection (the so-called *back channel*) without the user's consent.

You might think that having a robust firewall between you and the bad guys would make malware a problem of the past. Unfortunately, that's not true. These programs piggyback on other legitimate programs that users actually *want* to download, such as file-sharing programs, download managers, and screensavers. A *drive-by download* is the download and installation of a program without a user's knowledge or consent. This relates closely to a *pop-up download*—the download and installation of a program after the user clicks an option in a pop-up browser window, particularly when the option's intent is vaguely or misleadingly worded.

To make matters even worse, most spyware embeds itself deep into a system, and removing it is a delicate and time-consuming operation beyond the abilities of even some experienced users. Some programs actually come with an Uninstall option, but it's nothing but a ruse, of course. The program appears to remove itself from the system, but what it actually does is a *covert reinstall*—it surreptitiously reinstalls a fresh version of itself when the computer is idle.

All this means that you need to buttress your firewall with an antispyware program that can watch out for these unwanted programs and prevent them from getting their hooks into your system. In early versions of Windows, you needed to install a third-party program. However, Windows 7 and Vista come with an antispyware program named Windows Defender.

> **TIP**
>
> Many security experts recommend installing multiple antispyware programs on the premise that one program may miss one or two examples of spyware, but two or three programs are highly unlikely to miss any. So, in addition to Windows Defender, you might consider installing antispyware programs such as SuperAntiSpyware (www.super-antispyware.com), Lavasoft Ad-Aware (www.lavasoft.com), and PC Tools Spyware Doctor (www.pctools.com).

To open Windows Defender, select Start, type **defender**, and then click Windows Defender in the search results. You end up at the Windows Defender Home screen, shown in Figure 11.12. This window shows you the date, time, and results of your last scan, as well as the current Windows Defender status.

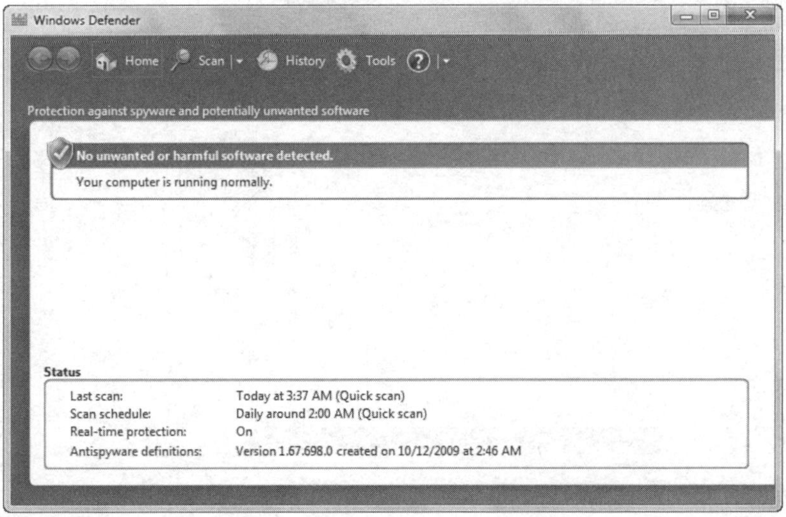

FIGURE 11.12 Windows Defender removes spyware from your system and keeps your system safe by preventing spyware installations.

Spyware Scanning

Windows Defender protects your computer from spyware in two ways. It can scan your system for evidence of installed spyware programs (and remove or disable those programs, if necessary), and it can monitor your system in real time to watch for activities that indicate the presence of spyware (such as a drive-by download or data being sent via a back channel).

For the scanning portion of its defenses, Windows Defender supports three different scan types:

▶ **Quick Scan**—This scan checks just those areas of your system where it is likely to find evidence of spyware. This scan usually takes just a couple of minutes. Quick Scan is the default, and you can initiate one at any time by clicking the Scan link.

▶ **Full Scan**—This scan checks for evidence of spyware in system memory, all running processes, and the system drive (usually drive C:), and it performs a deep scan on all folders. This scan might take 30 minutes or more, depending on your system. To run this scan, pull down the Scan menu and click Full Scan.

▶ **Custom Scan**—This scan checks just the drives and folders that you select. The length of the scan depends on the number of locations you select and the number of objects in those locations. To run this scan, pull down the Scan menu and click Custom Scan, which displays the Select Scan Options page shown in Figure 11.13. Click Select, activate the check boxes for the drives you want scanned, and then click OK. Click Scan Now to start the scan.

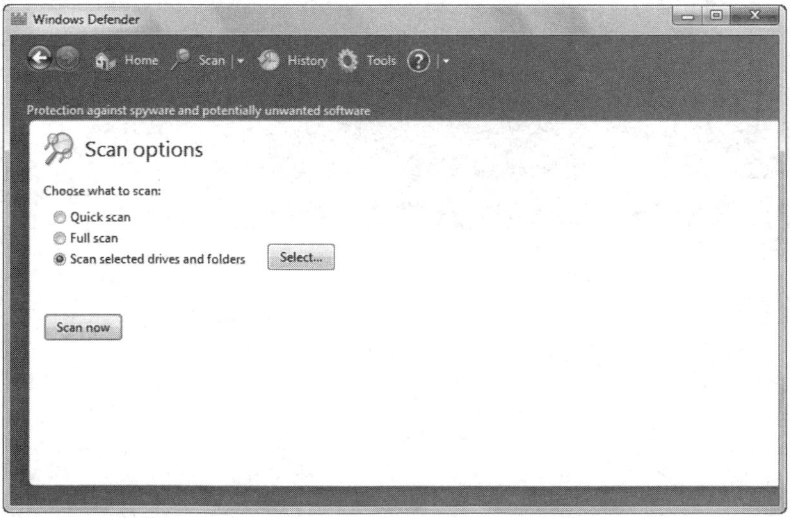

FIGURE 11.13   In the Scan menu, select Custom Scan to see the Scan Options page.

Windows Defender Settings

By default, Windows Defender is set up to perform a Quick Scan of your system every morning at 2:00 a.m. To change this, click Tools, and then click Options to display the Options page shown in Figure 11.14. Use the controls in the Automatic Scanning section to specify the scan frequency time and type.

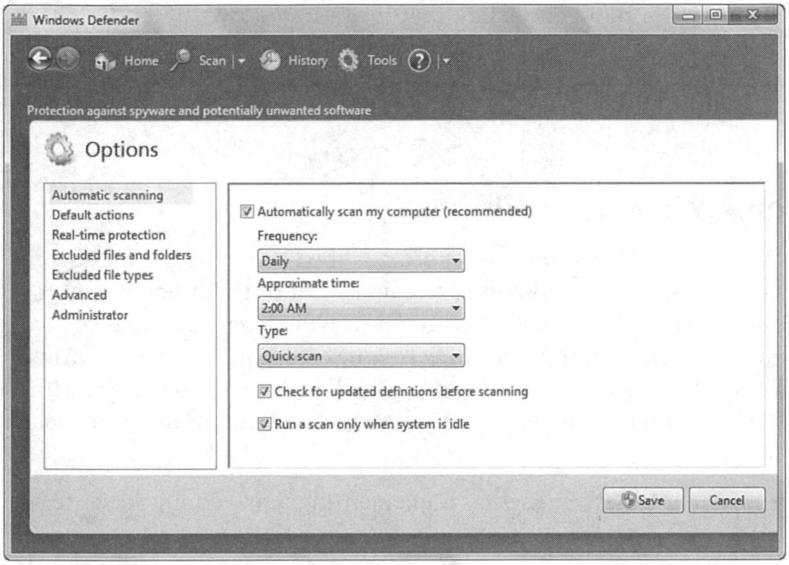

FIGURE 11.14   Use the Options page to set up a spyware scan schedule.

The rest of the Options page offers options for customizing Windows Defender. The remaining options include the following:

▶ **Default Actions**—Set the action that Windows Defender should take if it finds alert items (potential spyware) in the High, Medium, and Low categories: Default Action (the action prescribed in the definition file for the detected spyware), Ignore, or Remove.

▶ **Real-Time Protection**—Enables and disables real-time protection. You can also toggle security agents on and off. *Security agents* monitor Windows components that are frequent targets of spyware activity. For example, activating the Auto Start security agent tells Windows Defender to monitor the list of startup programs to ensure that spyware doesn't add itself to this list and run automatically at startup.

TIP

Windows Defender often warns you that a program might be spyware and asks whether you want to allow the program to operate normally or to block it. If you accidentally allow an unsafe program, click Tools, Allowed Items; select the program in the Allowed Items list; and then click Remove from List. Similarly, if you accidentally blocked a safe program, click Tools, Quarantined Items; select the program in the Quarantined Items list; and then click Remove.

▶ **Advanced**—Use these options to enable scanning inside compressed archives. In Windows 7, you can also elect to scan email and removable drives; in Windows Vista, you can prevent Windows Defender from scanning specific folders.

▶ **Administrator**—This section has a check box that toggles Windows Defender on and off. In Windows 7, you can activate a check box that lets you see other users' Windows Defender items; in Windows Vista, you see a check box that, when activated, allows all non-Administrators to use Windows Defender.

Protecting Yourself Against Email Viruses

By far the most productive method for viruses to replicate is the humble email message. The list of email viruses and Trojan horses is a long one, but most of them operate more or less the same way: They arrive as a message attachment, usually from someone you know. When you open the attachment, the virus infects your computer and then, without your knowledge, uses your email client and your address book to ship out messages with more copies of itself attached. The nastier versions also mess with your computer by deleting data or corrupting files.

You can avoid infection by one of these viruses by implementing a few common sense procedures:

▶ Never open an attachment that comes from someone you don't know.

▶ Even if you know the sender, if the attachment isn't something you're expecting, assume that the sender's system is infected. Write back and confirm that the sender emailed the message.

▶ Some viruses come packaged as scripts hidden within messages that use the Rich Text (HTML) format. This means that the virus can run just by your viewing the message! If a message looks suspicious, don't open it—just delete it. (Note that you'll need to turn off your email client's Preview pane before deleting the message. Otherwise, when you highlight the message, it appears in the Preview pane and sets off the virus. In Windows Mail, select View, Layout, deactivate the Show Preview Pane check box, and click OK. If you're using Windows Live Mail, select View, Layout, deactivate the Show the Reading Pane check box, and click OK.)

> **CAUTION**
>
> It's particularly important to turn off the Preview pane before displaying your email client's Junk E-Mail folder. Because many junk messages also carry a virus payload, your chances of initiating an infection are highest when working with messages in this folder.

▶ Install a top-of-the-line antivirus program, particularly one that checks incoming email. In addition, be sure to keep your antivirus program's virus list up-to-date. As you read this, there are probably dozens, maybe even hundreds, of morally challenged scumnerds designing even nastier viruses. Regular updates will help you keep up. Here are some security suites to check out:

Microsoft Security Essentials (http://www.microsoft.com/security_essentials/)

Norton Internet Security (www.symantec.com/index.jsp)

McAfee Internet Security Suite (http://mcafee.com/us)

AVG Internet Security (http://free.avg.com/)

In addition to these general procedures, Windows Mail comes with its own set of virus protection features. Here's how to use them:

1. In Windows Mail, select Tools, Options. (In Windows Live Mail, select Menus, Safety Options, or Tools, Safety Options if you have the menu bar displayed.)

2. Display the Security tab.

3. In the Virus Protection group, you have the following options:

Select the Internet Explorer Security Zone to Use—You use the security zones to determine whether to allow active content inside an HTML-format message to run:

   ▸ **Internet Zone**—If you choose this zone, active content is allowed to run.

   ▸ **Restricted Sites Zone**—If you choose this option, active content is disabled. This is the default setting and the one I recommend.

Warn Me When Other Applications Try to Send Mail as Me—As I mentioned earlier, it's possible for programs and scripts to send email messages without your knowledge. This happens by using Simple MAPI (*Messaging Application Programming Interface*) calls, which can send messages via your computer's default mail client— and it's all hidden from you. With this check box activated, Windows Mail displays a warning dialog box when a program or script attempts to send a message using Simple MAPI.

Do Not Allow Attachments to Be Saved or Opened That Could Potentially Be a Virus—With this check box activated, Windows Mail monitors attachments to look for file types that could contain viruses or destructive code. If it detects such a file, it disables your ability to open and save that file, and it displays a note at the top of the message to let you know about the unsafe attachment.

NOTE

Internet Explorer's built-in unsafe-file list defines the file types that Windows Mail disables. That list includes file types associated with the following extensions: `.ad`, `.ade`, `.adp`, `.bas`, `.bat`, `.chm`, `.cmd`, `.com`, `.cpl`, `.crt`, `.exe`, `.hlp`, `.hta`, `.inf`, `.ins`, `.isp`, `.js`, `.jse`, `.lnk`, `.mdb`, `.mde`, `.msc`, `.msi`, `.msp`, `.mst`, `.pcd`, `.pif`, `.reg`, `.scr`, `.sct`, `.shb`, `.shs`, `.url`, `.vb`, `.vbe`, `.vbs`, `.vsd`, `.vss`, `.vst`, `.vsw`, `.wsc`, `.wsf`, `.wsh`.

> **TIP**
>
> What do you do if you want to send a file that's on the Windows Mail unsafe file list and you want to make sure that the recipient will be able to open it? The easiest workaround is to compress the file into a `.zip` file—a file type not blocked by Windows Mail, Outlook, or any other mail client that blocks file types.

4. Click OK to put the new settings into effect.

Implementing Parental Controls

On your home network, there's a good chance that you have children who share your computer or who have their own computer. Either way, it's smart to take precautions regarding the content and programs they can access. Locally, this might take the form of blocking access to certain programs (such as your financial software), using ratings to control which games they can play, and setting time limits on when the computer is used. If the computer has Internet access, you might also want to allow (or block) specific sites, block certain types of content, and prevent file downloads.

All this sounds daunting, but the Parental Controls in Windows 7 and Windows Vista make things a bit easier by offering an easy-to-use interface that lets you set all the afore-mentioned options and lots more. (You get Parental Controls in the Home Basic, Home Premium, and Ultimate editions of Windows 7 and Vista.)

Creating Accounts for the Kids

Before you begin, be sure to create a standard user account for each child who uses the computer. Here are the steps to follow:

1. Select Start, Control Panel, Add or Remove User Accounts, and then enter your UAC credentials. Windows displays the Manage Accounts window.

2. Click Create a New Account. The Create New Account window appears.

3. Type the name for the account. The name can be up to 20 characters and must be unique on the system.

4. Make sure the Standard User option is activated.

5. Click Create Account. Windows returns you to the Manage Accounts window.

6. Repeat steps 2–5 to add standard user accounts for all your kids.

Activating Parental Controls and Activity Reporting

With the kids' accounts in place, you get to Parental Controls using either of the following methods:

▶ If you still have the Manage Accounts window open, click Set Up Parental Controls.

▶ Select Start, Control Panel, Set Up Parental Controls.

In Vista, enter your UAC credentials to get to the Parental Controls window, and then click the user you want to work with to get to the User Controls window.

You should activate two options here (see Figure 11.15, which shows the Windows Vista version of the Parental Controls window):

- **Parental Controls**—Click On, Enforce Current Settings. This enables the links in the Settings area.

- **Activity Reporting**(Windows Vista only)—Click On, Collect Information About Computer Usage. This tells Vista to track system events such as blocked logon attempts and attempted changes to user accounts, the system date and time, and system settings.

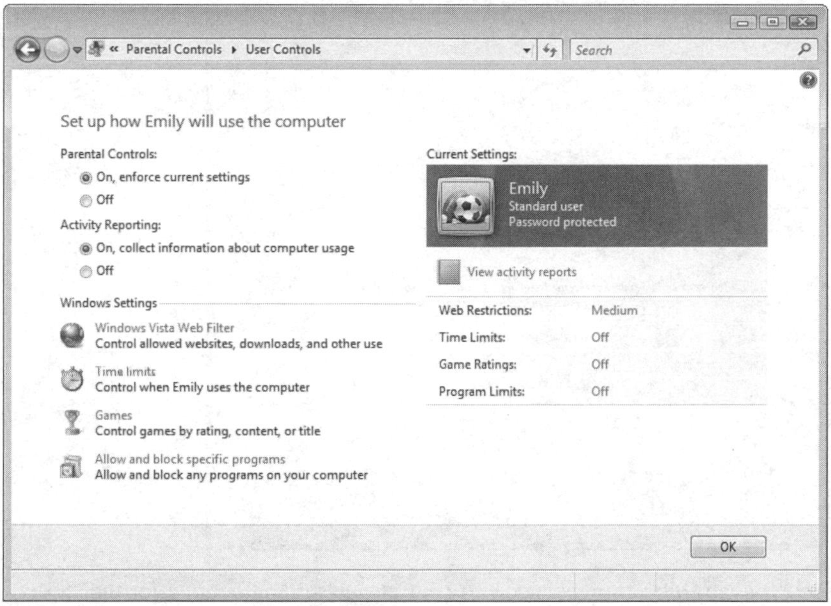

FIGURE 11.15   The User Controls window enables you to set up web, time, game, and program restrictions for the selected user.

The Windows Settings section has links that you use to set up the controls on the selected user. Two of these are security related—Windows Vista Web Filter (available only in Windows Vista) and Allow and Block Specific Programs—so I discuss them in the next two sections.

Controlling Web Use

In the Windows Vista version of the User Controls window, click Windows Vista Web Filter to display the Web Restrictions page, shown in Figure 11.16. Make sure the Block Some Websites or Content option is activated.

You can control websites, web content, and file downloads:

Allow and Block Specific Websites	Click the Edit the Allow and Block List to open the Allow Block Webpages window. For each safe site that the user can visit, type the website address and click Allow to add the site to the Allowed Websites list; for each unsafe site that the user can't visit, type the website address and click Block to add the site to the Blocked Websites list. Because there are so many possible sites to block, consider activating the Only Allow Websites Which Are on the Allow List check box.

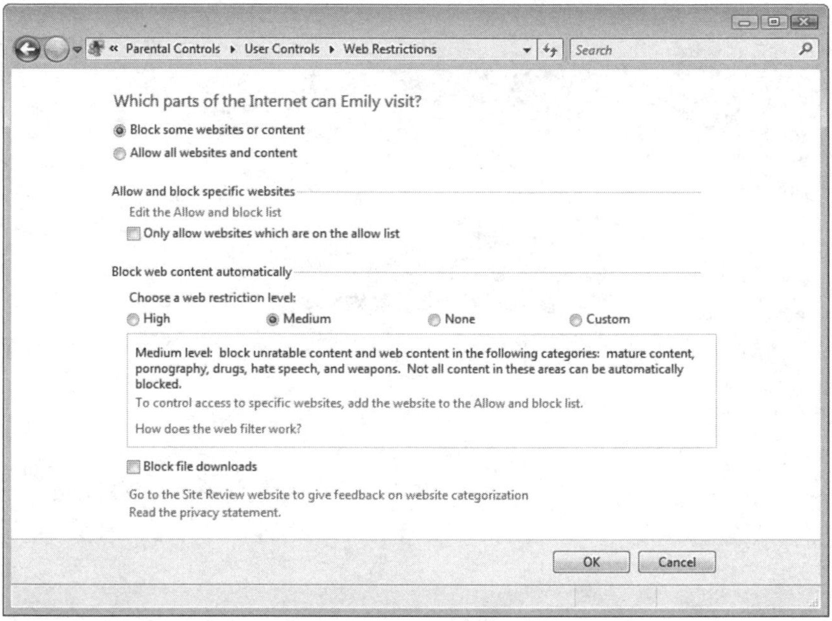

FIGURE 11.16   Use the Web Restrictions window to control web surfing actions for the selected user.

TIP

To make your life easier, you can import lists of allowed or blocked sites. First, create a new text file and change the extension to `Web Allow Block List` (for example, `MyURLs.Web Allow Block List`). Open the file and add the following text to start:

```
<WebAddresses>
</WebAddresses>
```

Between these lines, add a new line for each site using the following format:

```
<URL AllowBlock="n">address</URL>
```

Replace n with 1 for a site you want to allow, or 2 for a site you want to block, and replace address with the site URL. Here's an example:

```
<WebAddresses>
<URL AllowBlock="1">http://goodcleanfun.com</URL>
<URL AllowBlock="1">http://wholesomestuff.com</URL>
<URL AllowBlock="2">http://smut.com</URL>
<URL AllowBlock="2">http://depravity.com</URL>
</WebAddresses>
```

Block Web Content Automatically	Select the option you want to use to restrict site content: High, Medium, None, or Custom. If you select the Custom Web restriction level, Vista adds a number of check boxes that enable you to block specific content categories (such as Pornography, Mature Content, and Bomb Making).
Block File Downloads	Activate this check box to prevent the user from downloading files via the web browser.

Allowing and Blocking Programs

In the User Controls window, click Allow and Block Specific Programs to display the Application Restrictions page. Activate the *User* Can Only Use the Programs I Allow option. Windows 7 or Vista then populates the Check the Programs That Can Be Used list with the applications on your computer, as shown in Figure 11.17. Activate the check boxes for the programs you want to allow the person to use.

Avoiding Phishing Scams

Phishing refers to creating a replica of an existing web page to fool a user into submitting personal, financial, or password data. The term comes from the fact that Internet scammers are using increasingly sophisticated lures as they "fish" for users' financial information and password data. The most common ploy is to copy the web page code from a major site—such as AOL or eBay—and use it to set up a replica page that appears to be part of the company's site. (This is why another name for phishing is *spoofing*.) Phishers send out a fake email with a link to this page, which solicits the user's credit card data or password. When a recipient submits the form, it sends the data to the scammer and leaves the user on an actual page from the company's site so that he doesn't suspect a thing.

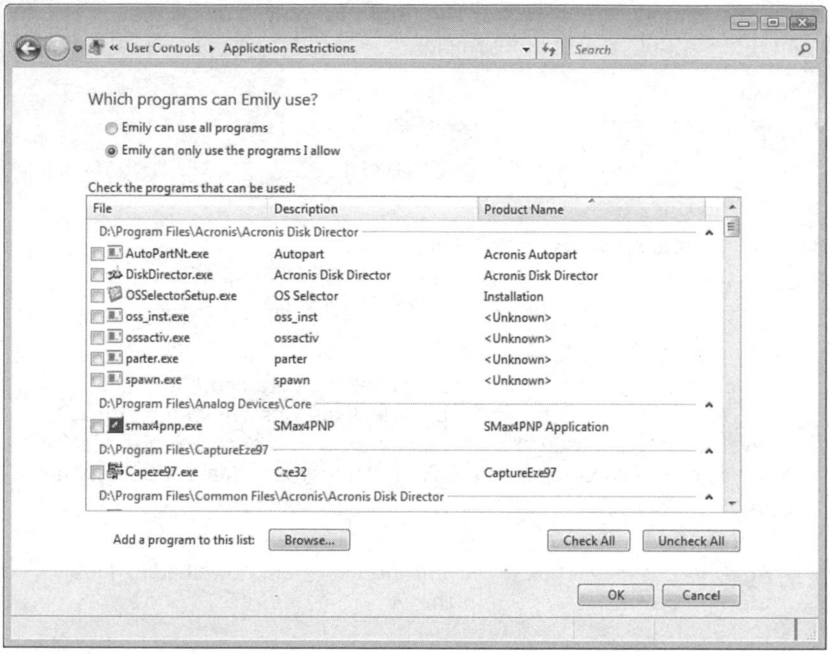

FIGURE 11.17   Use the Application Restrictions window to control the programs that the selected user can run.

A phishing page looks identical to a legitimate page from the company because the phisher has simply copied the underlying source code from the original page. However, no spoof page can be a perfect replica of the original. Here are five things to look for:

▶ **The URL in the address bar**—A legitimate page will have the correct domain—such as aol.com or ebay.com—whereas a spoofed page will have only something similar—such as aol.whatever.com or blah.com/ebay.

NOTE

The URL in the address bar is usually the easiest way to tell whether a site is trustworthy. For this reason, Internet Explorer 8 makes it impossible to hide the address bar in almost all browser windows, even simple pop-ups.

▶ **The URLs associated with page links**—Most links on the page probably point to legitimate pages on the original site. However, some links might point to pages on the phisher's site.

▶ **The form-submittal address**—Almost all spoof pages contain a form into which you're supposed to type whatever sensitive data the phisher seeks from you. Select View, Source, and look at the value of the <form> tag's action attribute—the form submits your data to this address. Clearly, if the form is not sending your data to the legitimate domain, you're dealing with a phisher.

▶ **Text or images that aren't associated with the trustworthy site**—Many phishing sites are housed on free web hosting services. However, many of these services place an advertisement on each page, so look for an ad or other content from the hosting provider.

▶ **Internet Explorer's lock icon in the status bar and Security Report area**—A legitimate site would transmit sensitive financial data only using a secure HTTPS connection, which Internet Explorer indicates by placing a lock icon in the status bar and in the address bar's new Security Report area. If you don't see the lock icon on a page that asks for financial data, the page is almost certainly a spoof.

If you watch for these things, you'll probably never be fooled into giving up sensitive data to a phisher. However, it's often not as easy as it sounds. For example, some phishers employ easily overlooked domain-spoofing tricks such as replacing the lowercase letter *L* with the number *1*, or the uppercase letter *O* with the number *0*. Still, phishing sites don't fool most experienced users, so this isn't a big problem for them.

Novice users, on the other hand, need all the help they can get. They tend to assume that if everything they see on the Web looks legitimate and trustworthy, it probably is. And even if they're aware that scam sites exist, they don't know how to check for telltale phishing signs. To help these users, Internet Explorer 8 comes with a tool called the *SmartScreen Filter*. This filter alerts you to potential phishing scams by doing two things each time you visit a site:

▶ Analyzes the site content to look for known phishing techniques (that is, to see whether the site is *phishy*). The most common of these is a check for domain spoofing. This common scam also goes by the names *homograph spoofing* and the *lookalike attack*. Internet Explorer 8 also supports Internationalized Domain Names (IDN), which refers to domain names written in languages other than English, and it checks for *IDN spoofing*, domain name ambiguities in the user's chosen browser language.

▶ Checks a global database of known phishing sites to see whether it lists the site. This database is maintained by a network of providers, such as Cyota, Inc., Internet Identity, and MarkMonitor, as well as by reports from users who find phishing sites while surfing. According to Microsoft, this "URL reputation service" updates several times an hour with new data.

Here's how the SmartScreen Filter works:

▶ If you visit a site that Internet Explorer *knows* is a phishing scam, it changes the background color of the address bar to red and displays an `Unsafe Website` message in the Security Report area, as shown in Figure 11.18. It also blocks navigation to the site by displaying a separate page telling you that the site is a known phishing scam. A link is provided to navigate to the site, if you so choose.

Security Report area

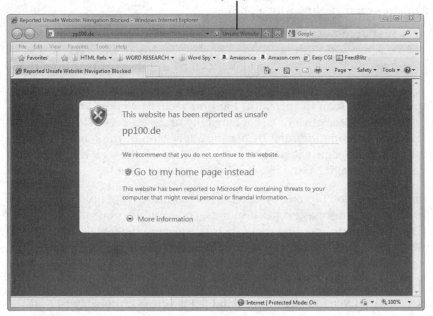

FIGURE 11.18   If Internet Explorer 8 detects a known phishing site, it displays `Unsafe Website` in the Security Report area and blocks access to the site.

> **NOTE**
>
> The Security Report area is another Internet Explorer security innovation. Clicking whatever text or icon appears in this area produces a report on the security of the site. For example, if you navigate to a secure site, you see the lock icon in this area. Click the lock to see a report that shows the site's digital certificate information.

▶ If you visit a site that Internet Explorer *thinks* is a potential phishing scam, it changes the background color of the address bar to yellow and displays a `Suspicious Website` message in the Security Report area.

Sharing a Computer Securely

If you're the only person who uses your computer, you don't have to worry all that much about the security of your user profile—that is, your files and Windows settings. However, if you share your computer with other people, either at home or at the office, you need to set up some kind of security to ensure that each user has his "own" Windows and can't mess with anyone else's (either purposely or accidentally). Here's a list of security precautions to set up when sharing your computer:

▶ **Create an account for each user**—All those who use the computer, even if they use it only occasionally, should have their own user account. (If a user needs to access the computer rarely, or only once, activate the Guest account and let him use that. You should disable the Guest account after the user finishes his session.)

NOTE

To activate the Guest account in Windows 7 or Vista, select Start, Control Panel, Add or Remove User Accounts, and enter your UAC credentials. In the Manage Accounts window, click Guest, and then click Turn On. To activate the Guest account in Windows XP, select Start, Control Panel, User Accounts. In the User Accounts window, click Guest, and then click Turn On the Guest Account.

▶ **Remove unused accounts**—If you have accounts set up for users who no longer require access to the computer, you should delete those accounts.

▶ **Limit the number of administrators**—Members of the Administrators group can do *anything* in Windows 7 or Vista simply by clicking Continue in the User Account Control dialog box. These powerful accounts should be kept to a minimum. Ideally, your system should have just one (besides the built-in Administrator account).

▶ **Rename the Administrator account**—Renaming the Administrator account ensures that no other user can be certain of the name of the computer's top-level user.

▶ **Put all other accounts in the Users (Standard users) group**—Users can perform almost all their everyday chores with the permissions and rights assigned to the Users group, so that's the group you should use for all other accounts.

▶ **Use strong passwords on all accounts**—Supply each account with a strong password so that no user can access another's account by logging on with a blank or simple password. **SEE** "Building a Strong Password," **P. 34.**

▶ **Set up each account with a screensaver, and be sure the screensaver resumes to the Welcome screen**—To do this, right-click the desktop, click Personalize (in Windows 7 or Vista) or Properties (in XP), and then click Screen Saver. Choose an item in the Screen Saver list, and then activate the On Resume, Display Welcome Screen check box.

▶ **Lock your computer**—When you leave your desk for any length of time, be sure to lock your computer; either select Start, Lock in Windows 7 or Vista, or press Windows Logo+L in Windows 7, Vista, or XP. This displays the Welcome screen; no one else can use your computer without entering your password.

Implementing Wireless Network Security

Wireless networks are less secure than wired ones because the wireless connection that enables you to access the network from afar can also enable an intruder from outside your home or office to access the network. In particular, *wardriving* is an activity in which a person drives through various neighborhoods with a portable computer or another device set up to look for available wireless networks. If the person finds a nonsecured network, he uses it for free Internet access or to cause mischief with shared network resources.

> **NOTE**
>
> If you don't believe that your wireless signals extend beyond your home or office, you can prove it to yourself. Unplug any wireless-enabled notebook and take it outside for a walk in the vicinity of your house. View the available wireless networks as you go, and you'll probably find that you can travel a fair distance (several houses, at least) away from your wireless access point and still see your network.

Here are a few tips and techniques you can easily implement to enhance the security of your wireless network:

▶ **Enable encryption**—First and foremost, enable encryption for wireless data so that an outside user who picks up your network packets can't decipher them. Be sure to use the strongest encryption that your equipment supports. For most home routers, this is *Wi-Fi Protected Access* (*WPA*), particularly WPA2, which is more secure than regular WPA.

> **NOTE**
>
> If you change your access point encryption method as described in the previous tip, you also need to update each wireless client to use the same form of encryption. In the Network Connections window, right-click your wireless network connection, and then click Properties. Display the Wireless Networks tab, click your network in the list, and then click Properties. Change the following three settings, and then click OK:
>
> ▶ **Network Authentication**—Select WPA-PSK.
>
> ▶ **Data Encryption**—Select TKIP.
>
> ▶ **Network Key**—Type your shared key here and in the Confirm Network Key text box.

▶ **Disable network broadcasting**—Windows sees your wireless network because the access point broadcasts the network's security set identifier (SSID). However, Windows remembers the wireless networks that you have successfully connected to. Therefore, after all your computers have accessed the wireless network at least once, you no longer need to broadcast the network's SSID. Therefore, you should use your AP setup program to disable broadcasting and prevent others from seeing your network.

11

CAUTION

You disable SSID broadcasting by accessing the wireless access point's configuration page and deactivating the broadcast setting. (Exactly how you do that varies depending on the manufacturer; see your documentation or just poke around in the settings page.) However, when previously authorized devices attempt to connect to a nonbroadcasting network, they include the network's SSID as part of the probe requests they send out to see whether the network is within range. The SSID is sent in unencrypted text, so it would be easy for a snoop with the right software (easily obtained from the Internet) to learn the SSID. If the SSID is not broadcasting to try to hide a network that is unsecure or uses an easily breakable encryption protocol, such as Wired Equivalent Privacy (WEP), hiding the SSID in this way actually makes the network *less* secure.

▶ **Change the default SSID**—Even if you disable broadcasting of your network's SSID, users can still attempt to connect to your network by guessing the SSID. All wireless access points come with a predefined name, such as linksys or default, and a would-be intruder will attempt these standard names first. Therefore, you can increase the security of your network by changing the SSID to a new name that is difficult to guess.

▶ **Change the access point username and password**—Any person within range of your wireless access point can open the device's setup page by entering http://192.168.1.1 or http://192.168.0.1 into a web browser. The person must log on with a username and password, but the default logon values (usually **admin**) are common knowledge among wardrivers. To prevent access to the setup program, be sure to change the access point's default username and password.

▶ **Consider static IP addresses**—Dynamic Host Configuration Protocol (DHCP) makes it easy to manage IP addresses, but it also gives an IP address to *anyone* who accesses the network. To prevent this, turn off DHCP in the access point and assign static IP addresses to each of your computers.

▶ **Enable MAC (Media Access Control) address filtering**—The *MAC address* is the physical address of a network adapter. This is unique to each adapter, so you can enhance security by setting up your access point to allow connections from only specified MAC addresses. (Unfortunately, MAC address filtering isn't a particularly robust form of security. The problem is that wireless network packets use a nonencrypted header that includes the MAC address of the device sending the packet! So any reasonably sophisticated cracker can sniff your network packets, determine the MAC address of one of your wireless devices, and then use special software to spoof that address so that the AP thinks the hacker's packets are coming from an authorized device.)

> **NOTE**
>
> To find out the MAC address of your wireless network adapter, open a Command Prompt session and enter the following command:
>
> `ipconfig /all`
>
> Find the data for the wireless adapter and look for the `Physical Address` value. (Alternatively, right-click the wireless connection, click Status, display the Support tab, and click Details.)

▶ **Avoid windows**—When positioning your access point within your home or office, don't place it near a window, if possible; otherwise, the access point sends a strong signal out of the building. Try to position the access point close to the center of your house or building.

From Here

▶ To learn what constitutes a strong password, **SEE** "Building a Strong Password," **P. 34.**

▶ To learn more about Windows Home Server's health notifications, **SEE** "Monitoring Network Health Alerts," **P. 240.**

CHAPTER 12

Setting Up a Windows Home Server Website

IN THIS CHAPTER

▶ Understanding the Windows Home Server Default Website

▶ Adding Folders and Files to the Default Website

▶ Creating a New Website

▶ Configuring a Website

Most of the features and techniques that I've talked about thus far in the book have been directly related to Windows Home Server (rightly so, what with the book's title and all). However, it's sometimes easy to forget the powerful server underpinnings upon which Windows Home Server does its thing. I speak, of course, of the Windows Server 2008 R2 code that underlies Windows Home Server 2011 and that has, until now, merely lurked in the background.

This chapter changes all that by tackling a subject that takes you well beyond the standard features of Windows Home Server and into brand new territory. Here you get a chance to play with one of Windows Home Server's most useful and most powerful features: Internet Information Services (IIS), the Windows Server 2008 R2 web server. Yes, you can use one of the many thousands of web hosting companies to put up your site, but if you want complete control over the site, you need to roll up your sleeves and get hands on with IIS.

Books bigger than this one have been written on the seemingly endless features and properties of this world-class web server, so I'm under no illusion that a single chapter will be even remotely exhaustive. However, Windows Home Server is designed as a family-oriented product, so my goal here is to show you how to get one or more websites online for you and your family members to put their best digital feet forward on the web.

Understanding the Windows Home Server Default Website

So far in this book you've seen two instances of the default Windows Home Server website:

▶ In Chapter 3, "Adding Devices to the Windows Home Server Network," you saw that you can start the Windows Home Server Connector installation by using your web browser to surf to the address `http://server/connect` (where *server* is the name of your Windows Home Server PC).

▶ In Chapter 7, "Making Connections to Network Computers," you saw that you can display the Remote Web Access logon page by using your web browser to navigate to `http://server/remote`.

> ▶ **SEE** "Displaying the Remote Web Access Page," **P. 160**.

The folders `connect` and `remote` are part of the Windows Home Server default website that's created, configured, and started automatically when you install Windows Home Server.

Viewing the Default Web Application Folders

Actually, it's more accurate to describe the `connect` and `remote` resources as *applications* that run within IIS. To get a feel for what's behind these applications, you need to head for the following folder:

`C:\ProgramFiles\Windows Server\Bin\WebApps`

This folder contains several subfolders, including `Client` (used by the Connect application) and `RemoteAccess` (used by the Remote Web Access application). The other folders—such as `Root` and `Site`—are used internally by IIS and Windows Home Server. Figure 12.1 shows the contents of the `Client` folder.

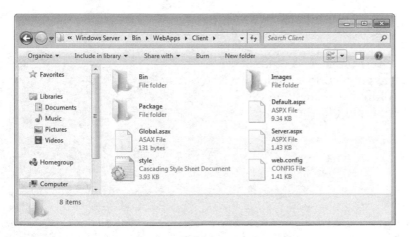

FIGURE 12.1   The contents of the IIS `Client` folder.

The `Client` folder contains the following subfolders and files:

▶ **Bin**—This folder contains a couple of dynamic-link libraries (DLLs) that contain code used by the Connect application.

▶ **Images**—This folder contains the images used on the Connect page.

▶ **Package**—This folder contains files that the Connect application uses.

▶ **default.aspx**—This file contains the Hypertext Markup Language (HTML) tags, cascading stylesheet (CSS) properties, and ASP.NET programming code that creates and configures the Connect page.

▶ **Global.asax**—This file contains references to .NET resources used globally in the Windows Home Server's default application pool.

▶ **Server.aspx**—This is an ASP.NET web page that gives instructions on using the Connect application.

▶ **style.css**—This file is the CSS that the Connect page uses.

▶ **web.config**—This file contains configuration data for the Connect folder's ASP.NET application.

Figure 12.2 shows the contents of the `RemoteAccess` folder. This folder contains quite a few files used internally by Windows Home Server's Remote Web Access application, so I'll just list the most important subfolders:

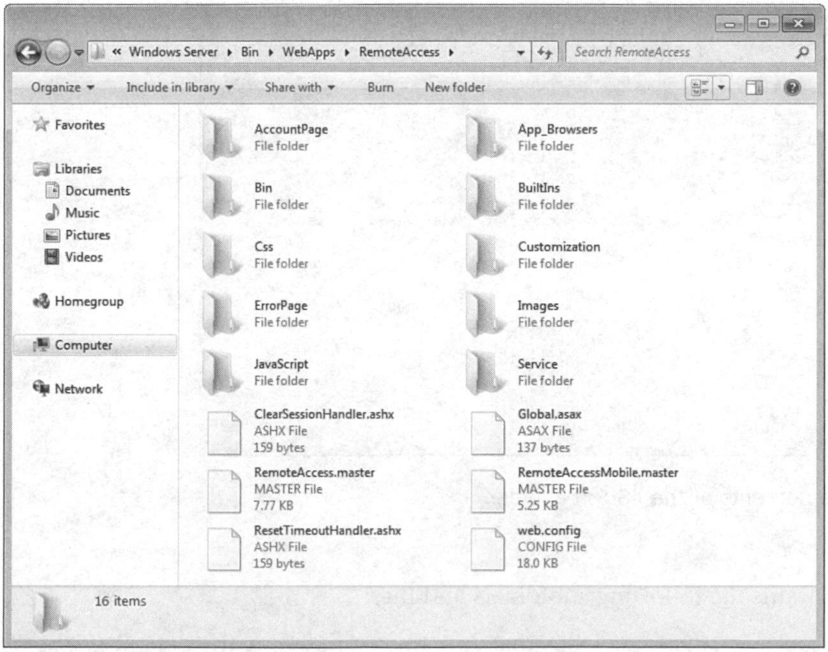

FIGURE 12.2   The contents of the IIS `RemoteAccess` folder.

▶ **AccountPage**—This folder contains the files that have the HTML tags, CSS properties, and ASP.NET programming code that create and configure the Remote Web Access logon page.

▶ **Bin**—This folder contains a bunch of DLLs that contain code used by the Remote Web Access application.

▶ **BuiltIns**—This folder contains the files that have the HTML tags, CSS properties, and ASP.NET programming code that creates and configures the Remote Web Access Home page, Remote Desktop feature, shared folder pages, media pages, and media streaming.

▶ **Css**—This folder contains the CSS files used by the Remote Web Access pages.

▶ **Images**—This folder contains the images used on the Remote Web Access pages.

Viewing the Default IIS Website

The Client and RemoteAccess folders are internal Windows Home Server applications, so you don't want to mess with them unless you know your way around HTML, CSS, and ASP.NET. For our purposes in this chapter, you're going to work with the default IIS website, which you'll find at C:\Program Files\Windows Server\Bin\WebApps\Site. Figure 12.3 shows the subfolders and files that you'll find here.

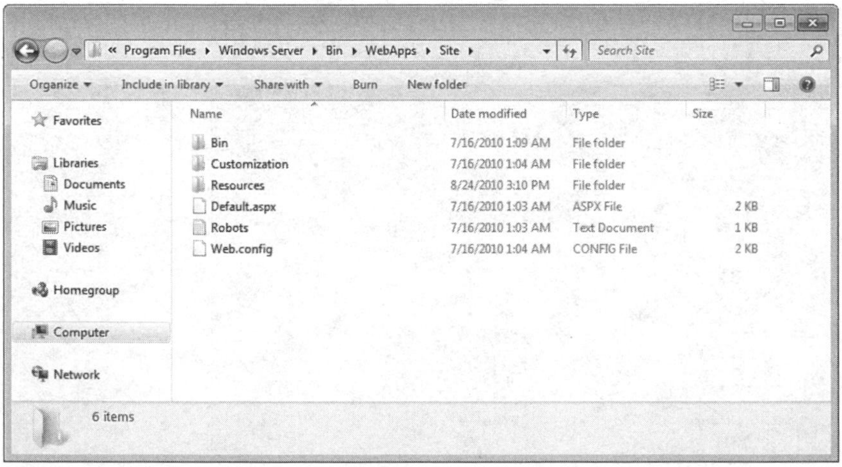

FIGURE 12.3   The contents of the IIS Site folder.

The Site folder contains the following subfolders and files:

▶ **Bin**—This folder contains some DLLs that contain code used by the default site.

▶ **Customization**—This folder contains an XML file used by the default site.

▶ **Resources**—This folder contains the images used on the default site, as well as a CSS file and security certificate.

▶ **default.aspx**—This file runs when you surf to http://*server*, and if Remote Web Access is turned on, the file redirects you to https://*server*/remote.

▶ **Robots.txt**—This file is read by search engine crawlers (automated programs that search the web for content to index), and it's used to define which aspects of the site the crawlers are allowed to index.

▶ **web.config**—This file contains configuration data for the site's ASP.NET application.

Viewing the Default Website with Internet Information Services Manager

The Client, RemoteAccess, and Site folders enable you to examine the physical files and subfolders associated with the Windows Home Server default website. However, you probably won't often deal with these folders (or any folder) directly when creating and configuring your own web pages and websites. Instead, you'll most often use a Microsoft Management Console snap-in called the IIS Manager.

To display this snap-in, select Start, Administrative Tools, Internet Information Server (IIS) Manager. When the snap-in loads, open the *SERVER*, Sites, Default Web Site branch (where *SERVER* is the name of your Windows Home Server PC), and then click Content View at the bottom of the window. This branch (see Figure 12.4) shows the contents of the default IIS website, the Connect and Remote applications, plus a few other applications that Windows Home Server uses.

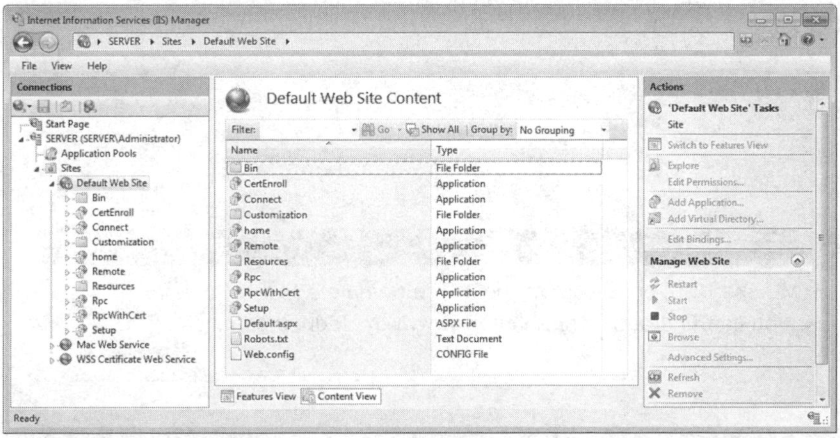

FIGURE 12.4   In the IIS Manager snap-in, the Default Web Site represents the Windows Home Server default site.

> **TIP**
>
> You can also launch IIS Manager by selecting Start, typing **inetmgr**, and pressing Enter.

Much of the rest of this chapter shows you how to use IIS Manager to create and configure Windows Home Server website content.

Adding Folders and Files to the Default Website

By far, the easiest way to set up your own web content on Windows Home Server is to add that content to the existing default website. This requires no reconfiguration of the server, of IIS, of the Windows Home Server firewall, of the client computers, or of the router. You simply add the content, and it's ready for browsing.

Adding a File to a Default Website Folder

If you have just a few web content files that you want to add to the Windows Home Server website, you can add them directly to the IIS folders. First, create your web content file (HTML, ASP, or whatever). Here's a sample HTML file—which I've named HelloWorld.htm—that I'll use as an example:

```
<html>
<head>
<title>Hello World!</title>
</head>
<body>
<p>
<font style="size: 20pt; font-family: Verdana; color:DarkBlue">
Hello Windows Home Server World!
<font>
</p>
</body>
</html>
```

> **NOTE**
>
> For a primer on HTML and CSS, check out my book *The Complete Idiot's Guide to Creating a Website*. You can find out more about it at www.mcfedries.com/CreatingAWebsite/.

> **TIP**
>
> Don't use spaces in the names of files (or folders) that you add to any IIS website. Although Internet Explorer might display such resources successfully, other browsers might not.

Next, save the file to one of Windows Home Server's default website folders:

Site	Add your web content to this folder to view the content without having to log on to Windows Home Server. To browse to the content, use Internet Explorer to navigate to `http://server/content`, where *server* is the Windows Home Server name and *content* is the name of the web content file.
RemoteAccess	Add your web content to this folder if you want users to have to log on to Windows Home Server before they can view the content. To browse to the content, use Internet Explorer to first navigate to `https://server/remote/` (where *server* is the Windows Home Server name), log on to Windows Home Server, and then navigate to `https://server/remote/content` (where *content* is the name of the web content file).

CAUTION

If your web content file references other files—for example, an HTML file that uses the `<img>` tag to reference an image file—be sure to copy those files to the `home` or `remote` folder (whichever folder you're using for the main file). You can either put the files in the root, or you can store them in a subfolder. For example, you might want to store image files in the `Resources` subfolder. If you store the files in subfolders, make sure you adjust the path in your code, as required. For example, if you place a file named `HelloWorld.jpg` in the `Resources` subfolder, you need to add the subfolder to the `<img>` tag, like so:

```
<img src="/Resources/HelloWorld.jpg" />
```

Figure 12.5 shows the `HelloWorld.htm` file copied to the `home` folder, and Figure 12.6 shows the file displayed with Internet Explorer.

Adding a Folder to the Default Website

To add a folder to the Windows Home Server default website, you have two choices:

▶ Add the folder manually.

▶ Use the Virtual Directory Creation Wizard in the IIS Manager.

The next two sections provide the details.

Adding a Folder Manually

Adding a folder to the Windows Home Server default website is not all that different from adding a file. That is, you can create a new subfolder within the `Site` or `RemoteAccess` folder, or you can copy or move an existing folder and paste it within `Site` or `RemoteAccess`. To access web content within the new folder, tack the folder name and file-name to the default website address. For example, if you create a subfolder named `photos`

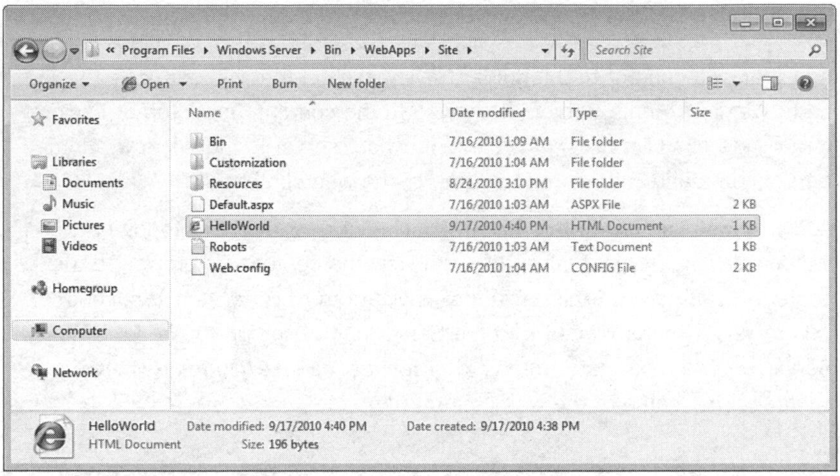

FIGURE 12.5   You can add individual files directly to the `Site` or `RemoteAccess` folder.

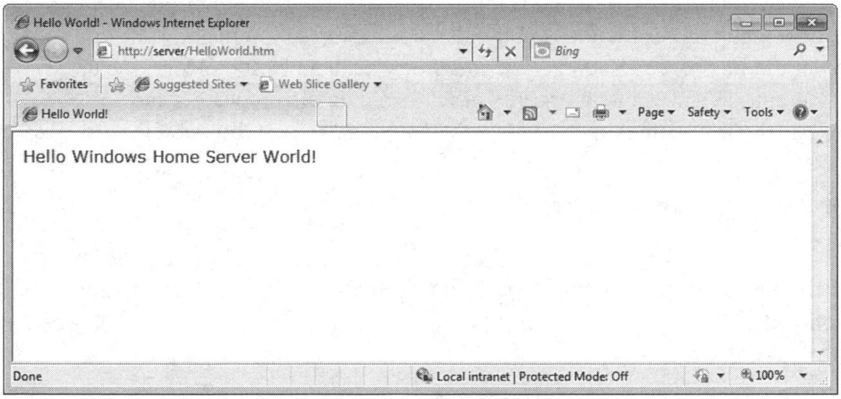

FIGURE 12.6   The `HelloWorld.htm` file displayed with Internet Explorer.

within the `Site` folder, and the main page is named `photos.htm`, you access the content by entering the following address into the browser:

http://*server*/photos/photos.htm

Note that you can save some wear and tear on your typing fingers by changing the name of the main content file to one of the following:

```
default.htm
default.asp
index.htm
index.html
default.aspx
```

When you use one of these names, IIS displays the file by default if you don't specify a filename as part of the URL. For example, if you rename the photos.htm file to default.htm, you can access the file just by specifying the folder path in the URL:

http://*server*/photos/

I discuss default content files in more detail later on in this chapter (see "Setting the Default Content Page").

Adding a Folder Using the Virtual Directory Creation Wizard

When you add a folder manually, IIS Manager detects the new folder and adds it to the folder content. However, you can also use IIS Manager to create a new folder with the default website. Here are the steps to follow:

1. In IIS Manager, open the *SERVER*, Sites, Default Web Site branch (where *SERVER* is the name of your Windows Home Server PC).

2. If you want to create a subfolder within the Remote folder, click Remote.

3. In the Actions pane, click View Virtual Directories. IIS Manager displays the Virtual Directories page.

4. In the Actions pane, click Add Virtual Directory. IIS Manager displays the Add Virtual Directory dialog box.

5. Use the Alias text box to type an alias for the folder. The alias is the name that appears in IIS Manager, within either the root branch or the Remote branch. Note that this is *not* the same (nor does it have to be the same) as the name of the directory.

6. Use the Physical Path text box to specify the location of the folder. You have three choices:

   ▶ If the folder exists and you know the full pathname (drive and folders), type it in the Physical Path text box.

   ▶ If the folder exists and you're not sure of the full pathname (or it's too long to type), click Browse, use the Browse for Folder dialog box to select the folder, and then click OK.

   ▶ If the folder doesn't exist, click Browse, use the Browse for Folder dialog box to select the folder within which you want the new folder to appear, click Make New Folder, type the folder name, press Enter, and then click OK.

7. Click OK.

Creating a New Website

With the powerful capabilities of IIS at your disposal, you're not stuck with using just the default Windows Home Server website. For all practical purposes, you can create as many websites as you want. You can create a website for each member of the family; you can create a website to display family photos; or you can create a website that hosts the family blog, which might be a record of your family's activities (a sort of year-round Christmas newsletter).

You can do all this and much more because IIS is capable of hosting multiple sites on a single Windows Home Server PC. The secret behind this is that you can use one or more of the following items to construct a unique address for each site:

IP address	You can assign multiple IP addresses to the Windows Home Server computer and then apply each address to a new website.
Port number	The Windows Home Server site uses ports 80, 443, 808, 5010, 8001, 55000, and 56000, but you can assign port numbers such as 81, 82, 8080, and so on to each new website. This enables you to host multiple websites on a single IP address.
Host header name	This is a unique name that you assign to each new website. This name enables you to host multiple websites on a single IP address and port number.

You can mix and match these techniques, as needed. For example, you could use nothing but unique IP addresses or port numbers for each website, or combinations of IP addresses and port numbers. The method you use depends on the number of websites you want to set up and the number of computers on your network. As you can see over the next few sections, the methods require varying amounts of effort on your part and varying levels of complexity for users to access the sites. Read through and try each method before deciding which one to implement.

Creating a New Website Using a Different IP Address

Back in Chapter 1, "Setting Up Your Windows Home Server Network," you learned how to set up Windows Home Server with a static IP address. This enables you to consistently access the server using an IP address that you know will never change, and it enables you to set up your router to forward ports to the server's IP address.

▶ **SEE** "Configuring Windows Home Server with a Static IP Address," **P. 8**.

However, there's nothing to stop you from assigning a second (or a third or a fourth) static IP address to Windows Home Server. This means that you can have the same benefits that come from a static IP address for your own websites (plus get the capability to host multiple sites on a single server in the first place) by adding more IP addresses to Windows Home Server and then using those addresses to define the location of your new websites.

Assigning an Additional IP Address to Windows Home Server

The first step here is to assign another IP address to Windows Home Server. Here are the steps to follow:

1. Right-click the Network icon in the notification area, click Network and Sharing Center, and then click Change Adapter Settings to open the Network Connections window.

12

TIP

You can also open Network Connections by clicking Start, typing **network conn**, and then clicking View Network Connections.

---

2. Right-click the icon for the connection to your local area network (LAN), and then click Properties. The connection's property sheet appears.

3. In the Networking tab, double-click Internet Protocol Version 4 (TCP/IPv4) to display the Internet Protocol Version 4 (TCP/IPv4) Properties dialog box.

4. Make sure the connection is set up to use a static IP address (again, as explained in Chapter 1).

5. Click Advanced to display the Advanced TCP/IP Settings dialog box.

6. In the IP Settings tab, click Add to display the TCP/IP Address dialog box.

7. Type the IP address you want to use. Be sure to use an address that doesn't conflict with an existing static IP address on the server or with the other DHCP clients on your network. A good idea is to start with the highest possible address (usually 192.168.1.254) for the first static IP address and then work down (so the second static IP address would be 192.168.1.253, the third would be 192.168.1.252, and so on).

8. Type the subnet mask. (Windows Home Server should fill this in automatically.)

9. Click Add. Windows Home Server returns you to the Advanced TCP/IP Settings dialog box and displays the new IP address in the IP Addresses list, as shown in Figure 12.7.

10. Click OK in all the open dialog boxes to put the new settings into effect.

Note that you can repeat these steps as often as you like (with the only practical limit being the number of available IP addresses) to add more static IP addresses as you need them.

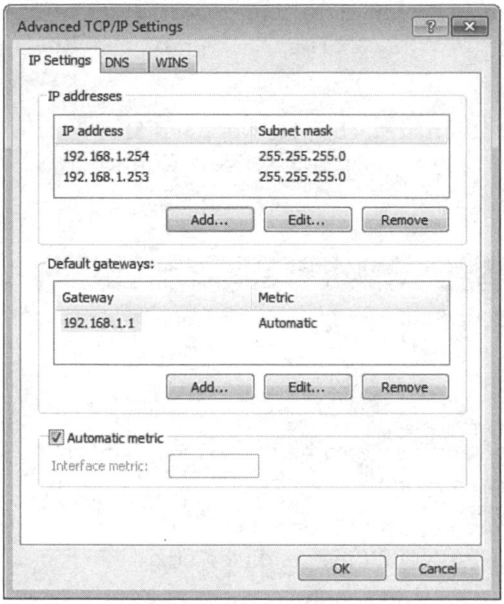

FIGURE 12.7   You can assign two or more static IP addresses to Windows Home Server.

Creating a Website Using a Different IP Address

With your newly minted IP address at the ready, you can now create your website. Here are the steps to follow:

1. In IIS Manager, open the *SERVER*, Sites branch (where *SERVER* is the name of your Windows Home Server PC).

2. In the Actions pane, click Add Web Site. IIS Manager opens the Add Web Site dialog box.

3. Use the Site Name text box to type a name for the website. This is the name that appears in IIS Manager, within the Sites branch.

4. Either type the full pathname (drive and folders) in the Physical Path text box, or click Browse and use the Browse for Folder dialog box to select the folder or create a new folder.

5. In the IP Address list, select the IP address you created in the previous section, as shown in Figure 12.8.

6. Leave the Port value at 80.

7. Click OK. IIS Manager adds the new site to the Sites branch, as shown in Figure 12.9 (see the Family Photos site).

From here, add content to the folder you specified in step 4, including a file that uses one of the IIS default names.

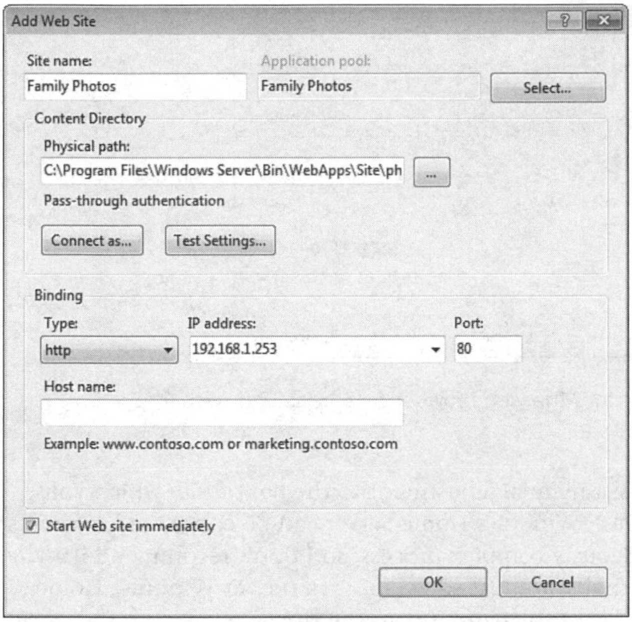

FIGURE 12.8   Select the other static IP address that you assigned to Windows Home Server.

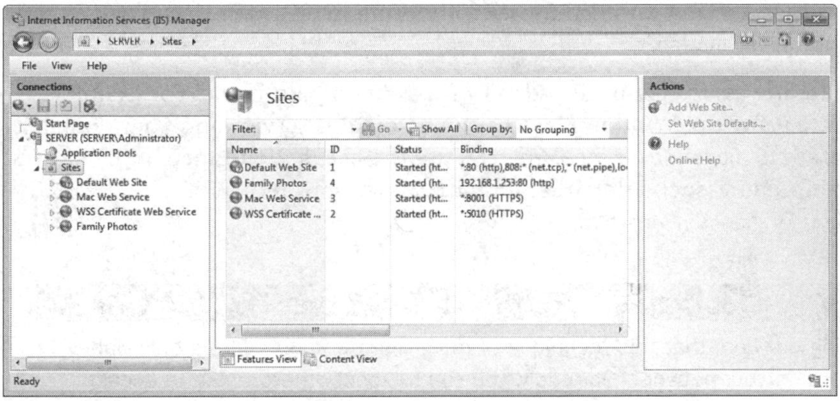

FIGURE 12.9   IIS Manager displays your new site in the Sites branch.

Associating the IP Address with a Hostname

Your new website now works, but the only way you can access it is to browse to
http://*IP*, where *IP* is the IP address that you created earlier, as shown in Figure 12.10.

That's fine, but you probably don't want some members of your family having to deal
with the complexities of IP addresses. To avoid that, you can associate a hostname (such
as FamilyPhotos) with the IP address.

FIGURE 12.10   Enter the IP address into the web browser to access your website.

The easiest way to do this is to make a manual adjustment to the hosts file, which you use to map IP addresses to hostnames. (Windows Home Server can be configured to use its built-in DNS server, but this is a hideously complex process, so I don't recommend it.) The only downside to this technique is that you must edit the hosts file on Windows Home Server and every computer that you want to give access to the site.

Before proceeding, note that you can use the hosts file to set up both local and remote (that is, Internet) mappings:

▶ A local mapping associates an IP addresses with a simple hostname, such as FamilyPhotos or KarensWeb.

▶ A remote mapping associates an IP address with a subdomain name. For example, suppose you're using the Windows Live Custom Domains service and your domain name is ourfamily.homeserver.com. You can use the hosts file to map an IP address to a subdomain name, such as photos.ourfamily.homeserver.com or karen.ourfamily.homeserver.com.

NOTE

It's worth pointing out here that this technique of modifying the hosts file is only viable for the computers on your network. Obviously, you can't expect others trying to access your site from the Internet to modify their hosts file.

Follow these steps to open the hosts file on computers running Windows XP or earlier:

1. Select Start, Run (or press Windows Logo+R) to open the Run dialog box.

2. Type the following command in the Open text box:

        notepad %systemroot%\System32\drivers\etc\hosts

3. Click OK. The hosts file opens in Notepad.

Windows 7 and Vista require elevated permissions to edit any file in the `%SystemRoot%` folder or any of its subfolders. Therefore, you need to follow these steps to open `hosts` in Notepad:

1. Select Start, All Programs, Accessories.

2. Right-click Command Prompt, and then click Run as Administrator.

3. Enter your UAC credentials to continue.

4. At the command prompt, type the following:

   `notepad %systemroot%\system32\drivers\etc\hosts`

5. Press Enter. The `hosts` file opens in Notepad.

With the `hosts` file open, start a new line at the end of the file. Then enter the mapping using the following general format:

`IP    hostname`

Here, replace *IP* with the address you assigned to your website, and replace *hostname* with the hostname you want to associate with the IP address. In the following example, I've assigned both a local name and a subdomain name to 192.168.1.253:

```
192.168.1.253     photos
192.168.1.253     photos.ourfamily.homeserver.com
```

Figure 12.11 shows the website from Figure 12.10 being accessed using the local hostname as the address (`http://photos`).

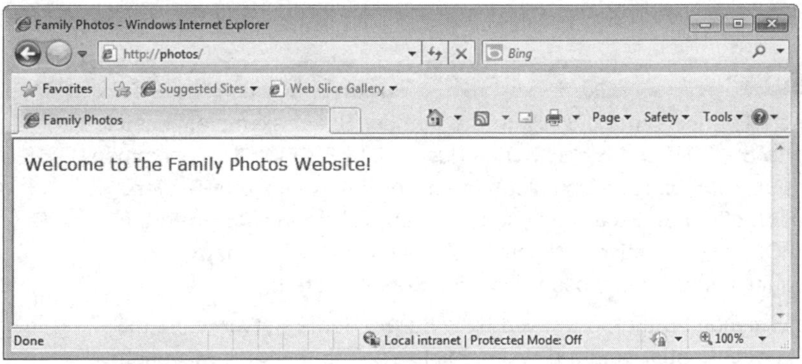

FIGURE 12.11   After you map an IP address to a hostname using the `hosts` file, you can access the website using the hostname.

Creating a New Website Using a Different Port

For IIS, the TCP port is the communications channel that is set up between the web browser and the web server. The traditional port used for the HTTP protocol is port 80, and that's the port used by the Windows Home Server default website and by any website you create using a different IP address, as described in the previous section. However, you don't have to use port 80. In fact, you can host multiple websites on a single server by assigning each of those websites a different port.

To access a site on a different port, you specify the port number in the address, after the host or domain name, as in the following general case:

```
http://server:port
```

Here, *server* is the hostname or domain name of the website, and `port` is the port number. In most cases, the *server* name is the same as the name you use to access the default site on port 80. In Windows Home Server, this means you specify the name of the server. For example, suppose your Windows Home Server PC is named SERVER, and you set up a new website and assign it to port 81. Then to access that site, you'd use the following address:

```
http://server:81
```

Similarly, if you have a Windows Live Custom Domains name of ourfamily.homeserver.com, you can access a website on port 81 as follows:

```
http://ourfamily.homeserver.com:81
```

Note, too, that you can also use an IP address instead of the host or domain name, which means you can set up a website that uses a different IP address *and* a different port. For example, here's the address you'd use to access a website using IP address 192.168.1.253 and port 81:

```
http://192.168.1.253:81
```

NOTE

It's traditional to use HTTP ports that begin with the number 8. For example, because IIS already uses ports 80, 808, and 8001, you can use 81 to 89. 8080 is a commonly used custom HTTP port number. For a complete list of ports that Windows Server systems use, Microsoft offers an Excel workbook that you can download. Go to the Microsoft Download Center (www.microsoft.com/downloads/en/default.aspx), and search for "Port Requirements for Microsoft Windows Server System."

You can also get information on the ports used by Windows Home Server using the Port Reporter tool. For information and a download link, see the following Microsoft Knowledge Base article at support.microsoft.com/kb/837243.

Creating a Website Using a Different Port

Here are the steps to follow to create a website that uses a different port number:

1. In IIS Manager, open the *SERVER*, Sites branch (where *SERVER* is the name of your Windows Home Server PC).

2. In the Actions pane, click Add Web Site. IIS Manager opens the Add Web Site dialog box.

3. Use the Site Name text box to type a name for the website. This is the name that appears in IIS Manager, within the Sites branch.

4. Either type the full pathname (drive and folders) in the Physical Path text box, or click Browse and use the Browse for Folder dialog box to select the folder or create a new folder.

5. Use the IP Address list to select the main IP address assigned to your Windows Home Server PC.

6. Enter a new value in the Port text box, as shown in Figure 12.12.

7. Click OK. IIS Manager adds the new site to the Sites branch.

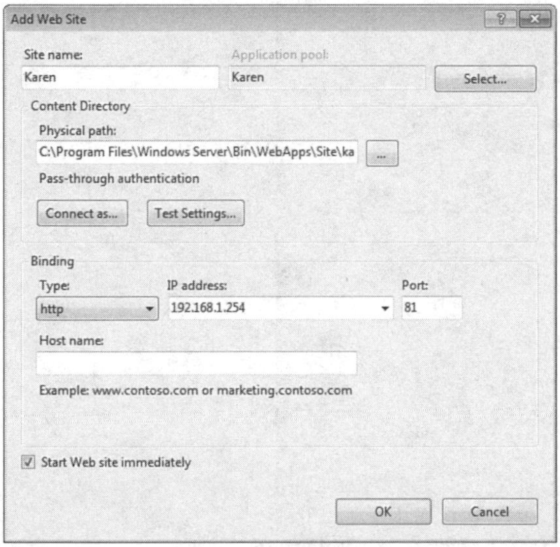

FIGURE 12.12   Type a new value in the Port text box.

Adding a Firewall Exception for the Website Port

As things stand now, your new website will work properly when you access it using a web browser running on the Windows Home Server PC. If you try to access the site on any other computer (or from a location outside your network), you get an error message.

The problem is that the Windows Firewall on Windows Home Server hasn't been configured to allow data traffic using the port you assigned to your new website. For your site to work from any remote location, you need to set up an exception for the port in Windows Firewall. Here are the steps to follow:

1. Log on to Windows Home Server.

2. Select Start, Control Panel, Windows Firewall.

3. Click Advanced Settings to open the Windows Firewall with Advanced Security snap-in.

4. Click Inbound Rules.

5. In the Actions pane, click New Rule to start the New Inbound Rule Wizard.

6. Activate the Port option, and then click Next. The wizard displays the Protocol and Ports dialog box.

7. Activate the TCP option, and use the Specific Local Ports text box to type the port you assigned to the site. Figure 12.13 shows the dialog box set up to allow traffic on port 81.

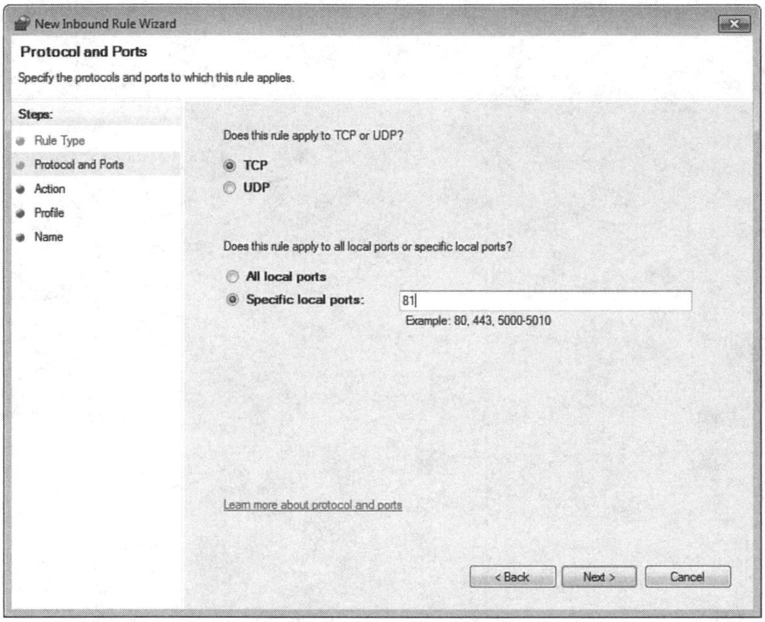

FIGURE 12.13   Configure Windows Firewall on Windows Home Server to allow traffic on the port you assigned to your new website.

8. Click Next. The wizard displays the Action dialog box.

9. Make sure the Allow the Connection option is activated, and then click Next. The wizard displays the Profile dialog box.

10. You have two choices. (You can ignore the Domain option.)

   ▶ **Private**—Select this option if you only want computers on your network to access the website.

   ▶ **Public**—Select this option if you want to be able to access this website from the Internet.

11. Click Next. The wizard displays the Name dialog box.

12. In the Name text box, type **`TCP Port`** *n*, where *n* is the port number you assigned to your website.
13. Click Finish.

You can now access the site on port 81, as shown in Figure 12.14.

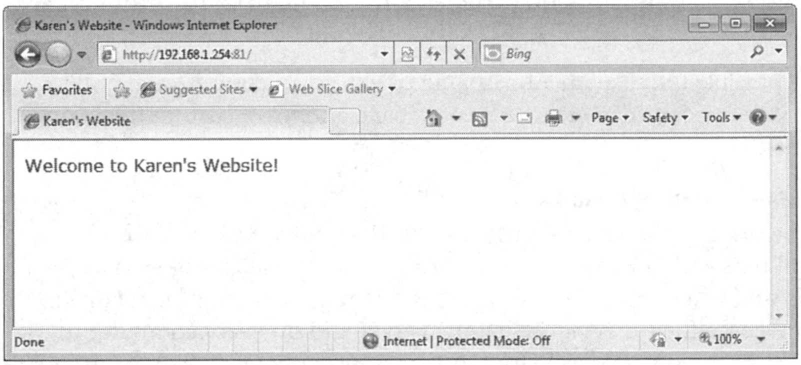

FIGURE 12.14 With the Windows Firewall exception in place on Windows Home Server, you can now access the site on the different port.

Forwarding the Port in Your Router

In the previous section, you may have set up the Windows Firewall port exception with the Any Computer scope to allow Internet access to your new website. However, users still can't access the site because your network's router doesn't know that it's supposed to allow data to come through the port you assigned to the website.

To allow traffic on that port, you need to configure the router to forward any data that comes in on that port to the IP address of the Windows Home Server PC. How you do this depends on the router. Figure 12.15 shows the Port Forwarding screen of the D-Link router on my system. In this case, I've forwarded TCP port 81 to the address 192.168.1.254, which is the static IP address of my Windows Home Server. Consult your device documentation for information on configuring port forwarding.

VIRTUAL SERVERS LIST

Enable	Name	IP Address	Protocol Private Port/Public Port	Inbound Filter	Schedule
☑	HTTP	192.168.1.254	TCP 80/80	Allow All	Always
☑	KarensWeb	192.168.1.253	TCP 81/81	Allow All	Always
☑	RPD 4125	192.168.1.254	TCP 4125/4125	Allow All	Always
☑	RDP 443	192.168.1.254	TCP 443/443	Allow All	Always

FIGURE 12.15 On your router, you need to forward the port associated with your new website to the Windows Home Server IP address.

Creating a New Website Using a Host Header

When a web browser opens a TCP communications channel with a web server, the HTTP data that is passed to the server comes with a header that includes information such as the date and a string that identifies the browser. The header also includes a hostname field, which identifies the location of the resource the browser seeks. The host header is usually either a domain name (for an Internet connection) or a network name (for a LAN connection).

Interestingly, it's also possible to make up a hostname of your own choosing: KatysBlog, FamilyWeb, or whatever. You can then create a new website and use a custom hostname as the identity of your site.

Associating the Host Header with an IP Address

Custom host headers work because you map them to an IP address. As before (see "Associating the IP Address with a Hostname"), you can set up the mapping yourself by editing the hosts file, and you can set up both local and remote mappings. Remember that you must edit the hosts file on Windows Home Server and on every computer that you want to give access to the site. (So, as before, this method only really works for your local computers, not for anyone outside your network.)

You modify the hosts file in the same way that I described in the earlier section. That is, you open the hosts file, start a new line at the end of the file, and then enter the mapping using the following general format:

IP   hostheader

In this case, you replace *IP* with the IP address of your Windows Home Server PC, and you replace *hostheader* with the host header name you want to use for the website. In the following example, I've assigned both a local name and a subdomain name to 192.168.1.254:

```
192.168.1.254    katysblog
192.168.1.254    katysblog.ourfamily.homeserver.com
```

Creating a Website Using a Host Header

Here are the steps to follow to create a website that uses a host header:

1. In IIS Manager, open the *SERVER*, Web branch (where *SERVER* is the name of your Windows Home Server PC).

2. In the Actions pane, click Add Web Site. IIS Manager opens the Add Web Site dialog box.

3. Use the Site Name text box to type a name for the website. This is the name that appears in IIS Manager, within the Sites branch.

4. Either type the full pathname (drive and folders) in the Physical Path text box, or click Browse and use the Browse for Folder dialog box to either select the folder or create a new folder.

5. In the IP Address list, select the main IP address assigned to your Windows Home Server PC. Leave the Port value as is.

6. Use the Host Name text box to type the host header, as shown in Figure 12.16.

7. Click OK. IIS Manager adds the new site to the Sites branch.

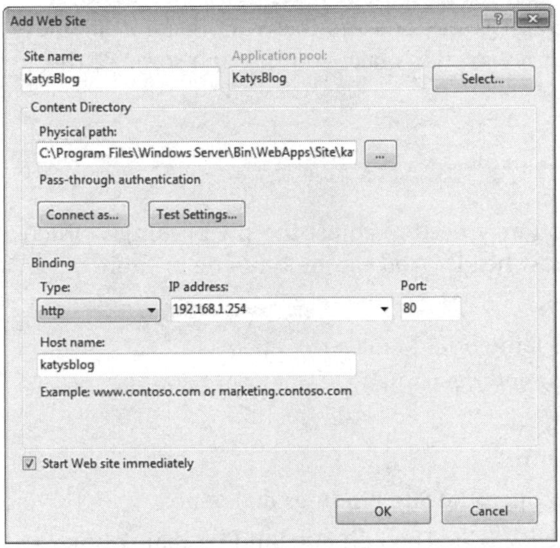

FIGURE 12.16   Type the host header in the Host Name text box.

From here, add content to the folder you specified in step 4, including a file that uses one of the IIS default names. Figure 12.17 shows Internet Explorer displaying a new website using the host header `katysblog` (`http://katysblog`).

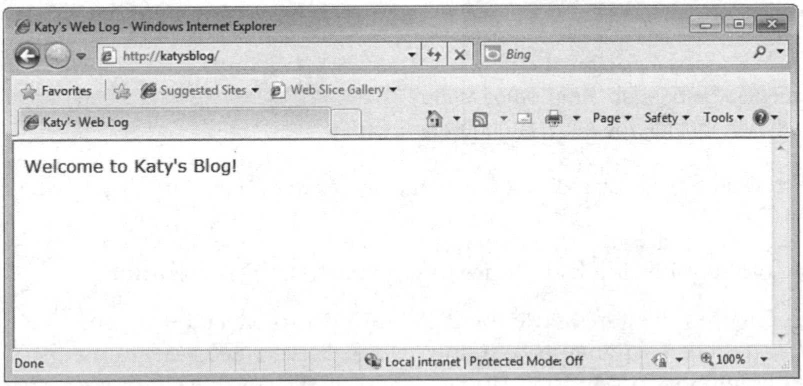

FIGURE 12.17   A website accessed using a host header name.

Configuring a Website

After you've set up one or more websites—either by adding folders to the Windows Home Server default website or by creating your own websites using the IIS Manager—you may need to adjust certain site properties. For example, you may need to change the website identification (IP address, port number, or host header), modify the website location, adjust the site permissions, and so on. All of these options and many more are available using the website's property sheet. The next few sections take you through some of the more common and useful properties.

Modifying the Website Bindings

If you've added your own website to IIS, you may need to adjust the site bindings, which include the IP address, port number, and host header. You can modify one or more of these bindings. Here are the steps to follow:

1. Log on to Windows Home Server and launch IIS Manager.

2. Open the *SERVER*, Sites branch (where *SERVER* is the name of your Windows Home Server PC).

3. Click the website you want to work with.

4. In the Actions pane, click Bindings to open the Site Bindings dialog box.

5. Select the current binding, and then click Edit. The Edit Site Binding dialog box appears, as shown in Figure 12.18.

FIGURE 12.18   Use the Edit Site Binding dialog box to modify the site's identity.

6. Use one or more of the following techniques to modify the website identity:

   ▶ To change the site's IP address, use the IP Address list to select a different address that has been assigned to Windows Home Server. (See "Assigning an Additional IP Address to Windows Home Server," earlier in this chapter.)

   ▶ To change the site's port, use the Port text box to specify a different port number.

CAUTION

If you assign the site a new port, you also need to set up a Windows Firewall exception on Windows Home Server to allow data through that port; see "Adding a Firewall Exception for the Website Port," earlier in this chapter. If you or others will be accessing the site from the Internet, be sure to configure your router to forward the port to the site's IP address; see "Forwarding the Port in Your Router," earlier in this chapter.

▶ To change the site's host header, type the new host header in the Host Name text box.

CAUTION

If you give the site a new host header, you must modify the hosts file to map the host header to the site's IP address; see "Associating the Host Header with an IP Address," earlier in this chapter.

7. Click OK.
8. Click Close to put the new identity into effect.

Giving a Website Multiple Identities

There's no rule that says a website must use only a single identity. In fact, you can assign as many separate identities as you like to a single website. These identities can be any combination of IP address, TCP port, and host header, although each combination must be unique.

Why use multiple identities for a single website? One common reason is that you want to change the site's current identity, but you don't want to go through the hassle of letting other users know about the change (or reconfiguring their PCs to handle the change). In this case, you can leave the existing identity intact so that users who know that identity can still use it. You can then create a second identity and supply that identity to any new users who need to access the site.

Here are the steps to follow to add another identity to a website:

1. Launch IIS Manager.
2. Open the *SERVER*, Sites branch (where *SERVER* is the name of your Windows Home Server PC).
3. Click the website you want to work with.
4. In the Actions pane, click Bindings to open the Site Bindings dialog box.
5. Click Add. The Add Site Binding dialog box appears.

6. Use one or more of the following techniques to set up the new website identity:

   ▶ Use the IP Address list to select an address that has been assigned to Windows Home Server.

   ▶ Use the Port text box to specify a port number.

CAUTION

If you assign the site a port other than 80, you also need to set up a Windows Firewall exception on Windows Home Server to allow data through that port; see "Adding a Firewall Exception for the Website Port," earlier in this chapter. If you or others will be accessing the site from the Internet, be sure to configure your router to forward the port to the site's IP address; see "Forwarding the Port in Your Router," earlier in this chapter.

   ▶ Use the Host Name text box to type the site's host header.

CAUTION

If you give the site a host header, you must modify the hosts file to map the host header to the site's IP address; see "Associating the Host Header with an IP Address," earlier in this chapter

---

7. Click OK.

8. Click Close to put the new identity into effect. Figure 12.19 shows a site with several identities.

Type	Host Name	Port	IP Address	Binding Informa...
http	katysblog	80	192.168.1.254	
http		80	192.168.1.252	
http		82	192.168.1.254	
http	katyshome	80	192.168.1.254	

FIGURE 12.19   You can configure a website with multiple identities.

Changing the Website Location

The home folder (or home directory, as IIS calls it) that you specified when you created a website isn't necessarily permanent. You may decide to move a website to a different home folder, or you may decide to rename the existing folder. In either case, you must use IIS Manager to specify the new home folder. Here are the steps to follow:

1. Launch IIS Manager.

2. Open the *SERVER*, Sites branch (where *SERVER* is the name of your Windows Home Server PC).

3. Click the website you want to work with.

4. In the Actions pane, click Basic Settings. The Edit Site dialog box appears.

5. Either type the full pathname (drive and folders) in the Physical Path text box, or click Browse and use the Browse for Folder dialog box to either select the folder or create a new folder.

6. Click OK.

Setting the Default Content Page

A normal website URL looks like the following:

http://*name*/*folder*/*file*

Here, `name` is a domain name or hostname, `folder` is a folder path, and `file` is the file-name of the web page or other resource. Here's an example:

http://server/photos/default.htm

Intriguingly, you can view the same web page by entering the following address into the browser:

http://server/photos/

This works because IIS defines `default.htm` as one of its default content page filenames. Here are the others:

```
default.asp
index.htm
index.html
default.aspx
```

This means that as long as a folder contains a file that uses one of these names, you can view the corresponding page without specifying the filename in the URL.

Note, too, that these default content pages have an assigned priority, with `default.htm` having the highest priority, followed by `default.asp`, then `index.htm`, then `index.html`, and finally `default.aspx`. This priority defines the order in which IIS looks for and displays the default content pages. That is, IIS first looks for `default.htm`; if that file doesn't exist in a folder, IIS next looks for `default.asp`, and so on.

For your own websites, you can add new content pages (for example, `index.htm` and `index.asp`), remove existing content pages, and change the priority of the content pages. Here are the steps to follow:

1. Launch IIS Manager.

2. Open the *SERVER*, Sites branch (where *SERVER* is the name of your Windows Home Server PC).

3. Click the website you want to work with.

4. Click Features View.

5. Double-click the Default Document icon. IIS Manager opens the Default Document page, shown in Figure 12.20.

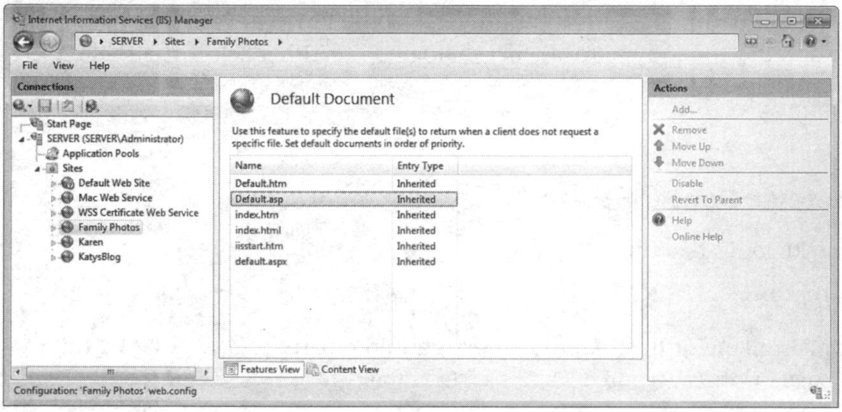

FIGURE 12.20   Use the Default Document page to add, remove, and reorder a site's default content pages.

TIP

Using a default content page is usually a good idea because it enables users to access your site without knowing the name of any file. However, for security reasons, you might want to allow access to the site only to users who know a specific filename on the site (for example, through a URL that you've provided). In that case, you have two choices: either don't include a file that uses one of the default content page names, or click Disable in the Default Document page (which appears in the Actions pane when no default documents are selected). Either way, be sure to deny directory browsing permission to all users: In the site's Home page in IIS Manager, double-click the Directory Browsing icon and then make sure this feature is disabled.

---

6. To specify a new default content page, click Add to open the Add Default Document dialog box, type the filename, and then click OK. IIS Manager adds the new filename to the Default Document list.

7. To delete a default content page, select it in the Default Document list and click Remove.

8. To change the default content page priority order, click the content page you want to work with, and then click either Move Up or Move Down.

9. Click OK to put the new settings into effect.

Disabling Anonymous Access

When you create a new site, IIS Manager allows anonymous access to the site by default. This is desirable for most websites because it enables users to most easily access the site content. IIS provides anonymous access via the IUSR accouπnt, which is a member of the Guest security group, so it has read-only access to the site.

However, you might have a site with content that you want to restrict to people who have user accounts on Windows Home Server. In that case, you need to disable anonymous access for the website and switch to Windows Authentication, which means IIS prompts each user for a username and password before allowing access to the site.

Follow these steps to disable anonymous access:

1. Launch IIS Manager.

2. Open the *SERVER*, Sites branch (where *SERVER* is the name of your Windows Home Server PC).

3. Click the website you want to work with.

4. Click Features View.

5. Double-click the Authentication icon. IIS Manager displays the Authentication page.

6. Click Anonymous Authentication, and then click Disable in the Actions pane. IIS Manager disables anonymous access to the site.

7. Click Windows Authentication, and then click Enable in the Actions pane. IIS Manager enables Windows account access to the site, as shown in Figure 12.21.

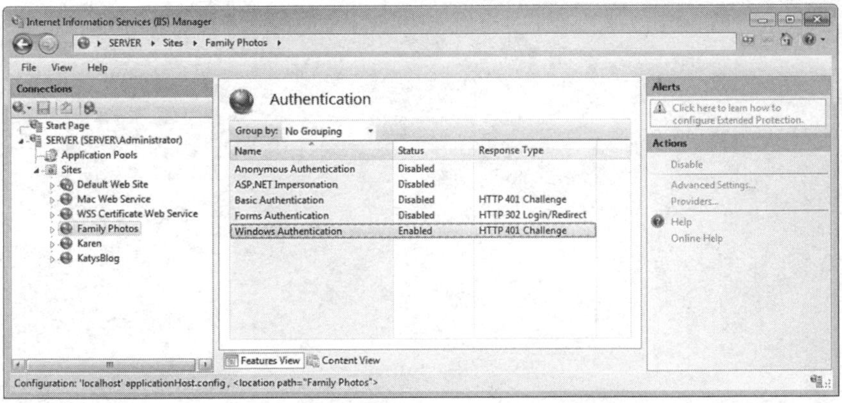

FIGURE 12.21   To secure a website, disable anonymous access and enable Windows Authentication.

> **TIP**
>
> Switching to Windows Authentication means that any user with a valid account on Windows Home Server can access the website. What if there are one or more users with Windows Home Server accounts that you do *not* want to view the website? In that case, you must adjust the security of the website's home folder directly. Use Windows Explorer to display the website's home folder, right-click the folder, and then click Properties. In the Security tab, click Edit, click Add, type the name of the user, and then click OK. Select the user, and then activate the Full Control check box in the Deny column. This tells Windows Home Server not to allow that user to view the folder, thus barring the user from viewing the website.

From Here

▶ To learn the details of applying a static IP address to the server, **SEE** "Configuring Windows Home Server with a Static IP Address," **P. 8.**

▶ For more information on installing the Connector software, **SEE** "Installing Windows Home Server Connector on the Client Computers," **P. 49.**

▶ For more information on connecting to Windows Home Server's home site and Remote Access site, **SEE** "Displaying the Remote Web Access Page," **P. 160.**

▶ You can also use Windows Home Server to host a SharePoint website; **SEE** Chapter 13, "Running a SharePoint Site on Windows Home Server."

Running a SharePoint Site on Windows Home Server

IN THIS CHAPTER

▶ Installing and Configuring Windows SharePoint Foundation 2010

▶ Adding Sites to SharePoint

▶ Working with Site Settings

▶ Creating Content for a SharePoint Site

One of the major (but hidden) advantages you get with Windows Home Server is the ability to use software that *only* installs and runs on Windows Server 2008. Now, granted, most such software programs and services are high-end tools for network administrators, IT personnel, and developers. However, a few powerful programs are useful for home networks as well as corporate shops. This chapter looks at one of the best examples of such software: Windows SharePoint Foundation 2010, which is normally used as a powerful and robust tool for business collaboration. However, SharePoint is loaded with features for sharing data among family members: picture libraries, calendars, contact lists, web page link lists, and more. You can also use SharePoint to set up a blog, run a wiki, and plan an upcoming social event.

As you see in this chapter, it takes a few steps to ensure that Windows Home Server and SharePoint get along well together, but after that's done, the full power of SharePoint is at your disposal. This chapter introduces you to SharePoint and shows you at least a bit of what you can do with it. However, SharePoint is a massive program with tons of features. As a result, this chapter can really only scratch the SharePoint surface. Fortunately, the SharePoint interface is intuitive and easy to use, so after you get up to speed with this chapter's techniques, you shouldn't have trouble figuring out the rest.

Installing and Configuring Windows SharePoint Foundation 2010

Windows SharePoint Foundation 2010 is not difficult to install and configure, but it does break (temporarily) the default Windows Home Server website. The next few sections take you through the steps for downloading, installing, and configuring Windows SharePoint Foundation 2010, including how to get the Windows Home Server default website back on its feet.

> **NOTE**
>
> To run Windows SharePoint Foundation 2010, your server must have a 64-bit quad-core CPU, and at least 4GB of RAM.

Downloading and Installing Windows SharePoint Foundation 2010

To download Windows SharePoint Foundation 2010, first head for the Microsoft Download Center at www.microsoft.com/downloads/, and then search for SharePoint Foundation. (Or you can go directly to the download page at www.microsoft.com/downloads/en/details.aspx?FamilyID=944d282d-f8f8-46fb-b951-fc650a384462.)

> **NOTE**
>
> If you want to download Windows SharePoint Foundation 2010 directly using your Windows Home Server machine, you'll need to configure the Internet Explorer Enhanced Security Configuration (ESC) feature. By default, this feature makes it a hassle to navigate any site that's not in your Trusted Sites security zone, so you need to disable it for Administrators. Click the Server Manager icon in the taskbar, and then click Configure IE ESC in the Security Information section. In the dialog box that appears, select Off in the Administrators section, and then click OK.

Follow these steps to install Windows SharePoint Foundation 2010 on Windows Home Server:

1. Launch the file that you downloaded, and click Run when prompted.
2. Click Install Software Prerequisites. The Products Preparation Tool appears.
3. Click Next. The license agreement appears.
4. Click I Accept the Terms of This Agreement, and then click Next. The Products Preparation Tool installs the software required for SharePoint.
5. Click Finish.
6. Click Install SharePoint Foundation. After a few moments, the license agreement appears.
7. Click I Accept the Terms of This Agreement, and then click Continue. SharePoint asks you to choose the installation you want.

8. Click Standalone. Windows Home Server installs Windows SharePoint Foundation 2010.

9. When the install is complete, leave the Run the SharePoint Products Configuration Wizard Now check box activated, and then click Close.

Running the Initial Windows SharePoint Foundation 2010 Configuration

When you click the Close button to end the installation, SharePoint launches the Products Configuration Wizard. This wizard runs through a series of 10 configuration tasks that get Windows SharePoint Foundation 2010 ready to run. Follow these steps to perform this configuration:

1. Click Next. The wizard displays a list of services and asks if these services can be restarted, if necessary, during the configuration.

2. Click Yes. The wizard then runs through the configuration tasks, which takes several minutes.

3. When the configuration is complete, click Finish. SharePoint then attempts to load the default site (http://server, where server is the name of your Windows Home Server).

4. If you see the Connect to Server dialog box, click Cancel.

5. Close the web browser window.

Creating a New SharePoint Web Application

During the initial SharePoint configuration, two things happen that cause the Windows Home Server default website to go offline and be replaced by the SharePoint default website:

▶ SharePoint stops the Windows Home Server default website.

▶ SharePoint creates its own default website and configures it to use TCP port 80.

This means that the http://server now loads the SharePoint default site instead of the Windows Home Server default site, as shown in Figure 13.1.

To fix this, you can't simply configure the default SharePoint site to use a different port or IP address, as you might expect. Instead, the solution is to create a new SharePoint web application that runs through a TCP port other than port 80. (In SharePoint, a *web application* is an object that acts as a container for one or more SharePoint sites.) You then shut down the default SharePoint site and restart the Windows Home Server default site.

For now, here are the steps to create a new SharePoint web application:

1. Select Start, All Programs, Microsoft SharePoint 2010 Products, SharePoint 2010 Central Administration. The SharePoint Central Administration site appears, as shown in Figure 13.2. (Note that in the address of this site, the port number you see will be different from the one shown in Figure 13.2 because the port number is assigned randomly at setup.)

FIGURE 13.1   SharePoint takes over the http://*server* site.

FIGURE 13.2   You use the Central Administration site to configure SharePoint.

2. Under Application Management, click Manage Web Applications.

3. In the Ribbon, click New. SharePoint loads the Create New Web Application page, shown in Figure 13.3.

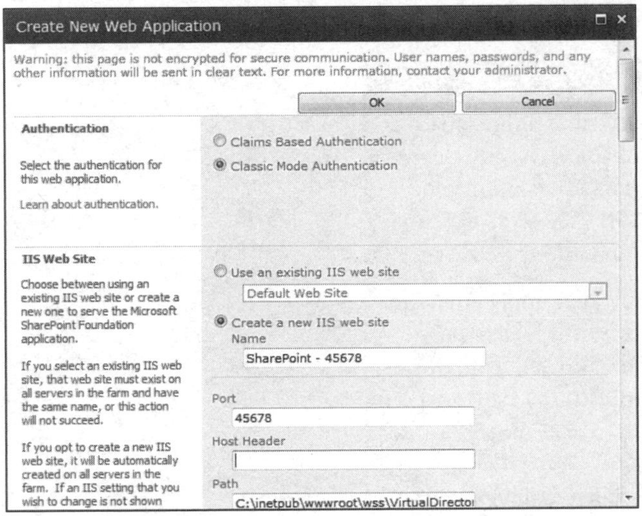

Create New Web Application

Warning: this page is not encrypted for secure communication. User names, passwords, and any other information will be sent in clear text. For more information, contact your administrator.

OK   Cancel

Authentication

Select the authentication for this web application.

Learn about authentication.

○ Claims Based Authentication
● Classic Mode Authentication

IIS Web Site

Choose between using an existing IIS web site or create a new one to serve the Microsoft SharePoint Foundation application.

If you select an existing IIS web site, that web site must exist on all servers in the farm and have the same name, or this action will not succeed.

If you opt to create a new IIS web site, it will be automatically created on all servers in the farm. If an IIS setting that you wish to change is not shown

○ Use an existing IIS web site
Default Web Site

● Create a new IIS web site
Name
SharePoint - 45678

Port
45678

Host Header

Path
C:\inetpub\wwwroot\wss\VirtualDirectoi

FIGURE 13.3   Use the Create New Web Application page to set up your new SharePoint web application.

4. For the most part, you can (and should) leave the settings as is on this page. If you want, you can make a couple of tweaks:

   ▶ **Port**—Enter any unused port that you prefer to use.

   ▶ **Select Windows SharePoint Foundation Search Server**—Choose your Windows Home Server computer here.

5. In the Application Pool section, click the Predefined option (and leave Network Service chosen in the list).

6. Click OK. SharePoint creates your new site, which might take a minute or two. When that's done, you see the Application Created page.

7. Click the Create Site Collection link to open the Create Site Collection page. You learn how to fill in this page in the next section.

Creating a Top-Level SharePoint Site

With the new SharePoint web application created, your next task is to add a top-level SharePoint site—called a *site collection*—to the application. You can use the top-level site by itself, or you can add sites to it later on. (See "Adding Sites to SharePoint," later in this chapter.)

Here are the steps to follow to create the top-level site:

1. In the Create Site Collection page (see Figure 13.4), enter the site title and description. The title appears in the upper-left corner of all site pages, and the description appears on the home page.

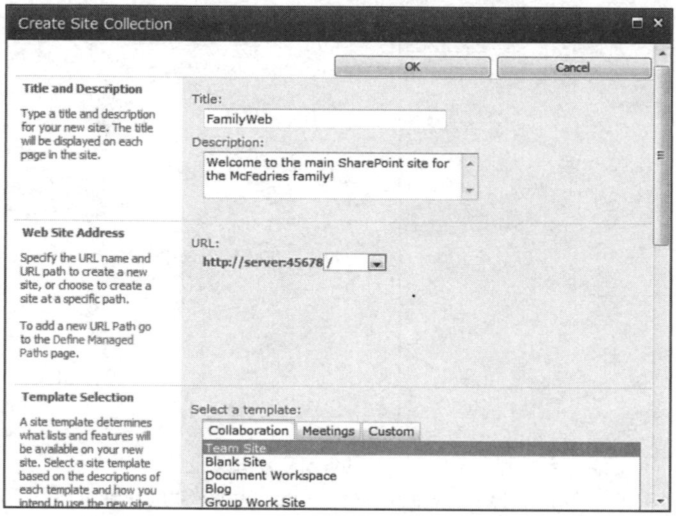

FIGURE 13.4   Use the Create Site Collection page to set up your new SharePoint site.

2. In the Web Site Address section, use the uniform resource locator (URL) list to define the path used for new sites that you add to the site collection. You have two choices:

   ▶ /—Choose this path if you won't be adding other sites to the collection, or if you want to place all new sites in the root folder of the site collection. For example, if your SharePoint web application address is http://*server*:45678/ and you later add a site that uses a folder named wedding, that site's URL will be http://server:45678/wedding/.

   ▶ /sites/—Choose this path if you want to place all new sites in the sites subfolder of the site collection. SharePoint adds an extra text box so that you can add a folder name for the site collection. If your SharePoint web application address is http://*server*:45678/ and you specify the site collection folder name as main, your site's URL will be http://server:45678/sites/main/.

TIP

You might prefer to store some or all of your SharePoint sites in a subfolder other than sites. For example, if you'll be creating several blogs, you might want to set up a blogs subfolder. To specify another subfolder, click the Define Managed Paths link to open the Define Managed Paths page. In the Add a New Path section, type / followed by the folder name, click OK, and then click the Back button until you return to the Create Site Collection page. To see the new folder in the URL list, you need to refresh the page. (If you made a long entry in the Description box, copy it before refreshing the page; otherwise, you'll lose the text and have to retype it.)

3. In the Template Selection section, select either the Collaboration or Meetings tab, and then select the template you want to use as a starting point for the site. When you click a template, a description of the template appears in the Template Selection section, as shown in Figure 13.5. If you're not sure which template to use, a good all-purpose choice is Team Site.

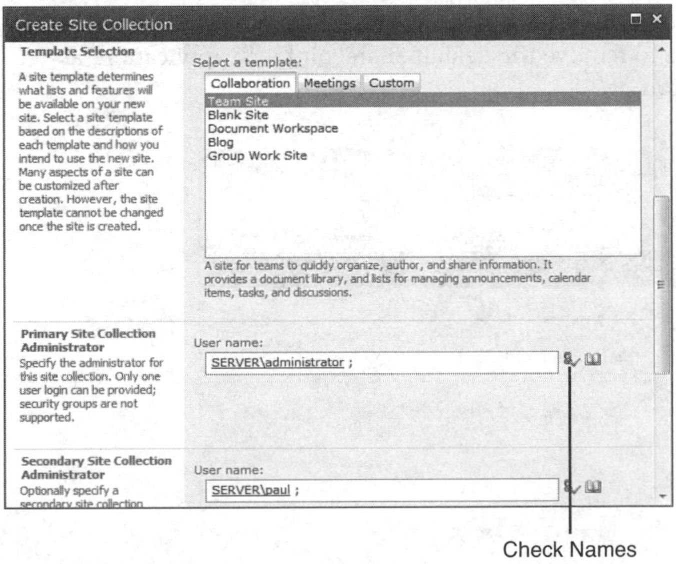

Check Names

FIGURE 13.5   Select the template you want to use as a starting point for your site.

4. In the Primary Site Collection Administrator section, type the name of the user who will be the main administrator of the site collection. Click the Check Names icon to ensure that you've entered an existing username.

5. (Optional) If you want to designate a second user as an administrator of the site collection, in the Secondary Site Collection Administrator section, type the name of the user. (Again, click Check Names to ensure that you've entered an existing username.)

6. Click OK to create the site collection. When the operation is complete, SharePoint displays the Top-Level Site Successfully Created page, which includes a link to the site, as shown in Figure 13.6.

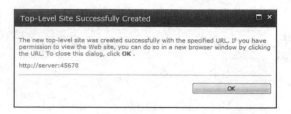

Top-Level Site Successfully Created   ☐ ✕

The new top-level site was created successfully with the specified URL. If you have permission to view the Web site, you can do so in a new browser window by clicking the URL. To close this dialog, click **OK** .

http://server:45678

[OK]

FIGURE 13.6   You see this page when SharePoint has successfully created the site collection.

7. Click OK to return to the Web Application Management page. You should now see three Web applications listed, as shown in Figure 13.7: the default application on port 80; the new application you just created; and the Central Administration application. You'll use this page to remove the default SharePoint web application, as described in the next section.

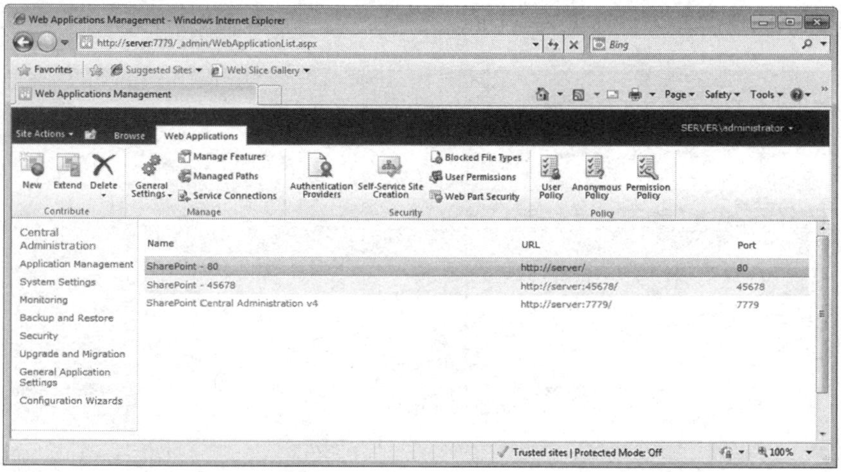

FIGURE 13.7   The Web Applications Management page now shows three applications.

Deleting the Default SharePoint Web Application

The next step in getting SharePoint and the Windows Home Server default website to operate successfully together is to delete the default SharePoint web application. Here are the steps required:

1. In the Web Application Management page, click the SharePoint - 80 web application.

2. In the Ribbon, click Delete. The Delete Web Application window appears, as shown in Figure 13.8.

3. In the Delete Content Databases option, click Yes.

4. In the Delete IIS Web Sites option, click Yes.

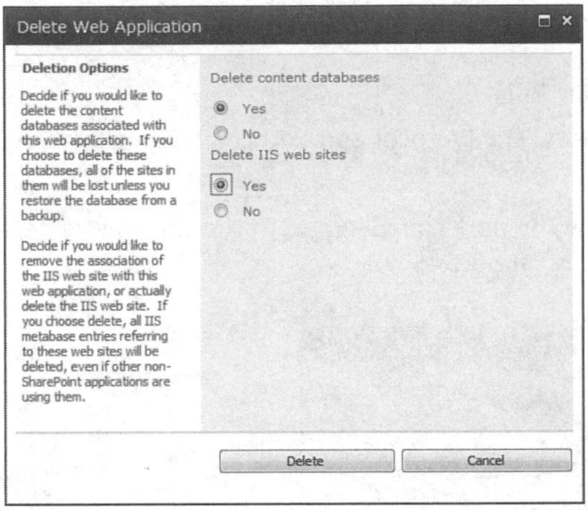

FIGURE 13.8   Use the Delete Web Application page to remove the default SharePoint Web application.

5. Click Delete. SharePoint asks you to confirm.

6. Click OK. SharePoint deletes the default site and its content.

Restarting the Windows Home Server Default Website

With SharePoint's default site deleted, you can now restart the Windows Home Server default site. Follow these steps:

1. Select Start, Administrative Tools, Internet Information Server (IIS) Manager.

2. Open the *SERVER*, Sites branch (where *SERVER* is the name of your Windows Home Server PC).

3. Click Default Web Site.

4. In the Actions pane, click Start. IIS Manager restarts the Windows Home Server default website.

Adding a Firewall Exception for the SharePoint Web Application Port

You can access your new SharePoint web application on Windows Home Server, but you won't be able to access it from a client computer. The problem is that Windows Home Server's firewall won't let traffic through on the TCP port associated with the web application. To fix this, you must add an exception for the port in Windows Firewall. Here are the steps to follow:

1. Log on to Windows Home Server.

2. Select Start, Control Panel, Windows Firewall.

3. Click Advanced Settings to open the Windows Firewall with Advanced Security window.

4. Click Inbound Rules, and then click New Rule.

5. Select the Port option, and then click Next. The Protocol and Ports dialog box appears.

6. Make sure the TCP option is activated.

7. In the Specific Local Ports text box, type the port you assigned to the site. Figure 13.9 shows the rule set up to allow traffic on port 45678.

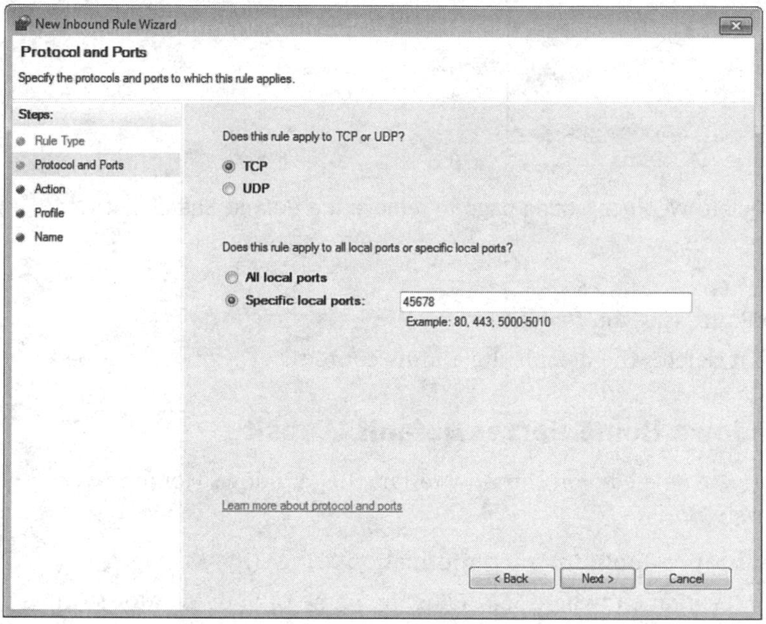

FIGURE 13.9   Set up a Windows Firewall exception to allow traffic on the TCP port associated with your SharePoint web application.

8. Click Next to display the Action dialog box.

9. Select the Allow the Connection option, and then click Next. The Profile dialog box appears.

10. Leave the check boxes activated, and click Next to display the Name dialog box.

11. In the Name text box, type TCP Port n, where n is the port number associated with your SharePoint web application, and then type an optional description for the rule.

12. Click Finish.

Forwarding the SharePoint Port in Your Router

If you configured the Windows Firewall port exception for your SharePoint web application with the Any Computer scope, Internet users won't be able to access the site because your network's router won't forward data through the port you associated with the web application.

You need to configure the router to forward any data that comes in on that port to the IP address of the Windows Home Server computer. The steps for doing this vary depending on the manufacturer of the router. As an example, Figure 13.10 shows the Port Forwarding screen for a D-Link router. Here, I've forwarded TCP port 45678 to the address 192.168.1.254, which is the static IP address of my Windows Home Server. Consult your device documentation for information on configuring port forwarding.

VIRTUAL SERVERS LIST

Enable	Name	IP Address	Protocol Private Port/Public Port	Inbound Filter	Schedule		
☑	SharePoint	192.168.1.254	TCP 45678/45678	Allow All	Always		
☑	HTTP	192.168.1.254	TCP 80/80	Allow All	Always		
☑	RPD 4125	192.168.1.254	TCP 4125/4125	Allow All	Always		
☑	RDP 443	192.168.1.254	TCP 443/443	Allow All	Always		

FIGURE 13.10   Configure your network's router to forward the SharePoint web application port to the Windows Home Server IP address.

Adding Users to the Top-Level SharePoint Site

You can now log on to the top-level SharePoint site (as described next in the "Logging On to the Top-Level SharePoint Site" section) using the primary site collection administration account. If you specified a secondary site collection administration account, you can log on to the top-level site under that account, as well. However, if you try to log on using any other Windows Home Server account, you get an Access Denied error.

To solve the problem, you must add users to the top-level SharePoint site. SharePoint enables you to add users to one of the following groups:

  ▶ **Visitors**—Users in this group have Read permission, which enables them only to view the contents of the site, not change the site in any way.

  ▶ **Members**—Users in this group have Contribute permission, which enables them to view, change, add, and delete content.

  ▶ **Owners**—Users in this group have Full Control permission, which enables them to perform any action on the site, including adding users, changing permissions, and adding sites.

You can also designate a specific permission level for a user: Read, Contribute, Full Control, or Design. (The latter includes the same permissions as the Contribute level but also allows the user to customize the site.)

Here are the steps to follow to add a user to the site:

  1. Log on to the top-level SharePoint site using the primary (or secondary) site collection administration account.

2. Click Site Actions, and then click Site Settings.

3. In the Site Settings page, click the People and Groups link.

4. In the Groups list, click the group to which you want to assign the new user.

5. Click New, and then click Add Users to open the site's Grant Permissions dialog box, shown in Figure 13.11.

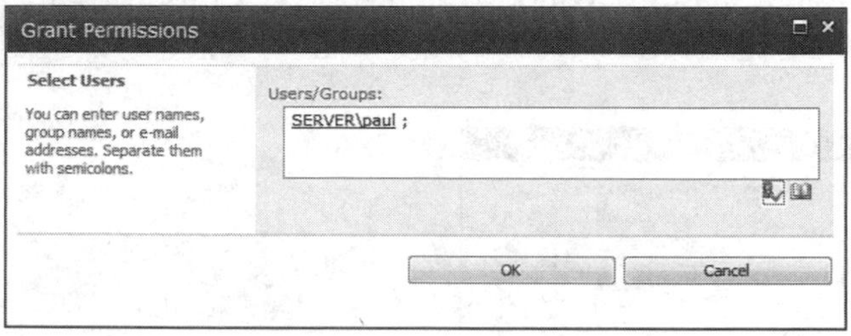

FIGURE 13.11   Use the Grant Permissions page to add users to the SharePoint top-level site.

6. Type the username in the Users/Groups box, and then click the Check Name icon to verify the name. (You can also enter the name of a Windows Home Server security group.)

7. Repeat step 6 to specify other users or groups.

8. Click OK. SharePoint adds the users or groups to the site.

Logging On to the Top-Level SharePoint Site

With the Windows Firewall exception in place and users added, you can access the top-level SharePoint site from any network computer by following these steps:

1. Open your web browser.

2. In the address bar, type the URL of the top-level SharePoint site. This is the URL that SharePoint displayed in the Create Site Collection page. (Refer to step 2 in the section "Creating a Top-Level SharePoint Site," earlier in this chapter.) The browser prompts you to enter your username and password.

3. Type the username and password, and then click OK.

The browser loads the home page of the top-level site. Your username appears in the top-right corner of the home page, as shown in Figure 13.12. (Note that the design of your top-level site may be quite different from the one you see in Figure 13.12, depending on the template you chose for the site.)

FIGURE 13.12   The home page of a top-level SharePoint site.

Adding Sites to SharePoint

With your SharePoint top-level site in place, you're ready to start using it for sharing, collaborating, and any other tasks you can think of. Before going further, however, you need to decide whether you want a single SharePoint site or multiple sites. SharePoint actually gives you three options:

▶ **Single top-level site**—This option means that you add all your content to the top-level site that you just created. Use this setup if your collaboration requirements are fairly basic. With a single site, you can add content such as a calendar, picture library, discussion board, lists for contacts, announcements, links, web pages, and more. (See "Creating Content for a SharePoint Site," later in this chapter, for the details of adding and working with these SharePoint content types.) In this case, you usually access your SharePoint site using an address of the form `http://server:port/`, where *server* is your Windows Home Server computer name and *port* is the TCP port associated with the SharePoint web application. An example is `http://server:45678/`.

▶ **Multiple top-level sites**—This option means that you create two or more top-level sites, each of which contains different content. Use multiple top-level sites if your collaboration needs are more complex. For example, you might want to create one site for the whole family, separate sites for each of the kids, and another site for your home business. In this case, you access the other top-level sites using an address of the form `http://server:port/sites/folder/`, where *server* is your Windows Home Server computer name, *port* is the TCP port associated with the SharePoint web application, and *folder* is the folder used by the top-level site. An example is `http://server:45678/sites/katysblog/`.

▶ **Single top-level site with subsites**—This option means that you augment the top-level site that you just created with one or more secondary SharePoint sites. Again, this is useful for more elaborate collaboration needs, but navigating between the sites is easier (which I'll explain in a moment). In this case, you access the subsites using an address of the form `http://server:port/folder/`, where *server* is your Windows Home Server computer name, *port* is the TCP port associated with the SharePoint web application, and *folder* is the folder the subsite uses. An example is `http://server:45678/wedding/`.

TIP

If you want to view a SharePoint site on a mobile device such as a handheld PC or smartphone, add `m/` to the URL to see a version suitable for the small screens on most mobile devices. Here are some examples:

http://server:45678/m/

http://server:45678/sites/katysblog/m/

http://server:45678/wedding/m/

In the previous item, I mentioned that using a single top-level site with subsites makes site navigation easier. To see what I mean, you need to know that if you set up multiple top-level sites, the sites can't "see" each other. That is, there's no default method for linking from one site to another. Instead, to navigate to another site, you must enter that site's URL into the browser. This isn't necessarily a bad thing because you (or your family) might *want* to keep the sites separate.

However, when you use a single top-level site with subsites, SharePoint gives you the option of adding links to the subsites in various navigation aids that are part of the top-level site. A good example is the SharePoint Central Administration site, shown earlier in Figure 13.2. Examine the tabs near the top of the page. (This section of the page is called the *top link bar*; see Figure 13.15.) The Home tab represents the top-level Central Administration site, whereas the Operations and Application Management tabs represent subsites within the top-level site. Links to these subsites also appear in Quick Launch, which is on the left side of the home page (again, see Figure 13.15).

Adding a Top-Level Site

Here are the steps to follow to add another top-level site to your SharePoint web application:

1. Select Start, All Programs, Microsoft SharePoint 2010 Products, SharePoint 2010 Central Administration.

2. Under Application Management, click the Create Site Collections link to display the Create Site Collection page.

3. Follow the steps I outlined earlier in the "Creating a Top-Level SharePoint Site" section. In this case, when you specify the site URL, you must use the `sites` folder and specify a subfolder for your site. (Again, you can also click Defined Managed Paths to create a folder other than `sites`.)

Adding a Subsite

If you prefer to use a single top-level SharePoint site, follow these steps to add a subsite:

1. Log on to the top-level SharePoint site using the primary (or secondary) site collection administration account.

2. Click Site Actions and then New Site to display the New SharePoint Site page, shown in Figure 13.13.

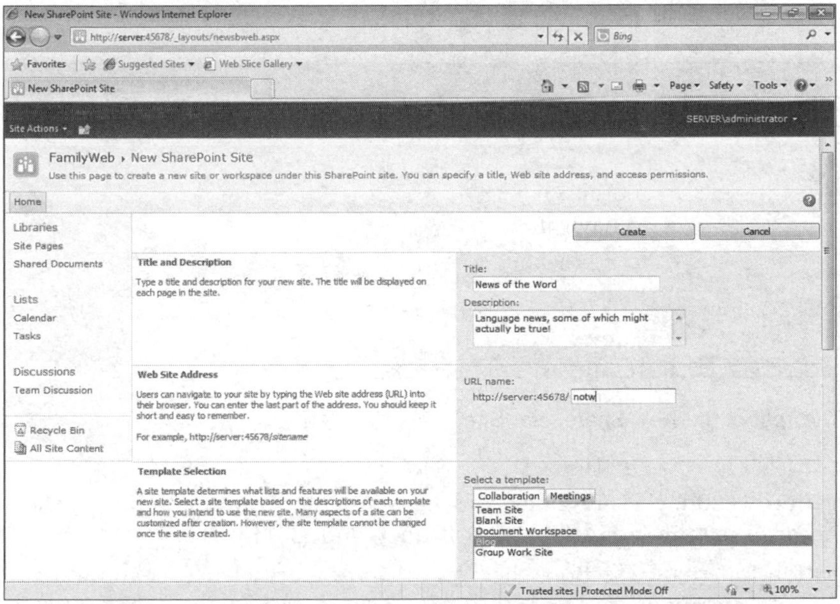

FIGURE 13.13 Use the New SharePoint Site page to set up a subsite.

3. Enter the site title and description.

4. In the Web Site Address section, use the URL Name text box to type the name of the folder you want to use to hold the site's contents. If the name consists of two or more words, separate each word with an underscore (_) instead of a space.

5. Use the Template Selection section to select the template you want to use as a starting point for the site.

6. In the Permissions section (see Figure 13.14), select a User Permissions option:

   ▶ **Use Same Permissions as Parent Site**—Select this option to configure the subsite with the same permissions that are configured on the top-level site.

   ▶ **Use Unique Permissions**—Select this option to configure the secondary site with its own permissions.

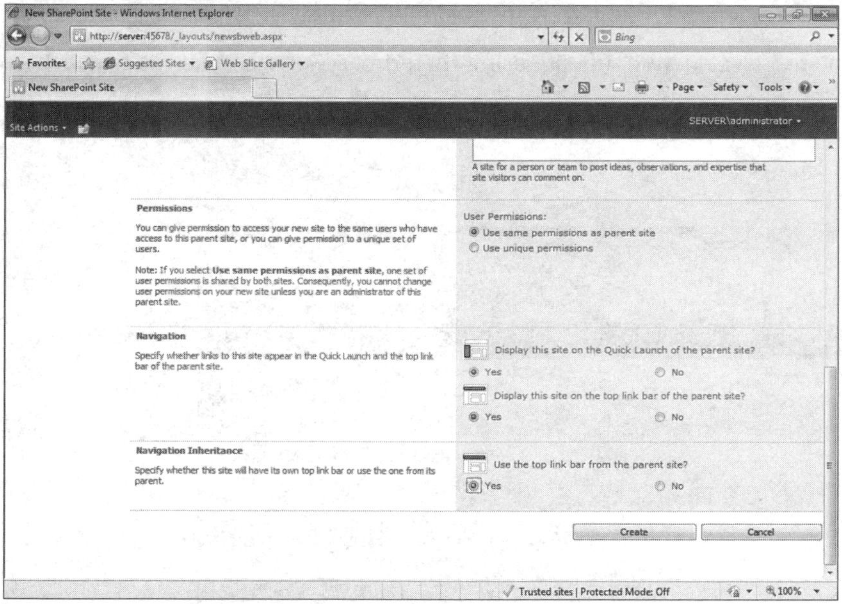

FIGURE 13.14   The rest of the New SharePoint Site page.

7. In the Navigation section, click Yes or No to specify whether you want a link to the subsite to appear in the top-level site's Quick Launch and top link bar.

8. In the Navigation Inheritance section, click Yes or No to specify whether you want the top-level site's top link bar to remain onscreen when you navigate to the subsite.

9. Click Create to create the subsite.

10. If you selected the Use Unique Permissions option, you see the Set Up Groups for This Site page. Click OK when you're done.

Figure 13.15 shows a top-level site with a subsite added. Note the extra tab in the links bar and the link to the subsite in Quick Launch's Sites section.

Top link bar   Links to subsite

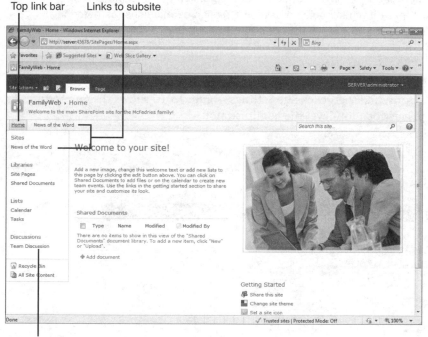

Quick Launch

FIGURE 13.15   A top-level site showing links to a subsite.

Working with Site Settings

Windows SharePoint Foundation 2010 gives you a tremendous number of settings that you can use to configure almost any aspect of a site. Space limitations prevent me from discussing all 30 or so settings, but the next few sections take you through some of the most useful tweaks you can make to a site.

Customizing a Site

The look and feel of a SharePoint site is governed by settings that control the title, the description, the visual theme, the top link bar and Quick Launch, and more. Follow these steps to adjust some or all of these settings:

1. Log on to the top-level SharePoint site as the primary or secondary site administrator, or use an account in the site's Owners group.

> **NOTE**
>
> Logging on as a site administrator or owner is ideal because it gives you access to the full range of customization settings. However, there are also a few aspects of a site that you can customize if you log on as a user with Design permissions (as noted in step 4, which follows).

2. If you want to customize a subsite, navigate to that site.

3. Click Site Actions, and then click Site Settings. Figure 13.16 shows the Site Settings page that appears for a top-level site administrator.

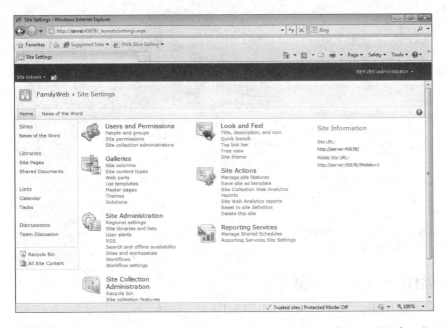

FIGURE 13.16   Use the Site Settings page to customize all aspects of a site.

4. Use the links in the Look and Feel section to customize the site.

The next few sections describe what you can do with each link.

Editing a Site's Title and Description

You specified the site's title and description when you first set up the site, but you're not stuck with the original values if you're tired of them or you feel they no longer reflect the site's content. Follow these steps:

1. In the Site Settings page, click the Title, Description, and Icon link.

2. Use the Title text box to edit the site title.

3. Use the Description text box to edit the site description.

4. Click OK to put the new settings into effect.

Displaying a Custom Site Icon

When you navigate to a site, you see an icon for the site to the left of the site title. This icon is the same for all sites, so you can inject some individuality into a site by specifying a custom icon. The image file (smaller images are better) can reside in a local folder, a shared network folder, or on a website. Here are the steps to follow:

1. In the Site Settings page, click the Title, Description, and Icon link.

2. In the Logo URL and Description section, use the URL text box to enter the address of the image file you want to use as the site's icon. Enter a local pathname, a UNC (Universal Naming Convention) pathname, or a web URL.

TIP

After you enter the image address, click the Click Here to Test link to open the image in a browser window. If you see the image, you know your address is accurate.

3. Use the Enter a Description text box to type text that describes the image. This text appears when a user points at the image, displays the site with image display turned off in his browser, or views the site using a screen-reading device.

4. Click OK to put the new settings into effect.

Changing a Subsite's Folder

If the name you originally supplied for a subsite's folder is no longer relevant or is too long, you can change it to something more suitable or shorter. Follow these steps:

1. In the Site Settings page for the subsite, click the Title, Description, and Icon link.

2. Use the URL Name text box to enter the new folder name you want to use.

3. Click OK to put the new settings into effect.

Adding a Tree View

A *tree view* is a method of displaying items that have a hierarchical relationship. The topmost item acts as the "trunk" of the tree, second-level items are the main branches, third-level items are subbranches, and so on. For example, the Folders list in Windows Explorer is a tree view, with a drive's root folder as the trunk, the root's folders as the branches, and so on.

13

> **NOTE**
>
> Some SharePoint sites (such as a blog) don't have hierarchical content by default, so adding the tree view won't do anything.

Here are the steps to follow to add a tree view control to your site:

1. In the Site Settings page, click the Tree View link.
2. Activate the Enable Tree View check box.
3. Click OK to put the new setting into effect.

Click the site's home page to see the tree view. Figure 13.17 shows a top-level site with a tree view added to the left side of the page.

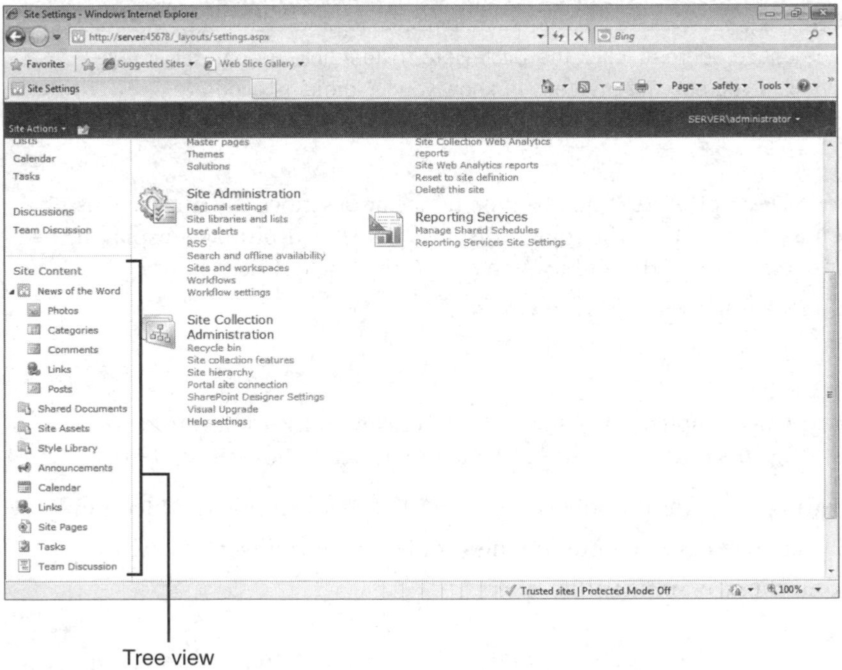

FIGURE 13.17   Use the Site Settings page to customize all aspects of a site.

Changing the Site Theme

The overall look of a site is determined by the site theme, which governs the following visual factors in the site's design:

▶ The color of the regular page text

▶ The color of the page headings

- ▸ The color of the links
- ▸ The background color of the page
- ▸ The background color of the top link bar
- ▸ The color of the Quick Launch headings
- ▸ The background color of the entire Quick Launch

SharePoint defines 20 themes to offer a variety of looks for your site. Here are the steps to follow to select a new theme:

1. In the Site Settings page, click the Site Theme link.

NOTE

The Site Theme link is available to group members who have at least Design permission.

2. Click the theme you want to use. (The Preview section gives you an idea what the theme looks like.)
3. Click OK to apply the theme to the site.

Adding Links to the Top Link Bar

As you know, the top link bar displays the Home tab, which represents the top-level SharePoint site, as well as tabs for each subsite. However, you can also add your own links to the top link bar. This is convenient because the top link bar is visible from any page in any SharePoint site, so you can put your favorite sites a mere mouse click away.

Here are the steps to follow to add a link to the top link bar:

1. In the Site Settings page, click the Top Link Bar link to open the Top Link Bar page.

NOTE

The Top Link Bar link is available to group members who have at least Design permission.

2. Click New Navigation Link.
3. Use the Type the Web Address text box to enter the URL of the site. If you'd rather see text instead of the URL in the top link bar, enter a name or short description in the Type the Description box.
4. Click OK to return to the Top Link Bar page.
5. Repeat steps 2 through 4 to add more links.
6. If you want to modify the order in which the links appear, click Change Order, specify the order for each link, and then click OK.
7. Click OK to put the new settings into effect.

> **NOTE**
>
> To remove a link from the top link bar, open the Site Settings page and click the Top Link Bar link. Click the Edit icon that appears beside the link you want to remove, click Delete, and then click OK when SharePoint asks you to confirm.

Customizing Quick Launch

Quick Launch is a useful area that gives you quick access to the main areas of a SharePoint site. However, you can make Quick Launch even more useful by deleting links and sections you never use, reordering the headings and links, and adding your own headings and links. Follow these steps:

1. In the Site Settings page, click the Quick Launch link.

> **NOTE**
>
> The Quick Launch link is available to group members who have at least Design permission.

2. Use one or more of the following techniques to customize Quick Launch:

   ▶ To delete a link, click the Edit icon to the left of the link, click Delete, and then click OK.

   ▶ To delete a heading (and all its links), click the Edit icon to the left of the heading, click Delete, and then click OK.

   ▶ To change the order of the headings, click Change Order, use the numerical lists beside each heading to set the order, and then click OK.

   ▶ To change the order in which the links appear within a particular heading, click Change Order, use the numerical lists beside each link to set the order, and then click OK.

   ▶ To create a new heading, click New Heading, type the address that you want the heading to link to and the heading description (this is the name that appears in Quick Launch), and then click OK.

   ▶ To add your own links to a heading, click New Navigation Link, type the address of the link and the link description (this is the link text that appears in Quick Launch), choose the heading under which you want the link to appear, and then click OK.

3. Click OK.

Working with Users

Unlike a typical website where any user can browse anything on the site, a SharePoint site is restricted to just those Windows Home Server users who have been granted access to the site. So, it's important not only that you grant access to the appropriate users but that you apply the appropriate permissions to those users. You learned earlier how to add users to a top-level SharePoint site. (See "Adding Users to the Top-Level SharePoint Site.") You use the same technique to add users to a subsite, except that you navigate to the subsite before adding the users.

However, SharePoint has user-related features behind basic site access. You can record user information such as the person's real name, picture, and email address. You can use the email address to send a message to a user, and more. The next few sections take you through some of these features.

Editing User Information

When you add a user to a SharePoint site, the only bit of information you supply is the user's account name. However, SharePoint can record quite a bit more data for each user, as the following steps show:

1. Log on to the top-level SharePoint as an administrator.
2. If you want to work with a user in a subsite, navigate to that subsite.
3. Select Site Actions, Site Settings.
4. Click the People and Groups link.
5. In the Quick Launch Groups header, click the group that contains the user.
6. Click the name of the user you want to edit.
7. Click Edit Item. SharePoint displays the Edit Personal Settings page, shown in Figure 13.18.

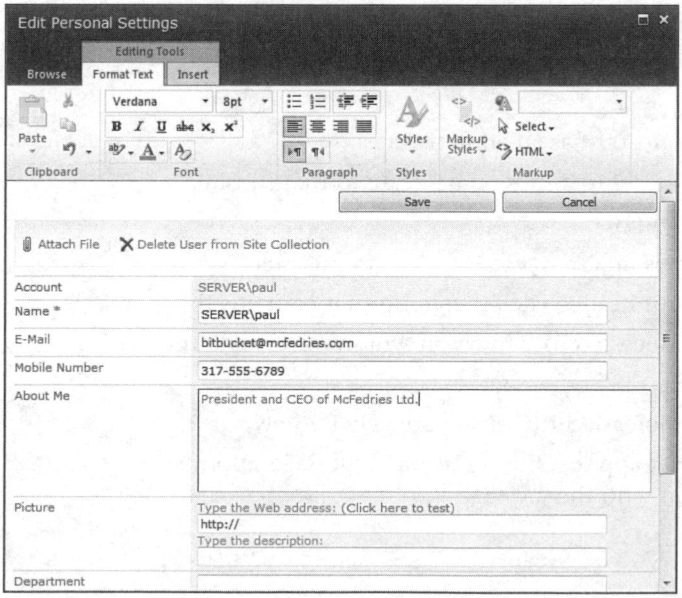

FIGURE 13.18   Use the Edit Personal Settings page to add to or edit the user's data.

8. Add or edit the data in the editable fields.

9. Click Save.

TIP

You're not restricted to just the fields (or *columns*, as SharePoint calls them) that you see in the User Information page. You can add your own custom columns to record data such as birthdays, MySpace or Facebook addresses, and cell phone numbers. Log on to the top-level SharePoint as an administrator, and then select Site Actions, Site Settings, People and Groups. In any group list, select Settings, List Settings to open the List Settings page, and then click the Create Column link. Type the Column Name and select a data type (such as Single Line of Text, Number, or Date and Time). Fill in the other settings, as necessary (these vary depending on the data type you selected), and then click OK.

Sending an Email to Users

In the previous section, you saw that SharePoint includes an E-Mail field in the user information. If you fill in that field for one or more users, you can send an email message to some or all of those users.

NOTE

I'm assuming here that you're accessing the site using a home computer that has an email client installed; this won't work on the Windows Home Server box because, by default, it doesn't come with an email client.

Here are the steps to follow:

1. Log on to the top-level SharePoint as an administrator.

2. If you want to work with a user in a subsite, navigate to that subsite.

3. Select Site Actions, Site Settings.

4. Click the People and Groups link.

5. In the Quick Launch Groups header, click the group that contains the user.

6. Activate the check box beside each user to whom you want to send the message.

7. Select Actions, E-Mail Users.

8. If you see the Internet Explorer Security dialog box, click Allow.

9. In the message window that appears, fill in the usual message information (subject, body, and so on), and then send the message.

Deleting a User from a SharePoint Group

If you've added a user to a SharePoint site, you may decide that you no longer want that person to access the site. In that case, you need to remove the user from whatever SharePoint group to which you assigned the user originally. Similarly, if you want to move a user to another group, you need to first remove the user from the existing group and then add him to the other group.

In either case, here are the steps required to remove a user from a SharePoint group:

1. Log on to the top-level SharePoint as an administrator.
2. If you want to work with a user in a subsite, navigate to that subsite.
3. Select Site Actions, Site Settings.
4. Click the People and Groups link.
5. In the Quick Launch Groups header, click the group that contains the user.
6. Activate the check box beside each user you want to remove from the group.
7. Select Actions, Remove Users from Group. SharePoint asks you to confirm.
8. Click OK.

Working with Groups

Like the security groups in Windows Home Server, the groups in a SharePoint site serve to simplify user management and user permissions. You've seen how to add a user to one of the three predefined groups—Visitors, Members, or Owners; see "Adding Users to the Top-Level SharePoint Site"—but SharePoint offers several other group features. For example, you can change group settings, such as the group name and permissions. You can also create your own custom groups, and you can apply different groups to visitors, members, and owners. The next few sections take you through these useful features.

Modifying Group Settings

For each group, SharePoint maintains settings such as the group name and description, the user or group that owns the group, and who can view and edit the group membership. You can modify all these settings and more by following these steps:

1. Log on to the top-level SharePoint as an administrator.
2. If you want to work with a group in a subsite, navigate to that subsite.
3. Select Site Actions, Site Settings.
4. Click the People and Groups link.
5. In the Quick Launch Groups header, click the group you want to work with.
6. Select Settings, Group Settings. The Change Group Settings page appears, as shown in Figure 13.19.

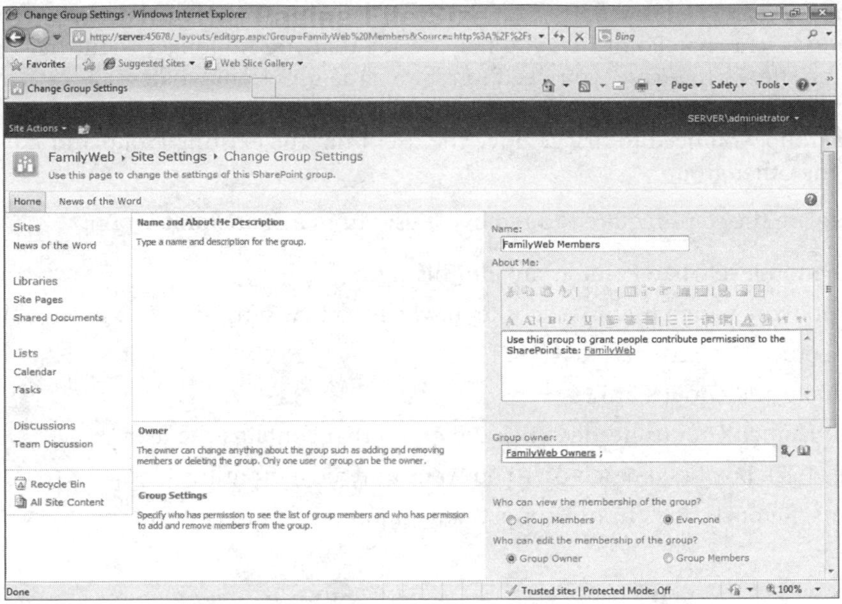

FIGURE 13.19   Use the Change Group Settings page to modify a group's settings.

7. Use the Name and About Me boxes to edit the group's name and description.

8. Use the Group Owner list to select the group's owner. (This can be a user or a group.)

9. Under Who Can View the Membership of the Group, select either Group Members or Everyone.

10. Under Who Can Edit the Membership of the Group, select either Group Owner or Group Members.

> **NOTE**
>
> Ignore the options in the Membership Requests section. These options require that an email server be configured on the system, and Windows Home Server doesn't come with an email server.

11. Click OK to put the new settings into effect.

Creating a New Group

If none of SharePoint's predefined groups has exactly the settings you want (and you don't want to reconfigure an existing group), you can add your own custom group to the SharePoint site. Follow these steps:

1. Log on to the top-level SharePoint as an administrator.

2. If you want to work with a group in a subsite, navigate to that subsite.

3. Select Site Actions, Site Settings.

4. Click the People and Groups link.

5. Click More to display the All Groups page.

6. Select New, New Group. SharePoint displays the New Group page, which has the same controls as the Change Group Settings page, shown earlier in Figure 13.19.

7. Fill in the settings you want for your new group.

8. In the Give Group Permissions to This Site section, use the check boxes to specify the permissions for the group membership: Full Control, Design, Contribute, or Read.

9. Click Create to add the group to the site.

Deleting a Group

If a SharePoint site has a group that you no longer need, you should delete it to reduce clutter in the Quick Launch Groups header. Follow these steps to delete a group:

1. Log on to the top-level SharePoint as an administrator.

2. If you want to work with a group in a subsite, navigate to that subsite.

3. Select Site Actions, Site Settings.

4. Click the People and Groups link.

5. In the Quick Launch Groups header, click the group you want to work with.

6. Select Settings, Group Settings to open the Change Group Settings page.

7. Click Delete. SharePoint asks you to confirm.

8. Click OK.

Working with Permissions

A site's permissions specify what a user or group can access on the site and what actions a user or group can perform on the site's content and other items that are part of the site (such as users and even permissions themselves). As a site administrator, you can alter permissions in two ways: You can change the permission level assigned to a user or group, and you can create custom permission levels. The next two sections provide the details.

Changing the Permission Level of a User or Group

Here are the steps to follow to change the current permission level that has been assigned to one or more users or groups:

1. Log on to the top-level SharePoint as an administrator.

2. If you want to work with a group in a subsite, navigate to that subsite.

3. Select Site Actions, Site Permissions. SharePoint displays the site's Permission Tools page, which lists the defined groups as well as any user who has been assigned a specific permission level (such as Full Control or Design) instead of a group permission level; see Figure 13.20.

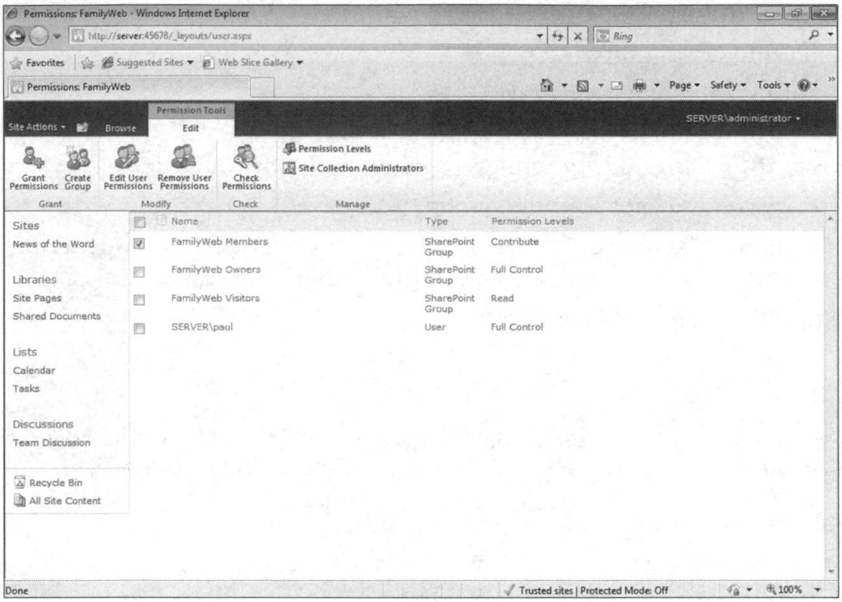

FIGURE 13.20   Use the Permission Tools page to modify the permission level for a user or group.

4. Activate the check box beside each group or user you want to work with. SharePoint displays the Edit Permissions page for the group or user.

5. In the Ribbon, click Edit User Permissions. SharePoint displays the Edit Permissions dialog box for the group or user, as shown in Figure 13.21.

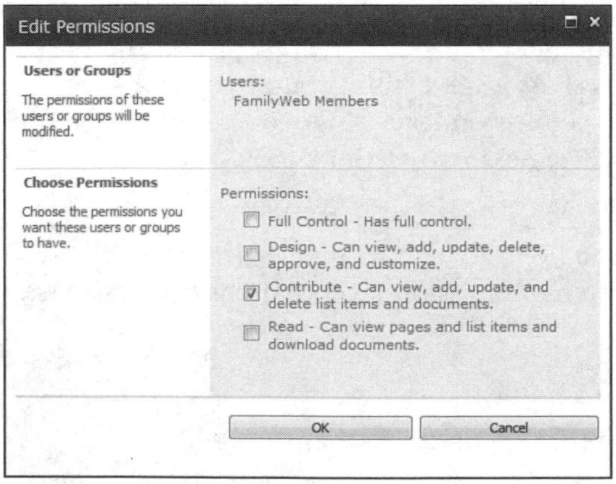

FIGURE 13.21   Use the Edit Permissions dialog box to set the permission level for a user or group.

6. Activate the check box beside each permission level you want to apply to the group or user.

7. Click OK.

Creating a Custom Permission Level

SharePoint's predefined permission levels—Full Control, Design, Contribute, and Read—should satisfy most of your needs. However, if none of these levels gives you exactly the permissions you want, you can create your own level. The following steps show you how it's done:

> **NOTE**
>
> SharePoint actually defines a fifth permission level called Limited Access. This level is used to give users permission to view specific lists, libraries, and other content.

1. Log on to the top-level SharePoint site as an administrator.

2. If you want to work with permissions in a subsite, navigate to that subsite.

3. Select Site Actions, Site Permissions to display the Permission Tools page.

4. In the Ribbon, click Permission Levels to open the Permission Levels page.

5. Click Add a Permission Level.

6. Type a name and description for the new permission level.

7. Activate the check box beside each type of permission you want to apply to this level, as shown in Figure 13.22.

8. Click Create.

Deleting a Site

If you have a site that you no longer use, you should delete it to save disk space and, in the case of subsites, reduce clutter on the top link bar and Quick Launch. Follow these steps:

1. Log on to the top-level SharePoint site as an administrator.

2. If you want to delete a subsite, navigate to that subsite.

3. Select Site Actions, Site Settings.

4. Under Site Actions, click the Delete This Site link.

5. In the Delete This Site page, click Delete. SharePoint asks you to confirm.

6. Click OK. SharePoint deletes the site.

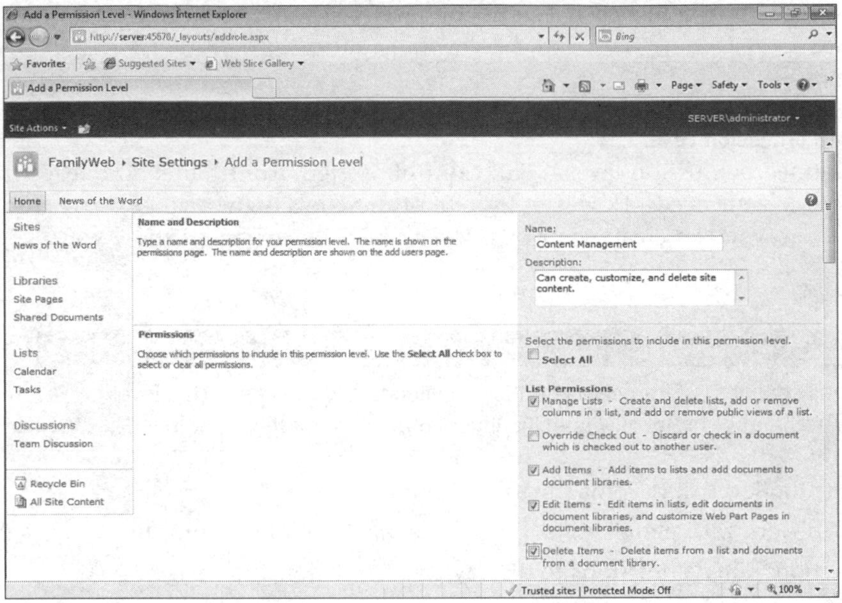

FIGURE 13.22   Use the Add a Permission Level page to create a custom permission level for your site.

Creating Content for a SharePoint Site

Administering even a small SharePoint site is a reasonably big responsibility, which is why I've devoted so much of this chapter to administrative chores. However, the value of any SharePoint site is always found in its content. SharePoint is designed for business users, so most of its content categories have a business feel to them, but there is plenty for families to enjoy. The next few sections take you through four content types that you might want to add to your site: a picture library, a calendar, a contacts list, and a links list.

Storing Images in a Picture Library

A SharePoint picture library is a storage area for images. You can use the library to view an image slide show, and you can edit the images if your computer has an image-editing program installed. If you have Office installed on the client computer, you can also email images via Outlook and edit and download images to your computer using the Microsoft Office Picture Manager.

To create a picture library, follow these steps:

1. Log on to the top-level SharePoint site using the primary (or secondary) site collection administration account.

2. Click Site Actions, and then click More Options to display the Create page.

3. Under Libraries, click the Picture Library link.

4. Type a name and description for the new library.

5. In the Navigation section, click Yes if you want to include a link to the picture library on Quick Launch.

6. If you want SharePoint to keep track of versions of pictures as they're editing in the library, click Yes in the Picture Version History section.

7. Click Create. SharePoint builds the new library and (if you clicked Yes in the Navigation section) adds a link to the picture library in the Pictures heading of Quick Launch. Figure 13.23 shows a sample picture library. Here's a summary of the most useful commands available in a picture library:

   ▶ **Upload Picture**—(Upload menu) Displays the Add Picture page, which you use to upload an image from your computer or network to the library.

   ▶ **Delete**—(Actions menu) Deletes those library images that have their check box activated.

   ▶ **View Slide Show**—(Actions menu) Displays the library images in a separate slide window.

   ▶ **Open with Windows Explorer**—(Actions menu) Opens the picture library in Windows Explorer. This enables you to click and drag images from another folder window and drop them inside the picture library.

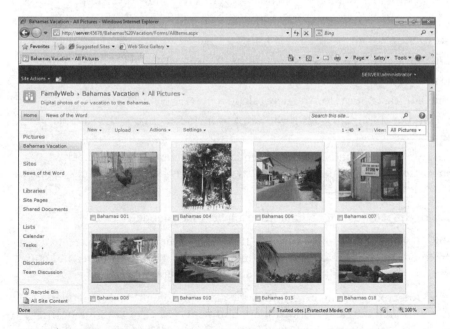

FIGURE 13.23   A SharePoint picture library.

If you have Microsoft Office installed, you also get the following commands:

▶ **Upload Multiple Pictures**—(Upload menu) Displays the Microsoft Office Picture Manager's Uploading Selected Pictures window, which enables you to select and upload multiple images to the library.

▶ **Edit**—(Action menu) Displays the Microsoft Office Picture Manager's Editing Selected Pictures window, which enables you to modify image properties such as brightness, contrast, and color, as well as crop, rotate, and resize the image.

▶ **Download**—(Action menu) Enables you to select and download multiple images from the library to your computer using the Microsoft Office Picture Manager program.

▶ **Send To**—(Action menu) Attaches the selected images to an Outlook email message.

Tracking Appointments with a Calendar

A SharePoint calendar, similar to the Outlook Calendar, is a special list that keeps track of your appointments and events. It can even synchronize with Outlook so that you don't have to maintain two separate lists of appointments.

SharePoint includes a calendar by default in many site templates. If your site doesn't have a calendar, or if you want to add another calendar to your site, follow these steps:

1. Log on to the top-level SharePoint site using the primary (or secondary) site collection administration account.
2. Click Site Actions, and then click More Options to display the Create page.
3. Under Tracking, click the Calendar link.
4. Type a name and description for the new calendar.
5. In the Navigation section, click Yes if you want to include a link to the calendar on Quick Launch.
6. Click Create. SharePoint builds the new calendar and (if you clicked Yes in the Navigation section) adds a link to the calendar in the Lists heading of Quick Launch. Figure 13.24 shows a sample calendar.

Here's a summary of the most useful commands available in a calendar:

▶ **New Event**—(Events tab) Displays the New Item page, which you use to create a new appointment by specifying the appointment title, location, start time, and end time. You can also create an all-day event and a recurring appointment.

▶ **Connect to Outlook**—(Calendar tab) Adds the calendar to Outlook's Calendar folder. You can then create and work with appointments either in Outlook or in SharePoint. Note, however, that you need Outlook 2003 or later for this to work.

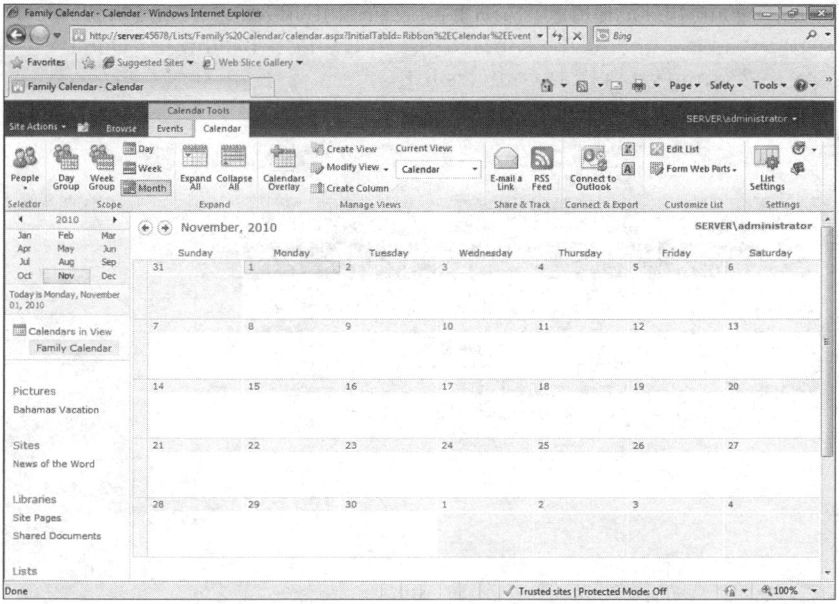

FIGURE 13.24   A SharePoint calendar.

> **TIP**
>
> It's easy to keep the SharePoint and Outlook calendars synchronized. If you change the data in Outlook, refresh the SharePoint window (by pressing F5) to see the new data; if you change the data in SharePoint, select the calendar in Outlook and then select Tools, Send/Receive, This Folder (or press Shift+F9).

Maintaining a List of Contacts

A SharePoint contacts list keeps track of your appointments and events. It's similar to the Outlook Contacts feature and can even synchronize with Outlook so that you don't have to maintain two separate lists of contacts.

SharePoint includes a contact list by default in many site templates. If your site doesn't have a contacts list, or if you want to add another contacts list to your site, follow these steps:

1. Log on to the top-level SharePoint site using the primary (or secondary) site collection administration account.

2. Click Site Actions, and then click More Options to display the Create page.

3. Under Communications, click the Contacts link.

4. Type a name and description for the new contacts list.

5. In the Navigation section, click Yes if you want to include a link to the contacts list on Quick Launch.

6. Click Create. SharePoint builds the contacts list and (if you clicked Yes in the Navigation section) adds a link to the contacts list in the Lists heading of Quick Launch. Figure 13.25 shows a sample contacts list.

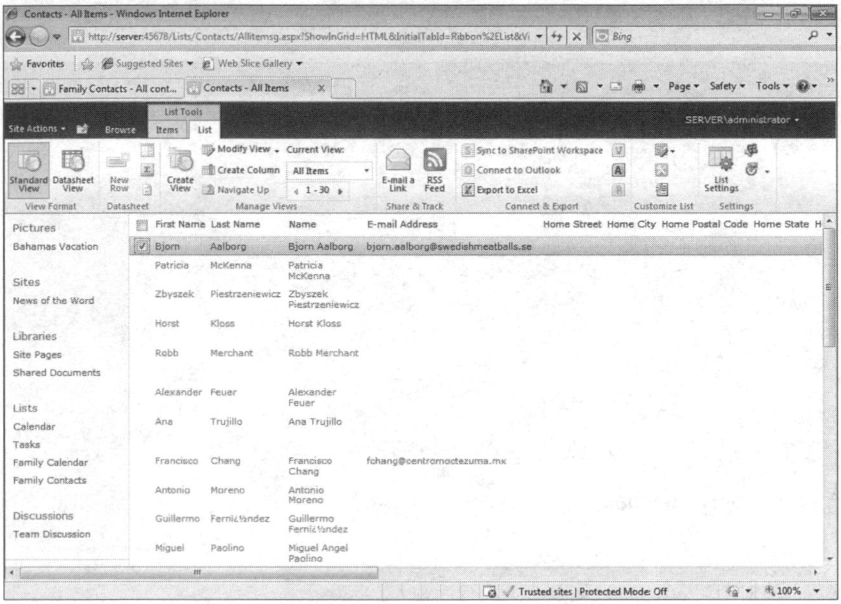

FIGURE 13.25   A SharePoint contacts list.

Here's a summary of the most useful commands available in a contacts list:

▶ **New Item**—(Items tab) Displays the New Item page, which you use to create a new contact. The Last Name field is required, but you can also enter a first name, email address, and company name, as well as the person's address and phone number.

▶ **Datasheet View**—(List tab; Office only) Displays the contacts in an Access datasheet for easier editing.

▶ **Connect to Outlook**—(List tab; Office only) Adds the contacts list to Outlook's Contacts folder. You can then create and work with contacts either in Outlook or in SharePoint.

TIP

Unfortunately, SharePoint doesn't offer a command for importing contacts from other programs. You can work around this by using Microsoft Access, if you have it. If your contacts are in a program other than Outlook, use the program's Export feature to export the contacts to a comma-separated values (CSV) text file. In Access, open or create a database, select the External Data tab, and then, in the Import group, select either More, Outlook Folder (to import Outlook's Contacts folder) or Text File (to import the CSV file). When the import is complete, select the table containing the contacts data, and then select External Data, SharePoint List in the Export group. You then specify and log on to your SharePoint site and export the contacts.

Keeping a List of Web Page Links

You can use your SharePoint site as a handy repository for links to your favorite or most-often-viewed websites. SharePoint often includes a list of links by default in many site templates, and you view and work with the links on the site's home page. If your site doesn't have a links list, or if you want to add another links list to your site, follow these steps:

1. Log on to the top-level SharePoint site using the primary (or secondary) site collection administration account.
2. Click Site Actions, and then click More Options to display the Create page.
3. Under Tracking, click Links.
4. Type a name and description for the new library.
5. In the Navigation section, click Yes if you want to include a link to the list of links on Quick Launch.
6. Click Create. SharePoint builds the links list and (if you clicked Yes in the Navigation section) adds a link to the list in the Lists heading of Quick Launch.

Here's a summary of the most useful commands available in a links list:

▶ **New Item**—(Items tab) Displays the New Item page, which you use to create a new link. You specify the link URL, as well as an options description and notes.

▶ **New Folder**—(Items tab) Enables you to create a subfolder for storing related links.

▶ **Change Order**—(Items tab) Displays the Change Item Order page, which enables you to specify the order the links appear in the list.

▶ **Datasheet View**—(List tab; Office only) Displays the contacts in an Access datasheet for easier editing.

Deleting Content from a Site

If you no longer use a particular list or library, you should delete it to recapture the disk space and make Quick Launch navigation easier. Here are the steps required:

1. Log on to the top-level SharePoint as an administrator.
2. If you want to delete content from a subsite, navigate to that subsite.
3. Select Site Actions, Site Settings.
4. Under Site Administration, click the Site Libraries and Lists link.

5. Click the Customize *Name* link, where *Name* is the name of the content you want to delete.

6. Under Permissions and Management, click Delete This *Content*, where *Content* is the type of content you're deleting (list, picture library, and so on). SharePoint asks you to confirm.

7. Click OK. SharePoint deletes the content.

From Here

▶ For Internet access to your SharePoint site, you need a static IP address for your server so that you can forward to the SharePoint port; **SEE** "Configuring Windows Home Server with a Static IP Address," **P. 8**.

▶ SharePoint uses the Windows Home Server user account database for permissions and site access; to learn how to create more accounts, **SEE** "Adding a New User," **P. 32**.

▶ To keep SharePoint secure, it's important to use strong passwords; **SEE** "Building a Strong Password," **P. 34**.

▶ For Internet access to SharePoint, it helps to use a dynamic DNS service to map a domain name to the dynamic IP address that your ISP supplies; **SEE** "Connecting with a Domain Name Maintained by a Dynamic DNS Service," **P. 168**.

▶ For dynamic DNS, you can also set up a Windows Live Custom Domain; **SEE** "Connecting with a Domain Name Maintained by Windows Home Server," **P. 169**.

▶ For the details on setting up a general website on Windows Home Server, **SEE** Chapter 12, "Setting Up a Windows Home Server Website."

CHAPTER 14

Patching Home Computers with WSUS

IN THIS CHAPTER

▸ Installing WSUS

▸ Configuring WSUS

▸ Synchronizing Updates

▸ Connecting Home Computers to WSUS

▸ Approving Updates

Windows Home Server removes many networking burdens from your shoulders: client backups, server backup, file sharing, media streaming, and more. However, if you're the administrator of your network, even if it's just a small home or office network, you already know that your biggest headache is keeping the network client computers patched with the latest updates. This is a crucial task because, without the latest updates, your client machines are vulnerable to software problems, hardware headaches, and, most crucially, security holes that black-hat hackers are only too eager to take advantage of.

If you just have one or two clients to tend, keeping them fully patched isn't a major burden. However, if you have more than just a few clients, keeping them updated can be a real hassle. To eliminate most of this hassle from your life, you can install on Windows Home Server a piece of server software called Windows Server Update Services (WSUS). WSUS acts as a central database of updates. WSUS connects with the Windows Update website to look for available updates, and then it stores them on the server. You can then configure your clients to look to the WSUS server for updates.

WSUS is a complex piece of software, but in a Windows Home Server environment where you're dealing with just a few clients and a fairly limited set of updates, it's actually straightforward to configure and use WSUS. This chapter tells you everything you need to know.

Installing WSUS

To download WSUS, first head for technet.microsoft.com/en-us/wsus/default.aspx.

Click the Download link, click the Download button for the 64-bit version of WSUS 3.0 SP2, click Run to download the setup file, and then click Run again to launch the WSUS Setup Wizard.

> **NOTE**
>
> If you want to download WSUS directly using your Windows Home Server machine, you'll need to turn off Internet Explorer Enhanced Security Configuration (ESC) for your Administrator account. Click the Server Manager icon in the taskbar and then click Configure IE ESC in the Security Information section. In the dialog box that appears, select Off in the Administrators section, and then click OK.

Next, follow these steps:

1. In the wizard's initial dialog box, click Next. The wizard asks what type of installation you want.

2. Select the Full Server Installation option, and then click Next. The wizard displays the license agreement.

3. Select the I Accept the Terms of the License Agreement option, and then click Next.

4. If the wizard tells you that you don't have required components installed (such as Microsoft Report Viewer 2008 Redistributable), make a note of what you'll need to install later, and then click Next. The wizard asks if you want to store the updates locally.

5. If you don't have much free space left on drive C:, deactivate the Store Updates Locally check box, which tells WSUS to store updates on the Microsoft Update website; otherwise, leave the Store Updates Locally check box activated, and change the path to C:\WSUS. Click Next. The wizard prompts you to choose a database option.

6. Leave the Install Windows Internal Database on this Computer option selected, and then click Next. The wizard prompts you to choose a website for WSUS.

7. Select the Create a Windows Server Update Services 3.0 SP2 Web Site option, which creates a new IIS website at http://*SERVER*:8530 (where *SERVER* is the name of your Windows Home Server machine). Click Next. The wizard tells you that it's ready to install WSUS.

8. Click Next to start the installation.

9. When the installation is complete, click Finish. The Windows Server Update Services Configuration Wizard appears. See the next section for the details on this wizard.

10. If the wizard warned you about required software that you need to install, go to Microsoft.com to locate and install the necessary programs.

Configuring WSUS

After WSUS is installed, the Windows Server Update Services Configuration Wizard appears. (If you don't have this wizard onscreen, select Start, Administrative Tools, Windows Server Update Services, open the Update Services, *SERVER* branch [where *SERVER* is the name of your Windows Home Server computer], click Options, and then click WSUS Server Configuration Wizard.) Follow these steps to use this wizard to configure WSUS for your Windows Home Server network:

1. In the wizard's initial dialog box, click Next. The wizard asks if you want to join the Microsoft Update Improvement Program.

2. Activate or deactivate the Yes, I Would Like to Join the Microsoft Update Improvement Program, as desired, and then click Next. The wizard prompts you to choose the server from which your WSUS server will synchronize the updates.

3. Select the Synchronize from Microsoft Update option, and then click Next. The wizard asks if your WSUS server requires a proxy server.

4. Your home network doesn't use a proxy server, so click Next to move on. The wizard prompts you to connect to the update server.

5. Click Start Connecting. The wizard connects to Windows Update and then downloads information about the available updates, which might take a few minutes.

6. Click Next. The wizard prompts you to select the languages you want to download.

7. Activate the check box beside each language you need, and then click Next. The wizard asks you to select the products for which you want updates downloaded.

8. Activate the check box beside each product you want updated (see Figure 14.1), and then click Next. The wizard prompts you to select the update classifications you want to include in the synchronization.

9. Activate the check box beside each type of classification you want to sync:

   ▶ **Critical Updates**—These are fixes that address critical, nonsecurity-related problems.

   ▶ **Definition Updates**—These are updates to the definition databases of software programs, particularly security-related software. Definition databases include virus lists for antivirus software; spyware and other malicious code for antispyware programs; and junk email filters for email programs.

   ▶ **Drivers**—These are updated device drivers for existing hardware, and new device drivers for recently released hardware.

   ▶ **Feature Packs**—These are updates that include new product features, particularly features that are intended to be included in the product's next release.

   ▶ **Security Updates**—These are fixes that address product-specific security issues.

   ▶ **Service Packs**—These are broad updates that include a cumulative set of all hotfixes, security updates, critical updates, new features, and other updates that have been created since the product was released.

▶ **Tools**—These are utilities designed to accomplish some task.

▶ **Update Rollups**—These are broad, product-specific updates that include a cumulative set of hotfixes, security updates, critical updates, and other updates that have been created since the product was released.

▶ **Updates**—These are fixes that address noncritical, nonsecurity-related problems.

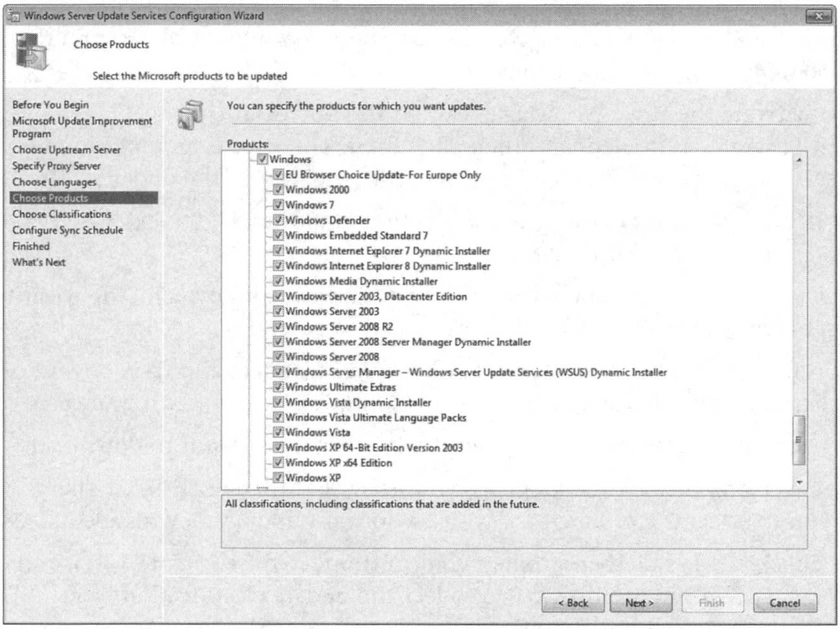

FIGURE 14.1   In the Choose Products dialog box, activate the check box beside each product you want WSUS to update.

> **NOTE**
>
> If you elected to store updates locally and disk space is tight, you don't need to sync every update type. At a minimum, however, you should sync Critical Updates, Definition Updates, and Security Updates.

10. Click Next. The wizard asks whether you want to synchronize manually or on a schedule.

11. If you prefer to run the sync yourself, leave the Synchronize Manually option selected; otherwise, select Synchronize Automatically, and then use the First Synchronization spin boxes to set the sync time you want to use, as shown in

Figure 14.2. Note, too, that you can leave the Synchronizations Per Day value set to 1, which is often enough. When you're ready to move on, click Next.

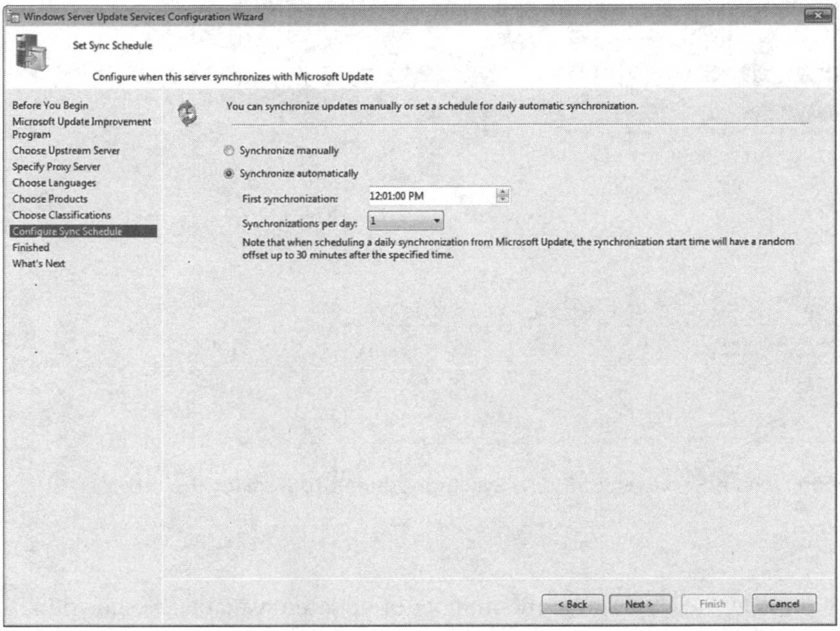

FIGURE 14.2   Select Synchronize Automatically to have WSUS automatically look for new updates.

12. In the Finished dialog box, leave the Launch the Windows Server Update Services Administration Console and the Begin Initial Synchronization check boxes activated, and then click Finish.

NOTE

The initial synchronization may take quite some time, depending on your connection speed and the number of products and update types you included in the sync.

Synchronizing Updates

If you elected to run the initial synchronization using the Windows Server Update Services Configuration Wizard, the sync begins immediately. To monitor the progress of the initial sync, select Start, Administrative Tools, Windows Server Update Services, open the Update Services, *SERVER* branch (where *SERVER* is the name of your Windows Home Server computer), click Synchronizations, and then click the running sync. (If you didn't ask the wizard to launch the initial sync automatically, you can start the sync yourself by clicking

Synchronize Now in the Actions pane.) As you can see in Figure 14.3, the Update Services snap-in shows you the status of the sync and the sync progress.

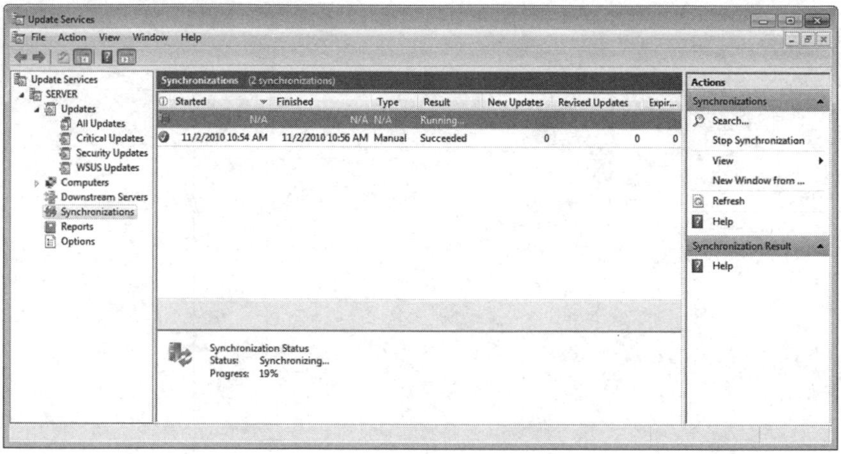

FIGURE 14.3   Open Update Services, *SERVER*, Synchronizations to monitor the progress of a running sync.

Once the sync is complete, WSUS displays the number of updates available, as shown in Figure 14.4.

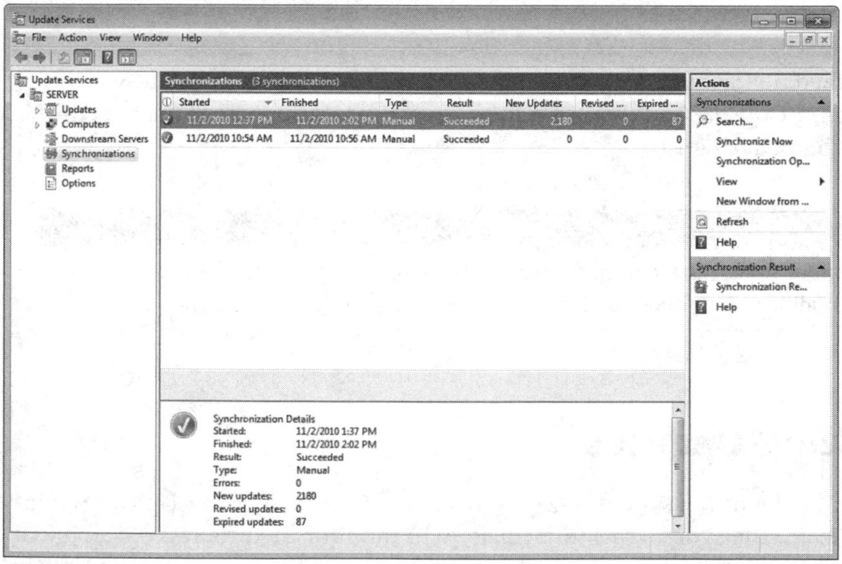

FIGURE 14.4   When the sync is complete, you see the number of available updates.

If you want to make changes to the way WSUS synchronizes updates, click Options, and then click Synchronization Schedule. You can then use the Synchronization Schedule dialog box (which has the same options as the wizard dialog box shown earlier in Figure 14.2) to choose a manual sync or to set up a schedule for an automatic sync.

> **NOTE**
>
> If a synchronization is currently running, you can't make changes to the sync options. Either cancel the running sync (click the Synchronization branch, click the running sync, and then click Stop Synchronization) or wait until the sync is complete before opening the Synchronization Schedule dialog box.

Connecting Home Computers to WSUS

To connect a client machine to the WSUS server, you must configure the client to check the server for updates instead of Windows Update. That is, you want the clients to use your *intranet*—your local network running Internet Protocol (IP) services and technologies to communicate with the server—to handle the updates. Here's how it's done:

1. On the client computer, click Start, type **gpedit.msc**, and then press Enter to launch the Local Group Policy Editor.
2. Open the Computer Configuration, Administrative Templates, Windows Components, Windows Update branch.
3. Double-click the Specify Intranet Microsoft Update Service Location policy.
4. Select the Enabled option.
5. In the Set the Intranet Update Service for Detecting Updates text box, type the address of your WSUS server: http://*SERVER*:8530 (where *SERVER* is the name of your Windows Home Server machine).
6. In the Set the Intranet Statistics Server text box, type the address of your WSUS server: http://*SERVER*:8530 (where *SERVER* is the name of your Windows Home Server machine). Figure 14.5 shows a sample policy ready to go.
7. Click OK to put the policy into effect.

If you're using a Windows client that doesn't come with the Group Policy Editor, you can also edit the Registry to connect the client to the WSUS server. Click Start, type **regedit**, and then press Enter to open the Registry Editor. Open the following key:

HKLM\SOFTWARE\Policies\Microsoft\Windows\WindowsUpdate

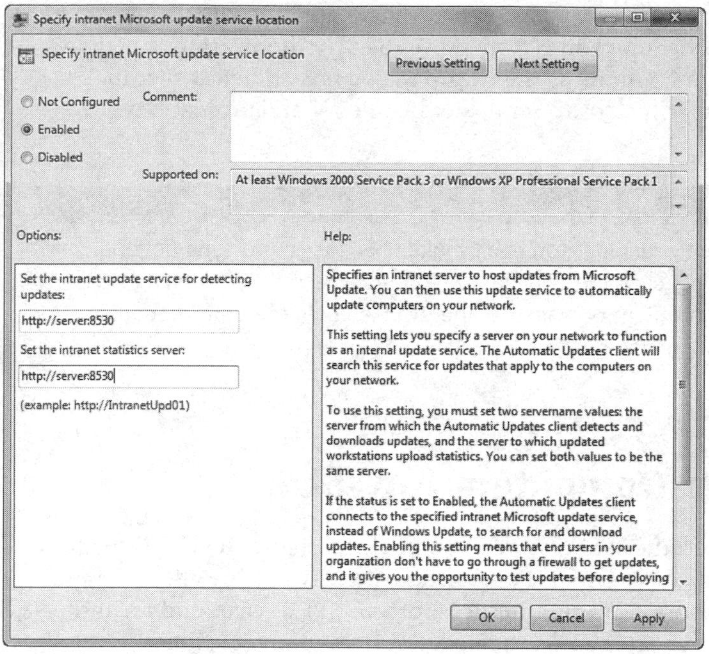

FIGURE 14.5   Use the Specify Intranet Microsoft Update Service Location policy to connect a client computer to the WSUS server.

Now create two settings:

- ▶ Select Edit, New, String Value, type **WUServer**, and press Enter. Press Enter again to open the new setting, type `http://SERVER:8530` (where *SERVER* is the name of your Windows Home Server machine), and click OK.

- ▶ Select Edit, New, String Value, type **WUStatusServer**, and press Enter. Press Enter again to open the new setting, type `http://SERVER:8530` (where *SERVER* is the name of your Windows Home Server machine), and click OK.

To confirm that a client is getting updates over the network from WSUS instead of from Windows Update, select Start, Control Panel and then open the Windows Update item. In the Windows Update window, the You Receive Updates value should read `Managed by Your System Administrator`, as shown in Figure 14.6.

Approving Updates

Before an update is sent to a client, the system administrator (that would be you) must approve it. WSUS gives you a hard way to do this (by hand), and an easy way (using a rule).

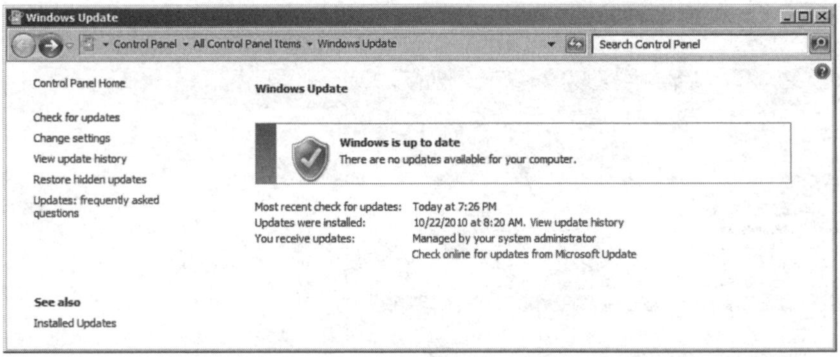

FIGURE 14.6   The Windows Update window should now say that the client's updates are being managed by the system administrator.

Approving Updates by Hand

Use the hard way if you want to maintain complete control over the updates that are sent to your client computers. Here's how it works:

1. In the Update Services snap-in, open the Update Services, *SERVER*, Updates branch.
2. Click the type of updates you want to work with: All Updates, Critical Updates, Security Updates, or WSUS Updates.
3. In the Approval list, select Unapproved.
4. In the Status list, select Any.
5. Click Refresh to see a list of unapproved updates, as shown in Figure 14.7.
6. Select the update or updates you want to approve.
7. In the Actions pane, click Approve. The Approve Updates dialog box appears.
8. Click the arrow to the right of All Computers, and then click Approved for Install.
9. Click OK. WSUS approves the updates.
10. Click Close.
11. Repeat steps 2 through 10 to approve other updates.

Approving Updates Using a Rule

The easy route is to take advantage of the approval rules that you can set up in WSUS. In fact, WSUS comes with a default rule that you can run to automatically approve all critical and security updates for all computers.

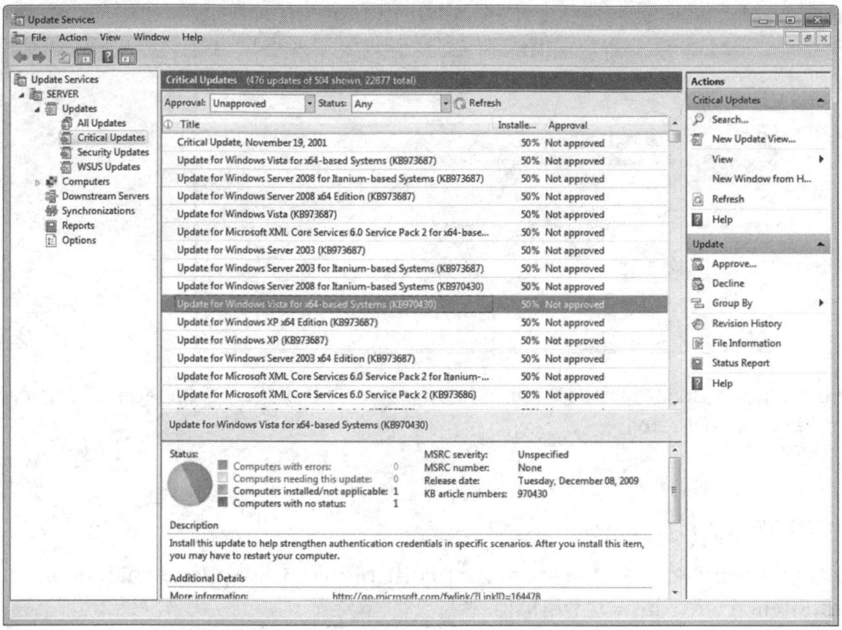

FIGURE 14.7   Display the list of updates awaiting approval.

First, follow these steps to edit the rule to include all the update classifications you want to approve automatically:

1. In the Update Services snap-in, open the Update Services, *SERVER*, Options branch.

2. Click Automatic Approvals to open the Automatic Approvals dialog box.

3. Select Default Automatic Approval Rule.

4. Click Edit to open the Edit Rule dialog box.

5. In the Step 2: Edit the Properties text box, click the Critical Updates, Security Updates link. The Choose Update Classifications dialog box appears.

6. Activate the check box beside each type of update classification you want to approve automatically, and then click OK.

7. Click OK to save the rule.

To run the rule, activate the check box beside Default Automatic Approval Rule, and then click Run Rule. WSUS automatically approves all the updates in the classifications you selected.

From Here

▶ To learn how to update Windows Home Server, **SEE** "Configuring Windows Update," **P. 85**.

▶ For the details on editing the Registry, **SEE** Chapter 18, "Working with the Windows Home Server Registry."

14

CHAPTER 15

Tuning Windows Home Server Performance

IN THIS CHAPTER

▶ Monitoring Performance
▶ Optimizing the Hard Disk
▶ Optimizing Virtual Memory
▶ Optimizing Applications
▶ More Optimization Tricks

How hard Windows Home Server works depends on many factors, but it mostly depends on how you and the others on your network use the server. If you mostly use Windows Home Server for nightly backups and nobody on the network generates tons of content each day, Windows Home Server's workload will always be fairly light (particularly after every client has been backed up at least once). In this kind of situation, server performance is not a big issue. However, if you use Windows Home Server not only for backups, but for file storage; recording TV shows directly to the server; streaming music, video, and other media; remote access; running several websites; and perhaps even running a SharePoint site, Windows Home Server's workload becomes decidedly heavy. In this case, you definitely want not only a fast computer as the server, but to monitor and tweak Windows Home Server's performance to eke out every ounce of horsepower in the machine.

This chapter shows you a number of methods for monitoring performance. Some of these no doubt seem like overkill for a home network, but you can always just pick out the ones that give you the information you require. The rest of the chapter takes you through specific techniques for improving the overall performance of Windows Home Server.

Monitoring Performance

Performance optimization is a bit of a black art in that every user has different needs, every configuration has different operating parameters, and every system can react in a unique and unpredictable way to performance tweaks.

What this means is that if you want to optimize your system, you have to get to know how it works, what it needs, and how it reacts to changes. You can do this just by using the system and paying attention to how things look and feel, but a more rigorous approach is often called for. To that end, the next few sections take you on a tour of Windows Home Server's performance monitoring capabilities.

Monitoring Performance with Task Manager

The Task Manager utility is excellent for getting a quick overview of the current state of the system. To get it onscreen, press Ctrl+Alt+Delete, and then click Task Manager.

TIP

For faster service, either press Ctrl+Shift+Esc or right-click an empty section of the taskbar and then click Task Manager.

Monitoring Processes

The Processes tab, shown in Figure 15.1, displays a list of the programs, services, and system components that are currently running on your system. The processes appear in the order in which they were started, but you can change their order by clicking the column headings. (To return to the original, chronological order, you must close and restart Task Manager.)

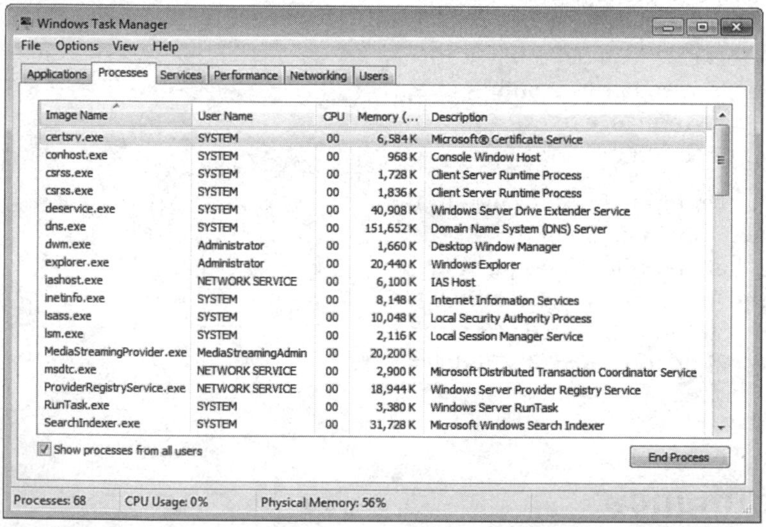

FIGURE 15.1   The Processes tab lists your system's running programs and services.

NOTE

A *process* is a running instance of an executable program.

NOTE

In the list of processes, you'll likely see several instances of svchost.exe. This is a program that acts as a host process for services that run from dynamic-link libraries (DLLs) instead of from executable files. To see which services the various instances of svchost.exe are running, start a command prompt session and enter the following command:

```
tasklist /svc
```

This displays a list of all the running processes and includes a column that displays the services that are hosted in each process.

In addition to the name of each process and the user who started the process, you see two performance measures:

- ▶ **CPU**—The values in this column tell you the percentage of CPU resources that each process is using. If your system seems sluggish, look for a process that is consuming all or nearly all the CPU's resources. Most programs monopolize the CPU occasionally for short periods, but a program that is stuck at 100 (percent) for a long time most likely has some kind of problem. In that case, try shutting down the program. If that doesn't work, click the program's process and then click End Process. Click Yes when Windows Home Server asks whether you're sure that you want to do this.

- ▶ **Memory (Private Working Set)**—This value tells you approximately how much memory the process is using. (See the following discussion for a more detailed explanation.) This value is less useful because a process might genuinely require a lot of memory to operate. However, if this value is steadily increasing for a process that you're not using, it could indicate a problem, and you should shut down the process.

TIP

You can control how often Task Manager refreshes its data. Select View, Update Speed, and then select High (Task Manager refreshes the data twice per second), Normal (Task Manager refreshes the data every 2 seconds; this is the default), or Low (Task Manager refreshes the data every 4 seconds). If you want to freeze the current data, select Paused. You can also refresh the data at any time by selecting View, Refresh Now.

The four default columns in the Processes tab aren't the only data available to you. Select the View, Select Columns command. As you can see in Figure 15.2, the Select Columns dialog box that Task Manager opens has a long list of values that you can monitor. To add a value to the Processes tab, activate its check box and click OK.

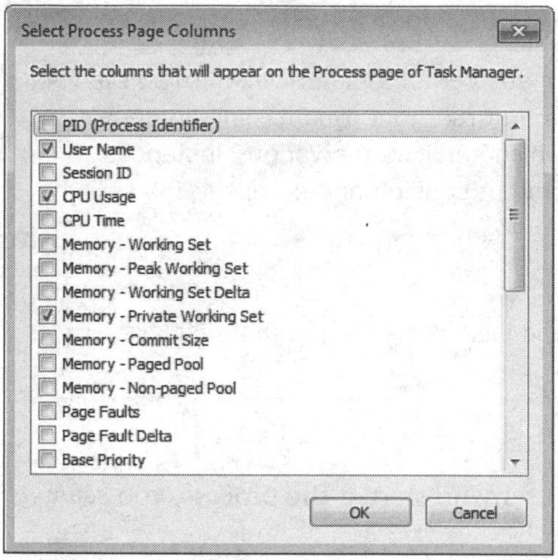

FIGURE 15.2   Use the Select Columns dialog box to choose which values you want to monitor using the Processes tab.

Here's a summary of the columns you can add:

▸ **PID (Process Identifier)**—This is a unique numerical value that Windows Home Server assigns to the process while it's running.

▸ **User Name**—This value tells you the name of the user or service that launched the process.

▸ **Session ID**—This is a unique numerical value that Windows Home Server assigns to the process while it's running within a Terminal Services session (such as if a user is running Windows Home Server Dashboard or has logged on to Windows Home Server via Remote Desktop).

TIP

To see the Session ID values, activate the Show Processes from All Users check box.

▸ **CPU Usage**—This is the CPU value discussed earlier in this section.

▸ **CPU Time**—This column shows the total time (in hours, minutes, and seconds) that the process has used the CPU since the process was launched. Because most computers (including Windows Home Server) don't access the processor constantly, the CPU is usually idle, which means the System Idle Process almost always shows the lion's share of the CPU Time value. However, if you see another process that seems to have used an inordinate amount of CPU time (for example, hours of CPU time, when all other processes have used only minutes or seconds of CPU time), it could mean that the process is frozen or out of control and should be shut down.

▶ **Memory - Working Set**—This value tells you the size (in kilobytes) of the *working set*, which is the number of kilobytes the process currently has resident in memory).

▶ **Memory - Peak Working Set**—This value tells you the maximum amount of memory (in kilobytes) used by each process. For most processes, the current working set value should be quite a bit less than the peak working set value. If a process is showing a current working set value at or very near the peak over a long period of time, it could be a sign that the process is stuck or has a memory leak.

▶ **Memory - Working Set Delta**—This value tells you how much the Memory Usage value changed (in kilobytes) since the last time Task Manager updated the processes. You see a positive value when memory use increases and a negative value when memory usage decreases. Under normal conditions, a program might show gradually increasing memory usage as more resources are used, and gradually decreasing memory usage as files and other objects are closed. If you see a process that has a constantly positive Delta value, particularly when it's not obvious that the process is being used, it might be the sign of a memory leak in the process.

▶ **Memory - Private Working Set**—This value tells you the amount of working set memory that is dedicated to the process and cannot be shared with other processes. The difference between the full working set and the private working set is the amount of memory that the process is using that can be shared with other processes. Because shareable memory is, in a sense, available memory, the private working set is more useful as a measure of how much memory a process is currently consuming (hence, this value's status as a default Task Manager column).

▶ **Memory - Commit Size**—This value shows the total amount of virtual memory, in kilobytes, that Windows Home Server has allocated to each process. If page faults are high (see the Page Faults bullet), it could be due to a process using a large amount of virtual memory. Consider ending and restarting that process.

15

▶ **Memory - Paged Pool**—This value is the amount of virtual memory, in kilobytes, that Windows Home Server has allocated to the process in the *paged pool*—the system memory area that Windows Home Server uses for objects that can be written back to the disk when the system doesn't need them. The most active processes have the largest paged pool values, so it's normal for this value to increase over time. However, it's unusual for any one process to have a significantly large paged pool value. You can improve performance by shutting down and restarting such a process.

▶ **Memory - Non-Paged Pool**—This value is the amount of virtual memory, in kilobytes, that Windows Home Server has allocated to the process in the *nonpaged pool*—the system memory area that Windows Home Server uses for objects that must remain in memory and so can't be written back to the disk when the system doesn't need them. Because the nonpaged pool takes up physical RAM on the system, if memory is running low, processes that require a lot of nonpaged pool memory could generate lots of page faults and slow down the system. Consider closing some programs to reduce memory usage.

▶ **Page Faults**—This value tells you how often each process has requested a page from virtual memory and the system couldn't find the page. (A page is an area of virtual memory used to transfer data between virtual memory and a storage medium, usually the hard disk.) The system then either retrieves the data from another virtual memory location (this is called a soft page fault) or from the hard disk (this is called a hard page fault). Lots of hard page faults can slow down overall system performance and may be a sign that your system doesn't have enough memory or that the virtual memory paging file isn't big enough.

NOTE

Unfortunately, Task Manager doesn't give you any way to differentiate between soft page faults and hard page faults. For this, you need to use System Monitor, as described later in the "Monitoring Performance with Performance Monitor" section.

NOTE

If you display the Page Faults column, you may notice that the Windows shell process (`explorer.exe`) seems to constantly accumulate page faults. (To see this, it helps to display the Page Faults Delta column, described next.) In fact, the Page Fault value increases every 2 seconds. Does this mean `explorer.exe` has a problem? Not at all. The page faults are caused by Task Manager, which causes an `explorer.exe` page fault every time it updates the CPU Usage value. Because that happens every 2 seconds (assuming that Task Manager's update speed is set to Normal), the `explorer.exe` Page Faults value also increases every 2 seconds.

▶ **Page Faults Delta**—This value tells you how much the Page Faults value changed since the last time Task Manager updated the processes. Because the total number of page faults can never decrease, this will always be either 0 or a positive number. A process that shows a consistently high Page Faults Delta value might not have enough memory to run properly. Consider shutting down the process and starting it again.

▶ **Base Priority**—This value shows you the priority level that each process uses. For more on this, see "Setting the Program Priority in Task Manager," later in this chapter.

▶ **Handles**—This value shows you the number of object handles in the object table associated with each process. An *object handle* is an index that points to an entry in a table of available objects, and it enables programs to interface with those objects. Handles take up memory, so a process with an inordinately large handle count could adversely affect system performance.

▶ **Threads**—This value tells you the number of threads that each process is using. A *thread* is a program task that can run independently of and (usually) concurrently with other tasks in the same program (in which case, the program is said to support *multithreading*). Multithreading improves program performance, but programs that have an unusually large number of threads can slow down the server because Windows has to spend too much time switching from one thread of execution to another.

▶ **USER Objects**—This value tells you the number of interface objects (which are part of User, a core system component used by applications and other processes that impact the user) that the process is using. Interface objects include windows, menus, cursors, icons, monitors, keyboard layouts, and other internal objects. If performance is slow, look for the process that has the highest USER Objects value and close it. (The exception here is the explorer.exe process, which usually has a high number of USER objects, but because it represents the Windows Home Server shell, you should never close it.)

▶ **GDI Objects**—This value shows the number of graphics device interface (GDI) objects that each process is currently using. The GDI is a core Windows component that manages the operating system's graphical interface. It contains routines that draw graphics primitives (such as lines and circles), manage colors, display fonts, manipulate bitmap images, and interact with graphics drivers. A process that uses an unusually large number of GDI objects can slow down the system.

▶ **I/O Reads**—This value shows the total number of input/output (I/O) operations that the process has used to read data since the process was started. The total includes reads from local files, network files, and devices, but not reads from the console input object, which includes the keyboard. Some processes generate tens or even hundreds of thousands of I/O reads, so this value isn't very useful in monitoring performance.

▶ **I/O Writes**—This value shows the total number of input/output operations that the process has used to write data since the process was started. The total includes writes to local files, network files, and devices, but not writes to the console input object, which includes the monitor. Some processes generate tens or even hundreds of thousands of I/O writes, so this value isn't very useful in monitoring performance.

15

▶ **I/O Other**—This value shows the total number of non-read and non-write input/output operations that the process has used since the process was started. Examples include starting another process, stopping a running process, requesting the status of a device, and other control functions.

▶ **I/O Read Bytes**—This value shows the total number of bytes generated by the read in input/output operations since the process was started. Again, because you often see I/O Ready Bytes values in the hundreds of millions or even billions, this value isn't much use for performance monitoring.

▶ **I/O Write Bytes**—This value shows the total number of bytes generated by the write input/output operations since the process was started. Because you often see I/O Write Bytes values in the hundreds of millions or even billions, this value isn't much use for performance monitoring.

▶ **I/O Other Bytes**—This value shows the total number of bytes generated by non-read and non-write input/output operations since the process was started.

▶ **Image Path Name**—This column informs you of the full path name (drive, folder, and filename) of the process executable.

▶ **Command Line**—This column tells you the command that was used to launch the process.

▶ **User Account Control (UAC) Virtualization**—This column tells you whether the process is allowed to be virtualized, which means that Windows Home Server creates virtual copies of the process for use during a program install where no user credentials have been given.

▶ **Description**—This default column specifies the name of the process.

▶ **Data Execution Prevention**—This column tells you whether DEP is enabled for the process.

Monitoring System Performance

The Performance tab, shown in Figure 15.3, offers even more performance data, particularly for that all-important component: your system's memory.

The graphs show you both the current value and the values over time for the CPU Usage (the total percentage of CPU resources that your running processes are using) and the Physical Memory Usage. If you also want to monitor the amount of CPU time used by the system files (the kernel), select View, Show Kernel Times. Windows Home Server adds red line graphs to each chart to represent the kernel time usage.

NOTE

If your server has multiple CPUs (or a multicore processor), the CPU Usage History section shows a separate graph for each processor (as shown in Figure 15.3). If you prefer to see a single graph for all the processors, select View, CPU History, One Graph, All CPUs.

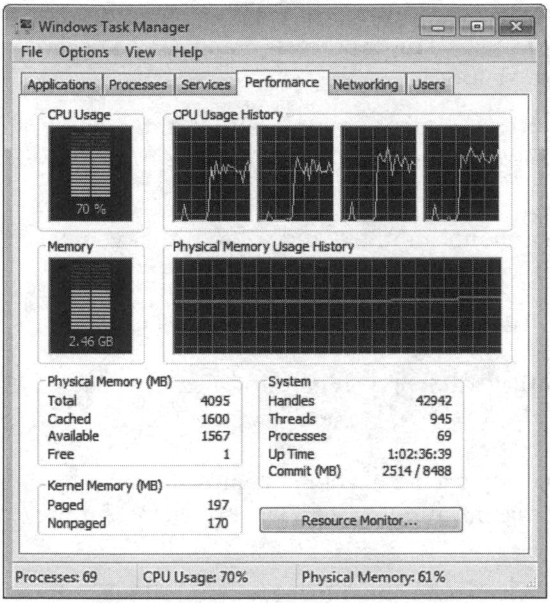

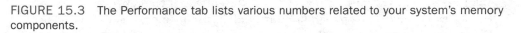

FIGURE 15.3   The Performance tab lists various numbers related to your system's memory components.

Below the graphs are various numbers. Here's what they mean:

▶ **Physical Memory Total**—The total amount of physical RAM in your system.

▶ **Physical Memory Cached**—The amount of physical RAM that Windows Home Server has set aside to store recently used programs and documents.

▶ **Physical Memory Available**—The amount of physical RAM that Windows Home Server has available for your programs. This includes not only the unallocated memory (described next), but memory that can be shared with other programs.

▶ **Physical Memory Free**—The amount of physical RAM that Windows Home Server has not allocated to any programs. Note that Windows Home Server does not include the system cache (described above) in this total.

▶ **Kernel Memory Paged**—The amount of kernel memory mapped to pages in virtual memory.

▶ **Kernel Memory Nonpaged**—The amount of kernel memory that cannot map to pages in virtual memory.

▶ **System Handles**—The number of object handles that all running processes use. A handle is a pointer to a resource. For example, if a process wants to use a particular service offered by a particular object, the process asks the object for a handle to that service.

▶ **System Threads**—The number of threads that all running processes use. A *thread* is a single processor task executed by a process, and most processes can use two or more threads at the same time to speed up execution.

▶ **System Processes**—The number of processes currently running (that is, the number of items you see in the Processes tab if you activate the Show Processes from All Users control).

▶ **System Up Time**—The number of days, hours, minutes, and seconds that you have been logged on to Windows Home Server in the current session.

▶ **System Commit (MB)**—The minimum and maximum values of the page file.

Here are some notes related to these values that will help you monitor memory-related performance issues:

▶ If the Physical Memory Available value approaches 0, your system is starved for memory. You might have too many programs running, or a large program is using lots of memory.

▶ If the Physical Memory Cached value is much less than half the Physical Memory Total value, your system isn't operating as efficiently as it could because Windows Home Server can't store enough recently used data in memory. Because Windows Home Server gives up some of the system cache when it needs RAM, close programs you don't need.

▶ If the Commit value remains higher than the Physical Memory Total value, Windows Home Server is doing a lot of work swapping data to and from the paging file, which greatly slows performance.

▶ If the Commit peak value is higher than the Physical Memory Total value, Windows Home Server had to use the paging file at some point in the current session. The peak value might have been a temporary event, but you should monitor the peak over time, just to make sure.

In all these situations, the quickest solution is to reduce the system's memory footprint either by closing documents or by closing applications. For the latter, use the Processes tab to determine which applications are using the most memory, and then shut down the ones you can live without for now. The better, but more expensive, solution is to add more physical RAM to your system. This decreases the likelihood that Windows Home Server will need to use the paging file, and it enables Windows Home Server to increase the size of the system cache, which greatly improves performance.

TIP

If you're not sure which process corresponds to which program, display the Applications tab, right-click a program, and then click Go to Process. Task Manager displays the Processes tab and selects the process that corresponds to the program.

Monitoring Network Performance

If your network feels sluggish, it could be that the server or node you're working with is sharing data slowly or that network traffic is exceptionally high. To see whether the latter situation is the cause of the problem, you can check out the current *network utilization* value, which is the percent of available bandwidth that your network adapter is currently using.

To check network utilization, open Task Manager, and then display the Networking tab, shown in Figure 15.4. If you have multiple adapters, click the one you want to check in the Adapter Name list. Now use the graph or the Network Utilization column to monitor the current network utilization value. Notice that this value is a percentage. This means that the utilization is a percentage of the bandwidth shown in the Link Speed column. So, for example, if the current network utilization is 10 percent and the Link Speed value is 1Gbps, the network is currently using about 100Mbps bandwidth.

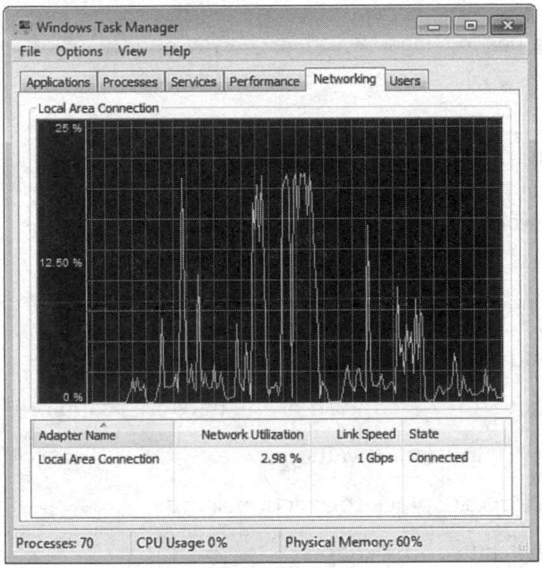

FIGURE 15.4   Use Task Manager's Networking tab to check the current network utilization percentage.

The Network Utilization value combines the data sent by the server and the data received by the server. If the utilization is high, it's often useful to break down the data stream into the separate sent and received components. To do that, select View, Network Adapter History, and then select Bytes Sent (which displays as a red line on the graph) or Bytes Received (which displays as a yellow line on the graph).

As with the Processes tab, you can view much more information than what you see in the default Networking tab. Select the View, Select Columns command. As shown in Figure 15.5, the Select Columns dialog box offers a long list of networking measures that you can monitor. To add a value to the Networking tab, activate its check box and click OK.

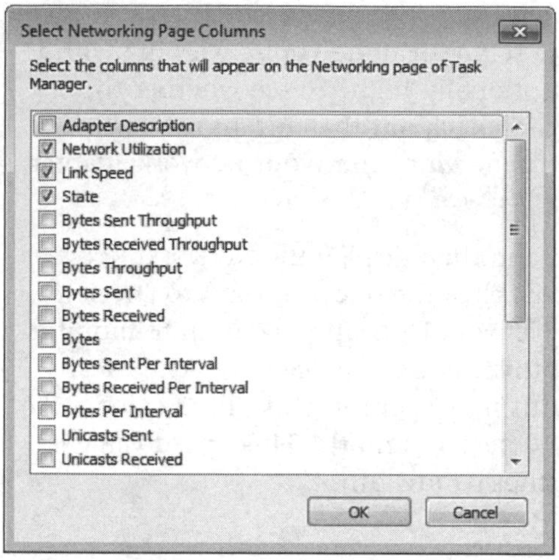

FIGURE 15.5   Use the Select Columns dialog box to choose which values you want to monitor using the Networking tab.

TIP

By default, the Networking tab doesn't collect data when you're viewing some other Task Manager tab. If you prefer that the Networking tab always collects data, select Options, Tab Always Active.

Here's a summary of the columns you can add:

▶ **Adapter Description**—This column shows the description of the network adapter.

▶ **Network Utilization**—This is the network utilization value.

▶ **Link Speed**—This value shows the network adapter's connection speed.

▶ **State**—This column displays the general state of the adapter.

▶ **Bytes Sent Throughput**—This value shows the percentage of connection bandwidth used by traffic sent from Windows Home Server.

▶ **Bytes Received Throughput**—This value shows the percentage of connection bandwidth used by traffic received by Windows Home Server.

▶ **Bytes Throughput**—This value shows the percentage of connection bandwidth used by traffic both sent from and received by Windows Home Server.

▶ **Bytes Sent**—This column tells you the total number of bytes sent from Windows Home Server over the network adapter during the current session (that is, since the last boot).

▶ **Bytes Received**—This column tells you the total number of bytes received by Windows Home Server over the network adapter during the current session.

▶ **Bytes**—This column tells you the total number of bytes sent from and received by Windows Home Server over the network adapter during the current session.

▶ **Bytes Sent Per Interval**—This value shows the total number of bytes sent from Windows Home Server over the network adapter during the most recent update interval. (For example, if the Update Speed value is set to Low, the display updates every 4 seconds, so the Bytes Sent/Interval value is the number of bytes sent during the most recent 4-second interval.)

▶ **Bytes Received Per Interval**—This value shows the total number of bytes received by Windows Home Server over the network adapter during the most recent update interval.

▶ **Bytes Per Interval**—This value shows the total number of bytes sent from and received by Windows Home Server over the network adapter during the most recent update interval.

▶ **Unicasts Sent**—This column tells you the total number of unicasts sent from Windows Home Server over the network adapter during the current session (that is, since the last boot). A *unicast* is a packet exchanged between a single sender and a single receiver.

▶ **Unicasts Received**—This column tells you the total number of unicasts received by Windows Home Server over the network adapter during the current session.

▶ **Unicasts**—This column tells you the total number of unicasts sent from and received by Windows Home Server over the network adapter during the current session.

▶ **Unicasts Sent Per Interval**—This value shows the total number of unicasts sent from Windows Home Server over the network adapter during the most recent update interval.

▶ **Unicasts Received Per Interval**—This value shows the total number of unicasts received by Windows Home Server over the network adapter during the most recent update interval.

▶ **Unicasts Per Interval**—This value shows the total number of unicasts sent from and received by Windows Home Server over the network adapter during the most recent update interval.

▶ **Nonunicasts Sent**—This column tells you the total number of nonunicast packets sent from Windows Home Server over the network adapter during the current session (that is, since the last boot). A *nonunicast* is a packet exchanged between a single sender and multiple receivers.

▶ **Nonunicasts Received**—This column tells you the total number of nonunicasts received by Windows Home Server over the network adapter during the current session.

▶ **Nonunicasts**—This column tells you the total number of nonunicasts sent from and received by Windows Home Server over the network adapter during the current session.

15

▶ **Nonunicast Sent Per Interval**—This value shows the total number of nonunicasts sent from Windows Home Server over the network adapter during the most recent update interval.

▶ **Nonunicast Received Per Interval**—This value shows the total number of nonunicasts received by Windows Home Server over the network adapter during the most recent update interval.

▶ **Nonunicast/Interval**—This value shows the total number of nonunicasts sent from and received by Windows Home Server over the network adapter during the most recent update interval.

Monitoring Performance with Resource Monitor

Windows Home Server 2011 comes with a new tool for monitoring your system: the Resource Monitor. You load this tool by selecting Start, typing **monitor**, and then choosing Resource Monitor in the search results. Figure 15.6 shows the Resource Monitor window.

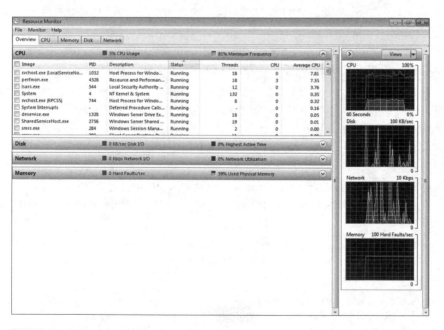

FIGURE 15.6   The new Resource Monitor enables you to monitor various aspects of your system.

The Resource Monitor is divided into five tabs:

▶ **Overview**—This section shows a couple of basic metrics in four categories: CPU, Disk, Network, and Memory, as well as graphs that show current activity in each of these categories. To see more data about a category (as with the CPU category in Figure 15.6), click the downward-pointing arrow on the right side of the category header.

▶ **CPU**—This section (see Figure 15.7) shows the CPU resources that your system is using. In two lists named Processes and Services, you see for each item the current status (such as Running), the number of threads used, the CPU percentage currently being used, and the average CPU percentage. You also get graphs for overall CPU usage, service CPU usage, and CPU usage by processor (or by core).

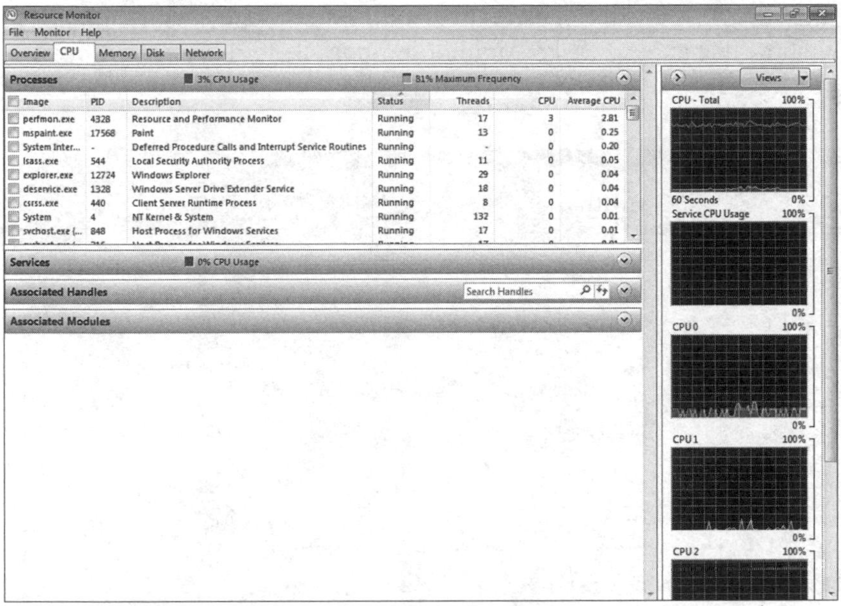

FIGURE 15.7   The CPU tab breaks down CPU usage by processes and by services.

▶ **Memory**—This tab displays a list of processes, and for each one it shows the average number of hard memory faults per minute, the total memory committed to the process, the working set (the number of kilobytes resident in memory), the amount of shareable memory (memory that other processes can use if needed), and the amount of private memory (memory that is dedicated to the process and cannot be shared).

TIP

A memory fault does not refer to a physical problem. Instead, it means that the system could not find the data it needed in the file system cache. If it finds the data elsewhere in memory, it is a soft fault; if the system has to go to the hard disk to retrieve the data, it is a hard fault.

▶ **Disk**—This tab shows the total hard disk I/O transfer rate (disk reads and writes in bytes per minute), as well as separate read and write transfer rates.

▶ **Network**—This tab shows the total network data-transfer rate (data sent and received in bytes per minute).

Monitoring Performance with Performance Monitor

For more advanced performance monitoring, Windows Home Server offers the Performance Monitor tool, which you can get to by selecting Start, typing **perf**, and pressing Enter. In the window that appears, select Monitoring Tools, Performance Monitor, as shown in Figure 15.8.

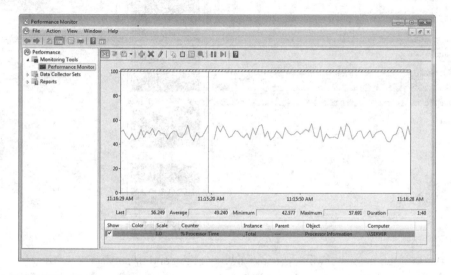

FIGURE 15.8   Use Performance Monitor to keep an eye on various system settings and components.

Performance Monitor's job is to provide you with real-time reports on how various system settings and components are performing. Each item is called a *counter*, and the displayed counters are listed at the bottom of the window. Each counter is assigned a different colored line, and that color corresponds to the colored lines shown in the graph. Note, too, that you can get specific numbers for a counter—the most recent value, the average, the minimum, and the maximum—by clicking a counter and reading the boxes just below the graphs.

The idea is that you should configure Performance Monitor to show the processes you're interested in (paging file size, free memory, and so on) and then keep Performance Monitor running while you perform your normal chores. By examining the Performance Monitor readouts from time to time, you gain an appreciation of what is typical on your system. Then, if you run into performance problems, you can check Performance Monitor to see whether you've run into any bottlenecks or anomalies.

> **TIP**
>
> By default, Performance Monitor samples the performance data every second. To change the sample interval, right-click Performance Monitor and then select Properties. (You can also press Ctrl+Q or click the Properties button in the toolbar.) In the Performance Monitor Properties dialog box, display the General tab, and modify the value in the Sample Automatically Every *X* Seconds text box. Click OK to put the new sample interval into effect.

Adding Performance Counters

By default, Performance Monitor shows a single counter, % Processor Time, which is the percentage of time the processor is busy. A consistently high value (say, more than 80%) probably indicates a rogue program that needs to be shut down. However, it may also indicate that the Windows Home Server CPU is too slow to keep up with the network demand (although this is unlikely on a home network).

To add another setting to the Performance Monitor window, follow these steps:

1. Right-click a counter and then click Add Counters. (You can also press Ctrl+I or click the Add button in the toolbar.) The Add Counters dialog box appears, as shown in Figure 15.9.

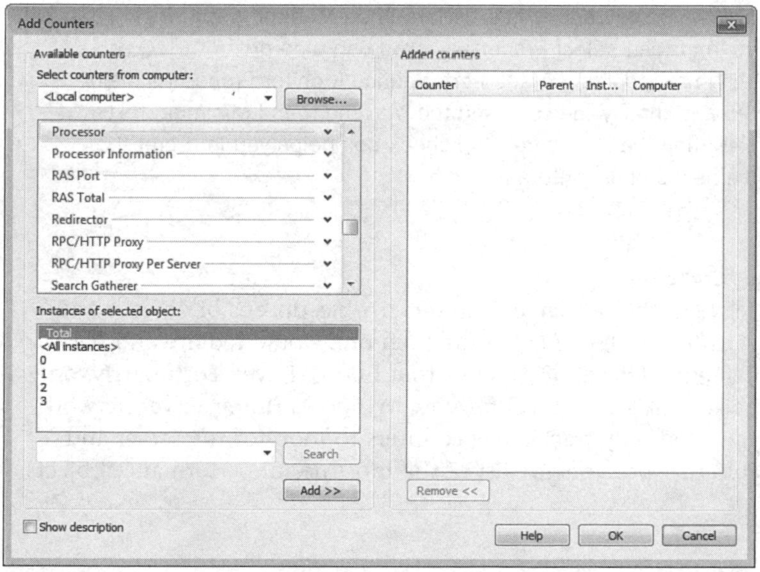

FIGURE 15.9   Use the Add Counters dialog box to add more counters to Performance Monitor.

2. In the Available Counters list, click the arrow to the right of the counter category you want to work with.

3. Select the counter you want. If you need more information about the item, activate the Show Description check box.

4. If the counter has multiple instances, select the one you want from the Instances of Selected Object list. (For example, if you choose Processor as the performance object and your system has either multiple processors or a multiple-core processor, you need to choose which processor you want to monitor. You can also usually select _Total to monitor the total of all the instances.)

5. Click Add.

6. Repeat steps 2 through 5 to add any other counters you want to monitor.

7. Click OK.

TIP

The graph is only useful if you can see the results properly. Unfortunately, sometimes the scale of the graph isn't appropriate for the numbers generated by a particular counter. The default scale is from 0 to 100, so if a counter regularly generates numbers larger than 100, all you'll see is a straight line across the top of the graph. Similarly, if a counter regularly generates small numbers, the counter's graph will be a straight line across the bottom of the graph.

To fix this, you can change the scale used by the Performance Monitor graph. Right-click Performance Monitor and then select Properties. (You can also press Ctrl+Q or click the Properties button in the toolbar.) In the Performance Monitor Properties dialog box, display the Graph tab and modify the values in the Maximum and Minimum text boxes. I also find that activating the Horizontal Grid check box helps you interpret the graph. Click OK to put the new settings into effect.

Understanding Performance Counters

In the Add Counters dialog box, the Available Counters list has dozens of objects, and each object can have dozens of counters. Explaining each one would require another book this size (and would require a level of patience that I don't have). Fortunately, only a few of the performance objects are truly useful for your Windows Home Server network, and in most situations, you need only track a few counters to monitor the server and network performance. Table 15.1 presents my list of the most useful performance objects and counters.

TABLE 15.1   Useful Performance Monitor Counters for Monitoring Server and Network
Performance

Object/Counter	Description
Cache	This performance object represents Windows Home Server's file system cache, which it uses to hold frequently used bits of data. The more data that Windows Home Server can read from the cache, the faster the system's performance. See also the Memory\Cache Bytes and Memory\Cache Faults/Sec counters.
Cache\Copy Reads/Sec	This counter tells you the number of times per second that Windows Home Server attempts to locate data in the cache instead of on the disk. Use this counter in conjunction with Copy Read Hits %.
Cache\Copy Read Hits %	This counter tells you the percentage of cache read requests that successfully retrieved data from the cache instead of from the disk. The higher the percentage (anything over 80% is very good), the better the system performance.
Cache\Data Flush Pages/Sec	This counter monitors the number of cache pages that are written back (flushed) to disk per second. If this value is steadily increasing, it might mean that Windows Home Server is having to reduce the size of the cache because memory is getting low.
LogicalDisk/Avg. Disk Queue Length	This value tells you the average number of read and write requests queued for the system's hard disks during the sample interval. If this value is consistently 2.0 or higher, it probably means that at least one of your hard disks is too slow to keep up with the demand being placed on it. You might want to replace the disk with a faster one.
Memory	This performance object represents Windows Home Server's memory, which includes both physical RAM and virtual memory.
Memory\Available MBytes	This counter tracks the number of megabytes that are currently available for processes. As this number gets lower, system performance slows because Windows Home Server must reduce the size of the system cache and read more data from the disk. Windows Home Server may also reduce the memory used by services, which can slow performance. If this number drops below 4MB, your system is seriously low on memory. Use the Task Manager to see if a process is using excessive amounts of memory. Otherwise, you may need to add RAM to your system.
Memory\Cache Bytes	This counter tells you the size, in bytes, of the system cache. If the system cache size is falling, it may indicate that Windows Home Server is running low on memory (so it reduces the cache size to free up memory for processes). For content, examine the Memory\Cache Bytes Peak value to see the largest value of the cache size since the system was last booted.

15

TABLE 15.1   Useful Performance Monitor Counters for Monitoring Server and Network
Performance

Object/Counter	Description
Memory\Cache Faults/sec	This counter monitors the number of times per second that the system looked for data in the system cache but didn't find it. A steady increase in this value may indicate that the system cache is too small.
Memory\Committed Bytes	This counter measures the number of bytes of physical and virtual memory that the system has committed to running processes. If this value is always close to the value of the Memory\Commit Limit counter—which measures the total amount of physical and virtual memory that can be assigned to processes—it means that either your paging file's maximum value is too small (see "Customizing the Paging File Size," later in this chapter), or your system doesn't have enough physical RAM.
Memory\Page Faults/Sec	This counter tells you the average number of page faults that occur per second. This value combines soft page faults and hard page faults.
Memory\Pages Input/Sec	This counter tells you the average number of pages per second that the system is reading to resolve hard page faults. A large number of hard page faults degrades performance because the system must retrieve data from the relatively slow hard disk. You need to either shut down some running programs or services or add RAM. Note, too, that the difference between this value and the Memory\Page Faults/Sec value tells you the number of soft page faults per second.
Memory\Page Reads/Sec	This counter monitors the number of read operations per second that the system is performing to resolve hard page faults. This doesn't tell you all that much by itself. However, if you divide the Memory\Pages Input/Sec value by Memory\Page Reads/Sec, you learn how many pages the system is retrieving per read operation. A large number of pages per read operation is a sign that your system is low on physical memory.
Memory\Pages Output/Sec	This counter tells you the number of times per second the system writes data to the disk to free up memory. If this value is increasing, your system doesn't have enough physical RAM.
Memory\Pages/Sec	This value shows the number of pages per second that are retrieved from or written to disk to resolve hard page faults. A consistently large number here (say, more than 2,500 pages per second) probably means that the server doesn't have enough memory. This counter shows the total for all your hard disks. To narrow down which disk is causing the problem, display separate counters for each instance of the Avg. Disk Queue Length value, as described in the previous steps. (In this case, each instance is a separate hard disk on the server.)

TABLE 15.1   Useful Performance Monitor Counters for Monitoring Server and Network Performance

Object/Counter	Description
Memory\Pool Nonpaged Bytes	This counter tracks the number of bytes allocated to the nonpaged pool.
Memory\Pool Paged Bytes	This counter tracks the number of bytes allocated to the *paged pool*, the system memory area that Windows Home Server uses for objects that can be written back to the disk when the system doesn't need them. (The current size of the paged pool is given by the Memory\Pool Paged Resident Bytes value.) The nonpaged pool and paged pool take memory away from other processes, so if these values are large relative to the total amount of physical memory, you should add more RAM to the system.
Network Interface	This performance object represents Windows Home Server's network adapter and its connection to the network. For the object instances, select the network adapter you want to monitor (if your system has more than one).
Network Interface\Current Bandwidth	This counter tells you the current network bandwidth, in bits per second.
Network Interface\Bytes Total/Sec	This counter tells you the total number of bytes received and bytes sent over the network connection per second. (This is the sum of the Network Interface\Bytes Received/Sec and Network Interface\Bytes Sent/Sec values.) Multiply this value by 1,024 to calculate the number of bits per second that are passing through the adapter. Under load (say, while streaming media), the result should be close to the Network Interface\Current Bandwidth value. If it's substantially less, you have a network bottleneck.
Paging File	This performance object represents Windows Home Server's paging file.
Paging File\% Usage	This counter tracks the current size of the paging file as a percentage of the maximum paging file size. If this value is consistently high—say, 70 percent or more—you either need to increase the maximum size of the paging file, or you need to add more RAM to the system.
Paging File\% Usage Peak	This counter tells you the maximum size of the Paging File\% Usage value in the current session.
PhysicalDisk	This performance object represents Windows Home Server's hard disks. For the object instances, you can monitor individual hard disks or all the hard disks combined. See also the System\Processor Queue Length counter.

TABLE 15.1   Useful Performance Monitor Counters for Monitoring Server and Network Performance

Object/Counter	Description
PhysicalDisk\% Disk Time	This counter tracks the percentage of the sample interval that the disk spent processing read and write requests. On your home network, this value should be quite small (usually less than 1%). If you see a larger value, you may have a hard disk that's too slow.
Processor	This performance object represents Windows Home Server's CPU. If your system has multiple processors or a multiple-core processor, you can select an individual processor or core as an instance.
Processor\% Idle Time	This counter tells you the percentage of time during the sample interval that the processor was idle.
Processor\% Interrupt Time	This counter shows the percentage of time during the sample interval that the processor was processing interrupt requests from devices.
Processor\% Privileged Time	This counter tells you the percentage of time during the sample interval that the processor spent running code in *privileged mode*, a processing mode that gives operating system programs and services full access to system hardware.
Processor\% User Time	This counter tells you the percentage of time during the sample interval that the processor spent running code in user mode. On your Windows Home Server network, this value—as well as the values for Processor\% Idle Time, Processor\% Interrupt Time, and Processor\% Privileged Time—should be at or near 0 most of the time. If any one of these values is consistently high, you might need to upgrade to a faster processor or a processor with more cores, or add a second processor if your system motherboard supports this.
System	This object represents the Windows Home Server system as a whole.
System\Processor Queue Length	This counter tells you the number of threads that are waiting to be executed by the processor (or processors; there is just one queue for all CPUs). If this value is consistently 10 or more, your processor isn't doing its job, and you should consider upgrading it or adding a second processor (if possible).
System\System Up Time	This counter shows the time, in seconds, that Windows Home Server has been running since the most recent boot.

Rather than comparing the Memory\Committed Bytes value and the Memory\Commit Limit value, you can monitor the Memory\% Committed Bytes in Use counter. Performance Monitor derives this value by dividing Memory\Committed Bytes by Memory\Commit Limit. The Memory\% Committed Bytes in Use is considered to be too high when it reaches 85% or more.

Optimizing the Hard Disk

Windows Home Server uses the hard disk to fetch application data and documents as well as to temporarily store data in the paging file. Therefore, optimizing your hard disk can greatly improve Windows Home Server's overall performance, as described in the next few sections.

Examining Hard Drive Performance Specifications

If you're looking to add another drive to your system, your starting point should be the drive itself: specifically, its theoretical performance specifications. Compare the drive's average seek time with other drives. (The lower the value, the better.) Also, pay attention to the rate at which the drive spins the disk's platters. A 7,200 RPM (or higher) drive has noticeably faster performance than, say, a 5,400 RPM drive. Most drives today spin at 7,200 RPM, although you can find faster if you're willing to pay a premium. (Beware of so-called "green" hard drives, which are designed to save power but do so at the cost of performance because most of them spin at a measly 5,400 RPM.)

Finally, the drive type can make a big speed difference. For example, USB 2.0 has a theoretical data transfer rate of up to 480Mbps, whereas the data transfer rates for FireWire 400 and FireWire 800 are about 400Mbps and 800Mbps, respectively. However, compare these speeds with the theoretical data transfer rate of USB 3.0 drives, which can sling data at up to 5Gbps, and eSATA (external SATA) drives, which can achieve up to 2.4Gbps. (Of course, you can only use an eSATA drive if your Windows Home Server computer's motherboard supplies an eSATA connector or if you add a controller card that offers one or more eSATA ports.)

Performing Hard Drive Maintenance

For an existing drive, optimization is the same as maintenance, so you should implement the maintenance plan discussed in Chapter 16, "Maintaining Windows Home Server." For a hard disk, this means doing the following:

▶ Keeping an eye on the disk's free space to make sure that it doesn't get too low

▶ Periodically cleaning out any unnecessary files on the disk

▶ Uninstalling any programs or devices you no longer use

▶ Frequently checking all partitions for errors

▶ Regularly defragmenting partitions

Disabling Compression and Encryption

Windows Home Server's partitions use the NTFS file system, which means they support compressing files to save space, as well as encrypting files for security. From a performance point of view, however, you shouldn't use compression and encryption on a partition.

15

Both technologies slow down disk accesses because of the overhead involved in the compression/decompression and encryption/decryption processes.

Turning Off Windows Search

Windows Search is a service that indexes the contents of the Windows Home Server shared folders as well as the contents of `%SystemDrive%\Documents and Settings`. Windows Search indexes these locations on-the-fly as you add or delete data. This greatly speeds up content-based file searches because Windows Home Server knows the contents of each file. However, if you frequently transfer data to Windows Home Server, you may find that the indexer (it's the `searchindexer.exe` process in Task Manager) uses a great deal of resources. If you never use the Windows Search service, or if you never use the Search box that appears in the Shared Folders tab of the Remote Access website, you should consider turning off the Windows Search service. To do this, follow these steps:

1. Select Start, Administrative Tools, Services to open the Services snap-in.
2. Double-click the Windows Search service.
3. Click Stop.
4. In the Startup Type list, select Disabled.
5. Click OK.

Enabling Write Caching

You should also make sure that your hard disk has *write caching* enabled. Write caching means that Windows Home Server doesn't flush changed data to the disk until the system is idle, which improves performance. The downside is that a power outage or system crash means the data never gets written, so the changes are lost. The chances of this happening are minimal because changed data is flushed to the hard drive quite frequently, so I recommend leaving write caching enabled, which is the Windows Home Server default.

You can get even more of a performance boost if your system uses a serial ATA (SATA) hard drive, because SATA drives include extra cache features. This hard drive performance improvement is theoretical because on most systems Windows doesn't activate write caching. However, because the advanced SATA drive write caching is more aggressive, losing data is a distinct possibility unless your system is protected by an uninterruptible power supply (UPS) or a battery backup.

To make sure the write caching setting is activated for a hard drive and to turn on a SATA drive's advanced caching features, follow these steps:

1. Select Start, type `device`, and then click Device Manager in the search results. Windows Home Server displays the Device Manager window.
2. Open the Disk Drives branch and double-click the hard disk you want to work with to display its property sheet.
3. In the Policies tab, make sure that the Enable Write Caching on the Device check box is activated.

4. For maximum performance with a SATA drive, activate the Turn Off Windows Write-Cache Buffer Flushing on the Device check box.

5. Click OK.

CAUTION

Let me reiterate here that activating the Turn Off Windows Write-Cache Buffer Flushing on the Device option tells Windows Home Server to use an even more aggressive write-caching algorithm. However, an unscheduled power shutdown means you will almost certainly lose some data. Activate this option only if your system is running off a UPS or has a battery backup.

Optimizing Virtual Memory

No matter how much main memory your system boasts, Windows Home Server still creates and uses a paging file for virtual memory. To maximize paging file performance, ensure that Windows Home Server is working with the paging file optimally. The next few sections present some techniques that help you do just that.

Storing the Paging File Optimally

The location of the paging file can have a major impact on its performance. There are three things you should consider:

▶ **If you have multiple physical hard disks, store the paging file on the hard disk that has the fastest access time**—You'll see later in this section that you can tell Windows Home Server which hard disk to use for the paging file.

▶ **Store the paging file on an uncompressed partition**—Windows Home Server is happy to store the paging file on a compressed NTFS partition. However, as with all file operations on a compressed partition, the performance of paging file operations suffers because of the compression and decompression required. Therefore, you should store the paging file on an uncompressed partition.

▶ **If you have multiple hard disks, store the paging file on the hard disk that has the most free space**—Windows Home Server expands and contracts the paging file dynamically depending on the system's needs. Storing the paging file on the disk with the most space gives Windows Home Server the most flexibility.

See "Changing the Paging File's Location and Size," later in this chapter, for the information about moving the paging file.

Customizing the Paging File Size

By default, Windows Home Server sets the initial size of the paging file to 1.5 times the amount of RAM in your system, and it sets the maximum size of the paging file to 3 times the amount of RAM. For example, on a system with 1GB RAM, the paging file's initial size will be 1.5GB, and its maximum size will be 3GB. The default values work well on most systems, but you might want to customize these sizes to suit your own configuration. Here are some notes about custom paging file sizes:

▶ The less RAM you have, the more likely it is that Windows Home Server will use the paging file, so the Windows Home Server default paging file sizes make sense. If your computer has less than 1GB RAM (unlikely, because that is the minimum amount of RAM required for Windows Home Server 2011) you should leave the paging file sizes as is.

▶ The more RAM you have, the less likely it is that Windows Home Server will use the paging file. Therefore, the default initial paging file size is too large and the disk space reserved by Windows Home Server is wasted. On systems with more than 1GB RAM, you should set the initial paging file size to half the RAM size, while leaving the maximum size at three times the RAM, just in case.

▶ If disk space on drive C: is at a premium, set the initial paging file size to 16MB (the minimum size supported by Windows Home Server). This should eventually result in the smallest possible paging file, but you'll see a bit of a performance drop because Windows Home Server often has to dynamically increase the size of the paging file as you work with your programs.

▶ You might think that setting the initial size and the maximum size to the same (relatively large; say, two or three times the RAM) value would improve performance because it would mean that Windows Home Server would never resize the paging file. In practice, however, it has been shown that this trick does *not* improve performance, and in some cases, it can actually decrease performance.

▶ If you have a large amount of RAM (at least 4GB), you might think that Windows Home Server would never need virtual memory, so it would be okay to turn off the paging file. This won't work, however, because Windows Home Server needs the paging file anyway, and some programs might crash if no virtual memory is present.

As you can see, certain circumstances could lead you to deviate from the default settings. See the section after next to learn how to change the paging file size.

Watching the Paging File Size

Monitor the paging file performance to get a feel for how it works under normal conditions, where "normal" means while running your usual collection of applications and your usual number of open windows and documents.

Start all the programs you normally use (and perhaps a few extra, for good measure), and then watch Performance Monitor's Process\Page File Bytes and Process\Page File Bytes Peak counters.

Changing the Paging File's Location and Size

The paging file is named pagefile.sys and it's stored in the root folder of Drive C. Here's how to change the hard disk that Windows Home Server uses to store the paging file, and how to adjust the paging file size:

NOTE

The pagefile.sys file is a hidden system file. To see it, open any folder window and select Organize, Folder and Search Options. In the Folder Options dialog box, click the View tab, activate the Show Hidden Files and Folders option, and deactivate the Hide Protected Operating System Files check box. When Windows Home Server asks you to confirm the display of protected operating system files, click Yes, and then click OK.

1. If necessary, defragment the hard disk that you'll be using for the page file, as described in Chapter 16.

2. Select Start, right-click Computer, and then click Properties to display the System window. (You can also press Windows Logo+Pause/Break.)

3. Click Advanced System Settings to open the System Properties dialog box with the Advanced tab displayed.

4. In the Performance group, click Settings to display the Performance Options dialog box.

5. Display the Advanced tab.

6. In the Virtual Memory group, click Change. Windows Home Server displays the Virtual Memory dialog box.

7. Deactivate the Automatically Manage Paging File Size for All Drives check box, as shown in Figure 15.10.

8. Use the Drive list to select the hard drive you want to use.

TIP

If you want to move the page file to another drive, first select the original drive and then activate the No Paging File option to remove the page file from that drive. Select the other drive and choose either Custom Size or System Managed Size to add a new page file to that drive.

9. Select the Custom Size option.

10. Use the Initial Size (MB) text box to enter the initial size, in megabytes, that Windows Home Server should use for the paging file.

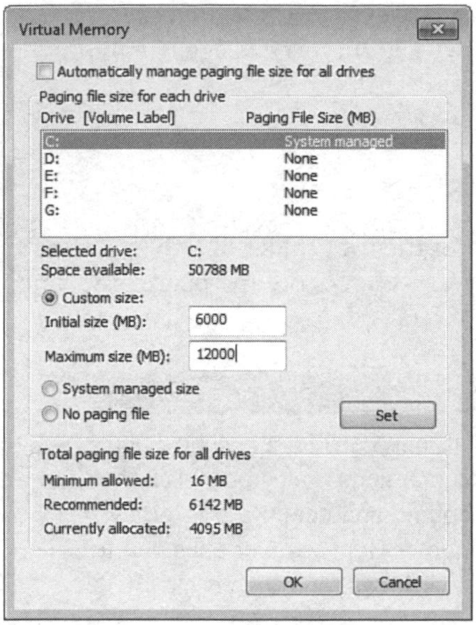

FIGURE 15.10   Use the Virtual Memory dialog box to select a different hard disk to store the paging file.

11. Use the Maximum Size (MB) text box to enter the largest size, in megabytes, that Windows Home Server can use for the paging file.

> **CAUTION**
>
> To ensure that Windows Home Server is able to dynamically resize the paging file as needed, specify a maximum size that's larger than the initial size.

12. Click Set.
13. Click OK in all the open dialog boxes. If you decreased either the initial size or the maximum size, Windows Home Server asks if you want to restart the computer.
14. Click Yes.

Optimizing Applications

Unless you use Windows Home Server as your main workstation, it's unlikely that you want or need to optimize applications. However, if you do run programs on Windows Home Server, you can do a few things to improve the performance of those applications. The next few sections offer some pointers for improving the performance of applications under Windows Home Server.

Adding More Memory

All applications run in RAM, of course, so the more RAM you have, the less likely it is that Windows Home Server has to store excess program or document data in the paging file on the hard disk, which is a real performance killer. In Task Manager or Performance Monitor, watch the Available Memory value. If it starts to get too low, consider adding RAM to your system.

Optimizing Application Launching

Prefetching is a Windows Home Server performance feature that analyzes disk usage and then reads into memory the data that you or your system accesses most frequently. You can use the prefetcher to speed up booting, application launching, or both. You configure the prefetcher using the following Registry key:

```
HKLM\SYSTEM\CurrentControlSet\Control\SessionManager\Memory Management\
↪PrefetchParameters\
```

Select Edit, New, DWORD (32-bit) Value, type **EnablePrefetcher**, and press Enter. Once again, select Edit, New, DWORD (32-bit) Value, type **EnableSuperfetch**, and press Enter.

Initialize these settings as follows:

- ▶ 1—Use this value for application-only prefetching.

- ▶ 2—Use this value for boot-only prefetching.

- ▶ 3—Use this value for both application and boot prefetching.

I normally recommend configuring both settings to 2 for boot-only prefetching. This value improves boot performance and, on most systems, has little or no effect on application performance because commonly used application launch files are probably in the RAM cache anyway. However, you can experiment with setting the values to 1 to optimize application launching.

Getting the Latest Device Drivers

If your application works with a device, check with the manufacturer or Windows Update to see whether a newer version of the device driver is available—in general, the newer the driver, the faster its performance. You learn how to update device drivers later in this chapter; see the section titled "Upgrading Your Device Drivers."

Setting the Program Priority in Task Manager

You can improve the performance of a program by adjusting the priority given to the program by your computer's processor. The processor enables programs to run by doling out thin slivers of its computing time to each program. These time slivers are called *cycles* because they are given to programs cyclically. For example, if you have three programs running—A, B, and C—the processor gives a cycle to A, one to B, another to C, and then one back to A again. This cycling happens quickly, appearing seamless when you work with each program.

The *base priority* is a ranking that determines the relative frequency with which a program gets processor cycles. A program given a higher frequency gets more cycles, which improves the program's performance. For example, suppose that you raise the priority of program A. The processor might give a cycle to A, one to B, another to A, one to C, another to A, and so on.

Follow these steps to change a program's priority:

1. Launch the program you want to work with.
2. Open Task Manager, as described earlier in this chapter. (Refer to "Monitoring Performance with Task Manager.")
3. Display the Processes tab.
4. Right-click your application's process to display its shortcut menu.
5. Click Set Priority, and then click (from highest priority to lowest) Realtime, High, or AboveNormal.

> **TIP**
>
> After you've changed the priority of one or more programs, you might forget the values that you have assigned to each one. To help, you can view the priority for all the items in the Processes tab. Click View, and then click Select Columns to display the Select Columns dialog box. Activate the Base Priority check box and click OK. This adds a Base Priority column to the Processes list.

More Optimization Tricks

The rest of this chapter takes you through several techniques and tricks for eking out a bit more performance from your system.

Adjusting Power Options

Windows Home Server's power management options can shut down your system's monitor (assuming you're not running Windows Home Server with a headless setup) or hard disk to save energy. Unfortunately, it takes a few seconds for the system to power up these devices again, which can be frustrating when you want to get back to work. You can do two things to eliminate or reduce this frustration:

▶ **Don't let Windows Home Server turn off the monitor and hard disk**—By default, Windows Home Server doesn't turn off the monitor or hard disks, and it doesn't go into a system standby state. To make sure, select Start, Control Panel, Power Options to display the Power Options window. Select the High Performance power plan, and then click Change Plan Settings. In the Turn Off Display list, select never. Click Change Advanced Power Settings, select the Hard Disk, Turn Off Hard Disk After branch, and make sure the Setting value is 0.

▶ **Don't use a screensaver**—Again, it can take a few seconds for Windows Home Server to recover from a screensaver. To ensure that you're not using one, select Start, Control Panel, Personalization, click Screen Saver, and choose (None) in the Screen Saver list. If you're worried about monitor wear and tear, use the Blank screensaver, which is relatively lightweight and exits quickly. Also, if you're not worried about security, you can deactivate the On Resume, Display Logon Screen check box to avoid having to log on each time you stop the screensaver.

Eliminate the Use of Visual Effects

Unless you use Windows Home Server for day-to-day work, there's no reason for it to be using visual effects. For example, effects such as animating the movement of windows when you minimize or maximize them, fading or scrolling menus and tooltips, and adding shadows under menus and the mouse pointer are merely cosmetic and are drains on system performance.

15

NOTE

To keep things in perspective, I should point out that these visual effects only affect system performance slightly, and most modern systems should be able to handle them without slowing noticeably. However, if you're running Windows Home Server on an older system that's already slower than you want it to be, or if you just want every last processor cycle to go to Windows Home Server's core functions, by all means lose the eye candy.

You can use various methods to turn off visual effects:

▶ Select Start, Control Panel, Display, Change Display Settings, Advanced Settings, select the Monitor tab, and then choose High Color (16 bit) in the Colors list. Using fewer colors gives your graphics card less to do, which should speed up video performance. Also, display the Troubleshoot tab, click Change Settings, and make sure the Hardware Acceleration slider is set to Full.

▶ Select Start, Control Panel, System, click Advanced System Settings, and click Settings in the Performance group. In the Visual Effects tab of the Performance Options dialog box (see Figure 15.11), activate the Adjust for Best Performance option (which deactivates all the check boxes).

▶ Open the Registry Editor, and set the following Registry value to 0:

    HKCU\Control Panel\Desktop\MenuShowDelay

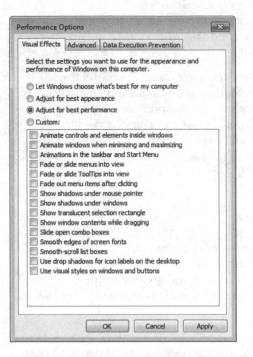

FIGURE 15.11   Turn off the check boxes in the Visual Effects tab to improve performance.

Optimizing Windows Home Server for Services

You can set up Windows Home Server so that it's optimized to run services. This involves configuring the processor scheduling, which determines how much time the processor allocates to the computer's activities. In particular, processor scheduling differentiates between programs and background services. The latter are the processes that Windows Home Server uses behind the scenes, such as performing backups and monitoring network health. Clearly, background services are what Windows Home Server is all about, so it should be optimized to give more processor cycles to these services.

Optimizing Windows Home Server performance means configuring it to give more CPU time to background services and using a large system cache. This is the default configuration in Windows Home Server, but it's worth your time to make sure this is still the case on your system. Here are the steps to follow:

1. Select Start, Control Panel, System to display the System window.

2. Click Advanced System Settings.

3. In the Performance group, click Settings to display the Performance Options dialog box.

4. Display the Advanced tab, shown in Figure 15.12.

5. In the Processor Scheduling group, activate the Background Services option.

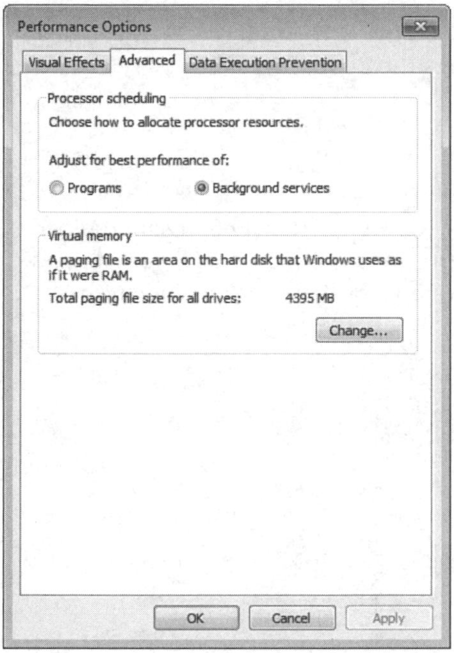

FIGURE 15.12   In the Performance Options dialog box, use the Advanced tab to optimize Windows Home Server for programs.

6. Click OK.

7. When Windows Home Server tells you the changes require a restart, click OK to return to the System Properties dialog box.

8. Click OK. Windows Home Server asks whether you want to restart your system.

9. Click Yes.

Upgrading Your Device Drivers

Device drivers that are designed to work with Windows Home Server (or Windows Server 2008 R2) generally load faster than older drivers. Therefore, you should check each of your device drivers to see whether a 64-bit version exists that's designed to work with Windows Home Server 2011 (or Windows Server 2008 R2) and, where available, upgrade to that driver.

The next few sections take you through Windows Home Server's various methods for updating a device driver.

Launching the Hardware Update Wizard

To get started, you need to run the Hardware Update Wizard, as described in the following steps:

1. If you have a disk or CD with the updated driver, insert the disk or CD. If you downloaded the driver from the Internet, decompress the driver file, if necessary.

2. Select Start, Control Panel, System.

3. Click Device Manager.

4. Locate and select the device you want to upgrade.

5. Select Action, Update Driver Software, or click the Update Driver Software toolbar button. (You can also open the device's property sheet, display the Driver tab, and click Update Driver.) The Update Driver Software Wizard appears, as shown in Figure 15.13.

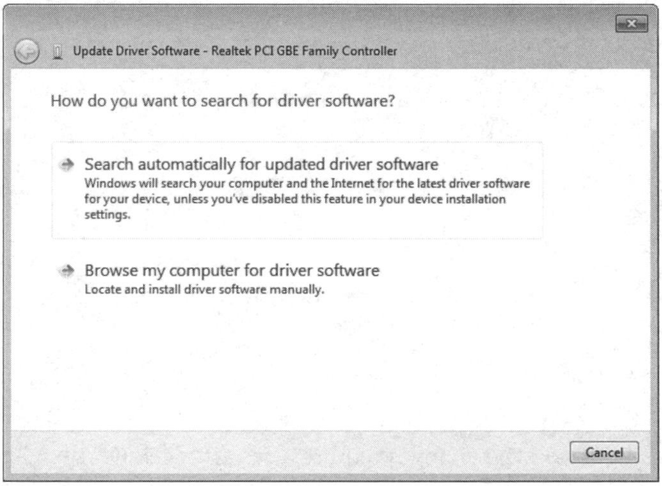

FIGURE 15.13   Use the Update Driver Software Wizard to upgrade your device driver.

From here, you can install the driver automatically, install the driver from a disc or downloaded file, or use a built-in Windows Home Server driver. These choices are covered in the next three sections.

Installing the Driver Automatically

If you have a disk or CD that has the updated driver and that driver is Windows Home Server-compatible, you can usually get Windows Home Server to upgrade the driver automatically. Follow these steps:

1. Insert the disk or CD that contains the upgraded driver.

2. In the initial Update Driver Software Wizard dialog box, click the Search Automatically for Updated Driver Software option, and then click Next. Windows Home Server examines the system's disk drives, locates the driver, and then installs it.

3. If the wizard finds more than one driver, it asks you to choose the one you want from a list. Click the driver you want, and then click Next. Windows Home Server installs the driver.

4. Click Finish.

Installing the Driver from a Disc or Download

If the Hardware Update Wizard couldn't find the driver on the disc, or if you've downloaded the driver file, here are the steps to follow to upgrade the driver:

1. If the driver is on a disc, insert the disc.

CAUTION

If the downloaded driver is contained within a compressed file (such as a ZIP file), be sure to decompress the file before moving on to the next wizard step.

---

2. In the initial Update Driver Software Wizard dialog box, click Browse My Computer for Driver Software. You see the dialog box shown in Figure 15.14.

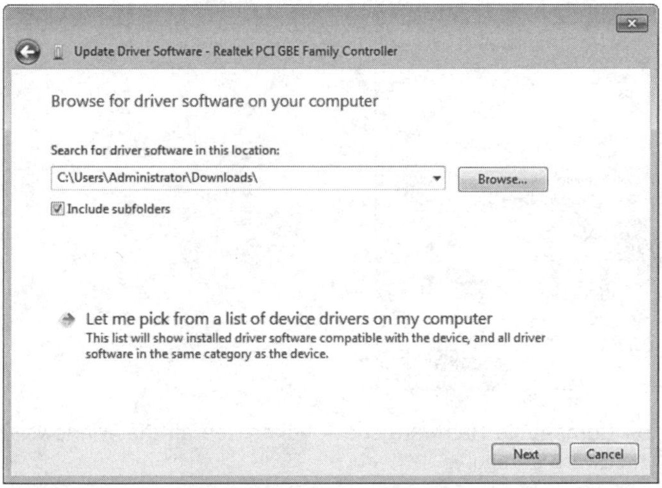

FIGURE 15.14   This dialog box appears if you elected to install the device driver from a list or a specific location.

3. In the Search for Driver Software in This Location text box, enter the full path of the folder that contains the driver (or click Browse to choose the location from a dialog box).

4. Click Next. Windows Home Server installs the driver from the location you specified.

5. Click Finish.

Installing a Built-In Windows Home Server Driver

If you don't have a disc or download, you can try installing one of Windows Home Server's built-in drivers, although in practice this is more useful for fixing driver problems than it is for improving performance. Follow these steps:

1. In the initial Update Driver Software Wizard dialog box, click Browse My Computer for Driver Software.

2. Click Let Me Pick from a List of Device Drivers on My Computer. The wizard displays a list of compatible drivers for the device.

3. If you don't see an updated (or even a different) driver, you're probably out of luck. If you want, you can deactivate the Show Compatible Hardware check box. The wizard then displays a complete list of its built-in drivers for the device's hardware category, as shown in Figure 15.15.

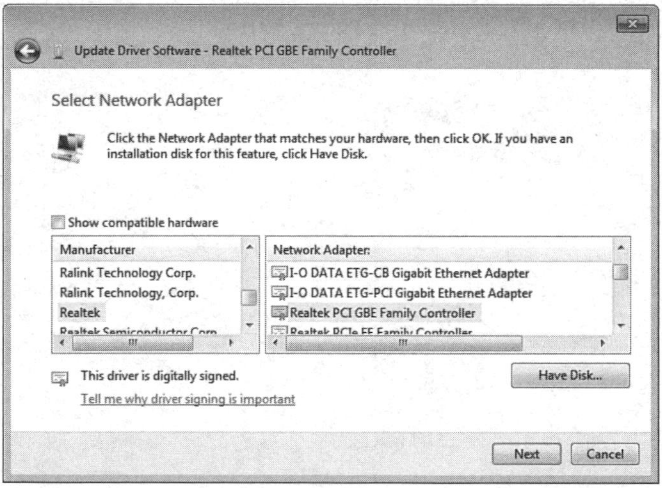

FIGURE 15.15   Deactivate the Show Compatible Hardware check box to see all the Windows Home Server drivers in the device's hardware category.

4. Use the Manufacturer list to select the manufacturer of your device.

5. Use the model list to select the device model.

6. Click Next. Windows Home Server installs the driver.

7. Click Finish.

From Here

- ▶ To learn how to check for hard disk problems, **SEE** "Checking Your Hard Disk for Errors," **P. 411.**

- ▶ For information on checking hard disk free space, **SEE** "Checking Free Disk Space on the System Drive," **P. 416.**

- ▶ To learn how to delete files that your system no longer uses, **SEE** "Deleting Unnecessary Files from the System Drive," **P. 419.**

15

CHAPTER **16**

Maintaining Windows Home Server

IN THIS CHAPTER

▶ Checking System Uptime

▶ Checking Your Hard Disk for Errors

▶ Checking Free Disk Space on the System Drive

▶ Deleting Unnecessary Files from the System Drive

▶ Defragmenting the System Drive

▶ Reviewing Event Viewer Logs

▶ Setting Up a Maintenance Schedule

Computers are useful beasts that do some pretty amazing tricks. However, one trick they haven't yet mastered is self-maintenance. Most of our other appliances run for years without much tending, but our computer appliances, being much more complex than your average microwave, require near-constant doses of digital TLC to keep them humming and happy. Fortunately, we're starting to see a trend toward self-maintenance in the PC world:

▶ Windows 7 and Windows Vista machines automatically defragment themselves once a week, and a background service monitors hard disk health and reports on problems that it finds.

▶ You learned in Chapter 9, "Backing Up and Restoring Network Computers," that Windows Home Server automatically deletes old backups and installs updates every Sunday. (**SEE** "Client Computer Backup Retention," **P. 212.**)

▶ In this chapter, you learn that Windows Home Server automatically checks for errors on your installed hard drives.

These are a good beginning, but we're still an awfully long way from reaching the Holy Grail of self-maintaining computers. For example, if it's no big deal for Windows 7 and Windows Vista machines to defragment themselves regularly, why didn't Microsoft add the same capability to Windows Home Server? Not to worry, though: In this chapter, you learn not only how to perform a few essential maintenance chores in Windows Home Server, but how to automate most of those chores so that you have a few less things to keep on your to-do list.

Checking System Uptime

In networking parlance, *uptime* refers to the amount of time that some system has been running continuously since the last time the system was started. From the standpoint of Windows Home Server, the longer the uptime the better, because that means the server has been available for clients longer, which means that shared folders, media streaming, and remote access have all been available. Checking the system uptime isn't a crucial system maintenance skill, but it does give you some indication of how the system is running overall. These next few sections take you through various methods for checking the current uptime value.

Displaying Uptime with the Task Manager

Probably the easiest way to get the current system uptime is to use Task Manager. Log in to the Windows Home Server desktop, right-click the taskbar, and then click Start Task Manager. Display the Performance tab, and look for the Up Time value in the System section (see Figure 15.3, in the previous chapter, for an example).

Displaying Uptime with the SYSTEMINFO Command

The SYSTEMINFO command-line utility gives you a tremendous amount of information about your computer, including data about the manufacturer, processor, and memory, what hotfixes are installed, and what network devices are installed. It also tells you the date and time when the system was last booted:

```
System Boot Time:      9/23/2011, 7:26:41 AM
```

Unfortunately, the output of the SYSTEMINFO command is quite long, so locating that one line can take some time. To make things faster, pipe the output of SYSTEMINFO through a case-insensitive FIND command, like so:

```
systeminfo ¦ FIND  /i "boot time"
```

This forces Windows Home Server to display just the System Boot Time line.

> ▶ **SEE** "SYSTEMINFO: Returning System Configuration Data," **P. 526.**

> ▶ **SEE** "FIND: Locating a Text String in a File," **P. 509.**

Displaying Uptime with Performance Monitor

In Chapter 15, "Tuning Windows Home Server Performance," you learned how to monitor Windows Home Server's performance using counters that you add to the Performance Monitor. One of those counters also tells you the current system uptime. Follow these steps to add it:

> ▶ **SEE** "Monitoring Performance with Performance Monitor," **P. 384.**

1. Select Start, Run, type **perf**, and press Enter. The Performance Monitor appears.

2. Select Monitoring Tools, Performance Monitor.

3. Right-click the Performance Monitor graph, and then click Add Counters. (Alternatively, press Ctrl+I or click the Add button in the toolbar.) The Add Counters dialog box appears.

4. In the Available Counters list, double-click System.

5. Select the System Up Time counter.

6. Click Add.

7. Click OK.

TIP

The System Up Time counter displays the uptime in seconds. To convert this value to days, divide it by 86,400 (the number of seconds in a day).

If you prefer a command-line solution, you can use the TYPEPERF utility to display performance counters in a Command Prompt window. Here's the command to run:

```
typeperf "\system\system up time" -sc 1
```

The -sc switch specifies the number of samples that you want TYPEPERF to collect and display. We need just one sample in this case.

▶ **SEE** "TYPEPERF: Monitoring Performance," **P. 528**.

Displaying Uptime with a Script

The problem with the System Up Time counter (whether you display it in Performance Monitor or at the command line) is that it displays the uptime in seconds, so you have to convert the value (to, say, days) to get a meaningful number. To avoid that, either use Task Manager, instead (which shows the uptime in days, hours, minutes, and seconds) or you can use the script in Listing 16.1, which does the conversion for you.

NOTE

You can download the scripts in this chapter from my website at www.mcfedries.com/HomeServerUnleashed3E/.

LISTING 16.1   A Script That Displays the System Uptime in Days, Hours, and Minutes

```
Option Explicit
    Dim objOS, dateLastBoot, nSystemUptime
    Dim nDays, nHours, nMinutes
```

```
    ' Get the Windows Home Server OS object
    '
    For Each objOS in GetObject( _
        "winmgmts:").InstancesOf ("Win32_OperatingSystem")
        '
        ' Return the last boot up time and
        ' convert it to a Date object
        '
        dateLastBoot = ConvertToDate(objOS.LastBootUpTime)
        '
        ' Calculate the number of minutes between then and now
        '
        nSystemUptime = DateDiff("n", dateLastBoot, Now)
        '
        ' Convert the total minutes into hours, days, and minutes
        '
        nDays = Int(nSystemUptime / 1440)
        nHours = Int (((nSystemUptime / 1440) - nDays) * 24)
        nMinutes = nSystemUptime Mod 60
        '
        ' Display the result
        '
        Wscript.Echo "Last Boot: " & dateLastBoot & vbCrLf & _
                     "System Uptime: " & _
                     nDays & " days and " & _
                     nHours & " hours and " & _
                     nMinutes & " minutes"
    Next
    '
    ' This function takes a datetime string and converts
    ' it to a real date and time object
    '
    Function ConvertToDate(strDate)
        Dim strYear, strMonth, strDay
        Dim strHour, strMinute, strSecond
        strYear = Left(strDate, 4)
        strMonth = Mid(strDate, 5, 2)
        strDay = Mid(strDate, 7, 2)
        strHour = Mid(strDate, 9, 2)
        strMinute = Mid(strDate, 11, 2)
        strSecond = Mid(strDate, 13, 2)
        ConvertToDate = DateSerial(strYear, strMonth, strDay) & " " & _
                     TimeSerial(strHour, strMinute, strSecond)
    End Function
```

This script references the `Win32_OperatingSystem` class, which has just one member object: the Windows Home Server operating system, represented in the `For Each...Next` loop by `objOS`. The script gets the `LastBootUpTime` property and converts the resulting string to a `Date` object using the `ConvertToDate` function. `DateDiff` returns the number of minutes between the last boot and `Now`. (This difference is the raw value for the system uptime.) Then the script converts the total minutes into the corresponding number of days, hours, and minutes and displays the result. Figure 16.1 shows sample output.

FIGURE 16.1   Sample output from the script in Listing 16.1.

Checking Your Hard Disk for Errors

Our hard disks store our programs and, most importantly, our precious data, so they have a special place in the computing firmament. We ought to pamper and coddle them to ensure a long and trouble-free existence, but that's rarely the case, unfortunately. Just consider everything that a modern hard disk has to put up with:

▶ **General wear and tear**—If your computer is running right now, its hard disk is spinning away at between 5,400 and 10,000 revolutions per minute. That's right—even though you're not doing anything, the hard disk is hard at work. Because of this constant activity, most hard disks simply wear out after a few years.

▶ **Head/platter collisions**—Your hard disk includes *read/write heads* that are used to read data from and write data to the disk. These heads float on a cushion of air just above the spinning hard disk platters. A bump or jolt of sufficient intensity can send them crashing onto the surface of the disk, which could easily result in trashed data. If the heads happen to hit a particularly sensitive area, the entire hard disk could crash. Notebook computers are particularly prone to this problem.

▶ **Power surges**—The current that is supplied to your PC is, under normal conditions, relatively constant. It's possible, however, for your computer to be assailed by massive power surges (such as during a lightning storm). These surges can wreak havoc on a carefully arranged hard disk.

So, what can you do about it? Windows Home Server comes with a program called Check Disk that can check your hard disk for problems and repair them automatically. It might not be able to recover a totally trashed hard disk, but it can at least let you know when a hard disk might be heading for trouble.

Check Disk performs a battery of tests on a hard disk. It looks for invalid filenames, invalid file dates and times, bad sectors, and invalid compression structures. In the hard disk's file system, Check Disk also looks for the following errors:

- Lost clusters
- Invalid clusters
- Cross-linked clusters
- File system cycles

The next few sections explain these errors in more detail.

Understanding Clusters

Large hard disks are inherently inefficient. When you format a disk, the disk's magnetic medium is divided into small storage areas called *sectors*, which usually hold up to 512 bytes of data. A large hard disk can contain tens of millions of sectors, so it would be too inefficient for Windows Home Server to deal with individual sectors. Instead, Windows Home Server groups sectors into *clusters*, the size of which depends on the file system and the size of the partition, as shown in Table 16.1.

TABLE 16.1   Default Cluster Sizes for Various File Systems and Partition Sizes

Partition Size	FAT16 Cluster Size	FAT32 Cluster Size	NTFS Cluster Size
7MB–16MB	2KB	N/A	512 bytes
17MB–32MB	512 bytes	N/A	512 bytes
33MB–64MB	1KB	512 bytes	512 bytes
65MB–128MB	2KB	1KB	512 bytes
129MB–256MB	4KB	2KB	512 bytes
257MB–512MB	8KB	4KB	512 bytes
513MB–1,024MB	16KB	4KB	1KB
1,025MB–2GB	32KB	4KB	2KB
2GB–4GB	64KB	4KB	4KB
4GB–8GB	N/A	4KB	4KB
8GB–16GB	N/A	8KB	4KB
16GB–32GB	N/A	16KB	4KB
32GB–2TB	N/A	N/A	4KB

Still, each hard disk has many thousands of clusters, so it's the job of the file system to keep track of everything. In particular, for each file on the disk, the file system maintains an entry in a *file directory*, a sort of table of contents for your files. (On an NT File System [NTFS] partition, this is called the *Master File Table*, or *MFT*.)

Understanding Lost Clusters

A *lost cluster* (also sometimes called an *orphaned cluster*) is a cluster that, according to the file system, is associated with a file but has no link to an entry in the file directory. Lost clusters are typically caused by program crashes, power surges, or power outages.

If Check Disk comes across lost clusters, it offers to convert them to files in either the file's original folder (if Check Disk can determine the proper folder) or in a new folder named Folder.000 in the root of the %SystemDrive%. (If that folder already exists, Check Disk creates a new folder named Folder.001 instead.) In that folder, Check Disk converts the lost clusters to files with names like File0000.chk and File0001.chk.

You can take a look at these files (using a text editor) to see whether they contain any useful data and then try to salvage the data. Most often, however, these files are unusable, and most people just delete them.

Understanding Invalid Clusters

An *invalid cluster* is one that falls under one of the following three categories:

- ▶ A file system entry with an illegal value. (In the FAT16 file system, for example, an entry that refers to cluster 1 is illegal because a disk's cluster numbers start at 2.)
- ▶ A file system entry that refers to a cluster number larger than the total number of clusters on the disk.
- ▶ A file system entry that is marked as unused but is part of a cluster chain.

In this case, Check Disk asks whether you want to convert these lost file fragments to files. If you say yes, Check Disk truncates the file by replacing the invalid cluster with an end of file (EOF) marker and then converts the lost file fragments to files. These are probably the truncated portion of the file, so you can examine them and try to piece everything back together. More likely, however, you just have to trash these files.

Understanding Cross-Linked Clusters

A *cross-linked cluster* is a cluster that has somehow been assigned to two different files (or twice in the same file). Check Disk offers to delete the affected files, copy the cross-linked cluster to each affected file, or ignore the cross-linked files altogether. In most cases, the safest bet is to copy the cross-linked cluster to each affected file. This way, at least one of the affected files should be usable.

Understanding Cycles

In an NTFS partition, a *cycle* is a corruption in the file system whereby a subfolder's parent folder is listed as the subfolder. For example, a folder named C:\Data should have C:\ as its parent; if C:\Data is a cycle, C:\Data—the same folder—is listed as the parent instead.

This creates a kind of loop in the file system that can cause the cycled folder to "disappear." In this case, Check Disk restores the correct parent folder, and all is well again.

Understanding Windows Home Server's Automatic Disk Checking

In Chapter 5, "Setting Up and Using Home Server Storage," you learned how to use the Windows Home Server Dashboard to check hard drive status and, if needed, repair a hard drive. How does Windows Home Server know when a hard drive needs fixing? It uses a behind-the-scenes service to periodically run the Check Disk tool in read-only mode. This means that Check Disk does not try to repair errors. Instead, if Check Disk reports that a drive is generating errors, it changes the drive's status to Failing, changes the overall network health status to Warning (orange), and enables the drive's Repair option in Windows Home Server Dashboard.

▶ **SEE** "Repairing Storage," **P. 115**.

All this means that you probably don't have to run a basic Check Disk by hand very often, particularly if your system is showing no signs of possible hard disk failure (such as intermittent system lock-ups, program crashes, and corrupt documents). However, if you *do* notice any of this behavior, it's always a good idea to run Check Disk as soon as possible, as described in the next section.

What you *will* do with Check Disk is run the more thorough scan that performs a sector-by-sector check of the physical disk. If you do this about once a month, you can give yourself a heads-up about potential problems.

Running Check Disk

Check Disk has two versions: a graphical user interface (GUI) version and a command-line version. See Chapter 19, "Using Windows Home Server's Command-Line Tools," to learn how to use the command-line version. Here are the steps to follow to run the GUI version of Check Disk:

▶ **SEE** "CHKDSK: Checking for Hard Disk Errors," **P. 502**.

> **NOTE**
>
> The GUI version of Check Disk only works with local partitions that have assigned drive letters. In Windows Home Server, this means you can use Check Disk on the system partition (C:) and the primary data partition (D:). However, you can't use Check Disk on secondary data partitions because these exist as mount points in Windows Home Server, so they don't have drive letters. To check mount points for errors, you need to use the CHKDSK command-line utility (again, see Chapter 19).

1. Select Start, Computer.
2. Right-click the drive you want to check, and then click Properties. The drive's property sheet appears.
3. Display the Tools tab.

4. Click the Check Now button. The Check Disk window appears, as shown in Figure 16.2.

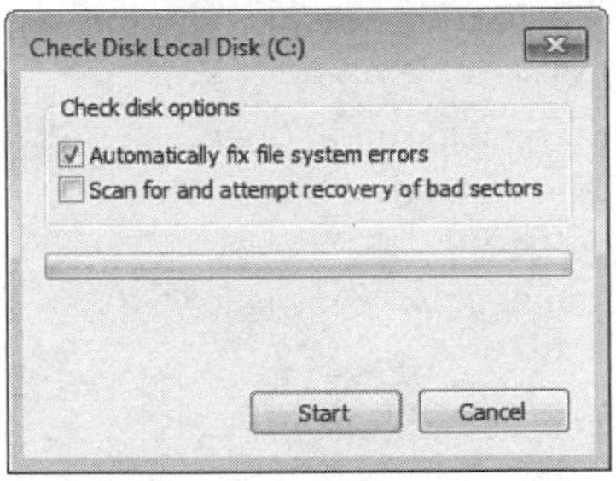

Check Disk Local Disk (C:)

Check disk options

☑ Automatically fix file system errors
☐ Scan for and attempt recovery of bad sectors

[Start]   [Cancel]

FIGURE 16.2   Use Check Disk to scan a hard disk partition for errors.

5. Activate one or both of the following options, if desired:

▶ **Automatically Fix File System Errors**—If you activate this check box, Check Disk automatically repairs any file system errors that it finds. If you leave this option deactivated, Check Disk runs in read only mode and just reports on any errors it finds.

▶ **Scan for and Attempt Recovery of Bad Sectors**—If you activate this check box, Check Disk performs a sector-by-sector surface check of the hard disk surface. If Check Disk finds a bad sector, it automatically attempts to recover any information stored in the sector and marks the sector as defective so that no information can be stored there in the future.

CAUTION

A sector-by-sector check can take several hours or more, depending on the size of the partition. Therefore, only run this more intensive check when you won't be using Windows Home Server for a while.

6. Click Start.

7. If you activated the Automatically Fix File System Errors check box and are checking a partition that has open system files, Check Disk tells you that it can't continue because it requires exclusive access to the disk. It then asks whether you want to schedule the scan to occur the next time you boot the computer. Click Yes to schedule the disk check.

8. When the scan is complete, Check Disk displays a message letting you know and provides a report on the errors it found, if any.

The AUTOCHK Utility

If you click Yes when Check Disk asks whether you want to schedule the scan for the next boot, the program adds the AUTOCHK utility to the following Registry setting:

    HKLM\SYSTEM\CurrentControlSet\Control\Session Manager\BootExecute

This setting specifies the programs that Windows Home Server should run at boot time when the Session Manager is loading. AUTOCHK is the automatic version of Check Disk that runs at system startup. If you want the option of skipping the disk check, you need to specify a timeout value for AUTOCHK. You change the timeout value by using the AutoChkTimeOut setting in the same Registry key:

    HKLM\SYSTEM\CurrentControlSet\Control\Session Manager\BootExecute

When AUTOCHK is scheduled with a timeout value greater than 0, you see the following the next time you restart the computer:

    A disk check has been scheduled.

    To skip disk checking, press any key within 10 second(s).

You can bypass the check by pressing a key before the timeout expires.

▶ **SEE** "CHKNTFS: Scheduling Automatic Disk Checks," **P. 503**.

Checking Free Disk Space on the System Drive

Hard disks with capacities measured in the hundreds of gigabytes are commonplace even in low-end systems nowadays, so disk space is much less of a problem than it used to be. However, remember that Windows Home Server has a system partition—drive C:—and that volume comes with a fixed 60GB size. With Windows Home Server taking up about 10- to 16GB (depending on the size of the paging file), you only have so much space left over to install other programs or store data in the Administrator account's local folders. Therefore, it's a good idea to keep track of how much free space you have on drive C:.

One way to check disk free space is to select Start, Computer. The Tiles view (select View, Tiles to see it) tells you the free space and the total size and displays the used portion of the disk in a graph, as shown in Figure 16.3. Alternatively, right-click drive C: in Windows Explorer and then click Properties. The system partition's total capacity, as well as its current used and free space, appear in the General tab of the property sheet, as shown in Figure 16.4.

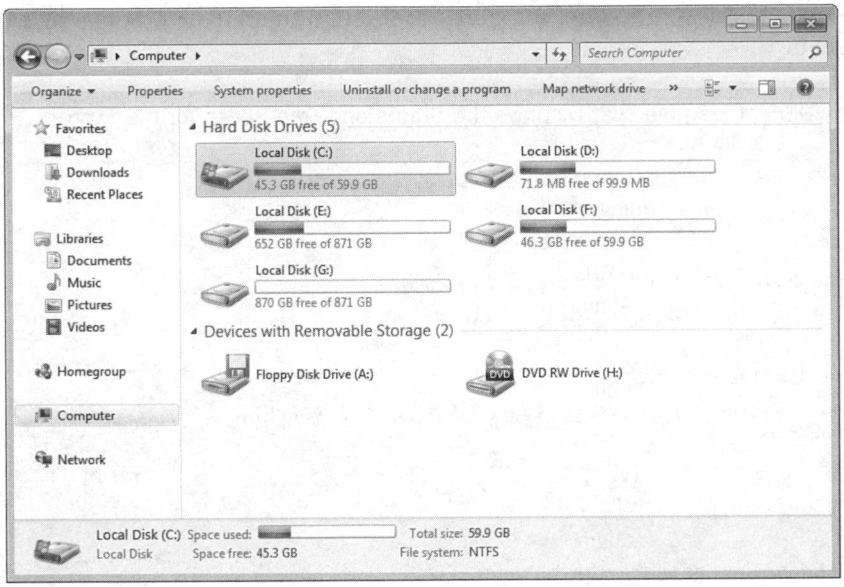

FIGURE 16.3   In Windows Explorer, display the Computer window in Details view to see the total size and free space on your system's disks.

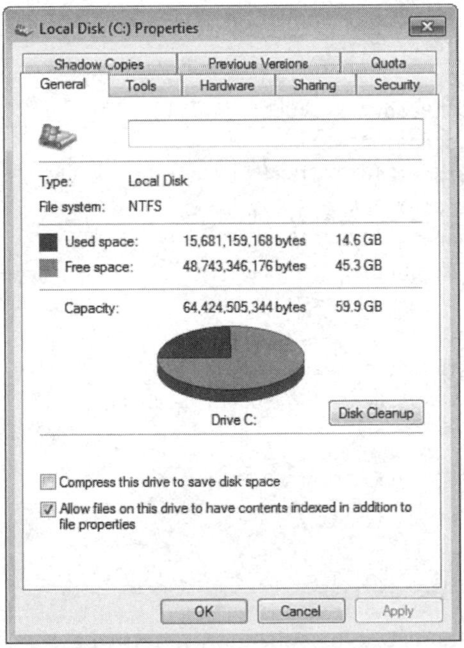

FIGURE 16.4   Right-click drive C:, and then click Properties to see the system drive's total size and free space.

Listing 16.2 presents a VBScript procedure that displays the status and free space for each drive on your system.

LISTING 16.2   A VBScript Example That Displays the Status and Free Space for the System Drive (C:)

```vbscript
Option Explicit
    Dim objFSO, strMessage

    ' Create the File System Object
    Set objFSO = CreateObject("Scripting.FileSystemObject")

    ' Start the display string
    strMessage = "Status Report for Drive C" & vbCrLf & vbCrLf

    ' Get the properties of drive C
    With objFSO.Drives("C")

        ' Add the volume name to the message
        strMessage = strMessage & "Volume Name: " & .VolumeName & vbCrLf

        ' Check the drive status
        If .IsReady = True Then

            ' If it's ready, add the status, total size,
            ' and the free space to the message
            strMessage = strMessage & "Status: Ready" & vbCrLf
            strMessage = strMessage & "Total space: " & _
                        FormatNumber(.TotalSize / 1073741824, 2) & " GB" & vbCrLf
            strMessage = strMessage & "Free space: " & _
                        FormatNumber(.FreeSpace / 1073741824, 2) & " GB"
            strMessage = strMessage & vbCrLf & vbCrLf
        Else

            ' Otherwise, just add the status to the message
            strMessage = strMessage & "Status: Not Ready" & vbCrLf & vbCrLf
        End If
    End With

    ' Display the message
WScript.Echo strMessage
```

This script creates a `FileSystemObject` and then uses its `Drives` collection to return a reference to the system drive: `Drives("C")`. Then the script checks the `Drive` object's `IsReady` property. If the drive is available (there's no reason why it wouldn't be, but you never know), a series of property values is added to the message: `VolumeName`, `TotalSize`, and `FreeSpace`. (Note that the last two are converted from bytes to gigabytes by dividing the property value by 1,073,741,824.) The script finishes by displaying the drive data, as shown in Figure 16.5.

```
Windows Script Host                    [x]

  Status Report for Drive C

  Volume Name:
  Status: Ready
  Total space: 60.00 GB
  Free space: 43.48 GB


                    [    OK    ]
```

FIGURE 16.5   The script displays the name, status, total space, and free space for the system drive.

Deleting Unnecessary Files from the System Drive

In the previous section, I mentioned that with hard drive capacities now regularly weighing in at several hundred gigabytes (with terabyte—1,000 gigabytes—and larger drives now readily available), free hard disk is not the problem it once was. Or is it? Just as these massive hard drives became affordable, it also became commonplace to create huge, multi-gigabyte files from DVD rips and recorded TV shows. In other words, no matter how humongous our hard drives are, we always seem to find a way to fill them up.

On your Windows Home Server system, you probably store any large data files in the shared folders, where your storage space should be large enough to handle them. However, that doesn't mean your system drive (C:) is in no danger of filling up. You only get 60GB to play with, and if you install large programs such as SharePoint Foundation (see Chapter 13, "Running a SharePoint Site on Windows Home Server") and programming tools such as Visual Studio Express, you may find that it doesn't take you all that long to fill up the system drive.

If you find that the system partition is getting low on free space, you should delete any unneeded files and programs. Windows Home Server comes with a Disk Cleanup utility that enables you to remove certain types of files quickly and easily. Before discussing this utility, let's look at a few methods you can use to perform a spring cleaning on your hard disk by hand:

▶ **Uninstall programs you don't use**—If you have an Internet connection, you know it's easier than ever to download new software for a trial run. Unfortunately, that also means it's easier than ever to have unused programs cluttering your hard disk. Use the Control Panel's Add or Remove Programs icon to uninstall these and other rejected applications.

▶ **Delete downloaded program archives**—Speaking of program downloads, your hard disk is also probably littered with ZIP files or other downloaded archives. For those programs you use, consider moving the archive files to a removable medium for storage. For programs you don't use, delete the archive files.

▶ **Remove Windows Home Server components that you don't use**—If you don't use some Windows Home Server components, use the Control Panel's Add or Remove Programs icon to remove those components from your system.

▶ **Move documents to the shared folders**—Your Administrator account on Windows Home Server has its own My Documents folder, and it's fine to use that folder to store scripts and other local files. However, if you use Windows Home Server to rip audio CDs and DVDs, record TV shows, or work with large database files, your documents can eat up a lot of disk space. If your Windows Home Server storage space is large, you should probably move some or all of your My Documents contents to the shared folders.

After you've performed these tasks, you should run the Disk Cleanup utility, which can automatically remove some of the preceding file categories, as well as several other types of files. Here's how it works:

1. Select Start, All Programs, Accessories, System Tools, Disk Cleanup. The Select Drive dialog box appears.

2. In the Drives list, select drive C:. (It should be selected by default.) Disk Cleanup scans the drive to see which files can be deleted and then displays a window similar to the one shown in Figure 16.6.

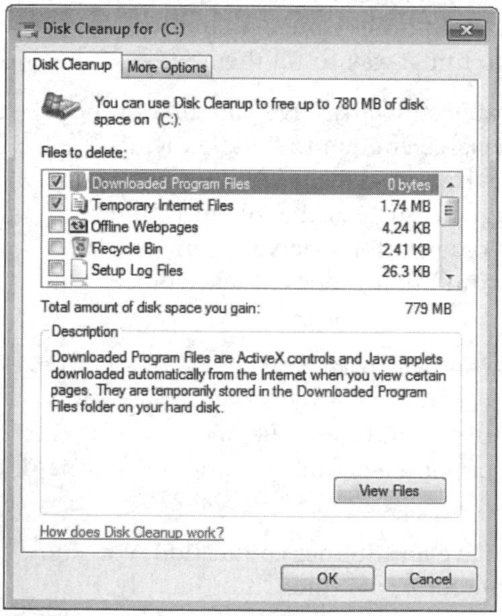

FIGURE 16.6   Disk Cleanup can automatically and safely remove certain types of files from a disk drive.

TIP

Windows Home Server offers two methods for bypassing the Select Drive dialog box. One method is to right-click drive C: in Windows Explorer, click Properties, and then click the Disk Cleanup button in the General tab of the drive's property sheet. The other method is to select Start, Run, type `cleanmgr /dc`, and then click OK.

3. In the Files to Delete list, activate the check box beside each category of file you want to remove. If you're not sure what an item represents, select it and read the text in the Description box. Note, too, that for most of these items, you can click View Files to see what you'll be deleting. In most cases, you see the following items in this list:

   ▶ **Downloaded Program Files**—These are ActiveX controls and Java applets used by some web pages. Internet Explorer downloads the objects and stores them on your system.

   ▶ **Temporary Internet Files**—These are copies of web pages that Internet Explorer keeps on hand so that the pages view faster the next time you visit them. Note that deleting these files slows down your web surfing slightly, but you probably won't notice this much if you have a broadband connection.

   ▶ **Offline Webpages**—These are web pages that you've set up as favorites and for which you've activated the "Make available offline" feature. This means that Internet Explorer stores updated copies of these pages on your computer for offline surfing. Deleting them means that you have to go online to view them.

   ▶ **Recycle Bin**—These are the files that you've deleted recently. Windows Home Server stores them in the Recycle Bin for a while just in case you delete a file accidentally. If you're sure you don't need to recover a file, you can clean out the Recycle Bin and recover the disk space.

   ▶ **Setup Log Files**—These are files that Windows Home Server created while it was installing itself on your computer. If your computer is running well, you'll never need to refer to these logs, so you can toss them.

   ▶ **Temporary Files**—These are files that some programs use to store temporary information. Most programs delete these files automatically, but a program or computer crash could prevent that from happening. You can delete these files at will.

   ▶ **Thumbnails**—These are smaller versions of pictures, videos, and documents that Windows Home Server stores to display the contents of each folder more quickly. You can delete these safely, but note that Windows Home Server re-creates them anyway when you next visit a folder.

   ▶ **Microsoft Error Reporting Files**—Windows Home Server keeps track of several kinds of files that it uses for reporting errors and checking for solutions to problems. For example, there are Per User Archived Microsoft Error Reporting

Files (error reporting files for individual user accounts) and System Archived Microsoft Error Reporting Files (error reporting files for all users). These are temporary files that the Error Reporting service uses. You can safely delete these files.

4. Click OK. Disk Cleanup asks whether you're sure that you want to delete the files.

5. Click Yes. Disk Cleanup deletes the selected files.

Saving Disk Cleanup Settings

It's possible to save your Disk Cleanup settings and run them again at any time. This is handy if, for example, you want to delete all your downloaded program files and temporary Internet files at shutdown. Select Start, Command Prompt, and then enter the following command:

```
cleanmgr /sageset:1
```

Note that the number 1 in the command is arbitrary. You can enter any number between 0 and 65535. This launches Disk Cleanup with an expanded set of file types to delete. Make your choices, and click OK. What this does is save your settings to the Registry; it doesn't delete the files. To delete the files, open the command prompt and enter the following command:

```
cleanmgr /sagerun:1
```

You can also create a shortcut for this command, add it to a batch file, or schedule it with the Task Scheduler.

Defragmenting the System Drive

Windows Home Server comes with a utility called Disk Defragmenter that's an essential tool for tuning your hard disk. Disk Defragmenter's job is to rid your hard disk of file fragmentation.

File fragmentation means that a file is stored on your hard disk in scattered, noncontiguous bits. This is a performance drag because it means that when Windows Home Server tries to open such a file, it must make several stops to collect the various pieces. If a lot of files are fragmented, it can slow even the fastest hard disk to a crawl.

Why doesn't Windows Home Server just store files contiguously? Recall that Windows Home Server 2011 stores files on disk in clusters, and these clusters have a fixed size, depending on the disk's capacity. Most NTFS partitions use 4KB clusters, which is a small enough value that it more or less ensures that most files will be stored in multiple clusters.

Suppose, then, that a file requires 100 clusters to store everything. When you go to save that file (or when the system decides to write the file back to disk from memory or the paging file), you might think that Windows Home Server would examine the hard disk and look for a spot large enough to place all 100 clusters in a row. However, that's not the case. Windows Home Server is constantly writing files to disk, and if it took the time to find the perfect disk location every time, your system would feel extremely slow and sluggish.

To speed things up, Windows Home Server stores the first part of the file in the first available cluster, the second part in the next available cluster, and so on. Because available clusters can appear anywhere on the disk (for example, after you delete a file, its clusters become available for use by other files), you almost always end up with bits of the file scattered around the hard disk. That's *file fragmentation*, and that's what Disk Defragmenter is designed to fix.

Before using Disk Defragmenter on the system drive, you should perform a couple of housekeeping chores:

▶ **Delete any files from drive** C that you don't need, as described in the previous section. Defragmenting junk files only slows down the whole process.

▶ **Check drive** C and drive E for errors by running Check Disk, as described earlier in this chapter (refer to "Checking Your Hard Disk for Errors").

Follow these steps to use Disk Defragmenter:

1. Select Start, All Programs, Accessories, System Tools, Disk Defragmenter. (Alternatively, in Windows Explorer, right-click the hard drive partition, click Properties, display the Tools tab in the dialog box that appears, and then click the Defragment Now button.) The Disk Defragmenter window appears.

2. Select drive C.

3. Click Analyze Disk. Disk Defragmenter analyzes the fragmentation of the drive and then displays the percentage of defragmentation. If the value is 10 percent or more, you should defragment. If you don't want to defragment the drive, click Close and skip the rest of these steps.

4. Click Defragment Disk. Disk Defragmenter begins defragmenting the drive and displays the progress of the defrag in the Progress column.

5. When the defrag is done, click Close.

TIP

In some cases, you can defragment a drive even further by running Disk Defragmenter on the drive twice in a row. (That is, run the defragment, and when it's done, immediately run a second defragment on the same drive.)

TIP

You can avoid the tedium of manual defragments by turning on automatic defragmentation. In the Disk Defragmenter window, click Turn on Schedule, activate the Run on a Schedule check box, and then use the lists to configure the frequency, day, and time of the schedule, and the disks you want to include in the defragment.

16

Reviewing Event Viewer Logs

Windows Home Server constantly monitors your system for unusual or noteworthy occurrences, such as a service that doesn't start, the installation of a device, or an application error. These occurrences are called *events*, and Windows Home Server tracks them in four main event logs:

▶ **Application**—This log stores events related to applications, including Windows Home Server programs and third-party applications.

▶ **Security**—This log stores events related to system security, including logons, user accounts, and user privileges. I discussed this log in detail in Chapter 11, "Implementing Windows Home Server Security." SEE "Tracking Auditing Events," P. 266.

▶ **System**—This log stores events generated by Windows and components, such as system services and device drivers.

▶ **Windows Server**—This log stores events related to specific Windows Home Server features, such as the backup service and remote access.

NOTE

The System log catalogs device driver errors, but remember that Windows Home Server has other tools that make it easier to see device problems. As you see in Chapter 17, "Troubleshooting Windows Home Server," Device Manager displays an icon on devices that have problems, and you can view a device's property sheet to see a description of the problem. Also, the System Information utility (`Msinfo32.exe`) reports hardware woes in the System Information, Hardware Resources, Conflicts/Sharing branch and the System Information, Components, Problem Devices branch.

▶ **SEE** "Troubleshooting with Device Manager," **P. 442**.

You should scroll through the Application and System event logs regularly to look for existing problems or for warnings that could portend future problems. The Security log isn't as important for day-to-day maintenance. You need to use it only if you suspect a security issue with your machine, such as if you want to keep track of who logs on to the computer. To examine these logs, you use the Event Viewer snap-in, available by selecting Start, Administrative Tools, Event Viewer.

Figure 16.7 shows a typical Event Viewer window. Use the tree in the left pane to select the log you want to view, such as Application, Security, System, or Windows Server.

When you select a log, the middle pane displays the available events, including the event's date, time, and source; its type (Information, Warning, or Error); and other data. To see a description of an event, double-click it or select it and press Enter.

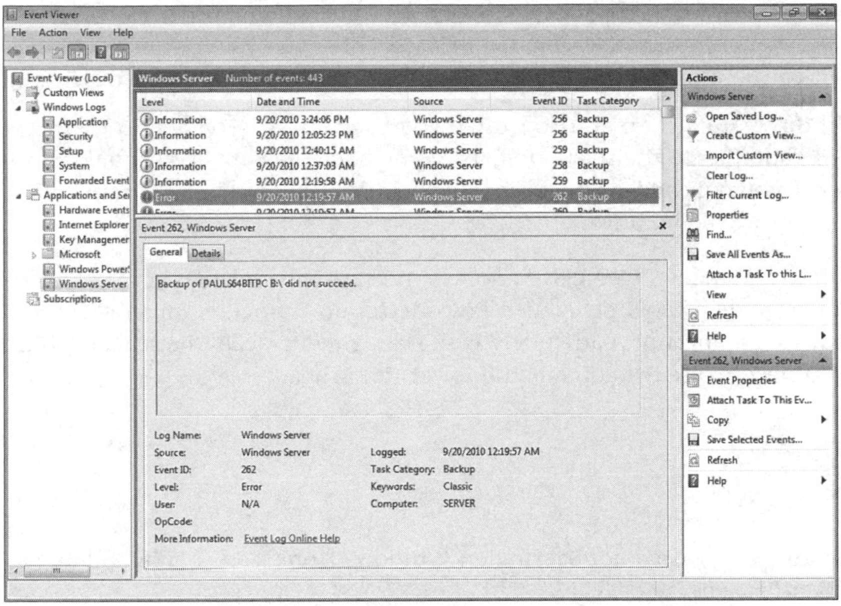

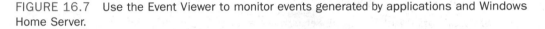

FIGURE 16.7   Use the Event Viewer to monitor events generated by applications and Windows Home Server.

Setting Up a Maintenance Schedule

Maintenance is effective only if it's done regularly, but there's a fine line to be navigated. If maintenance is performed too often, it can become a burden and interfere with more interesting tasks; if it's performed too seldom, it becomes ineffective. So, how often should you perform the maintenance chores I discussed in this chapter? Here's a suggested schedule:

▶ **Check your hard disk for errors**—As I mentioned earlier, Windows Home Server runs automatic disk checks daily, so you only need to run a basic scan when you think your system is having problems that Windows Home Server hasn't noticed yet. Run the more thorough disk surface scan about once a month. The surface scan takes a long time, so run it when you won't be using your computer for a while.

▶ **Check free disk space on the system drive**—Do this about once a month. If the free space on your system drive is getting low, check it weekly.

▶ **Delete unnecessary files on the system drive**—If free disk space isn't a problem on drive C:, run this chore once every two or three months.

▶ **Defragment the system drive**—How often you defragment your hard disk depends on how often you use your computer. Your Windows Home Server machine probably gets a pretty good workout every day, so you should run Disk Defragmenter about once a week.

▶ **Review Event Viewer logs**—If your system appears to be working fine, you need only check the Application and System log files weekly or every couple of weeks. If the system has a problem, check the logs daily to look for Warning or Error events.

▶ **Back up Windows Home Server**—How often you back up the server depends on how often you add files to the shared folders. If you add data daily, you should run a daily backup; if you only add files occasionally, you probably only need to back up every few days or even once a week.

Remember, as well, that Windows Home Server offers the Task Scheduler (select Start, All Programs, Accessories, System Tools, Scheduled Tasks) to set up a program on a regular schedule. Note that some programs, particularly Disk Defragmenter, can't be scheduled in their GUI form. You need to use the command-line version instead.

From Here

▶ To learn how to set up a drive for backing up Windows Home Server, **SEE** "Adding a Drive for Server Backups," **P. 103.**

▶ For more on repairing a drive, **SEE** "Repairing Storage," **P. 115.**

▶ For details on Windows Home Server's automatic backup deletions, **SEE** "Client Computer Backup Retention," **P. 212.**

▶ For the specifics of the Security event log, **SEE** "Tracking Auditing Events," **P. 266.**

▶ For more information on Device Manager's troubleshooting features, **SEE** "Troubleshooting with Device Manager," **P. 442.**

▶ You can run Check Disk from the command line; **SEE** "CHKDSK: Checking for Hard Disk Errors," **P. 502.**

▶ You can also use the CHKNTFS command-line to set the AUTOCHK timeout value; **SEE** "CHKNTFS: Scheduling Automatic Disk Checks," **P. 503.**

▶ For a discussion of the FIND command, **SEE** "FIND: Locating a Text String in a File," **P. 509.**

▶ For details on the SYSTEMINFO command, **SEE** "SYSTEMINFO: Returning System Configuration Data," **P. 526.**

▶ For the specifics of using TYPEPERF, **SEE** "TYPEPERF: Monitoring Performance," **P. 528.**

CHAPTER 17

Troubleshooting Windows Home Server

IN THIS CHAPTER

▶ Replacing Your System Hard Drive

▶ Checking for Solutions to Problems

▶ Understanding Troubleshooting Strategies

▶ General Troubleshooting Tips

▶ Troubleshooting Using Online Resources

▶ Troubleshooting Device Problems

▶ Troubleshooting Startup

One of the most compelling aspects of Windows Home Server is that after it's on your network and your other computers are connected to it, the safety of your data is immediately and dramatically increased:

▶ The Windows 7, Windows Vista, and Windows XP network computers are automatically added to the Windows Home Server backup system and will be completely backed up by the next morning.

▶ If you've configured the server backup, Windows Home Server backs up (by default) the entire system, the shared folders, the shared folder shadow copies, and the client computer backups twice a day (again by default).

In short, if you're sleeping better at night these days, it's at least in part because you know Windows Home Server is safeguarding your most important data. If a client computer goes down, or even if the server itself goes belly-up, you can recover without too much fuss.

Not that I want to wreck your good night's sleep, but the Achilles' heel in this rosy scenario is when other kinds of trouble rear up: software woes, hardware glitches, startup snags, and so on. Fortunately, there *are* some techniques you can use to recover from these kinds of problems. This chapter shows you a few techniques that are specific to Windows Home Server. It also takes you through some general troubleshooting tips that you can apply to Windows Home Server and to any computer on your network.

Replacing Your System Hard Drive

What happens if your system hard drive—the drive that stores the system partition and the operating system files—fails? That's quite problematic not only because you no longer have access to Windows Home Server, but because you lose access to the shared data and client backups. The good news is that, as long as you have at least one complete system backup, you can replace the hard drive with another one and then use the Windows Home Server DVD to make a complete recovery.

Determining the System Hard Drive

Before going any further, if you have multiple internal hard drives installed on your Windows Home Server machine, you do need to know which of them holds the system partition. In previous versions of Windows Home Server, you could use the Console to determine the system drive, but the Windows Home Server 2011 Dashboard doesn't offer this feature, so you need to follow these steps, instead:

1. Click the Server Manager icon in the taskbar to launch the Server Manager.
2. Open the Diagnostics, Device Manager branch.
3. In Device Manager, open the Disk Drives branch.
4. Double-click a hard drive to open the drive's Properties dialog box.
5. Click the Volumes tab.
6. Click Populate. Device Manager populates the Volumes section with a list of the partitions on the drive. If you see drive C: in that list (as shown in Figure 17.1), then you've found your system hard drive. If not, click Cancel and repeat steps 4-6 until you find the system drive.

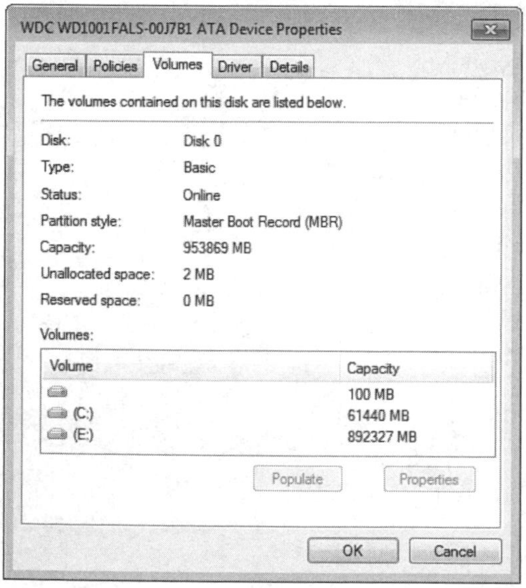

FIGURE 17.1   Drive C appears in the Volumes list of the system hard drive.

Replacing the System Drive

Here are the steps to follow to replace your system hard drive and reinstate Windows Home Server:

1. Shut down the Windows Home Server computer, if you haven't done so already.

2. Replace the failed system hard drive with a new hard drive.

CAUTION

The order in which the drives' data cables are connected to the motherboard determines the order of the drives on the system. Because your new hard drive must be the first hard drive, be sure to connect the new drive in the same position as the old drive.

---

3. If the system image backup of the server resides on an external drive, make sure that drive is attached to the server and powered up.

4. Turn on the computer, and insert the Windows Home Server installation DVD.

5. Boot from the DVD when your system prompts you. Setup loads the installation files and then displays the Installing Windows dialog box.

6. Click Repair an Existing Installation. The Select a System Image Backup dialog box appears.

7. Select the Use the Latest Available System Image option, and then click Next. Setup displays the Choose Additional Restore Options dialog box.

NOTE

The most recent system image backup is usually your best bet, but you can use an earlier backup if you prefer. In the Select a System Image Backup dialog box, choose the Select a System Image option, click Next, and then click the backup you want to use. If the backup resides on a network share, click Advanced and then click Search for a System Image on the Network.

---

8. If your replacement system drive is not new, you should select the Format and Repartition Disks check box. If you have multiple hard drives and you don't want Windows Home Server to format one or more of these drives, click Exclude Disks, activate the check box beside each drive you want to exclude, and then click OK.

9. If your server has multiple hard drives, you can save time by telling Setup to only restore the system drive by activating the Only Restore System Drives check box.

10. Click Next.

11. Click Finish. Windows Home Server begins restoring your system.

17

Checking for Solutions to Problems

Microsoft constantly collects information about Windows Home Server from users. When a problem occurs, Windows Home Server usually asks whether you want to send information about the problem to Microsoft and, if you do, it stores these tidbits in a massive database. Engineers then tackle the "issues" (as they euphemistically call them) and hopefully come up with solutions.

One of Windows Home Server's most promising features is called Problem Reporting, and it's designed to make solutions available to anyone who goes looking for them. Windows Home Server keeps a list of problems your computer is having, so you can tell it to go online and see whether a solution is available. If there's a solution waiting, Windows Home Server downloads it, installs it, and fixes your system.

Here are the steps to follow to check for solutions to problems:

1. Select Start, Control Panel, and then click Action Center. The Action Center window appears.
2. Click Maintenance to view the maintenance-related tools and messages.
3. Click Check for Solutions. Windows Home Server begins checking for solutions.
4. If you see a dialog box asking whether you want to send more information about your problems, you can click View Problem Details to see information about the problems, as shown in Figure 17.2. When you're ready to move on, click Send Information.

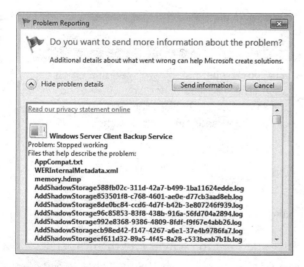

FIGURE 17.2   If Windows Home Server tells you it needs more information, click View Problem Details to see the problems.

If a solution exists for your computer, you see it listed in the Maintenance section of the Action Center window. Click View Message Details, and then follow the solution instructions.

By default, when a problem occurs, Windows Home Server does two things:

▶ It automatically checks for a solution to the problem.

▶ It asks whether you want to send more information about the problem to Microsoft.

You can control this behavior by configuring a few settings:

1. Select Start, Control Panel, Action Center.

2. Click Change Action Center Settings.

3. Click Problem Reporting Settings. The Problem Reporting Settings window appears.

4. Click Change Report Settings for All Users. This opens the Problem Reporting dialog box shown in Figure 17.3.

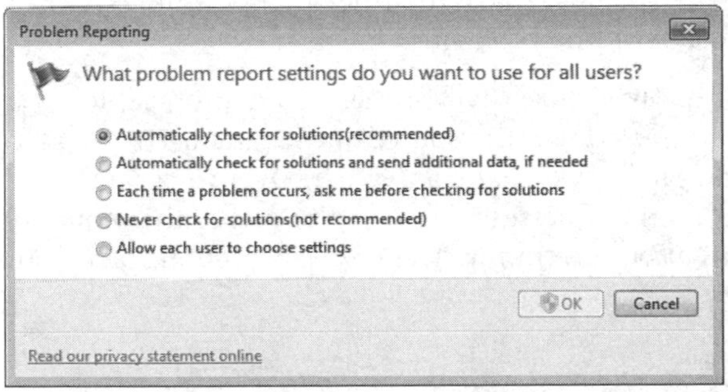

FIGURE 17.3   Use the Problem Reporting dialog box to configure the Problem Reporting feature if Windows Home Server tells you it needs more information.

5. To configure problem reporting, click one of the following options:

▶ **Automatically Check for Solutions**—Activate this option (it's the default) to have Windows Home Server automatically check online for an existing solution to a problem.

▶ **Automatically Check for Solutions and Send Additional Data, If Needed**— Activate this option to have Windows Home Server automatically check online for an existing solution to a problem and to automatically send extra information about the problem.

▶ **Each Time a Problem Occurs, Ask Me Before Checking for Solutions**— Activate this option to have Windows Home Server prompt you to check for solutions and to send additional information about the problem.

- ▸ **Never Check for Solutions**—Activate this option if you don't want to report problems at all.

- ▸ **Allow Each User to Choose Settings**—This option doesn't apply to Windows Home Server.

6. Click OK to return to the Problem Reporting Settings window.

7. Click OK to put the new settings into effect.

Understanding Troubleshooting Strategies

One of the ongoing mysteries that all Windows Home Server users experience at one time or another is what might be called the now-you-see-it-now-you-don't problem. This is a glitch that plagues you for a while and then mysteriously vanishes without intervention on your part. (This also tends to occur when you ask someone else to look at the problem. Like the automotive problem that goes away when you take the car to a mechanic, computer problems often resolve themselves as soon as a knowledgeable user sits down at the keyboard.) When this happens, most people just shake their heads and resume working, grateful to no longer have to deal with the problem.

Unfortunately, most computer ills aren't resolved so easily. For these more intractable problems, your first order of business is to track down the source of the glitch. This is, at best, a black art, but it can be done if you take a systematic approach. Over the years, I've found that the best approach is to ask a series of questions designed to gather the required information or to narrow down what might be the culprit. The next few sections take you through these questions.

Did You Get an Error Message?

Unfortunately, most computer error messages are obscure and do little to help you resolve a problem directly. However, error codes and error text can help you down the road, either by giving you something to search for in an online database (see "Troubleshooting Using Online Resources," later in this chapter) or by providing information to a tech support person. Therefore, you should always write down the full text of any error message that appears.

TIP

If the error message is lengthy and you can still use other programs on your computer, don't bother writing down the full message. Instead, while the message is displayed, press Print Screen to place an image of the current screen on the Clipboard. Then open Paint (select Start, All Programs, Accessories, Paint) or some other graphics program, press Ctrl+V to paste the screen into a new image, and save the image. If you think you'll be sending the image via email to a tech support employee or someone else who can help with the problem, consider saving the image as a monochrome or 16-color bitmap or, if possible, a JPEG file, to keep the image size small.

TIP

If the error message appears before Windows Home Server starts, but you don't have time to write it down, press the Pause Break key to pause the startup. After you record the error, press Ctrl+Pause Break to resume the startup.

Does an Error or Warning Appear in the Event Viewer Logs?

Open the Event Viewer (click Start, Administrative Tools, Event Viewer) and examine the Application and System logs. In particular, look in the Level column for Error or Warning events. If you see any, double-click each one to read the event description. Figure 17.4 shows an example.

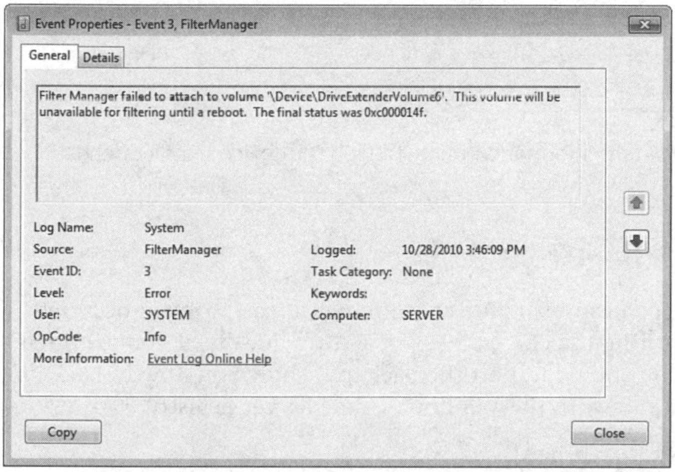

FIGURE 17.4   In the Event Viewer, look for Error events (like the one shown here) or Warning events in the Application and System logs.

▶ **SEE** "Reviewing Event Viewer Logs," **P. 424**.

If you see multiple errors or warnings associated with a particular application, consider either repairing or reinstalling the program or check to see if a patch is available from the software vendor. In extreme cases, you may need to uninstall the program. If you see multiple errors or warnings associated with a particular device, see if a device driver upgrade is available.

Does an Error Appear in System Information?

Select Start, type **system**, and then click System Information in the results to launch the System Information utility. In the Hardware Resources, Conflicts\Sharing category, look for device conflicts. Also, see whether any devices are listed in the Components\Problem Devices category, as shown in Figure 17.5. As with event errors, if you see errors associated with a particular device, your best bet is to check the vendor's website to see if a device driver upgrade is available.

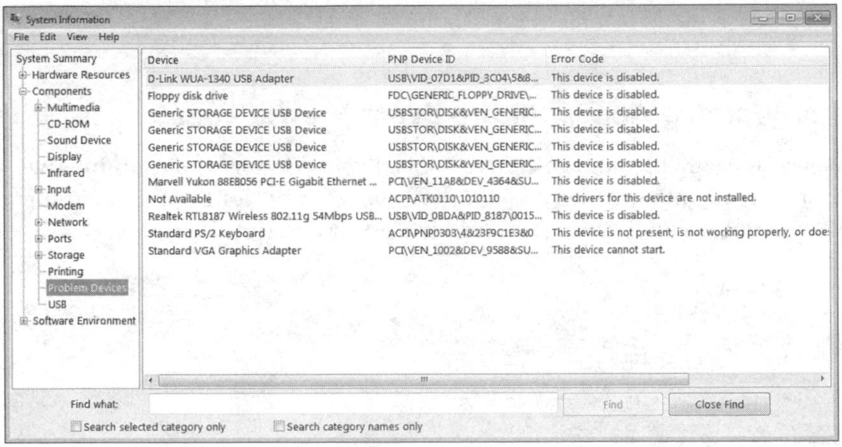

FIGURE 17.5   You can use the System Information utility to look for device conflicts and problems.

Did You Recently Edit the Registry?

Improper Registry modifications can cause all kinds of mischief. If the problem occurred after editing the Registry, try restoring the changed key or setting. Ideally, if you exported a backup of the offending key, you should import the backup. I show you how to back up the Registry in Chapter 18, "Working with the Windows Home Server Registry."

▶ **SEE** "Keeping the Registry Safe," **P. 463**.

Did You Recently Change Any Windows Settings?

If the problem started after you changed your Windows configuration, try reversing the change no matter how trivial. Even something as seemingly innocent as activating the screensaver can cause problems, so don't rule anything out. Actually, if your screen is garbled or the display is frozen, a screensaver should be your prime suspect. (There's something about the mode switch from regular video to screensaver video that, at least in my experience, has always been problematic. This shouldn't be an issue if you use the simple Blank screensaver that comes with Windows Home Server, but if you use anything fancier, you may have display troubles.)

Did Windows Home Server "Spontaneously" Reboot?

When certain errors occur, Windows Home Server reboots itself. This apparently random behavior is actually built into the system in the event of a system failure (also called a *stop error* or a *blue screen of death*—BSOD). By default, Windows Home Server writes an error event to the system log, dumps the contents of memory into a file, and then reboots the system. So, if your system reboots, check the Event Viewer to see what happened.

You can control how Windows Home Server handles system failures by following these steps:

1. Select Start, right-click Computer, and then click Properties to open the System window. (Alternatively, select Start, Control Panel, System.)

2. Click Advanced System Settings. This opens the System Properties dialog box with the Advanced tab displayed.

3. In the Startup and Recovery group, click Settings. Figure 17.6 shows the Startup and Recovery dialog box that appears.

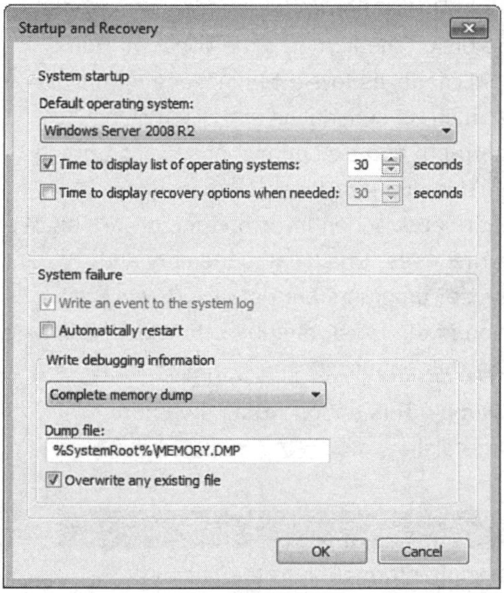

FIGURE 17.6   Use the Startup and Recovery dialog box to configure how Windows Home Server handles system failures.

4. Configure how Windows Home Server handles system failures using the following controls in the System Failure group:

Write an Event to the System Log	This option (which you can't deactivate in Windows Home Server) ensures that the system failure is recorded in the system log. This enables you to view the event in the Event Viewer.
Automatically Restart	This is the option that, when activated, causes your system to reboot when a stop error occurs. Deactivate this check box to avoid the reboot.

Write Debugging
Information

This list determines what information Windows Home Server saves to disk (in the folder specified in the text box below the list) when a system failure occurs. This information—it's called a *memory dump*—contains data that can help a tech support employee determine the cause of the problem. You have five choices:

▶ **None**—No debugging information is written.

▶ **Small Memory Dump (64 KB)**—This option writes the minimum amount of useful information that can be used to identify what caused the stop error. This 64KB file includes the stop error number and its description, the list of running device drivers, and the processor state.

▶ **Kernel Memory Dump**—This option writes the contents of the kernel memory to the disk. (The kernel is the Windows Home Server component that manages low-level functions for processor-related activities, such as scheduling and dispatching threads, handling interrupts and exceptions, and synchronizing multiple processors.) This dump includes memory allocated to the kernel, the hardware abstraction layer, and the drivers and programs that the kernel uses. Unallocated memory and memory allocated to user programs are not included in the dump. This information is the most useful for troubleshooting, so I recommend using this option.

▶ **Complete Memory Dump**—This option writes the entire contents of RAM to the disk.

CAUTION

Windows Home Server first writes the debugging information to the paging file—pagefile.sys in the root folder of Drive C: When you restart the computer, Windows Home Server transfers the information to the dump file. Therefore, you need to have a large enough paging file to handle the memory dump. This is particularly true for the Complete Memory Dump option, which requires the paging file to be as large as the physical RAM, plus one megabyte. The file size of the Kernel Memory Dump is typically about one-third of physical RAM, although it may be as large as 800MB. I showed you how to check and adjust the size of the paging file in Chapter 15, "Tuning Windows Home Server Performance."

▶ **Overwrite Any Existing File**—When this option is activated, Windows Home Server overwrites any existing dump file with the new dump information. If you deactivate this check box, Windows Home Server creates a new dump file with each system failure. Note that this option is enabled only for the Kernel Memory Dump and the Complete Memory Dump (which by default write to the same file: %SystemRoot%\Memory.dmp).

Did You Recently Change Any Application Settings?

If you did just change application settings, try reversing the change to see whether doing so solves the problem. If that doesn't help, check to see whether an upgrade or patch is available. Also, some applications come with a "Repair" option that can fix corrupted files. To try this out, follow these steps:

1. Select Start, Control Panel, Add or Remove Programs.
2. Make sure the Change or Remove Programs tab is displayed.
3. Click the program you're having trouble with.
4. Click the Change button. (You may need to click the Change/Remove button, instead. If you only see a Remove button, it means the program doesn't offer a repair option.) The application's install program launches.
5. Select the Repair option, if one exists.
6. Click Next to run the repair.

If repairing the program doesn't work, try reinstalling the program.

17

NOTE

If a program freezes, you can't shut it down using conventional methods. If you try, you might see a dialog box warning you that the program is not responding. If so, click End Now to force the program to close. Alternatively, right-click the taskbar and then click Task Manager. When you display the Applications tab, you should see your stuck application listed, and the Status column will likely say Not responding. Click the program, and then click End Task.

Did You Recently Install a New Program?

If you suspect that a new program is causing system instability, restart Windows Home Server and try operating the system for a while without using the new program. (If the program has components that load at startup, be sure to deactivate them, as I describe later in this chapter in the section titled "Troubleshooting Startup Using the System Configuration Utility.") If the problem doesn't recur, the new program is likely the culprit. Try using the program without other programs running.

You should also examine the program's readme file (if it has one) to look for known problems and possible workarounds. It's also a good idea to check for a version of the program designed to work with either Windows Home Server or Windows Server 2008. Again, you can also try the program's Repair option, or you can reinstall the program.

Similarly, if you recently upgraded an existing program, try uninstalling the upgrade.

> **TIP**
>
> One common cause of program errors is having one or more program files corrupted because of bad hard disk sectors. Before you reinstall a program, run a surface check on your hard disk to identify and block off bad sectors. I showed you how to do a hard disk surface scan in Chapter 16, "Maintaining Windows Home Server."

Did You Recently Install a New Device?

If you recently installed a new device or if you recently updated an existing device driver, the new device or driver might be causing the problem. Check Device Manager to see whether there's a problem with the device. Follow my device troubleshooting suggestions later in this chapter; see the section titled "Troubleshooting Device Problems."

Did You Recently Install an Incompatible Device Driver?

Windows Home Server enables you to install drivers that aren't Windows Home Server-certified, but it also warns you that this is a bad idea. Incompatible drivers are one of the most common sources of system instability, so whenever possible, download and install a driver that is designed for Windows Home Server.

▶ **SEE** "Upgrading Your Device Drivers," **P. 401**.

If you can't find a compatible driver, the next best thing is to roll back the driver you just installed. Here are the steps to follow:

1. Select Start, Administrative Tools, Computer Management to open the Computer Management snap-in.
2. Select Device Manager.
3. Display the device for the driver that's causing the problem.
4. Double-click the device to open its property sheet.
5. Display the Driver tab.
6. Click Roll Back Driver.

Did You Recently Apply an Update from Windows Update?

If your system becomes unstable after installing an update from Windows Update, in many cases you can uninstall the update. Here are the steps to follow:

1. Select Start, Control Panel, Programs and Features. Windows Home Server opens the Programs and Features window.

2. Click View Installed Updates.

3. Select the update you recently installed. (See Figure 17.7 for an example.)

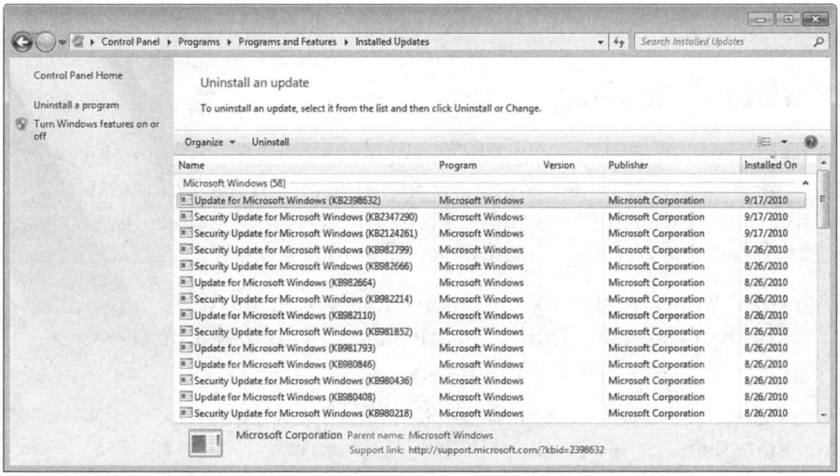

FIGURE 17.7   If you suspect that an update is causing problems, uninstall the update.

4. Click Uninstall. Windows Home Server asks you to confirm.

5. Click Yes to confirm that you want to remove the update. In most cases, Windows Home Server prompts you to restart the computer to complete the uninstall.

6. Click Restart Now.

TIP

If you have Windows Home Server set up to perform automatic updating, you can keep tabs on the changes made to your system by viewing the update history. Select Start, Control Panel, Windows Update, and then click the View Update History link.

Did You Recently Install a Windows Home Server Update?

It's ironic that updates designed to increase system stability occasionally do the opposite and cause more problems than they fix:

▶ If you've applied a hotfix, you can often remove it using the Control Panel's Programs and Features icon. Click View Installed Updates, and then look for a Windows Home Server Hotfix entry in the updates list. If you have multiple hotfixes listed, make sure that you remove the correct one. To be sure, check with either the

Microsoft Security site or the Microsoft Knowledge Base, both of which I discuss in the next section. Note, however, that you cannot uninstall most hotfixes.

▶ If you installed another type of update, you can uninstall it using the Control Panel's Programs and Features icon. Look for a Windows Home Server update entry in the installed programs list.

General Troubleshooting Tips

Figuring out the cause of a problem is often the hardest part of troubleshooting, but by itself, it doesn't do you much good. When you know the source, you need to parlay that information into a fix for the problem. I discussed a few solutions in the previous section, but here are a few other general fixes you need to keep in mind:

▶ **Close all programs**—You can often fix flaky behavior by shutting down all your open programs and starting again. This is a particularly useful fix for problems caused by low memory or low system resources.

▶ **Log off Windows Home Server**—Logging off clears the RAM and gives you a slightly cleaner slate than merely closing all your programs.

▶ **Reboot the computer**—If there are problems with some system files and devices, logging off won't help because these objects remain loaded. By rebooting the system, you reload it, which is often enough to solve many computer problems.

▶ **Turn off the computer and restart**—You can often solve a hardware problem by first shutting off your machine. Wait for 30 seconds to give all devices time to spin down, and then restart.

▶ **Check connections, power switches, and so on**—Some of the most common (and some of the most embarrassing) causes of hardware problems are the simple physical things: making sure that a device is turned on, checking that cable connections are secure, and ensuring that insertable devices are properly inserted. If you have pets, check for cables that have been chewed or otherwise damaged.

Troubleshooting Using Online Resources

The Internet is home to an astonishingly wide range of information, but its forte has always been computer knowledge. Whatever problem you have, there's a good chance that someone out there has run into the same thing, knows how to fix it, and has posted the solution on a website or newsgroup or would be willing to share it with you if asked. True, finding what you need is sometimes difficult, and you often can't be sure how accurate some of the solutions are. However, if you stick to the more reputable sites and if you get second opinions on solutions offered by complete strangers, you'll find the online world to be an excellent troubleshooting resource. Here's my list of favorite online resources:

Microsoft Product Support	This is Microsoft's main online technical support site.
Services	Through this site, you can access frequently asked questions about Windows Home Server, see a list of known problems, download files, and send questions to Microsoft support personnel: support.microsoft.com/
Microsoft Knowledge Base	The Microsoft Product Support Services site has links that enable you to search the Microsoft Knowledge Base, which is a database of articles related to all Microsoft products including, of course, Windows Home Server. These articles provide you with information about Windows Home Server and instructions on using Windows Home Server features. But the most useful aspect of the Knowledge Base is for troubleshooting problems. Many of the articles were written by Microsoft support personnel after helping customers overcome problems. By searching for error codes or key words, you can often get specific solutions to your problems: support.microsoft.com/search/
Windows Home Server Forums	Many Windows Home Server experts prowl this site, and you can usually get help with a problem quickly: social.microsoft.com/Forums/en/category/WindowsHomeServer/
Microsoft TechNet	This Microsoft site is designed for IT professionals and power users. It contains a huge number of articles on all Microsoft products. These articles give you technical content, program instructions, tips, scripts, downloads, and troubleshooting ideas: www.microsoft.com/technet/
Windows Update	Check this site for the latest device drivers, security patches, Service Packs, and other updates: windowsupdate.microsoft.com/
Microsoft Security	Check this site for the latest information on Microsoft's security and privacy initiatives, particularly security patches: www.microsoft.com/security/
Vendor websites	All but the tiniest hardware and software vendors maintain websites with customer support sections that you can peruse for upgrades, patches, workarounds, frequently asked questions, and sometimes chat or bulletin board features.

17

| The Web | Whatever problem you're facing, chances are that someone else has not only faced the same problem, but created a web page that explains the solution. Use your favorite search engine to search for your problem. This works best if you're getting a specific error message because you can then use some or all of the message as the search text. Google works great for this kind of searching: www.google.com/ |
| Newsgroups | There are computer-related newsgroups for hundreds of topics and products. Microsoft maintains its own newsgroups via the msnews.microsoft.com server, and Usenet has a huge list of groups in the alt and comp hierarchies. Before asking a question in a newsgroup, be sure to search Google Groups to see whether your question has been answered in the past: groups.google.com/ |

Troubleshooting Device Problems

Windows Home Server has good support for most newer devices, and it's likely that most major hardware vendors will take steps (eventually) to update their devices and drivers to run properly with Windows Home Server. If you use only recent, Plug and Play-compliant devices that are compatible with either Windows Home Server or Windows Server 2008, you should have a trouble-free computing experience (at least from a hardware perspective). Of course, putting *trouble-free* and *computing* next to each other is just asking for trouble. Hardware is not foolproof—far from it. Things still can, and will, go wrong, and, when they do, you'll need to perform some kind of troubleshooting. (That's assuming, of course, that the device doesn't have a physical fault that requires a trip to the repair shop.) Fortunately, Windows Home Server also has some handy tools to help you both identify and rectify hardware ills.

Troubleshooting with Device Manager

Windows Home Server stores all its hardware data in the Registry, but it provides Device Manager to give you a graphical view of the devices on your system. To display Device Manager, first use either of the following techniques:

▶ Select Start, Control Panel, System (or click Start, right-click Computer, and then click Properties), and then click Device Manager.

▶ Select Start, right-click Computer, and click Manage. In the Computer Management window, click the Device Manager branch.

TIP

A quick way to go directly to the Device Manager snap-in is to select Start, Run (or press Windows Logo+R) to open the Run dialog box, type `devmgmt.msc`, and click OK.

Device Manager's default display is a tree-like outline that lists various hardware types. To see the specific devices, click the arrow to the left of a device type. For example, opening the Network Adapters branch displays all the network adapter drives attached to your computer, as shown in Figure 17.8.

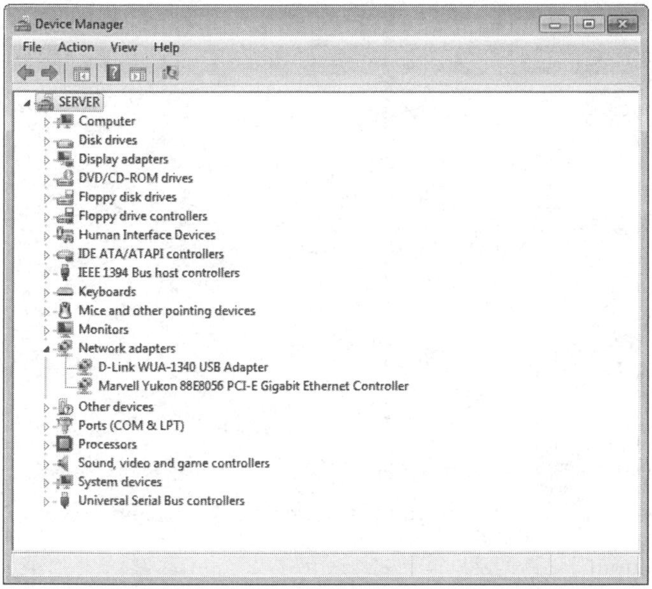

FIGURE 17.8 Device Manager organizes your computer's hardware in a tree-like hierarchy by hardware type.

Device Manager not only provides you with a comprehensive summary of your system's hardware data, it also doubles as a decent troubleshooting tool. To see what I mean, check out the Device Manager tab shown in Figure 17.9. See how the icon for the Standard VGA Graphics Adapter device has an exclamation mark superimposed on it? This tells you that there's a problem with the device.

If you examine the device's properties, as shown in Figure 17.10, the Device Status area tells you a bit more about what's wrong. As you can see, the problem here is that the device won't start. Either try Device Manager's suggested remedy or click the Check for Solutions button to see whether Microsoft has a fix for the problem.

NOTE

Device Manager has several dozen error codes. See the following Microsoft Knowledge Base article for a complete list of the codes, as well as solutions to try in each case: support.microsoft.com/kb/310123.

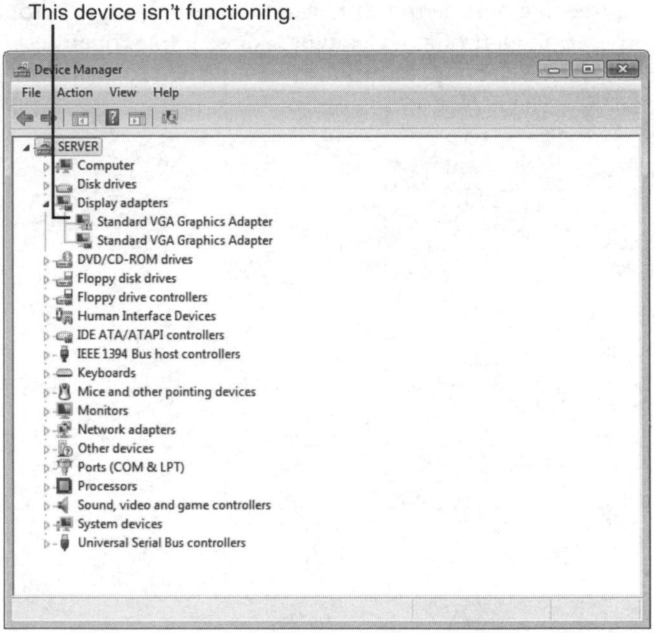

This device isn't functioning.

FIGURE 17.9   The Device Manager uses icons to warn you if a device has a problem.

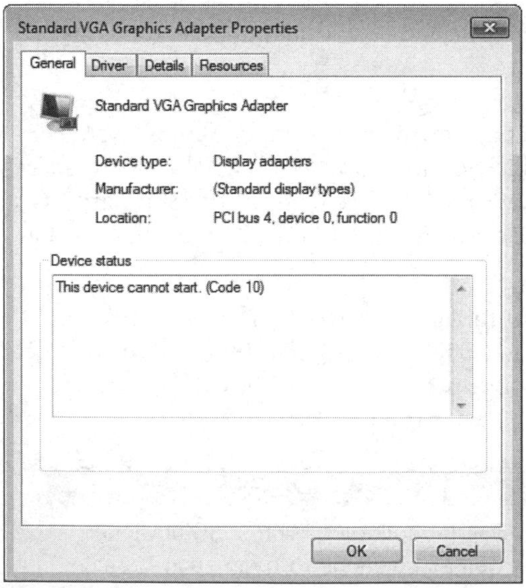

FIGURE 17.10   The Device Status area tells you if the device isn't working properly.

Device Manager uses three different icons to indicate the device's current status:

▶ A black exclamation mark (!) on a yellow field tells you that the device has a problem.

▶ A red X tells you that the device is disabled or missing.

▶ A blue i on a white field tells you that the device's Use Automatic Settings check box (on the Resources tab) is deactivated and that at least one of the device's resources was selected manually. Note that the device might be working just fine, so this icon doesn't indicate a problem. If the device isn't working properly, however, the manual setting might be the cause. (For example, the device might have a DIP switch or jumper set to a different resource.)

If your system flags a device but you don't notice problems, you can usually get away with just ignoring the flag. I've seen lots of systems that run perfectly well with flagged devices, so this falls under the "If it ain't broke" school of troubleshooting. The danger here is that tweaking your system to try to get rid of the flag can cause other—usually more serious—problems.

Troubleshooting Device Driver Problems

Other than problems with the hardware, device drivers are the cause of most device woes. For example, because Windows Home Server 2011 is a 64-bit operating system, it's possible that a device doesn't even have 64-bit drivers available. However, even a 64-bit driver can cause trouble, and this is true even if your device doesn't have one of the problem icons that I mentioned in the previous section. That is, if you open the device's properties sheet, Windows Home Server may tell you that the device is "working properly," but all that means is that Windows Home Server can establish a simple communications channel with the device. So if your device isn't working right, but Windows Home Server says otherwise, suspect a driver problem. Here are a few tips and pointers for correcting device driver problems:

▶ **Reinstall the driver**—A driver might be malfunctioning because one or more of its files have become corrupted. You can usually solve this by reinstalling the driver. Just in case a disk fault caused the corruption, you should check for errors in the partition where the driver is installed before reinstalling (see Chapter 16).

▶ **Upgrade to a signed driver**—Unsigned drivers are accidents waiting for a place to happen in Windows Home Server, so you should upgrade to a signed driver, if possible. How can you tell whether an installed driver is unsigned? Open the device's properties sheet, and display the Driver tab. Signed driver files display a name beside the Digital Signer label, whereas unsigned drivers display Not digitally signed instead. See Chapter 15 for the steps on updating a device driver.

17

NOTE

How is it possible to install an unsigned driver when 64-bit Windows operating systems (such as Windows Home Server 2011) require driver signing? It's possible because you can turn off mandatory driver signing (for example, to install an unsigned driver that you really need to use). You do this using the Local Group Policy Editor, which you start by select Start, typing `gpedit.msc`, and then pressing Enter. Open the User Configuration, Administrative Templates, System, Driver Installation branch, and then double-click the Code Signing for Device Drivers policy. Select the Enabled option, use the list to choose Ignore, and then click OK.

▶ **Disable an unsigned driver**—If an unsigned driver is causing system instability and you can't upgrade the driver, try disabling the device. Right-click the device, and then click Disable.

▶ **Use the Signature Verification Tool**—This program checks your entire system for unsigned drivers. To learn how it works, see "Verifying Digitally Signed Files," later in this chapter.

▶ **Try the manufacturer's driver supplied with the device**—If the device came with its own driver, try either updating to the manufacturer's driver or running the device's setup program.

▶ **Download the latest driver from the manufacturer**—Device manufacturers often update drivers to fix bugs, add new features, and tweak performance. Go to the manufacturer's website to see whether an updated driver is available. (See "Tips for Downloading Device Drivers," next.)

▶ **Try Windows Update**—The Windows Update website often has updated drivers for downloading. Select Start, All Programs, Windows Update and let the site scan your system. Then click the Driver Updates link to see which drivers are available for your system.

▶ **Roll back a driver**—If the device stops working properly after you update the driver, try rolling it back to the old driver. (Refer to "Did You Recently Install an Incompatible Device Driver?," earlier in this chapter.)

Tips for Downloading Device Drivers

Finding device drivers on the World Wide Web is an art in itself. I can't tell you how much of my life I've wasted rooting around manufacturer websites trying to locate a device driver. Most hardware vendor sites seem to be optimized for sales rather than service, so although you can purchase, say, a new printer with just a mouse click or two, downloading a new driver for that printer can take a frustratingly long time. To help you avoid such frustration, here are some tips from my hard-won experience:

▶ If the manufacturer offers different sites for different locations (such as different countries), always use the company's "home" site. Most mirror sites aren't true mirrors, and (Murphy's Law still being in effect) it's usually the driver you're looking for that a mirror site is missing.

▶ The temptation when you first enter a site is to use the search feature to find what you want. This works only sporadically for drivers, and the site search engines almost always return marketing or sales material first. Note, too, that occasionally these searches are case-sensitive, so bear that in mind when you enter your search text.

▶ Instead of the search engine, look for an area of the site dedicated to driver downloads. The good sites have links to areas called Downloads or Drivers, but it's far more common to have to go through a Support or Customer Service area first.

▶ Don't try to take shortcuts to where you *think* the driver might be hiding. Trudge through each step the site provides. For example, it's common to have to select an overall driver category, and then a device category, and then a line category, and then the specific model you have. This is tedious, but it almost always gets you where you want to go.

▶ If the site is particularly ornery, the preceding method might not lead you to your device. In that case, try the search engine. Note that device drivers seem to be particularly poorly indexed, so you might have to try lots of search text variations. One thing that usually works is searching for the exact filename. How can you possibly know that? I've had good luck using Google (www.google.com), Google Groups (groups.google.com), or some other web search engine to search for a driver. Chances are someone else has looked for your file and will have the filename (or, if you're really lucky, a direct link to the driver on the manufacturer's site).

▶ When you get to the device's download page, be careful which file you choose. Make sure that it's a 64-bit Windows Home Server (or Windows Server 2008 R2) driver, and make sure that you're not downloading a utility program or some other nondriver file.

▶ When you finally get to download the file, be sure to save it to your computer rather than opening it. If you reformat your system or move the device to another computer, you'll be glad you have a local copy of the driver so that you don't have to wrestle with the whole download rigmarole all over again.

Verifying Digitally Signed Files

I mentioned earlier that digitally unsigned drivers are often the cause of system instabilities. To ensure that you don't accumulate unsigned drivers on your system, you should regularly run the Signature Verification tool. This program scans your entire system (or, optionally, a specific folder) for unsigned drivers. Follow these steps to run this tool:

1. Select Start, type **sigverif**, and press Enter. The File Signature Verification window appears.

2. Click Advanced to display the Advanced File Signature Verification Settings dialog box.

3. Activate the Save the File Signature Verification Results to a Log File check box (it should be activated by default), and then click OK.

4. Click Start to begin the verification process.

When the verification is complete, the program displays a list of the unsigned driver files, if any. The results for all the scanned files are written to the log file `Sigverif.txt`, which is copied to the `C:\\Windows` folder when you close the window that shows the list of unsigned drivers. In the Status column of `Sigverif.txt`, look for files listed as `Not Signed`. If you find any, consider upgrading these drivers to signed versions.

> ▶ **SEE** "Upgrading Your Device Drivers," **P. 401**.

Troubleshooting Startup

Computers are often frustrating beasts, but few things in computing are as frustrating as an operating system that won't operate. This section outlines a few common startup difficulties and their solutions.

When to Use the Various Advanced Startup Options

You saw back in Chapter 4, "Configuring Windows Home Server," that Windows Home Server has some useful options on its Advanced Options menu. But under what circumstances should you use each option? That's not such an easy question to answer because there is some overlap in what each option brings to the table, so there are no hard and fast rules. It is possible, however, to lay down some general guidelines.

> ▶ **SEE** "Configuring Startup with the Advanced Boot Options Menu," **P. 90**.

Using Safe Mode

You should use the Safe Mode option if one of the following conditions occurs:

▶ Windows Home Server doesn't start after the Power On Self Test (POST) ends.

▶ Windows Home Server seems to stall for an extended period.

▶ Windows Home Server doesn't work correctly or produces unexpected results.

▶ You can't print to a local printer.

▶ Your video display is blank or is distorted and possibly unreadable.

▶ Your computer stalls repeatedly.

▶ Your computer suddenly slows down.

▶ You need to test an intermittent error condition.

Using Safe Mode with Networking

You should use the Safe Mode with Networking option if one of the following situations occurs:

▶ Windows Home Server fails to start using any of the other Safe mode options.

▶ The drivers or programs you need to repair a problem exist on a shared network resource.

▶ You need access to email or other network-based communications for technical support.

Using Safe Mode with Command Prompt

You should use the Safe Mode with Command Prompt option if one of the following situations occurs:

▶ Windows Home Server fails to start using any of the other Safe mode options.

▶ The programs you need to repair a problem can be run from the command prompt.

▶ You can't load the Windows Home Server graphical user interface (GUI).

Using Enable Boot Logging

You should use the Enable Boot Logging option in the following situations:

▶ The Windows Home Server startup hangs after switching to Protected mode.

▶ You need a detailed record of the startup process.

▶ You suspect (after using one of the other Startup menu options) that a Protected-mode driver is causing Windows Home Server startup to fail.

After starting (or attempting to start) Windows Home Server with this option, you end up with a file named NTBTLOG.TXT in the %SystemRoot% folder. This is a text file, so you can examine it with any text editor. For example, you could boot to the command prompt (using the Save Mode with Command Prompt option) and then use EDIT.COM to examine the file.

Move to the end of the file, and you might see a message telling you which device driver failed. You probably need to reinstall or roll back the driver.

Using Enable VGA Mode

You should use the Enable VGA Mode option in the following situations:

▶ Windows Home Server fails to start using any of the Safe mode options.

▶ You recently installed a new video card device driver, and the screen is garbled or the driver is balking at a resolution or color depth setting that's too high.

▶ You can't load the Windows Home Server GUI.

After Windows Home Server has loaded, you can either reinstall or roll back the driver, or you can adjust the display settings to values that the driver can handle.

Using Last Known Good Configuration

Use the Last Known Good Configuration option under the following circumstances:

▶ You suspect the problem is hardware related, but you can't figure out the driver that's causing the problem.

▶ You don't have time to try out the other more detailed inspections.

Each time Windows Home Server starts successfully in Normal mode, the system makes a note of which *control set*—the system's drivers and hardware configuration—was used. Specifically, it enters a value in the following Registry key:

```
HKLM\SYSTEM\Select\LastKnownGood
```

For example, if this value is 1, control set 1 was used to start Windows Home Server successfully:

```
HKLM\SYSTEM\ControlSet001
```

If you make driver or hardware changes and then find that the system won't start, you can tell Windows Home Server to load using the control set that worked the last time (that is, the control set that doesn't include your most recent hardware changes). This is called the *last known good configuration*, and the theory is that by using the previous working configuration, your system should start because it's bypassing the changes that caused the problem.

Using Directory Services Restore Mode

The Directory Services Restore Mode option is only for domain controllers. That means you'll never need to use it, because you can't configure Windows Home Server as a domain controller.

Using Debugging Mode

Use the Debugging Mode option if you receive a stop error during startup and a remote technical support professional has asked you to send debugging data.

What to Do If Windows Home Server Won't Start in Safe Mode

If Windows Home Server is so intractable that it won't even start in Safe mode, your system is likely afflicted with one of the following problems:

▶ Your system is infected with a virus. You need to run an antivirus program (usually from a bootable disc) to cleanse your system.

▶ Your system has incorrect BIOS settings. Run the machine's BIOS setup program to see whether any of these settings need to be changed or whether the CMOS battery needs to be replaced. (To access the setup program, shut down and then restart the Windows Home Server computer. Look for a message that tells you which key or key combination to press to access the settings.)

▶ Your system has a hardware conflict. See "Troubleshooting Device Problems," earlier in this chapter, for hardware troubleshooting procedures.

Troubleshooting Startup Using the System Configuration Utility

If Windows Home Server won't start, troubleshooting the problem usually involves trying various advanced startup options. It's almost always a time-consuming and tedious business.

However, what if Windows Home Server *will* start, but you encounter problems along the way? Or what if you want to try a few different configurations to see whether you can eliminate startup items or improve Windows Home Server's overall performance? For these scenarios, don't bother trying out different startup configurations by hand. Instead, take advantage of Windows Home Server's System Configuration Utility which, as you saw in Chapter 4, gives you a graphical front-end that offers precise control over how Windows Home Server starts.

▶ **SEE** "Configuring Startup with the System Configuration Editor," **P. 92**.

To launch the System Configuration Utility, select Start, type `msconfig`, and then press Enter. In the System Configuration Utility windows, display the General tab, which has the following three startup options:

Normal Startup	This option loads Windows Home Server normally.
Diagnostic Startup	This option loads only those device drivers and system services that are necessary for Windows Home Server to boot. This is equivalent to deactivating all the check boxes associated with the Selective Startup option, discussed next.

Selective Startup	When you activate this option, the check boxes below become available, as shown in Figure 17.11. Use these check boxes to select which portions of the startup should be processed.

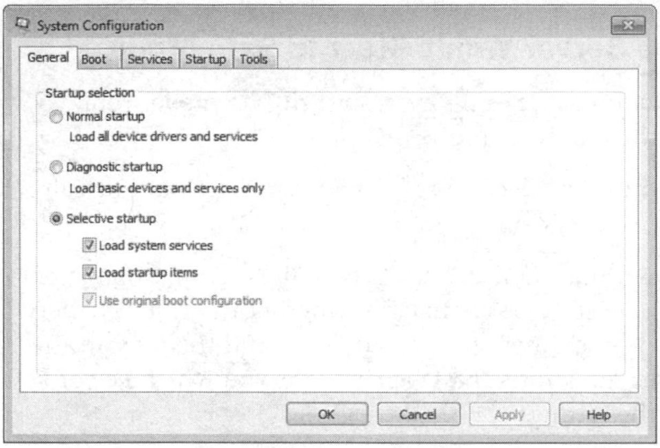

FIGURE 17.11   Use the System Configuration Utility to select different startup configurations.

For a selective startup, you control how Windows Home Server processes items using two categories:

Load System Services	This category refers to the system services that Windows Home Server loads at startup. The specific services loaded by Windows Home Server are listed in the Services tab.

NOTE

A *service* is a program or process that performs a specific, low-level support function for the operating system or for an installed program. For example, Windows Home Server's Automatic Updates feature is a service.

NOTE

The Services tab has an Essential column. Only those services that have Yes in this column are loaded when you choose the Selective Startup option.

Load Startup Items	This category refers to the items in your Windows Home Server Startup group and to the startup items listed in the Registry. For the latter, the settings are stored in one of the following keys:

```
HKCU\SOFTWARE\Microsoft\Windows\CurrentVersion\Run
HKLM\SOFTWARE\Microsoft\Windows\CurrentVersion\Run
```

The specific items loaded from the Startup group or the Registry are listed in the Startup tab.

To control these startup items, the System Configuration utility gives you two choices:

▶ To prevent Windows Home Server from loading every item in a particular category, activate Selective Startup in the General tab, and then deactivate the check box for the category you want. For example, to disable all startup items, deactivate the Load Startup Items File check box.

▶ To prevent Windows Home Server from loading only specific items in a category, display the category's tab, and then deactivate the check box beside the item or items you want to bypass at startup. For example, to prevent only certain startup items from loading, use the check boxes in the Startup tab.

Here's a basic procedure you can follow to use the System Configuration Utility to troubleshoot a startup problem (assuming that you can start Windows Home Server by using some kind of Safe mode boot, as described earlier):

1. In the System Configuration Utility, activate the Diagnostic Startup option, and then reboot the computer. If the problem did not occur during the restart, you know the cause lies in the system services or the startup items.

2. Activate the Selective Startup option.

3. Activate one of the two check boxes, and then reboot the computer.

4. Repeat step 3 for the other check box. When the problem occurs, you know that whatever item you activated just before rebooting is the source of the problem.

5. Display the tab of the item that is causing the problem. For example, if the problem recurred after you activated the Load Startup Items check box, display the Startup tab.

6. Click Disable All to clear all the check boxes.

7. Activate one of the check boxes to enable an item, and then reboot the computer.

8. Repeat step 7 for each of the other check boxes until the problem recurs. When this happens, you know that whatever item you activated just before rebooting is the source of the problem.

Troubleshooting by Halves

If you have a large number of check boxes to test (such as in the Services tab), activating one check box at a time and rebooting can quickly become tedious. A faster method is to begin by activating the first half of the check boxes and rebooting. One of two things will happen:

▶ **The problem won't recur**—This means that one of the items represented by the deactivated check boxes is the culprit. Clear all the check boxes, activate half the other check boxes, and then reboot.

▶ **The problem will recur**—This means that one of the activated check boxes is the problem. Activate only half of those check boxes and reboot.

Keep halving the number of activated check boxes until you isolate the offending item.

17

9. In the System Configuration Utility's General tab, activate the Normal Startup option.

10. Fix or work around the problem:

   ▶ If the problem is a system service, you can disable the service. Select Start, Control Panel, Administrative Tools, Services. Then double-click the problematic service to open its property sheet. In the Startup Type list, select Disabled, and then click OK.

   ▶ If the problem is a Startup item, either delete the item from the Startup group or delete the item from the appropriate Run key in the Registry. If the item is a program, consider uninstalling or reinstalling it. For more detailed information on the Registry's Run key, see the Chapter 4 section "Launching Items Using the Registry."

From Here

▶ To learn some network troubleshooting techniques, **SEE** "Troubleshooting Network Problems," **P. 14.**

▶ For details on the Advanced Options menu, **SEE** "Configuring Startup with the Advanced Boot Options Menu," **P. 90.**

▶ For information on the System Configuration Utility, **SEE** "Configuring Startup with the System Configuration Editor," **P. 92.**

▶ For more detailed information on the Registry's Run key, **SEE** "Launching Items Using the Registry," **P. 95.**

▶ To learn how to modify the paging file size, **SEE** "Changing the Paging File's Location and Size," **P. 395.**

▶ For information on installing driver updates, **SEE** "Upgrading Your Device Drivers," **P. 401.**

▶ To learn how to run a hard disk check, **SEE** "Checking Your Hard Disk for Errors," **P. 411.**

▶ For details on backing up the Registry and its keys, **SEE** "Keeping the Registry Safe," **P. 463.**

CHAPTER 18

Working with the Windows Home Server Registry

IN THIS CHAPTER

▶ Starting the Registry Editor
▶ Navigating the Registry
▶ Keeping the Registry Safe
▶ Working with Registry Entries
▶ Finding Registry Entries

The Windows Home Server Registry comes up a fair number of times in this book. In Chapter 2, "Setting Up and Working with User Accounts," I showed you how to modify a Registry setting to customize Windows Home Server's minimum password length requirement.

> ▶ **SEE** "Customizing the Password Length Requirement,"
> **P. 33**.

In Chapter 4, "Configuring Windows Home Server," you learned how to use the Registry's Run and RunOnce keys to launch a program at startup.

> ▶ **SEE** "Launching Applications and Scripts at Startup,"
> **P. 94**.

In Chapter 19, "Using Windows Home Server's Command-Line Tools," I show you how to use the Registry to customize the folder shortcut menu to include a command for opening a folder at the command prompt.

> ▶ **SEE** "Opening a Folder in a Command Prompt Session,"
> **P. 481**.

You can do these and many other useful and powerful Windows Home Server tweaks only by modifying the Registry. So just what is the Registry? It's a central repository that Windows Home Server uses to store almost everything that applies to the configuration of your system, including all the following:

▶ Information about all the hardware installed on your computer

    ▶ The resources those devices use

    ▶ A list of the device drivers that Windows Home Server loads at startup

    ▶ Settings that Windows Home Server uses internally

    ▶ File type data that associates a particular type of file with a specific application

    ▶ Wallpaper, color schemes, and other interface customization settings

    ▶ Other customization settings for things such as the Start menu and the taskbar

    ▶ Settings for accessories such as Windows Explorer and Internet Explorer

    ▶ Internet and network connections and passwords

    ▶ Settings and customization options for many applications

It's all stored in one central location, and, thanks to a handy tool called the Registry Editor, it's yours to play with (carefully!) as you see fit. No, the Registry doesn't have a pretty interface like most of the other customization options, and many aspects of the Registry give new meaning to the word *arcane*, but it gives you unparalleled access to facets of Windows Home Server that would be out of reach otherwise. This chapter introduces you to the Registry and its structure, and it shows you how to make changes to the Registry by wielding the Registry Editor.

Starting the Registry Editor

As you see a bit later, the Registry's files are binary files, so you can't edit them directly. Instead, you use a program called the Registry Editor, which enables you to view, modify, add, and delete any Registry setting. It also has a search feature to help you find settings and export and import features that enable you to save settings to and from a text file.

To launch the Registry Editor, follow these steps:

1. Log on to Windows Home Server.
2. Select Start.
3. In the Start menu Search box, type `regedit`.
4. Press Enter.

Figure 18.1 shows the Registry Editor window that appears. (Your Registry Editor window might look different if someone else has used the program previously. Close all the open branches in the left pane to get the view shown in Figure 18.1.)

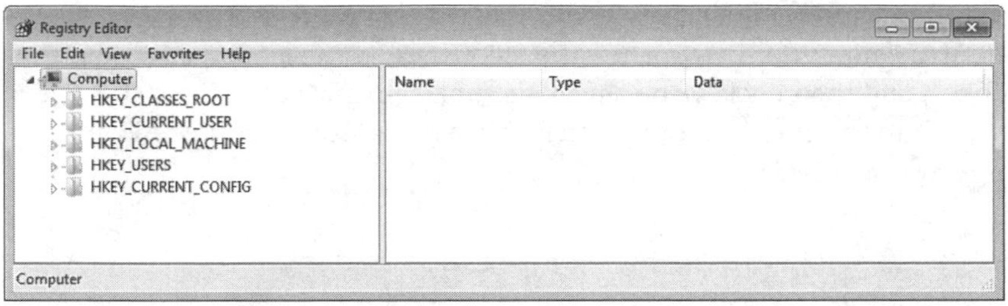

FIGURE 18.1   Running the REGEDIT command launches the Registry Editor, a program that enables you to view and edit the Registry's data.

Navigating the Registry

The Registry Editor is reminiscent of Windows Explorer, and it works in basically the same way. The left side of the Registry Editor window is similar to Explorer's Folders pane, except that rather than folders, you see *keys*. In this chapter, I'll call the left pane the *Keys pane*.

> **CAUTION**
>
> The Registry Editor is arguably the most dangerous tool in the Windows Home Server arsenal. The Registry is so crucial to the smooth functioning of Windows Home Server that a single imprudent change to a Registry entry can bring your system to its knees. Therefore, just because you have the Registry Editor open, don't start tweaking settings willy-nilly. Instead, read the section titled "Keeping the Registry Safe," later in this chapter, for some advice on protecting this precious and sensitive resource.

Navigating the Keys Pane

The Keys pane, like Explorer's Folders pane, is organized in a treelike hierarchy. The five keys that are visible when you open the Registry Editor are special keys called *handles* (which is why their names all begin with HKEY). These keys are collectively referred to as the Registry's *root keys*. I'll tell you what to expect from each of these keys later. (See the section called "Getting to Know the Registry's Root Keys," later in this chapter.)

All these keys contain subkeys, which you can display by clicking the arrow to the left of each key or by highlighting a key and pressing the plus-sign key on your keyboard's numeric keypad. To close a key, click the arrow, or highlight the key and press the minus-sign key on the numeric keypad. Again, this is just like navigating folders in Explorer.

18

You often have to drill down several levels to get to the key you want. For example, Figure 18.2 shows the Registry Editor after I've opened the HKEY_CURRENT_USER key, and then the Control Panel subkey, and then clicked the Keyboard subkey. Notice how the status bar tells you the exact path to the current key, and that this path is structured just like a folder path.

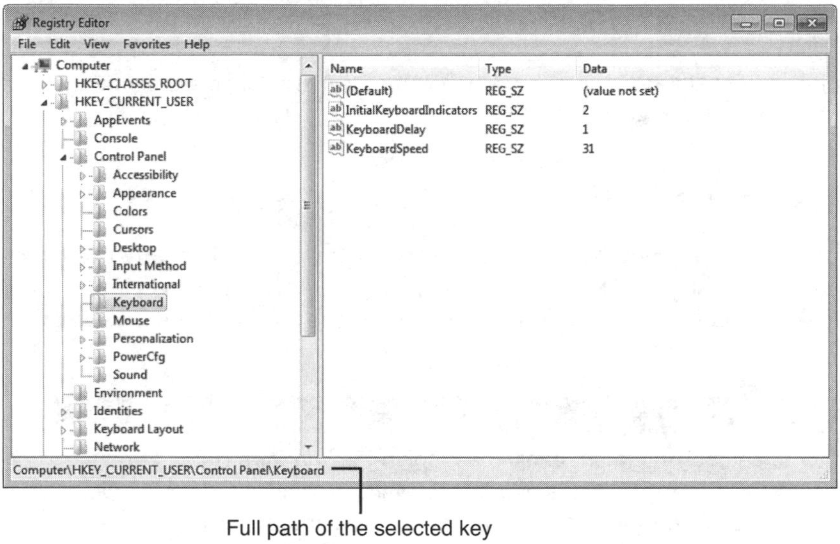

Full path of the selected key

FIGURE 18.2   Open the Registry's keys and subkeys to find the settings you want to work with.

> **TIP**
>
> To see all the keys properly, you likely will have to increase the size of the Keys pane. To do this, use your mouse to click and drag the split bar to the right. Alternatively, select View, Split, use the Right Arrow key to adjust the split bar position, and then press Enter.

Understanding the Registry Settings

If the left side of the Registry Editor window is analogous to Explorer's Folders pane, the right side is analogous to Explorer's Contents pane. In this case, the right side of the Registry Editor window displays the settings contained in each key (so I'll call it the *Settings pane*). The Settings pane is divided into three columns:

Name   This column tells you the name of each setting in the currently selected key (analogous to a filename in Explorer).

Type   This column tells you the data type of the setting. There are six possible data types:

REG_SZ—This is a string value.

REG_MULTI_SZ—This is a series of strings.

REG_EXPAND_SZ—This is a string value that contains an environment variable name that gets "expanded" into the value of that variable. For example, the %SystemRoot% environment variable holds the folder in which Windows Home Server was installed. So, if you see a Registry setting that includes the value %SystemRoot%\System32\ (see Figure 18.3 for an example), and Windows Home Server is installed in C:\Windows, the setting's expanded value is C:\Windows\System32\.

REG_DWORD—This is a double word value: a 32-bit hexadecimal value arranged as eight digits. For example, 11 hex is 17 decimal, so this number would be represented in DWORD form as 0x00000011 (17). (Why "double word"? A 32-bit value represents four bytes of data, and because a *word* in programming circles is defined as two bytes, a four-byte value is a *double word*.)

REG_QWORD—This is a quadruple word value: a 64-bit hexadecimal value arranged as 16 digits. Note that leading zeros are suppressed for the high 8 digits. Therefore, 11 hex appears as 0x00000011 (17), and 100000000 hex appears as 0x1000000000 (4294967296).

REG_BINARY—This value is a series of hexadecimal digits.

Data   This column displays the value of each setting.

Getting to Know the Registry's Root Keys

The root keys are your Registry starting points, so you need to become familiar with what kinds of data each key holds. The next few sections summarize the contents of each key.

HKEY_CLASSES_ROOT

HKEY_CLASSES_ROOT—usually abbreviated as HKCR—contains data related to file extensions and their associated programs, the objects that exist in the Windows Home Server system, as well as applications and their Automation information. There are also keys related to shortcuts and other interface features.

The top part of this key contains subkeys for various file extensions. You see .bmp for BMP (Paint) files, .doc for DOC (Word or WordPad) files, and so on. In each of these subkeys, the Default setting tells you the name of the registered file type associated with the extension. For example, the .txt extension is associated with the txtfile file type.

These registered file types appear as subkeys later in the HKEY_CLASSES_ROOT branch, and the Registry keeps track of various settings for each registered file type. In particular, the shell subkey tells you the actions associated with this file type. For example, in the shell\open\command subkey, the Default setting shows the path for the executable file that opens. Figure 18.3 shows this subkey for the txtfile file type.

18

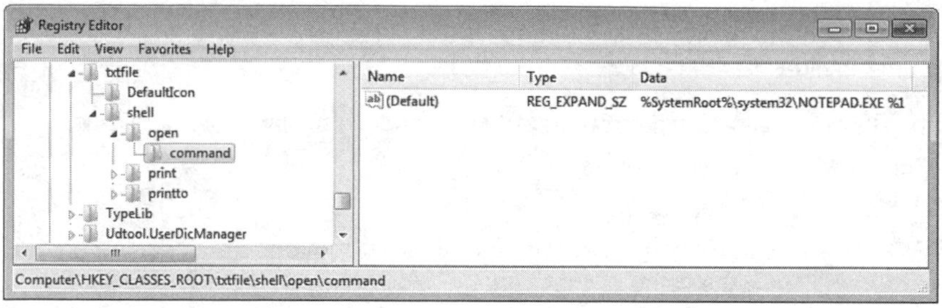

FIGURE 18.3   The registered file type subkeys specify various settings associated with each file type, including its defined actions.

HKEY_CLASSES_ROOT is actually a copy (or an *alias*, as these copied keys are called) of the following HKEY_LOCAL_MACHINE key:

HKEY_LOCAL_MACHINE\Software\Classes

The Registry creates an alias for HKEY_CLASSES_ROOT to make these keys easier for applications to access and to improve compatibility with legacy programs.

HKEY_CURRENT_USER

HKEY_CURRENT_USER—usually abbreviated as HKCU—contains data that applies to the user who's currently logged on (which with Windows Home Server is almost always the Administrator account). It contains user-specific settings for Control Panel options, network connections, applications, and more.

Here's a summary of the most important HKEY_CURRENT_USER subkeys:

AppEvents	Contains sound files that play when particular system events occur (such as maximizing of a window).
Control Panel	Contains settings related to certain Control Panel icons.
Keyboard Layout	Contains the keyboard layout as selected via Control Panel's Keyboard icon.
Network	Contains settings related to mapped network drives.
Software	Contains user-specific settings related to installed applications and Windows.

HKEY_LOCAL_MACHINE

HKEY_LOCAL_MACHINE (HKLM) contains non–user-specific configuration data for your system's hardware and applications. This is by far the most important key, and it's where you'll perform most of your Registry edits. You'll use the following subkeys most often:

Software   Contains computer-specific settings related to installed applications. The `Classes` subkey is aliased by `HKEY_CLASSES_ROOT`. The `Microsoft` subkey contains settings related to Windows (as well as any other Microsoft products you have installed on your computer).

System   Contains subkeys and settings related to Windows startup.

HKEY_USERS

HKEY_USERS (HKU) contains settings that are similar to those in `HKEY_CURRENT_USER`. HKEY_USERS is used to store the settings for users with group policies defined, as well as the default settings (in the `.DEFAULT` subkey) that are mapped to a new user's profile.

HKEY_CURRENT_CONFIG

HKEY_CURRENT_CONFIG (HKCC) contains settings for the current hardware profile. If your machine uses only one hardware profile, `HKEY_CURRENT_CONFIG` is an alias for `HKEY_LOCAL_MACHINE\SYSTEM\ControlSet001`. If your machine uses multiple hardware profiles, `HKEY_CURRENT_CONFIG` is an alias for `HKEY_LOCAL_MACHINE\SYSTEM\ControlSet`*nnn*, where *nnn* is the numeric identifier of the current hardware profile. This identifier is given by the *Current* setting in the following key:

`HKLM\SYSTEM\CurrentControlSet\Control\IDConfigDB`

Understanding Hives and Registry Files

The Registry database actually consists of a number of files that contain a subset of the Registry called a *hive*. A hive consists of one or more Registry keys, subkeys, and settings. Each hive is supported by several files that use the extensions listed in Table 18.1.

TABLE 18.1   Extensions Used by Hive-Supporting Files

Extension	File Contains
None	A complete copy of the hive data
log1	A log of the changes made to the hive data
.log, .log2	Files that are created during the Windows Home Server setup but remain unchanged as you work with the system

Table 18.2 shows the supporting files for each hive. (Note that all these files might not appear on your system.)

NOTE

To see all these files, you must display hidden files on your system. In Windows Explorer, select Organize, Folder and Search Options, select the View tab, and then activate the Show Hidden Files, Folder, and Drives option. While you're here, you can also deactivate the Hide Extensions for Known File Types check box. Click OK.

18

TABLE 18.2   Supporting Files Used by Each Hive

Hive	Files
HKLM\BCD00000000	%SystemRoot%\System32\config\BCD-Template
HKLM\COMPONENTS	%SystemRoot%\System32\config\COMPONENTS
	%SystemRoot%\System32\config\COMPONENTS.LOG
	%SystemRoot%\System32\config\COMPONENTS.LOG1
	%SystemRoot%\System32\config\COMPONENTS.LOG2
HKLM\SAM	%SystemRoot%\System32\config\SAM
	%SystemRoot%\System32\config\SAM.LOG
	%SystemRoot%\System32\config\SAM.LOG1
	%SystemRoot%\System32\config\SAM.LOG2
HKLM\SECURITY	%SystemRoot%\System32\config\SECURITY
	%SystemRoot%\System32\config\SECURITY.LOG
	%SystemRoot%\System32\config\SECURITY.LOG1
	%SystemRoot%\System32\config\SECURITY.LOG2
HKLM\SOFTWARE	%SystemRoot%\System32\config\SOFTWARE
	%SystemRoot%\System32\config\SOFTWARE.LOG
	%SystemRoot%\System32\config\SOFTWARE.LOG1
	%SystemRoot%\System32\config\SOFTWARE.LOG2
HKLM\SYSTEM	%SystemRoot%\System32\config\SYSTEM
	%SystemRoot%\System32\config\SYSTEM.LOG
	%SystemRoot%\System32\config\SYSTEM.LOG1
	%SystemRoot%\System32\config\SYSTEM.LOG2
HKU\.DEFAULT	%SystemRoot%\System32\config\DEFAULT
	%SystemRoot%\System32\config\DEFAULT.LOG
	%SystemRoot%\System32\config\DEFAULT.LOG1
	%SystemRoot%\System32\config\DEFAULT.LOG2

Also, the Administrator account has its own hive, which maps to HKEY_CURRENT_USER during logon. The supporting files for each user hive are stored in C:\Users\ Administrator. The NTUSER.DAT file contains the hive data, and the NTUSER.DAT.LOG1 file tracks the hive changes.

NOTE

To see the Administrator's hive files, you must display the protected operating system (OS) files on your system. In Windows Explorer, select Organize, Folder and Search Options, select the View tab, deactivate the Hide Protected Operating System Files check box, click Yes when Windows Home Server asks you to confirm, and then click OK.

Keeping the Registry Safe

The sheer wealth of data stored in one place makes the Registry convenient, but it also makes it precious. If your Registry went missing somehow, or if it became corrupted, Windows Home Server simply would not work. With that scary thought in mind, let's take a moment to run through several protective measures. The techniques in this section should ensure that Windows Home Server never goes down for the count because you made a mistake while editing the Registry.

Backing Up the Registry

In Chapter 5, "Setting Up and Using Home Server Storage," you learned how to add a hard drive to your system to use as a backup device for the server itself, and I took you through the process of configuring the server backup. In particular, you learned how to select the items you wanted to include in the backup. For our purposes here, the list of items includes an Operating System item, which (among many other things) includes the Registry hive files. So as long as you're running server backup regularly and the Operating System item is included in the backup, your Windows Home Server Registry is safe.

To make sure your server's Registry files are included in the server backups, follow these steps:

1. Launch the Windows Home Server Dashboard.
2. Click Computers and Backup.
3. In the list of computers, click your server.
4. Click Customize Backup for the Server. The Dashboard runs the Customize Server Backup Wizard.
5. Click Next.
6. Click Change Server Backup Settings.
7. (Optional) Change the backup destination, and then click Next.
8. (Optional) Change the backup label, and then click Next.
9. (Optional) Change the backup schedule, and then click Next.
10. In the Select Which Items to Back Up dialog box, activate the Operating System check box, as shown in Figure 18.4.
11. Click Next.
12. Click Apply Settings.

Protecting Keys by Exporting Them to Disk

If you're just making a small change to the Registry, backing up all its files might seem like overkill. Another approach is to back up only the part of the Registry that you're working on. For example, if you're about to make changes within the HKEY_CURRENT_USER key, you could back up just that key, or even a subkey within HKCU. You do that by exporting the key's data to a registration file, which is a text file that uses the .reg extension. That way, if the change causes a problem, you can import the .reg file back into the Registry to restore things the way they were.

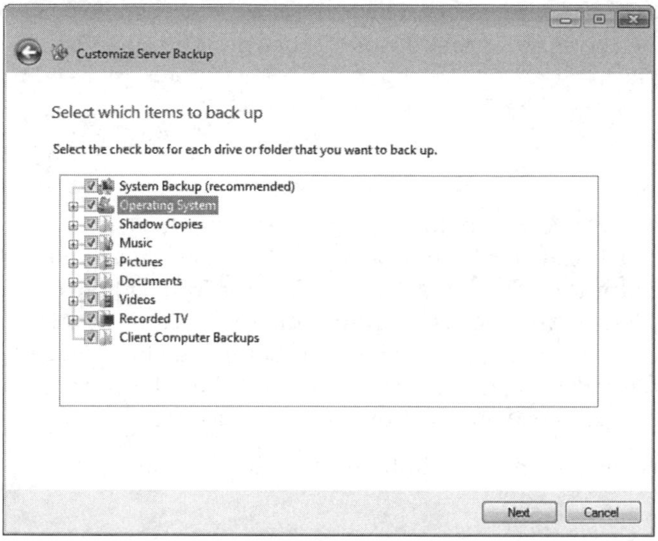

FIGURE 18.4   Select the Operating System check box to back up the Windows Home Server Registry files.

Exporting the Entire Registry to a .reg File

The easiest way to protect the entire Registry is to export the whole thing to a .reg file on a separate hard drive or network share. Note that the resulting file will be about 50MB, and possibly larger, so make sure the target destination has enough free space. Here are the steps to follow:

1. Open the Registry Editor.
2. Select File, Export to display the Export Registry File dialog box.
3. Select a location for the file.
4. Use the File Name text box to type a name for the file.
5. Activate the All option.
6. Click Save.

Exporting a Key to a .reg File

Here are the steps to follow to export a key to a registration file:

1. Open the Registry Editor, and select the key you want to export.
2. Select File, Export (or right-click the key and then click Export) to display the Export Registry File dialog box.

3. Select a location for the file.

4. Use the File Name text box to type a name for the file.

5. Activate the Selected Branch option.

6. Click Save.

TIP

You can save time by creating a batch file that uses the REG utility to export one or more keys to a .reg file. Here's the general syntax to use:

```
reg export rootkey\subkey destination [/y]
```

Here, you replace *rootkey* with one of the following root key values: HKCR, HKCU, HKLM, HKU, or HKCC; you replace *subkey* with the path to the key you want to export; and you replace *destination* with the full pathname of the file to which the key should be exported. (Add the /y switch to force Windows Home Server to overwrite the destination file, if one exists.) Here are some examples:

```
reg export HKCU \\paulspc\backups\whs_hkcu.reg

reg export HKLM\Software\Microsoft\Windows

➥\\paulspc\backups\whs_hklm.reg
```

Finding Registry Changes

One common Registry scenario is to make a change to Windows Home Server using a tool such as the Group Policy editor and then try to find which Registry setting (if any) was affected by the change. However, because of the sheer size of the Registry, this is usually a needle-in-a-haystack exercise that ends in frustration. One way around this is to export some of or all of the Registry before making the change and then export the same key or keys after making the change. You can then use the file compare (FC) utility at the command prompt to find out where the two files differ. Here's the FC syntax to use for this:

```
FC /U pre_edit.reg post-edit.reg > reg_changes.txt
```

Change *pre_edit.reg* to the name of the registration file you exported before editing the Registry; change *post_edit.reg* to the name of the registration file you exported after editing the Registry; and change *reg_changes.txt* to the name of a text file to which the FC output is redirected. Note that the /U switch is required because registration files use the Unicode character set.

Importing a .reg File

If you need to restore the key that you backed up to a registration file, follow these steps:

1. Open the Registry Editor.

2. Select File, Import to display the Import Registry File dialog box.

3. Find and select the file you want to import.

4. Click Open.

5. When Windows Home Server tells you the information has been entered into the Registry, click OK.

TIP

You also can import a `.reg` file by locating it in Windows Explorer and then double-clicking the file. Yet another way to import a `.reg` file is by using the `REG` utility:

```
reg import file
```

Here, you replace *file* with the full pathname of the `.reg` file that you want to import. Here's an example:

```
reg import \\paulspc\backups\whs_hklm.reg
```

CAUTION

Many applications ship with their own `.reg` files for updating the Registry. Unless you're sure that you want to import these files, avoid double-clicking them. They might end up overwriting existing settings and causing problems with your system.

Working with Registry Entries

Now that you've had a look around, you're ready to start working with the Registry's keys and settings. In this section, I'll give you the general procedures for basic tasks, such as modifying, adding, renaming, deleting, and searching for entries.

Changing the Value of a Registry Entry

Changing the value of a Registry entry is a matter of finding the appropriate key, displaying the setting you want to change, and editing the setting's value. Unfortunately, finding the key you need isn't always a simple matter. Knowing the root keys and their main subkeys, as described earlier, will certainly help, and the Registry Editor has a Find feature that's invaluable. (I'll show you how to use it later; see "Finding Registry Entries.")

To illustrate how this process works, let's look at an example: changing your registered owner name and company name. In other versions of Windows, the installation process often asks you to enter your name and, optionally, your company name. These registered names appear in several places as you work with Windows:

▶ If you select Help, About in most Windows programs, your registered names appear in the About dialog box.

▶ If you install an application, the installation program uses your registered names for its own records (although you usually get a chance to make changes).

Unfortunately, Windows Home Server doesn't ask you for this data. Instead, it uses the generic values `Owner` for the owner name and `Organization` for the organization name.

With these names appearing in so many places, it's good to know that you can change either or both names. The secret lies in the following key:

`HKLM\SOFTWARE\Microsoft\WindowsNT\CurrentVersion`

To get to this key, you open the branches in the Registry Editor's tree pane: `HKEY_LOCAL_MACHINE`, and then `SOFTWARE`, and then `Microsoft`, and then `Windows NT`. Finally, click the `CurrentVersion` subkey to select it. Here you see a number of settings, but two are of interest to us (see Figure 18.5).

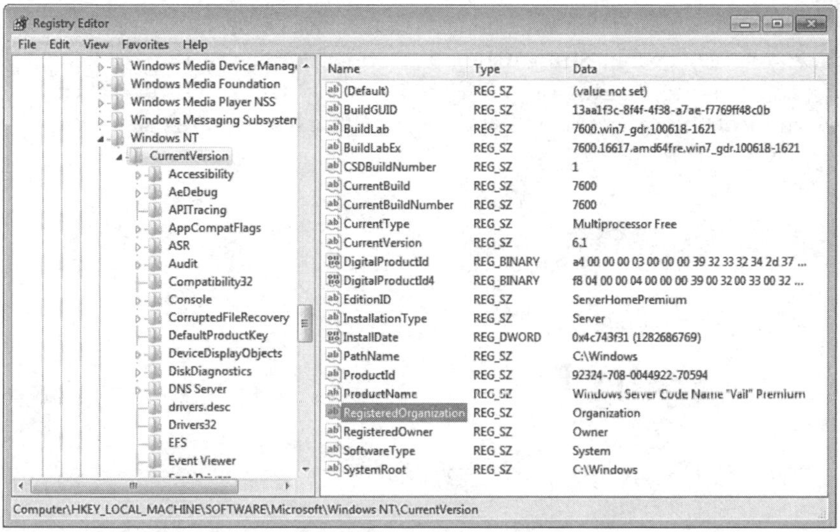

FIGURE 18.5   Navigate to `HKLM\SOFTWARE\Microsoft\Windows NT\CurrentVersion` to see your registered names.

TIP

If you have keys that you visit often, you can save them as favorites to avoid trudging through endless branches in the Keys pane. To do this, navigate to the key and then select Favorites, Add to Favorites. In the Add to Favorites dialog box, edit the Favorite Name text box, if desired, and then click OK. To navigate to a favorite key, pull down the Favorites menu and select the key name from the list that appears at the bottom of the menu.

RegisteredOrganization	This setting contains your registered company name.
RegisteredOwner	This setting contains your registered name.

18

Now you open the setting for editing by using any of the following techniques:

▶ Select the setting name and either select Edit, Modify or press Enter.

▶ Double-click the setting name.

▶ Right-click the setting name, and click Modify from the context menu.

The dialog box that appears depends on the value type you're dealing with, as discussed in the next few sections. Note that edited settings are written to the Registry right away, but the changes might not go into effect immediately. In many cases, you need to exit the Registry Editor and then either log off or restart Windows Home Server.

Editing a String Value

If the setting is a REG_SZ value (as it is in our example), a REG_MULTI_SZ value, or a REG_EXPAND_SZ value, you see the Edit String dialog box, shown in Figure 18.6. Use the Value Data text box to enter a new string or modify the existing string, and then click OK. (For a REG_MULTI_SZ multistring value, Value Data is a multiline text box.) Type each string value on its own line.

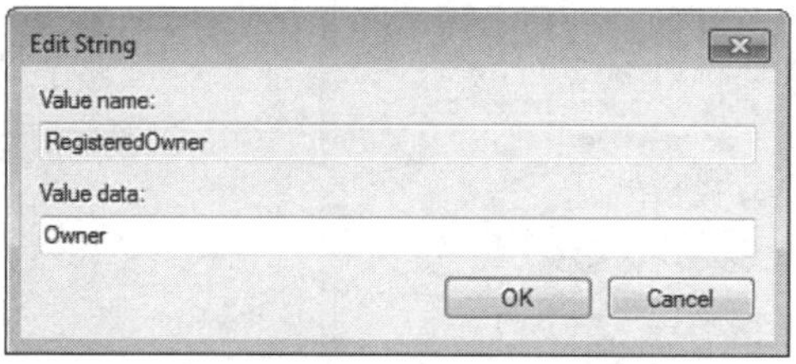

FIGURE 18.6   You see the Edit String dialog box if you're modifying a string value.

Editing a DWORD or QWORD Value

If the setting is a REG_DWORD, you see the Edit DWORD (32-Bit) Value dialog box shown in Figure 18.7. In the Base group, select either Hexadecimal or Decimal, and then use the Value Data text box to enter the new value of the setting. (If you chose the Hexadecimal option, enter a hexadecimal value; if you chose Decimal, enter a decimal value.) Note that editing a QWORD value is identical, except that the dialog box is named Edit QWORD (64-Bit) Value, instead.

Editing a Binary Value

If the setting is a REG_BINARY value, you see an Edit Binary Value dialog box like the one shown in Figure 18.8.

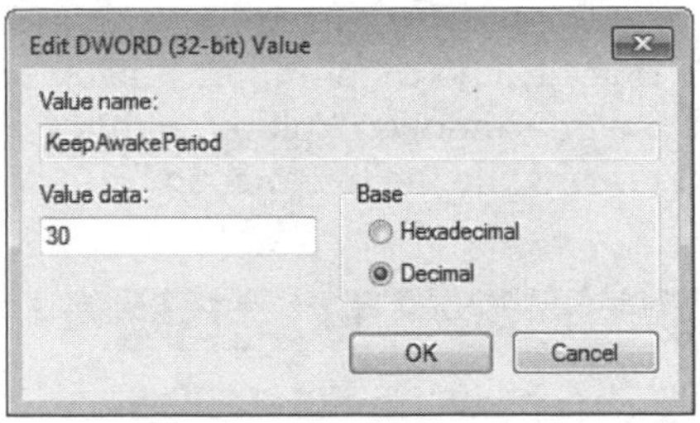

FIGURE 18.7   You see the Edit DWORD Value dialog box if you're modifying a double word value.

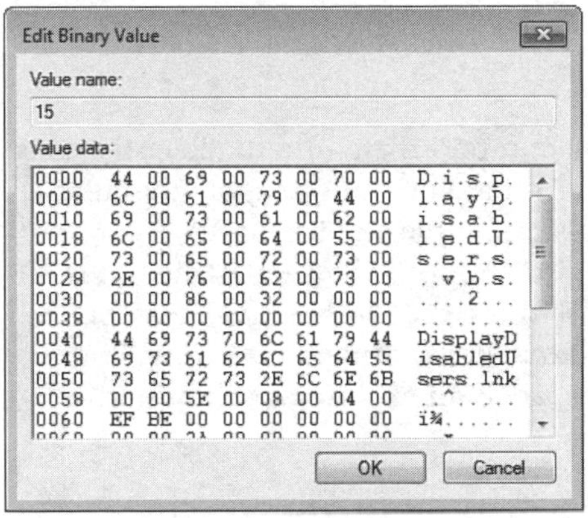

FIGURE 18.8   You see the Edit Binary Value dialog box if you're modifying a binary value.

For binary values, the Value Data box is divided into three vertical sections:

Starting Byte Number	The four-digit values on the left of the Value Data box tell you the sequence number of the first byte in each row of hexadecimal numbers. This sequence always begins at 0, so the sequence number of the first byte in the first row is 0000. There are eight bytes in each row, so the sequence number of the first byte in the second row is 0008, and so on. You can't edit these values.
Hexadecimal Numbers (Bytes)	The eight columns of two-digit numbers in the middle section display the setting's value, expressed in hexadecimal numbers, where each two-digit number represents a single byte of information. You can edit these values.
ANSI Equivalents	The third section on the right side of the Value Data box shows the American National Standards Institute (ANSI) equivalents of the hexadecimal numbers in the middle section. For example, the first byte of the first row is the hexadecimal value 44, which represents the upper-case letter D. You can also edit the values in this column.

18

Editing a .reg File

If you exported a key to a registration file, you can edit that file and then import it back into the Registry. To change a registration file, find the file in Windows Explorer, right-click the file, and then click Edit. Windows Home Server opens the file in Notepad.

> **TIP**
>
> If you need to make global changes to the Registry, export the entire Registry and then load the resulting registration file into WordPad or some other word processor or text editor. Use the application's Replace feature (carefully!) to make changes throughout the file. If you use a word processor for this, be sure to save the file as a text file when you're done. You can then import the changed file back into the Registry.

Creating a .reg File

You can create registration files from scratch and then import them into the Registry. This is a handy technique if you have some customizations that you want to apply to multiple systems. To demonstrate the basic structure of a registration file and its entries, Figure 18.9 shows two windows. The bottom window is the Registry Editor with a key named Test highlighted. The settings pane contains six sample settings: the (Default) value and one each of the five types of settings (binary, DWORD, expandable string, multistring, and string). The top window shows the Test key in Notepad as an exported registration file (Test.reg).

> **NOTE**
>
> The file that contains the test Registry code (test.reg) is available on my website at www.mcfedries.com/HomeServerUnleashed3E.

Windows Home Server registration files always start with the following header:

```
Windows Registry Editor Version 5.00
```

> **TIP**
>
> If you're building a registration file for a Windows 9x, Me, or NT 4 system, change the header to the following:
>
> ```
> REGEDIT4
> ```

Next is an empty line followed by the full path of the Registry key that will hold the settings you're adding, surrounded by square brackets:

```
[HKEY_CURRENT_USER\Test]
```

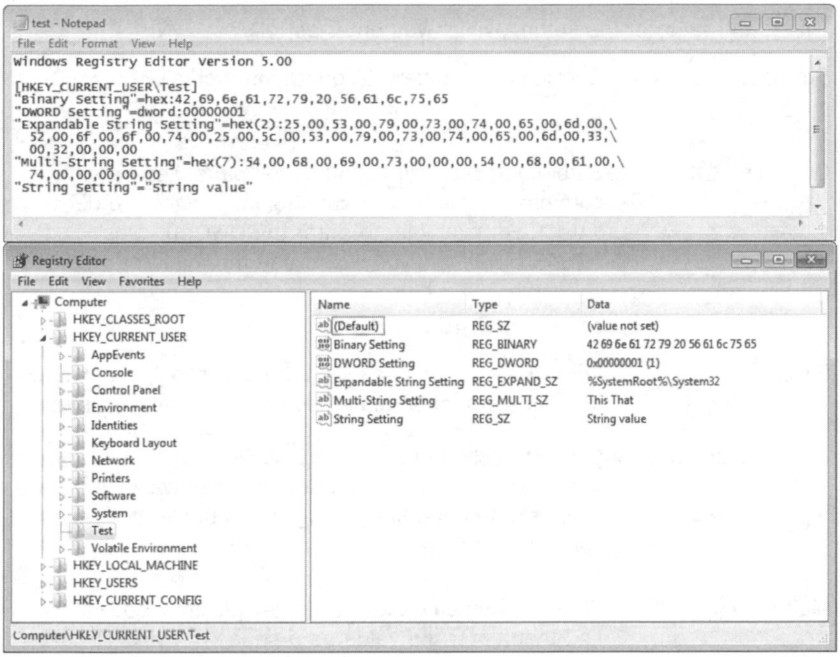

FIGURE 18.9   The settings in the `Test` key shown in the Registry Editor correspond to the data shown in the `Test.reg` file in Notepad.

Below the key are the setting names and values, which use the following general form:

TIP

If you want to add a comment to a .reg file, start a new line and begin the line with a semicolon (;).

`"SettingName"=identifier:SettingValue`

SettingName	The name of the setting. Note that you use the @ symbol to represent the key's `Default` value.
identifier	A code that identifies the type of data. REG_SZ values don't use an identifier, but the other five types do:

dword	Use this identifier for a DWORD value.
hex(b)	Use this identifier for a QWORD value.
hex	Use this identifier for a binary value.
hex(2)	Use this identifier for an expandable string value.
hex(7)	Use this identifier for a multistring value.

18

SettingValue   This is the value of the setting, which you enter as follows:

String	Surround the value with quotation marks.
DWORD	Enter an eight-digit DWORD value.
QWORD	Enter eight two-digit hexadecimal pairs, separated by commas, with the pairs running from highest order to lowest. For example, to enter the QWORD value 123456789abcd, you would use the following value: cd,ab,89,67,45,23,01,00
Binary	Enter the binary value as a series of two-digit hexadecimal numbers, separating each number with a comma.
Expandable string	Convert each character to its hexadecimal equivalent, and then enter the value as a series of two-digit hexadecimal numbers, separating each number with a comma, and separating each character with 00.
Multistring	Convert each character to its hexadecimal equivalent, and then enter the value as a series of two-digit hexadecimal numbers, separating each number with a comma, and separating each character with 00, and separating each string with space (00 hex).

TIP

To delete a setting using a `.reg` file, set its value to a hyphen (-), as in this example:

```
Windows Registry Editor Version 5.00


[HKEY_CURRENT_USER\Test]
"BinarySetting"=-
```

To delete a key, add a hyphen to the start of the key name, as in this example:

```
Windows Registry Editor Version 5.00


[-HKEY_CURRENT_USER\Test]
```

Renaming a Key or Setting

You won't often need to rename existing keys or settings. Just in case, though, here are the steps to follow:

   1. In the Registry Editor, find the key or setting you want to work with, and then highlight it.

2. Select Edit, Rename, or press F2.

3. Edit the name, and then press Enter.

CAUTION

Rename only those keys or settings that you created yourself. If you rename any other key or setting, Windows Home Server might not work properly.

Creating a New Key or Setting

Many Registry-based customizations don't involve editing an existing setting or key. Instead, you have to create a new setting or key. Here's how you do it:

1. In the Registry Editor, select the key in which you want to create the new subkey or setting.

2. Select Edit, New. (Alternatively, right-click an empty section of the Settings pane and then click New.) A submenu appears.

3. If you're creating a new key, select the Key command. Otherwise, select the command that corresponds to the type of setting you want: String Value, Binary Value, DWORD (32-bit) Value, QWORD (64-bit) Value, Multi-String Value, or Expandable String Value.

4. Type a name for the new key or setting.

5. Press Enter.

Deleting a Key or Setting

Here are the steps to follow to delete a key or setting:

1. In the Registry Editor, select the key or setting that you want to delete.

2. Select Edit, Delete, or press Delete. The Registry Editor asks whether you're sure.

3. Click Yes.

CAUTION

Again, to avoid problems, you should delete only those keys or settings that you created. If you're not sure about deleting a setting, try renaming it instead. If a problem arises, you can return the setting to its original name.

Finding Registry Entries

The Registry contains only five root keys, but they contain hundreds of subkeys. The fact that some root keys are aliases for subkeys in a different branch only adds to the confusion. If you know exactly where you're going, the Registry Editor's treelike hierarchy is a reasonable way to get there. If you're not sure where a particular subkey or setting resides, however, you could spend all day poking around in the Registry's labyrinthine nooks and crannies.

To help you get where you want to go, the Registry Editor has a Find feature that enables you to search for keys, settings, or values. Here's how it works:

1. In the Keys pane, select Computer at the top of the pane (unless you're certain of which root key contains the value you want to find; in this case, you can highlight the appropriate root key instead).

2. Select Edit, Find or press Ctrl+F. The Registry Editor displays the Find dialog box, shown in Figure 18.10.

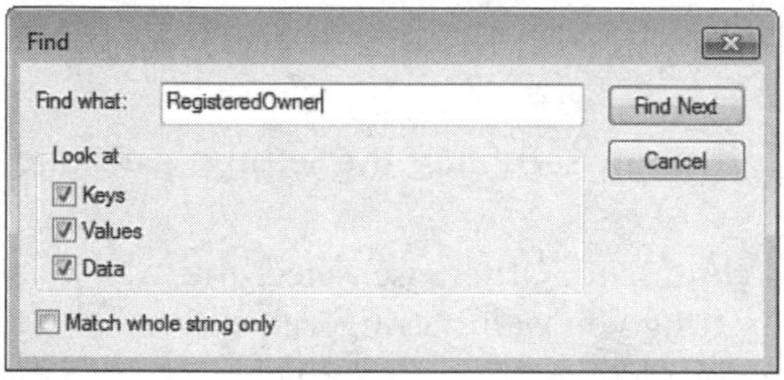

FIGURE 18.10   Use the Find dialog box to search for Registry keys, settings, or values.

3. Use the Find What text box to enter your search string. You can enter partial words or phrases to increase your chances of finding a match.

4. In the Look At group, activate the check boxes for the elements you want to search. For most searches, you want to leave all three check boxes activated.

5. If you want to find only those entries that exactly match your search text, activate the Match Whole String Only check box.

6. Click the Find Next button. The Registry Editor highlights the first match.

7. If this isn't the item you want, select Edit, Find Next (or press F3) until you find the setting or key you want.

When the Registry Editor finds a match, it displays the appropriate key or setting. Note that if the matched value is a setting name or data value, Find doesn't highlight the current key. This is a bit confusing, but remember that the current key always appears at the bottom of the Keys pane.

From Here

▶ To learn how to modify a Registry setting to customize Windows Home Server's minimum password length requirement, **SEE** "Customizing the Password Length Requirement," **P. 33.**

▶ To learn how to use the Registry's Run and RunOnce keys to launch a program at startup, **SEE** "Launching Applications and Scripts at Startup," **P. 94.**

▶ For details on using the Registry to customize the folder shortcut menu, **SEE** "Opening a Folder in a Command Prompt Session," **P. 481.**

▶ To learn how to read, add, and modify Registry entries programmatically, **SEE** "Working with Registry Entries," **P. 611.**

18

CHAPTER 19

Using Windows Home Server's Command-Line Tools

IN THIS CHAPTER

▶ Getting to the Command Line

▶ Working at the Command Line

▶ Understanding Batch File Basics

▶ Working with the Command-Line Tools

All versions of Windows have at their core a basic premise: It's easier, faster, and more intuitive to work and play using a graphical user interface (GUI) than using an old-fashioned command-line interface, such as the kind we saw way back in the days when MS-DOS and its variants ruled the PC world. Few, if any, people today would dispute that premise; the last of the Windows versus MS-DOS battles was fought a long time ago.

However, that doesn't mean that a GUI is the *only* way to operate a PC. All versions of Windows still come with a command prompt utility that gives you access to the command line. That's not surprising, but what *is* surprising is that the command line is a source of tremendous power and flexibility. After you have that blinking cursor in front of you, a huge and potent arsenal of commands, tools, and utilities becomes available. With these features at your disposal, you can perform amazing tricks in the areas of disk and file management, performance monitoring, network administration, system maintenance, and much more. This chapter introduces you to the Windows Home Server command line and takes you through quite a few of the available command-line tools.

Getting to the Command Line

To take advantage of the command line and all its many useful commands, you need to start a command-line session. Windows Home Server offers a number of ways to get to the command prompt:

▶ Select Start, Command Prompt.

▶ Press Windows Logo+R (or select Start, Run), type **cmd** in the Run dialog box, and click OK. (You can also click Start, type **cmd,** and then press Enter.)

▶ Create a shortcut for %SystemRoot%\system32\cmd.exe on your desktop (or some other convenient location, such as the taskbar), and then launch the shortcut.

▶ Reboot your computer, press F8 to display Windows Home Server's Advanced Boot Options menu, and select the Safe Mode with Command Prompt item.

> **NOTE**
>
> It's also possible to configure Windows Home Server's Folder file type to open the command prompt in Windows Explorer's current folder. To see how, refer to the "Opening a Folder in a Command Prompt Session" section, later in this chapter.

Running CMD

For the methods that use the CMD executable, you can specify extra switches after the cmd.exe filename. Most of these switches aren't particularly useful, so let's start with the simplest syntax that you'll use most often:

CMD [[/S] [/C ¦ /K] command]

/S   Strips out the first and last quotation marks from the command, provided that the first quotation mark is the first character in command.

/C   Executes the command and then terminates.

/K   Executes the command and remains running.

command   Specifies the command to run.

For example, if your Internet service provider (ISP) provides you with a dynamic Internet Protocol (IP) address, you can often solve some connection problems by asking the IP for a fresh address. You do that by running the command ipconfig /renew at the command line. In this case, you don't need the Command Prompt window to remain open, so you can specify the /C switch to shut down the command-line session automatically when the IPCONFIG utility finishes:

cmd /c ipconfig /renew

On the other hand, you often either want to see the results of the command, or want to leave the Command Prompt window open so that you can run other commands. In those cases, use the /K switch. For example, the following command runs the SET utility (which displays the current values of the Windows Home Server environment variables) and then leaves the command-line session running:

cmd /k set

Here's the full syntax of cmd.exe:

```
CMD [/A ¦ /U] [/Q] [/D] [/T:bf] [/E:ON ¦ /E:OFF] [/F:ON ¦ /F:OFF]
➥[/V:ON ¦ /V:OFF] [[/S] [/C ¦ /K] command]
```

/Q   Turns off command echoing. If command is a batch file, you won't see any of the batch file commands as they're executed. This is the same as adding the statement @ECHO OFF at the beginning of a batch file.

/D   Disables the execution of AutoRun commands from the Registry. These are commands that run automatically when you start any command-line session. You can find the settings here:

```
HKLM\Software\Microsoft\Command Processor\AutoRun
HKCU\Software\Microsoft\Command Processor\AutoRun
```

> **NOTE**
>
> If you do not see an AutoRun setting in one or both keys, select the key; select File, New, String Value; type AutoRun; and press Enter.

> **TIP**
>
> The AutoRun Registry settings are handy if you always run a particular command at the beginning of each command-line session. If you run multiple commands to launch a session, you can add those commands to either AutoRun setting. In that case, you must separate each command with the command separator string: &&. For example, to run the IPCONFIG and SET utilities at the start of each command-line session, change the value of an AutoRun setting to the following:
>
>   ipconfig&&set

/A   Converts the output of internal commands to a pipe or file to the American National Standards Institute (ANSI) character set.

/U   Converts the output of internal commands to a pipe or file to the Unicode character set.

/T:bf   Sets the foreground and background colors of the Command Prompt window, where f is the foreground color and b is the background color. Both f and b are hexadecimal digits that specify the color as follows:

0	Black	8	Gray
1	Blue	9	Light Blue
2	Green	A	Light Green
3	Aqua	B	Light Aqua
4	Red	C	Light Red

19

5	Purple	D	Light Purple
6	Yellow	E	Light Yellow
7	White	F	Bright White

TIP

You can also set the foreground and background colors during a command-line session by using the COLOR *bf command,* where *b* and *f* are hexadecimal digits specifying the colors you want. To revert to the default command prompt colors, run *COLOR* without the bf parameter.

/E:ON   Enables *command extensions*, which are extra features added to the following commands. (At the command line, type the command name followed by a space and /? to see the extensions.)

ASSOC	IF
CALL	MD or MKDIR
CD or CHDIR	POPD
COLOR	PROMPT
DEL or ERASE	PUSHD
ENDLOCAL	SET
FOR	SETLOCAL
FTYPE	SHIFT
GOTO	START

/E:OFF   Disables command extensions.

/F:ON   Turns on file and directory name completion, which enables you to press special key combinations to scroll through a list of files or subdirectories in the current directory that match the characters you've already typed. For example, suppose that the current directory contains files named budget2009.doc, budget2010.doc, and budget2011.doc. If you type start budget in a command-line session started with /F:ON, pressing Ctrl+F tells Windows Home Server to display the first file (or subfolder) in the current folder with a name that starts with budget. Pressing Ctrl+F again displays the next file with a name that starts with budget, and so on. You can do the same thing with just subfolder names by pressing Ctrl+D instead.

> **TIP**
>
> You don't need to start the command prompt with the /F:ON switch to use file and directory name completion. The command prompt offers a similar feature called *AutoComplete* that's turned on by default. At the prompt, type the first letter or two of a file or subfolder name, and then press the Tab key to see the first object that matches your text in the current folder. Keep pressing Tab to see other matching objects. If, for some reason, you prefer to turn off AutoComplete, pull down the Command Prompt window's control menu (right-click the title bar), select Defaults, and then deactivate the AutoComplete check box in the Options tab.

/F:OFF   Turns off file and directory name completion.

/V:ON   Enables delayed environment variable expansion using ! as the delimiter: !*var*!, where *var* is an environment variable. This is useful for batch files in which you want to delay the expansion of an environment variable. Normally, Windows Home Server expands all environment variables to their current values when it reads the contents of a batch file. With delayed expansion enabled, Windows Home Server doesn't expand a particular environment variable within a batch file until it executes the statement containing that variable.

/V:OFF   Disables delayed environment expansion.

/S   Strips out the first and last quotation marks from *command*, provided the first quotation mark is the first character in *command*.

/C   Executes the *command* and then terminates.

/K   Executes the *command* and remains running.

command   Specifies the command to run.

Opening a Folder in a Command Prompt Session

When you're working in Windows Explorer, you might find that you need to do some work at the command prompt. For example, the current folder might contain multiple files that need to be renamed—a task that's most easily done within a command-line session. Selecting Start, Command Prompt starts the session in the %USERPROFILE% folder, so you have to use one or more CD commands to get to the folder you want to work in.

An easier way is to create a new action for the Folder file type that launches the command prompt and automatically displays the current Windows Explorer folder. To do this, follow these steps:

1. Select Start, Run (or press Windows Logo+R), type **regedit**, and then click OK to open the Registry Editor.
2. Navigate to the following key:

   HKCR\Folder\shell

3. Select Edit, New, Key. Type **Open with Command Prompt**, and press Enter.

4. Make sure that the key you created in step 3 is selected, and then select Edit, New, Key. Type **command**, and press Enter.

5. With the new command key selected, double-click the `Default` value to open the Edit String dialog box.

6. Type the following:

   ```
   cmd.exe /k cd "%L"
   ```

NOTE

In the command string, cd represents the command prompt's internal CD (change directory) command, which changes the prompt to another folder. The %L placeholder represents the full pathname of the current folder.

---

7. Click OK.

Figure 19.1 displays two windows. The top window is the Registry Editor showing the new `Open with Command Prompt` action added to the `HKCR\Folder\shell` key; in the bottom window, I right-clicked a folder. Notice how the new action appears in the shortcut menu.

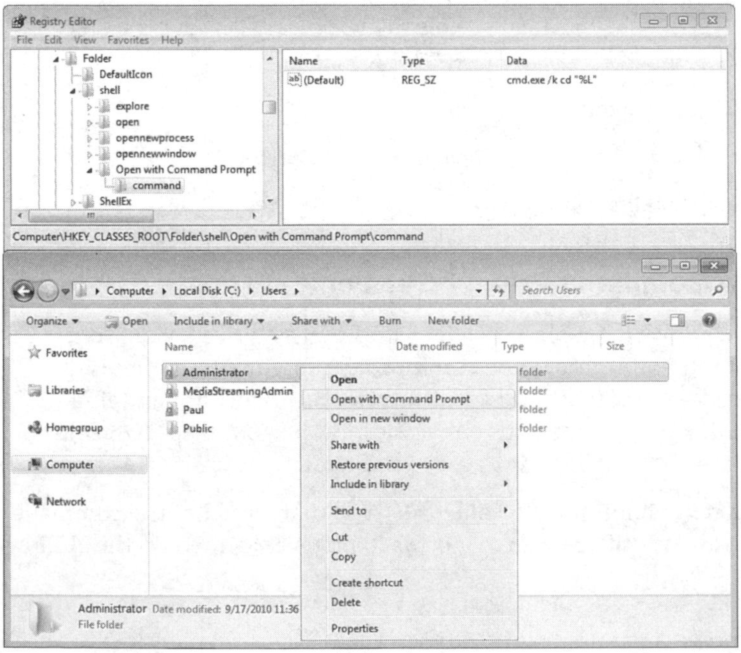

FIGURE 19.1   After you add the new action to the `HKCR\Folder\shell` key, the action appears in the folder file type's shortcut menu.

Working at the Command Line

When you have your command-line session up and running, you can run commands and programs, create and launch batch files, perform file maintenance, and so on. If you haven't used the command prompt since the days of DOS, you'll find that the Windows Home Server command prompt offers a few extra command-line goodies. The next few sections highlight some of the more useful ones.

> **CAUTION**
>
> When you're working in the command prompt, be warned that any files you delete aren't sent to the Recycle Bin but are purged from your system.

Running Commands

Although many of the Windows Home Server accessories provide more powerful and easier-to-use replacements for nearly all commands, a few commands still have no Windows Home Server peer. These include the REN command, as well as the many Command Prompt-specific commands, such as CLS, DOSKEY, and PROMPT.

> **NOTE**
>
> Command-line commands that exist as separate executable files—such as CHKDSK, DEFRAG, and XCOPY—are called *external commands*; all other command-line commands—such as DIR, CD, and CLS—are part of the CMD shell and are known as *internal commands*.

The way you run a command depends on whether it's an internal or external command and on what you want Windows Home Server to do after the command is finished. For an internal command, you have two choices: You can either enter the command in the command prompt, or you can include it as a parameter with CMD. As you saw earlier, you can run internal commands with CMD by specifying either the /C switch or the /K switch. If you use the /C switch, the command executes, and then the command-line session shuts down. This is fine if you're running a command for which you don't need to see the results. For example, if you want to redirect the contents of drive C:'s root folder in the text file root.txt, entering the following command in the Run dialog box (for example) will do the job:

```
cmd.exe /c dir c:\ > root.txt
```

On the other hand, you might want to examine the output of a command before the Command Prompt window closes. In that case, you need to use the /K switch. The following command runs DIR on drive C:'s root folder and then drops you off in the command prompt:

```
cmd.exe /k dir c:\
```

For an external command, you have three choices: Enter the command in the command prompt, enter the command by itself from within Windows Home Server, or include it as a parameter with `CMD`.

Entering a command by itself from within Windows Home Server means launching the command's file in Explorer, entering the command in the Start menu or Run dialog box, or creating a shortcut for the command. For the latter two methods, you can embellish the command by adding parameters and switches. The problem with this method is that Windows Home Server automatically closes the Command Prompt window when the command completes. To change this behavior, follow these steps:

> **NOTE**
>
> When you use the command prompt or the Run dialog box to start an external command prompt command, you don't need to use the command's full pathname. For example, the full pathname for `mem.exe` is `%SystemRoot%\System32\mem.exe`, but to run this command, you need to enter only `mem`. The reason is that the `%SystemRoot%\System32` subfolder is part of the `PATH` statement for each command-line session.

1. Find the command's executable file in the `%SystemRoot%\System32` folder.
2. Right-click the executable file, and then click Properties to display the command's properties sheet.
3. Display the Program tab. (Note that this tab doesn't appear for all commands.)
4. Deactivate the Close on Exit check box.
5. Click OK.

Working with Long Filenames

If you want to use long filenames in a command, you need to be careful. If the long filename contains a space or any other character that's illegal in an 8.3 filename, you need to surround the long name with quotation marks. For example, if you run the following command

```
copy Fiscal Year 2011.doc Fiscal Year 2012.doc
```

Windows Home Server tells you this:

```
The syntax of the command is incorrect:
```

Instead, you need to enter this command as follows:

```
copy "Fiscal Year 2011.doc" "Fiscal Year 2012.doc"
```

Long filenames are, of course, long, so they tend to be a pain to type in the command prompt. Fortunately, Windows Home Server offers a few methods for knocking long names down to size:

▶ In Explorer, drag a folder or file and drop it inside the Command Prompt window. Windows Home Server pastes the full pathname of the folder or file to the end of the prompt.

▶ In Windows Explorer, navigate to the folder you want to work with, and then select and copy the folder path in the address bar. Return to the Command Prompt window, type the command up to the point where you want the path to appear, right-click the title bar, and then select Edit, Paste.

▶ If you're trying to run a program that resides in a folder with a long name, add the folder to the PATH. This technique enables you to run programs from the folder without having to specify the full pathname.

TIP

To edit the PATH environment variable, you have two choices. At the command line, enter the following command (where *folder* is the path of the folder you want to add to the PATH variable):

```
path %path%;folder
```

Alternatively, select Start, Control Panel, System (or select Start, right-click Computer, and then click Properties), and then click Advanced System Settings to open the System Properties dialog box. In the Advanced tab, click Environment Variables. In the System Variables list, click Path, click Edit, and then append the folder to the end of the Variable Value string. Be sure to separate each folder path with a semicolon (;).

Use the SUBST command to substitute a virtual drive letter for a long pathname. For example, the following command substitutes drive S: for the Start menu's System Tools folder:

```
subst s: "%AllUsersProfile%\Microsoft\Windows\Start Menu\Programs\
➥ Accessories\System Tools"
```

Changing Folders Faster

I mentioned earlier that you use the CD command to change to a different folder on the current drive. However, the command prompt has a few short forms you can use to save time.

You might know that both the command prompt and Windows Home Server use the dot symbol (.) to represent the current folder, and the double-dot symbol (..) to represent its parent folder. You can combine the CD command and the dot notation to jump immediately to a folder's parent folder, or even higher.

To make this more concrete, suppose that the current folder is C:\Animal\Mammal\Dolphin. Table 19.1 demonstrates the techniques you can use to navigate to this folder's parent, grandparent (two levels up), and great-grandparent (three levels up) folders.

TABLE 19.1 Combining the CD Command with Dot Notation

Current Folder	Command	New Folder
C:\Animal\Mammal\Dolphin	Cd..	C:\Animal\Mammal
C:\Animal\Mammal\Dolphin	Cd..\..	C:\Animal
C:\Animal\Mammal\Dolphin	Cd..\..\..	C:\
C:\Animal\Mammal\Dolphin	Cd..\Baboon	C:\Animal\Mammal\Baboon

TIP

If you want to return to the root folder of any drive, type cd\ and press Enter.

Taking Advantage of DOSKEY

Windows Home Server loads the DOSKEY utility by default when you start any command-line session. This useful little program brings a number of advantages to your command-line work:

▶ You can recall previously entered commands with just a keystroke or two.

▶ You can enter multiple commands on a single line.

▶ You can edit commands instead of retyping them.

The next few sections take you through the specifics.

Recalling Command Lines

The simplest DOSKEY feature is command recall. DOSKEY maintains a *command history buffer* that keeps a list of the commands you enter. To scroll through your previously entered commands in reverse order, press the up-arrow key; when you've done that at least once, you can change direction and run through the commands in the order you entered them by pressing the down-arrow key. To rerun a command, use the arrow keys to find it, and then press Enter.

TIP

If you don't want to enter commands from the history buffer, press Esc to get a clean command line.

Table 19.2 lists all the command-recall keys you can use.

TABLE 19.2   DOSKEY Command-Recall Keys

Press	To
Up arrow	Recall the previous command in the buffer.
Down arrow	Recall the next command in the buffer.
Page Up	Recall the oldest command in the buffer.
Page Down	Recall the newest command in the buffer.
F7	Display the entire command buffer.
Alt+F7	Delete all commands from the buffer.
F8	Have DOSKEY recall a command that begins with the letter or letters you've typed on the command line.
F9	Have DOSKEY prompt you for a command list number. (You can see the numbers with the F7 key.) Type the number and press Enter to recall the command.

> **TIP**
>
> The command history buffer holds 50 commands by default. If you need a larger buffer, run DOSKEY with the /LISTSIZE=*buffers* switch, where *buffers* is the number of commands you want to store. You also need to include the /REINSTALL switch to install a new copy of DOSKEY, which puts the new history buffer setting into effect. For example, to change the buffer size to 100, enter the following command:
>
> ```
> doskey /listsize=100 /reinstall
> ```

Entering Multiple Commands on a Single Line

DOSKEY enables you to run multiple commands on a single line. To do this, insert the characters && between commands. For example, a common task is to change to a different drive and then run a directory listing. Normally, you'd do this with two separate commands:

```
e:
dir
```

With DOSKEY, however, you can do it on one line, like so:

```
e:&&dir
```

> **TIP**
>
> You can enter as many commands as you like on a single line, but just remember that the total length of the line can't be more than 8,191 characters, which should be plenty!

19

Editing Command Lines

Rather than simply rerunning a previously typed command, you might need to run the command again with slightly different switches or parameters. Rather than retyping the whole thing, DOSKEY enables you to edit any recalled command line. You use various keys to move the cursor to the offending letters and replace them. Table 19.3 summarizes DOSKEY's command-line editing keys.

TABLE 19.3   DOSKEY Command-Line Editing Keys

Press	To
Left arrow	Move the cursor one character to the left.
Right arrow	Move the cursor one character to the right.
Ctrl+left arrow	Move the cursor one word to the left.
Ctrl+right arrow	Move the cursor one word to the right.
Home	Move the cursor to the beginning of the line.
End	Move the cursor to the end of the line.
Delete	Delete the character over the cursor.
Backspace	Delete the character to the left of the cursor.
Ctrl+Home	Delete from the cursor to the beginning of the line.
Ctrl+End	Delete from the cursor to the end of the line.
Insert	Toggle DOSKEY between Insert mode (your typing is inserted between existing letters on the command line) and Overstrike mode (your typing replaces existing letters on the command line).

Redirecting Command Output and Input

Windows Home Server is always directing things here and there. This generally falls into two categories:

▶ Directing data into its commands from a device called *standard input*

▶ Directing data out of its commands to a device called *standard output*

A device called *CON* (*console*) normally handles standard input and standard output, which is your keyboard and monitor. Windows Home Server assumes that all command input comes from the keyboard and that all command output (such as a DIR listing or a system message) goes to the screen. Redirection is just a way of specifying different input and output devices.

Redirecting Command Output

To send command output to somewhere other than the screen, you use the *output redirection operator* (>). One of the most common uses for output redirection is to capture the results of a command in a text file. For example, you might want to use the report produced by the SYSTEMINFO command as part of a word-processing document. (For the details on this command, see "SYSTEMINFO: Returning System Configuration Data," later in this chapter.) You could use the following command to first capture the report as the file systeminfo.csv:

```
systeminfo /fo csv > c:\systeminfo.csv
```

When you run this command, the usual SYSTEMINFO data doesn't appear onscreen. That's because you directed it away from the screen and into the systeminfo.csv file.

You can use this technique to capture DIR listings, CHKDSK reports, and more. One caveat: If the file you specify as the output destination already exists, Windows Home Server overwrites it without warning. To avoid this, you can use the *double output redirection symbol* (>>). This tells Windows Home Server to append the output to the end of the file if the file exists. For example, suppose you used the following command to output the results of the CHKDSK C: command to chkdsk.txt:

```
chkdsk c: > c:\chkdsk.txt
```

If you then want to append the results of the CHKDSK D: command to chkdsk.txt, you'd enter the following command:

```
chkdsk d: >> c:\chkdsk.txt
```

You can also redirect output to different devices. Table 19.4 lists the various devices that Windows Home Server installs each time you start your system.

TABLE 19.4 Devices Installed by Windows Home Server When You Start Your System

Device Name	Device
AUX	Auxiliary device (usually COM1)
CLOCK$	Real-time clock
COMn	Serial port (COM1, COM2, COM3, or COM4)
CON	Console (keyboard and screen)
LPTn	Parallel port (LPT1, LPT2, or LPT3)
NUL	NUL device (nothing)
PRN	Printer (usually LPT1)

19

For example, you can send a DIR listing to the printer with the following command. (Of course, you need to be sure that your printer is on before doing this. Also note that this only works for a printer attached to a parallel port; it doesn't work for USB printers.)

```
dir > prn
```

The NUL device usually throws people for a loop when they first see it. This device (affectionately known as the *bit bucket*) is, literally, nothing. Batch files normally use it to suppress the usual messages Windows Home Server displays when it completes a command. For example, Windows Home Server normally says 1 file(s) copied when you copy a file. However, the following command sends that message to *NUL*, so you wouldn't see it onscreen:

```
copy somefile.doc \\server\users\paul\ > nul
```

> **TIP**
>
> Unfortunately, Windows Home Server gives you no way to redirect output to a USB port. However, there's a workaround you can use if you're trying to redirect output to a USB printer. Assuming that the printer is shared and that no other device is using the port LPT2, run the following command:
>
> ```
> NET USE LPT2 \\server\printer
> ```
>
> Here, replace *server* with the name of your Windows Home Server computer and *printer* with the share name of the USB printer. Now, when you redirect output to LPT2, Windows Home Server sends the output to the USB printer.

Redirecting Command Input

The *input redirection operator* (<) handles getting input to a Windows Home Server command from somewhere other than the keyboard. Input redirection is almost always used to send the contents of a text file to a Windows Home Server command. The most common example is the MORE command, which displays one screen of information at a time. If you have a large text file that scrolls off the screen when you use TYPE, the following command, which sends the contents of BIGFILE.TXT to the MORE command, solves the problem:

```
more < bigfile.txt
```

When you run this command, the first screen of text appears, and the following line shows up at the bottom of the screen:

```
- More -
```

Just press any key, and MORE displays the next screen. (Whatever you do, don't mix up < and > when using MORE. The command more > bigfile.txt erases BIGFILE.TXT!) MORE is an example of a *filter* command. Filters process whatever text is sent through them. The other Windows Home Server filters are SORT and FIND, which I discuss in a moment.

Another handy use for input redirection is to send keystrokes to Windows Home Server commands. For example, create a text file called enter.txt that consists of a single press of the Enter key, and then try this command:

```
date < enter.txt
```

Windows Home Server displays the current date, and instead of waiting for you to either type in a new date or press Enter, it just reads enter.txt and uses its single carriage return as input. (For an even easier way to input the Enter key to a command, check out the next section.)

One common recipient of redirected input is the SORT command. SORT, as you might guess from its name, sorts the data sent to it and displays the results onscreen. So, for example, here's how you would sort a file called JUMBLED.TXT:

```
sort < jumbled.txt
```

Instead of merely displaying the results of the sort onscreen, you can use > to redirect them to another file.

TIP

SORT normally starts with the first column and works across. To start with any other column, use the /+n switch, where n is the number of the column you want to use. To sort a file in reverse order (that is, a descending sort—Z to A, then 9 to 0—instead of an ascending sort—0 to 9, then A to Z), use the /R switch.

Piping Commands

Piping is a technique that combines both input and output redirection. Using the pipe operator (¦), the output of one command is captured and sent as input to another command. For example, the SYSTEMINFO command displays about five screens of data, so you usually need to scroll back to see the data you're looking for. However, you can pause the output by piping it to the MORE command:

```
systeminfo ¦ more
```

The pipe operator captures the SYSTEMINFO output and sends it as input to MORE, which then displays the SYSTEMINFO results one screen at a time.

NOTE

Piping works by first redirecting the output of a command to a temporary file. It then takes this temporary file and redirects it as input to the second command. A command such as SYSTEMINFO ¦ MORE is approximately equivalent to the following two commands:

```
SYSTEMINFO > tempfile
MORE < tempfile
```

I showed you in the preceding section how to use input redirection to send keystrokes to a Windows Home Server command. But if you have to send only a single key, piping offers a much nicer solution. The secret is to use the ECHO command to echo the character you need and then pipe it to the Windows Home Server command.

For example, if you use the command DEL *.*, Windows Home Server always asks whether you're sure that you want to delete all the files in the current directory. This is a sensible precaution, but you can override it if you do things this way:

```
echo y ¦ del *.*
```

Here, the y that would normally be echoed to the screen is sent to DEL instead, which interprets it as a response to its prompt. This is a handy technique for batch files in which you want to reduce or even eliminate user interaction.

> **TIP**
>
> You can even use this technique to send an Enter keypress to a command. The command ECHO. (that's ECHO followed by a period) is equivalent to pressing Enter. So, for example, you could use the following command in a batch file to display the time without user input:
>
> ```
> ECHO. ¦ TIME
> ```

Understanding Batch File Basics

As you've seen so far, the command line is still an often-useful and occasionally indispensable part of computing life, and most power users will find themselves doing at least a little work in the Command Prompt window. Part of that work might involve writing short batch file programs to automate routine chores, such as performing simple file backups and deleting unneeded files. And if you throw in any of the commands that enhance batch files, you can do many other interesting and useful things.

When you run a command in a command-line session, the command prompt executes the command or program and returns to the prompt to await further orders. If you tell the command prompt to execute a batch file, however, things are a little different. The command prompt goes into *Batch mode*, where it takes all its input from the individual lines of a batch file. These lines are just commands that (in most cases) you otherwise have to type in yourself. The command prompt repeats the following four-step procedure until it has processed each line in the batch file:

1. It reads a line from the batch file.
2. It closes the batch file.
3. It executes the command.
4. It reopens the batch file and reads the next line.

The main advantage of Batch mode is that you can lump several commands together in a single batch file and tell the command prompt to execute them all simply by typing the name of the batch file. This is great for automating routine tasks such as backing up the Registry files or deleting leftover .tmp files at startup.

Creating Batch Files

Before getting started with some concrete batch file examples, you need to know how to create them. Here are a few things to bear in mind:

▶ Batch files are simple text files, so using Notepad (or some other text editor) is probably your best choice.

▶ If you decide to use WordPad or another word processor, make sure that the file you create is a text-only file.

▶ Save your batch files using the .bat extension.

▶ When naming your batch files, don't use the same name as a command prompt command. For example, if you create a batch file that deletes some files, don't name it Del.bat. If you do, the batch file will never run! Here's why: When you enter something at the prompt, CMD first checks to see whether the command is an internal command. If it's not, CMD then checks for (in order) a .com, .exe, .bat, or .cmd file with a matching name. Because all external commands use a .com or .exe extension, CMD never bothers to check whether your batch file even exists!

After you've created the batch file, the rest is easy. Just enter any commands exactly as you would at the command line, and include whatever batch instructions you need.

> **TIP**
>
> If you find yourself creating and using a number of batch files, things can get confusing if you have the files scattered all over your hard disk. To remedy this, it makes sense to create a new folder to hold all your batch files. To make this strategy effective, however, you have to tell the command prompt to look in the batch file folder to find these files. To do that, you need to add the batch file folder to the PATH variable, as described earlier (see "Working with Long Filenames").

REM: Adding Comments to a Batch File

The first of the batch file–specific commands is REM (which stands for *remark*). This simple command tells the command prompt to ignore everything else on the current line. Batch file mavens use it almost exclusively to add short comments to their files:

```
REM This batch file changes to drive C
REM folder and starts CHKDSK in automatic mode.
C:
CHKDSK /F
```

Why would anyone want to do this? Well, it's probably not all that necessary with short, easy-to-understand batch files, but some of the more complex programs you'll be seeing later in this chapter can appear incomprehensible at first glance. A few pithy REM state-ments can help clear things up (not only for other people, but for you if you haven't looked at the file in a couple of months).

CAUTION

It's best not to go overboard with REM statements. Having too many slows a batch file to a crawl. You really need only a few REM statements at the beginning to outline the purpose of the file and one or two to explain each of your more cryptic commands.

ECHO: Displaying Messages from a Batch File

When it's processing a batch file, Windows Home Server normally lets you know what's going on by displaying each command before executing it. That's fine, but it's often better to include more expansive descriptions, especially if other people will be using your batch files. The ECHO batch file command makes it possible for you to do just that.

For example, here's a simple batch file that deletes all the text files in the current user's Cookies and Recent folders and courteously tells the user what's about to happen:

```
ECHO This batch file will now delete all your cookie text files
DEL "%LocalAppData%\Microsoft\Windows\Temporary Internet Files\cookie*"
ECHO This batch file will now delete your Recent Items list
DEL "%AppData%\Microsoft\Windows\Recent Items\*.lnk"
```

The idea here is that when Windows Home Server stumbles on the ECHO command, it simply displays the rest of the line onscreen. Sounds pretty simple, right? Well, here's what the output looks like when you run the batch file:

```
C:\>ECHO This batch file will now delete all your cookie text files
This batch file will now delete all your cookie text files
C:\>DEL "%LocalAppData%\Microsoft\Windows\Temporary Internet Files\cookie*""
C:\>ECHO This batch file will now delete your Recent Items list
This batch file will now delete your Recent Items list
C:\>DEL "%AppData%\Microsoft\Windows\Recent Items\*.lnk"
```

What a mess! The problem is that Windows Home Server is displaying the command and ECHOing the line. Fortunately, Windows Home Server provides two solutions:

▶ To prevent Windows Home Server from displaying a command as it executes, precede the command with the @ symbol:

```
@ECHO This batch file will now delete all your cookie text files
```

▶ To prevent Windows Home Server from displaying commands, place the following at the beginning of the batch file:

```
@ECHO OFF
```

Here's what the output looks like with the commands hidden:

```
This batch file will now delete all your cookie text files
This batch file will now delete your Recent Items list
```

> **TIP**
>
> You might think that you can display a blank line simply by using ECHO by itself. That would be nice, but it doesn't work. (Windows Home Server just tells you the current state of ECHO: on or off.) Instead, use ECHO. (ECHO followed by a period).

PAUSE: Temporarily Halting Batch File Execution

Sometimes you want to see something that a batch file displays (such as a folder listing produced by the DIR command) before continuing. Or, you might want to alert users that something important is about to happen so that they can consider the possible ramifications (and bail out if they get cold feet). In both cases, you can use the PAUSE command to halt the execution of a batch file temporarily. When Windows Home Server comes across PAUSE in a batch file, it displays the following:

```
Press any key to continue . . .
```

To continue processing the rest of the batch file, press any key. If you don't want to continue, you can cancel processing by pressing Ctrl+C or Ctrl+Break. Windows Home Server then asks you to confirm:

```
Terminate batch job (Y/N)?
```

Either press Y to return to the prompt or N to continue the batch file.

Using Batch File Parameters

Most command-line utilities require extra information such as a filename (for example, when you use COPY or DEL) or a folder path (such as when you use CD or MD). These extra pieces of information—they're called *parameters*—give you the flexibility to specify exactly how you want a command to work. You can add the same level of flexibility to your batch files. To understand how this works, first look at the following example:

```
@ECHO OFF
ECHO.
ECHO The first parameter is %1
ECHO The second parameter is %2
ECHO The third parameter is %3
```

As you can see, this batch file doesn't do much except ECHO four lines to the screen (the first of which is just a blank line). Curiously, however, each ECHO command ends with a percent sign (%) and a number. Type and save this batch file as Parameters.bat. Then, to see what these unusual symbols mean, enter the following at the command line:

parameters A B C

This produces the following output:

```
C:\>parameters A B C

The first parameter is A
The second parameter is B
The third parameter is C
```

The following ECHO command in Parameters.bat produces the first line in the output (after the blank line):

```
ECHO The first parameter is %1
```

When Windows sees the %1 symbol in a batch file, it examines the original command, looks for the first item after the batch filename, and then replaces %1 with that item. In the example, the first item after parameters is A, so Windows uses that to replace %1. Only when it has done this does it proceed to ECHO the line to the screen.

NOTE

If your batch file command has more parameters than the batch file is looking for, it ignores the extras. For example, adding a fourth parameter to the parameters command line has no effect on the file's operation. Note, too, that you can't use more than nine replaceable parameters in a batch file (%1 through %9). However, a tenth replaceable parameter (%0) holds the name of the batch file.

TIP

If the replaceable parameter is a string that includes one or more spaces, surround the parameter with quotation marks (for example, "%1").

FOR: Looping in a Batch File

The FOR command is a batch file's way of looping through an instruction:

```
FOR %%parameter IN (set) DO command
```

%%parameter   This is the parameter that changes each time through the loop. You can use any single character after the two % signs (except 0 through 9). There are two % signs because Windows deletes single ones as it processes the batch file.

IN (*set*)   This is the list (it's officially called the *set*) of choices for *%%parameter*. You can use spaces, commas, or semicolons to separate the items in the set, and you must enclose them in parentheses.

DO *command*   For each item in the set, the batch file performs whatever instruction is given by command. The *%%parameter* is normally found somewhere in *command*.

Here's an example of the FOR command in a simple batch file that might help clear things up:

```
@ECHO OFF
FOR %%B IN (A B C) DO ECHO %%B
```

This batch file (call it Parameters.bat) produces the following output:

```
C:\BATCH>parameters2
A
B
C
```

All this does is loop through the three items in the set (A, B, and C) and substitute each one for %%B in the command ECHO %%B.

GOTO: Jumping to a Line in a Batch File

Your basic batch file lives a simple, linear existence. The first command is processed, and then the second, the third, and so on to the end of the file. It's boring, but that's all you need most of the time.

However, sometimes the batch file's usual one-command-after-the-other approach breaks down. For example, depending on a parameter or the result of a previous command, you might need to skip over a line or two. How do you do this? With the GOTO batch command:

```
...
... (the opening batch commands)
...
GOTO NEXT
...
... (the batch commands that get skipped)
...
:NEXT
...
... (the rest of the batch commands)
...
```

Here, the GOTO command is telling the batch file to look for a line that begins with a colon and the word NEXT (this is called a *label*) and to ignore any commands in between.

19

GOTO is useful for processing different batch commands depending on a parameter. Here's a simple example:

```
@ECHO OFF
CLS
GOTO %1
:A
ECHO This part of the batch file runs if A is the parameter.
GOTO END
:B
ECHO This part of the batch file runs if B is the parameter.
:END
```

Suppose that this file is named GOTOTest.BAT and you enter the following command:

gototest a

In the batch file, the line GOTO %1 becomes GOTO A. That makes the batch file skip down to the :A label, where it then runs the commands (in this example, just an ECHO statement) and skips to :END to avoid the rest of the batch file commands.

IF: Handling Batch File Conditions

Batch files sometimes have to make decisions before proceeding. Here are a few examples of what a batch file might have to decide:

▶ If the %2 parameter equals /Q, jump to the QuickFormat section. Otherwise, do a regular format.

▶ If the user forgets to enter a parameter, cancel the program. Otherwise, continue processing the batch file.

▶ If the file that the user wants to move already exists in the new folder, display a warning. Otherwise, proceed with the move.

▶ If the last command failed, display an error message and cancel the program. Otherwise, continue.

For these types of decisions, you need to use the IF batch command. IF has the following general form:

IF *condition command*

condition	This is a test that evaluates to a yes or no answer ("Did the user forget a parameter?").
command	This is what is executed if the *condition* produces a positive response ("Cancel the batch file").

For example, one of the most common uses of the IF command is to check the parameters that the user entered and proceed accordingly. From the previous section, the simple batch file that used GOTO can be rewritten with IF as follows:

```
@ECHO OFF
CLS
IF "%1"=="A" ECHO This part of the batch file runs if A is the parameter.
IF "%1"=="B" ECHO This part of the batch file runs if B is the parameter.
```

The condition part of an IF statement is a bit tricky. Let's look at the first one: "%1"=="A". Remember that the condition is always a question with a yes or no answer. In this case, the question boils down to the following:

```
Is the first parameter (%1) equal to A?
```

The double equal sign (==) looks weird, but that's just how you compare two strings of characters in a batch file. If the answer is yes, the command executes. If the answer is no, the batch file moves on to the next IF, which checks to see whether the parameter is "B".

> **NOTE**
>
> Strictly speaking, you don't need to include the quotation marks ("). Using %1==A accomplishes the same thing. However, I prefer to use them for two reasons: First, it makes it clearer that the IF condition is comparing strings; second, as you'll see in the next section, the quotation marks enable you to check whether the user forgot to enter a parameter.

> **CAUTION**
>
> This batch file has a serious flaw that will prevent it from working under certain conditions. Specifically, if you use the lowercase "a" or "b" as a parameter, nothing happens because, to the IF command, "a" is different from "A". The solution is to add extra IF commands to handle this situation:
>
> ```
> IF "%1"=="a" ECHO This part of the batch file runs if a is the parameter
> ```

Proper batch file techniques require you to check to see not only what a parameter is, but whether one exists. This can be vital because a missing parameter can cause a batch file to crash and burn. For example, here's a batch file called DontCopy.bat designed to copy all files in the current folder to a new destination (given by the second parameter) except those you specified (given by the first parameter):

```
@ECHO OFF
CLS
ATTRIB +H %1
ECHO.
```

```
ECHO Copying all files to %2 except %1:
ECHO.
XCOPY *.* %2
ATTRIB -H %1
```

What happens if the user forgets to add the destination parameter (%2)? Well, the XCOPY command becomes XCOPY *.*, which terminates the batch file with the following error:

```
File cannot be copied onto itself
```

The solution is to add an IF command that checks to see whether %2 exists:

```
@ECHO OFF
CLS
IF "%2"=="" GOTO ERROR
ATTRIB +H %1
ECHO.
ECHO Copying all files to %2 except %1:
ECHO.
XCOPY32 *.* %2
ATTRIB -H %1
GOTO END
:ERROR
ECHO You didn't enter a destination!
ECHO Please try again...
:END
```

The condition "%2"=="" is literally comparing %2 to nothing (""). If this proves to be true, the program jumps (using GOTO) to the :ERROR label, and a message is displayed to admonish the user. Notice, too, that if everything is okay (that is, the user entered a second parameter), the batch file executes normally and jumps to the :END label to avoid displaying the error message.

Another variation of IF is the IF EXIST command, which checks for the existence of a file. This is handy, for example, when you're using COPY or MOVE. First, you can check whether the file you want to copy or move exists. Second, you can check whether a file with the same name already exists in the target folder. (As you probably know, a file that has been copied over by another of the same name is downright impossible to recover.) Here's a batch file called SafeMove.bat, which uses the MOVE command to move a file but first checks the file and then the target folder:

```
@ECHO OFF
CLS
IF EXIST %1 GOTO SO_FAR_SO_GOOD
ECHO The file %1 doesn't exist!
GOTO END
:SO_FAR_SO_GOOD
```

```
IF NOT EXIST %2 GOTO MOVE_IT
ECHO The file %1 exists on the target folder!
ECHO Press Ctrl+C to bail out or, to keep going,
PAUSE
:MOVE_IT
MOVE %1 %2
:END
```

To explain what's happening, I'll use a sample command:

```
safemove moveme.txt "%userprofile%\documents\moveme.txt"
```

The first IF tests for the existence of %1 (MOVEME.TXT in the example). If there is such a file, the program skips to the :SO_FAR_SO_GOOD label. Otherwise, it tells the user that the file doesn't exist and then jumps down to :END.

The second IF is slightly different. In this case, I want to continue only if MOVEME.TXT doesn't exist in the current user's Documents folder, so I add NOT to the condition. (You can include NOT in any IF condition.) If this proves true (that is, the file given by %2 doesn't exist), the file skips to :MOVE_IT and performs the move. Otherwise, the user is warned and given an opportunity to cancel.

Working with the Command-Line Tools

The real power of the command line shines through when you combine the techniques you've learned so far with any of Windows Home Server's dozens of command-line tools. I don't have enough space to cover every tool (that would require a book in itself), so the rest of this chapter takes you through the most useful and powerful command-line tools in three categories: disk management, file management, and system management.

Working with Disk Management Tools

Windows Home Server comes with a large collection of command-line disk management tools that enable you to check disks or partitions for errors, as well as defragment, format, partition, and convert disks. Table 19.5 lists the disk management tools that you can use with Windows Home Server.

TABLE 19.5 Windows Home Server's Command-Line Disk Management Tools

Tool	Description
CHKDSK	Checks a specified volume for errors.
CHKNTFS	Configures automatic disk checking.
CONVERT	Converts a specified volume to a different file system.
DEFRAG	Defragments a specified volume.
DISKCOMP	Compares the contents of two floppy disks. (This tool does not compare hard disks or other types of removable media, such as memory cards.)

DISKCOPY   Copies the contents of one floppy disk to another. (This tool does not copy hard disks or other types of removable media, such as memory cards.)

DISKPART   Enables you to list, create, select, delete, and extend disk partitions.

EXPAND   Extracts one or more files from a compressed file, such as a .cab file found on some installation discs.

FORMAT   Formats the specified volume.

FSUTIL   Performs a number of file system tasks.

LABEL   Changes or deletes the name of a specified volume.

MOUNTVOL   Creates, displays, or deletes a mount point.

VOL   Displays the name and serial number of a specified volume.

NOTE

In this section, I'll use the word *volume* to refer to any disk, partition, or mount point.

The next four sections give you more detailed coverage of the CHKDKS and CHKNTFS tools.

CHKDSK: Checking for Hard Disk Errors

In Chapter 16, "Maintaining Windows Home Server," you learned how to use the Check Disk utility to check a hard disk for errors. Check Disk also comes with a command-line version called CHKDSK that you can run in a Command Prompt window.

▶ **SEE** "Checking Your Hard Disk for Errors," **P. 411**.

Here's the syntax for CHKDSK:

CHKDSK [*volume* [*filename*]] [/F] [/V] [/R] [/X] [/I] [/C] [/B] [/L:[*size*]]

volume   The drive letter (followed by a colon) or mount point.

filename   On FAT16 and FAT32 disks, the name of the file to check for errors. Include the path if the file isn't in the current folder.

/F   Tells CHKDSK to automatically fix errors. This is the same as running the Check Disk GUI with the Automatically Fix File System Errors option activated.

/V   Runs CHKDSK in verbose mode. On FAT16 and FAT32 drives, CHKDSK displays the path and name of every file on the disk; on NTFS drives, CHKDSK displays cleanup messages, if any.

/R	Tells CHKDSK to scan the disk surface for bad sectors and recover data from the bad sectors, if possible. (The /F switch is implied.) This is the same as running the Check Disk GUI with the Scan for and Attempt Recovery of Bad Sectors option activated.
/X	On NTFS nonsystem disks that have open files, forces the volume to dismount, invalidates the open file handles, and then runs the scan. (The /F switch is implied.)
/I	On NTFS disks, tells CHKDSK to check only the file system's index entries.
/C	On NTFS disks, tells CHKDSK to skip the checking of cycles within the folder structure. This is a rare error, so using /C to skip the cycle check can speed up the disk check.
/B	On NTFS disks, tells CHKDSK to recheck bad clusters. (The /R switch is implied.)
/L:[*size*]	On NTFS disks, tells CHKDSK to set the size of its log file to the specified number of kilobytes. The default size is 65,536, which is big enough for most systems, so you should never need to change the size. Note that if you include this switch without the size parameter, Check Disk tells you the current size of the log file.

For example, to run a read-only check—that is, a check that doesn't repair errors—on drive C:, you enter the following command:

```
chkdsk c:
```

Note that when you use the /F switch to fix errors, CHKDSK must lock the volume to prevent running processes from using the volume during the check. If you use the /F switch on drive C:, which is the Windows Home Server system drive, CHKDSK can't lock the drive, and you see the following message:

```
Cannot lock current drive.

Chkdsk cannot run because the volume is in use by another
process. Would you like to schedule this volume to be
checked the next time the system restarts? (Y/N)
```

If you press Y and Enter, CHKDSK schedules a check for drive C: to run the next time you reboot Windows Home Server.

CHKNTFS: Scheduling Automatic Disk Checks

You saw in the previous section that CHKDSK prompts you to schedule an automatic disk check during the next reboot if you run CHKDSK /F on the system drive (drive C: in

19

Windows Home Server). If you press Y and Enter at this prompt, CHKDSK adds the AUTOCHK utility to the following Registry setting:

```
HKLM\SYSTEM\CurrentControlSet\Control\Session Manager\BootExecute
```

This setting specifies the programs that Windows Home Server should run at boot time when the Session Manager is loading. AUTOCHK is the automatic version of CHKDSK that runs at system startup.

Windows Home Server also comes with a command-line tool named CHKNTFS that enables you to cancel pending automatic disk checks, schedule boot-time disk checks without using CHKDSK, and set the time that AUTOCHK counts down before running the automatic disk checks.

Here's the syntax for CHKNTFS:

```
CHKNTFS [volume ][/C volume:] [/X volume:] [/D] [/T:[time]]
```

volume	A drive letter (followed by a colon) or mount point.
/C volume	Tells CHKNTFS to schedule an automatic startup disk check for the specified volume. You can specify multiple volumes (separated by spaces).
/X volume	Tells CHKNTFS to exclude the specified volume from an automatic startup disk check. You can specify multiple volumes (separated by spaces).
/D	Tells CHKNTFS to exclude all volumes from an automatic startup disk check.
/T:[time]	Specifies the time that AUTOCHK counts down before starting the automatic disk checks.

When you run CHKNTFS with just a volume name, you see one of the following:

▶ If the volume is not scheduled for a startup disk check, you see the volume's file system:

```
The type of the file system is NTFS.
```

▶ If the volume is scheduled for a startup disk check, you see the following message:

```
Chkdsk has been scheduled manually to run on next reboot.
```

▶ If Windows Home Server's Storage Manager has detected an error on the volume, it marks the volume as *dirty*, so in this case, you see the following message (using drive C: as an example):

```
C: is dirty. You may use the /C option to schedule chkdsk for this drive.
```

This last message is confusing because Windows Home Server *always* performs an automatic startup disk check of any volume that's marked as dirty. What you can do with

CHKNTFS is bypass the automatic startup disk check of any volume that is marked as dirty. To do that, run CHKNTFS with the /X switch, as in this example:

```
chkntfs /x c:
```

NOTE

To manually mark a volume as dirty, use the FSUTIL DIRTY SET *volume* command, where *volume* is the drive you want to work with. For example, the following command marks drive C: as dirty:

```
fsutil dirty set c:
```

If you're not sure whether a drive is dirty, either run CHKNTFS *volume* or run FSUTIL DIRTY QUERY *volume*, as in this example:

```
fsutil dirty query c:
```

Note, however, that FSUTIL doesn't give you a way to unmark a drive as dirty.

If a volume isn't already marked as dirty, you can force CHKDSK to check a volume at startup by running CHKNTFS with the /C switch. For example, the following command sets up an automatic start check for drive C:

```
chkntfs /c c:
```

Note that the /C switch is cumulative, meaning that if you run it multiple times and specify a different volume each time, CHKNTFS adds each new volume to the list of volumes to check at startup. Instead of running multiple commands, however, you can specify multiple volumes in a single command, like so:

```
chkntfs /c c: t: w:
```

If you know that a volume has been scheduled for a startup check, but you want to cancel that check, run CHKNTFS with the /X switch, as in this example:

```
chkntfs /x c:
```

If you know that multiple volumes are scheduled for automatic startup checks, you can cancel all the checks by running CHKNTFS with the /D switch:

```
chkntfs /d
```

If you've scheduled a startup check for one or more volumes, or if a volume is marked as dirty, the next time you reboot Windows Home Server, you see a message similar to the following (which uses drive C: as an example):

```
Checking file system on C:
The type of the file system is NTFS.
Volume label is SYS.

One of your disks needs to be checked for consistency. You
may cancel the disk check, but it is strongly recommended
that you continue.
To skip disk checking, press any key within 10 second(s).
```

The number of seconds in the last line counts down to 0. If you press a key before the countdown ends, Windows Home Server skips the disk check; otherwise, it continues with CHKDSK.

CAUTION

Pressing any key to skip the disk check usually only works with wired keyboards. On most wireless keyboards, pressing a key has no effect.

You can change the initial countdown value by running CHKNTFS with the /T switch, followed by the number of seconds you want to use for the countdown. For example, the following command sets the countdown to 30 seconds:

```
chkntfs /t:30
```

Note that if you run the command CHKNTFS /T (that is, you don't specify a countdown value), CHKNTFS returns the current countdown value.

Working with File and Folder Management Tools

Windows Explorer is the GUI tool of choice for most file and folder operations. However, Windows Home Server comes with an impressive collection of command-line file and folder tools that let you perform all the standard operations such as renaming, copying, moving, and deleting, as well as more interesting chores such as changing file attributes and comparing the contents of two files. Table 19.6 lists the file management tools that you can use with Windows Home Server.

TABLE 19.6 Windows Home Server's Command-Line File and Folder Management Tools

Tool	Description
ATTRIB	Displays, applies, or removes attributes for the specified file or folder.
CD or CHDIR	Changes to the specified folder.
COMP	Compares the contents of two specified files byte by byte.
COMPACT	Displays or modifies the compression settings for the specified file or folder (which must be located on an NTFS partition).

COPY	Creates a copy of the specified file or folder in another location.
DEL	Deletes the specified file or folder.
DIR	Displays a directory listing for the current folder or for the specified file or folder.
FC	Compares the content of two specified files.
FIND	Searches for and displays all the instances of a specified string in a file.
FINDSTR	Uses a regular expression to search for and display all the instances of a specified string in a file.
FTYPE	Displays or modifies file types.
MD or MKDIR	Creates the specified folder.
MOVE	Moves the specified file or folder to another location.
REN	Changes the name of the specified file or folder.
REPLACE	Replaces files in the destination folder with files in the source folder that have the same name.
	Deletes the specified folder.
SORT	Sorts the specified file and then displays the results.
SFC	Runs the System File Checker, which scans and verifies the protected Windows Home Server files.
TAKEOWN	Enables an administrator to take ownership of the specified file.
TREE	Displays a graphical tree diagram showing the subfolder hierarchy of the current folder or the specified folder.
WHERE	Searches for and displays all the files that match a specified pattern in the current folder and in the PATH folders.
XCOPY	Creates a copy of the specified file or folder in another location. This tool offers many more options than the COPY command.

19

The next few sections take a closer look at a half dozen of these tools: ATTRIB, FIND, REN, REPLACE, SORT, and XCOPY.

Before getting to the tools, I should mention that most of the file and folder management tools work with the standard wildcard characters: ? and *. In a file or folder specification, you use ? to substitute for a single character, and you use * to substitute for multiple characters. Here are some examples:

File Specification	Matches
Budget201?.xlsx	Budget2011.xlsx, Budget2012.xlsx, and so on
Memo.doc?	Memo.doc, Memo.docx, Memo.docm, and so on
*.txt	ReadMe.txt, log.txt, to-do.txt, and so on
*201?.pptx	Report2011.pptx, Budget2012.pptx, Conference2012.pptx, and so on
.	Every file

ATTRIB: Modifying File and Folder Attributes

A file's *attributes* are special codes that indicate the status of the file. There are four attributes you can work with:

Archive   When this attribute is turned on, it means the file has been modified since it was last backed up.

Hidden   When this attribute is turned on, it means the file doesn't show up in a DIR listing and isn't included when you run most command-line tools. For example, if you run DEL *.* in a folder, Windows Home Server deletes all the files in that folder, except the hidden files.

Read-only   When this attribute is turned on, it means the file can't be modified or erased.

System   When this attribute is turned on, it means the file is an operating system file (that is, a file that was installed with Windows Home Server).

The ATTRIB command lets you turn these attributes on or off. Here's the syntax:

ATTRIB [+A ¦ -A] [+H ¦ -H] [+R ¦ -R] [+S ¦ -S] *filename* [/S [/D]]

+A   Sets the archive attribute.

-A   Clears the archive attribute.

+H   Sets the hidden attribute.

-H   Clears the hidden attribute.

+R   Sets the read-only attribute.

-R   Clears the read-only attribute.

+S   Sets the system attribute.

-S   Clears the system attribute.

filename   The file or files you want to work with.

/S	Applies the attribute change to the matching files in the current folder and all of its subfolders.
/D	Applies the attribute change only to the current folder's subfolders. You must use this switch in conjunction with /S.

For example, if you'd like to hide all the DOC files in the current directory, use the following command:

```
attrib +h *.doc
```

As another example, if you've ever tried to delete or edit a file and gotten the message Access denied, the file is likely read-only. You can turn off the read-only attribute by running ATTRIB with the -R switch, as in this example:

```
attrib -r readonly.txt
```

> **NOTE**
>
> If you want to check out a file's attributes, use the DIR command's /A switch. Use /AA to see files with their archive attribute set, /AH for hidden files, /AR for read-only, and /AS for system files.

You can also use ATTRIB for protecting important or sensitive files. When you hide a file, it doesn't show up in a listing produced by the DIR command. Out of sight is out of mind, so someone taking a casual glance at your files won't see the hidden ones and, therefore, won't be tempted to display or erase them.

Although a hidden file is invisible, it's not totally safe. Someone who knows the name of the file can attempt to modify the file by opening it with the appropriate program. As an added measure of safety, you can also set the file's read-only attribute. When you do this, the file can't be modified. You can set both attributes with a single command:

```
attrib +h +r payroll.xlsx
```

FIND: Locating a Text String in a File

You use the FIND command to search for a string inside a file. Here's the syntax:

```
FIND [/C] [/I] [/N] [/V] [/OFF[LINE]] "string" filename
```

/C	Displays the number of times that *string* appears in *filename*.
/I	Performs a case-insensitive search.
/N	Displays each match of *string* in *filename* with the line number in *filename* where each match occurs.
/V	Displays the lines in *filename* that don't contain *string*.

19

/OFF[LINE]   Searches *filename* even if the file's offline attribute is set.

string   The string you want to search for.

filename   The file you want to search in. (Note that you can't use wildcards with the FIND command.) If the filename contains one or more spaces, surround it with double quotation marks.

NOTE

The FIND command doesn't work with the Office 2007 (and later) file formats. However, it works fine with most documents created in earlier versions of Office.

For example, to find the string *DVD* in a file named WishList.txt, you use the following command:

```
find "DVD" WishList.txt
```

If the string you want to find contains double quotation marks, you need to place two quotation marks in the search string. For example, to find the phrase *Dave "The Hammer" Schultz* in the file players.doc, use the following command:

```
find "Dave ""The Hammer"" Schultz" players.doc
```

TIP

The FIND command doesn't accept wildcard characters in the *filename* parameter. That's too bad, because it's often useful to search multiple files for a string. Fortunately, you can work around this limitation by using a FOR loop, in which the command you run on each file is FIND. Here's the general syntax to use:

```
FOR %f IN (filespec) DO FIND "string" %f
```

Replace *filespec* with the file specification you want to use, and *string* with the string you want to search for. For example, the following command runs through all the .doc files in the current folder and searches each file for the string *Thanksgiving*:

```
FOR %f IN (*.doc) DO FIND "Thanksgiving" %f
```

If the file specification matches files with spaces in their names, you need to surround the last %f parameter with quotation marks, like so:

```
FOR %f IN (*.doc) DO FIND "Thanksgiving" "%f"
```

One of the most common uses of the FIND command is as a filter in pipe operations. (See "Piping Commands," earlier in this chapter.) In this case, instead of a filename, you pipe the output of another command through FIND. In this case, FIND searches this input for a specified string and, if it finds a match, it displays the line that contains the string.

For example, the last line of a DIR listing tells you the number of bytes free on the current drive. Rather than wade through the entire DIR output just to get this information, use this command instead:

```
dir | find "free"
```

You'll see something like the following:

```
2 Dir(s) 28,903,331,184 bytes free
```

FIND scours the DIR listing piped to it and looks for the word *free*. You can use this technique to display specific lines from, say, a CHKDSK report. For example, searching for bad finds the number of bad sectors on the disk.

REN: Renaming a File or Folder

You use the REN (or RENAME) command to change the name of one or more files and folders. Here's the syntax:

```
REN old_filename1 new_filename
```

old_filename	The original filename
new_filename	The new filename

For example, the following command renamed Budget 2011.xlsx to Budget 2012.xlsx:

```
ren "Budget 2011.xlsx" "Budget 2012.xlsx"
```

A simple file or folder rename such as this probably isn't something you'll ever fire up a command-line session to do because renaming a single object is faster and easier in Windows Explorer. However, the real power of the REN command is that it accepts wildcards in the file specifications. This enables you to rename several files at once, something you can't do in Windows Explorer.

For example, suppose you have a folder full of files, many of which contain 2011 somewhere in the filename. To rename all those files by changing 2011 to 2012, you'd use the following command:

```
ren *2011* *2012*
```

Similarly, if you have a folder full of files that use the .htm extension and you want to change each extension to .asp, you'd use the following command:

```
ren *.htm *.asp
```

Note that for these multiple-file renames to work, in most cases the original filename text and the new filename text must be the same length. For example, digital cameras often supply photos with names such as img_1234.jpg and img_5678.jpg. If you have a number of related photos in a folder, you might want to give them more meaningful names. If the photos are from a vacation in Rome, you might prefer names such as

Rome_Vacation1234.jpg and Rome_Vacation5678.jpg. Unfortunately, the REN command can't handle this. However, it can rename the files to Rome1234.jpg and Rome5678.jpg:

```
ren img_* Rome*
```

The exception to the same length rule is if the replacement occurs at the end of the filenames. For example, the following command renames all files with the .jpeg extension to .jpg:

```
ren *.jpeg *.jpg
```

REPLACE: Smarter File Copying

If there was such a thing as a Most Underrated Command award, REPLACE would win it hands down. This command, which you almost never hear about, can do three *very* useful (and very different) things:

▶ It copies files, but only if their names match those in the target directory.

▶ It copies files, but only if their names don't exist in the target directory.

▶ It copies files, but only if their names match those in the target directory and the matching files in the target directory are older than the files being copied.

Here's the syntax:

```
REPLACE source_files target /A /U /P /R /S /W
```

source_files	The path and file specification of the files you want to copy.
target	The folder to which you want to copy the files.
/A	Copies only new files to the target folder. You can't use this switch in conjunction with /S or /U.
/U	Copies files that have the same name in the target folder and that are newer than the matching files in the target folder. You can't use this switch in conjunction with /A.
/P	Prompts you for confirmation before replacing files.
/R	Replaces read-only files.
/S	Replaces files in the target folder's subfolders. You can't use this switch in conjunction with /A.
/W	Waits for you to insert a disk before starting.

If you don't specify switches, REPLACE copies a file from the source folder to the target folder if and only if it finds a file with a matching name in the target.

More useful is the REPLACE command's updating mode, where it copies a file from the source folder to the target folder if and only if it finds a file with a matching name in the target and that target file is older than the source file. A good example where updating comes in handy is when you copy some files to a disk or memory card so you can use them on another machine (such as taking files from your computer at work to use them at home). When you need to copy the files back to the first machine, the following REPLACE command does the job. (This assumes the disk or memory card is in drive G:.)

```
replace g:*.* %UserProfile% /s /u
```

For each file on drive G:, REPLACE looks for matching filenames anywhere in the %UserProfile% folder and its subfolders (thanks to the /S switch) and replaces only the ones that are newer (the /U switch).

What if you created some new files on the other computer? To copy those to the first machine, use the /A switch, like so:

```
replace g:*.* %UserProfile%\Documents /a
```

In this case, REPLACE only copies a file from G if it doesn't exist in the %UserProfile%\Documents folder. (You have to specify a target folder because you can't use the /S switch with /A.)

SORT: Sorting the Contents of a File

When you obtain a file from the Internet or some other source, the data in the file may not appear in the order you want. What I usually do in such cases is import the file into Word or Excel and then use the program's Sort feature. This sometimes involves extra steps (such as converting text to a table in Word), so it's not always an efficient way to work.

If the file is text, it's often easier and faster to run the SORT command-line tool. By default, SORT takes the content of the file, sorts it in ascending alphanumeric order (0 to 9, then a to z, and then A to Z) starting at the beginning of each line in the file, and then displays the sorted results. You can also run descending order sorts, write the results to the same file or another file, and more. Here's the syntax:

```
SORT [input_file] [/+n] [/R] [/L locale] [/M kilobytes] [/REC characters] [/T
➥ temp_folder] [/O output_file]
```

input_file	The file you want to sort.
/+n	Specifies the starting character position (n) of the sort. The default is 1 (that is, the first character on each line in the file).
/R	Sorts the file in descending order (Z to A, then z to a, and then 9 to 0).
/L locale	Specifies a locale for sorting other than the default system locale. Your only choice here is to use "C" to sort the file using the binary values for each character.
/M kilobytes	Specifies the amount of memory, in kilobytes, that SORT uses during the operation. If you don't specify this value, SORT uses a minimum of 160KB and a maximum of 90% of available memory.

19

/REC *characters*	Specifies the maximum length, in characters, of each line in the file. The default value is 4,096 characters, and the maximum value is 65,535 characters.
/T *temp_folder*	Specifies the folder that SORT should use to hold the temporary files it uses during the sort.
/O *output_file*	Specifies the file that SORT should create to store the results of the sort. You can specify a different file or the input file.

For example, the following SORT command sorts the data in records.txt and stores the results in sorted_records.txt:

```
sort records.txt sorted_records.txt
```

XCOPY: Advanced File Copying

The XCOPY command is one of the most powerful of the file management command-line tools, and you can use it for some fairly sophisticated file copying operations.

Here's the syntax for XCOPY:

```
XCOPY source destination [/A ¦ /M] [/C] [/D[:mm-dd－yyyy]]
➥ [/EXCLUDE:file1[+file2[+file3]]] [/F] [/G] [/H] [/I] [/K] [/L] [/N]
➥ [/O] [/P] [/Q] [/R] [/S [/E]] [/T] [/U] [/V] [/W] [/X] [/Y ¦ -Y] [/Z] [/B] [/J]
```

source	The path and names of the files you want to copy.
destination	The location where you want the source files copied.
[/A]	Tells XCOPY to copy only those source files that have their archive attribute turned on. The archive attribute is not changed. If you use /A, you can't also use /M.
[/M]	Tells XCOPY to copy only those source files that have their archive attribute turned on. The archive attribute is turned off. If you use /M, you can't also use /A.
[/C]	Tells XCOPY to ignore any errors that occur during the copy operation. Otherwise, XCOPY aborts the operation if an error occurs.
[/D[:*mm-dd-yyyy*]]	Copies only those source files that changed on or after the date specified by *mm-dd-yyyy*. If you don't specify a date, using /D tells XCOPY to copy those source files that are newer than destination files that have the same name.
[/EXCLUDE:*file1* [+*file2*[+*file3*]]]	Tells XCOPY not to copy the files or file specification given by *file1*, *file2*, *file3*, and so on.

[/F]	Displays the source and destination filename during the copy operation.
[/G]	Creates decrypted copies of encrypted source files.
[/H]	Tells XCOPY to include in the copy operation any hidden and system files in the *source* folder.
[/I]	Tells XCOPY to create the destination folder. For this to work, the *source* value must be a folder or a file specification with wildcards.
[/K]	For each *source* file that has its read-only attribute set, tells XCOPY to maintain the read-only attribute on the corresponding *destination* file.
[/L]	Displays a list of the files that XCOPY will copy. (No files are copied if you use /L.)
[/N]	Tells XCOPY to use 8.3 filenames in the *destination* folder. Use this switch if the *destination* folder is a FAT partition that doesn't support long filenames.
[/O]	Tells XCOPY to also copy ownership and discretionary access control list data to the *destination*.
[/P]	Prompts you to confirm each file copy.
[/Q]	Tells XCOPY not to display messages during the copy.
[/R]	Overwrites read-only files when copying.
[/S]	Tells XCOPY to also include the *source* folder's subfolders in the copy.
[/E]	Tells XCOPY to include empty subfolders in the copy if you specify the /S or /T switch.
[/T]	Tells XCOPY to copy the *source* folder subfolder structure. (No files are copied, just the subfolders.)
[/U]	Only copies those *source* files that exist in the *destination* folder.
[/V]	Tells XCOPY to verify that each *destination* copy is identical to the original source file.
[/W]	Displays the message Press any key to begin copying file(s) before copying. You must press a key to launch the copy (or press Ctrl+C to cancel).
[/X]	Tells XCOPY to also copy file audit settings and system access control list data to the *destination*. (This switch implies /O.)

19

[/Y]	Tells XCOPY not to ask you whether you want to overwrite existing files in the *destination*.
[/-Y]	Tells XCOPY to ask you whether you want to overwrite existing files in the *destination*. Use this switch if you've set the %COPYCMD% environment variable to /Y, which suppresses overwrite prompts for XCOPY, COPY, and MOVE.
[/Z]	If you're copying to a network *destination*, this switch tells XCOPY to restart to the copy if the network connection goes down during the operation.
[/B]	Normally, if the next *source* file to be copied is a symbolic link—that is, a file that points to the location of another file—XCOPY does not copy the symbolic link itself, but instead it copies the file that is referenced by the symbolic link. However, if you include the [/B] switch, XCOPY copies the symbolic link itself instead of the file that it references.
[/J]	Tells XCOPY to use *unbuffered I/O* (input/output) for the copy. This is useful if you're copying very large files, because it's more efficient to write large files directly to the destination rather than using a memory location as a temporary storage area (that is, a *buffer*) when copying (this is called *buffered I/O*, and it's the method that XCOPY uses if you omit the [/J] switch).

In its basic form, XCOPY works just like COPY. So, for example, to copy all the .doc files in the current folder to a folder called Documents in drive G:, use the following command:

```
xcopy *.doc g:\documents
```

Besides being faster, XCOPY also contains a number of features not found in the puny COPY command. Think of it as COPY on steroids. (The X in XCOPY means that it's an extended COPY command.) For example, suppose you want to copy all the .doc files in the current folder and all the .doc files in any attached subfolders to G:\Documents. With COPY, you first have to create the appropriate folders on the destination partition and then perform separate COPY commands for each folder, which is not very efficient, to say the least. With XCOPY, all you do is add a single switch:

```
xcopy *.doc g:\documents /s
xcopy *.bat d:\batch /s
```

The /S switch tells XCOPY to copy the current folder and all non-empty subfolders and to create the appropriate folders in the destination, as needed. (If you want XCOPY to copy empty subfolders, include the /E switch, as well.)

Another useful feature of XCOPY is the ability to copy files by date. This is handy for performing incremental backups of files that you modified on or after a specific date. For example, suppose you keep your word processing documents in

%UserProfile%\Documents and you want to make backup copies in your Windows Home Server user share of all the .doc files that have changed since August 23, 2011. You can do this with the following command:

```
xcopy %userprofile%\documents\*.doc \\server\users\%Username%\ /d:08-23-2011
```

It's common to use XCOPY in batch files, but take care to handle errors. For example, what if a batch file tries to use XCOPY, but there's not enough memory? Or what if the user presses Ctrl+C during the copy? It might seem impossible to check for these kinds of errors; yet it is not only possible, it's really quite easy.

When certain commands finish, they always file a report on the progress of the operation. This report, or *exit code*, is a number that specifies how the operation went. For example, Table 19.7 lists the exit codes that the XCOPY command uses.

TABLE 19.7   XCOPY Exit Codes

Exit Code	What It Means
0	Everything's okay; the files were copied.
1	Nothing happened because no files were found to copy.
2	The user pressed Ctrl+C to abort the copy.
4	The command failed because there wasn't enough memory or disk space or because there was something wrong with the command's syntax.
5	The command failed because of a disk error.

What does all this mean for your batch files? You can use a variation of the IF command—IF ERRORLEVEL—to test for these exit codes. For example, here's a batch file called CheckCopy.bat, which uses some of the XCOPY exit codes to check for errors:

```
@ECHO OFF
XCOPY %1 %2
IF ERRORLEVEL 4 GOTO ERROR
IF ERRORLEVEL 2 GOTO CTRL+C
IF ERRORLEVEL 1 GOTO NO_FILES
GOTO DONE
:ERROR
ECHO Bad news! The copy failed because there wasn't
ECHO enough memory or disk space or because there was
ECHO something wrong with your file specs . . .
GOTO DONE
:CTRL+C
ECHO Hey, what gives? You pressed Ctrl+C to abort . . .
GOTO DONE
```

19

```
:NO_FILES
ECHO Bad news! No files were found to copy . . .
:DONE
```

As you can see, the ERRORLEVEL conditions check for the individual exit codes and then use GOTO to jump to the appropriate label.

> **NOTE**
>
> How does a batch file know what a command's exit code was? When Windows Home Server gets an exit code from a command, it stores it in a special data area set aside for exit code information. When Windows Home Server sees the IF ERRORLEVEL command in a batch file, it retrieves the exit code from the data area so that it can be compared to whatever is in the IF condition.

One of the most important things to know about the IF ERRORLEVEL test is how Windows Home Server interprets it. For example, consider the following IF command:

```
IF ERRORLEVEL 2 GOTO CTRL+C
```

Windows Home Server interprets this command as "If the exit code from the last command is equal to or greater than 2, jump to the CTRL+C label." This has two important consequences for your batch files:

- ▶ The test IF ERRORLEVEL 0 doesn't tell you much because it's always true. If you simply want to find out whether the command failed, use the test IF NOT ERRORLEVEL 0.

- ▶ To get the correct results, always test the *highest* ERRORLEVEL first and then work your way down.

Working with System Management Tools

System Management is one of those catch-all terms that encompasses a range of tasks, from simple adjustments such as changing the system date and time to more complex tweaks such as modifying the Registry. Windows Home Server's command-line system management tools also enable you to monitor system performance, shut down or restart the computer, and even modify the huge Windows Management Instrumentation (WMI) interface. Table 19.8 lists the system management command-line tools that apply to Windows Home Server.

The next few sections take more detailed looks at five of these command-line tools: REG, SHUTDOWN, SYSTEMINFO, TYPEPERF, and WHOAMI.

TABLE 19.8   Windows Home Server's Command-Line System Management Tools

Tool	Description
CHCP	Displays or changes the number of active console code pages.
DATE	Displays or sets the system date.
EVENTCREATE	Creates a custom event in an event log.
REG	Adds, modifies, displays, and deletes Registry keys and settings.
REGSVR32	Registers dynamic-link library (DLL) files as command components in the Registry.
SHUTDOWN	Shuts down or restarts Windows Home Server or a remote computer.
SYSTEMINFO	Displays a wide range of detailed configuration information about the computer.
TIME	Displays or sets the system time.
TYPEPERF	Monitors a performance counter.
WHOAMI	Displays information about the current user, including the domain name (not applicable to Windows Home Server), computer name, username, security group membership, and security privileges.
WMIC	Operates the Windows Management Instrumentation command-line tool that provides command-line access to the WMI interface.

REG: Working with Registry Keys and Settings

In Chapter 18, "Working with the Windows Home Server Registry," you learned how to view, add, and modify Registry keys and settings using the Registry Editor. That's the easiest and safest way to make Registry changes. However, there may be some settings that you change quite often. In such cases, it can become burdensome to frequently launch the Registry Editor and change the settings. A better idea is to create a shortcut or batch file that uses the REG command-line tool to make your Registry changes for you.

REG actually consists of 11 subcommands, each of which enables you to perform different Registry tasks:

REG ADD	Adds new keys or settings to the Registry. You can also use this command to modify existing settings.
REG QUERY	Displays the current values of one or more settings in one or more keys.
REG COMPARE	Compares the values of two Registry keys or settings.
REG COPY	Copies Registry keys or settings to another part of the Registry.
REG DELETE	Deletes a key or setting.
REG EXPORT	Exports a key to a .reg file.

19

REG IMPORT   Imports the contents of a `.reg` file.

REG SAVE   Copies Registry keys or settings to a hive (`.hiv`) file.

REG RESTORE   Writes a hive file into an existing Registry key. The hive file must be created using REG SAVE.

REG LOAD   Loads a hive file into a new Registry key. The hive file must be created using REG SAVE.

REG UNLOAD   Unloads a hive file that was loaded using REG LOAD.

I won't go through all these commands. Instead, I'll focus on the three most common Registry tasks: viewing, adding, and modifying Registry data.

Viewing Registry Data   To view the current value of the Registry setting, you use the REG QUERY command:

```
REG QUERY KeyName [/V SettingName ¦ /VE] [/C] [/D] [/E] [/F data] [/K ¦ [/S]
➥ [/SE separator] [/T type] [/Z]
```

KeyName   The Registry key that contains the setting or settings that you want to view. The *KeyName* must include a root key value: HKCR, HKCU, HKLM, HKU, or HKCC. Place quotation marks around key names that include spaces.

/V ValueName   The Registry setting in *KeyName* that you want to view.

/VE   Tells REG to look for empty settings (that is, settings with a null value).

/F data   Specifies the data that REG should match in the *KeyName* settings.

/C   Runs a case-sensitive query.

/E   Returns only exact matches.

/K   Queries only key names, not settings.

/S   Tells REG to query the subkeys of *KeyName*.

/SE separator   Defines the separator to search for in REG_MULTI_SZ settings.

/T type   Specifies the setting type or types to search: REG_SZ, REG_MULTI_SZ, REG_EXPAND_SZ, REG_DWORD, REG_BINARY, or REG_NONE.

/Z   Tells REG to include the numeric equivalent of the setting type in the query results.

For example, if you want to know the current value of the RegisteredOwner setting in HKLM\Software\Microsoft\Windows NT\CurrentVersion, you'd run the following command:

```
reg query "hklm\software\microsoft\windows nt\currentversion" /v registeredowner
```

The Registry Editor has a Find command that enables you to look for text within the Registry. However, it would occasionally be useful to see a list of the Registry keys and settings that contains a particular bit of text. You can do this using the /F switch. For example, suppose you want to see a list of all the HKLM keys and settings that contain the text *Home Server*. Here's a command that will do this:

```
reg query hklm /f "Home Server " /s
```

Adding Registry Data   To add a key or setting to the Registry, use the REG ADD command:

```
REG ADD KeyName [/V SettingName ¦ /VE] [/D data] [/F ¦ [/S separator] [/T type]
```

KeyName	The Registry key that you want to add or to which you want to add a setting. The *KeyName* must include a root key value: HKCR, HKCU, HKLM, HKU, or HKCC. Place quotation marks around key names that include spaces.
/V ValueName	The setting that you want to add to *KeyName*.
/VE	Tells REG to add an empty setting.
/D data	Specifies the data that REG should use as the value for the new setting.
/F	Modifies an existing key or setting without prompting to confirm the change.
/S separator	Defines the separator to use between multiple instances of data in a new REG_MULTI_SZ setting.
/T type	Specifies the setting type: REG_SZ, REG_MULTI_SZ, REG_EXPAND_SZ, REG_DWORD, REG_BINARY, or REG_NONE.

For example, the following command adds a key named MySettings to the HKCU root key:

```
reg add hkcu\MySettings
```

Here's another example that adds a setting named CurrentProject to the new MySettings key and sets the value of the new settings to WHS Unleashed:

```
reg add hkcu\MySettings /v CurrentProject /d "WHS Unleashed"
```

19

Modifying Registry Data   If you want to make changes to an existing setting, run REG ADD on the setting. For example, to change the HKCU\MySettings\CurrentProject setting to Windows Home Server Unleashed, you run the following command:

```
reg add hkcu\MySettings /v CurrentProject /d "Windows Home Server Unleashed"
```

Windows Home Server responds with the following prompt:

```
Value CurrentProject exists, overwrite (Yes/No)?
```

To change the existing value, press Y and press Enter.

TIP

To avoid being prompted when changing existing settings, add the /F switch to the REG ADD command.

SHUTDOWN: Shutting Down or Restarting a Computer

You can use the SHUTDOWN command to restart or shut down either the Windows Home Server computer or a remote computer on your network. Here's the syntax:

```
SHUTDOWN [[/R] ¦ [/S] ¦ [/L] ¦ [/H] ¦ [/I] ¦ [/P] ¦ [/E] ¦ [/A]] [/F¦
➥ [/T seconds] [/D [P:]xx:yy] [/M \\ComputerName] [/C "comment"]
```

/R	Restarts the computer.
/S	Shuts down the computer.
/L	Logs off the current user immediately.
/H	Puts the computer into hibernation, if the computer supports hibernation mode.
/I	Displays the Remote Shutdown dialog box, which enables you to specify many of the options provided by these switches.
/P	Turns off the local computer immediately (that is, without the usual warning interval).
/E	Enables you to document the reason for an unexpected shutdown. (Note that this switch does not work in Windows Home Server.)
/A	Cancels the pending restart or shutdown.
/F	Forces all running programs on the target computer to shut down without warning. This, obviously, is dangerous and should only be used as a last resort.
/D [P:]major:minor]	Specifies the reason for the shutdown. Include P: to indicate the shutdown is planned. Use values between 0 and 255 for major and between 0 and 65535 for minor. Windows Home Server also defines a number of predefined values for the major and minor parameters:

major	minor	Reason
0	0	Other (Planned)
0	5	Other Failure: System Unresponsive
1	1	Hardware: Maintenance (Unplanned)
1	1	Hardware: Maintenance (Planned)
1	2	Hardware: Installation (Unplanned)

1	2	Hardware: Installation (Planned)
2	3	Operating System: Upgrade (Planned)
2	4	Operating System: Reconfiguration (Unplanned)
2	4	Operating System: Reconfiguration (Planned)
2	16	Operating System: Service Pack (Planned)
2	17	Operating System: Hot Fix (Unplanned)
2	17	Operating System: Hot Fix (Planned)
2	18	Operating System: Security Fix (Unplanned)
2	18	Operating System: Security Fix (Planned)
4	1	Application: Maintenance (Unplanned)
4	1	Application: Maintenance (Planned)
4	2	Application: Installation (Planned)
4	5	Application: Unresponsive
4	6	Application: Unstable
5	15	System Failure: Stop Error
5	19	Security Issue
5	19	Security Issue
5	19	Security Issue
5	20	Loss of Network Connectivity (Unplanned)
6	11	Power Failure: Cord Unplugged
6	12	Power Failure: Environment
7	0	Legacy API Shutdown

/M *ComputerName*	Specifies the remote computer you want to shut down.
/T *seconds*	Specifies the number of seconds after which the computer is shut down. The default is 30 seconds, and you can specify any number up to 600.
/C "*comment*"	The *comment* text (which can be a maximum of 127 characters) appears in the dialog box and warns the user of the pending shutdown. This *comment* text also appears in the shutdown event that is added to the System log in Event Viewer. (Look for an Event ID of 1074.)

19

For example, to restart the local computer in 60 seconds, use the following command:

```
shutdown /r /t 60
```

When you enter the SHUTDOWN command, a System Shutdown dialog box appears and counts down to the shutdown time (see Figure 19.4, later in this section).

To document the shutdown, add the /D and /C switches, as in this example:

```
shutdown /s /d p:1:2 /c "Installing internal hard drive"
```

The reason code given by the /D switch and the comment specified by the /C switch appear in the event that Windows Home Server generates for the shutdown. You can see this event by launching Event Viewer (select Start, Administrative Tools, Event Viewer), opening the System log, and looking for a recent item with Event ID of 1074. Figure 19.2 shows an example.

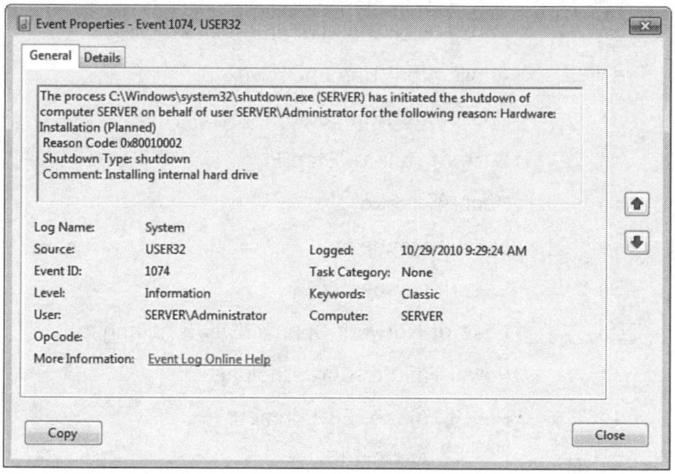

FIGURE 19.2   A shutdown event records the reason and comment that you specified with the SHUTDOWN command's /P and /C switches.

To shut down or restart a remote computer, you must run SHUTDOWN using the *remote* computer's Administrator account. This requires you to use the RUNAS command-line tool:

```
RUNAS /user:ComputerName\UserName cmd
```

ComputerName	The name of the remote computer.
UserName	The name of the account under which you want to run *cmd*.
cmd	The command you want to run.

For running SHUTDOWN with the /M switch, *UserName* will be Administrator and *cmd* will be the SHUTDOWN command, enclosed in quotation marks. Here's an example that shuts down a remote computer named OFFICEPC in 120 seconds:

```
runas /user:officepc\administrator "shutdown /s /m \\officepc /t 120"
```

When you enter the RUNAS command, Windows Home Server prompts you for the account password:

```
Enter the password for officepc\administrator:
```

Type the password (it doesn't appear onscreen), and press Enter.

TIP

If you need to embed a quotation mark in the *cmd* portion of RUNAS, precede it with a backslash (\). Here's an example:

```
runas /user:officepc\administrator "shutdown /s /m \\officepc
➥ /c \"Comment\""
```

This works fine on XP machines but not on Windows 7 and Vista PCs, because the Administrator account is disabled by default on Windows 7 and Vista systems. Here are the steps to follow to enable this account and set its password:

1. On the Windows 7 or Vista machine, press Windows Logo+R (or select Start, All Programs, Accessories, Run) to open the Run dialog box, type **lusrmgr.msc**, and click OK.
2. If you see the User Account Control dialog box, enter your credentials to continue.
3. In the Local User and Groups snap-in, click Users.
4. Double-click the Administrator account to open its property sheet.
5. Deactivate the Account Is Disabled check box, and then click OK.
6. Right-click the Administrator account, and then click Set Password. Windows warns you that changing an account password can cause problems.
7. You can ignore the warning in this case, so click Proceed to open the Set Password for Administrator dialog box.
8. Type the password in the New Password and Confirm Password text boxes, and then click OK.

Figure 19.3 shows an example of the dialog box that Windows 7 users see when the shutdown event is launched. Figure 19.4 shows the XP dialog box, which is also what the dialog box looks like on Windows Home Server.

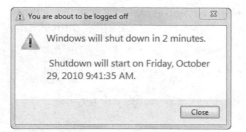

FIGURE 19.3   This is what a Windows 7 user sees when you start the shutdown process from a remote computer.

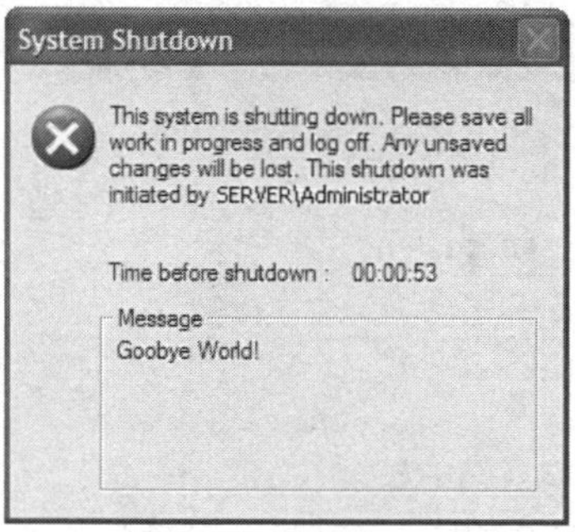

FIGURE 19.4   This is what a Windows XP user sees when you start the shutdown process from a remote computer.

If you need to cancel a pending shutdown on a remote computer, run SHUTDOWN with the /A switch before the timeout interval is over:

```
runas /user:officepc\administrator "shutdown /a /m \\officepc"
```

SYSTEMINFO: Returning System Configuration Data

If you want to get information about various aspects of your computer, a good place to start is the SYSTEMINFO command-line tool, which displays data about the following aspects of your system:

▶ The operating system name, version, and configuration type

▶ The registered owner and organization

▶ The original install date

▶ The system uptime

▶ The computer manufacturer, make, and model

▶ The system processors

▶ The BIOS version

▶ The total and available physical memory

▶ The paging file's maximum size, available size, in-use value, and location

▶ The installed hotfixes

▶ The network interface card data, such as the name, connection, Dynamic Host Configuration Protocol (DHCP) status, and IP address (or addresses)

You can see all this data (and more), as well as control the output, by running SYSTEMINFO with the following syntax:

```
SYSTEMINFO [/S ComputerName] [/U [Domain]\UserName] [/P Password]
➡ [/FO Format] [/NH]
```

/S ComputerName   The name of the remote computer for which you want to view the system configuration.

/U [Domain]\UserName The username and, optionally, the domain, of the account under which you want to run the SYSTEMINFO command.

/P Password   The password of the account you specified with /U.

/FO Format   The output format, where format is one of the following values:

                      table—The output is displayed in a row-and-column format, with headers in the first row and values in subsequent rows.

                      list—The output is displayed in a two-column list, with the headers in the first column and values in the second column.

                      csv—The output is displayed with headers and values separated by commas. The headers appear on the first line.

/NH   Tells SYSTEMINFO not to include column headers when you use the /FO switch with either table or csv.

The output of SYSTEMINFO is quite long, so pipe it through the MORE command to see the output one screen at a time:

```
systeminfo ¦ more
```

If you want to examine the output in another program or import the results into Excel or Access, redirect the output to a file and use the appropriate format. For example, Excel can read .csv files, so you can redirect the SYSTEMINFO output to a .csv file while using csv as the output format:

```
systeminfo /fo csv > systeminfo.csv
```

19

TYPEPERF: Monitoring Performance

In Chapter 15, "Tuning Windows Home Server Performance," you learned how to use the System Monitor utility to track the real-time performance of counters in various categories, such as processor and memory.

▶ **SEE** "Monitoring Performance with Performance Monitor," **P. 384**.

You can get the same benefit without the System Monitor GUI by using the powerful TYPEPERF command-line tool. Here's the syntax:

```
TYPEPERF [counter1 [counter2 ...]] [-CF file] [-O file] [-F format]
➡ [-SI interval] [-SC samples] [-Q [object]] [-QX [object]]
➡ [-CONFIG file] [-S computer]
```

counter1 [*counter2* ...]	Specifies the path of the performance counter to monitor. If you want to track multiple counters, separate each counter path with a space. If any path includes spaces, surround the path with quotation marks.
-CF *file*	Loads the counters from *file*, where *file* is a text file that lists the counter paths on separate lines.
-O *file*	Specifies the path and name of the file that will store the performance data.
-F *format*	Specifies the format for the output file format given by the /O switch, where *format* is one of the following values:
	csv—The output is displayed with each counter separated by a comma and each sample on its own line. This is the default output format.
	tsv—The output is displayed with each counter separated by a tab and each sample on its own line.
	bin—The output is displayed in binary format.
	sql—The output is displayed in SQL log format.
-SI *interval*	Specifies the time interval between samples. The *interval* parameter uses the form [mm:]ss. The default interval is 1 second.
-SC *samples*	Specifies the number of samples to collect. If you omit this switch, TYPEPERF samples continuously until you press Ctrl+C to cancel.
-Q [*object*]	Lists the available counters for *object* without instances.
-QX [*object*]	Lists the available counters for *object* with instances.
-CONFIG *file*	Specifies the pathname of the settings file that contains the TYPEPERF parameters you want to run.
-S *computer*	Specifies that the performance counters should be monitored on the PC named *computer* if no computer name is specified in the counter path.
-Y	Answers yes to any prompts generated by TYPEPERF.

The official syntax of a counter path looks like this:

```
[\\Computer]\Object([Parent/][Instance][#Index])\Counter
```

Computer	The computer on which the counter is to be monitored. If you omit a computer name, TYPEPERF monitors the counter on the local computer.
Object	The performance object—such as Processor, Memory, or PhysicalDisk—that contains the counter.
Parent	The container instance of the specified *Instance*.
Instance	The instance of the *Object*, if it has multiple instances. For example, in a two- (or dual-core) processor system, the instances are 0 (for the first processor), 1 (for the second processor), or _Total (for both processors combined). You can also using an asterisk (*) to represent all the instances in *Object*.
Index	The index number of the specified *Instance*.
Counter	The name of the performance counter. You can also use an asterisk (*) to represent all the counters in *Object* (*Instance*).

In practice, however, you rarely use the *Computer, Parent,* and *Index* parts of the path, so most counter paths use one of the following two formats:

```
\Object\Counter
\Object(Instance)\Counter
```

For example, here's the path for the Memory object's Available MBytes counter:

```
\Memory\Available MBytes
```

Here's a TYPEPERF command that displays five samples of this counter:

```
typeperf "\Memory\Available Mbytes" -sc 5
```

Similarly, here's the path for the Processor object's % Processor Time counter, using the first processor instance:

```
\Processor(0)\% Processor Time
```

Here's a TYPEPERF command that displays 10 samples of this counter every 3 seconds and saves the results to a file named ProcessorTime.txt:

```
typeperf "\Processor(0)\% Processor Time" -sc 10 -si 3 -o ProcessorTime.txt
```

To use the -CONFIG parameter with TYPEPERF, you need to create a text file that stores the command-line parameters you want to use. This configuration file consists of a series of parameter/value pairs that use the following general format:

19

```
[Parameter]
Value
```

Here, *Parameter* is text that specifies a TYPEPERF parameter—such as F for the -F parameter and S for the -S parameter. Use C to specify one or more counter paths—and *Value* as the value you want to assign to the parameter.

For example, consider the following command:

```
typeperf "\PhysicalDisk(_Total)\% Idle Time" -si 5 -sc 10 -o idletime.txt
```

To run the same command using the -CONFIG parameter, you first need to create a file with the following text:

```
[c]
\PhysicalDisk(_Total)\% Idle Time
[si]
5
[sc]
10
[o]
idletime.txt
```

If this file is named IdleTimeCounter.txt, you can run it at any time with the following command (assuming IdleTimeCounter.txt resides in the current folder):

```
typeperf -config IdleTimeCounter.txt
```

WHOAMI: Getting Information About the Current User

The WHOAMI command gives you information about the user who is currently logged on to the computer:

```
WHOAMI [/UPN ¦ /FQDN ¦ LOGONID] [/USER ¦ /GROUPS ¦ /PRIV] [/ALL] [/FO format]
```

/UPN	(Domains only) Returns the current user's name using the user principal name (UPN) format.
/FQDN	(Domains only) Returns the current user's name using the fully qualified domain name (FQDN) format.
/LOGONID	Returns the current user's security identifier (SID).
/USER	Returns the current username using the *computer\user* format.
/GROUPS	Returns the groups of which the current user is a member.
/PRIV	Returns the current user's privileges.
/ALL	Returns the current user's SID, username, groups, and privileges.

/FO *format*   The output format, where *format* is one of the following values:

> table—The output is displayed in a row-and-column format, with headers in the first row and values in subsequent rows.

> list—The output is displayed in a two-column list, with the headers in the first column and values in the second column.

> csv—The output is displayed with headers and values separated by commas. The headers appear on the first line.

You probably won't use this command often on the Windows Home Server computer because you'll almost always be logged on as Administrator. However, WHOAMI is useful when you're working on a client computer and you're not sure who is currently logged on.

For example, the following command redirects the current user's SID, username, groups, and privileges to a file named whoami.txt using the list format:

```
whoami /all /fo list > whoami.txt
```

From Here

- ▶ For details on setting up a time server using the command line, **SEE** "Specifying the Time Server at the Command Prompt," **P. 81.**

- ▶ To learn more about the Advanced Options menu, **SEE** "Configuring Startup with the Advanced Boot Options Menu," **P. 90.**

- ▶ To learn how to use the CONVERT tool to convert a FAT32 drive to NTFS, **SEE** "Run the CONVERT Utility," **P. 214.**

- ▶ To learn how to use System Monitor, **SEE** "Monitoring Performance with Performance Monitor," **P. 384.**

- ▶ For details on viewing system uptime with SYSTEMINFO, **SEE** "Displaying Uptime with the SYSTEMINFO Command," **P. 408.**

- ▶ For information on Check Disk and the types of errors it looks for, **SEE** "Checking Your Hard Disk for Errors," **P. 411.**

19

CHAPTER **20**

Using Other Windows Home Server Power Tools

IN THIS CHAPTER

▶ Using the Local Group Policy Editor

▶ Getting More Out of Control Panel

▶ Configuring the Microsoft Management Console

▶ Controlling Services

▶ Setting Up a Fax Server

One of the main themes of this book has been that getting the most out of Windows Home Server often means eschewing the Windows Home Server Dashboard program and getting your hands on the operating system (OS) itself, particularly because that OS is really just Windows Server 2008 R2 in disguise. Throughout the book, I've shown you how to use various OS tools to tweak, improve, and customize your system. These tools have included Device Manager, Event Viewer, Internet Information Services Manager, Network Diagnostics, Registry Editor, Remote Desktop Connection, System Configuration Manager, System Information, Performance Monitor, Task Manager, and Remote Desktop Services Manager, to name but a few.

That's a long list, but we're not done—not by a long shot. Windows Home Server still has a few other power tools that will be welcome additions to your Windows Home Server workshop, and this chapter shows you how to use them. The chapter begins by taking a closer look at several tools that you've used already in this book: Local Group Policy Editor, Control Panel, and the Microsoft Management Console (MMC). You also learn how to control services and configure a fax server.

Using the Local Group Policy Editor

Group policies are settings that control how Windows Home Server works. You can use them to customize the Windows Home Server interface, enable or disable features, specify security settings, and much more.

Group policies are mostly used by system administrators who want to make sure that novice users don't have access to dangerous tools (such as the Registry Editor) or who want to ensure a consistent computing experience across multiple machines. Group policies are also ideally suited to situations in which multiple users share a single computer. However, group policies are also useful on single-user standalone machines, as you've seen in several places in this book.

▶ In Chapter 4, "Configuring Windows Home Server," you learned how to use group policies to set up programs or scripts to launch at startup. **SEE** "Launching Items Using Group Policies," **P. 96.**

▶ In Chapter 11, "Implementing Windows Home Server Security," I showed you how to activate Windows Home Server's security auditing policies. **SEE** "Activating the Auditing Policies," **P. 258.**

▶ In Chapter 14, "Patching Home Computers with WSUS," you learned how to enable a group policy that forces client computers to check for updates on a WSUS server. **SEE** "Connecting Home Computers to WSUS," **P. 363.**

In this section, you learn the details of working with group policies using the Local Group Policy Editor, and I take you through a few more useful group policy settings.

Working with Group Policies

You implement group policies using the Local Group Policy Editor, which is a Microsoft Management Console snap-in. To start the Local Group Policy Editor, select Start (or Start, Run), type `gpedit.msc`, and then press Enter.

The Local Group Policy Editor window that appears is divided into two sections:

▶ **Left pane**—This pane contains a treelike hierarchy of policy categories, which is divided into two main categories: Computer Configuration and User Configuration. The Computer Configuration policies apply to all users and are implemented before the logon. The User Configuration policies apply only to the current user and, therefore, are not applied until that user logs on.

▶ **Right pane**—This pane contains the policies for whichever category is selected in the left pane.

The idea, then, is to open the tree's branches to find the category you want. When you click the category, its policies appear in the right pane. For example, Figure 20.1 shows the Local Group Policy Editor window with the Computer Configuration, Administrative Templates, System, Logon category selected.

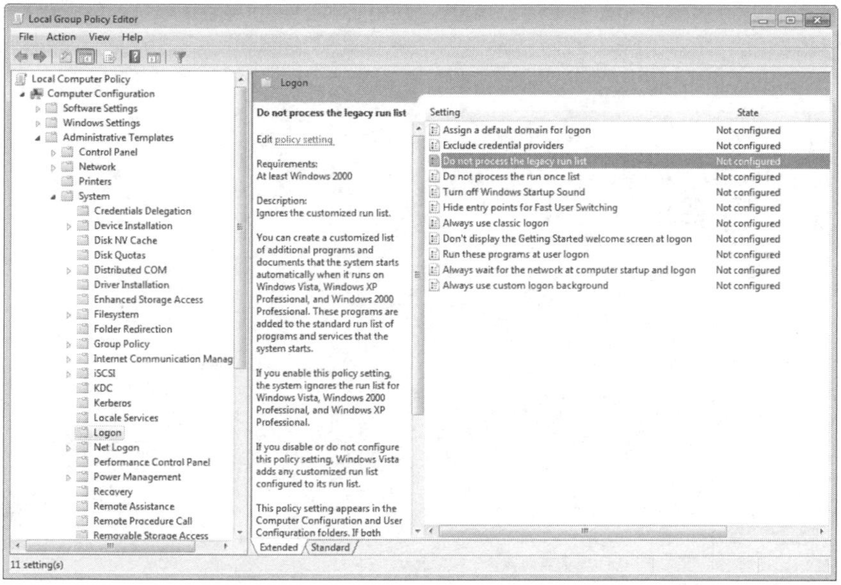

FIGURE 20.1   When you select a category in the left pane, the category's policies appear in the right pane.

TIP

Windows Home Server comes with another snap-in, Local Security Settings, which displays only the policies found in the Local Group Policy Editor's Computer Configuration, Windows Settings, Security Settings branch. To launch the Local Security Settings snap-in, select Start (or Start, Run), type `secpol.msc`, and press Enter. You can also select Start, Administrative Tools, Local Security Policy.

In the right pane, the Setting column tells you the name of the policy, and the State column tells you the current state of the policy. Click a policy to see its description on the left side of the pane, as shown in Figure 20.1. To configure a policy, double-click it. The type of window you see depends on the policy:

▶ For simple policies, you see a window similar to the one shown in Figure 20.2. These kinds of policies take one of three states: Not Configured (the policy is not in effect), Enabled (the policy is in effect and its setting is enabled), and Disabled (the policy is in effect but its setting is disabled).

▶ Other kinds of policies also require extra information when the policy is enabled. For example, Figure 20.3 shows the window for the Run These Programs at User Logon policy. When Enabled is activated, the Show button appears; you use it to specify one or more programs that run when the computer starts.

20

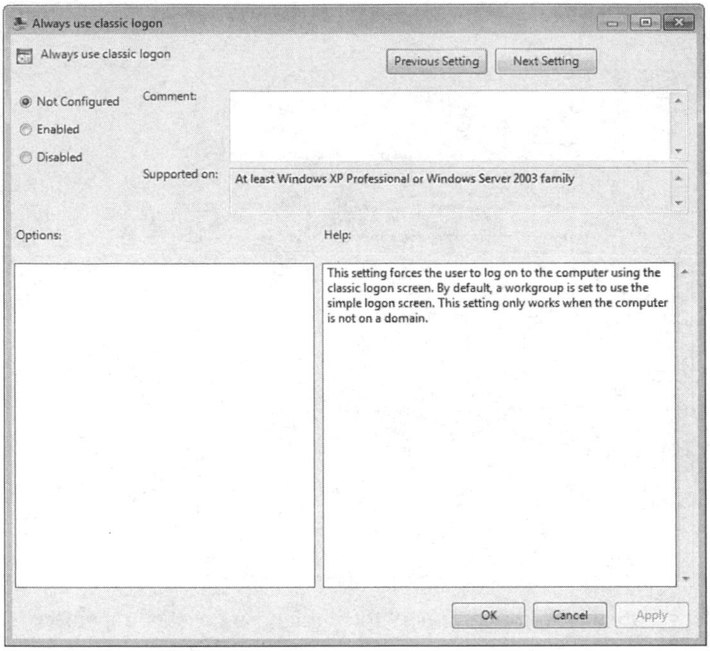

FIGURE 20.2   Simple policies are Not Configured, Enabled, or Disabled.

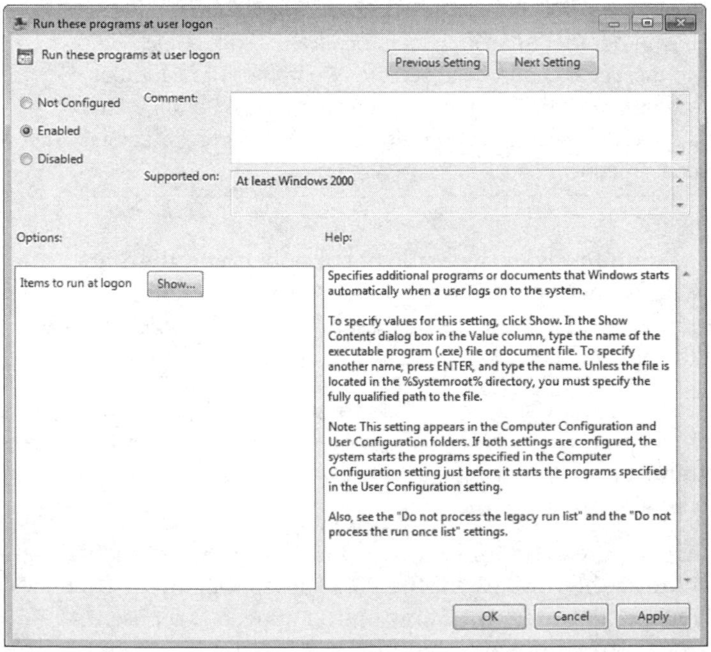

FIGURE 20.3   More complex policies also require extra information such as, in this case, a list of programs to run at logon.

TIP

After you apply some group policies, you may forget which ones you applied, or you may want to see a summary of the applied policies. You can see such a summary by opening the Resultant Set of Policy snap-in. (Select Start, Run, type `rsop.msc,` and click OK.) The snap-in looks much like the Local Group Policy Editor, except the only sub-branches you see are those that have applied policies.

Customizing the Windows Security Screen

When you press Ctrl+Alt+Delete while logged on to Windows Home Server, you see the Windows Security screen, which contains the following links, as shown in Figure 20.4:

Lock This Computer

Click this link to hide the desktop and display the Computer Locked screen. To return to the desktop, you must press Ctrl+Alt+Delete and then enter your Windows Home Server password. This is useful if you're going to leave Windows Home Server unattended and don't want another person accessing the desktop. However, Windows Home Server offers a faster way to lock the computer: Press Windows Logo+L.

Switch User

Click this link to log on with another user account while keeping the Administrator account logged on in the background. Most Windows Home Server systems use only the Administrator account, so it's unlikely you'll find this link useful.

Log Off

Click this link to log off the Administrator account. You can also log off by selecting Start, Log Off.

Change a Password

Click this link to specify a new password for the Administrator account. In Windows Home Server, you're better off doing this through the Windows Home Server Dashboard application.

▶ **SEE** "Changing the Windows Home Server Password," **P. 88**.

Start Task Manager

Click this link to open Task Manager. You've seen elsewhere in this book that Task Manager is a useful tool, but Windows Home Server offers two faster methods to open it: Press Ctrl+Shift+Esc, or right-click the taskbar and then click Task Manager.

▶ **SEE** "Monitoring Performance with Task Manager," **P. 370**.

Shut Down

Click this button in the lower-right corner of the screen to shut down Windows Home Server. Alternatively, click the arrow and then click Restart to reboot the server. You can also restart or turn off Windows Home Server by selecting Start, Shut Down.

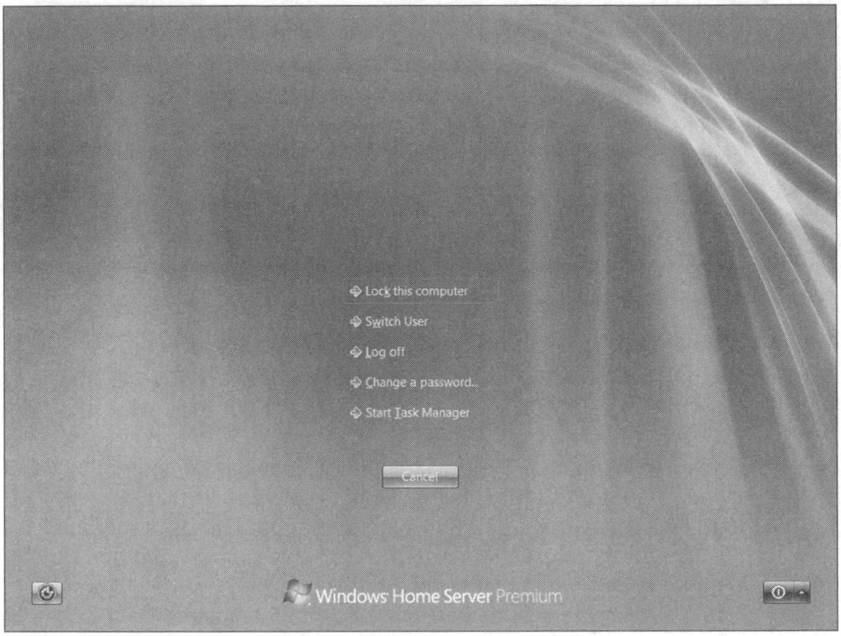

FIGURE 20.4   In Windows Home Server, press Ctrl+Alt+Delete to display the Windows Security screen.

Of these five commands, the four (all except Switch User) are customizable using group policies. So if you find that you never use one or more of those commands, you can use group policies to disable them in the Windows Security screen. Here are the steps to follow:

1. Open the Local Group Policy Editor window, as described earlier in this chapter.

2. Open the User Configuration, Administrative Templates, System, Ctrl+Alt+Del Options branch.

3. Double-click one of the following policies:

   ▶ **Remove Change Password**—You can use this policy to disable the Change a Password link in the Windows Security screen.

   ▶ **Remove Lock Computer**—You can use this policy to disable the Lock this Computer link in the Windows Security screen.

   ▶ **Remove Task Manager**—You can use this policy to disable the Start Task Manager link in the Windows Security screen.

   ▶ **Remove Logoff**—You can use this policy to disable the Log Off link in the Windows Security screen.

4. In the policy dialog box that appears, click Enabled, and then click OK.

5. Repeat steps 3 and 4 to disable all the buttons you don't need.

Figure 20.5 shows the Windows Security screen box with the four links disabled.

Switch User

Cancel

Windows Home Server Premium

FIGURE 20.5   You can use group policies to disable most of the buttons in the Windows Security dialog box.

Customizing the Places Bar

Most file-based applications in Windows Home Server use the common Save As dialog box that's employed to save a file in an application (usually by selecting File, Save or by pressing Ctrl+O for a new, unsaved file, or by selecting File, Save As for a saved file). The common Save As dialog box is a scaled-down version of Explorer, so it presents an easy and familiar interface.

However, many legacy applications use an older version of the Save As dialog box that looks like the one shown in Figure 20.6.

> **NOTE**
>
> The same Places Bar also appears in the older version of the common Open dialog box, which appears when you select File, Open or press Ctrl+O when using a legacy application.

Notice in Figure 20.6 that the left side of the common Save As dialog box contains a strip called the Places Bar, which contains icons for five shell folders: Recent Places, Desktop, Libraries, Computer, and Network. These icons are handy navigation tools, but only if you use the default folders.

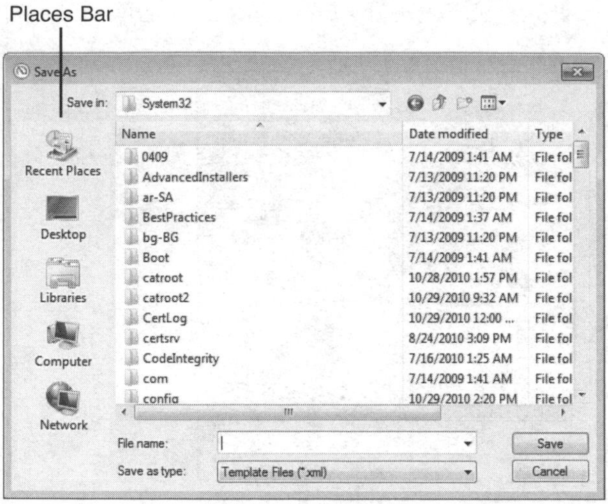

Places Bar

FIGURE 20.6 Many legacy applications display this older version of the Save As dialog box when you select the File, Save As command.

Fortunately, if you have other folders that you use more frequently, you can use a group policy to customize the Places Bar icons. You can replace the existing Places Bar icons with up to five items, which can be any combination of the following:

▶ **A local folder path**—For example, someone who writes a lot of scripts for Windows Home Server might set up a `Scripts` folder within `My Documents`. In that case, you could add `%UserProfile%\My Documents\Scripts` to the Places Bar. Note that in this case, only the name of the subfolder appears in the Places Bar. (That is, you don't see the entire folder path.)

▶ **A UNC path to a shared network folder**—For example, this would be ideal for accessing those Windows Home Server shares that you use most often. In this case, Windows Home Server displays the Places Bar icon with the name *Share on Computer*, where *Share* is the name of the shared folder and *Computer* is the name of the computer that's sharing the folder. (The exception to this is when you add a subfolder of the share to the Places Bar. In that case, you see just the subfolder name.)

▶ **A Windows Home Server shell folder**—The following table lists some of the common shell folders.

Shell Folder	Path
CommonDocuments	%Public%\Public Documents
CommonMusic	%Public%\Public Music
CommonPictures	%Public%\Public Pictures
Desktop	%UserProfile%\Desktop
MyComputer	Computer folder

Shell Folder	Path
MyDocuments	%UserProfile%\My Documents
MyFavorites	%UserProfile%\Favorites
MyMusic	%UserProfile%\My Music
MyNetworkPlaces	%AppData%\Microsoft\Windows\Network Shortcuts
MyPictures	%UserProfile%\My Pictures
Printers	Control Panel, Printers
ProgramFiles	C:\Program Files\
Recent	%UserProfile%\Recent

Follow these steps to use a group policy to customize the Places Bar:

1. Open the Local Group Policy Editor window, as described earlier in this chapter.
2. Navigate to the User Configuration, Administrative Templates, Windows Components, Windows Explorer, Common Open File Dialog branch.
3. Double-click the Items Displayed in Places Bar policy.
4. Activate the Enabled option.
5. Use the text boxes in the Places to Display section to specify the local folders, network paths, or shell folders that you want to include in the Places Bar.
6. Click OK.

Figure 20.7 shows the Items Displayed in Places Bar policy enabled and with some custom items added, and Figure 20.8 shows the resulting Places Bar in the legacy common Save As dialog box. (The same customized Places Bar also appears in the legacy common Open dialog box.)

> **NOTE**
>
> If you don't use the Places Bar at all, you might prefer to hide it to give yourself more room in the legacy Open and Save As dialog boxes. To do that, open the Local Group Policy Editor and navigate to the User Configuration, Administrative Templates, Windows Components, Windows Explorer, Common Open File Dialog branch. Double-click the Hide the Common Dialog Places Bar, click Enabled, and then click OK.

Increasing the Size of the Recent Documents List

If you work with files on the Windows Home Server machine, you can customize the Windows Home Server Start menu to include the Recent Items menu, which displays a list of the 15 documents you worked on most recently. Right-click Start, click Properties, click Customize, activate the Recent Items check box, and then click OK.

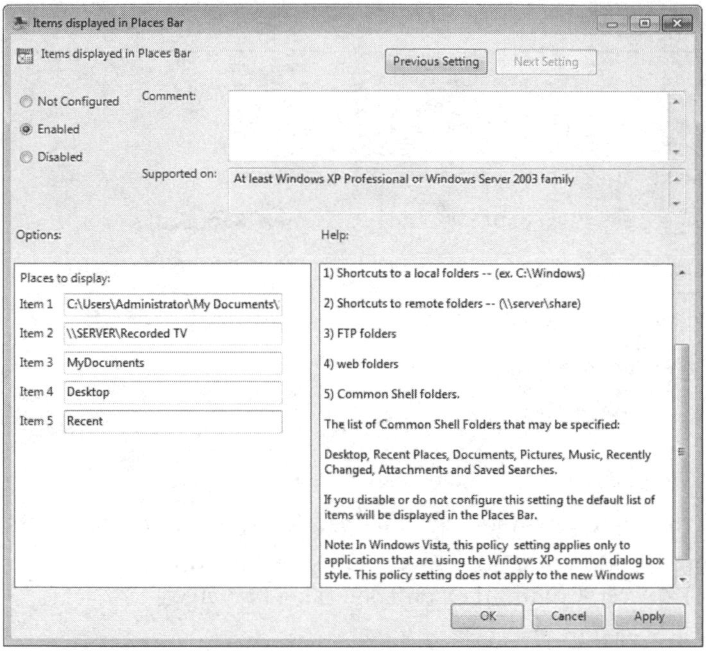

FIGURE 20.7   Use the Items Displayed in Places Bar policy to customize the Places Bar.

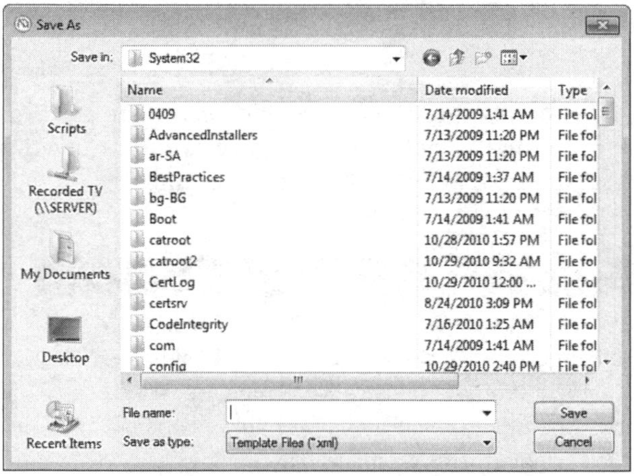

FIGURE 20.8   The legacy common Save As dialog box showing the custom Places Bar items specified in Figure 20.7.

Fifteen documents should be plenty on any Windows Home Server machine that you use purely as a server. However, if you also use Windows Home Server as a workstation or development platform, you may find that 15 documents isn't enough. In that case, you can use a group policy to configure Windows Home Server to display a higher number of recent documents.

Here are the steps to follow to customize the size of the My Recent Documents list:

1. Open the Local Group Policy Editor window, as described earlier in this chapter.

2. Navigate to the User Configuration, Administrative Templates, Windows Components, Windows Explorer branch.

3. Double-click the Maximum Number of Recent Documents policy.

4. Click Enabled.

5. Use the Maximum Number of Recent Documents spin box to specify the number of documents you want Windows Home Server to display (see Figure 20.9).

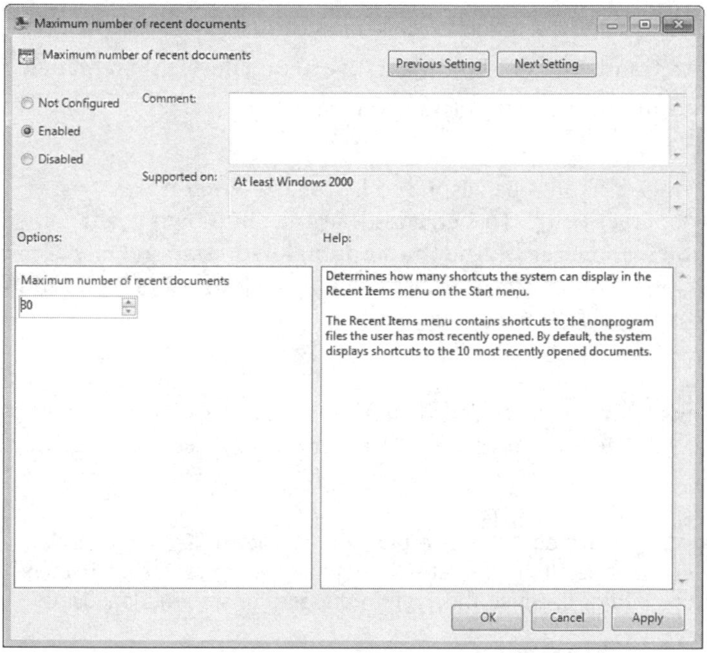

FIGURE 20.9   Use the Maximum Number of Recent Documents policy to customize the size of the Start menu's Recent Items list.

6. Click OK.

NOTE

You can specify a value between 1 and 9999 (!) in the Maximum Number of Recent Documents spin box. If you specify more documents than can fit vertically on your screen, Windows Home Server adds scroll buttons to the top and bottom of the Recent Items menu.

Enabling the Shutdown Event Tracker

In Windows Home Server, when you select Start, Shut Down (or click the Shut Down button in the Windows Security screen as described earlier; see "Customizing the Windows Security Screen"), Windows Home Server goes right ahead and shuts down the system.

If you want to keep track of why you shut down or restarted Windows Home Server, you can enable a feature called Shutdown Event Tracker. With this feature, you can document the shutdown event by specifying whether it is planned or unplanned, selecting a reason for the shutdown, and adding a comment that describes the shutdown.

Here are the steps to follow to use a group policy to enable the Shutdown Event Tracker feature:

1. Open the Local Group Policy Editor window, as described earlier in this chapter.
2. Navigate to the Computer Configuration, Administrative Templates, System branch.
3. Double-click the Display Shutdown Event Tracker policy.
4. Click Enabled.
5. In the Shutdown Event Tracker Should Be Displayed list, select either Always (as shown in Figure 20.10) or Server Only. (This ensures that the Shutdown Event Tracker appears in Windows Home Server; the third option—Workstation Only— displays the Tracker only on computers running as a client, such as XP or Vista, so it doesn't apply to Windows Home Server.)
6. Click OK.

Now when you select Start, Shut Down, you see the version of the Shut Down Windows dialog box shown in Figure 20.11. The Shutdown Event Tracker group gives you three new controls to operate:

Planned   Leave this check box activated if this is a planned shutdown. If you didn't plan on shutting down Windows Home Server (for example, you're restarting because a program has crashed or because the system appears unstable), deactivate this check box.

Option   Use this list to select the reason for the shutdown. (Note that the items you see in this list change depending on the state of the Planned check box.)

Comment   Use this text box to describe the shutdown event. If you choose either Other (Planned) or Other (Unplanned) in the Option list, you must add a comment to enable the OK button; for all other items in the Option list, the Comment text is optional.

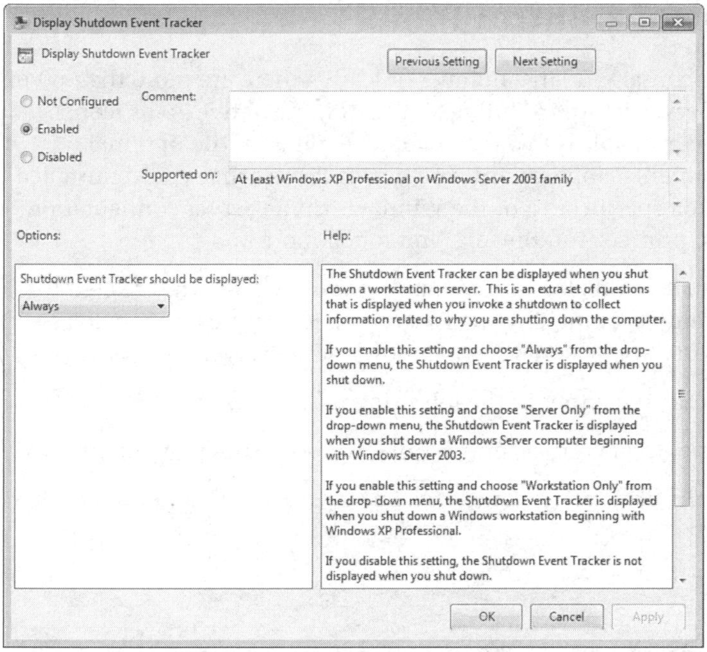

FIGURE 20.10   To document Windows Home Server shutdowns, enable the Display Shutdown Event Tracker policy.

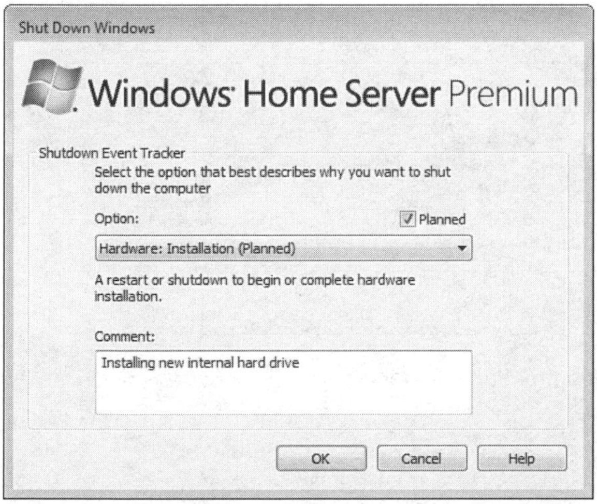

FIGURE 20.11   The Shut Down Windows dialog box with the Shutdown Event Tracker feature enabled.

20

Getting More Out of Control Panel

Control Panel is a folder that contains a large number of icons—there are more than 60 in the default Windows Home Server setup (including all the Administrative Tools icons). However, more icons could be available on your system depending on the optional Windows Home Server components, applications, and device drivers that you've installed. Each of these icons deals with a specific area of the Windows Home Server configuration: hardware, applications, fonts, printers, multimedia, and much more.

Opening an icon displays (usually) a dialog box containing various properties related to that area of Windows. For example, launching the Programs and Features icon enables you to install or uninstall third-party applications and Windows Home Server components.

To view the Control Panel icons, use either of the following techniques:

▶ Select Start, Control Panel to open the Control Panel window, shown in Figure 20.12.

▶ In Explorer, right-click the Navigation pane, click Show All Folders, and then click Control Panel.

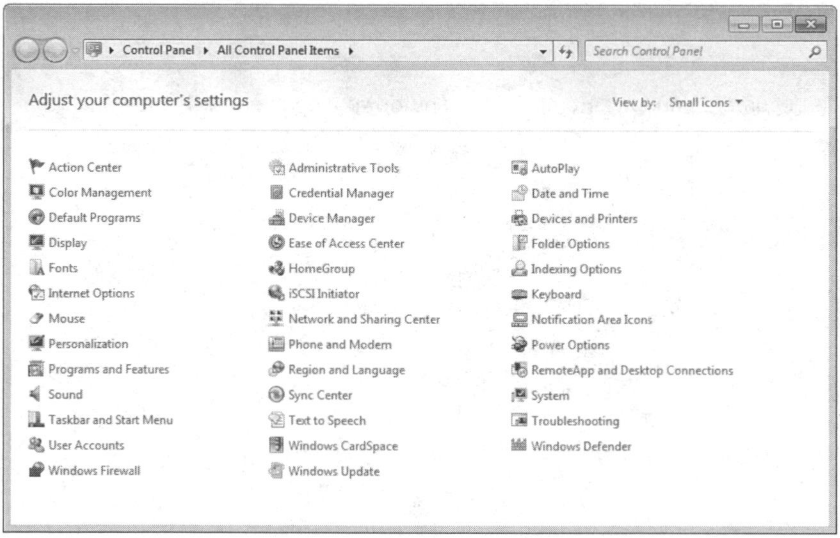

FIGURE 20.12   Windows Home Server's Control Panel folder.

Reviewing Control Panel Icons

To help you familiarize yourself with what's available in Control Panel, this section offers summary descriptions of the Control Panel icons found in a standard Windows Home Server installation. Note that your system might have extra icons, depending on your system's configuration and the programs you have installed.

▶ **Action Center**—Displays a list of your computer's current security issues and hardware and software problems.

▶ **Administrative Tools**—Displays a window with more icons, each of which enables you to administer a particular aspect of Windows Home Server. Many of these apply only to Windows Server 2008 machines operating in a domain environment. Here are the icons that work with Windows Home Server:

  ▶ **Remote Desktop Services**—Contains icons that enable you to configure and create Remote Desktop connections to network clients.

  ▶ **Certification Authority**—Enables you to view and work with security certificates.

  ▶ **Component Services**—Enables you to configure and administer Component Object Model (COM) components and COM+ applications.

  ▶ **Computer Management**—Enables you to manage a local or remote computer. You can examine hidden and visible shared folders, set group policies, access Device Manager, manage hard disks, and much more.

  ▶ **Data Sources (ODBC)**—Enables you to create and work with data sources, which are connection strings that you use to connect to local or remote databases.

  ▶ **Event Viewer**—Enables you to examine Windows Home Server's list of *events*, which are unusual or noteworthy occurrences on your system. An event might be a service that doesn't start, the installation of a device, or an application error.

  ▶ **Internet Information Services (IIS) Manager**—Enables you to create and configure websites hosted on Windows Home Server, as described in Chapter 12, "Setting Up a Windows Home Server Website."

  ▶ **iSCSI Initiator**—Displays the iSCSI Initiator property sheet, which enables you to manage connections to iSCSI devices such as tape drives.

  ▶ **Local Security Policy**—Displays the Local Security Settings snap-in, which enables you to set up security policies on your system.

  ▶ **Network Policy Server**—Enables you to create and configure network-wide access policies.

  ▶ **Performance Monitor**—Enables you to monitor the performance of your system using Performance Monitor, performance logs, and alerts as explained in Chapter 15, "Tuning Windows Home Server Performance."

  ▶ **Security Configuration Wizard**—Runs a wizard that enables you to create a security policy for network servers.

  ▶ **Server Manager**—Enables you to add and configure roles, features, storage, and other aspects of the server.

20

- ▸ **Services**—Displays a list of the system services available with Windows Home Server. See "Controlling Services," later in this chapter.

- ▸ **Share and Storage Management**—Enables you to view and control the server's shared folders and storage.

- ▸ **Storage Explorer**—Enables you to view advanced storage technologies on the server.

- ▸ **System Configuration**—Opens the System Configuration utility.

- ▸ **Task Scheduler**—Runs the Task Scheduler console, which enables you to run programs or scripts on a schedule.

- ▸ **Windows Firewall with Advanced Security**—Enables you to control every aspect of Windows Home Server's bidirectional firewall.

- ▸ **Windows Memory Diagnostic**—Runs the Windows Memory Diagnostics Tool, which checks your computer's memory chips for problems.

- ▸ **Windows PowerShell Modules**—Loads the system's PowerShell modules.

- ▸ **Windows Server Backup**—Runs the Windows Server Backup program. You should use the backup feature that comes with Windows Home Server, instead.

- ▸ **AutoPlay**—Opens the AutoPlay window, which enables you to configure AutoPlay defaults for various media.

- ▸ **Color Management**—Enables you to configure the colors of your monitor and printer to optimize color output.

- ▸ **Credential Manager**—This new tool enables you to store and work with usernames and passwords for servers, websites, network shares, and other secure resources.

- ▸ **Date and Time**—Enables you to set the current date and time, select your time zone, and set up an Internet time server to synchronize your system time.

- ▸ **Default Programs**—Displays the Default Programs window, which enables you to change the programs that are associated with Windows Home Server's file types.

- ▸ **Device Manager**—Launches Device Manager, which enables you to view and work with your system devices and their drivers. See Chapter 17, "Troubleshooting Windows Home Server," for more information.

- ▸ **Devices and Printers**—Displays a list of the major devices connected to your computer. This is the same as selecting Start, Devices and Printers.

- ▸ **Display**—Offers a large number of customization options for the desktop, screensaver, video card, monitor, and other display components.

- ▸ **Ease of Access Center**—Enables you to customize input—the keyboard and mouse—and output—sound and display—for users with special mobility, hearing, or vision requirements

▶ **Folder Options**—Enables you to customize the display of Windows Home Server's folders, set up whether Windows Home Server uses single- or double-clicking, work with file types, and configure offline files.

▶ **Fonts**—Displays the Fonts folder, from which you can view, install, and remove fonts.

▶ **HomeGroup**—Enables you to join a home group, which is a user account-free networking technology introduced with Windows 7.

▶ **Indexing Options**—Enables you to configure the indexing settings used by Windows Desktop Search.

▶ **Internet Options**—Displays a large collection of settings for modifying Internet properties (how you connect, the Internet Explorer interface, and so on).

▶ **iSCSI Initiator**—Displays the iSCSI Initiator property sheet, which enables you to manage connections to iSCSI devices such as tape drives.

▶ **Keyboard**—Enables you to customize your keyboard, work with keyboard languages, and change the keyboard driver.

▶ **Mouse**—Enables you to set various mouse options and to install a different mouse device driver.

▶ **Network and Sharing Center**—Displays general information about your network connections and sharing settings.

▶ **Notification Area Icons**—Gives you access to notification area customization options.

▶ **Personalization**—Offers a large number of customization options for the current Windows Home Server theme: glass effects, colors, desktop background, screensaver, sounds, mouse pointers, and display settings.

▶ **Phone and Modem**—Enables you to configure telephone dialing rules and to install and configure modems.

▶ **Power Options**—Enables you to configure power management properties for powering down system components (such as the monitor and hard drive), defining low-power alarms for notebook batteries, enabling hibernation, and configuring an uninterruptible power supply.

▶ **Programs and Features**—Enables you to install and uninstall applications, add and remove Windows Home Server components, and view installed updates.

▶ **Region and Language**—Enables you to configure international settings for country-dependent items, such as numbers, currencies, times, and dates.

▶ **RemoteApp and Desktop Connections**—Enables you to create and work with remote programs and desktops.

▶ **Sound**—Enables you to control the system volume; map sounds to specific Windows Home Server events (such as closing a program or minimizing a window); and specify settings for audio, voice, and other multimedia devices.

▶ **Sync Center**—Enables you to set up and maintain synchronization with other devices and with offline files.

▶ **System**—Gives you access to a large number of system properties, including the computer name and workgroup; Device Manager and hardware profiles; and settings related to performance, startup, Automatic Updates, Remote Assistance, and Remote Desktop.

▶ **Taskbar and Start Menu**—Enables you to customize the taskbar and Start menu.

▶ **Text to Speech**—Enables you to configure Windows Home Server's text-to-speech feature.

▶ **Troubleshooting**—Displays a collection of tasks related to troubleshooting various aspects of your system.

▶ **User Accounts**—Enables you to set up and configure user accounts.

▶ **Windows CardSpace**—Enables you to use Microsoft's new CardSpace system to manage your personal online data.

▶ **Windows Defender**—Launches Windows Defender, Windows Home Server's anti-spyware program.

▶ **Windows Firewall**—Enables you to activate and configure Windows Firewall.

▶ **Windows Updates**—Enables you to configure Windows Home Server's Automatic Updates feature, including setting up a schedule for the download and installation of updates.

Understanding Control Panel Files

Many of the Control Panel icons are represented by Control Panel extension files, which use the .cpl extension. These files reside in the %SystemRoot%\System32 folder. When you open Control Panel, Windows Home Server scans the System32 folder, looking for CPL files, and then displays an icon for each one.

The CPL files offer an alternative method for launching individual Control Panel dialog boxes. The idea is that you open the Run dialog box (by selecting Start, Run; you could also use the command line if you have a Command Prompt session going; note that this doesn't work in the Start menu's Search box) and use it to launch control.exe and specify the name of a CPL file as a parameter. This bypasses the Control Panel folder and opens the icon directly. Here's the syntax:

```
control CPLfile [,option1 [, option2]]
```

CPLfile   The name of the file that corresponds to the Control Panel icon you want to open. (See Table 20.1 later in this chapter.)

option1   This option is obsolete and is included only for backward compatibility with batch files and scripts that use Control.exe for opening Control Panel icons.

option2   The tab number of a multitabbed dialog box. Many Control Panel icons open a dialog box that has two or more tabs. If you know the specific tab you want to work with, you can use the option2 parameter to specify an integer that corresponds to the tab's relative position from the left side of the dialog box. The first (leftmost) tab is 0, the next tab is 1, and so on.

NOTE

If the dialog box has multiple rows of tabs, count the tabs from left to right and from bottom to top. For example, if the dialog box has two rows of four tabs each, the tabs in the bottom row are numbered 0 to 3 from left to right, and the tabs in the top row are numbered 4 to 7 from left to right.

Also, note that even though you no longer use the option1 parameter, you must still display its comma in the command line.

For example, to open Control Panel's System icon with the Hardware tab displayed, run the following command:

```
control sysdm.cpl,,2
```

Table 20.1 lists the various Control Panel icons and the appropriate command line to use. (Note, however, that you can't access certain Control Panel icons—such as Taskbar and Start Menu—by running Control.exe.)

TABLE 20.1   Command Lines for Launching Individual Control Panel Icons

Control Panel Icon	Command
Action Center	control wscui.cpl
Administrative Tools	control admintools
Data Sources	control odbccp32.cpl
Date and Time	control timedate.cpl
Device Manager	control hdwwiz.cpl
Devices and Printers	control printers
Ease of Access Center	control access.cpl

20

TABLE 20.1   Command Lines for Launching Individual Control Panel Icons

Control Panel Icon	Command
Folder Options	`control folders`
Fonts	`control fonts`
Internet Options	`control inetcpl.cpl`
Keyboard	`control keyboard`
Mouse	`control mouse`
Network Connections	`control ncpa.cpl`
Phone and Modem	`control telephon.cpl`
Power Options	`control powercfg.cpl`
Programs and Features	`control appwiz.cpl`
Region and Language	`control intl.cpl`
Scanners and Cameras	`control scannercamera`
Scheduled Tasks	`control schedtasks`
Screen Resolution	`control desk.cpl`
Sound	`control mmsys.cpl`
System	`control sysdm.cpl`
Windows CardSpace	`control infocardcpl.cpl`
Windows Firewall	`control firewall.cpl`
Windows Update	`control wuaucpl.cpl`

Alternative Methods for Opening Control Panel Icons

Access to many Control Panel icons is scattered throughout the Windows Home Server interface, meaning that there's more than one way to launch an icon. Many of these alternative methods are faster and more direct than using the Control Panel folder. Here's a summary:

- ▶ **Computer Management**—Click Start, right-click Computer, and then click Manage.

- ▶ **Date and Time**—Click the clock in the taskbar's notification area, and then click Change Date and Time Settings.

- ▶ **Default Programs**—Select Start, Default Programs.

▶ **Devices and Printers**—Select Start, Devices and Printers.

▶ **Folder Options**—In Windows Explorer, either select Organize, Folder and Search Options, or press Alt and then select Tools, Folder Options.

▶ **Fonts**—In Windows Explorer, open the `%SystemRoot%\Fonts` folder.

▶ **Internet Options**—In Internet Explorer, select Tools, Internet Options.

▶ **Network and Sharing Center**—Right-click the notification area's Network icon, and then click Open Network and Sharing Center.

▶ **Notification Area Icons**—Right-click an empty section of the taskbar's notification area, and then click Customize Notification Area.

▶ **Personalization**—Right-click the desktop, and then click Personalize.

▶ **Scheduled Tasks**—Select Start, All Programs, Accessories, System Tools, Task Scheduler. Alternatively, in Windows Explorer, open the `%SystemRoot%\Tasks` folder.

▶ **Sound**—Right-click the Volume icon in the notification area, and then click Sounds.

▶ **System**—Click Start, right-click Computer, and then click Properties. You can also press Windows Logo+Pause/Break.

▶ **Taskbar and Start Menu**—Right-click an empty section of the taskbar or Start button, and then click Properties.

▶ **Troubleshooting**—Right-click the Action Center icon in the notification area, and then click Troubleshoot a Problem.

▶ **Windows Update**—Click Start, All Programs, Windows Update, or right-click the Action Center icon in the notification area and then click Open Windows Update.

Another relatively easy way to get at a Control Panel icon is to use the Windows Home Server search engine, which indexes the Control Panel. Select Start, type some or all of the Control Panel icon name, and then click the icon that appears in the Control Panel section of the search results. For example, in Figure 20.13 I typed **ease** in the Search box, and you can see that Ease of Access Center shows up at the top of the results. Several other related Control Panel items also appear in the results.

TIP

You can create a special shell folder that displays every Control Panel command, organized by topic. Create a new folder on the desktop or some other convenient location, and give the folder the following name:

Full Control Panel.{ED7BA470-8E54-465E-825C-99712043E01C}

20

FIGURE 20.13   You can use the Start menu's Search box to search for Control Panel icons.

Putting a Control Panel Submenu on the Start Menu

You can turn the Start menu's Control Panel command into a menu that displays the
Control Panel icons by following these steps:

1. Right-click the Start button, and then click Properties. The Taskbar and Start Menu
   Properties dialog box appears with the Start Menu tab displayed.
2. Click Customize. The Customize Start Menu dialog box appears.
3. In the list of Start menu items, find the Control Panel item, and activate the Display
   as a Menu option.
4. Click OK.

Figure 20.14 shows the Start menu with the Control Panel item configured as a menu.
Depending on the screen resolution you are using, some of the Control Panel icons might
not fit on the screen. In that case, hover the mouse pointer over the downward-pointing
arrow at the bottom of the menu to scroll through the rest of the icons. (To scroll up,
hover the pointer over the upward-pointing arrow that appears at the top of the menu.)

Removing an Icon from Control Panel

You might find that you don't use some Control Panel icons. For example, if your
Windows Home Server computer doesn't have any iSCSI devices, you'll never need to use
Control Panel's iSCSI Initiator icon. Because Control Panel contains so many icons, it

FIGURE 20.14   The Start menu's Control Panel item configured as a menu.

makes sense to remove those you never use. Doing that makes it easier to find the icon you want and faster to navigate the icons.

Here are the steps for using a group policy to remove icons from Control Panel:

1. Open the Local Group Policy Editor window, as described earlier in this chapter.

2. Navigate to the User Configuration, Administrative Templates, Control Panel branch.

3. Double-click the Hide Specified Control Panel applets.

4. Activate the Enabled option.

5. Click Show to display the Show Contents dialog box.

6. Click Add to open the Add Item dialog box.

7. Use the Enter the Item to Be Added text box to specify the Control icon you want to hide. You have two choices:

   ▶ Type the name of the CPL file that corresponds to the Control Panel icon you want to hide. (See Table 20.1, earlier in this chapter.)

   ▶ Type the icon caption as it appears in Control Panel. For example, to hide the iSCSI Initiator icon, type **iSCSI Initiator**.

20

> **NOTE**
>
> You can only hide icons that appear in the main Control Panel folder. You can't hide icons that appear in the Control Panel subfolders, such as Administrative Tools.

8. Click OK. The Local Group Policy Editor adds the CPL file to the Show Contents dialog box.

9. Repeat steps 6 to 8 to remove other icons.

10. Click OK.

Showing Only Specified Control Panel Icons

Control Panel is so useful that you'll probably use most of the icons at least some of the time. However, it's possible that you may only use a few of the icons most of the time. In that case, you might want to really streamline the Control Panel view by displaying only those few icons you use. Here's how to do this using a group policy:

1. Open the Local Group Policy Editor window, as described earlier in this chapter.

2. Navigate to the User Configuration, Administrative Templates, Control Panel branch.

3. Double-click the Show Only Specified Control Panel Applets policy.

4. Activate the Enabled option.

5. Click Show to display the Show Contents dialog box.

6. Click Add to open the Add Item dialog box.

7. Use the Enter the Item to Be Added text box to specify the Control icon you want to show. You have two choices:

    ▶ Type the name of the CPL file that corresponds to the Control Panel icon you want to show. (See Table 20.1, earlier in this chapter.)

    ▶ Type the icon caption as it appears in Control Panel. For example, to show the Programs and Features icon, type **Programs and Features.**

8. Click OK. The Local Group Policy Editor adds the CPL file to the Show Contents dialog box.

9. Repeat steps 6 to 8 to show other icons.

10. Click OK.

> **NOTE**
>
> Group policies also enable you to customize the behavior of some Control Panel icons. When you open the User Configuration, Administrative Templates, Control Panel branch, you'll see six subbranches that correspond to six Control Panel icons: Add or Remove Programs, Display, Personalization, Printers, Programs, and Regional and Language Options. In each case, you use the policies in a particular subbranch to hide dialog box tabs, specify default settings, and more.

Configuring the Microsoft Management Console

The MMC is a system administration program that can act as a host application for a variety of tools. The advantage of MMC is that it displays each tool as a *console*—a two-pane view that has a treelike hierarchy in the left pane (this is called the *tree pane*) and a *taskpad* in the right pane that shows the contents of each branch (this is called the *results pane*). This gives each tool a similar interface, which makes it easier to use the tools. You can also customize the console view in a number of ways, create custom taskpad views, and save a particular set of tools to reuse later. These tools are called *snap-ins*, because you can "attach" them to the console root.

When you work with the MMC interface, what you're really doing is editing a Microsoft Common Console Document, an .msc file that stores one or more snap-ins, the console view, and the taskpad view used by each snap-in branch. You learn how to create custom MSC files in this section, but you should know that Windows Home Server comes with a large number of predefined MSC snap-ins. I've summarized them in Table 20.2.

TABLE 20.2   The Default Windows Home Server Snap-Ins

Snap-In	File	Description
Active X Control	N/A	Launches the Insert ActiveX Control Wizard, which enables you to choose an ActiveX control to display as a node. I haven't been able to find a good use for this one yet!
Authorization Manager	azman.msc	Used by developers to set permissions on applications.
Certificate Templates	certtmpl.msc	Enables you to create and manage certificate templates. This snap-in requires domain access, so it doesn't work with Windows Home Server.
Certificates	certmgr.msc	Enables you to browse the security certificates on your system.
Certification Authority	certsrv.msc	Enables you to manage Certificate Services. This service is not available in Windows Home Server.
Component Services	comexp.msc	Enables you to view and work with Component Object Model (COM) services.
Computer Management	compmgmt.msc	Contains a number of snap-ins for managing various aspects of Windows Home Server. You can examine hidden and visible shared folders, set group policies, access Device Manager, manage hard disks, and much more.
Device Manager	devmgmt.msc	Enables you to add and manage your system hardware. See Chapter 17.

20

TABLE 20.2   The Default Windows Home Server Snap-Ins

Snap-In	File	Description
Disk Management	`diskmgmt.msc`	Enables you to view and manage all the disk drives on your system.
Distributed File System	N/A	Enables you to combine multiple shared network folders from multiple network clients under a single logical folder called a *root*.
Enterprise PKI	`pkiview.msc`	Enables you to monitor the health of components in a public key infrastructure.
Event Viewer	`eventvwr.msc`	Enables you to view the Windows Home Server event logs. See Chapter 16, "Maintaining Windows Home Server."
Folder	N/A	Enables you to add a folder node to the root to help you organize your nodes.
Group Policy Object Editor	`gpedit.msc`	Enables you to work with group policies. See "Using the Local Group Policy Editor," earlier in this chapter.
Internet Information Services (IIS) Manager	`iis.msc`	Runs the IIS Manager, which I described in detail in Chapter 12.
IP Security Monitor	N/A	Enables you to monitor Internet Protocol (IP) security settings.
IP Security Policy Management	N/A	Enables you to create IP Security (IPSec) policies.
Link to Web Address	N/A	Adds a node that displays the contents of a specified web page.
Local Security Policy	`secpol.msc`	Enables you to view, enable, and configure Windows Home Server's security-related group policies.
Local Users and Groups	`lusrmgr.msc`	Enables you to add, modify, and delete user accounts. See Chapter 2, "Setting Up and Working with User Accounts."
NAP Client Configuration	`napclcfg.msc`	Enables you to configure Network Access Protection (NAP) for a computer.
Network Policy Server	`nps.msc`	Enables you to create and configure network-wide access policies.
Performance Monitor	`perfmon.msc`	Enables you to monitor one or more performance counters.
Remote Desktop Services Manager	`tsadmin.msc`	Enables you to manage Remote Desktop connections to network clients.

TABLE 20.2 The Default Windows Home Server Snap-Ins

Snap-In	File	Description
Remote Desktop Session Host Configuration	`tsconfig.msc`	Enables you to configure Windows Home Server as a Remote Desktop host.
Remote Desktops	`tsmmc.msc`	Enables you to create Remote Desktop connections to network clients.
Resultant Set of Policy	`rsop.msc`	Shows the applied group policies for the current user.
Routing and Remote Access	`rrasmgmt.msc`	Enables you to configure Windows Home Server to accept remote dial-up or virtual private network (VPN) connections.
Security Configuration and Analysis	N/A	Enables you to open an existing security database or build a new security database based on a security template you create using the Security Templates snap-in.
Security Templates	N/A	Enables you to create a security template in which you enable and configure one or more security-related policies.
Server Manager	`ServerManager.msc`	Enables you to add and configure roles, features, storage, and other aspects of the server.
Services	`services.msc`	Enables you to start, stop, enable, and disable services. See "Controlling Services," later in this chapter.
Share and Storage Management	`StorageMgmt.msc`	Enables you to view and control the server's shared folders and storage.
Shared Folders	`fsmgmt.msc`	Enables you to monitor activity on the Windows Home Server shared folder.
Storage Explorer	`StorExpl.msc`	Enables you to view advanced storage technologies on the server.
Task Scheduler	`taskschd.msc`	Enables you to schedule programs, scripts, and other items to run on a schedule.
Telephony	`tapimgmt.msc`	Displays the current status of the telephony hardware on your system.
TPM Management	`tpm.msc`	Enables you to configure work with Trusted Platform Module (TPM) security devices.
Windows Firewall with Advanced Security	`wf.msc`	Presents an advanced Windows Firewall interface.

20

TABLE 20.2   The Default Windows Home Server Snap-Ins

Snap-In	File	Description
Windows Server Backup	`wbadmin.msc`	Enables you to configure Windows Home Server backups outside of the Dashboard.
WMI Control	`wmimgmt.msc`	Enables you to configure properties related to Windows Management Instrumentation (WMI). See Chapter 21, "Scripting Windows Home Server."

Launching the MMC

To get the MMC onscreen, you have two choices:

▶ To start with a blank console, select Start, Run to open the Run dialog box, type **mmc**, and then click OK.

▶ To start with an existing snap-in, select Start, Run to open the Run dialog box, type the name of the .msc file you want to load (see Table 20.2), and then click OK.

The initial MMC window is blank. I show you how to add snap-ins to the console in the next section.

Adding a Snap-In

You start building your console file by adding one or more snap-ins to the console root, which is the top-level MMC container. (Even if you loaded the MMC by launching an existing snap-in, you can still add more snap-ins to the console.) Here are the steps to follow:

1. Select File, Add/Remove Snap-In (or press Ctrl+M). The MMC displays the Add/Remove Snap-In dialog box.
2. Click Add. The MMC opens the Add Standalone Snap-In dialog box.
3. Select the snap-in you want to use, and then click Add.

> **TIP**
>
> You can help organize your snap-ins by adding subfolders to the console root. In the list of snap-ins, select Folder and then click Add. When you return to the MMC, right-click the new subfolder and then click Rename to give the subfolder a useful name. To add a snap-in inside this subfolder, select File, Add/Remove Snap-In (or press Ctrl+M) to open the Add or Remove Snap-Ins dialog box, click Advanced, activate Allow Changing the Parent Snap-In, and then click OK. Use the Parent Snap-In list to choose the subfolder. See Figure 20.16 for some sample subfolders.

4. If the snap-in can work with remote computers, you see a dialog box similar to the one shown in Figure 20.15. To have the snap-in manage a remote machine, select Another Computer, type the computer name in the text box, and then click Finish.
5. Repeat steps 3 and 4 to add other snap-ins to the console.

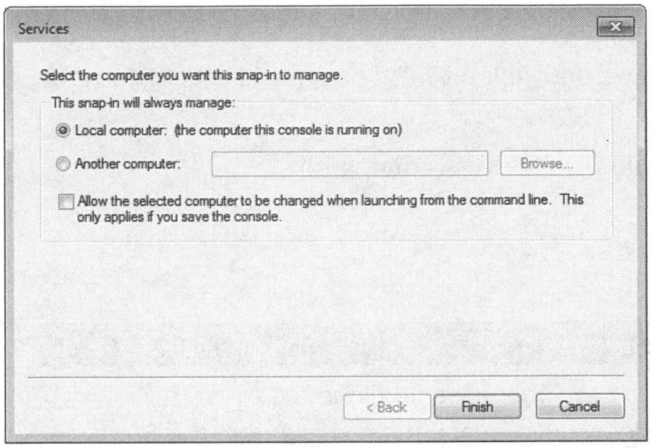

FIGURE 20.15   Some snap-ins can manage remote computers as well as the local machine.

6. Click Close to return to the Add/Remove Snap-In dialog box, which displays a list of the snap-ins you added.

7. Click OK.

Figure 20.16 shows the MMC with a custom console consisting of several snap-ins and subfolders.

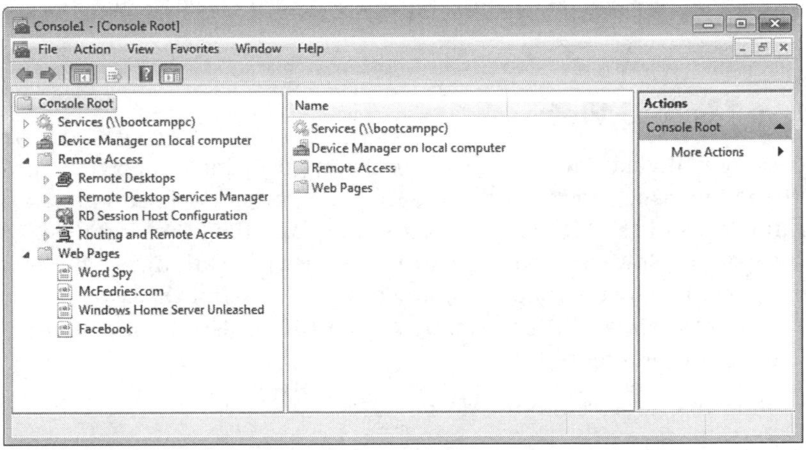

FIGURE 20.16   The MMC with a custom console.

NOTE

In Figure 20.16, the items in the Web Pages subfolder are based on the Link to Web Address snap-in, which is a special snap-in that displays the current version of whatever web page you specify. When you add the snap-in, the MMC runs the Link to Web Address Wizard. Type the web page address (either an Internet URL or a path to a local or network page), click Next, type a name for the snap-in, and then click Finish.

Saving a Console

If you think you want to reuse your custom console later on, you should save it to an `.msc` file. Here are the steps to follow:

1. Select File, Save (or press Ctrl+S) to open the Save As dialog box.
2. Type a filename for the console.
3. Select a location for the console file.

TIP

By default, MMC assumes that you want to save your console file in the `Administrative Tools` folder. This enables you to launch the console from the Start menu. (Select Start, All Programs, Administrative Tools, and then click the console name.) However, if you want to be able to launch your console file from the Run dialog box, you should save it in the `%SystemRoot%\System32` folder, along with the pre-defined snap-ins.

4. Click Save.

NOTE

To make changes to a custom taskpad view, right-click the snap-in and then click Edit Taskbar View.

Creating a Custom Taskpad View

A taskpad view is a custom configuration of the MMC results (right) pane for a given snap-in. By default, the results pane shows a list of the snap-in's contents—for example, the list of categories and devices in the Device Manager snap-in and the list of installed services in the Services snap-in. However, you can customize this view with one or more tasks that run commands defined by the snap-in, or any program or script that you specify. You can also control the size of the list, whether the list is displayed horizontally or vertically in the results pane, and more.

Here are the steps to follow to create a custom taskpad view:

1. Select a snap-in in the tree pane, as follows:
   ▶ If you want to apply the taskpad view to a specific snap-in, select that snap-in.
   ▶ If you want to apply the taskpad view to a group of snap-ins that use the same snap-in type, specify one snap-in from the group. For example, if you want to customize all the folders, select any folder (such as the Console Root folder); similarly, if you want to customize all the Link to Web Address snap-ins, select one of them.
2. Select Action, New Taskpad View to launch the New Taskpad View Wizard.
3. Click Next to open the Taskpad Style dialog box, shown in Figure 20.17.

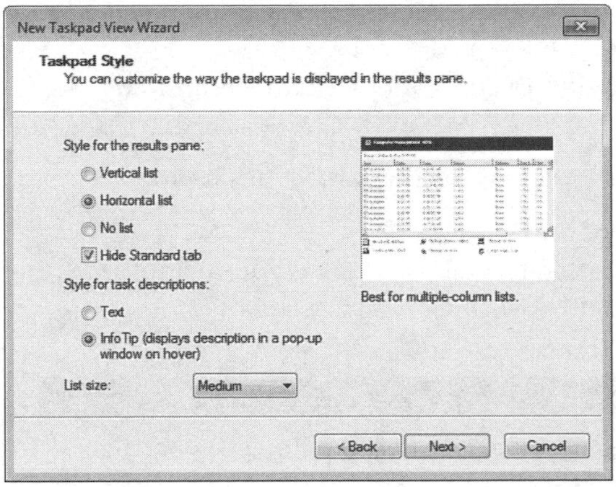

FIGURE 20.17   Use the New Taskpad View Wizard to create your custom taskpad view.

4. Use the following controls to set up the style of taskpad you want:

   ▶ **Style for Results Pane**—Select an option for displaying the snap-in's results:
     Vertical List (this is best for lists with a large number of items), Horizontal List
     (this is best for web pages or lists with a large number of columns), or No List
     (choose this option if you want only tasks to appear in the results pane).

   ▶ **Hide Standard Tab**—After you create the new taskpad view, the MMC displays
     two tabs in the results pane: The Extended tab shows your custom taskpad
     view, and the Standard tab shows the default view. To keep the option of
     displaying the default view, deactivate the Hide Standard Tab check box.

   ▶ **Style for Task Descriptions**—When you add descriptions for your tasks later
     on, you can have the MMC display each description either as text below the
     task link or as an InfoTip that appears when you hover the mouse over the
     task link.

   ▶ **List Size**—Choose the size of the list: Small (good if you add lots of tasks),
     Medium (this is the default), or Large (good if you have few or no tasks).

5. Click Next. The Taskpad Reuse dialog box appears.

6. The wizard assumes that you want to apply the new taskpad view to all snap-ins of
   the same type. If you only want to apply the taskpad view to the current snap-in,
   select the Selected Tree Item option.

7. Click Next. The Name and Description dialog box appears.

8. Type a name and optional description for the taskpad view, and then click Next. The
   final wizard dialog box appears.

9. If you don't want to add tasks to the new view, deactivate the Add New Tasks to This
   Taskpad After the Wizard Closes check box.

20

10. Click Finish. If you elected to add tasks to the view, the New Task Wizard appears.

11. Click Next. The Command Type dialog box appears.

12. Select one of the following command types:

    ▶ **Menu Command**—Select this option to create a task that runs an MMC or snap-in menu command.

    ▶ **Shell Command**—Select this option to create a task that runs a program, script, or batch file.

    ▶ **Navigation**—Select this option to create a task that takes you to another snap-in that's in your MMC Favorites list.

NOTE

To add a snap-in to the MMC Favorites list, select the snap-in in the tree pane and then select Favorites, Add to Favorites.

---

13. Click Next.

14. How you proceed from here depends on the command type you selected in step 12:

    ▶ **Menu Command**—In the Menu Command dialog box, first select an item from the Command Source list. Choose Item Listed in the Results Pane to apply the command to whatever item is currently selected in the results pane; choose Node in the Tree to select a command based on an item in the MMC tree pane.

    ▶ **Shell Command**—In the Command Line dialog box, use the Command text box to specify the path to the program executable, script, or batch file that you want the task to run. You can also specify startup Parameters, the Start In folder, and a Run window type.

    ▶ **Navigation**—In the Navigation dialog box, select the items from the MMC Favorites list.

15. Click Next. The Name and Description dialog box appears.

16. Edit the task name and description, and then click Next. The Task Icon dialog box appears, as shown in Figure 20.18.

17. Click Next. The final New Task Wizard dialog box appears.

18. If you want to add more tasks, activate the When I Click Finish, Run This Wizard Again check box.

19. Click Finish.

20. If you elected to add more tasks, repeat steps 11 through 19, as needed.

Figure 20.19 shows the MMC with a custom taskpad view applied to a Link to Web Address snap-in.

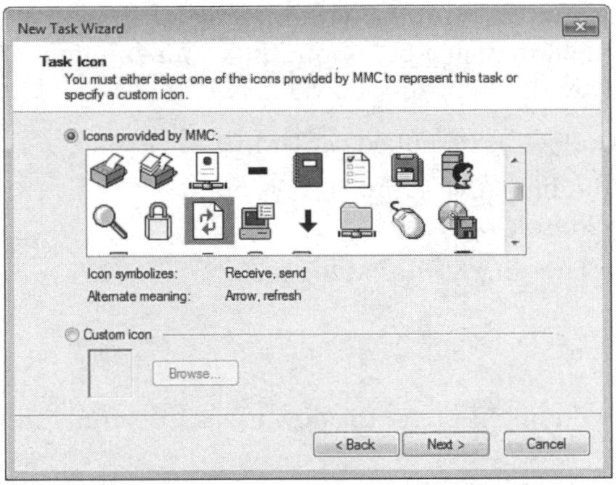

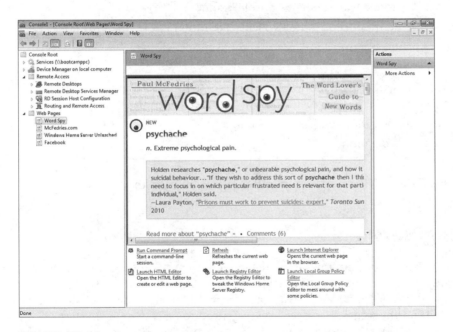

FIGURE 20.18   Use the Task Icon dialog box to choose an icon to display with your task.

FIGURE 20.19   A custom taskpad view.

Controlling Snap-Ins with Group Policies

If you share Windows Home Server with other people, you can control which snap-ins they're allowed to use, and you can prevent users from adding snap-ins to the MMC.

The latter is the simpler of the two options, so let's begin with that. The MMC has an *author mode* that enables you to add snap-ins to it. If you prevent the MMC from entering author mode, you prevent users from adding snap-ins. You can do this using a group policy. Note, too, that this policy prevents users from entering author mode for those snap-ins that can be opened directly (from the Run dialog box, from the command line, from Administrative Tools, and so on). Here are the steps to follow:

1. Open the Local Group Policy Editor window, as described earlier in this chapter.
2. Navigate to the User Configuration, Administrative Templates, Windows Components, Microsoft Management Console branch.
3. Double-click the Restrict the User from Entering Author Mode policy.
4. Activate the Enabled option.
5. Click OK.

Rather than blocking off the MMC entirely, you might prefer to allow users access only to specific snap-ins. Here are the steps to follow:

1. Open the Local Group Policy Editor window, as described earlier in this chapter.
2. Navigate to the User Configuration, Administrative Templates, Windows Components, Microsoft Management Console branch.
3. Double-click the Restrict Users to the Explicitly Permitted List of Snap-Ins policy.
4. Activate the Enabled option.
5. Click OK.
6. Navigate to the User Configuration, Administrative Templates, Windows Components, Microsoft Management Console, Restricted/Permitted Snap-Ins branch.
7. Double-click a snap-in that you want users to access.
8. Activate the Enabled option.
9. Click OK.
10. Repeat steps 7 through 9 for each snap-in that you want users to access.

Controlling Services

System services are background routines that enable the system to perform tasks such as logging on to the network, managing disks, collecting performance data, and writing event logs. Windows Home Server comes with more than 100 installed services. Services usually operate behind the scenes. However, you may need to pause, stop, and start services, as well as configure the way a service loads at startup. The next few sections show you the various methods you can use to control services.

Controlling Services with the Services Snap-In

The standard interface for the Windows Home Server services is the Services snap-in, which you can load by using either of the following techniques:

▶ Select Start, Administrative Tools, Services.

▶ Select Start, Run to open the Run dialog box, type **services.msc**, and click OK.

The Services snap-in that appears displays a list of the installed services, and for each service, it displays the name of the service and a brief description, the current status of the service (Started, Paused, or blank for a stopped service), the service's startup type (such as Automatic or Manual), and the name of the system account that the service uses to log on at startup. When you select a service, the Extended tab of the taskpad view shows the service name and description and offers links to control the service status (such as Start, Stop, or Restart). Figure 20.20 shows an example.

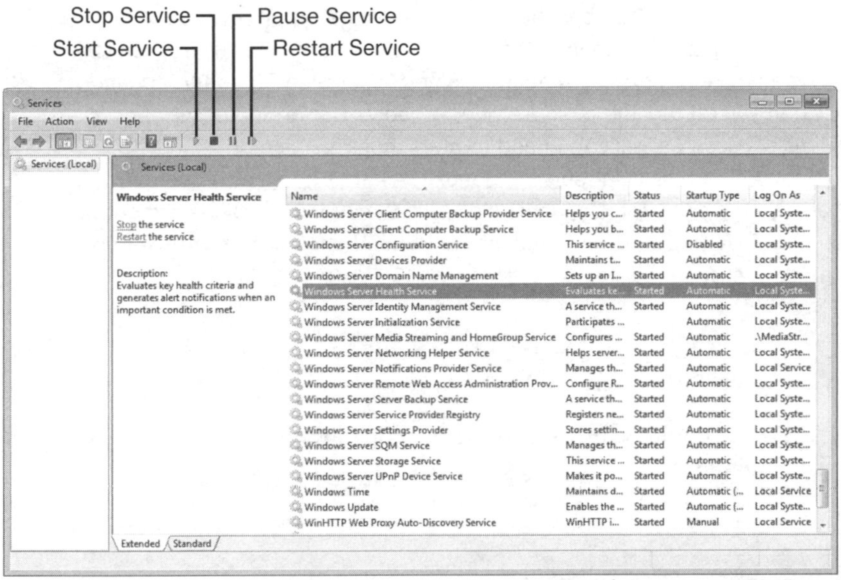

FIGURE 20.20   You can use the Services snap-in to control the Windows Home Server services.

To change the status of a service, select it and then use one of the following techniques:

▶ To start a stopped service, either click the Start link in the taskpad or click the Start Service toolbar button.

▶ To stop a running service, either click the Stop link in the taskpad or click the Stop Service toolbar button.

▶ To pause a running service, either click the Pause link in the taskpad or click the Start Service toolbar button. (Note that only a few services support the Pause task.)

▶ To resume a paused service, either click the Restart link in the taskpad or click the Restart Service toolbar button.

20

NOTE

If a service is started but it has no Stop link and the Stop toolbar button is disabled, it means the service is essential to Windows Home Server and can't be stopped. Examples of essential services include Plug and Play, Remote Procedure Call (RPC), and Security Accounts Manager.

CAUTION

It's possible that a service might be dependent on one or more other services, and if those services aren't running, the dependent service will not work properly. If you stop a service that has dependent services, Windows Home Server also stops the dependents. However, when you restart the main service, Windows Home Server may not start the dependent services as well. You need to start those services by hand. To see which services depend on a particular service, double-click that service to open its property sheet, and then display the Dependencies tab. Dependent services are shown in the field under The Following System Components Depend on This Service. The field is grayed out if no dependencies exist.

To change the way a service starts when you boot Windows Home Server, follow these steps:

1. Double-click the service you want to work with to open its property sheet. Figure 20.21 shows an example.

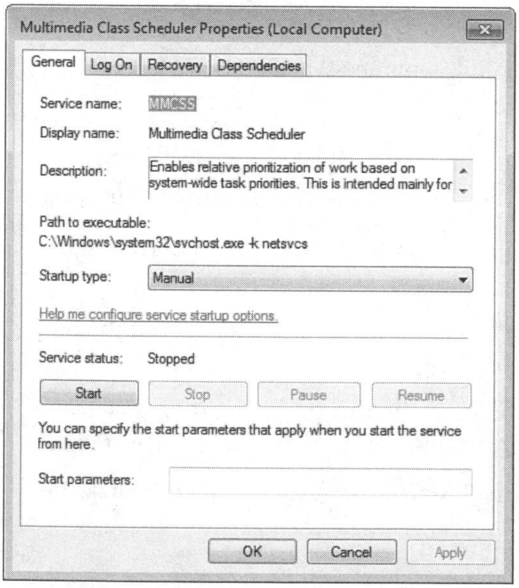

FIGURE 20.21   You use a service's property sheet to control its startup type.

2. Use the Startup Type list to select one of the following types:

Automatic	The service starts automatically when Windows Home Server boots. The service is started before the Welcome to Windows dialog box appears.
Automatic (Delayed Start)	The service starts automatically when Windows Home Server boots. The service does not start until you log on.
Manual	The service does not start when Windows Home Server boots. You must start the service yourself.
Disabled	The service does not start when Windows Home Server boots, and you can't start the service manually.

3. Click OK.

NOTE

If the Startup Type list is disabled, it means the service is essential to Windows Home Server and must be started automatically when the system boots.

NOTE

All the services that Windows Home Server requires to perform its core functions use the Automatic startup type. This explains how Windows Home Server can run on a headless device. When you turn on the headless device, the "boot" only goes as far as the Welcome to Windows prompt. However, all the essential services are started by that point, so Windows Home Server can perform its core duties without the need for a local logon.

TIP

If you make changes to service startup types and you find that your system is unstable or causing problems, the best thing to do is return each service to its default startup type. If you're not sure of the default for a service, open the Services snap-in, select Help, Help Topics, and then select the Services, Concepts, Default Settings for Services branch.

Controlling Services at the Command Prompt

If you regularly stop and start certain services, loading the Services snap-in and manually stopping and then restarting each service can be time-consuming. A better method is to take advantage of the NET STOP and NET START command-line tools, which enable you to stop and start any service that isn't disabled. If a service can be paused and restarted, you can also use the NET PAUSE and NET CONTINUE commands to control the service. Each of these commands uses the same syntax:

20

```
NET STOP Service
NET START Service
NET PAUSE Service
NET CONTINUE Service
```

> *Service*   The name of the service you want to control. Use the same value that appears in the Name column of the Services snap-in. If the name contains a space, surround the name with quotation marks.

Here are some examples:

```
net start Telephony
net stop "Themes"
net pause "World Wide Web Publishing Service"
net continue "Windows Management Instrumentation"
```

You can combine multiple commands in a batch file to easily control several services with a single task.

TIP

To see a list of the currently running services, open a command-line session and enter the command **net start** without the *Service* parameter.

Controlling Services with a Script

If you want to automate service control, but you want to also control the startup type, you need to go beyond the command line and create scripts that manage your services. WMI has a class called `Win32_Service` that represents a Windows service. You can return an instance of this class to work with a specific service on Windows Home Server. After you have the service object, you can query its current status with the `State` property; determine whether the service is running with the `Started` property; and return the service's startup type with the `StartMode` property. You can also change the service state using the `StartService`, `StopService`, `PauseService`, and `ResumeService` methods.

> ▶ **SEE** "Programming the Windows Management Instrumentation Service," **P. 617**.

Listing 20.1 presents a script that uses most of these properties and methods.

NOTE

You can find this script on my website at www.mcfedries.com/HomeServerUnleashed3E.

LISTING 20.1   A WMI Script That Toggles a Service's State Between Started and Stopped

```
Option Explicit
Dim strComputer, strServiceName, intReturn
Dim objWMI, objServices, objService
'
' Get the WMI service
'
strComputer = "localhost"
Set objWMI = GetObject("winmgmts:{impersonationLevel=impersonate}!\\" & _
    strComputer & "\root\cimv2")
'
' Specify the service name
'
strServiceName = "Distributed File System"
'
' Get the service instance
'
Set objServices = objWMI.ExecQuery("SELECT * FROM Win32_Service " & _
                  "WHERE DisplayName = '" & strServiceName & "'")
For Each objService In objServices
    '
    ' Save the service name
    '
    strServiceName = objService.DisplayName
    '
    ' Is the service started?
    '
    If objService.Started Then
        '
        ' Can it be stopped?
        '
        If objService.AcceptStop Then
            '
            ' Attempt to stop the service
            '
            intReturn = objService.StopService
            '
            ' Check the return value
            '
            If intReturn <> 0 Then
                '
                ' Display the error message
                '
                WScript.Echo "ERROR: The " & strServiceName & " service " & _
                            "failed to stop. The return code is " & intReturn
```

20

```
                Else
                    '
                    ' Display the current state
                    '
                    WScript.Echo "The " & strServiceName & " service is now " & _
                            objService.State
                End If
            Else
                '
                ' Display the error message
                '
                WScript.Echo "ERROR: The " & strServiceName & " service " & _
                        "cannot be stopped."
            End If
        Else
            '
            ' Attempt to start the service
            '
            intReturn = objService.StartService
            '
            ' Check the return value
            '
            If intReturn <> 0 Then
                '
                ' Display the error message
                '
                WScript.Echo "ERROR: The " & strServiceName & " service " & _
                        "failed to start. The return code is " & intReturn
            Else
                '
                ' Display the current state
                '
                WScript.Echo "The " & strServiceName & " service is now " & _
                        objService.State
            End If
        End If
    Next
    '
    ' Release the objects
    '
    Set objWMI = Nothing
    Set objServices = Nothing
    Set objService = Nothing
```

This script gets the WMI service object and uses its ExecQuery method to return an instance of the Win32_Service class by using the WHERE clause to look for a specific service name. That name was earlier stored in the strServiceName variable. In the For Each...Next loop, the script first checks to see if the service is currently started by checking its Started property:

▶ If the Started property returns True, the service is running, so we want to stop it. The script then checks the service's AcceptStop property, which returns False for essential Windows Home Server services that can't be stopped. In this case, the script returns an error message. If AcceptStop returns True, the script attempts to stop the service by running the StopService method.

▶ If the Started property returns False, the service is stopped, so we want to start it. The script attempts to start the service by running the StartService method.

The StopService and StartService methods generate the return codes shown in Table 20.3.

TABLE 20.3   Return Codes Generated by the StartService and StopService Methods

Return Code	Description	Return Code	Description
0	Success	13	Service dependency failure
1	Not supported	14	Service disabled
2	Access denied	15	Service logon failed
3	Dependent services running	16	Service marked for deletion
4	Invalid service control	17	Service no thread
5	Service cannot accept control	18	Status circular dependency
6	Service not active	19	Status—duplicate name
7	Service request timeout	20	Status—invalid name
8	Unknown failure	21	Status—invalid parameter
9	Path not found	22	Status—invalid service account
10	Service already stopped	23	Status—service exists
11	Service database locked	24	Service already paused
12	Service dependency deleted		

20

For both the StopService and StartService methods, the script stores the return code in the intReturn variable and then checks to see if it's a number other than 0. If it is, the script displays an error message that includes the return code; otherwise, the script displays the new state of the service (as given by the State property).

Setting Up a Fax Server

Perhaps I'm dating myself, but I still remember when the fax machine (or the *facsimile machine*, as it was called back then) was the hottest thing around—the new kid on the telecommunications block. How amazing it seemed that we could send a letter or memo or even a picture through the phone lines and have it emerge seconds later across town or even across the country. Sure, the fax that came slithering out the other end was a little fuzzier than the original, and certainly a lot slimier, but it sure beat using the post office.

The faxing fad has come and gone, and with so many other ways to share documents nowadays (email, the web, SharePoint sites, and so on), faxing is becoming increasingly rare. But reports of the demise of the fax have been greatly exaggerated, which is why Windows Home Server continues to provide fax services.

Most Windows clients come with some faxing capabilities built in, but Windows Home Server does them one better by enabling you to share a fax with the network and to route incoming faxes to an email address. The rest of this chapter shows you how to configure the Fax service and how to use it to send and receive faxes. Note that I'm assuming here that your Windows Home Server machine either comes with a fax modem built in or you've connected an external fax modem. If you're thinking about purchasing a fax modem for use with Windows Home Server, be sure to get one that's compatible with Windows Server 2008 R2.

Adding the Fax Server Role

If you want to get into the fax fast lane, look no further than the Fax Server role. If you haven't yet added this role to your server, follow these steps to install it:

1. Log on to the Windows Home Server desktop.
2. Click the taskbar's Server manager icon to open the Server Manager window.
3. Click Roles.
4. Click Add Roles. The Add Roles Wizard appears.
5. Click Next. The wizard asks which role you'd like to install.
6. Activate the Fax Server check box. The wizard asks if you want to add the Print and Document Services role, and the Print Server role, both of which are required for the Fax Server.
7. Click Add Required Role Services. The wizard selects the required roles.
8. Click Next. The wizard displays introductory information about the Fax Server role.
9. Click Next. The wizard prompts you to specify users or groups that will be allowed to use the fax service.
10. The Administrator account is added by default, and you probably don't need to add any other users and groups, so just click Next. The wizard asks you to specify who can access the Fax Server's Inbox.

11. Select the All Users Can Access the Fax Server Inbox option, and then click Next. The wizard displays introductory information about the Print and Document Services role.

12. Click Next. The wizard prompts you to select services for the Print and Document Services role.

13. Make sure the Print Server role service is selected, and then click Next.

14. Click Install. The wizard installs the Fax Server and Print and Document Services roles.

15. Click Close.

Configuring a Shared Fax Printer

You can send faxes directly from Windows Home Server using the Windows Fax and Scan application. However, if you want network users to also be able to send faxes through the Fax Server, you need to configure and share a fax printer.

First, follow these steps to create a fax printer:

1. Select Start, All Programs, Windows Fax and Scan. The Windows Fax and Scan window appears.

2. Select Tools, Fax Accounts to open the Fax Accounts dialog box.

3. Click Add to launch the Fax Setup Wizard.

4. Click Connect to a Fax Modem. The wizard prompts you to enter a name for the fax modem.

5. Edit the default name, if you feel like it, and then click Next. The wizard asks you to select how you want to receive faxes.

6. Click Answer Automatically, which configures the fax modem to answer incoming calls after five rings. If you prefer to control when the fax modem answers incoming calls, click Notify Me, instead. The wizard adds your fax modem to the Fax Accounts dialog box.

7. Click Close.

Next, follow these steps to share the fax printer:

1. Select Start, Devices and Printers to open the Devices and Printers window.

2. In the Printers and Faxes group, right-click Fax and then click Printer Properties. The Fax Properties dialog box appears.

3. Click the Sharing tab.

4. Activate the Share This Printer check box.

5. Edit the default Share Name, if needed.

6. Click Additional Drivers.

7. Activate the x86 check box, and then click OK. Windows Home Server prompts you to specify the location of the printer drivers.

20

8. Click Browse, navigate to a 32-bit Windows client, open the `%WinDir%\System32\DriverStore\FileRepository` folder, open the folder with the name that begins with `prnms002.inf_x86`, click `prnms002.inf`, and then click Open.

9. Click OK. Windows Home Server installs the extra printer drivers.

10. Click Close.

▶ **SEE** "Connecting to the Shared Fax Printer," later in this chapter, to learn how to connect to the shared fax.

Starting the Fax Service Manager

You begin your faxing duties at the Fax Service Manager, which you open by selecting Start, Administrative Tools, Fax Service Manager. The first time you do this, the Fax Configuration Wizard appears. The next section takes you through this wizard's steps.

Configuring the Fax Modem

Follow these steps to use the Fax Service Manager to configure the fax modem:

1. In the Fax Service Manager, open the Devices and Providers, Devices branch.

2. Right-click the fax modem, and then click Properties. The fax modem's property sheet appears.

3. (Optional) Enter a description for the fax modem.

4. If you want to use the fax modem to send faxes, activate the Send Faxes check box.

5. Use the Transmitting Subscriber ID (TSID) text box to type the sending ID (such as your name or your company name).

NOTE

Windows Home Server assigns a name to your fax machine. This is known in the trade as the TSID—Transmitting Subscriber Identification (or sometimes Transmitting Station Identifier). When the other person receives your fax, your TSID is displayed at the top of each page. If the other person is receiving on a computer, the TSID appears in the TSID line (or some similar field, depending on the program the recipient is using). Unfortunately, the default TSID in Windows Home Server is *Fax*, which redefines the word *uninspiring*. To fix this, edit the TSID as described in step 5. For example, it's common to change it to a name—such as your company name, your department name, or your own name—followed by your fax number.

---

6. If you want to use the fax modem to receive faxes, activate the Receive Faxes check box.

7. Use the Called Subscriber ID (CSID) text box to type the receiving ID, which is used to identify your computer to the fax sender. This isn't as important as the TSID, so enter whatever you like (or leave the default).

8. Select the way you want incoming faxes to be handled:

Manual Answer   Activate this option to answer incoming calls manually (as
                     described in the "Answering Calls Manually" section, later in this
                     chapter).

Automatic Answer   Activate this option to have the Fax Server answer incoming calls
                     automatically (as described in the "Answering Calls Automatically"
                     section, later in this chapter). Use the Rings Before Answering field
                     to specify the number of rings.

9. Click OK.

Starting Windows Fax and Scan

You'll do most of your server-based fax work using Windows Fax and Scan, which you
load by selecting Start, All Programs, Windows Fax and Scan. Figure 20.22 shows the
Windows Fax and Scan window.

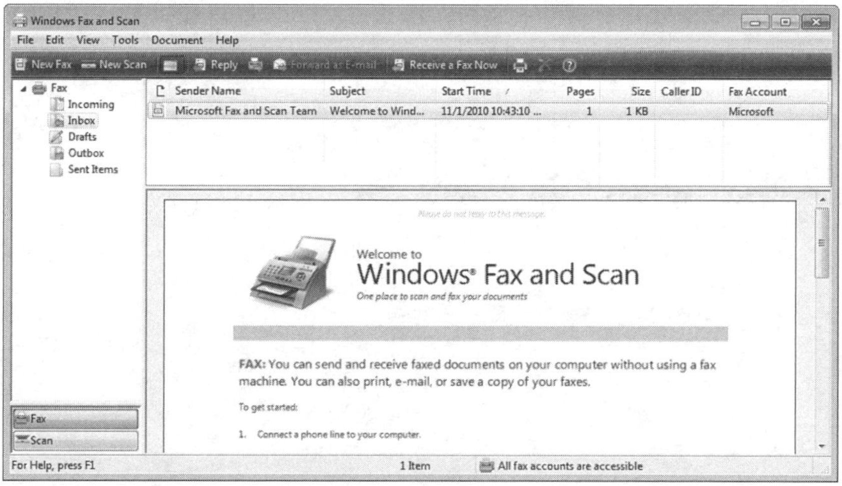

FIGURE 20.22   Windows Fax and Scan is your home base for Windows Home Server faxing.

Windows Fax and Scan includes five folders that store fax-related things:

Incoming   This folder displays information about the fax that is currently being received. For
            example, during fax reception, the Status column displays In progress and the
            Extended Status column displays Answered and then Receiving.

Inbox   This folder stores the incoming faxes that were received successfully. Note that
            the TSID column shows the name or phone number of the sender.

Drafts   This folder stores data faxes that you're working on but haven't yet sent.

Outbox   This folder stores data about the fax that is currently being sent. For example, during the send, the Status column displays In progress and the Extended Status column displays Transmitting.

Sent Items   This folder stores a copy of the faxes that you have sent successfully.

Sending a Fax

To fax something to a friend or colleague (or, heck, even a total stranger), Windows Home Server gives you two ways to proceed:

▸ You can fax a simple note by sending just a cover page.

▸ You can fax a more complex document by sending it to the Windows Home Server fax "printer."

Sending a Cover Page Fax

Let's start with the simple cover page route:

1. In Windows Fax and Scan, either click New Fax or select File, New, Fax. The New Fax window appears, as shown in Figure 20.23.

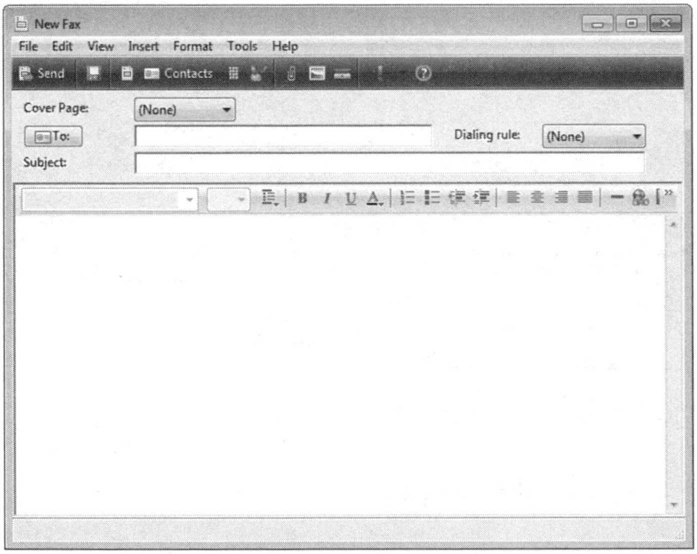

FIGURE 20.23   Use the New Fax window to send a simple cover page fax.

2. Use the Cover Page list to select the cover page you want to use. You have four default choices:

▸ **Confidential**—This cover page includes the word *Confidential*, so use it for faxes that contain sensitive data.

- ▶ **FYI**—This cover page includes the phrase *FOR YOUR INFORMATION*, so use it for faxes that don't require a response or action.

- ▶ **Generic**—This cover page does not contain special text, so it's useful for regular fax messages.

- ▶ **Urgent**—This cover page includes the word *Urgent* in large (52-point) type, so use it for faxes that require immediate attention or action.

3. Use the To box to type the recipient's fax number.

TIP

If the recipient is in your Contacts folder and you have the Fax field filled in (in either the Work or the Home tab), click To, select the recipient, click To, and then click OK. If the person's name appears in the To box in red type, it means Fax and Scan can't find a fax number. Double-click the recipient to open the contact properties sheet, fill in the Fax number in either the Work or Home tab, and then click OK.

4. Type a subject for the fax.
5. Use the large text box to type the message you want to appear on the cover page.
6. Select Tools, Options to open the Options dialog box.
7. Choose when you want to send the fax:

- ▶ **Now**—Sends the fax right away

- ▶ **When Discount Rates Apply**—Sends the fax as soon as possible after your discount rates begin

- ▶ **At This Time**—Sends the fax at the time you specify use the spin box

NOTE

If you want to send faxes when your phone rates are discounted (such as after midnight), open the Fax Services Manager, right-click Fax (Local), and then click Properties. Display the Outbox tab, use the Discount Rate Start spin box to specify the start time for your discounted phone rates, use the Discount Rate End spin box to specify the end time for your discounted phone rates, and then click OK.

8. In the Priority group, use the Send Fax As list to set the fax priority to High, Normal, or Low.
9. Click OK.
10. When you're ready to ship the fax, click Send.

Faxing from an Application

The other (and probably more common) method of sending a fax is to send a document directly from an application. You don't need applications with special features to do this, either. That's because when you install the Fax Server, it adds a new printer driver to Windows Home Server. This printer driver, however, doesn't send a document to the printer. Instead, it renders the document as a fax and sends it to your modem.

To try this, follow these steps:

1. Create the document that you want to send.
2. Select the program's File, Print command to get to the Print dialog box.
3. Select Fax as the printer, and then click Print. The New Fax window appears.
4. Follow the steps outlined in the previous section to set the fax options. With this method, you don't have to bother with a cover page, although you can still include one of you like.

Connecting to the Shared Fax Printer

When you configured the Fax service earlier, you shared the Windows Home Server Fax printer with the network. This means that anyone else on the network can use the Fax printer to send a fax. Here are the steps clients must follow to connect to this printer:

1. Double-click the Shared Folders on *Server* icon on the desktop. (Alternatively, open Windows Explorer and navigate to the *Server* folder.)
2. Right-click the Fax printer and click Connect.
3. If you're asked to confirm. Click Yes.

Windows connects to the Fax printer and adds it to your list of printers. In the Print dialog box of any local application, use the Fax on *SERVER* printer to fax a document.

Receiving Faxes

This section explains how the Fax service handles incoming faxes and shows you how to view those faxes when they're sitting in your Inbox.

Answering Calls Automatically

Enabling the Automatic Answer option (see "Configuring the Fax Modem," earlier in this chapter) is the easiest way to handle incoming calls. In this mode, the Fax service constantly polls the modem's serial port for calls. When it detects a call coming in, it waits for whatever number of rings you specified (which can be as few as one ring or as many as 99) and then leaps into action. Without prodding from you, Automatic Answer answers the phone and immediately starts conversing with the remote fax machine. To follow the progress of the transfer, in the Fax and Scan window, select Tools, Fax Status Monitor to open the Fax Status Monitor window, as shown in Figure 20.24.

Answering Calls Manually

If you work with Fax and Scan in manual mode, when a call comes in you hear a ringing tone, and the taskbar's notification area pops up a message that says Incoming call from

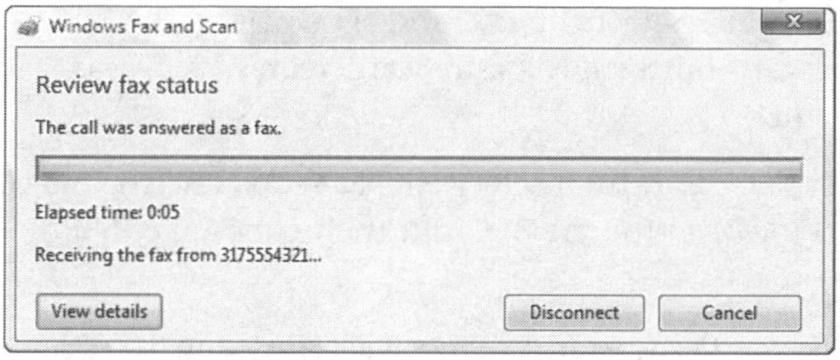

FIGURE 20.24 You can display the Fax Status Monitor to follow the progress of an incoming fax.

fax, where *fax* is the Called Subscriber ID (CSID) of the remote fax. To answer the call, you have three choices:

▶ Click the taskbar message.

▶ In Windows Fax and Scan, either select Tools, Receive a Fax Now or click the Receive a Fax Now toolbar button.

▶ If you happen to have the Fax Status Monitor open already, click the Answer Call button.

This mode is ideal if you receive both voice calls and fax calls on the same phone line. Here's the basic procedure you need to follow for incoming calls:

1. When the phone rings, pick up the receiver.

2. If you hear a series of tones, you know that a fax is on its way. In this case, click the notification message or the Answer Now button, as described earlier.

3. Fax and Scan initializes the modem to handle the call. Wait until the Fax and Scan reports the call was answered as a fax in the Fax Status Monitor window, and then hang up the receiver. If you hang up before you see this message, you disconnect the call.

Working with Received Faxes
Depending on the size of the fax transmission, the Fax service takes from a few seconds to a few minutes to process the data. Eventually, though, your fax appears in the Inbox. From there, you can perform the following chores:

▶ **Read the fax**—Double-click the fax in the Fax Console's Inbox folder (or select the fax and then select File, View). This launches the Windows Picture and Fax Viewer, which displays your fax and enables you to annotate it.

▶ **Print the fax**—Select the fax, and then select File, Print.

▶ **Send a reply to the fax sender**—Select the fax, and then select Document, Reply (or click the Reply button). Fax and Scan creates a new fax message with the sender added to the To box.

20

▶ **Forward the fax to another fax number**—Select the fax, and then select Document, Forward (or click the Forward button). Fax and Scan creates a new fax message with the fax as an attachment.

▶ **Save the fax as an image**—Select the fax, and then select File, Save As. Use the Save As dialog box to choose a name and location for the file, and then click Save. Note that the fax is saved as a TIF image.

▶ **Email the fax as an attachment**—Select the fax, and then select File, Mail To. Use the New Message window to set up the email message, and then click Send.

▶ **Delete the fax**—Select the fax, and then select File, Delete (or just press the Delete key).

Routing a Received Fax

One of the nice features in Windows Home Server's version of the Fax service is that you can configure it to automatically route all incoming faxes to an address you specify. Here are the steps to follow to set this up:

1. Open the Fax Service Manager.

2. Open the Devices and Providers, Devices branch, open your modem branch, and then click Incoming Methods. You see three methods in the list:

Route Through E-Mail	This is the method we'll use here to send incoming faxes to an email address, as described in the rest of the steps in this section.
Store in a Folder	Use this method to have Windows Home Server store a second copy of each fax in the folder that you specify. (You may have done this earlier; see "Configuring the Fax Modem.") To change the folder, double-click this method and use the text box in the Store in Folder tab.
Print	Use this method to have Windows Home Server automatically print any received fax. Double-click this method, display the Print tab, and use the Printer Name list to choose the printer you want to use.

TIP

If you want others to have access to the incoming faxes, create a subfolder called, say, Faxes in Windows Home Server's `Public` shared folder. For this to work, you also need to add permissions for the Network Service, which is the system account that the Fax service uses. Right-click the new `Faxes` folder, click Sharing and Security, and then display the Security tab. Click Add, type **Network Service** in the Select Users or Groups dialog box, and then click OK to return to the Security tab. Click Network Service, and click Full Control under the Allow column. Click OK. You can now specify the `\\Server\Public\Faxes` folder in the Store a Copy in a Folder text box.

---

3. Double-click the Route Through E-Mail method.

4. Display the E-Mail tab, type an address in the Mail To text box, and then click OK.

5. In the tree pane, right-click the Fax (Local) item at the top of the tree, and then click Properties.

6. Display the Receipts tab, shown completed in Figure 20.25.

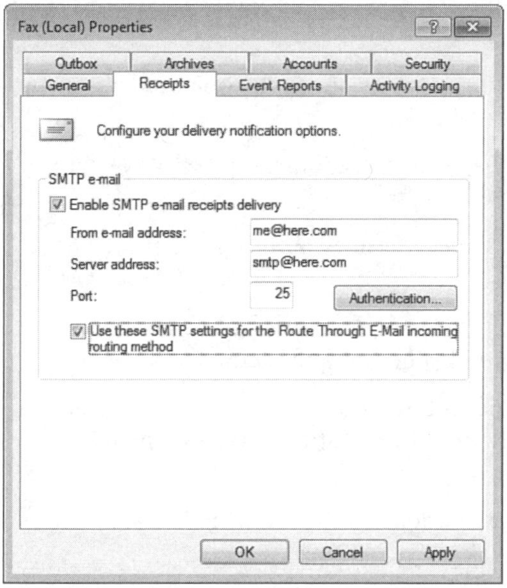

FIGURE 20.25   Use the Receipts tab to configure the routing of incoming faxes to an email address.

7. Activate the Enable SMTP E-Mail Receipts Delivery check box.

8. Fill in the fields for From E-Mail Address and the Server Address, which is the domain name of your ISP's or email host's SMTP server.

9. If your ISP or host requires you to use a port other than 25 for outgoing mail, enter that port number in the Port text box.

10. If your ISP or host requires authentication for outgoing mail, click Authentication, activate the Basic Authentication option, click Credentials, and then enter the username and password (twice) that you use to authenticate outgoing mail. (On most systems, this is the same as the login credentials you use for incoming mail.) Click OK until you return to the Microsoft Fax Service Manager.

11. Right-click the Route Through E-Mail method, and then click Enable.

12. Activate the Use These SMTP Settings for the Route Through E-Mail Incoming Routing Method check box.

13. Click OK.

Now when a fax comes in, the Fax service will use the address you specified in step 8 to send the fax as an attachment to the address you specified in step 4.

From Here

▶ To learn how to use the Windows Home Server Console program to change the Administrator password, **SEE** "Changing the Windows Home Server Password," **P. 88.**

▶ To learn how to use group policies to set up programs or scripts to launch at startup, **SEE** "Launching Items Using Group Policies," **P. 96.**

▶ For details on using Terminal Services Manager, **SEE** "Monitoring Remote Desktop Sessions," **P. 249.**

▶ To learn how to activate Windows Home Server's security auditing policies, **SEE** "Activating the Auditing Policies," **P. 258.**

▶ To learn how to enable a group policy that forces client computers to check for updates on a WSUS server, **SEE** "Connecting Home Computers to WSUS," **P. 363.**

▶ For details on using Control Panel's Internet Information Services (IIS) Manager icon, **SEE** "Viewing the Default Website with Internet Information Services Manager," **P. 297.**

▶ For a good example of what Task Manager can do, **SEE** "Monitoring Performance with Task Manager," **P. 370.**

CHAPTER 21

Scripting Windows Home Server

IN THIS CHAPTER

▶ Understanding Windows Script Host

▶ Running Scripts

▶ Programming Objects

▶ Programming the WScript Object

▶ Programming the WshShell Object

▶ Programming the WshNetwork Object

▶ Programming the Windows Management Instrumentation Service

You've seen throughout this book that unleashing the power of Windows Home Server involves understanding the technology behind Windows Home Server, getting in-depth explanations of the standard tools and features, and going behind the scenes to explore Windows Home Server's vast bounty of hidden tools, programs, and settings.

I've also helped you unlock Windows Home Server's potential by providing you with sample scripts that automate routine or cumbersome tasks and take advantage of the power that only scripting and programming can provide. This isn't a programming book, so I've tried not to overwhelm you with too many scripts. However, there have been quite a few, as this incomplete list shows:

▶ In Chapter 11, "Implementing Windows Home Server Security," you saw a script that extracted specific security events from the Windows Home Server Security events log. **SEE** "Viewing Auditing Events with a Script," **P. 268**.

▶ In Chapter 16, "Maintaining Windows Home Server," I showed you a script that displayed the current Windows Home Server uptime. **SEE** "Displaying Uptime with a Script," **P. 409**.

▶ Chapter 16 also provided a script for checking the free space on the Windows Home Server system drive. **SEE** "Checking Free Disk Space on the System Drive," **P. 416**.

▶ In Chapter 20, "Using Other Windows Home Server Power Tools," I showed you a script that toggled a service between started and stopped. **SEE** "Controlling Services with a Script," **P. 570.**

If you're looking to automate a wider variety of tasks in Windows, you need to supplement your knowledge with scripts that can deal with the Registry, shortcuts, files, and network drives, and that can even interact with Windows programs via Automation. The secret to these powerful scripts is the *Windows Script Host* (*WSH*). This chapter introduces you to the Windows Script Host, shows you how to execute scripts, and runs through the various elements in the Windows Script Host object model.

Understanding Windows Script Host

As you might know, Internet Explorer is really just an empty container application that's designed to host different data formats, including ActiveX controls, various file formats (such as Microsoft Word documents and Microsoft Excel worksheets), and several ActiveX scripting engines. A *scripting engine* is a dynamic-link library (DLL) that provides programmatic support for a particular scripting language. Internet Explorer supports two such scripting engines: VBScript (`VBScript.dll`) and JavaScript (`JSscript.dll`). This enables web programmers to write small programs—*scripts*—that interact with the user, control the browser, set cookies, open and close windows, and more. Although these scripting engines don't offer full-blown programmability (you can't compile scripts, for example), they do offer modern programming structures such as loops, conditionals, variables, objects, and more. In other words, they're a huge leap beyond what a mere batch file can do.

The WSH is also a container application, albeit a scaled-down application in that its only purpose in life is to host scripting engines. Right out of the box, the Windows Script Host supports both the VBScript and JavaScript engines. However, Microsoft designed the WSH to be a universal host that can support any ActiveX-based scripting engine. Therefore, third-party vendors also offer scripting engines for languages such as Perl, Tcl, and Rexx.

The key difference between Internet Explorer's script hosting and the WSH is the environment in which the scripts run. Internet Explorer scripts are web page–based, so they control and interact with either the web page or the web browser. The WSH runs scripts within the Windows Home Server shell or from the command prompt, so you use these scripts to control various aspects of Windows Home Server. Here's a sampling of the things you can do:

▶ Execute Windows programs.

▶ Create and modify shortcuts.

▶ Use Automation to connect and interact with Automation-enabled applications such as Microsoft Word, Outlook, and Internet Explorer.

21

▶ Read, add, and delete Registry keys and items.

▶ Access the VBScript and JavaScript object models, which give access to the file system, runtime error messages, and more.

▶ Use pop-up dialog boxes to display information to the user, and determine which button the user clicked to dismiss the dialog box.

▶ Read environment variables, which are system values that Windows Home Server keeps in memory, such as the folder into which Windows Home Server is installed—the %SystemRoot% environment variable—and the name of the computer—the %ComputerName% environment variable.

▶ Deal with network resources, including mapping and unmapping network drives, accessing user data (such as the username and user domain), and connecting and disconnecting network printers.

▶ Script the Windows Management Instrumentation (WMI) interface.

What about speed? After all, you wouldn't want to load something that's the size of Internet Explorer each time you need to run a simple script. That's not a problem because, as I've said, the WSH does nothing but host scripting engines, so it has much less memory overhead than Internet Explorer. That means that your scripts run quickly. For power users looking for a Windows-based batch language, the WSH is a welcome tool.

> **NOTE**
>
> This chapter does not teach you how to program in either VBScript or JavaScript and, in fact, assumes that you're already proficient in one or both of these languages. If you're looking for a programming tutorial, my book *VBA for the Office 2007 System* (Que, 2007) is a good place to start. (VBScript is a subset of Visual Basic for Applications, or VBA.) For JavaScript, try my book *Special Edition Using JavaScript* (Que, 2001).

Running Scripts

Scripts are simple text files that you create using Notepad or some other text editor. You can use a word processor such as WordPad to create scripts, but you must make sure that you save these files using the program's Text Only document type. For VBScript, a good alternative to Notepad is the editor that comes with either Visual Basic or any program that supports VBA (such as the Office suite). Just remember that VBScript is a subset of VBA (which is, in turn, a subset of Visual Basic), so it does not support all objects and features.

In a web page, you use the `<script>` tag to specify the scripting language you're using, as in this example:

```
<SCRIPT LANGUAGE="VBScript">
```

With the WSH, the script file's extension specifies the scripting language:

▶ For VBScript, save your text files using the .vbs extension (which is registered as the following file type: VBScript Script File).

▶ For JavaScript, use the .js extension (which is registered as the following file type: JScript Script File).

As described in the next three sections, you have three ways to run your scripts: by launching the script files directly, by using WSscript.exe, or by using CScript.exe.

Running Script Files Directly

The easiest way to run a script from within Windows is to launch the .vbs or .js file directly. That is, you either double-click the file in Windows Explorer or type the file's path and name in the Run dialog box. Note, however, that this technique does not work at the command prompt. For that, you need to use the CScript program described a bit later.

Using WScript for Windows-Based Scripts

The .vbs and .js file types have an open method that's associated with WScript (WScript.exe), which is the Windows-based front-end for the WSH. In other words, launching a script file named MyScript.vbs is equivalent to entering the following command in the Run dialog box:

```
wscript myscript.vbs
```

The WScript host also defines several parameters that you can use to control the way the script executes. Here's the full syntax:

```
WSCRIPT [filename] [arguments] [//B] [//D] [//E:engine] [//H:host] [//I]
➥ [//Job:xxxx] [//S] [//T:ss] [//X]
```

filename	Specifies the filename, including the path of the script file, if necessary.
arguments	Specifies optional arguments required by the script. An *argument* is a data value that the script uses as part of its procedures or calculations.
//B	Runs the script in batch mode, which means script errors and Echo method output lines are suppressed. (I discuss the Echo method later in this chapter.)
//D	Enables Active Debugging. If an error occurs, the script is loaded into the Microsoft Script Debugger (if it's installed), and the offending statement is highlighted.
//E:engine	Executes the script using the specified scripting *engine*, which is the scripting language to use when running the script.
//H:host	Specifies the default scripting host. For *host*, use either CScript or WScript.
//I	Runs the script in interactive mode, which displays script errors and Echo method output lines.

//Job:id   In a script file that contains multiple jobs, executes only the job with id attribute equal to id.

//S   Saves the specified WScript arguments as the default for the current user; uses the following Registry key to save the settings:

         HKCU\Software\Microsoft\Windows Script Host\Settings

//TT:ss   Specifies the maximum time in seconds (ss) that the script can run before it shuts down automatically.

//X   Executes the entire script in the Microsoft Script Debugger (if it's installed).

For example, the following command runs MyScript.vbs in batch mode with a 60-second maximum execution time:

```
wscript myscript.vbs //B //TT:60
```

Creating Script Jobs

A script *job* is a section of code that performs a specific task or set of tasks. Most script files contain a single job. However, it's possible to create a script file with multiple jobs. To do this, first surround the code for each job with the <script> and </script> tags, and then surround those with the <job> and </job> tags. In the <job> tag, include the id attribute and set it to a unique value that identifies the job. Finally, surround all the jobs with the <package> and </package> tags. Here's an example:

```
<package>
<job id="A">
<script language="VBScript">
    WScript.Echo "This is Job A."
</script>
</job>

<job id="B">
<script language="VBScript">
     WScript.Echo "This is Job B."
</script>
</job>
</package>
```

Save the file using the .wsf (Windows Script File) extension.

NOTE

If you write a lot of scripts, the Microsoft Script Debugger is an excellent programming tool. If there's a problem with a script, the debugger can help you pinpoint its location. For example, the debugger enables you to step through the script's execution one statement at a time. If you don't have the Microsoft Script Debugger, you can download a copy from www.microsoft.com/downloads/en/details.aspx?FamilyID=2f465be0-94fd-4569-b3c4-dffdf19ccd99. (To install this program on Windows 7 and Vista, right-click the downloaded file, and then click Run as Administrator.)

Using CScript for Command-Line Scripts

The WSH has a second host front-end application called CScript (`CScript.exe`), which enables you to run scripts from the command line. In its simplest form, you launch CScript and use the name of the script file (and its path, if required) as a parameter, as in this example:

```
cscript myscript.vbs
```

The WSH displays the following banner and then executes the script:

Microsoft (R) Windows Script Host Version 5.8 for Windows

Copyright (C) Microsoft Corporation. All rights reserved.

As with WScript, the CScript host has an extensive set of parameters you can specify:

```
CSCRIPT [filename] [arguments] [//B] [//D] [//E:engine] [//H:host] [//I]
➥ [//Job:xxxx] [//S] [//T:ss] [//X] [//LOGO ¦ //NOLOGO] [//U]
```

This syntax is almost identical to that of WScript, but it adds the following three parameters:

//LOGO	Displays the WSH banner at startup
//NOLOGO	Hides the WSH banner at startup
//U	Uses Unicode for redirected input/output from the console

Script Properties and .wsh Files

In the previous two sections, you saw that the WScript and CScript hosts have a number of parameters you can specify when you execute a script. It's also possible to set some of these options by using the properties associated with each script file. To see these properties, right-click a script file and then click Properties. In the properties sheet that appears, display the Script tab, shown in Figure 21.1. You have two options, as follows:

▶ **Stop Script After Specified Number of Seconds**—If you activate this check box, Windows shuts down the script after it has run for the number of seconds specified in the associated spin box. This is useful for scripts that might hang during execution. For example, a script that attempts to enumerate all the mapped network drives at startup might hang if the network is unavailable.

▶ **Display Logo When Script Executed in Command Console**—As you saw in the previous section, the CScript host displays some banner text when you run a script at the command prompt. If you deactivate this check box, the WSH suppresses this banner (unless you use the //LOGO parameter).

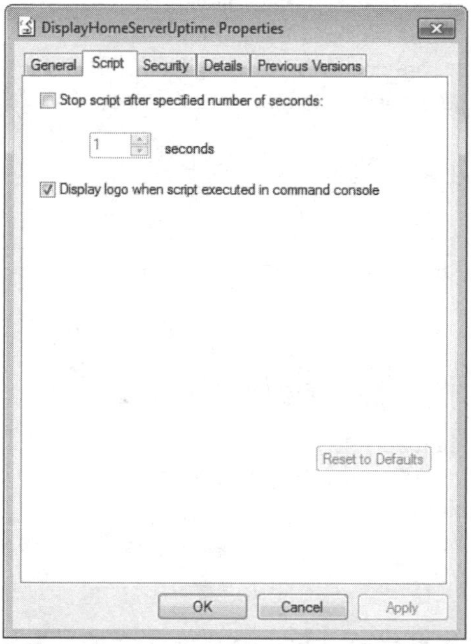

FIGURE 21.1 In a script file's properties sheet, use the Script tab to set some default options for the script.

When you make changes to these properties, the WSH saves your settings in a new file that has the same name as the script file, except with the .wsh (WSH Settings) extension. For example, if the script file is MyScript.vbs, the settings are stored in MyScript.wsh. These .wsh files are text files organized in sections, much like .ini files. Here's an example:

```
[ScriptFile]
Path=C:\Users\Administrator\My Documents\Scripts\
➥ DisplayHomeServerUptime.vbs
[Options]
Timeout=10
DisplayLogo=0
```

To use these settings when running the script, use either WScript or CScript and specify the name of the .wsh file:

```
wscript myscript.wsh
```

> **NOTE**
>
> Rather than setting properties for individual scripts, you might prefer to set global properties that apply to the WScript host. Those global settings then apply to every script that runs using the WScript host. To do this, run `WScript.exe` without parameters. This displays the properties sheet for WScript, which contains only the Script tab shown in Figure 21.1. The settings you choose in the properties sheet are stored in the following Registry key:
>
> ```
> HKLM\Software\Microsoft\Windows Script Host\Settings
> ```

Programming Objects

Although this chapter isn't a programming primer per se, I'd like to take some time now to run through a few quick notes about programming objects. This will serve you well throughout the rest of the chapter as I take you on a tour of the WSH object model.

The dictionary definition of an object is "anything perceptible by one or more of the senses, especially something that can be seen and felt." In scripting, an *object* is an application element that exposes an interface to the programmer, who can then perform the programming equivalent of seeing and feeling:

▶ You can make changes to the object's *properties*. (This is the seeing part.)

▶ You can make the object perform a task by activating a *method* associated with the object. (This is the feeling part.)

Working with Object Properties

Every programmable object has a defining set of characteristics. These characteristics are the object's *properties*, and they control the appearance and position of the object. For example, the WScript object (the top-level WSH object) has an `Interactive` property that determines whether the script runs in interactive mode or batch mode.

When you refer to a property, you use the following syntax:

Object.Property

Object   The name of the object

Property   The name of the property with which you want to work

For example, the following expression refers to the Interactive property of the WScript object:

```
WScript.Interactive
```

Setting the Value of a Property

To set a property to a certain value, you use the following syntax:

```
Object.Property = value
```

Here, *value* is an expression that specifies the value to which you want to set the property. As such, it can be any of the scripting language's recognized data types, which usually include the following:

▶ A numeric value

▶ A string value, enclosed in double quotation marks (such as "My Script Application")

▶ A logical value (in VBScript: True or False; in JavaScript: true or false)

For example, the following VBScript statement tells the WSH to run the script using interactive mode:

```
WScript.Interactive = True
```

Returning the Value of a Property

Sometimes you need to store the current value of a property or test that value before changing the property or performing some other action. You can store the current value of a property in a variable by using the following syntax:

```
variable = Object.Property
```

Here, *variable* is a variable name or another property. For example, the following statement stores the current script mode (batch or interactive) in a variable named currentMode:

```
currentMode = WScript.Interactive
```

Working with Object Methods

An object's *properties* describe what the object is, whereas its *methods* describe what the object *does*. For example, the WScript object has a Quit method that enables you to stop the execution of a script.

The way you refer to a method depends on whether the method requires arguments. If it doesn't, the syntax is similar to that of properties:

`Object.Method`

`Object`	The name of the object
`Method`	The name of the method you want to run

For example, the following statement shuts down a script:

`WScript.Quit`

If the method requires arguments, you use the following syntax:

`Object.Method (Argument1, Argument2, ...)`

NOTE

In VBScript, the parentheses around the argument list are necessary only if you'll be storing the result of the method in a variable or object property. In JavaScript, the parentheses are always required.

For example, the `WshShell` object has a `RegWrite` method that you use to write a key or value to the Registry. (I discuss this object and method in detail later in this chapter; see "Working with Registry Entries.") Here's the syntax:

`WshShell.RegWrite strName, anyValue[, strType]`

`strName`	The name of the Registry key or value
`anyValue`	The value to write, if `strName` is a Registry value
`strType`	The data type of the value

Argument Naming Conventions

When presenting method arguments in this chapter, I'll follow Microsoft's naming conventions, including the use of the following prefixes for the argument names:

Prefix	Data Type
any	Any type
b	Boolean
int	Integer
nat	Natural numbers
obj	Object
str	String

> For many object methods, not all the arguments are required. In the RegWrite
> method, for example, the *strName* and *anyValue* arguments are required, but the
> strType argument is not. Throughout this chapter, I differentiate between required and
> optional arguments by surrounding the optional arguments with square brackets—for
> example, *[strType]*.

For example, the following statement creates a new value named Test and sets it equal
to Foo:

```
WshShell.RegWrite "HKCU\Software\Microsoft\Windows Script Host\Test",
➥"Foo", "REG_SZ"
```

Assigning an Object to a Variable

If you're using JavaScript, you assign an object to a variable using a standard variable
assignment:

```
var variableName = ObjectName
```

variableName	The name of the variable
ObjectName	The object you want to assign to the variable

In VBScript, you assign an object to a variable by using the Set statement. Set has the
following syntax:

```
Set variableName = ObjectName
```

variableName	The name of the variable
ObjectName	The object you want to assign to the variable

You'll see later on that you must often use Automation to access external objects. For
example, if you want to work with files and folders in your script, you must access the
scripting engine object named FileSystemObject. To get this access, you use the
CreateObject method and store the resulting object in a variable, like so:

```
Set fs = CreateObject("Scripting.FileSystemObject")
```

Working with Object Collections

A *collection* is a set of similar objects. For example, WScript.Arguments is the set of all the
arguments specified on the script's command line. Collections are objects, too, so they
have their own properties and methods, and you can use these properties and methods to
manipulate one or more objects in the collection.

The members of a collection are *elements*. You can refer to individual elements by using an *index*. For example, the following statement refers to the first command-line argument. (Collection indexes always begin at 0.)

```
WScript.Arguments(0)
```

If you don't specify an element, the WSH assumes that you want to work with the entire collection.

VBScript: Using For Each...Next Loops for Collections

As you might know, VBScript provides the For...Next loop that enables you to cycle through a chunk of code a specified number of times. For example, the following code loops 10 times:

```
For counter = 1 To 10
    Code entered here is repeated 10 times
Next counter
```

A useful variation on this theme is the For Each...Next loop, which operates on a collection of objects. You don't need a loop counter because VBScript loops through the individual elements in the collection and performs on each element whatever operations are inside the loop. Here's the structure of the basic For Each...Next loop:

```
For Each element In collection
    [statements]
Next
```

element	A variable used to hold the name of each element in the collection
collection	The name of the collection
statements	The statements to execute for each element in the collection

The following code loops through all the arguments specified on the script's command line and displays each one:

```
For Each arg In WScript.Arguments
    WScript.Echo arg
Next
```

JavaScript: Using Enumerators and for Loops for Collections

To iterate through a collection in JavaScript, you must do two things: create a new Enumerator object, and use a for loop to cycle through the enumerated collection.

To create a new Enumerator object, use the new keyword to set up an object variable (where collection is the name of the collection you want to work with):

```
var enum = new Enumerator(collection)
```

Then set up a special for loop:

```
for (; !enumerator.atEnd(); enumerator.moveNext())
{
    [statements];
}
```

enumerator   The Enumerator object you created

statements   The statements to execute for each element in the collection

The `Enumerator` object's `moveNext` method runs through the elements in the collection, whereas the `atEnd` method shuts down the loop after the last item has been processed. The following code loops through all the arguments specified on the script's command line and displays each one:

```
var args = new Enumerator(WScript.Arguments);
for (; !args.atEnd(); args.moveNext())
{
    WScript.Echo(args.item());
}
```

Programming the WScript Object

The `WScript` object represents the WSH applications (`WScript.exe` and `CScript.exe`). You use this object to get and set certain properties of the scripting host, as well as to access two other objects: WshArguments (the `WScript` object's `Arguments` property) and WshScriptEngine (accessed via the `WScript` object's `GetScriptEngine` method). `WScript` also contains the powerful `CreateObject` and `GetObject` methods, which enable you to work with Automation-enabled applications.

Displaying Text to the User

The `WScript` object method that you'll use most often is `Echo`, which displays text to the user. Here's the syntax:

```
WScript.Echo [Argument1, Argument2,...]
```

Here, Argument1, Argument2, and so on are any number of text or numeric values that represent the information you want to display to the user. In the Windows-based host (`WScript.exe`), the information displays in a dialog box; in the command-line host (`CScript.exe`), the information displays at the command prompt (much like the command-line `ECHO` utility).

▶ **SEE** "ECHO: Displaying Messages from a Batch File," **P. 494.**

For example, here's a one-line script that uses the Echo method:

```
WScript.Echo "Hello Scripting World!"
```

Figure 21.2 shows the dialog box that appears when you run this script.

FIGURE 21.2   When you run the Echo method with WScript.exe, the message appears in a dialog box.

Shutting Down a Script

You use the WScript object's Quit method to shut down the script. You can also use Quit to have your script return an error code by using the following syntax:

```
WScript.Quit [intErrorCode]
```

intErrorCode   An integer value that represents the error code you want to return

You could then call the script from a batch file and use the ERRORLEVEL environment variable to deal with the return code in some way.

▶ **SEE** "XCOPY: Advanced File Copying," **P. 514**.

Scripting and Automation

Applications such as Internet Explorer and Word come with (or *expose*, in the jargon) a set of objects that define various aspects of the program. For example, Internet Explorer has an Application object that represents the program as a whole. Similarly, Word has a Document object that represents a Word document. By using the properties and methods that come with these objects, you can programmatically query and manipulate the applications. With Internet Explorer, for example, you can use the Application object's Navigate method to send the browser to a specified web page. With Word, you can read a Document object's Saved property to see whether the document has unsaved changes.

This is powerful stuff, but how do you get at the objects that these applications expose? You do that by using a technology called *Automation*. Applications that support Automation implement object libraries that expose the application's native objects to Automation-aware programming languages. Such applications are *Automation servers*, and the applications that manipulate the server's objects are *Automation controllers*. The WSH is an Automation controller that enables you to write script code to control any server's objects.

This means that you can use an application's exposed objects more or less as you use the WSH objects. With just a minimum of preparation, your script code can refer to and work with the Internet Explorer `Application` object, or the Microsoft Word `Document` object, or any of the hundreds of other objects exposed by the applications on your system. (Note, however, that not all applications expose objects. Outlook Express and most of the built-in Windows Home Server programs—such as WordPad and Paint—do not expose objects.)

Creating an Automation Object with the CreateObject Method

The `WScript` object's `CreateObject` method creates an Automation object (specifically, what programmers call an *instance* of the object). Here's the syntax:

```
WScript.CreateObject(strProgID)
```

strProgID   A string that specifies the Automation server application and the type of object to create. This string is a *programmatic identifier*, which is a label that uniquely specifies an application and one of its objects. The programmatic identifier always takes the following form:

> *AppName.ObjectType*

> Here, AppName *is the Automation name of the application and* ObjectType *is the object class type (as defined in the Registry's* HKEY_CLASSES_ROOT *key). For example, here's the programmatic ID for Word:

> `Word.Application`

Note that you normally use `CreateObject` within a `Set` statement, and that the function serves to create a new instance of the specified Automation object. For example, you could use the following statement to create a new instance of Word's `Application` object:

```
Set objWord = CreateObject("Word.Application")
```

You need to do nothing else to use the Automation object. With your variable declared and an instance of the object created, you can use that object's properties and methods directly. Listing 21.1 shows a VBScript example that works with Internet Explorer.

LISTING 21.1   A VBScript Example That Creates and Manipulates an Internet Explorer Application Object

```
Option Explicit
Dim objIE
'
' Create the Internet Explorer object
'
Set objIE = WScript.CreateObject("InternetExplorer.Application")
'
' Navigate to a page
'
objIE.Navigate "http://www.wordspy.com/"
'
' Make the browser window visible
```

```
'
objIE.Visible = True
'
' Release the object
'
Set objIE = Nothing
```

This script displays a website in Internet Explorer by working with Internet Explorer's `Application` object via Automation. The script begins by using the `CreateObject` method to create a new Internet Explorer `Application` object, and the object is stored in the `objIE` variable. From there, you can wield the `objIE` variable just as though it were the Internet Explorer `Application` object.

For example, the `objIE.Navigate` statement uses the `Navigate` method to navigate to the website given by the URL. Then the object's `Visible` property is set to `True` so that we can see the new browser window. Finally, the script sets the `objIE` object variable to `Nothing` to release the variable's memory (always a good idea when dealing with Automation objects).

For comparison, Listing 21.2 shows a JavaScript procedure that performs the same tasks.

LISTING 21.2   A JavaScript Example That Creates and Manipulates an Internet Explorer Application Object

```
// Create the Internet Explorer object
//
var objIE = WScript.CreateObject("InternetExplorer.Application");
//
// Navigate to a page
//
objIE.Navigate ("http://www.wordspy.com/");
//
// Make the browser window visible
//
objIE.Visible = true;
//
// Release the object
//
objIE = null;
```

Working with an Existing Object Using the GetObject Method

If you know that the object you want to work with already exists or is already open, the `CreateObject` method isn't the best choice. In the example in the previous section, if Word is already running, the code starts a second copy of Word, which is a waste of resources. For these situations, it's better to work directly with the existing object. To do that, use the `GetObject` method:

WScript.GetObject(*strPathname*[, *strProgID*])

strPathname   The pathname (drive, folder, and filename) of the file you want to work with (or the file that contains the object you want to work with). If you omit this argument, you have to specify the *strProgID* argument.

strProgID   The programmatic identifier that specifies the Automation server application and the type of object to work with (that is, the *App Name.ObjectType* class syntax).

Listing 21.3 shows a VBScript procedure that puts the GetObject method to work.

LISTING 21.3   A VBScript Example That Uses the GetObject Method to Work with an Existing Instance of a Word Document Object

```
Option Explicit
Dim objDoc
'
' Get the Word Document object
'
Set objDoc = WScript.GetObject("C:\Users\Administrator\" & _
                               "My Documents\GetObject.doc", "Word.Document")
'
' Get the word count
'
WScript.Echo objDoc.Name & " has " & objDoc.Words.Count & " words."
'
' We're done, so quit Word
'
objDoc.Application.Quit
```

The GetObject method assigns the Word Document object named GetObject.doc to the objDoc variable. After you've set up this reference, you can use the object's properties and methods directly. For example, the Echo method uses objDoc.Name to return the filename and objDoc.Words.Count to determine the number of words in the document.

Note that although you're working with a Document object, you still have access to Word's Application object. That's because most objects have an Application property that refers to the Application object. In the script in Listing 21.3, for example, the following statement uses the Application property to quit Word:

```
objDoc.Application.Quit
```

Exposing VBScript and JavaScript Objects
One of the most powerful uses for scripted Automation is accessing the object models exposed by the VBScript and JavaScript engines. These models expose a number of objects, including the local file system. This enables you to create scripts that work with files,

folders, and disk drives; read and write text files; and more. You use the following syntax to refer to these objects:

```
Scripting.ObjectType
```

Scripting is the Automation name of the scripting engine, and ObjectType is the class type of the object.

NOTE

This section gives you a brief explanation of the objects associated with the VBScript and JavaScript engines. For the complete list of object properties and methods, please see the following site: msdn.microsoft.com/en-us/library/d1wf56tt(VS.85).aspx.

Programming the FileSystemObject

FileSystemObject is the top-level file system object. For all your file system scripts, you begin by creating a new instance of FileSystemObject.

In VBScript:

```
Set fs = WScript.CreateObject("Scripting.FileSystemObject")
```

In JavaScript:

```
var fs = WScript.CreateObject("Scripting.FileSystemObject");
```

Here's a summary of the file system objects you can access via Automation and the top-level FileSystemObject:

▶ **Drive**—This object enables you to access the properties of a specified disk drive or UNC network path. To reference a Drive object, use either the Drives collection (discussed next) or the FileSystemObject object's GetDrive method. For example, the following VBScript statement references drive C:

```
Set objFS = WScript.CreateObject("Scripting.FileSystemObject")
Set objDrive = objFS.GetDrive("C:")
```

▶ **Drives**—This object is the collection of all available drives. To reference this collection, use the FileSystemObject object's Drives property:

```
Set objFS = WScript.CreateObject("Scripting.FileSystemObject")
Set objDrives = objFS.Drives
```

▶ **Folder**—This object enables you to access the properties of a specified folder. To reference a Folder object, use either the Folders collection (discussed next) or the FileSystemObject object's GetFolder method:

```
Set objFS = WScript.CreateObject("Scripting.FileSystemObject")
Set objFolder = objFS.GetFolder("C:\Users")
```

> ▶ **Folders**—This object is the collection of subfolders within a specified folder. To reference this collection, use the Folder object's Subfolders property:

```
Set objFS = WScript.CreateObject("Scripting.FileSystemObject")
Set objFolder = objFS.GetFolder("C:\Windows")
Set objSubfolders = objFolder.Subfolders
```

> ▶ **File**—This object enables you to access the properties of a specified file. To reference a File object, use either the Files collection (discussed next) or the FileSystemObject object's GetFile method:

```
Set objFS = WScript.CreateObject("Scripting.FileSystemObject")
Set objFile = objFS.GetFile("c:\Boot.ini")
```

> ▶ **Files**—This object is the collection of files within a specified folder. To reference this collection, use the Folder object's Files property:

```
Set objFS = WScript.CreateObject("Scripting.FileSystemObject")
Set objFolder = objFS.GetFolder("C:\Windows")
Set objFiles = objFolder.Files
```

> ▶ **TextStream**—This object enables you to use sequential access to work with a text file. To open a text file, use the FileSystemObject object's OpenTextFile method:

```
Set objFS = WScript.CreateObject("Scripting.FileSystemObject")
Set objTS= objFS.OpenTextFile("C:\ToDoList.txt")
```

Alternatively, you can create a new text file by using the FileSystemObject object's CreateTextFile method:

```
Set objFS = WScript.CreateObject("Scripting.FileSystemObject")
Set objTS= objFS.CreateTextFile("C:\ToDoList.txt")
```

Either way, you end up with a TextStream object, which has various methods for reading data from the file and writing data to the file. For example, the following script reads and displays the text from C:\ToDoList.txt:

```
Set objFS = WScript.CreateObject("Scripting.FileSystemObject")
Set objTS = objFS.OpenTextFile("C:\ToDoList.txt")
strContents = objTS.ReadAll
WScript.Echo strContents
objTS.Close
```

Programming the WshShell Object

WshShell is a generic name for a powerful object that enables you to query and interact with various aspects of the Windows shell. You can display information to the user, run applications, create shortcuts, work with the Registry, and control Windows' environment variables. The next few sections discuss each of those useful tasks.

Referencing the WshShell Object

WshShell refers to the Shell object exposed via the Automation interface of WScript. Therefore, you must use CreateObject to return this object:

```
Set objWshShell = WScript.CreateObject("WScript.Shell")
```

From here, you can use the objWshShell variable to access the object's properties and methods.

Displaying Information to the User

You saw earlier that the WScript object's Echo method is useful for displaying simple text messages to the user. You can gain more control over the displayed message by using the WshShell object's Popup method. This method is similar to the MsgBox function used in Visual Basic and VBA in that it enables you to control both the dialog box title and the buttons displayed, as well as to determine which of those buttons the user pressed. Here's the syntax:

```
WshShell.Popup(strText[, nSecondsToWait][, strTitle][, intType])
```

WshShell	The WshShell object.
strText	The message you want to display in the dialog box. You can enter a string up to 1,024 characters long.
nSecondsToWait	The maximum number of seconds the dialog box will be displayed.
strTitle	The text that appears in the dialog box title bar. If you omit this value, Windows Script Host appears in the title bar.
intType	A number or constant that specifies, among other things, the command buttons that appear in the dialog box (see the next section). The default value is 0.

For example, the following statements display the dialog box shown in Figure 21.3:

```
Set objWshShell = WScript.CreateObject("WScript.Shell")
objWshShell.Popup "Hello Popup World!", , "My Popup"
```

FIGURE 21.3   A simple message dialog box produced by the Popup method.

> **TIP**
>
> For long messages, VBScript wraps the text inside the dialog box. If you prefer to create your own line breaks, use VBScript's Chr function and the carriage return character (ASCII 13) between each line:
>
> ```
> WshShell.Popup "First line" & Chr(13) & "Second line"
> ```
>
> You can also use the vbCrLf constant, which does the same thing:
>
> ```
> WshShell.Popup "First line" & vbCrLf & "Second line"
> ```
>
> For JavaScript, use \n:
>
> ```
> WshShell.Popup("First line" + "\n" + "Second line");
> ```

Setting the Style of the Message

The default Popup dialog box displays only an OK button. You can include other buttons and icons in the dialog box by using different values for the intType parameter. Table 21.1 lists the available options.

TABLE 21.1   The Popup Method's intType Parameter Options

VBScript Constant	Value	Description
Buttons		
vbOKOnly	0	Displays only an OK button. This is the default.
vbOKCancel	1	Displays the OK and Cancel buttons.
vbAbortRetryIgnore	2	Displays the Abort, Retry, and Ignore buttons.
vbYesNoCancel	3	Displays the Yes, No, and Cancel buttons.
vbYesNo	4	Displays the Yes and No buttons.
vbRetryCancel	5	Displays the Retry and Cancel buttons.
Icons		
vbCritical	16	Displays the Critical Message icon.
vbQuestion	32	Displays the Warning Query icon.
vbExclamation	48	Displays the Warning Message icon.
vbInformation	64	Displays the Information Message icon.
Default Buttons		
vbDefaultButton1	0	The first button is the default (that is, the button selected when the user presses Enter).
vbDefaultButton2	256	The second button is the default.
vbDefaultButton3	512	The third button is the default.

You derive the `intType` argument in one of two ways:

▶ By adding the values for each option

▶ By using the VBScript constants separated by plus signs (+)

The script in Listing 21.4 shows an example, and Figure 21.4 shows the resulting dialog box.

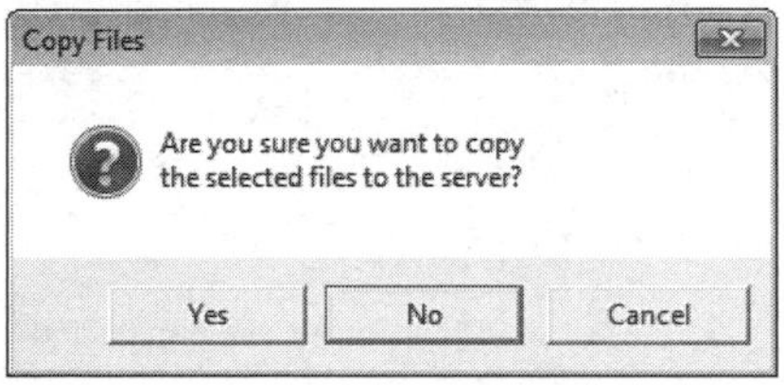

FIGURE 21.4   The dialog box that's displayed when you run the script.

LISTING 21.4   A VBScript Example That Uses the Popup Method to Display the Dialog Box Shown in Figure 21.4

```
Option Explicit
Dim strText, strTitle, intType, objWshShell, intResult
'
' First, set up the message
'
strText = "Are you sure you want to copy" & vbCrLf
strText = strText & "the selected files to the server?"
strTitle = "Copy Files"
intType = vbYesNoCancel + vbQuestion + vbDefaultButton2
'
' Now display it
'
Set objWshShell = WScript.CreateObject("WScript.Shell")
intResult = objWshShell.Popup(strText, ,strTitle, intType)
```

Here, three variables—`strText`, `strTitle`, and `intType`—store the values for the `Popup` method's `strText`, `strTitle`, and `intType` arguments, respectively. In particular, the following statement derives the `intType` argument:

```
intType = vbYesNoCancel + vbQuestion + vbDefaultButton2
```

You also could derive the `intType` argument by adding up the values that these constants represent (3, 32, and 256, respectively), but the script becomes less readable that way.

Getting Return Values from the Message Dialog Box

A dialog box that displays only an OK button is straightforward. The user either clicks OK or presses Enter to remove the dialog from the screen. The multibutton styles are a little different, however; the user has a choice of buttons to select, and your script should have a way to find out which button the user chose, which enables it to decide what to do next. You do this by storing the Popup method's return value in a variable. Table 21.2 lists the seven possible return values.

TABLE 21.2   The Popup Method's Return Values

VBScript Constant	Value	Button Selected
vbOK	1	OK
vbCancel	2	Cancel
vbAbort	3	Abort
vbRetry	4	Retry
vbIgnore	5	Ignore
vbYes	6	Yes
vbNo	7	No

To process the return value, you can use an If...Then...Else or Select Case structure to test for the appropriate values. For example, the script shown earlier used a variable called intResult to store the return value of the Popup method. Listing 21.5 shows a revised version of the script that uses a VBScript Select Case statement to test for the three possible return values.

LISTING 21.5   A Script That Uses a Select Case Statement to Process the Popup Method's Return Value

```
Option Explicit
Dim strText, strTitle, intType, objWshShell, intResult
'
' First, set up the message
'
strText = "Are you sure you want to copy" & Chr(13)
strText = strText & "the selected files to the server?"
strTitle = "Copy Files"
intType = vbYesNoCancel + vbQuestion + vbDefaultButton2
'
' Now display it
'
Set objWshShell = WScript.CreateObject("WScript.Shell")
intResult = objWshShell.Popup(strText, ,strTitle, intType)
'
' Process the result
'
```

```
Select Case intResult
    Case vbYes
        WScript.Echo "You clicked ""Yes""!"
    Case vbNo
        WScript.Echo "You clicked ""No""!"
    Case vbCancel
        WScript.Echo "You clicked ""Cancel""!"
End Select
```

Running Applications

When you need your script to launch another application, use the Run method:

WshShell.Run *strCommand*[, *intWindowStyle*][, *bWaitOnReturn*]

WshShell	The WshShell object.
strCommand	The name of the file that starts the application. Unless the file is in the Windows folder, you should include the drive and folder to make sure that the script can find the file.
intWindowStyle	A constant or number that specifies how the application window will appear:

intWindowStyle	Window Appearance
0	Hidden
1	Normal size with focus
2	Minimized with focus (the default)
3	Maximized with focus
4	Normal without focus
6	Minimized without focus

bWaitOnReturn	A logical value that determines whether the application runs asynchronously. If this value is True, the script halts execution until the user exits the launched application; if this value is False, the script continues running after it has launched the application.

Here's an example:

```
Set objWshShell = WScript.CreateObject("WScript.Shell")
objWshShell.Run "Control.exe Inetcpl.cpl", 1, True
```

This Run method launches the Control Panel's Internet Properties dialog box.

▶ **SEE** "Understanding Control Panel Files," **P. 550**.

Working with Shortcuts

The WSH enables your scripts to create and modify shortcut files. When writing scripts for other users, you might want to take advantage of this capability to display shortcuts for new network shares, Internet sites, instruction files, and so on.

Creating a Shortcut

To create a shortcut, use the CreateShortcut method:

WshShell.CreateShortcut(*strPathname*)

WshShell   The WshShell object.

strPathname   The full path and filename of the shortcut file you want to create. Use the .lnk
                extension for a file system (program, document, folder, and so on) shortcut; use
                the .url extension for an Internet shortcut.

The following example creates and saves a shortcut on a user's desktop:

```
Set WshShell = objWScript.CreateObject("WScript.Shell")
Set objShortcut = objWshShell.CreateShortcut("C:\Users\" & _
                "Administrator\Desktop\test.lnk")
objShortcut.Save
```

Programming the WshShortcut Object

The CreateShortcut method returns a WshShortcut object. You can use this object to manipulate various properties and methods associated with shortcut files.

This object contains the following properties:

▶ Arguments—Returns or sets a string that specifies the arguments used when launching the shortcut. For example, suppose that the shortcut's target is the following:

    C:\Windows\Notepad.exe C:\ToDoList.txt

In other words, this shortcut launches Notepad and loads a file named ToDoList.txt. In this case, the Arguments property would return the following string:

    C:\ToDoList.txt

▶ Description—Returns or sets a string description of the shortcut.

▶ FullName—Returns the full path and filename of the shortcut's target. This is the same as the *strPathname value used in the CreateShortcut* method.

▶ Hotkey—Returns or sets the hotkey associated with the shortcut. To set this value, use the following syntax:

```
WshShortcut.Hotkey = strHotKey
```

WshShortcut	The WshShortcut object.
strHotKey	A string value of the form *Modifier+Keyname*, where *Modifier* is any combination of Alt, Ctrl, and Shift, and *Keyname* is one of A through Z or 0 through *23*.

For example, the following statement sets the hotkey to Ctrl+Alt+7:

```
objShortcut.Hotkey = "Ctrl+Alt+7"
```

▶ IconLocation—Returns or sets the icon used to display the shortcut. To set this value, use the following syntax:

```
WshShortcut.IconLocation = strIconLocation
```

WshShortcut	The WshShortcut object.
strIconLocation	A string value of the form *Path,Index*, where *Path* is the full pathname of the icon file and *Index* is the position of the icon within the file (where the first icon is 0).

Here's an example:

```
objShortcut.IconLocation = "C:\Windows\System32\Shell32.dll,18"
```

TargetPath	Returns or sets the path of the shortcut's target.
WindowStyle	Returns or sets the window style used by the shortcut's target. Use the same values outlined earlier for the Run method's *intWindowStyle* argument.
WorkingDirectory	Returns or sets the path of the shortcut's working directory.

NOTE

If you're working with Internet shortcuts, bear in mind that they support only two properties: FullName and TargetPath (the URL target).

The WshShortcut object also supports two methods, as follows:

Save	Saves the shortcut file to disk.
Resolve	Uses the shortcut's TargetPath property to look up the target file. Here's the syntax: *WshShortcut*.Resolve = *intFlag*

WshShortcut	The WshShortcut object.
intFlag	Determines what happens if the target file is not found:

intFlag	**What Happens**
1	Nothing.
2	Windows continues to search subfolders for the target file.
4	Windows updates the TargetPath property if the target file is found in a new location.

Listing 21.6 shows a complete example of a script that creates a shortcut.

LISTING 21.6   A Script That Creates a Shortcut File

```
Option Explicit
Dim objWshShell, objShortcut
Set objWshShell = WScript.CreateObject("WScript.Shell")
Set objShortcut = objWshShell.CreateShortcut("C:\Users\" & _
                "Administrator\Desktop\Edit Hosts File.lnk")
With objShortcut
    .TargetPath = "C:\Windows\Notepad.exe"
    .Arguments = "C:\Windows\System32\Drivers\etc\hosts"
    .WorkingDirectory = "C:\"
    .Description = "Opens the hosts file in Notepad"
    .Hotkey = "Ctrl+Alt+7"
    .IconLocation = "C:\Windows\System32\Shell32.dll,18"
    .WindowStyle = 3
    .Save
End With
```

Working with Registry Entries

You've seen throughout this book that the Registry is one of the most crucial data structures in Windows. However, Windows isn't the only software that uses the Registry. Most 32-bit applications use the Registry as a place to store setup options, customization values the user selected, and much more. Interestingly, your scripts can get in on the act as well. Not only can your scripts read the current value of any Registry setting, but they can use the Registry as a storage area. This enables you to keep track of user settings, recently used files, and any other configuration data that you'd like to save between sessions. This section shows you how to use the WshShell object to manipulate the Registry from within your scripts.

Reading Settings from the Registry

To read any value from the Registry, use the WshShell object's RegRead method:

WshShell.RegRead(strName)

WshShell   The WshShell object.

strName   The name of the Registry value or key that you want to read. If strName
                  ends with a backslash (\), RegRead returns the default value for the key;
                  otherwise, RegRead returns the data stored in the value. Note, too, that
                  strName must begin with one of the following root key names:

Short Name	Long Name
HKCR	HKEY_CLASSES_ROOT
HKCU	HKEY_CURRENT_USER
HKLM	HKEY_LOCAL_MACHINE
N/A	HKEY_USERS
N/A	HKEY_CURRENT_CONFIG

The script in Listing 21.7 displays the name of the registered owner of this copy of Windows.

LISTING 21.7   A Script That Reads the RegisteredOwner Setting from the Registry

```
Set objWshShell = WScript.CreateObject("WScript.Shell")
strSetting = "HKLM\SOFTWARE\Microsoft\Windows NT\CurrentVersion\
➥ RegisteredOwner"
strRegisteredUser = objWshShell.RegRead(strSetting)
WScript.Echo strRegisteredUser
```

Storing Settings in the Registry

To store a setting in the Registry, use the WshShell object's RegWrite method:

WshShell.RegWrite strName, anyValue [, strType]

WshShell   The WshShell object.

strName   The name of the Registry value or key that you want to set. If strName ends with
              a backslash (\), RegWrite sets the default value for the key; otherwise, RegWrite
              sets the data for the value. strName must begin with one of the root key names
              detailed in the RegRead method.

anyValue   The value to be stored.

strType   The data type of the value, which must be one of the following: REG_SZ (the
              default), REG_EXPAND_SZ, REG_DWORD, or REG_BINARY.

The following statements create a new key named ScriptSettings in the
HKEY_CURRENT_USER root:

```
Set objWshShell = WScript.CreateObject("WScript.Shell")
objWshShell.RegWrite "HKCU\ScriptSettings\", ""
```

The following statements create a new value named NumberOfReboots in the
HKEY_CURRENT_USER\ScriptSettings key and set this value to 1:

```
Set objWshShell = WScript.CreateObject("WScript.Shell")
objWshShell.RegWrite "HKCU\ScriptSettings\NumberOfReboots", 1, "REG_DWORD"
```

Deleting Settings from the Registry

If you no longer need to track a particular key or value setting, use the RegDelete method
to remove the setting from the Registry:

WshShell.RegDelete(*strName*)

WshShell   The WshShell object.

strName   The name of the Registry value or key that you want to delete. If *strName* ends
with a backslash (\), RegDelete deletes the key; otherwise, RegDelete deletes the
value. *strName* must begin with one of the root key names detailed in the RegRead
method.

To delete the NumberOfReboots value used in the previous example, you would use the
following statements:

```
Set objWshShell = WScript.CreateObject("WScript.Shell")
objWshShell.RegDelete "HKCU\ScriptSettings\NumberOfReboots"
```

Working with Environment Variables

Windows Home Server keeps track of a number of environment variables that hold data,
such as the location of the Windows folder, the location of the temporary files folder, the
command path, the primary drive, and much more. Why would you need such data? One
example would be for accessing files or folders within the main Windows folder. Rather
than guessing that this folder is C:\Windows, it would be much easier to just query the
%SystemRoot% environment variable. Similarly, if you have a script that accesses files in a
user's Documents folder, hard-coding the username in the file path is inconvenient
because it means creating custom scripts for every possible user. Instead, it would be much
easier to create just a single script that references the %UserProfile% environment variable. This section shows you how to read environment variable data within your scripts.

The defined environment variables are stored in the Environment collection, which is a
property of the WshShell object. Windows Home Server environment variables are stored
in the "Process" environment, so you reference this collection as follows:

WshShell.Environment("Process")

Listing 21.8 shows a script that runs through this collection, adds each variable to a string, and then displays the string.

LISTING 21.8   A Script That Displays the System's Environment Variables

```
Option Explicit
Dim objWshShell, objEnvVar, strVariables
Set objWshShell = WScript.CreateObject("WScript.Shell")
'
' Run through the environment variables
'
strVariables = ""
For Each objEnvVar In objWshShell.Environment("Process")
    strVariables = strVariables & objEnvVar & vbCrLf
Next
WScript.Echo strVariables
```

Figure 21.5 shows the dialog box that appears. (The environment variables in your version of Windows Home Server may be different.)

FIGURE 21.5   A complete inventory of a system's environment variables.

If you want to use the value of a particular environment variable, use the following syntax:

```
WshShell.Environment("Process")("strName")
```

WshShell   The WshShell object

strName   The name of the environment variable

Listing 21.9 shows a revised version of the script from Listing 21.6 to create a shortcut. In this version, the Environment collection is used to return the value of the %UserProfile% variable, which constructs the path to the current user's Desktop folder, as well as the %SystemRoot% variable, which constructs the paths for Notepad and the hosts file.

LISTING 21.9   A Script That Creates a Shortcut File Using an Environment Variable

```
Option Explicit
Dim objWshShell, strUserProfile, strSystemRoot, objShortcut
Set objWshShell = WScript.CreateObject("WScript.Shell")
strUserProfile = objWshShell.Environment("Process")("UserProfile")
Set objShortcut = objWshShell.CreateShortcut(strUserProfile & _
                  "\Desktop\Edit Hosts File.lnk")
strSystemRoot = objWshShell.Environment("Process")("SystemRoot")
With objShortcut
    .TargetPath = strSystemRoot & "\Notepad.exe"
    .Arguments = strSystemRoot & "\System32\Drivers\etc\hosts"
    .WorkingDirectory = "C:\"
    .Description = "Opens the hosts file in Notepad"
    .Hotkey = "Ctrl+Alt+7"
    .IconLocation = strSystemRoot & "\System32\Shell32.dll,18"
    .WindowStyle = 3
    .Save
End With
```

Programming the WshNetwork Object

WshNetwork is a generic name for an object that enables you to work with various aspects of the Windows network environment. You can determine the computer name and user-name, enumerate the mapped network drives, map new network drives, and more. The next couple of sections show you how to work with this object.

Referencing the WshNetwork Object

WshNetwork refers to the Network object exposed via the Automation interface of WScript. This means you use CreateObject to return this object, as shown next:

```
Set objWshNetwork = WScript.CreateObject("WScript.Network")
```

From here, you use the WshNetwork variable to access the object's properties and methods.

WshNetwork Object Properties

The WshNetwork object supports three properties:

ComputerName   Returns the network name of the computer

UserDomain   Returns the network domain name of the current user

UserName   Returns the username of the current user

Mapping Network Printers

The WshNetwork object supports several methods for working with remote printers. For example, to map a network printer to a local printer resource, use the WshNetwork object's AddWindowsPrinterConnection method:

WshNetwork.AddPrinterConnection *strPrinterPath*

WshNetwork   The WshNetwork object

strPrinterPath   The UNC path to the network printer

Here's an example:

```
Set objWshNetwork = WScript.CreateObject("WScript.Network")
objWshNetwork.AddWindowsPrinterConnection "\\SERVER\printer"
```

To remove a remote printer mapping, use the WshNetwork object's RemovePrinterConnection method:

WshNetwork.RemovePrinterConnection *strPrinterPath* [, *bForce*] [, *bUpdateProfile*]

WshNetwork   The WshNetwork object.

strPrinterPath   The UNC path to the network printer.

bForce   If True, the resource is removed even if it is currently being used.

bUpdateProfile   If True, the printer mapping is removed from the user's profile.

Here's an example:

```
Set objWshNetwork = WScript.CreateObject("WScript.Network")
objWshNetwork.RemovePrinterConnection "\\SERVER\inkjet"
```

Mapping Network Drives

The WshNetwork object supports several methods for mapping network drives. To map a shared network folder to a local drive letter, use the WshNetwork object's MapNetworkDrive method:

WshNetwork.MapNetworkDrive *strLocalName*, *strRemoteName*
➥ [, *bUpdateProfile*][, *strUser*][, *strPassword*]

WshNetwork	This is the `WshNetwork` object.
strLocalName	This is the local drive letter to which the remote share will be mapped (for example, F:).
strRemoteName	This is the UNC path for the remote share.
bUpdateProfile	If `True`, the drive mapping is stored in the user's profile.
strUser	Use this value to enter a username that might be required to map the remote share (if you're logged on as a user who doesn't have the proper permissions, for example).
strPassword	Use this value to enter a password that might be required to map the remote drive.

Here's an example:

```
Set objWshNetwork = WScript.CreateObject("WScript.Network")
objWshNetwork.MapNetworkDrive "Z:", "\\SERVER\Music"
```

To remove a mapped network drive, use the `WshNetwork` object's `RemoveNetworkDrive`:

`WshNetwork.RemoveNetworkDrive strName[, bForce][, bUpdateProfile]`

WshNetwork	The WshNetwork object.
strName	The name of the mapped network drive you want removed. If you use a network path, all mappings to that path are removed; if you use a local drive letter, only that mapping is removed.
bForce	If `True`, the resource is removed even if it is currently being used.
bUpdateProfile	If `True`, the network drive mapping is removed from the user's profile.

Here's an example:

```
Set objWshNetwork = WScript.CreateObject("WScript.Network")
objWshNetwork.RemoveNetworkDrive "Z:"
```

Programming the Windows Management Instrumentation Service

WMI is a powerful tool that gives you access to just about every aspect of Windows Home Server and of remote computers. With WMI, your scripts can manage applications, systems, devices, networks, and much more. WMI consists of a series of classes that implement various properties and methods that you can access using your scripts. For example, the `Win32_OperatingSystem` class represents the computer's operating system. Its properties include `InstallDate`, the date and time the operating system (OS) was installed, and

LastBootUpTime, the date and time when the OS was last started; its methods include Reboot for restarting the computer and SetDateTime for setting the system's date and time.

NOTE

WMI is massive. It has hundreds of classes that you can use, although you'll mostly use the Win32 classes, which enable you to manage the operating system, hardware, and applications, and to monitor performance. For the complete WMI reference, see msdn.microsoft.com/en-us/library/aa394582(VS.85).aspx.

Referencing the WMI Service Object

Your WMI scripts will always begin by setting up a variable for the WMI service object. One way to do that is to create an SWbemLocator object and use it to connect to the WMI service. Here's the code:

```
strComputer = "localhost"
Set objLocator = CreateObject("WbemScripting.SWbemLocator")
Set objWMI = objLocator.ConnectServer(strComputer, "root\cimv2")
objWMI.Security.ImpersonationLevel = 3
```

That works fine, but most scripts use a shortcut method that reduces to just a couple of statements:

```
strComputer = "localhost"
Set objWMI = GetObject("winmgmts:{impersonationLevel=impersonate}!\\" & _
            strComputer & "\root\cimv2")
```

TIP

I like to use localhost to reference the local computer because it's straightforward and easy to read. However, you can also use just dot (.) to refer to the local machine:

```
strComputer = "."
Set objWMI = GetObject("winmgmts:{impersonationLevel=impersonate}!\\" & _
                strComputer & "\root\cimv2")
```

Returning Class Instances

After you have your WMI service object, you can use it to access a class. Each class is really a collection of instances, or actual implementations of the class. For example, the Win32_UserAccount class consists of all the user accounts defined on the computer. Each user account is an instance of the Win32_UserAccount class. To access the instances of a class, you can use either of the following WMI object methods: ExecQuery or InstancesOf.

The ExecQuery method executes a SELECT query using the WMI Query Language (WQL). In general, this method uses the following form:

```
object.ExecQuery("SELECT * FROM class")
```

object   A variable that references the WMI object

class   The WMI class you want to work with

For example, the following method assumes that the WMI object is referenced by the objWMI variable, and the query returns all the instances of the Win32_UserAccount class:

```
objWMI.ExecQuery("SELECT * FROM Win32_UserAccount")
```

The InstancesOf method uses the following syntax:

```
object.InstancesOf("class")
```

object   A variable that references the WMI object

class   The WMI class you want to work with

For example, the following method assumes the WMI object is referenced by the objWMI variable, and the code returns all the instances of the Win32_UserAccount class:

```
objWMI.InstancesOf("Win32_UserAccount")
```

Which method should you use? If you want to work with all instances of a particular class, either method is fine, and you may gravitate to the InstancesOf method only because it's slightly shorter. However, if you only want to work with a subset of the instances, the ExecQuery method is better because you can add a WHERE clause to the WQL statement. For example, if you just want to work with the account named Administrator, the following code returns just that instance from the Win32_UserAccounts class:

```
objWMI.ExecQuery("SELECT * FROM Win32_UserAccount " & _
                 "WHERE Name = 'Administrator'")
```

Both ExecQuery and InstancesOf return a collection object that contains the class instances. You usually store that collection in a variable, as in this example:

```
Set objUsers = objWMI.ExecQuery("SELECT * FROM Win32_UserAccount")
```

You could then use a For Each...Next loop to run through the collection and perform some action on each instance. For example, Listing 21.10 presents a script that runs through all the instances of the Win32_UserAccount class, stores the Name and Fullname properties for each user in a string, and then displays the string.

LISTING 21.10   A Script That Runs Through the Instances of the Win32_UserAccount Class

```
Option Explicit
Dim strComputer, strUserInfo
Dim objWMI, objUsers, objUser
'
' Work with the local computer
'
strComputer = "localhost"
'
' Get the WMI service
'
Set objWMI = GetObject("winmgmts:{impersonationLevel=impersonate}!\\" & _
                    strComputer & "\root\cimv2")
'
' Store the instances of the Win32_UserAccount class
'
Set objUsers = objWMI.ExecQuery("SELECT * FROM Win32_UserAccount")
'
' Initialize the display string
'
strUserInfo = ""
'
' Loop through the instances
'
For each objUser in objUsers
    strUserInfo = strUserInfo & objUser.Name & " (" & _
                            objUser.FullName & ")" & vbCrLf
Next
'
' Display the string
'
WScript.Echo strUserInfo
'
' Release the objects
'
Set objWMI = Nothing
Set objUsers = Nothing
Set objUsers = Nothing
```

In many cases, the class returns only a single instance, either because the class only has one instance or because you used the WQL WHERE clause to restrict the class to a particular instance. Either way, you still need to use a For Each...Next loop to extract the data from the instance.

As an example, consider the script in Listing 21.11.

LISTING 21.11   A Script That Displays BIOS Data

```
Option Explicit
Dim strComputer, strBIOS
Dim objWMI, objBIOS, objItem
'
' Get the WMI service
'
strComputer = "localhost"
Set objWMI = GetObject("winmgmts:{impersonationLevel=impersonate}!\\" & _
            strComputer & "\root\cimv2")
'
' Get the BIOS instance
'
Set objBIOS = objWMI.ExecQuery("SELECT * FROM Win32_BIOS " & _
                            "WHERE PrimaryBIOS = true")
'
' Initialize the display string
'
strBIOS = "BIOS Data for " & UCase(strComputer) & ":" & vbCrLf & vbCrLf
'
' Collect the BIOS data
'
For Each objItem in objBIOS
        strBIOS = strBIOS & _
            "BIOS Name:" & vbTab & objItem.Name & vbCrLf & _
            "Manufacturer:" & vbTab & objItem.Manufacturer & vbCrLf & _
            "BIOS Version:" & vbTab & objItem.Version & vbCrLf & _
            "SMBIOS Version:" & vbTab & objItem.SMBIOSBIOSVersion & vbCrLf & _
            "BIOS Date:" & vbTab & ConvertToDate(objItem.ReleaseDate)

Next
'
' Display the string
'
WScript.Echo strBIOS
'
' Release the objects
'
Set objWMI = Nothing
Set objBIOS = Nothing
Set objItem = Nothing
'
' This function takes a datetime string and
' converts it to a real date object
'
```

21

```
Function ConvertToDate(strDate)
    Dim strYear, strMonth, strDay
    strYear = Left(strDate, 4)
    strMonth = Mid(strDate, 5, 2)
    strDay = Mid(strDate, 7, 2)
    ConvertToDate = DateSerial(strYear, strMonth, strDay)
End Function
```

This script uses ExecQuery to return the instance of the Win32_BIOS class that represents the computer's primary BIOS (that is, where the PrimaryBIOS property equals true). Then a For Each...Next loop runs through the single instance and uses a string variable to store the values of five properties: Name, Manufacturer, Version, SMBBIOSBIOSVersion, and ReleaseDate. The last of these is converted to a proper date object using the ConvertToDate function. The script then uses the Echo method to display the results, as shown in Figure 21.6.

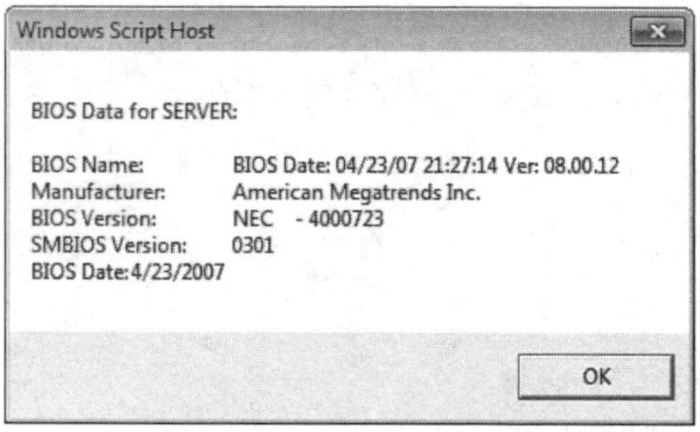

FIGURE 21.6   A computer's BIOS data displayed by the script in Listing 21.11.

From Here

▶ For a script that extracts specific security events from the Windows Home Server Security events log, **SEE** "Viewing Auditing Events with a Script," **P. 268.**

▶ For a script that displays the current Windows Home Server uptime, **SEE** "Displaying Uptime with a Script," **P. 409.**

▶ For a script that checks the free space on the Windows Home Server system drive, **SEE** "Checking Free Disk Space on the System Drive," **P. 416.**

▶ For more about the ECHO command-line tool, **SEE** "ECHO: Displaying Messages from a Batch File," **P. 494.**

▶ I discuss using ERRORLEVEL in relation to the XCOPY command in Chapter 19; **SEE** "XCOPY: Advanced File Copying," **P. 514.**

▶ To learn more about launching individual Control Panel icons using Control.exe, **SEE** "Understanding Control Panel Files," **P. 550.**

▶ For a script that toggles a service between stated and stopped, **SEE** "Controlling Services with a Script," **P. 570.**

Glossary

accelerator key   The underlined letter in a menu name or menu command.

active partition   A disk drive's bootable partition. Its boot sector tells the ROM BIOS at startup that this partition contains the operating system's bootstrap code. The active partition is usually the same as the primary partition.

ad hoc wireless network   A wireless network configuration that allows for direct wireless NIC-to-NIC communication. See also *infrastructure wireless network*.

add-in   A program that extends the functionality and features of Windows Home Server.

Address Resolution Protocol   A network protocol that handles the conversion of an IP address to a MAC address of a network interface card.

Alert Viewer   A client program that displays information about the current Windows Home Server network health alerts.

allocation unit   See *cluster*.

API   See *application programming interface*.

application programming interface   A set of procedures and other code that higher-level programs can call to perform lower-level functions.

archive bit   An attribute of a file or folder that is activated when the file or folder is created, when it's modified, or when it's renamed.

ARP   See *Address Resolution Protocol*.

ARP cache   A memory location that improves network performance by temporarily storing addresses that have been resolved by the Address Resolution Protocol.

auditing   Tracking Windows Home Server events such as logon failures and privilege use failures.

bit flip   A silent storage error in which a bit is written to the disk as a 1 instead of a 0, or vice versa.

block-based file system   A file system in which the operating system stores and tracks data using large sections of the hard drive, such as the 1GB blocks that Windows Home Server uses.

bps   Bits per second. The rate at which a communications device transmits data.

burn-in   Permanent damage to areas of a CRT monitor caused by continuously displaying a particular image over a long period. See also *persistence*.

cleanup   A weekly process that Windows Home Server uses to delete old backups.

client   In a client/server network, a computer that uses the services and resources provided to the network by a server.

client/server network   A network model that splits the computing workload into two separate but related areas. On the one hand, you have users working at intelligent "front-end" systems called clients. In turn, these client machines interact with powerful "back-end" systems called servers. The basic idea is that the clients have enough processing power to perform tasks on their own, but they rely on the servers to provide them with specialized resources or services, or access to information that would be impractical to implement on a client (such as a large database). See also *peer-to-peer network*.

Clipboard   A memory location used to store data that has been cut or copied from an application.

cluster   The basic unit of storage on a hard disk or floppy disk. On most systems, clusters are 4KB.

cluster chain   The sequence of clusters that defines an entire file.

codec   A compressor/decompressor device driver. During playback of audio or video data, the codec decompresses the data before sending it to the appropriate multimedia device. During recording, the codec decompresses the raw data so that it takes up less disk space. Most codecs offer a variety of compression ratios.

color quality   A measure of the number of colors available to display images on the screen. Color quality is usually expressed in either bits or total colors. For example, a 4-bit display can handle up to 16 colors (because 2 to the power of 4 equals 16). The most common values are 16-bit (65,536 colors; see *High Color*), 24-bit (16,777,216 colors; see *True Color*), and 32-bit (16,777,216 colors).

command extensions   Extra features added to commands such as DEL, MD, and SET.

compress   To reduce the size of a file by replacing redundant character strings with tokens.

concentrator   See *hub*.

connectionless protocol   See *Network Layer Protocol*.

connection-oriented protocol   See *Transport Layer Protocol*.

Connector   A Windows Home Server client program that connects a PC or Mac to Windows Home Server.

covert reinstall   When a malicious program surreptitiously reinstalls a fresh version of itself when the computer is idle.

cross-linked cluster   A cluster that has somehow been assigned to two different files or that has two FAT entries that refer to the same cluster.

Dashboard   A Windows Home Server client program that provides administrator-level access to the Windows Home Server user accounts, connected computers, backups, server folders, server hard drives, add-ins, and server settings.

data throughput   The collective term for network tasks involving client computers, users, and files.

datagram   An IP packet. The datagram header includes information such as the address of the host that sent the datagram and the address of the host that is supposed to receive the datagram.

DE   See *Drive Extender*.

device conflict   See *resource conflict*.

device driver   A small software program that serves as an intermediary between hardware devices and the operating system. Device drivers encode software instructions into signals that the device understands, and, conversely, the drivers interpret device signals and report them to the operating system.

Device Manager   A tab in the System properties sheet that provides a graphical outline of all the devices on your system. It can show you the current configuration of each device (including the IRQ, I/O ports, and DMA channel used by each device). It even lets you adjust a device's configuration (assuming that the device doesn't require you to make physical adjustments to, say, a DIP switch or jumper). The Device Manager actually gets its data from, and stores modified data in, the Registry.

DHCP   See *Dynamic Host Configuration Protocol*.

DHCP lease   An agreement from a DHCP server that allows a client computer to use a specified IP address for a certain length of time, typically 24 hours.

DHCP server   A computer or device that dynamically assigns IP addresses to client computers.

digital media receiver   A device that can access a media stream being sent over a wired or wireless network connection and then play that stream through connected equipment such as speakers, audio receivers, or a TV.

digital media server   A device that can distribute a media stream over a wired or wireless network connection.

directory entry   See *file directory*.

DMA   Direct Memory Access. See also *DMA channel*.

DMA channel   A connection that lets a device transfer data to and from memory without going through the processor. A DMA controller chip coordinates the transfer.

DMR   See *digital media receiver*.

DMS   See *digital media server*.

DNS   See *Domain Name System*.

Domain Name System   On the Internet, a hierarchical distributed database system that converts hostnames into IP addresses.

dotted-decimal notation   A format used to represent IP addresses. The 32 bits of the address are divided into quads of 8 bits, which are then converted into their decimal equivalent and separated by dots (for example, 205.208.113.1).

dotted-quad notation   See *dotted-decimal notation*.

double output redirection operator (>>)   A command-line operator that redirects the output of a command, program, or batch file to a location other than the screen. If the output is redirected to a file, the output is appended to the end of the file. See also *output redirection operator*.

Drive Extender   A Windows Home Server technology that combines all hard drives into a single storage pool with no drive letters, supports multiple hard drive types (internal Serial ATA or iSCSI and external, SATA, USB 3.0 or 2.0, and FireWire), and implements folder duplication.

drive-by download   The download and installation of a program without a user's knowledge or consent. See also *pop-up download*.

Dynamic Host Configuration Protocol   A system that manages the dynamic allocation of IP addresses.

environment   A small memory buffer that holds the DOS environment variables.

environment variables   Settings used to control certain aspects of DOS and DOS programs. For example, the PATH, the PROMPT, and the values of all SET statements are part of the environment.

extended partition   The hard disk space that isn't allocated to the primary partition. For example, if you have a 1.2GB disk and you allocate 300MB to the primary partition, the extended partition will be 900MB. You can then subdivide the extended partition into logical drives.

extensible markup language   See *XML*.

external IP address   The IP address that a device (particularly a router or gateway) uses to communicate with Internet resources. See also *internal IP address*.

FAT   See *File Allocation Table*.

File Allocation Table   A built-in filing system that is created on every formatted disk. The FAT contains a 16-bit entry for every disk cluster that specifies whether the cluster is empty or bad or points to the next cluster number in the current file.

file directory   A table of contents for the files on a disk that is maintained by the File Allocation Table. The entries in the file directory specify each file's name, extension, size, attributes, and more.

File Transfer Protocol   An Internet protocol that defines file transfers between computers. Part of the TCP/IP suite of protocols.

firewall   A security component that blocks unauthorized access and permits authorized access to the system.

folder duplication   The creation of redundant copies of data files spread across multiple physical hard drives so that if one hard drive fails, no data is lost. See also *Drive Extender*.

font   A unique set of design characteristics that is common to a group of letters, numbers, and symbols.

FTP   See *File Transfer Protocol*.

Full Access   Gives a user read/write permissions on a shared folder, meaning that the user can traverse subfolders, run programs, open documents, make changes to documents, create new files and folders, and delete files and folders. See also *No Access* and *Read Only*.

gateway   A network computer or other device that acts as a middleman between two otherwise-incompatible systems. The gateway translates the incoming and outgoing packets so that each system can work with the data.

GDI   See *graphical device interface*.

graphical device interface   A core Windows component that manages the operating system's graphical interface. It contains routines that draw graphics primitives (such as lines and circles), manage colors, display fonts, manipulate bitmap images, and interact with graphics drivers. See also *kernel* and *USER*.

graphics adapter   The internal component in your system that generates the output you see on your monitor.

handle   See *object handle*.

hard page fault   A type of page fault in which the system must retrieve the data from the hard disk. See also *soft page fault*.

High Color   A color quality of 16 bits, or 65,536 colors.

hostname   The unique name of a network or Internet computer expressed as an English-language equivalent of an IP address.

HTTP   See *Hypertext Transfer Protocol*.

hub   A central connection point for network cables. They range in size from small boxes with six or eight RJ-45 connectors to large cabinets with dozens of ports for various cable types.

hyperlink   In a World Wide Web page, an underlined word or phrase that takes you to a different website.

hypertext   A document that includes one or more *hyperlinks*.

Hypertext Transfer Protocol   An Internet protocol that defines the format of Uniform Resource Locator addresses and how World Wide Web data is transmitted between a server and a browser. Part of the TCP/IP suite of protocols.

infrastructure wireless network   A wireless network configuration that uses a wireless access point to receive and transmit signals from wireless computers. See also *ad hoc wireless network*.

input redirection operator (<)   A command-line operator that redirects input to a command, program, or batch file from somewhere other than the keyboard. See also *output redirection operator*.

internal IP address   The IP address that a device (particularly a router or gateway) uses to communicate with local network resources. See also external IP address.

Internet Protocol   A network layer protocol that defines the Internet's basic packet structure and its addressing scheme, and handles routing of packets between hosts. See also *TCP/IP* and *Transmission Control Protocol*.

interrupt request   An instruction to the CPU that halts processing temporarily so that another operation (such as handling input or output) can take place. Interrupts can be generated by either hardware or software.

invalid cluster   A cluster that falls under one of the following three categories:

  ▶ A FAT entry that refers to cluster 1. This is illegal, because a disk's cluster numbers start at 2.
  ▶ A FAT entry that refers to a cluster number larger than the total number of clusters on the disk.
  ▶ A FAT entry of 0 (which normally denotes an unused cluster) that is part of a cluster chain.

I/O port   A memory address that the processor uses to communicate with a device directly. Once a device has used its IRQ line to catch the processor's attention, the actual exchange of data or commands takes place through the device's I/O port address.

IP   See *Internet Protocol*.

IP address   The unique address assigned to every host and router on the Internet or on an internal TCP/IP network. IP addresses are 32-bit values that are usually expressed in dotted-decimal notation, such as 192.168.1.1. See also *hostname*.

IRQ line   A hardware line over which peripherals and software can send interrupt requests.

Kbps   One thousand bits per second (bps).

kernel   A core Windows component that loads applications (including any DLLs needed by the program), handles all aspects of file I/O, allocates virtual memory, and schedules and runs threads started by applications. See also *graphical device interface* and *USER*.

LAN   See *local area network*.

Launchpad   A client program that gives quick access to the Windows Home Server backups, Remote Web Access, shared folders, Dashboard, add-ins, and network health alerts.

lazy write   A file write process that waits until the CPU is free before copying or moving data to a disk. This process is used by Drive Extender Migrator.

local area network   A network in which all the computers occupy a relatively small geographical area, such as a department, office, home, or building. All the connections between computers are made via either network cables or wireless connections.

local resource   Any peripheral, file, folder, or application that either is attached directly to your computer or resides on your computer's hard disk. See also *remote resource*.

logical drive   A subset of an extended partition. For example, if the extended partition is 300GB, you could create three logical drives, each with 100GB, and they would use drive letters D:, E:, and F:. You can assign up to 23 logical drives to an extended partition (letters D: through Z:).

lost cluster   A cluster that, according to the File Allocation Table, is associated with a file but has no link to an entry in the file directory. Lost clusters are typically caused by program crashes, power surges, or power outages.

MAC address   The Media Access Control address, which is the unique physical address assigned to a device such as a network interface card or router.

malware   The generic term for malicious software such as viruses, Trojan horses, and spyware.

Mbps   One million bits per second (bps).

Media Access Control address   See *MAC address*.

Moore's Law   Processing power doubles every 18 months (from Gordon Moore, cofounder of Intel).

motherboard   The computer's main circuit board, which includes connectors for the CPU, memory chips, hard drives, ports, expansion slots, controllers, and BIOS.

multithreading   A multitasking model in which multiple threads run simultaneously.

name resolution   A process that converts a hostname into an IP address. See *Domain Name System*.

NAS   See *network attached storage*.

NetBIOS   An API that handles the conversion between the network names of computers and their IP addresses.

NetBIOS name cache   A memory location used to improve network performance by storing names resolved by NetBIOS.

network   A collection of computers connected via special cables or other network media (such as wireless) to share files, folders, disks, peripherals, and applications.

network adapter   See *network interface card*.

network attached storage   A device that contains one or more hard drives that plugs into a switch or router to enable computers on the network to store files on the device instead of on a network share.

network health alert   A fly-out message displayed by the Windows Home Server Status icon that tells you why the network health status has recently changed.

network interface card   An adapter that usually slips into an expansion bus slot inside a client or server computer. (There are also external NICs that plug into parallel ports or PC Card slots, and internal NICs that are integrated into the system's motherboard.) The NIC's main purpose is to serve as the connection point between the PC and the network. The NIC's backplate (the portion of the NIC that you can see after the card is installed) contains one or more ports into which you plug a network cable.

Network Layer Protocol   A protocol in which no communications channel is established between nodes. Instead, the protocol builds each packet with all the information required for the network to deliver each packet and for the destination node to assemble everything. See also *Transport Layer Protocol*.

network name   The unique name by which a computer is identified on the network.

network operating system   Operating system software that runs on a network server and provides the various network services for the network clients.

network redirector   A virtual device driver that lets applications find, open, read, write, and delete files on a remote drive.

network utilization   The percent of available bandwidth that the computer's network interface card is currently using.

NIC   See *network interface card*.

node   A computer on a network.

No Access   Prevents a user from accessing a shared folder. See also *Full Access* and *Read Only*.

nonpaged pool   The system memory area that Windows Home Server uses for objects that must remain in memory and thus can't be written back to the disk when the system doesn't need them. See also *paged pool*.

nonunicast   A network packet exchanged between a single sender and multiple receivers. See also *unicast*.

NOS   See *network operating system*.

notification area   The box on the right side of the taskbar that Windows uses to display icons that tell you the current state of the system (which is why it is also sometimes called the system tray).

object   A separate entity or component that is distinguished by its properties and methods.

object handle   An index that points to an entry in a table of available objects and enables programs to interface with those objects.

ODBC   See *Open Database Connectivity*.

OOBE   See *out-of-box experience*.

Open Database Connectivity   A database standard that enables a program or script to connect to and manipulate a data source.

out-of-box experience   What you must do to get a computer running after you take it out of the box.

output redirection operator (>)   A command-line operator that redirects the output of a command, program, or batch file to a location other than the screen. If the output is redirected to a file, that file is overwritten without warning. See also *double output redirection operator* and *input redirection operator*.

packet   The data transfer unit used in network and modem communications. Each packet contains not only data, but a "header" that contains information about which machine sent the data, which machine is supposed to receive the data, and a few extra tidbits that let the receiving computer put all the original data together in the correct order and check for errors that might have cropped up during the transmission.

page   An area of virtual memory used to transfer data between virtual memory and a storage medium, usually the hard disk.

page fault   An error that occurs when a running process requests data from a page in virtual memory and the system can't find the page in the requested memory location. See also *soft page fault* and *hard page fault*.

paged pool   The system memory area that Windows Home Server uses for objects that can be written back to the disk when the system doesn't need them. See also *nonpaged pool*.

paging file   A special file used by the Memory Pager to emulate physical memory. If you open enough programs or data files that physical memory becomes exhausted, the paging file is brought into play to augment memory storage. Also called a swap file.

Parkinson's Law of Data   Data expands to fill the space available for storage (from the original Parkinson's Law: Work expands to fill the time available).

peer-to-peer network   A network in which no one computer is singled out to provide special services. Instead, all the computers attached to the network have equal status (at least as far as the network is concerned), and all the computers can act as both servers and clients. See also *client/server network*.

permissions   Attributes applied to a user or security group that define the actions the user can take in a specified folder, usually a network share. See also *Full Access*, *No Access*, and *Read Only*.

persistence   A faint and usually temporary version of an image that has been continuously displayed on an LCD monitor over a long period. See also *burn-in*.

phishing   Creating a replica of an existing web page to fool a user into submitting personal, financial, or password data.

pipe operator (|)   A command-line operator that captures the output of one command and sends the data as input to another command.

pop-up download   The download and installation of a program after the user clicks an option in a pop-up browser window, particularly when the option's intent is vaguely or misleadingly worded. See also *drive-by download*.

port number   A 16-bit number that uniquely identifies each running process on a computer. See also *socket*.

POST   At system startup, the POST detects and tests memory, ports, and basic devices such as the video adapter, keyboard, and disk drives. If everything passes, your system emits a single beep.

Power-On Self Test   See *POST*.

previous version   A shadow copy of a file or folder that was taken prior to the current version of the file or folder.

primary partition   The first partition (drive C:) on a hard disk. See also *active partition* and *extended partition*.

process   A running instance of an executable program.

Process Scheduler   The Windows component that doles out resources to applications and operating system processes. In particular, the Process Scheduler organizes running applications so that they take advantage of multitasking and multithreading.

property sheet   A dialog box with controls that let you manipulate various properties of the underlying object.

protocol   A set of standards that define the way information is exchanged between two systems across a network connection. See also *Transport Layer Protocol* and *Network Layer Protocol*.

Read Only   Gives a user read-only permissions on a shared folder, meaning that the user can traverse subfolders, run programs, and open documents, but he cannot make changes to the shared folder or any of its contents. See also *Full Access* and *No Access*.

recovery key   A bootable USB flash drive that contains the data required to recover a client PC from a Windows Home Server backup.

redirector   A networking driver that provides all the mechanisms needed for an application to communicate with a remote device, including file reads and writes, print job submissions, and resource sharing.

Registry   A central repository that Windows Home Server uses to store anything and everything that applies to your system's configuration. This includes hardware settings, object properties, operating system settings, and application options.

remote resource   Any peripheral, file, folder, or application that exists somewhere on the network. See also *local resource*.

Remote Web Access   A Windows Home Server web server application that gives client computers access to other client machines, the Windows Home Server shared folders, and Windows Home Server media streaming over the network or over the Internet.

repeater   A device that boosts a network cable's signal so that the length of the network can be extended. Repeaters are needed because copper-based cables suffer from attenuation—a phenomenon in which the degradation of the electrical signal carried over the cable is proportional to the distance the signal has to travel.

resolution   See *screen resolution*.

resource conflict   A hardware glitch where two or more device are configured to use the same resource, such as an *IRQ line*.

router   A device that makes decisions about where to send the network packets it receives. Unlike a switch, which merely passes along any data that comes its way, a router examines the address information in each packet and then determines the most efficient route that the packet must take to reach its eventual destination.

routing   The process whereby packets travel from host to host until they eventually reach their destination.

Safe mode   A Windows Home Server startup mode that loads a minimal system configuration. Safe mode is useful for troubleshooting problems caused by incorrect or corrupt device drivers.

screen resolution   A measure of the density of the pixels used to display the screen image and usually expressed as rows by columns, where rows is the number of pixel rows and columns is the number of pixel columns (for example, 1024 by 768).

secondary partition   A partition created from an extra hard drive and used by Drive Extender to store data from the Windows Home Server shared folders. See also *primary partition*.

security group   A security object that is defined with a specific set of permissions, and any user added to the group is automatically granted that group's permissions.

server   In a client/server network, a computer that provides and manages services (such as file and print sharing and security) for the users on the network.

shadow copy   A copy of a file or folder taken at a specific time and stored for possible use as a previous version of the file or folder.

silent storage error   A file system error in which a file appears to be stored correctly, but in fact has a hidden error that might cause the file to become unreadable. See also *bit flip*.

Simple Mail Transport Protocol   An Internet protocol that describes the format of Internet email messages and how those messages are delivered. Part of the TCP/IP suite of protocols.

Single Instance Storage   The storage technology used by Windows Home Server's backup feature, in which backups are tracked at the cluster level, and only a single instance of a particular cluster—even if that cluster appears in multiple folders and multiple computers—is included in the backup.

SMTP   See *Simple Mail Transport Protocol*.

snap-in   A Microsoft Management Console tool that is wrapped in a Microsoft Common Console Document (.msc) file and can be added to the MMC interface.

socket   In the Transmission Control Protocol, a communications channel between two hosts that consists of their IP addresses and port numbers.

soft page fault   A type of page fault in which the system is able to retrieve the data from another virtual memory location. See also *hard page fault*.

spyware   Any malware program that surreptitiously monitors a user's computer activities—particularly the typing of passwords, PINs, and credit card numbers—or harvests sensitive data on the user's computer, and then sends that information to an individual or a company via the user's Internet connection without the user's consent.

storage pool   The combined hard drive storage space that Windows Home Server uses for the shared folders, shadow copies, and client computer backups.

subnet   A subsection of a network that uses related IP addresses.

subnet mask   A 32-bit value, usually expressed in *dotted-decimal notation* (for example, 255.255.255.0), that lets IP separate a network ID from a full IP address and thus determine whether the source and destination hosts are on the same network.

swap file   See *paging file*.

switch   A network device that forwards data from one part of the network to another, or across multiple network segments.

system drive   The hard drive partition on which Windows Home Server is installed.

TCP   See *Transmission Control Protocol*.

TCP/IP   Transmission Control Protocol/Internet Protocol. TCP/IP is the underlying language of most UNIX systems and the Internet as a whole. However, TCP/IP is also an excellent choice for other types of networks because it's routable, robust, and reliable.

thread   A program task that can run independently of other tasks in the same program. In a spreadsheet, for example, you might have one thread for recalculating, another for printing, and a third for accepting keyboard input. See also *multithreading*.

topology   Describes how the various nodes that comprise a network—which include not only the computers, but devices such as hubs and bridges—are connected.

Transmission Control Protocol   A Transport Layer Protocol that sets up a connection between two hosts and ensures that data is passed between them reliably. If packets are lost or damaged during transmission, TCP takes care of retransmitting the packets. See also *Internet Protocol* and *TCP/IP*.

Transport Layer Protocol   A protocol in which a virtual communications channel is established between two systems. The protocol uses this channel to send packets between nodes. See also *Network Layer Protocol*.

True Color   A color quality of 24 bits, or 16,777,216 colors.

unicast   A network packet exchanged between a single sender and a single receiver. See also *nonunicast*.

uptime   The amount of time that some system has been running continuously since the last time the system was started.

USER   A core Windows component that handles all user-related I/O tasks. On the input side, User manages incoming data from the keyboard, mouse, joystick, and any other input devices that are attached to your computer. For output, User sends data to windows, icons, menus, and other components of the Windows user interface. User also handles the sound driver, the system timer, and the communications ports. See also *graphical device interface* and *kernel*.

virtual memory   Memory created by allocating hard disk space and making it look to applications as though they are dealing with physical RAM.

wardriving   An activity in which a person drives through various neighborhoods with a portable computer or another device set up to look for available wireless networks.

web application   An object that acts as a container for one or more SharePoint sites.

wireless access point   A device that receives and transmits signals from wireless computers to form a wireless network.

wireless gateway   A wireless access point that has a built-in router to provide Internet access to all the computers on the network.

wireless range extender   A device used to boost signals going to and from a wireless access point.

XML   A markup language that creates a universal data format for defining complex documents and data structures using custom tags and text.

Windows Home Server Keyboard Shortcuts

If Windows Home Server is just another appliance in your home—that is, it's a headless device (no keyboard, no mouse, no monitor) that you rarely interact with directly or via Remote Desktop—then you have no reason to learn keyboard shortcuts because they simply don't apply. However, this book assumes that you're regularly interacting directly with Windows Home Server, so the keyboard comes into play. Fortunately, like all versions of Windows, Home Server is loaded with keyboard shortcuts that you can take advantage of to speed up your work and reduce the risk of "mouse elbow," a painful malady most often caused by excessive mouse use. This appendix presents you with a complete list of the Windows Home Server keyboard shortcuts.

TABLE B.1   General Windows Home Server Shortcut Keys

Press	To Do This
Ctrl+Esc	Open the Start menu.
Ctrl+Shift+Esc	Open Task Manager.
Windows Logo	Open the Start menu.
Ctrl+Alt+Delete	Display the Windows Security screen.
Print Screen	Copy the entire screen image to the Windows Clipboard.
Alt+Print Screen	Copy the active window's image to the Windows Clipboard.
Alt+double-click	Display the Properties dialog box for the selected item.
Alt+Enter	Display the Properties dialog box for the selected object.
Shift	Prevent an inserted CD from running its AutoPlay application. (Hold down Shift while inserting the CD.)
Shift+F10	Display the shortcut menu for the selected object. (This is the same as right-clicking the object.)
Shift+right-click	Display the shortcut menu with alternative commands for the selected object.

TABLE B.2   Shortcut Keys for Working with Program Windows

Press	To Do This
Alt	Activate or deactivate the program's menu bar.
Alt+Esc	Cycle through the open program windows.
Alt+F4	Close the active program window.
Alt+spacebar	Display the system menu for the active program window.
Alt+Tab	Cycle through icons for each of the running programs.
Shift+Alt+Tab	Cycle backward through icons for each of the running programs.
F1	Display context-sensitive help.
F10	Activate the application's menu bar.

TABLE B.3   Shortcut Keys for Working with Documents

Press	To Do This
Alt+-(hyphen)	Display the system menu for the active document window.
Alt+Print Screen	Copy the active window's image to the Clipboard.
Ctrl+F4	Close the active document window.
Ctrl+F6	Cycle through the open documents within an application.
Ctrl+N	Create a new document.
Ctrl+O	Display the Open dialog box.
Ctrl+P	Display the Print dialog box.
Ctrl+S	Save the current file. If the file is new, display the Save As dialog box.

TABLE B.4   Shortcut Keys for Working with Data

Press	To Do This
Backspace	Delete the character to the left of the insertion point.
Ctrl+C	Copy the selected data to memory.
Ctrl+F	Display the Find dialog box.
Ctrl+H	Display the Replace dialog box.
Ctrl+X	Cut the selected data to memory.
Ctrl+V	Paste the most recently cut or copied data from memory.
Ctrl+Z	Undo the most recent action.
Delete	Delete the selected data.
F3	Repeat the most recent Find operation.

B

TABLE B.5   Shortcut Keys for Moving the Insertion Point

Press	To Do This
Ctrl+End	Move the insertion point to the end of the document.
Ctrl+Home	Move the insertion point to the beginning of the document.
Ctrl+left arrow	Move the insertion point to the next word to the left.
Ctrl+right arrow	Move the insertion point to the next word to the right.
Ctrl+down arrow	Move the insertion point to the end of the paragraph.
Ctrl+up arrow	Move the insertion point to the beginning of the paragraph.

TABLE B.6   Shortcut Keys for Selecting Text

Press	To Do This
Ctrl+A	Select all the text in the current document.
Ctrl+Shift+End	Select from the insertion point to the end of the document.
Ctrl+Shift+Home	Select from the insertion point to the beginning of the document.
Ctrl+Shift+left arrow	Select the next word to the left.
Ctrl+Shift+right arrow	Select the next word to the right.
Ctrl+Shift+down arrow	Select from the insertion point to the end of the paragraph.
Ctrl+Shift+up arrow	Select from the insertion point to the beginning of the paragraph.
Shift+End	Select from the insertion point to the end of the line.
Shift+Home	Select from the insertion point to the beginning of the line.
Shift+left arrow	Select the next character to the left.
Shift+right arrow	Select the next character to the right.
Shift+down arrow	Select the next line down.
Shift+up arrow	Select the next line up.

TABLE B.7   Shortcut Keys for Working with Dialog Boxes

Press	To Do This
Alt+down arrow	Display the list in a drop-down list box.
Alt+underlined letter	Select a control.
Ctrl+Shift+Tab	Move backward through the dialog box tabs.
Ctrl+Tab	Move forward through the dialog box tabs.
Enter	Select the default command button or the active command button.
Spacebar	Toggle a check box on and off; select the active option button or command button.
Esc	Close the dialog box without making changes.
F1	Display help text for the control that has the focus.
F4	Display the list in a drop-down list box.
Backspace	In the Open and Save As dialog boxes, move up to the parent folder when the folder list has the focus.
Shift+Tab	Move backward through the dialog box controls.
Tab	Move forward through the dialog box controls.

TABLE B.8   Shortcut Keys for Drag-and-Drop Operations

Press	To Do This
Alt	Creates a shortcut for the dragged object.
Ctrl	Copy the dragged object.
Ctrl+Shift	Display a shortcut menu after dropping a left-dragged object.
Esc	Cancel the current drag.
Shift	Move the dragged object.

TABLE B.9   Shortcut Keys for Working in a Folder Window

Press	To Do This
Alt+D	Select the address bar text.
Alt+left arrow	Navigate backward to a previously displayed folder.
Alt+right arrow	Navigate forward to a previously displayed folder.
Backspace	Navigate to the parent folder of the current folder.
Ctrl+A	Select all the objects in the current folder.
Ctrl+C	Copy the selected objects.
Ctrl+V	Paste the most recently cut or copied objects.
Ctrl+X	Cut the selected objects.
Ctrl+Z	Undo the most recent action.
Delete	Delete the selected objects.
F2	Rename the selected object.
F5	Refresh the folder contents.
F6	Cycle between the address bar, the Folders list, and the folder contents.
letter	In the Folders list or folder contents, select the next item that begins with letter.
Shift+Delete	Delete the currently selected objects without sending them to the Recycle Bin.
Tab	Cycle between the address bar, the Folders list, and the folder contents.
Shift+Tab	Cycle backward between the address bar, the Folders list, and the folder contents.

TABLE B.10   Shortcut Keys for Working with Internet Explorer

Press	To Do This
Alt	Display the Classic menu bar (Internet Explorer 7 and 8).
Alt+Home	Go to the home page.
Alt+left arrow	Navigate backward to a previously displayed web page.
Alt+right arrow	Navigate forward to a previously displayed web page.

TABLE B.10   Shortcut Keys for Working with Internet Explorer

Press	To Do This
Ctrl+A	Select the entire web page.
Ctrl+B	Display the Organize Favorites dialog box.
Alt+C	Display the Favorites Center (Internet Explorer 7 and 8).
Ctrl+Shift+J	Pin the Feeds list to keep it permanently onscreen (Internet Explorer 7 and 8).
Ctrl+N	Open a new window.
Ctrl+T	Open a new tab (Internet Explorer 7 and 8).
Ctrl+W	Close the current tab (Internet Explorer 7 and 8).
Ctrl+Q	Display the Quick Tabs (Internet Explorer 7 and 8).
Ctrl+O	Display the Open dialog box.
Ctrl+P	Display the Print dialog box.
Ctrl+Tab	Cycle forward through the open tabs (Internet Explorer 7 and 8).
Ctrl+Shift+Tab	Cycle backward through the open tabs (Internet Explorer 7 and 8).
Ctrl+Enter	Add http://www. to the beginning of the Address bar text, .com to the end of the text, and then display the website.
Ctrl++	Zoom in on the current web page.
Ctrl+−	Zoom out on the current web page.
Esc	Stop downloading the web page.
F4	Open the Address toolbar's drop-down list.
F5	Refresh the web page.
F11	Toggle between Full Screen mode and the regular window.
Spacebar	Scroll down one screen.
Shift+spacebar	Scroll up one screen.
Shift+Tab	Cycle backward through the Address toolbar and the web page links.
Tab	Cycle forward through the web page links and the Address toolbar.
Ctrl+D	Add the current page to the Favorites list.
Ctrl+E	Activate the Instant Search box (Internet Explorer 7 and 8).

TABLE B.10   Shortcut Keys for Working with Internet Explorer

Press	To Do This
Ctrl+F	Display the Find dialog box.
Ctrl+H	Display the History list.
Ctrl+Shift+H	Pin the History list (Internet Explorer 7 and 8).
Ctrl+I	Display the Favorites list.
Ctrl+Shift+I	Pin the Favorites list (Internet Explorer 7 and 8).
Ctrl+J	Display the Feeds list (Internet Explorer 7 and 8).

TABLE B.11   Shortcut Keys for DOSKEY

Press	To Do This
Command Recall Keys	
Alt+F7	Delete all the commands from the recall list.
Arrow keys	Cycle through the commands in the recall list.
F7	Display the entire recall list.
F8	Recall a command that begins with the letter or letters you've typed on the command line.
F9	Display the Line number prompt. You then enter the number of the command (as displayed by F7) that you want.
Page Down	Recall the newest command in the list.
Page Up	Recall the oldest command in the list.
Command-Line Editing Keys	
Backspace	Delete the character to the left of the cursor.
Ctrl+End	Delete from the cursor to the end of the line.
Ctrl+Home	Delete from the cursor to the beginning of the line.
Ctrl+left arrow	Move the cursor one word to the left.
Ctrl+right arrow	Move the cursor one word to the right.
Delete	Delete the character over the cursor.
End	Move the cursor to the end of the line.

TABLE B.11   Shortcut Keys for DOSKEY

Press	To Do This
Home	Move the cursor to the beginning of the line.
Insert	Toggle DOSKEY between Insert mode (your typing is inserted between existing letters on the command line) and Overstrike mode (your typing replaces existing letters on the command line).
Left arrow	Move the cursor one character to the left.
Right arrow	Move the cursor one character to the right.

TABLE B.12   Windows Logo Key Shortcut Keys

Press	To Do This
Windows Logo	Open the Start menu.
Windows Logo+D	Minimize all open windows. Press Windows Logo+D again to restore the windows.
Windows Logo+E	Open the Computer folder.
Windows Logo+F	Display the Search Results window.
Windows Logo+L	Lock the computer.
Windows Logo+M	Minimize all open windows, except those with open modal windows.
Windows Logo+Shift+M	Undo minimize all.
Windows Logo+R	Display the Run dialog box.
Windows Logo+T	Cycle through the icons and running programs on the taskbar.
Windows Logo+U	Display the Ease of Access Center.
Windows Logo+*number*	Start or switch to the program pinned to the taskbar in the position indicated by *number* (counting from the left).
Shift+Windows Logo+*number*	Start a new instance of the program pinned to the taskbar in the position indicated by *number*.
Ctrl+Windows Logo+*number*	Switch to the last active windows of the program pinned to the taskbar in the position indicated by *number*.
Alt+Windows Logo+*number*	Display the jump list for the program pinned to the taskbar in the position indicated by *number*.

TABLE B.12   Windows Logo Key Shortcut Keys

Press	To Do This
Windows Logo+Up arrow	Maximize the active window.
Windows Logo+Down arrow	Minimize the active window; if the active window is currently maximized, restore the window to its original position.
Shift+Windows Logo+Up arrow	Size the active window to the height of the screen.
Shift+Windows Logo+Left arrow	Move a window from one monitor to another.
Windows Logo+Home	Minimize all open windows except the active window.
Windows Logo+spacebar	Scroll down one page (supported only in certain applications, such as Internet Explorer).
Windows Logo+Shift+spacebar	Scroll up one page (supported only in certain applications, such as Internet Explorer).
Windows Logo+Pause/Break	Display the System window.
Windows Logo+Tab	Cycle through the taskbar buttons.

APPENDIX C

Windows Home Server Online Resources

IN THIS APPENDIX

▶ Windows Home Server Websites

▶ Windows Home Server Blogs

▶ Windows Home Server for Developers

When Microsoft first announced Windows Home Server at the Consumer Electronics Show in January of 2007, it seemed like only minutes later that the web was awash in blogs, reviews, forums, and other online sites dedicated to Windows Home Server. I'm exaggerating, of course, but it's true that it didn't take long for Windows Home Server to have a significant presence on the web, and that presence has continued to grow. Lists of websites are always fraught with peril for a book author, because no sooner has the book rolled off the presses than some sites go belly-up (or *sneakers-up*, in the vernacular) and others spring up to take their places. But fortune favors the bold, or something like that, so this appendix offers a list of my favorite Windows Home Server sites and blogs.

Windows Home Server Websites

Here are some general websites devoted to Windows Home Server:

Windows Home Server—Microsoft's home page for Windows Home Server. It includes general information about the product and its features, links to other Windows Home Server sites, links to Windows Home Server resources, and more:

www.microsoft.com/windows/products/winfamily/windowshomeserver

Windows Home Server Forums—This Microsoft site offers several different groups for discussing all aspects of Windows Home Server. There's a Windows Home Server frequently asked questions list (FAQ), and you can discuss Windows Home Server software, hardware, and more. Here are the main forums:

social.microsoft.com/Forums/en-US/whsannouncements/threads

social.microsoft.com/Forums/en-US/whssoftware/threads

social.microsoft.com/Forums/en-US/whshardware/threads

MSWHS—This site offers lots of articles and resources for all aspects of Windows Home Server:

www.mswhs.com

Using Windows Home Server—This site gives you reviews of Home Server hardware, add-ins, and more:

www.usingwindowshomeserver.com

Home Server Land—Lots of news and views related to Windows Home Server, as well as a comprehensive list of add-ins available for Windows Home Server:

www.homeserverland.com

Windows Home Server Unleashed—The home page for this book on my website, which includes all the sample code used in the book:

www.mcfedries.com/HomeServerUnleashed3E

Windows Home Server Blogs

Name a topic, and there's almost certainly a blog devoted to it—probably more than one. Windows Home Server is no exception:

Windows Home Server Team Blog—The official Windows Home Server blog featuring posts directly from the Windows Home Server management and development teams:

blogs.technet.com/b/homeserver

Home Server Show—This blog offers lots of great tips and tricks for Windows Home Server:

www.homeservershow.com

We Got Served—This blog includes lots of great Windows Home Server info, hardware and software reviews, and more:

www.wegotserved.com

Windows Home Server for Developers

If you're interested in writing add-ins for Windows Home Server and accessing Windows Home Server objects in your VB.NET or C# code, here are some resources to help you get started:

Windows Home Server Software Development Kit (SDK) Documentation—This Microsoft Developer Network (MSDN) site has the documentation you need to get started writing code for Windows Home Server:

msdn.microsoft.com/en-us/library/bb425866.aspx

Windows Home Server Developers Forum—Use this section of the Windows Home Server forums to ask and answer questions about developing for Windows Home Server:

social.microsoft.com/Forums/en-US/whsdevelopers/threads

Index

Symbols

@ (backslash), 613
$ (dollar sign), 274
. (dot) notation, 485-486
== (double equal sign), 499
! (exclamation mark), 23, 445
< (input redirection operator), 490-491
> operator, 143
< operator, 143
<= operator, 143
>= operator, 143
> (output redirection operator), 489-490
| (pipe operator), 491-492
" (quotation marks), 499
? wildcard, 144
* wildcard, 144
.. wildcard, 144

A

/A option (CMD), 479
access levels, 30
access point username/password, 291
AccountPage folder, 296
accounts
    administrator account, renaming, 271
    user accounts, 29
Action menu commands, Refresh, 247
activating auditing policies, 258-259
Active X Control, 557
activity reporting (Parental Controls), 283
Adapter Description column
  (Task Manager), 380

Add a Folder Wizard, 123-124
Add a User Account Wizard, 36-39
Add Counters dialog box, 385, 409
Add Default Document dialog box, 318
Add Folder to Gallery dialog box, 197
Add Mirror dialog box, 111
Add Network Location Wizard, 131-133
Add or Edit DHCP Scopes dialog box, 12
Add or Remove Snap-Ins dialog box, 560
Add Roles Wizard, 12-13, 574-575
Add Scope dialog box, 12
Add Site Binding dialog box, 315
Add Standalone Snap-In dialog box, 560
Add to Library dialog box, 195, 203
Add Virtual Directory dialog box, 301
Add Web Site dialog box, 304, 308
Address Resolution Protocol (ARP) cache, flushing, 18
addresses (IP), 302
    assigning to websites, 304
    assigning to Windows Home Server, 303
    associating host headers with, 312
    associating with hostnames, 305-307
    determining, 164-165
    router's IP address, connecting with, 164-168
    static IP addresses, configuring, 8
AddWindowsPrinterConnection method, 616
ADMIN$ share, disabling, 274-275
administrative shares, hidden, 274-275
administrator account, renaming, 271
Administrators group, 30
Advanced Boot Options menu, 90-91
Advanced File Signature Verification Settings dialog box, 448
Advanced Security Settings dialog box, 177
Advanced Sharing dialog box, 121
Advanced TCP/IP Settings dialog box, 303
Alert Viewer, 242-244
alerts
    Alert Viewer, 242-244
    network health alerts, 240-242
Allow and Block Specific Websites, 284
AND operator, 144
anonymous access, disabling, 319-320

answering calls
    automatically, 580-584
    manually, 580-581
antispyware software. See Windows Defender
Application log, 424
applications. See also specific applications
    launching at startup, 94-95
        group policies, 96
        Registry, 95-97
        specifying startup and logon scripts, 97
        Startup folder, 95
        Task Scheduler, 98
    performance optimization
        application launching, 397
        device drivers, 397
        memory, 397
        program priority, 397-398
    restrictions, 285-286
    running, 608-609
    sending faxes from, 579-580
    troubleshooting
        application settings, 437
        new program installations, 437-438
Approve Updates dialog box, 365
approving updates
    manually, 365
    with rules, 365-366
archiving recorded TV, 204-206
argument naming conventions, 594-595
ARP (Address Resolution Protocol) cache, flushing, 18
arp -a command, 18
Assign Drive Letter or Path dialog box, 109
assigning
    IP addresses
        static IP addresses, 8
        to websites, 304
        to Windows Home Server, 303
    objects to variables, 594-595
    port numbers, 308-309
associating
    host headers with IP addresses, 312
    IP addresses with hostnames, 305-307
ATTRIB utility, 508-509
Audit Account Logon Events policy, 259-260

Audit Account Management policy, 260-262
Audit Logon Events policy, 261-263
Audit Policy Change policy, 263-264
Audit Process Tracking policy, 263-264
Audit System Events policy, 263-265
auditing, 257-258
    activating auditing policies, 258-259
    Audit Account Logon Events policy, 259-260
    Audit Account Management policy, 260-262
    Audit Logon Events policy, 261-263
    Audit Policy Change policy, 263-264
    Audit Process Tracking policy, 263-264
    Audit System Events policy, 263-265
    viewing auditing events
        with filter, 266-267
        with script, 268-270
authentication, anonymous, 319-320
Authorization Manager, 557
AutoAdminLogon setting (Registry), 41
AUTOCHK utility, 416, 503-504
Automatic Approvals dialog box, 366
automatic restart on system failure, 91
Automatically Log On dialog box, 40
automating
    call answering, 580-584
    client logons, 39-41
    disk checking, 414-416, 503-506
    scripts, 598-599
        creating Automation object, 599-600
        exposing VBScript and JavaScript objects, 601-602
        programming FileSystemObject, 602-603
        retrieving existing objects, 600-601
Automation object, 599-600
AutoRun Registry settings, 479
AVG Internet Security, 281
azman.msc, 557

B

backslash (\), 613
Backup Cleanup feature, 215
Backup Details dialog box, 228

Backup Now dialog box, 223
Backup Operators group, 32
Backup Properties dialog box, 225
backups, 209, 211-212. See also partitions, converting to NTFS
    adding hard drives to, 220-221
    backing up other systems to Windows Home Server, 224
    backup time, 215-216
    bootable USB recovery key, creating, 224-232
    canceling, 224
    cleaning up old backups, 230-231
    client computer backup retention, 212, 216-217
    configuring computers for, 217-218
    deleting, 230-231
    disabling, 221-222
    excluding disk drives from, 218
    excluding folders from, 219
    improvements in Windows Home Server 2011, 212-213
    manual backups, 223-225
    preventing deletion of, 230
    Registry, 463
    repairing, 232
    restoring from
        restoring backed-up files, 232-234
        restoring to previous configuration, 235-237
    Single Instance Storage, 210
    with Time Machine, 222
    viewing backup details, 227-230
    viewing list of, 226-227
    Windows Home Server backup system, 211-212
Backups folder, 224
Base Priority column (Task Manager), 375
Base Video boot option, 93
batch files, 492-493
    adding comments to, 493-494
    creating, 493
    displaying messages from, 494-495
    halting execution of, 495
    handling conditions in, 498-501
    jumping to lines in, 497-498

looping, 496-497

parameters, 495-496

Best password policy, 31

Bin folder, 295-296

binary values, editing, 468-469

bindings (website), configuring, 314-315

BIOS data, displaying, 621-622

blogs, 650

BOOT Advanced Options dialog box, 93-94

Boot Log, 93

bootable USB recovery keys creating, 231-232

Browse for Folder dialog box, 309, 312

built-in Windows Home Server drivers, 404

BuiltIns folder, 296

Bytes column (Task Manager), 381

Bytes Per Interval column (Task Manager), 381

Bytes Received column (Task Manager), 380

Bytes Received Per Interval column (Task Manager), 381

Bytes Received Throughput column (Task Manager), 380

Bytes Sent column (Task Manager), 380

Bytes Sent Per Interval column (Task Manager), 381

Bytes Sent Throughput column (Task Manager), 380

Bytes Throughput column (Task Manager), 380

C

/C option (CMD), 478, 481

C$ share, disabling, 274-275

cables, troubleshooting, 20-21

cache

ARP (Address Resolution Protocol) cache, flushing, 18

NetBIOS cache, flushing, 19

write caching, enabling, 392-393

Cache counter, 387

Cache\Copy Read Hits % counter, 387

Cache\Copy Reads/Sec counter, 387

Cache\Data Flush Pages/Sec counter, 387

Calendar Subscription Settings dialog box, 139

calendars, 118-137

publishing, 137-138

subscribing to, 138-140

working with, 140

Called Subscriber ID (CSID), 576

calls, answering

automatically, 580-584

manually, 580-581

canceling backups, 224

Certificate Services DCOM Access group, 32

Certificate Templates, 557

Certificates snap-in, 557

Certification Authority, 557

certmgr.msc, 557

certsrv.msc, 557

certtmpl.msc, 557

Change the Password Policy dialog box, 33

changing

access point username/password, 291

default Pictures import location, 198

default rip location, 199-200

default SSID, 291

paging file size/location, 395-396

password hints, 88

region, 83

scope, 77

shared folder permissions, 119-120

SharePoint permissions, 347-349

user account passwords, 35-36, 43-44

website location, 316-317

Windows Home Server password, 88

workgroup names, 8

Check Disk, 502-503

Check for Solutions feature, 430-432

checking

connection status, 15-17

free disk space, 416-419

network utilization, 17

for solutions to problems, 430-432

system uptime. See system uptime, checking

CHKDSK utility, 502-503

CHKNTFS utility, 503-506

Choose Additional Restore Options dialog box, 429

Choose File to Upload dialog box, **175**

Choose Products dialog box, **360**

Choose Update Classifications dialog box, **366**

choosing DMRs (digital media receivers), **183-184**

classes

    returning class instances, 618-622

    Win32_Service, 570

    Win32_UserAccount, 620

cleaning up old backups, **230-231**

Client Computer Backup Retention Policy, **216-217**

Client folder, **295**

clients

    backups

        client computer backup retention, 212, 216-217

        improvements in Windows Home Server 2011, 212-213

    connecting to WSUS (Windows Server Update Services), 363-365

    converting client partitions to NTFS, 213

        with CONVERT utility, 214-215

        formatting partitions as NTFS, 214

    logons, automating, 39-41

    Mac clients, 53-54

        connecting to Windows Home Server network, 54

        file sharing, 61-65

        MacConnector installation, 55-57

        Remote Desktop Connection Client for Mac, 153

        Remote Desktop connections, 59-61

        shared folders, mounting, 56-58

    preparing for Remote Desktop connections, 153

    Remote Desktop clients. *See* Remote Desktop connections

    Ubuntu clients, 65

        changing Samba workgroup name, 69

        defining Samba users, 67-69

        folder sharing, 70-71

        installing Samba, 67

        rdesktop, 153

        viewing Windows Home Server network, 65-66

Windows Home Server Connector. *See* Windows Home Server Connector

    Xbox 360, 72-73

closing user's session or file, **249**

clusters

    cross-linked clusters, 413

    explained, 412-413

    invalid clusters, 413

    lost clusters, 413

cmd.exe, **478-481**

collections, **595-596**

    Environment, 613-615

    iterating in JavaScript, 596-597

    iterating in VBScript, 596

color of Launchpad Status icon, **240**

comexp.msc, **557**

Command Line column (Task Manager), **376**

Command Line dialog box, **564**

command prompt. *See also* batch files; commands

    accessing, 477-478

    cmd.exe, 478-481

    controlling services with, 569-570

    opening folders in command prompt session, 481-482, 485-486

    running commands from, 483-484

Command Type dialog box, **564**

commands. *See also* batch files; *specific commands*

    editing command lines, 488

    entering multiple commands on single line, 487

    long filenames in, 484-485

    piping, 491-492

    recalling, 486-487

    redirecting command input, 490-491

    redirecting command output, 488-490

    running, 483-484

comments, adding to batch files, **493-494**

complexity of passwords, **31-33**

compmgmt.msc, **557**

Component Services, **557**

compression, disabling, **391-392**

computer command, **245**

Computer Management snap-in, 557
opening, 245-246
renaming administrator account, 271
ComputerName property (WshNetwork), 616
conditions in batch files, 498-501
Configure DHCPv6 Stateless Mode dialog box, 13
configuring. *See also* **customizing; enabling**
backups, 217-218
adding hard drives, 220-221
backing up other systems to Windows Home Server, 224
backup time, 215-216
client computer backup retention, 216-217
excluding disk drives, 218
excluding folders, 218
manual backups, 223-225
with Time Machine, 222
domains
existing domains, 163-171
new domains, 171-172
subdomains, 169-170
fax servers, 574
adding Fax Server role, 574-575
fax modems, 576-577
Fax Service Manager, 576
receiving faxes, 580-584
sending faxes, 578-580
shared fax printers, 575-576
Windows Fax and Scan, 577-578
networks, 7
DHCP servers, 11-13
Remote Desktop connections, 26-27
static IP addresses, 8-11
subnets, 24-26
Windows 7 homegroups, 13-14
workgroup names, 8
Parental Controls, 282-283
port forwarding, 165
program priority, 397-398
Remote Desktop hosts, 148
restricting connections, 151-152
Windows 7 or Vista hosts, 149-150
XP hosts, 150-151

routers
manually, 167
with Windows Home Server, 165-167
scopes, 12
SharePoint Foundation 2010, 323
startup, 89-90
Advanced Boot Options menu, 90-91
launching applications at, 94-98
System Configuration utility, 92-94
time servers, 81-82
user accounts. *See* user accounts
websites. *See* websites
Windows Firewall, 272-274
Windows Home Server, 75
Dashboard, 77-78
Launchpad, 76-77
passwords, 88
region, 83-84
time and date, 79-83
Windows Update, 85-88
Windows Home Server Media Server, 186-189
WSUS (Windows Server Update Services), 359-361
Confirm Password dialog box, 44
Confirm the Backup Settings dialog box, 106
Connect a Computer to the Network Wizard, 55-56
Connect a Computer to the Server Wizard, 52-53
Connect to Server dialog box, 58
connections
checking status of, 15-17
current connections, viewing, 246-247
Remote Desktop. *See* Remote Desktop connections
to shared folders, viewing, 247-248
console. *See* **MMC (Microsoft Management Console)**
Control Panel, 546
adding to Start menu, 554-555
files, 550-552
icons
opening, 549-553
removing, 554-556
showing only specified icons, 556

summary of, 546-550

viewing, 546

control userpasswords2 command, 40

controlling services

at command prompt, 569-570

with scripts, 570-573

with Services snap-in, 566

Convert to Dynamic Disk dialog box, 108

CONVERT utility, 214-215

converting client partitions to NTFS, 213

with CONVERT utility, 214-215

formatting partitions as NTFS, 214

ConvertToDate() function, 410

Copy File dialog box, 234

copying files

with REPLACE utility, 512-513

to shared folders, 135-136

with XCOPY utility, 514-518

cover pages (fax), 578-579

.cpl extension, 550

CPU column (Task Manager), 371

CPU tab (Resource Monitor), 383

CPU Time column (Task Manager), 372

CPU Usage column (Task Manager), 372

Create Computer Recovery Key Wizard, 224-232

Create New Web Application page, 325

Create Site Collection page, 325-328, 335

CreateObject method, 599-600

CreateShortcut method, 609

CreateTextFile method, 603

cross-linked clusters, 413

Cryptographic Operators group, 32

CScript, 590

CSID (Called Subscriber ID), 576

Css folder, 296

current connections, viewing, 246-247

custom consoles (MMC), 562

Custom Scan (Windows Defender), 278

custom taskpad views, 562-565

Customization folder, 296

Customize Backup Wizard, 218

Customize Format dialog box, 84

Customize Media Library dialog box, 187-188

Customize Remote Web Access dialog box, 178-179, 180-181

Customize Server Backup Wizard, 106, 463

Customize Start Menu dialog box, 554

customizing. See also configuring

paging file size, 394-395

Places Bar, 539-541

region formats, 83-84

Remote Web Access pages, 177-181

logon pages, 178-180

web page links, 179-181

SharePoint sites, 337-338

icons, 339

links, 341-342

Quick Launch, 342

themes, 340-341

title and description, 338-339

tree view, 339-340

user account password requirements, 33-34

Windows Security screen, 537-539

cycles, 413-414

D

/D option (CMD), 479

D$ share, disabling, 274-275

Dashboard

changing region, 83

changing Windows Home Server password, 88

opening, 77-78

restarting Windows Home Server, 89

shared folders

creating, 123-124

deleting, 127

moving, 124-125

shutting down Windows Home Server, 89

Data Execution Prevention column (Task Manager), 376

data redundancy, creating with mirrored volumes, 111-112

data shortcut keys, 641

databases, W32_NTLogEvent, 270
date
  setting current date, 79-81
  synchronizing with time server, 81-83
Date and Time dialog box, 80
Date and Time Settings dialog box, 80
Debugging Mode, 91, 451
default content pages, 317-318
Default Document page, 318
default Pictures import location, changing, 198
default rip location, changing, 199-200
default SSID, changing, 291
default website (Windows Home Server),
  293-294
  adding files to, 298-300
  adding folders to
    manually, 299-301
    with Virtual Directory Creation
      Wizard, 301
  default IIS website, 296-297
  restarting, 329
  viewing with IIS Manager, 297-298
  Web application folders, 294-296
default.aspx file, 295, 297
DefaultUserName setting (Registry), 41
defender command, 277
defragmenting hard drives, 422-423
Delete a User Account dialog box, 46
deleting
  backups, 230-231
  default SharePoint site, 328-329
  faxes, 582
  old/unnecessary files, 419-422
  Registry keys, 473
  shared folders, 127
  SharePoint groups, 347
  SharePoint sites, 349
  SharePoint users, 345
  user accounts, 46
Description column (Task Manager), 376
determining IP addresses, 164-165
developers, resources for, 651
device drivers
  built-in Windows Home Server drivers, 404
  downloading, 446-447

installing
  automatically, 402-403
  from disc or download, 403-404
performance optimization, 397, 401-404
troubleshooting, 438, 445-446
updating, 24
Device Manager, 442-445, 557
  updating device drivers, 23
  viewing NICs (network interface cards),
    22-23
devices. See also device drivers
  digitally signed files, verifying, 447-448
  troubleshooting, 442-445
devmgmt.msc, 557
DHCP (Dynamic Host Configuration
  Protocol), 8-9
  leases, 18
  servers, configuring Windows Home Server
    as, 11-13
DHCP Administrators group, 32
DHCP Server dialog box, 12
DHCP Server role, 11-13
DHCP Users group, 32
DHCPREQUEST message, 18
Diagnostic Startup (System Configuration
  utility), 451
dialog box shortcut keys, 643
dialog boxes. See specific dialog boxes
Digital Living Network Alliance (DLNA)
  devices, 184
digital media, 183
  music sharing, 198-199
    customizing Music share with template,
      199-200
    default rip location, changing, 200-201
    with Windows Media Player, 200-201
  photo sharing
    changing default Picture import
      location, 198
    customizing Pictures share with
      template, 193-194
    running slideshows from Pictures
      share, 198
    screensaver slideshows, 194-195
    with Windows Live Photo
      Gallery, 196-197
    with Windows Media Player, 195-196

streaming, 184

activating Windows Home Server Media Server, 186-189

over Internet, 191-193

playing streamed media in Windows Media Center, 190-191

playing streamed media in Windows Media Player, 188-191

preparing devices for, 184-186

video sharing

archiving recorded TV, 204-206

customizing Videos share with template, 201-202

with Windows Media Player, 202-204

digital media receivers (DMRs)

choosing, 183-184

preparing for streaming media, 184-186

digitally signed files, verifying, 447-448

Directory Services Restore Mode, 91, 450

disabling

anonymous access, 319-320

automatic restart on system failure, 91

backups, 221-222

compression, 391-392

driver signature enforcement, 91

encryption, 391-392

hidden administrative shares, 274-275

network broadcasting, 290-291

user accounts, 44-45

visual effects, 399-400

Windows Search, 392

disconnecting from server

mapped network folders, 131

with Remote Desktop, 27, 253-254

Remote Desktop connections, 158

Remote Web Access, 163

discs, installing device drivers from, 403-404

Disk Cleanup, 419-422

Disk Defragmenter, 422-423

Disk Management snap-in, 558

adding dynamic disks to spanned volumes, 110-111

combining dynamic disks into spanned volumes, 108-110

converting hard drives to dynamic disks, 108

creating mirrored volumes, 111-112

creating RAID 5 volumes, 112-115

disk management utilities

CHKDSK utility, 502-503

CHKNTFS utility, 503-506

table of, 501-502

Disk tab (Resource Monitor), 383

diskmgmt.msc. See Disk Management snap-in

Disks to Convert dialog box, 108

Display Shutdown Event Tracker policy, 544-545

Display tab (Remote Desktop Connection dialog box), 155

displaying. See viewing

Distributed COM Users group, 32

Distributed File System, 558

DLNA (Digital Living Network Alliance) devices, 184

DMRs (digital media receivers)

choosing, 183-184

preparing for streaming media, 184-186

DNS (Domain Name Service)

cache, flushing, 19

dynamic DNS, 168

Do Not Display Last User Name policy, 272

Do Not Process the Legacy Run List policy, 97

Do Not Process the Run Once List policy, 97

documents

recent documents list, increasing size of, 541-543

shortcut keys, 641

Documents folder, 118

dollar sign ($), 274

Domain Name Service (DNS) cache, flushing, 19

domains

configuring

existing domains, 163-171

new domains, 171-172

subdomains, 169-170

domain names, connecting with, 168

DOSKEY utility, 486

editing command lines, 488

entering multiple commands on single line, 487

recalling command lines, 486-487

shortcut keys, 646-647

dot (.) notation, 485-486

double equal sign (==), 499

downloading
  device drivers, 446-447
  SharePoint Foundation 2010, 322

downloads, installing device drivers
  from, 403-404

drag-and-drop
  shortcut keys, 643
  uploading, enabling, 176-177

Drive Extender, 99-100

Drive object, 602

driver signature enforcement, disabling, 91

drives. See hard drives

Drives object, 602

.dvr-ms extension, 204

DWORD values, editing, 468-469

dynamic disks
  adding to spanned volumes, 110-111
  combining into spanned volumes, 108-110
  converting hard drives to, 108

dynamic DNS, 168

Dynamic Host Configuration Protocol.
  See DHCP (Dynamic Host Configuration
  Protocol)

DynDNS, 168

E

/E option (CMD), 480

Easy File Upload Tool, 176

ECHO command, 492, 494-495

Echo method, 597-598

Edit Binary Value dialog box, 468-469

Edit Rule dialog box, 366

Edit Site Binding dialog box, 314

Edit Site dialog box, 317

editing
  command lines, 488
  file/folder attributes, 508-509
  PATH environment variable, 485

Registry, 466-468
  binary values, 468-469
  DWORD or QWORD values, 468-469
  keys or settings, 472-473
  .reg files, 468-472
  string values, 468
  SharePoint user information, 343-344

electromagnetic interference, 21

email
  emailing faxes, 582
  sending to SharePoint users, 344
  viruses, 280-282

Enable Boot Logging option, 449

Enable VGA Mode option, 450

enabling. See also configuring
  drag-and-drop uploading, 176-177
  encryption, 290
  guest accounts, 45
  Media Library Sharing, 186-189
  prefetching, 397
  Remote Web Access, 160
  Shutdown Event Tracker, 544-545
  user accounts, 45
  write caching, 392-393

encryption
  disabling, 391-392
  enabling, 290

Enterprise PKI, 558

Enumerator object, 592

Environment collection, 613-615

environment variables, accessing with
  WshShell, 613-615

equal sign (=), 499

error messages, 432-433

Event Log Readers group, 32

Event Viewer, 558
  logs, reviewing, 424
  troubleshooting, 433
  viewing auditing events, 266-267

events, audit
  viewing with filter, 266-267
  viewing with script, 268-270

eventvwr.msc. See Event Viewer

exclamation mark (!), 23, 445
excluding
    disk drives from backups, 218
    folders from backups, 218
ExecQuery method, 619
exit codes (XCOPY), 517
Experience tab (Remote Desktop Connection dialog box), 157
Export Registry File dialog box, 464
exporting .reg files, 464-465
exposing VBScript and JavaScript objects, 601-602
Extend Volume Wizard, 110-111

F

/F option (CMD), 480
Fax Accounts dialog box, 575
fax modems, configuring, 576-577
Fax Properties dialog box, 575
Fax Server role, 574-575
fax servers, 574
    adding Fax Server role, 574-575
    configuring fax modems, 576-577
    configuring shared fax printers, 575-576
    receiving faxes
        answering calls automatically, 580-581
        answering calls manually, 580-581
        routing received faxes, 582-584
        working with received faxes, 581-582
    sending faxes, 578
        from applications, 579-580
        connecting to shared fax printer, 580
        cover pages, 578-579
    starting Fax Service Manager, 576
    starting Windows Fax and Scan, 577-578
Fax Service Manager, 576
Fax Setup Wizard, 575
Fax Status Monitor window, 580-581
faxes
    deleting, 582
    emailing, 582
    forwarding, 582

printing, 581
reading, 581
receiving
    answering calls automatically, 580-584
    answering calls manually, 580-581
    routing received faxes, 582-584
    working with received faxes, 581-582
saving, 582
sending
    from applications, 579-580
    connecting to shared fax printer, 580
    cover pages, 578-579
FC (file compare) utility, 465
File object, 603
filenames in commands, 484-485
files
    adding to Windows Home Server default website, 298-300
    batch files, 492-493
        adding comments to, 493-494
        creating, 493
        displaying messages from, 494-495
        halting execution of, 495
        handling conditions in, 498-501
        jumping to lines in, 497-498
        looping, 496-497
        parameters, 495-496
    closing user's session or file, 249
    Control Panel files, 550-552
    copying
        with REPLACE utility, 512-513
        with XCOPY utility, 514-518
    copying to shared folders, 135-136
    default.aspx, 295, 297
    digitally signed files, verifying, 447-448
    file management tools
        ATTRIB utility, 508-509
        FIND utility, 509-511
        REN utility, 511-512
        REPLACE utility, 512-513
        SORT utility, 513-514
        table of, 506-508
        XCOPY utility, 514-518

files fragmentation, 422-423
finding text strings in, 509-511
Global.aspx, 295
hosts, 307
.js extension, 588
long filenames, 484-485
modifying attributes of, 508-509
.msc files, 557
old/unnecessary files, deleting, 419-422
paging file
    changing size/location of, 395-396
    customizing size of, 394-395
    storing, 393
.reg files, 461-462
    creating, 470-472
    editing, 468-470
    exporting, 464-465
    importing, 465-466
renaming, 511-512
restoring, 232-234
Robot.txt, 297
Server.aspx, 295
sharing
    Linux clients, 70-71
    Mac clients, 61-65
shortcut files, 609-611
    creating, 609
    WshShortcut object, 609-611
Sigverif.txt, 448
sorting contents of, 513-514
style.css, 295
.vbs extension, 588
viewing open files, 248
web.config, 295, 297
.wsh files, 590-592
Files object, 603
FileSystemObject, 602-603
Filter Current Log dialog box, 266
filters
MAC (Media Access Control) address
    filtering, 291-292
viewing auditing events with, 266-267
Find dialog box, 474
FIND utility, 509-511

finding
Registry changes, 465
Registry entries, 473-474
text strings, 509-511
firewalls
configuring SharePoint for, 329-330
Windows Firewall
    activating, 272-274
    configuring ports for, 309-311
/flushdns option (ipconfig command), 19
flushing
ARP (Address Resolution Protocol)
    cache, 18
DNS (Domain Name Service) cache, 19
NetBIOS cache, 19
Folder object, 602
Folder Sharing dialog box, 70
Folder snap-in, 558
folders
AccountPage, 296
adding to Windows Home Server default
  website
    manually, 299-301
    with Virtual Directory Creation
      Wizard, 301
Backups, 224
Bin, 295-296
BuiltIns, 296
Client, 295
Css, 296
Customization, 296
Documents, 118
excluding from backups, 218
folder management tools
    ATTRIB utility, 508-509
    REN utility, 511-512
    REPLACE utility, 512-513
    SORT utility, 513-514
    table of, 506-508
    XCOPY utility, 514-518
folder windows shortcut keys, 644
Images, 295-296
modifying attributes of, 508-509

Music, 118
   adding to Windows Media Player,
      200-201
   customizing Music share with template,
      199-200
opening in command prompt session,
   481-482, 485-486
Package, 295
Pictures, 118
   adding to Windows Live Photo Gallery,
      196-197
   adding to Windows Media Player,
      195-196
   changing default Picture import
      location, 198
Recorded TV, 118
RemoteAccess, 295-296, 299
renaming, 511-512
Resources, 297
restoring, 232-234
Sessions, 246
sharing. See shared folders
shell folders, 540-541
Site, 296-297, 299
Startup, 95
Videos, 118
   adding to Windows Media Player,
      202-204
   templates, 201-202
Windows Home Server default
   website, 294-296
Folders object, 603
FOR command, 496-497
Format dialog box, 214
Format Volume dialog box, 109
formatting partitions as NTFS, 214
For...Next loop, 596
forums
   Windows Home Server Developers
      Forum, 651
   Windows Home Server forums, 441, 650
forwarding
   faxes, 582
   ports, 165, 311, 330-331

fragmentation, 422-423
free disk space, checking, 416-419
fsmgmt.msc, 559
Full Access level, 30
Full Scan (Windows Defender), 278
Full System Restore Wizard, 235-237
functions. See specific functions

G

GDI Objects column (Task Manager), 375
general shortcut keys, 640
General tab (Remote Desktop Connection
   dialog box), 154
GetObject method, 600-601
Global.aspx file, 295
glossary, 625-637
gnome-network-admin package, 69
GOTO command, 497-498
gpedit.msc, 558
Grant Permissions dialog box, 332
group policies, 533-537
   customizing Places Bar, 539-541
   customizing Windows Security screen,
      537-539
   enabling Shutdown Event Tracker, 544-545
   increasing size of recent documents list,
      541-543
   launching applications at startup with, 96
Group Policy Object Editor, 558
groups (security). See security groups
groups (SharePoint)
   creating, 346-347
   deleting, 347
   settings, 345-346
Guest account, 45, 289
Guests group, 32

H

Handles column (Task Manager), 375
hard drives. *See also* storage
    adding to backups, 220-221
    clusters
        cross-linked clusters, 413
        explained, 412-413
        invalid clusters, 413
        lost clusters, 413
    converting to dynamic disks, 108
    cycles, 413-414
    defragmenting, 422-423
    determining system hard drive, 428
    Disk Cleanup, 419-422
    Drive Extender, 99-100
    excluding from backups, 218
    free disk space, checking, 416-419
    mapping, 616-617
    mapping shared folders to, 130-132
    performance optimization
        compression and encryption, 391-392
        hard drive performance specifications, 391
        maintenance, 391
        Windows Search, 392
        write caching, 392-393
    replacing, 429
    scanning
        AUTOCHK utility, 503-506
        CHKNTFS utility, 503-506
    scanning for errors, 411-412
        AUTOCHK utility, 416
        Check Disk, 414-416, 502-503
Hardware Update Wizard, 402
headers. *See* host headers
health alerts, 240-242
hidden administrative shares, disabling, 274-275
hiding
    network health alerts, 240-242
    usernames in Log On to Windows dialog box, 271-272
hives (Registry), 461-462
HKEY_CLASSES_ROOT, 459-460
HKEY_CURRENT_CONFIG, 461

HKEY_CURRENT_USER, 460
HKEY_LOCAL_MACHINE, 460-461
HKEY_USERS, 461
home computer security, 275
    application restrictions, 285-286
    email viruses, 280-282
    monitoring, 275-276
    Parental Controls, 282
        activating, 282-283
        activity reporting, 283
        creating childrens' accounts, 282
    phishing, 285-288
    shared computers, 288-290
    web restrictions, 283-285
    Windows Defender, 276-277
        settings, 278-280
        spyware scanning, 277-278
Home Server Land, 650
Home Server Show, 650
homegroups (Windows 7), connecting Windows Home Server to, 13-14
HomeUsers Security Group, 32
host headers, 312
    associating with IP addresses, 312
    creating websites with, 312-313
hostnames, associating IP addresses with, 305-307
hosts (Remote Desktop), configuring, 148
    restricting connections, 151-152
    Windows 7 or Vista hosts, 149-150
    XP hosts, 150-151
hosts file, 307
HTML tags. *See specific tags*

I

icons (Control Panel)
    opening, 549-553
    removing, 554-556
    showing only specified icons, 556
    summary of, 546-550
    viewing, 546
identities, adding to websites, 315-316
IF command, 498-501

IIS (Internet Information Services)
  default IIS website, 296-297
  IIS Manager
    viewing websites with, 297-298
    Virtual Directory Creation Wizard, 301
IIS_IUSRS group, 32
iis.msc, 558
Image Path Name column (Task Manager), 376
images. See icons (Control Panel)
Images folder, 295-296
Import Registry File dialog box, 465
importing .reg files, 465-466
increasing size of recent documents
  list, 541-543
indexing, 141
Indexing Options dialog box, 141
inetmgr command, 298
input redirection operator (<), 490-491
insertion point shortcut keys, 642
installing
  device drivers
    automatically, 402-403
    built-in Windows Home Server
      drivers, 404
    from disc or download, 403-404
  MacConnector, 55-57
  Samba, 67
  SharePoint Foundation 2010, 322-323
  Windows Home Server Connector, 51-53
  WSUS (Windows Server Update
    Services), 358
Installing Windows dialog box, 429
InstancesOf method, 619
Internet, streaming digital media over, 191-193
Internet connections, 163-164
  connecting to network computer, 173
  connecting with domain name maintained
    by dynamic DNS service, 168
  connecting with domain names, 169-173
  connecting with router's IP address,
    164-168
  drag-and-drop uploading, 176-177
  file sharing, 173-175
Internet Explorer shortcut keys, 645-646
Internet Information Services. See IIS (Internet
  Information Services)

Internet Information Services (IIS)
  Manager, 558
Internet Protocol. See IP (Internet Protocol)
Internet Protocol Version 4 (TCP/IPv4)
  Properties dialog box, 303
Internet Time Settings dialog box, 81
intType parameter, 605-606
invalid clusters, 413
I/O Other Bytes column (Task Manager), 376
I/O Other column (Task Manager), 376
I/O Reads column (Task Manager), 375
I/O Ready Bytes column (Task Manager), 376
I/O Write Bytes column (Task Manager), 376
I/O Writes column (Task Manager), 375
IP Address dialog box, 152
IP addresses, 302
  assigning to websites, 304
  assigning to Windows Home Server, 303
  associating host headers with, 312
  associating with hostnames, 305-307
  determining, 164-165
  router's IP address
    connecting with, 164-168
    determining, 167
  static IP addresses, 8-11
IP Security Monitor, 558
IP Security Policy Management, 558
ipconfig command, 478
  /all option, 9
  /flushdns option, 19
  /registerdns option, 19
Items Displayed in Places Bar policy, 541

J

JavaScript
  exposing JavaScript objects, 601-602
  iterating collections, 596-597
<job> tag, 589
jobs (script), creating, 589
joining Windows 7 homegroups, 13-14
.js extension, 588
jumping to lines in batch files, 497-498

K

/K option (CMD), 478, 481

Kernel Memory Nonpaged (Task Manager), 377

Kernel Memory Paged (Task Manager), 377

keyboard shortcuts, 639-648

    data shortcut keys, 641

    dialog box shortcut keys, 643

    document shortcut keys, 641

    DOSKEY shortcut keys, 487-488, 646-647

    drag-and-drop shortcut keys, 643

    folder window shortcut keys, 644

    general shortcut keys, 640

    insertion point shortcut keys, 642

    Internet Explorer shortcut keys, 645-646

    program window shortcut keys, 640

    text selection shortcut keys, 642

    Windows logo key shortcut keys, 647-648

Keys pane (Registry), 457-458

L

last known good configuration, booting to, 91, 450

launching. See opening

Launchpad

    Alert Viewer, 242-244

    features, 76-77

    network health alerts, 240-242

    Status icon, 240

Launchpad Settings dialog box, 77

Lavasoft Ad-Aware, 277

leases (DHCP), 18

length of passwords

    customizing requirements, 33-34

    setting, 31-33

Link Speed column (Task Manager), 380

Link to Web Address Wizard.558, 561

links

    adding to Remote Web Access pages, 179-181

    SharePoint sites, 341-342

Linux clients, 65

    changing Samba workgroup name, 69

    defining Samba users, 67-69

    folder sharing, 70-71

    installing Samba, 67

    rdesktop, 153

    viewing Windows Home Server network in Ubuntu, 65-66

LMCompatibilityLevel setting (Registry), 65

Local and Network scope, 77

Local Group Policy Editor, 34, 533-537

    customizing Places Bar, 539-541

    customizing Windows Security screen, 537-539

    enabling Shutdown Event Tracker, 544-545

    increasing size of recent documents list, 541-543

local logons, configuring, 47

Local Only scope, 77

Local Resources tab (Remote Desktop Connection dialog box), 155-156

Local Security Policy snap-in, 258-259, 558

Local Security Settings snap-in, 47, 271-272

Local Users and Groups snap-in, 42, 558

location (website), changing, 316-317

locking computer, 289

Log On to Windows dialog box, hiding usernames in, 271-272

LogicalDisk/Avg. Disk Queue Length counter, 387

logon pages (Remote Web Access), customizing, 178-180

logons

    automating, 39-41

    local logons, 47

    remote logons, 47-48

    to top-level SharePoint sites, 332-333

logs, Event Viewer, 424

long filenames, 484-485

looping batch files, 496-497

loops, For...Next, 596

lost clusters, 413

lusrmgr.msc, 558

M

MAC (Media Access Control) address filtering, 291-292

Mac clients, 53-54

accessing shared folders, 135

connecting Windows Home Server to, 54

file sharing, 61-65

MacConnector installation, 55-57

Remote Desktop Connection Client for Mac, 153

Remote Desktop connections, 59-61

shared folders, mounting, 56-58

Time Machine, 222

MacConnector, 55-57

maintenance, 407

Disk Cleanup, 419-422

Disk Defragmenter, 422-423

Event Viewer logs, reviewing, 424

free disk space, checking, 416-419

hard drives, scanning for errors, 391, 411-412

AUTOCHK utility, 416

Check Disk, 414-416

cross-linked clusters, 413

cycles, 413-414

invalid clusters, 413

lost clusters, 413

maintenance schedules, 425-426

system uptime, checking, 408

with Performance Monitor, 408-409

with script, 409-411

with SYSTEMINFO command, 408

with Task Manager, 408

manual backups, 223-225

manual router configuration, 167

manually answering calls, 580-581

manually approving updates, 365

MapNetworkDrive method, 616-617

mapping

network drives, 616-617

network printers, 616

shared folders to local drive letters, 130-132

Maverick Meerkat. See Ubuntu clients

McAfee Internet Security Suite, 281

Media Library Sharing, 186-189

Media Server, 186-189

Medium password policy, 31

Memory (Private Working Set) column (Task Manager), 371

memory, adding, 397

Memory - Commit Size column (Task Manager), 373

Memory - Non-Paged Pool column (Task Manager), 374

Memory - Paged Pool column (Task Manager), 374

Memory - Peak Working Set column (Task Manager), 373

Memory - Private Working Set column (Task Manager), 373

Memory - Working Set column (Task Manager), 373

Memory - Working Set Delta column (Task Manager), 373

Memory counter, 387

Memory tab (Resource Monitor), 383

Memory\Available MBytes counter, 387

Memory\Cache Bytes counter, 387

Memory\Cache Faults/sec counter, 388

Memory\Committed Bytes counter, 388

Memory\Page Faults/Sec counter, 388

Memory\Page Reads/Sec counter, 388

Memory\Pages Input/Sec counter, 388

Memory\Pages Output/Sec counter, 388

Memory\Pages/Sec counter, 388

Memory\Pool Nonpaged Bytes counter, 389

Memory\Pool Paged Bytes counter, 389

Menu Command dialog box, 564

messages

DHCPREQUEST, 18

displaying from batch files, 494-495

error messages, 432-433

sending to Remote Desktop clients, 252-253

methods, 593-594

AddWindowsPrinterConnection, 616

CreateShortcut, 609

CreateTextFile, 603

Echo, 597-598

ExecQuery, 619

GetObject, 600-601

InstancesOf, 619

MapNetworkDrive, 616-617

moveNext, 597

OpenTextFile, 603

Popup, 604-608

Quit, 598

RegDelete, 613

RegRead, 612

RegWrite, 594, 612-613

RemoveNetworkDrive, 617

RemovePrinterConnection, 616

StartService, 573

StopService, 573

Microsoft Common Console Documents, 557

Microsoft Knowledge Base, 441

Microsoft Management Console. *See* **MMC (Microsoft Management Console)**

Microsoft Product Support, 441

Microsoft Security Essentials, 281

Microsoft Security website, 441

Microsoft TechNet, 441

mirrored volumes, 111-112

MMC (Microsoft Management Console)

custom consoles, 562

custom taskpad views, 562-565

opening, 560

snap-ins

adding, 560-561

controlling with group policies, 565-566

default snap-ins, 557-560

modems (fax), configuring, 576-577

monitoring, 239

with Alert Viewer, 242-244

home computer security, 275-276

network health alerts, 240-242

network health status, 240

with Performance Monitor, 384-390

adding performance counters, 385-386

table of performance counters, 386-390

Remote Desktop connections, 249-255

disconnecting Remote Desktop sessions, 253-254

monitoring users via Task Manager, 254-255

sending messages to Remote Desktop clients, 252-253

starting Remote Desktop Services Manager, 250

viewing Remote Desktop sessions, 250-252

with Resource Monitor, 382-384

shared folders, 245-249

closing user's session or file, 249

launching Computer Management snap-in, 245-246

viewing connections to shared folders, 247-248

viewing current connections, 246-247

viewing open files, 248

with Task Manager

network performance, 379-382

processes, 370-376

system performance, 376-378

with TYPEPERF utility, 528-530

users with Task Manager, 254-255

More tab (Remote Desktop Connection dialog box), 156

mounting shared folders, 56-58

moveNext method, 597

moving shared folders, 124-125

.msc files, 557

MSWHS website, 650

multiple commands, entering on single line, 487

multiple identities, assigning to websites, 315-316

multiple-drive systems, storage on, 102-104

Music Album template, 199

Music Artist template, 199

Music Details template, 199

Music folder, 118

adding to Windows Media Player, 200-201

customizing Music share with template, 199-200

Music Icons template, 199

music sharing, 197
  customizing Music share with template, 199-200
  default rip location, changing, 199-200
  with Windows Media Player, 200-201
Music template, 199

N

Name and Description dialog box, 564
names
  argument naming conventions, 594-595
  UNC (universal naming convention), 128-130
  workgroup names, changing, 8, 69
NAP Client Configuration, 558
napclcfg.msc, 558
navigating Registry
  Keys pane, 457-458
  Settings pane, 458-459
Navigation dialog box, 564
nbtstat command
  -R option, 19
  -RR option, 19
NET CONTINUE command, 569-570
NET PAUSE command, 569-570
NET START command, 569-570
net start w32time command, 82
NET STOP command, 569-570
net stop w32time command, 82
NetBIOS, cache, flushing, 19
Network and Internet Troubleshooter, 19-20
network broadcasting, disabling, 290-291
Network Configuration Operators group, 32
Network Connection Bindings dialog box, 12
Network Connections window, 9
network interface cards (NICs), troubleshooting, 21-22
Network Interface counter, 389
Network Interface\Bytes Total/Sec counter, 389
Network Interface\Current Bandwidth, 389

network locations, creating
  Windows 7 and Vista, 131-133
  Windows XP, 133-135
Network Policy Server, 558
Network tab (Resource Monitor), 384
network utilization, checking, 17
Network Utilization column (Task Manager), 380
Networking tab (Task Manager)
  checking network utilization, 17
  monitoring network performance, 379-382
New Fax window, 578
New Inbound Rule Wizard, 310-311
New SharePoint Site page, 335-336
New Spanned Volume Wizard, 108-110
New Task Wizard, 564
NICs (network interface cards), troubleshooting, 21-22
No Access level, 30
No Access permissions, 119
No GUI Boot option, 93
No-IP.com, 168
None scope, 77
Nonunicast Received Per Interval column (Task Manager), 382
Nonunicast Sent Per Interval column (Task Manager), 382
Nonunicast/Interval column (Task Manager), 382
Nonunicasts column (Task Manager), 381
Nonunicasts Received column (Task Manager), 381
Nonunicasts Sent column (Task Manager), 381
Normal Startup (System Configuration utility), 451
Norton Internet Security, 281
NOT operator, 144
notifications
  Alert Viewer, 242-244
  network health alerts, 240-242
nps.msc, 558
NT LAN Manager version 2 (NTLMv2) authentication, 65

NTFS

converting client partitions to, 213

with CONVERT utility, 214-215

formatting partitions as NTFS, 214

NTFS Configuration Tool, 65

NTLMv2 (NT LAN Manager version 2) authentication, 65

O

objects

assigning to variables, 594-595

Automation, 599-600

collections, 595-596

iterating in JavaScript, 596-597

iterating in VBScript, 596

defined, 592

Drive, 602

Drives, 602

Enumerator, 592

exposing VBScript and JavaScript objects, 601-602

File, 603

Files, 603

FileSystemObject, 602-603

Folder, 602

Folders, 603

methods, 593-594. *See also specific methods*

properties, 592-593

SWbemLocator, 618

TextStream, 603

WMI service object, 617-618

ExecQuery method, 619

InstancesOf method, 619

referencing, 618

returning class instances, 618-622

WScript. *See WScript*

WshNetwork

mapping network drives, 616-617

mapping network printers, 616

methods. *See specific methods*

properties, 616

referencing, 615

WshShell

displaying text to user, 604-607

methods. *See specific methods*

referencing, 604

running applications, 608-609

shortcuts, 609-611

working with environment variables, 613-615

working with Registry entries, 611-613

WshShortcut, 609-611

Open Files command (Shared Folders menu), 248

open files, viewing, 248

opening

applications/scripts at startup, 94-95

group policies, 96

Registry, 95-97

specifying startup and logon scripts, 97

Startup folder, 95

Computer Management snap-in, 245-246

Control Panel icons, 549-553

Dashboard, 77-78

Fax Service Manager, 576

folders in command prompt session, 481-482, 485-486

MMC (Microsoft Management Console), 560

Network Connections window, 9

optimizing application launching, 397

Registry Editor, 456-457

Remote Desktop Services Manager, 250

Windows Fax and Scan, 577-578

OpenTextFile method, 603

operating systems, Windows Home Server Connector supported operating systems, 50-51

operators, 143-144

input redirection operator (<), 490-491

output redirection operator (>), 489-490

optimizing performance. *See performance optimization*

OR operator, 144

orphaned clusters, 413

OS Boot Information option, 93

output redirection operator (>), 489-490

Overview tab (Resource Monitor), 382

P

Package folder, 295

Page Faults column (Task Manager), 374

Page Faults Delta column (Task Manager), 374

paging file
  changing size/location of, 395-396
  customizing size of, 394-395
  storing, 393

Paging File counter, 389

Paging File\% Usage counter, 389

Paging File\% Usage Peak counter, 389

Parental Controls, 282
  activating, 282-283
  activity reporting, 283
  creating childrens' accounts, 282

partitions, converting to NTFS, 213
  with CONVERT utility, 214-215
  formatting partitions as NTFS, 214

passwords
  access point username/password, 291
  password complexity checker, 34
  password hints, 88
  Ubuntu clients, 68-69
  user account passwords
    changing, 35-36, 43-44
    choosing strong passwords, 34-35
    customizing requirements, 33-34
    length and complexity, 31-33
  Windows Home Server password, 88

PATH environment variable, editing, 485

PAUSE command, 495

PC Tools Spyware Doctor, 277

perfmon.msc, 558

performance counters
  adding, 385-386
  table of, 386-390

Performance Log Users group, 32

Performance Monitor, 384-390, 558
  adding performance counters, 385-386
  checking system uptime, 408-409
  table of performance counters, 386-390

Performance Monitor Users group, 32

performance optimization, 369
  application performance
    application launching, 397
    device drivers, 397
    memory, 397
    program priority, 397-398
  device drivers, 401-404
    built-in Windows Home Server drivers, 404
    Hardware Update Wizard, 402
    installing automatically, 402-403
    installing from disc or download, 403-404
  hard drive optimization
    compression and encryption, 391-392
    hard drive performance specifications, 391
    maintenance, 391
    Windows Search, 392
    write caching, 392-393
  paging file
    changing size/location of, 395-396
    customizing size of, 394-395
    storing, 393
  with Performance Monitor, 384-390
    adding performance counters, 385-386
    table of performance counters, 386-390
  power options, 398-399
  with Resource Monitor, 382-384
  for services, 387-401
  with Task Manager
    monitoring network performance, 379-382
    monitoring processes, 370-376
    monitoring system performance, 376-378
  TYPEPERF utility, 528-530
  visual effects, 399-400

Performance tab (Task Manager), 376-378

permissions
  changing, 119-120
  No Access, 119
  Read, 118-119
  Read/Write permissions, 118

setting, 118-119
SharePoint permissions
    changing, 347-349
    custom permission levels, 349
SharePoint site permissions, 335-336
Permissions dialog box, 121
phishing, 285-288
Photo Album template, 194
photo sharing
    changing default Picture import
        location, 198
    customizing Pictures share with
        template, 193-194
    running slideshows from Pictures
        share, 198
    screensaver slideshows, 194-195
    with Windows Live Photo Gallery, 196-197
    with Windows Media Player, 195-196
Physical Memory Available (Task Manager), 377
Physical Memory Cached (Task Manager), 377
Physical Memory Free (Task Manager), 377
Physical Memory Total (Task Manager), 377
PhysicalDisk counter, 389
PhysicalDisk\% Disk Time counter, 390
Picture and Videos template, 194
Picture Library Locations dialog box, 196
Pictures and Videos template, 202
Pictures folder, 118
    adding to Windows Live Photo
        Gallery, 196-197
    adding to Windows Media Player, 195-196
    changing default Picture import
        location, 198
    running slideshows from, 198
Pictures template, 194
**PID (Process Identifier) column (Task
    Manager), 372**
ping command, 89
pipe operator (|), 491-492
piping commands, 491-492
pkiview.msc, 558
Places Bar, customizing, 539-541
playing streamed media
    in Windows Media Center, 190-191
    in Windows Media Player, 188-191

policies
    activating, 258-259
    Audit Account Logon Events, 259-260
    Audit Account Management, 260-262
    Audit Logon Events, 261-263
    Audit Policy Change, 263-264
    Audit Process Tracking, 263-264
    Audit System Events, 263-265
    Client Computer Backup Retention Policy,
        216-217
    Display Shutdown Event Tracker, 544-545
    Do Not Process the Legacy Run List, 97
    Do Not Process the Run Once List, 97
    group policies, 96. See also Local Group
        Policy Editor
    Items Displayed in Places Bar, 541
    password policies, 31-33
    Remove Change Password, 538
    Remove Lock Computer, 538
    Remove Logoff, 538
    Remove Task Manager, 538
    Restrict the User from Entering Author
        Mode, 564
    Restrict Users to the Explicitly Permitted
        List of Snap-Ins, 566
    Run Logon Scripts Synchronously, 97
    Run Startup Scripts Asynchronously, 97
    Run Startup Scripts Visible, 97
    Run These Programs at User Logon, 96
    Show Only Specified Control Panel
        Applets, 556
    Specify Intranet Microsoft Update Service
        Location, 363-364
Popup method, 604-608
Port Reporter tool, 308
ports, 307-308
    assigning port numbers, 308-309
    firewall exceptions, 309-311
    port forwarding, 165, 311, 330-331
power, optimizing performance of, 398-399
Power Users group, 32
predefined shares, 118
prefetching, 397
PrefetchParameters (Registry), 397

previous versions of shares, accessing, 125-126
Print Operators group, 32
printers
    mapping, 616
    shared fax printers, 580
printing faxes, 581
priority (programs), 397-398
Problem Reporting dialog box, 431
Processes tab
    Remote Desktop Services Manager, 252
    Task Manager, 370-376
Processor counter, 390
Processor\% Idle Time counter, 390
Processor\% Interrupt Time counter, 390
Processor\% Privileged Time counter, 390
Processor\% User Time counter, 390
Products Configuration Wizard, 323
program window shortcut keys, 640
programs. *See specific programs*
Programs tab (Remote Desktop Connection dialog box), 156
properties
    of objects, 592-593
    of scripts, 590-592
    user account properties, 42-43
    of WshNetwork object, 616
Protocol and Ports dialog box, 310, 330
protocols. *See specific protocols*
Publish Calendar dialog box, 137-138
publishing calendars, 137-138

Q

/Q option (CMD), 479
Quick Launch, 342
Quick Scan (Windows Defender), 278
Quit method, 598
quotation marks ("), 499
QWORD values, editing, 468-469

R

-R option, nbtstat command, 19
RA_AllowAddInAccess, 30
RA_AllowComputerAccess, 30
RA_AllowDashboardAccess, 30
RA_AllowHomePageLinks, 30
RA_AllowMediaAccess, 30
RA_AllowNetworkAlertAccess, 31
RA_AllowRemoteAccess, 31
RA_AllowShareAccess, 31
RAID 5 volumes, 112-115
Read Only access, 30
Read permissions, 118-119
reading faxes, 581
Read/Write permissions, 118
reboots, troubleshooting, 432-437
recalling command lines, 486-487
receiving faxes
    answering calls automatically, 580-584
    routing received faxes, 582-584
    working with received faxes, 581-582
recent documents list, increasing size of, 541-543
recorded TV, archiving, 204-206
Recorded TV folder, 118
recovering shared folders, 125-126
redirecting
    command input, 490-491
    command output, 488-490
Redundant Array of Inexpensive Disks (RAID) 5 volumes, 112-115
referencing
    WMI service object, 618
    WshNetwork object, 615
    WshShell object, 604
Refresh command (Action menu), 247
.reg files
    creating, 470-472
    editing, 468-470
    exporting Registry to, 464-465
    importing, 465-466
REG utility, 519-521-522

REG_BINARY values, 468-469

REG_EXPAND_SZ values, 468

REG_MULTI_SZ values, 468

REG_SZ values, 468

RegDelete method, 613

region

    changing, 83

    customizing region formats, 83-84

Region and Language dialog box, 84

/registerdns option (ipconfig command), 19

Registry, 455-456

    accessing with WshShell, 611-613

    adding data to, 521-522

    backing up, 463

    clients

        automating client logon, 40-41

        connecting to WSUS (Windows Server Update Services), 363-364

    customizing synchronization interval, 82-83

    disabling hidden administrative shares, 274-275

    editing, 466-470

        binary values, 468-469

        DWORD or QWORD values, 468-469

        keys or settings, 472-473

        .reg files, 468-472

        string values, 468

    enabling prefetching, 397

    files, 461-462

    Find feature, 473-474

    finding changes, 465

    finding entries in, 473-474

    hives, 461-462

    Keys pane, 457-458

    launching applications at startup, 95-97

    LMCompatibilityLevel setting, 65

    modifying Registry data, 521-522

    .reg files

        creating, 470-472

        editing, 468-470

        exporting Registry to, 464-465

        importing, 465-466

    Registry Editor, starting, 456-457

root keys, 459

    HKEY_CLASSES_ROOT, 459-460

    HKEY_CURRENT_CONFIG, 461

    HKEY_CURRENT_USER, 460

    HKEY_LOCAL_MACHINE, 460-461

    HKEY_USERS, 461

    Settings pane, 458-459

    troubleshooting, 434

RegRead method, 612

RegWrite method, 594, 612-613

REM command, 493-494

Remote Desktop Connection Client for Mac, 59-61, 153

Remote Desktop Connection dialog box, 27, 60, 153

    Display tab, 155

    Experience tab, 157

    General tab, 154

    More tab, 156

    Programs tab, 156

Remote Desktop connections, 26, 148, 559

    connecting via, 153-158

    disconnecting, 27, 158, 253-254

    Internet connections, 163-164

        connecting to network computer, 173

        connecting with domain name maintained by dynamic DNS service, 168

        connecting with domain name maintained by Windows Home Server, 169-173

        connecting with router's IP address, 164-168

        drag-and-drop uploading, 176-177

        file sharing, 173-175

    Local Resources tab, 155-156

    Mac clients, 59-61

    making server connections, 27

    monitoring, 249-255

        starting Remote Desktop Services Manager, 250

        users via Task Manager, 254-255

        viewing Remote Desktop sessions, 250-252

    preparing client computer for, 153

    Remote Desktop Connection Client for Mac, 153

Remote Desktop Connection dialog box
    Display tab, 155
    Experience tab, 157
    General tab, 154
    Local Resources tab, 155-156
    More tab, 156
    Programs tab, 156
Remote Desktop hosts, configuring, 148
    restricting connections, 151-152
    Windows 7 or Vista hosts, 149-150
    XP hosts, 150-151
Remote Web Access, 158-159
    activating on server, 160
    configuring users for, 159
    connecting via, 162-163
    customizing Remote Web Access pages,
        177-181
    disconnecting from host, 163
    displaying Remote Web Access page,
        160-161
    sending messages to Remote Desktop
        clients, 252-253
    viewing, 250-252
Remote Desktop Services Manager, 558
    disconnecting Remote Desktop sessions,
        253-254
    monitoring users via Task Manager,
        254-255
    opening, 250
    sending messages to Remote Desktop
        clients, 252-253
    viewing Remote Desktop sessions, 250-252
Remote Desktop Session Host
    Configuration, 559
Remote Desktop Users dialog box, 27, 48, 150
Remote Desktop Users group, 30
remote logons, configuring, 47-48
Remote tab (System Properties dialog box), 26
Remote Web Access, 158-159
    activating on server, 160
    configuring users for, 159
    connecting via, 162-163
    customizing Remote Web Access pages,
        177-181
        logon pages, 178-180
        web page links, 179-181

disconnecting from host, 163
displaying Remote Web Access page,
    160-161
RemoteAccess folder, 295-296, 299
Remove Change Password policy, 538
Remove Lock Computer policy, 538
Remove Logoff policy, 538
Remove Task Manager policy, 538
RemoveNetworkDrive method, 617
RemovePrinterConnection method, 616
removing
    Control Panel icons, 554-556
    server backup drives, 106
    user accounts, 46
REN utility, 511-512
RENAME utility, 511-512
renaming
    administrator account, 271
    files/folders, 511-512
    Registry keys, 472-473
Repair the Backup Database Wizard, 232
repairing
    backups, 232
    network connection, 17-19
    storage, 115-116
REPLACE utility, 512-513
replacing hard drives, 429
Replicator group, 32
replying to faxes, 581
Reset User Password dialog box, 43
Resource Monitor, 382-384
resources
    blogs, 650
    developer resources, 651
    troubleshooting resources, 440-442
    websites, 649-650
Resources folder, 297
restarting
    Windows Home Server, 89, 522-526
    Windows Home Server default website, 329
Restore Files or Folder Wizard, 232-234
restoring
    backed-up files, 232-234
    to previous configuration, 235-237

Restrict the User from Entering Author Mode policy, 564

Restrict Users to the Explicitly Permitted List of Snap-Ins policy, 566

Resultant Set of Policy, 559

return codes (StopService/StartService methods), 573

returning class instances, 618-622

ReturnLogDate() function, 269

Robot.txt file, 297

roles
    Add Roles Wizard, 12-13
    DHCP Server role, 11-13
    Fax Server, 574-575

root keys (Registry), 459
    HKEY_CLASSES_ROOT, 459-460
    HKEY_CURRENT_CONFIG, 461
    HKEY_CURRENT_USER, 460
    HKEY_LOCAL_MACHINE, 460-461
    HKEY_USERS, 461

routers
    configuring
        manually, 167
        with Windows Home Server, 165-167
    IP addresses
        connecting with, 164-168
        determining, 167-168
    port forwarding, 165

Routing and Remote Access, 559

routing received faxes, 582-584

-RR option, nbtstat command, 19

rrasmgmt.msc, 559

rsop.msc, 559

rules, approving updates with, 365-366

Run dialog box, 39-41

Run key, 95-97

Run Logon Scripts Synchronously policy, 97

Run method, 608

Run Startup Scripts Asynchronously policy, 97

Run Startup Scripts Visible policy, 97

Run These Programs at User Logon policy, 96

running
    applications, 608-609
    commands, 483-484
    scripts, 587-588
        CScript, 590
        directly, 588
        WScript, 588-590

S

/S option (CMD), 478, 481

Safe Boot: Active Directory Repair, 93

Safe Boot: Alternate Shell, 92

Safe Boot: Minimal, 92

Safe Boot: Network, 93

Safe Mode, 90-91, 448-449

Safe Mode with Command Prompt, 91, 449

Safe Mode with Networking, 91, 449

Samba
    changing workgroup name, 69
    defining Samba users, 67-69
    installing, 67

saving
    custom taskpad views, 562-565
    Disk Cleanup settings, 422
    faxes, 582
    MMC consoles, 562

scanning hard drives, 411-412
    AUTOCHK utility, 416, 503-506
    Check Disk, 414-416, 502-503
    CHKNTFS utility, 503-506
    for spyware, 277-278

schedules (maintenance), 425-426

scopes
    adding, 12
    changing, 77
    Local and Network, 77
    Local Only, 77
    None, 77

screensavers
    performance optimization, 399
    screensaver slideshows, 194-195

<script> tag, 587
scripts, 585-586. *See also* objects
    automation, 598-599
        creating Automation object, 599-600
        exposing VBScript and JavaScript
            objects, 601-602
        programming FileSystemObject, 602-603
        retrieving existing objects, 600-601
    checking system uptime, 409-411
    controlling services with, 570-573
    launching at startup, 94-95
        group policies, 96
        Registry, 95-97
        specifying startup and logon scripts, 97
        Startup folder, 95
        Task Scheduler, 98
    properties, 590-592
    running, 587-588
        CScript, 590
        directly, 588
        WScript, 588-590
    script jobs, creating, 589
    shutting down, 598
    viewing auditing events with, 268-270
    WMI service object, 617-618
        ExecQuery method, 619
        InstancesOf method, 619
        referencing, 618
        returning class instances, 618-622
    WScript object. *See* WScript
    WSH (Windows Script Host), 586-587
    .wsh files, 590-592
    WshNetwork object
        mapping network drives, 616-617
        mapping network printers, 616
        methods. *See specific methods*
        properties, 616
        referencing, 615
    WshShell object
        displaying text to user, 604-607
        methods. *See specific methods*
        referencing, 604
        running applications, 608-609
        shortcuts, 609-611

        working with environment variables,
            613-615
        working with Registry entries, 611-613
Search feature, 140-144
searching
    Registry, 473-474
    shared folders, 140-144
secpol.msc, 558
security, 257. *See also* backups
    administrator account, renaming, 271
    application restrictions, 285-286
    auditing, 257-258
        activating auditing policies, 258-259
        Audit Account Logon Events policy,
            259-260
        Audit Account Management policy,
            260-262
        Audit Logon Events policy, 261-263
        Audit Policy Change policy, 263-264
        Audit Process Tracking policy, 263-264
        Audit System Events policy, 263-265
        viewing auditing events, 266-270
    email viruses, 280-282
    hidden administrative shares, disabling,
        274-275
    home computer security, 275-276
    network computers, 275
    Parental Controls, 282
        activating, 282-283
        activity reporting, 283
        creating childrens' accounts, 282
    passwords. *See* passwords
    phishing, 285-288
    Registry
        backups, 463
        .reg files, 464-466
    security groups. *See* security groups
    shared computers, 288-290
    usernames, hiding in Log On to Windows
        dialog box, 271-272
    web restrictions, 283-285
    WEP (Wired Equivalent Privacy), 184
    Windows Defender, 276-277
        settings, 278-280
        spyware scanning, 277-278

Windows Firewall, 272-274

wireless security, 290-292

access point username/password, 291

default SSID, changing, 291

encryption, 290

MAC (Media Access Control) address filtering, 291-292

network broadcasting, disabling, 290-291

static IP addresses, 291

WPA (Wi-Fi Protected Access), 184

Security Configuration and Analysis, 559

security groups, 29-31

access levels, 30

adding users to, 46

Administrators group, 30

Backup Operators, 32

Certificate Services DCOM Access, 32

Cryptographic Operators, 32

DHCP Administrators, 32

DHCP Users, 32

Distributed COM Users, 32

Event Log Readers, 32

Guests, 32

HomeUsers Security Group, 32

IIS_IUSRS, 32

Network Configuration Operators, 32

Performance Log Users, 32

Performance Monitor Users, 32

Power Users, 32

Print Operators, 32

RA_AllowAddInAccess, 30

RA_AllowComputerAccess, 30

RA_AllowDashboardAccess, 30

RA_AllowHomePageLinks, 30

RA_AllowMediaAccess, 30

RA_AllowNetworkAlertAccess, 31

RA_AllowRemoteAccess, 31

RA_AllowShareAccess, 31

Remote Desktop Users, 30

Replicator, 32

Users group, 30

Windows Media Center, 32

Security log, 424

Security Templates, 559

Select a System Image Backup dialog box, 429

Select Disks dialog box, 111

Select Drive dialog box, 420

Select Groups dialog box, 46

Select Users or Groups dialog box, 47, 122

selecting text, 642

Selective Startup (System Configuration utility), 452

sending

email to SharePoint users, 344

faxes

from applications, 579-580

connecting to shared fax printer, 580

cover pages, 578-579

messages to Remote Desktop clients, 252-253

Server Device icon, 14

Server Manager, 559

Server Settings dialog box, 169

Server Shared Folders icon, 14

Server Shared Media icon, 14

Server.aspx file, 295

servers

DHCP servers, configuring Windows Home Server as, 11-13

fax servers, 574

adding Fax Server role, 574-575

configuring fax modems, 576-577

configuring shared fax printers, 575-576

receiving faxes, 580-584

sending faxes, 578-580

starting Fax Service Manager, 576

server backup drives, 103-106

adding, 103-106

removing, 106

starting Windows Fax and Scan, 577-578

time servers, synchronizing time/date with, 81-83

services

controlling

at command prompt, 569-570

with scripts, 570-573

with Services snap-in, 566-569

performance optimization, 387-401

startup type, 569

Services snap-in, 566

Session ID column (Task Manager), 372

sessions

    closing, 249

    Remote Desktop connections. *See* Remote Desktop connections

Sessions command (Shared Folders menu), 246

Sessions folder, 246

Sessions tab (Remote Desktop Services Manager), 251-252

Set statement, 595

Set Up Server Backup Wizard, 103-106

Set Up Your Domain Name Wizard, 169-172

Settings pane (Registry), 458-459

Share and Storage Management, 559

shared fax printers

    configuring, 575-576

    connecting to, 580

        Mac clients, 61-65

shared folders, 117

    accessing

        with Internet connections, 173-175

        Mac clients, 135

        previous versions of, 125-126

        Windows clients, 127-129

    calendars, 118-137

        publishing, 137-138

        subscribing to, 138-140

        working with, 140

    copying files to, 135-136

    creating, 123-124

    deleting, 127

    disconnecting mapped network folders, 131

    hidden administrative shares, disabling, 274-275

    Linux clients, 70-71

    mapping to local drive letters, 130-132

    Media Library Sharing, 186-189

    monitoring, 245-249

        closing user's session or file, 249

        launching Computer Management snap-in, 245-246

        viewing connections to shared folders, 247-248

        viewing current connections, 246-247

        viewing open files, 248

mounting, 56-58

moving, 124-125

music sharing, 197

    customizing Music share with template, 199-200

    default rip location, changing, 199-200

    with Windows Media Player, 200-201

network locations, creating

    Windows 7 and Vista, 131-133

    Windows XP, 133-135

permissions

    changing, 119-120

    setting, 118-119

photo sharing

    changing default Picture import location, 198

    customizing Pictures share with template, 193-194

    running slideshows from Pictures share, 198

    screensaver slideshows, 194-195

    with Windows Live Photo Gallery, 196-197

    with Windows Media Player, 195-196

predefined shares, 118

recovering, 125-126

searching, 140-144

sharing outside Dashboard, 120-122

UNC (universal naming convention), 128-130

video sharing

    archiving recorded TV, 204-206

    customizing Videos share with template, 201-202

    with Windows Media Player, 202-204

Shared Folders menu

    Open Files command, 248

    Sessions command, 246

    Shares command, 247

Shared Folders snap-in, 559

SharePoint Foundation 2010

    configuring, 323

    downloading, 322

    groups

        creating, 346-347

        deleting, 347

        settings, 345-346

How can we make this index more useful? Email us at indexes@samspublishing.com

installing, 322-323

permissions
    changing, 347-349
    custom permission levels, 349

SharePoint sites
    adding, 333-337
    creating, 323
    custom site icons, 339
    default site, deleting, 328-329
    deleting, 349
    firewall exceptions, 329-330
    links, 341-342
    port forwarding, 330-331
    Quick Launch, 342
    settings, 337-338
    subsite folders, 339
    subsites, 335-337
    themes, 340-341
    title and description, 338-339
    top-level sites, 325-328, 331-333
    tree view, 339-340

users
    deleting, 345
    editing user information, 343-344
    sending email to, 344

SharePoint sites, 321
    creating, 323-325
    custom site icons, 339
    default site, deleting, 328-329
    deleting, 349
    firewall exceptions, 329-330
    groups
        creating, 346-347
        deleting, 347
        settings, 345-346
    links, 341-342
    permissions
        changing, 347-349
        custom permission levels, 349
    port forwarding, 330-331
    Quick Launch, 342
    settings, 337-338
    subsites
        adding, 335-337
        folders, 339

themes, 340-341
title and description, 338-339
top-level sites, 325-328, 333-334
    adding, 335
    adding users to, 331-332
    logging on to, 332-333
tree view, 339-340
users
    deleting, 345
    editing user information, 343-344
    sending email to, 344

shares. See shared folders
Shares command (Shared Folders menu), 247
shell folders, 540-541
shortcut files, 609-611
    creating, 609
    WshShortcut object, 609-611
shortcut keys, 639-648
    data shortcut keys, 641
    dialog box shortcut keys, 643
    document shortcut keys, 641
    DOSKEY shortcut keys, 487-488, 646-647
    drag-and-drop shortcut keys, 643
    folder window shortcut keys, 644
    general shortcut keys, 640
    insertion point shortcut keys, 642
    Internet Explorer shortcut keys, 645-646
    program window shortcut keys, 640
    text selection shortcut keys, 642
    Windows logo key shortcut keys, 647-648
Show Only Specified Control Panel Applets
    policy, 556
Shut Down Windows dialog box, 544-545
Shutdown Event Tracker, 544-545
SHUTDOWN utility, 522-526
shutting down
    scripts, 598
    Windows Home Server, 89, 522-526
Signature Verification Tool, 446
signatures, verifying, 447-448
Sigverif.txt file, 448
Single Instance Storage, 210
single-drive systems, storage on, 100-101
Site Bindings dialog box, 314
Site folder, 296-297, 299

slideshows
    running from Pictures share, 198
    screensaver slideshows, 194-195

SmartScreen Filter, 287-288

snap-ins. *See also specific snap-ins*
    adding, 560-561
    controlling with group policies, 565-566
    default snap-ins, 557-560

software. *See specific software*

solutions, checking for, 430-432

SORT utility, 513-514

sorting file contents, 513-514

spanned volumes, creating, 107
    adding dynamic disks to spanned volumes, 110-111
    combining dynamic disks into spanned volumes, 108-110
    converting hard drives to dynamic disks, 108
    creating storage pools, 107-108

SpecialPollInterval setting, 82

Specify Intranet Microsoft Update Service Location policy, 363-364

Specify IPv4 DNS Server Settings dialog box, 12

spyware, removing with Windows Defender, 276-277
    settings, 278-280
    spyware scanning, 277-278

SSIDs, changing, 291

Start menu, adding Control Panel submenu to, 554-555

starting. *See opening*

StartService method, 573

startup, 89-90
    configuring with Advanced Boot Options menu, 90-91
    configuring with System Configuration utility, 92-94
    launching applications at, 94-95
        group policies, 96
        Registry, 95-97
        specifying startup and logon scripts, 97
        Startup folder, 95
        Task Scheduler, 98

troubleshooting, 448
    Debugging Mode, 451
    Directory Service Restore Mode, 450
    Enable Boot Logging option, 449
    Enable VGA Mode option, 450
    inability to restart, 451
    last known good configuration, booting to, 450
    Safe Mode, 448-449
    Safe Mode with Command Prompt, 449
    Safe Mode with Networking, 449
    System Configuration utility, 445-454

Startup folder, 95

startup type (services), 569

State column (Task Manager), 380

static IP addresses, 8-11, 291

Status dialog box, 10, 16

Status icon (Launchpad), 240

stopping
    batch files, 495
    published calendars, 140

StopService method, 573

storage. *See also* hard drives
    explained, 99-100
    mirrored volumes, 111-112
    on multiple-drive systems, 102-104
    RAID 5 volumes, 112-115
    repairing, 115-116
    server backup drives
        adding, 103-106
        removing, 106
    on single-drive systems, 100-101
    spanned volumes, creating, 107
        adding dynamic disks to spanned volumes, 110-111
        combining dynamic disks into spanned volumes, 108-110
        converting hard drives to dynamic disks, 108
        creating storage pools, 107-108

Storage Explorer, 559

storage pools, 107-108

StorageMgmt.msc, 559

StorExpl.msc, 559

streaming digital media, **184**
  over Internet, 191-193
  playing streamed media
    in Windows Media Center, 190-191
    in Windows Media Player, 188-191
  preparing devices for, 184-186
string values, editing, 468
Strong password policy, 33
strong passwords, 34-35
style.css file, 295
subdomains, 169-170
subnet masks, 24-26
subnets, 24-26
Subscribe to a Calendar dialog box, 139
subscribing to calendars, 138-140
subsites (SharePoint)
  adding, 335-337
  folders, 339
SUBST command, 485
SuperAntiSpyware, 277
svchost.exe, 371
SWbemLocator object, 618
Synchronization Schedule dialog box, 363
synchronizing
  calendars, 140
  time/date with time server, 81-83
  updates (WSUS), 361-363
System Commit (Task Manager), 378
system configuration data, returning, 526-527
System Configuration utility, 92-94, 445-454
System counter, 390
System Handles (Task Manager), 377
system hard drive, determining, 428
System Information, troubleshooting, 433-434
System log, 424
system management tools
  REG utility, 519-521-522
  SHUTDOWN utility, 522-526
  SYSTEMINFO command, 526-527
  table of, 518
  TYPEPERF utility, 528-530
  WHOAMI utility, 530-531
system performance. *See **performance*
  optimization*
System Processes (Task Manager), 378

System Properties dialog box, 26, 149
system reboots, troubleshooting, 432-437
System Threads (Task Manager), 378
System Up Time (Task Manager), 378
system uptime, checking, 408
  with Performance Monitor, 408-409
  with script, 409-411
  with SYSTEMINFO command, 408
  with Task Manager, 408
SYSTEMINFO command, 408, 491, 526-527
System\Processor Queue Length counter, 390
System\System Up Time counter, 390

T

/T option (CMD), 479-480
tags. *See specific tags*
Task Icon dialog box, 564-565
Task Manager
  checking system uptime, 408
  monitoring network performance, 379-382
  monitoring processes, 370-376
  monitoring system performance, 376-378
  monitoring users with, 254-255
  Networking tab, 17
  setting program priority, 397-398
Task Scheduler, 98, 559
Taskbar and Start Menu Properties dialog
  box, 554
taskpad, custom taskpad views, 562-565
Taskpad Reuse dialog box, 563
Taskpad Style dialog box, 563
taskschd.msc, 559
TCP/IP Address dialog box, 303
templates
  customizing Music share with, 199-200
  customizing Pictures share with, 193-194
  customizing Videos share with, 201-202
text
  displaying to user
    WScript object, 597-598
    WshShell object, 604-607
  selecting, 642
  text strings, finding, 509-511

TextStream object, 603

themes for SharePoint sites, 340-341

This Computer Meets the Prerequisites dialog box, 52

Threads column (Task Manager), 375

Tiles view, 416

time

backup time, 215-216

setting current time, 79-81

synchronizing with time server, 81-83

Time Machine, 222

time servers

configuring at command prompt, 81-82

synchronizing time/date with, 81-83

Time Zone Settings dialog box, 80

title of SharePoint sites, 338-339

TodaysDate() function, 269

tools. See specific tools

top-level SharePoint sites, 325-328, 333-334

adding, 335

adding users to, 331-332

logging on to, 332-333

subsites, 335-337

TPM Management, 559

tpm.msc, 559

tree view (SharePoint), 339-340

troubleshooting, 427

application settings, 437

Check for Solutions feature, 430-432

device drivers, 438, 445-446

devices, 438, 442

with Device Manager, 442-445

digitally signed files, verifying, 447-448

error messages, 432-433

Event Viewer, 433

general troubleshooting tips, 440

hard drives

determining system hard drive, 428

replacing, 429

networks, 14-15

cables, 20-21

connection status, 15-17

device drivers, updating, 24

Device Manager, 22-23

Network and Internet Troubleshooter, 19-20

network connection, repairing, 17-19

network utilization, 17

NICs (network interface cards), 21-22

new program installations, 437-438

online resources, 440-442

questions to ask, 432-440

startup, 448

Debugging Mode, 451

Directory Service Restore Mode, 450

Enable Boot Logging option, 449

Enable VGA Mode option, 450

inability to restart, 451

last known good configuration, booting to, 450

Safe Mode, 448-449

Safe Mode with Command Prompt, 449

Safe Mode with Networking, 449

System Configuration utility, 445-454

System Information, 433-434

system reboots, 432-437

updates, 438-440

Windows settings, 434

tsadmin.msc, 558

tsconfig.msc, 559

tsmmc.msc, 559

tuning performance. See performance optimization

turning off. See disabling

turning on. See enabling

TV archiving, 204-206

TYPEPERF utility, 528-530

TZO, 168

U

/U option (CMD), 479

Ubuntu clients

changing Samba workgroup name, 69

defining Samba users, 67-69

folder sharing, 70-71

installing Samba, 67

viewing Windows Home Server network in, 65-66

Ubuntu Software Center, 65

UNC (universal naming convention), 128-130

Unicasts column (Task Manager), 381

Unicasts Per Interval column (Task Manager), 381

Unicasts Received column (Task Manager), 381

Unicasts Received Per Interval column (Task Manager), 381

Unicasts Sent column (Task Manager), 381

Unicasts Sent Per Interval column (Task Manager), 381

universal naming convention (UNC), 128-130

Universal Plug and Play (UPnP), 165

unpublishing calendars, 140

updates. *See also* Windows Home Server configuration; Windows Update

    calendars, 140

    device drivers, 24

    troubleshooting, 438-440

UPnP (Universal Plug and Play), 165

uptime, checking, 408

    with Performance Monitor, 408-409

    with script, 409-411

    with SYSTEMINFO command, 408

    with Task Manager, 408

USB recovery keys, creating, 224-232

User Account Control (UAC) Virtualization column (Task Manager), 376

user accounts, 29

    adding, 31, 36-39, 46

    client logons, 39-41

    closing user's session or file, 249

    configuring for Remote Web Access, 159

    creating for children, 282

    defining Samba users, 67-69

    disabling, 44-45

    enabling, 45

    Guest account, 45, 289

    local logons, 47

    modifying, 41-42

    monitoring with Task Manager, 254-255

    passwords

        changing, 35-36, 43-44

        choosing strong passwords, 34-35

        customizing requirements, 33-34

        length and complexity, 31-33

        password complexity checker, 34

    remote logons, 47-48

    removing, 46

    returning user information, 530-531

    security groups. See security groups

    SharePoint users

        deleting, 345

        editing user information, 343-344

        sending email to, 344

    viewing account properties, 42-43

User Accounts dialog box, 41

User Name column (Task Manager), 372

USER Objects column (Task Manager), 375

UserDomain property (WshNetwork), 616

UserName property (WshNetwork), 616

usernames, hiding in Log On to Windows dialog box, 271-272

users. *See user accounts*

Users group, 30

Users tab

    Remote Desktop Services Manager, 250-251

    Task Manager, 254-255

Using Windows Home Server website, 650

utilities. *See specific utilities*

V

/V option (CMD), 481

variables

    assigning objects to, 594-595

    environment variables, accessing with WshShell, 613-615

.vbs extension, 588

VBScript

    exposing VBScript objects, 601-602

    iterating collections, 596

verifying digitally signed files, 447-448

video sharing

    archiving recorded TV, 204-206

    customizing Videos share with template, 201-202

    with Windows Media Player, 202-204

Videos folder, **118**
    adding to Windows Media Player, 202-204
    templates, 201-202
Videos template, **202**
View Device Webpage command, **185**
View Workgroup Computers option, **14**
viewing
    auditing events
        with filter, 266-267
        with script, 268-270
    backups
        backup details, 227-230
        list of backups, 226-227
    connections to shared folders, 247-248
    Control Panel icons, 546, 556
    current connections, 246-247
    default IIS website, 296-297
    networks, 14
    open files, 248
    Remote Desktop sessions, 250-252
    Remote Web Access page, 160-161
    user account properties, 42-43
    Windows Home Server default website, 297-298
Virtual Directory Creation Wizard, **301**
virtual memory. *See* paging file
Virtual Memory dialog box, **395-396**
viruses, email, **280-282**
Vista. *See* Windows Vista
visual effects, disabling, **399-400**
volumes
    mirrored volumes, 111-112
    RAID 5 volumes, 112-115
    spanned volumes. *See* spanned volumes

W

W32_NTLogEvent database, **270**
wbadmin.msc, **560**
We Got Served, **650**
Weak password policy, **31**
Web access, restricting, **283-285**
web.config file, **295, 297**

websites. *See also* blogs
    adding identities to, 315-316
    anonymous access, disabling, 319-320
    creating, 301-302
    default content pages, 317-318
    Home Server Land, 650
    host headers, 312
        associating with IP addresses, 312
        creating websites with, 312-313
    IP addresses, 302
        assigning to websites, 304
        assigning to Windows Home Server, 303
        associating with hostnames, 305-307
    location, changing, 316-317
    MSWHS, 650
    ports, 307-308
        assigning port numbers, 308-309
        firewall exceptions, 309-311
        port forwarding, 311
    SharePoint sites. *See* SharePoint sites
    site bindings, 314-315
    troubleshooting resources, 440-442
    Using Windows Home Server, 650
    Windows Home Server, 649
    Windows Home Server default website, 293-294
        adding files to, 298-300
        adding folders to, 299-301
        default IIS website, 296-297
        restarting, 329
        viewing with IIS Manager, 297-298
        Web application folders, 294-296
    Windows Home Server Developers Forum, 651
    Windows Home Server forums, 650
    Windows Home Server Unleashed, 650
WEP (Wired Equivalent Privacy), **184**
wf.msc, **559**
WhatIsMyIP, **168**
WHOAMI utility, **530-531**
Wi-Fi Protected Access (WPA), **184**
wildcards, **143-144**
Win32_Service class, **570**
Win32_UserAccount class, **620**

windows. *See also specific windows*
folder window shortcut keys, 644
program window shortcut keys, 640

Windows 7
homegroups, connecting Windows Home
Server to, 13-14
network locations, 131-133
Remote Desktop hosts, 149-150

Windows Defender, 276-277
settings, 278-280
spyware scanning, 277-278

Windows Fax and Scan, starting, 577-578

Windows Firewall
activating, 272-274
Advanced Security, 559
configuring ports for, 309-311

Windows Home Server configuration, 75
Dashboard, 77-78
Launchpad, 76-77
passwords, 88
region
changing, 83
customizing region formats, 83-84
startup, 89-91
time and date, 79
setting current time and date, 79-81
synchronizing with time server, 81-83
Windows Update, 85
configuring, 85-87
updating Windows Home Server
with, 87-88

Windows Home Server Connector
explained, 49-50
installing, 51-53
preparing for installation, 51
supported operating systems, 50-51

Windows Home Server default website. *See*
default website (Windows Home Server)

Windows Home Server Developers Forum, 651

Windows Home Server forums, 441, 650

Windows Home Server home page, 649

Windows Home Server Team Blog, 650

Windows Home Server Unleashed website, 650

**Windows Live Photo Gallery, adding Pictures
folder to, 196-197**

Windows logo key shortcut keys, 647-648

Windows Media Center
archiving recorded TV, 204-206
playing streamed media in, 190-191

Windows Media Center group, 32

Windows Media Player
adding Music folder to, 200-201
adding Pictures folder to, 195-196
adding Videos folder to, 202-204
playing streamed media in, 188-191

Windows Script Host (WSH), 586-587

Windows Search, disabling, 392

Windows Security screen, customizing, 537-539

Windows Server Backup, 560

Windows Server log, 425

Windows Server Update Services. *See* WSUS
(Windows Server Update Services)

**Windows Server Update Services Configuration
Wizard, 358-361**

Windows Update, 85
configuring, 85-87
troubleshooting, 438-440
updating Windows Home Server with, 87-88

Windows Vista
network locations, 131-133
Remote Desktop hosts, 149-150

Windows Vista Web Filter, 283

Windows XP
network locations, 133-135
Remote Desktop hosts, 150-151

Wired Equivalent Privacy (WEP), 184

wireless security, 290-292
access point username/password, 291
default SSID, changing, 291
encryption, 290
MAC (Media Access Control) address
filtering, 291-292
network broadcasting, disabling, 290-291
Repair the Backup Database Wizard, 232
static IP addresses, 291

wizards
Add a Folder Wizard, 123-124
Add a User Account Wizard, 36-39
Add Network Location Wizard, 131-133
Add Roles Wizard, 12-13, 574-575
Connect a Computer to the Network Wizard,
55-56

Connect a Computer to the Server Wizard, 52-53

Create Computer Recovery Key Wizard, 224-232

Customize Backup Wizard, 106, 218

Customize Server Backup Wizard, 463

Extend Volume Wizard, 110-111

Fax Setup Wizard, 575

Full System Restore Wizard, 235-237

Hardware Update Wizard, 402

Link to Web Address Wizard, 561

New Inbound Rule Wizard, 310-311

New Spanned Volume Wizard, 108-110

New Task Wizard, 564

Products Configuration Wizard, 323

Restore Files or Folder Wizard, 232-234

Set Up Server Backup Wizard, 103-106

Set Up Your Domain Name Wizard, 169-172

Virtual Directory Creation Wizard, 301

Windows Server Update Services Configuration Wizard, 358-361

WMI Control, 560

WMI service object, 617-618

methods

ExecQuery, 619

InstancesOf, 619

referencing, 618

returning class instances, 618-622

wmimgmt.msc, 560

WORKGROUP group, 8

workgroups

changing name of, 8, 69

WORKGROUP group, 8

WPA (Wi-Fi Protected Access), 184

write caching, enabling, 392-393

WScript, 588-590, 597

automation, 598-599

creating Automation object, 599-600

exposing VBScript and JavaScript objects, 601-602

programming FileSystemObject, 602-603

retrieving existing objects, 600-601

displaying text to user, 597-598

methods

CreateObject, 599-600

Echo, 597-598

GetObject, 600-601

Quit, 598

shutting down scripts, 598

WSH (Windows Script Host), 586-587. *See also* **scripts**

.wsh files, 590-592

WshNetwork object

mapping network drives, 616-617

mapping network printers, 616

methods

AddWindowsPrinterConnection, 616

MapNetworkDrive, 616-617

RemoveNetworkDrive, 617

properties, 616

referencing, 615

WshShell object

displaying text to user, 604-607

methods

CreateShortcut, 609

Popup, 604-608

RegDelete, 613

RegRead, 612

RegWrite, 612-613

RemovePrinterConnection, 616

referencing, 604

running applications, 608-609

shortcuts, 609-611

creating, 609

WshShortcut object, 609-611

working with environment variables, 613-615

working with Registry entries, 611-613

WshShortcut object, 609-611

WSUS (Windows Server Update Services), 357

approving updates

manually, 365

with rules, 365-366

configuring, 359-361

connecting home computers to, 363-365

installing, 358

synchronizing updates, 361-363

X-Y-Z

Xbox 360, connecting to Windows Home Server
  network, 72-73
XCOPY utility, 514-518
XP. *See* Windows XP

UNLEASHED

Unleashed takes you beyond the basics, providing an exhaustive, technically sophisticated reference for professionals who need to exploit a technology to its fullest potential. It's the best resource for practical advice from the experts, and the most in-depth coverage of the latest technologies.

informit.com/unleashed

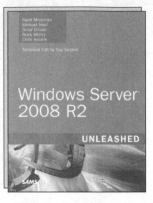

Windows Server 2008 R2 Unleashed
ISBN-13: 9780672330926

OTHER UNLEASHED TITLES

Macromedia Flash MX Professional 2004 Unleashed
ISBN-13: 9780672326066

Microsoft Internet Security and Acceleration (ISA) Server 2004 Unleashed
ISBN-13: 9780672327186

Microsoft SharePoint 2003 Unleashed
ISBN-13: 9780672328039

Microsoft Exchange Server 2003 Unleashed
ISBN-13: 9780672328077

Windows PowerShell Unleashed
ISBN-13: 9780672329531

Microsoft XNA Unleashed: Graphics and Game Programming for Xbox 360 and Windows
ISBN-13: 9780672329647

Adobe Dreamweaver CS3 Unleashed
ISBN-13: 9780672329449

Microsoft Office Project Server 2007 Unleashed
ISBN-13: 9780672329210

Adobe Dreamweaver CS4 Unleashed
ISBN-13: 9780672330391

Expression Blend 4 Unleashed
ISBN-13: 9780672331077

VMware Virtual Infrastructure Unleashed
ISBN-13: 9780672330032

Microsoft Dynamics AX 2011 Unleashed
ISBN-13: 9780672335488

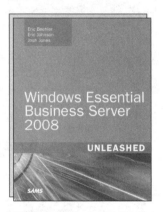

Windows Essential Business Server 2008 Unleashed
ISBN-13: 9780672330520

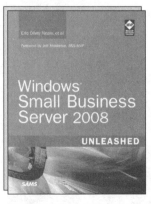

Windows Small Business Server 2008 Unleashed
ISBN-13: 9780672329579

informit.com/sams

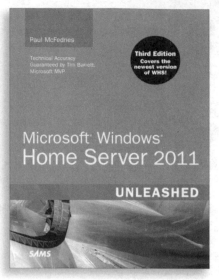

FREE Online Edition

Your purchase of *Microsoft® Windows® Home Server 2011 Unleashed* includes access to a free online edition for 45 days through the Safari Books Online subscription service. Nearly every Sams book is available online through Safari Books Online, along with more than 5,000 other technical books and videos from publishers such as Addison-Wesley Professional, Cisco Press, Exam Cram, IBM Press, O'Reilly, Prentice Hall, and Que.

SAFARI BOOKS ONLINE allows you to search for a specific answer, cut and paste code, download chapters, and stay current with emerging technologies.

Activate your FREE Online Edition at www.informit.com/safarifree

> **STEP 1:** Enter the coupon code: PILPFDB.

> **STEP 2:** New Safari users, complete the brief registration form.
> Safari subscribers, just log in.

If you have difficulty registering on Safari or accessing the online edition, please e-mail customer-service@safaribooksonline.com

Safari. Books Online

Addison Wesley   Adobe Press   ALPHA   Cisco Press   FT Press   IBM Press   lynda.com   Microsoft Press   New Riders

O'REILLY   Peachpit Press   PRENTICE HALL   QUE   Redbooks   SAMS   SAS Publishing   Sun   WILEY